The
Essential
ATLAS
of the
WORLD

The Essential ATLAS of the WORLD

Revised Edition

BARNES
& NOBLE
NEW YORK

Helicon Publishing
Research Machines plc
New Mill House
183 Milton Park
Abingdon
Oxon
OX14 4SE

e-mail: helicon@rm.com
Web site: http://www.helicon.co.uk

This edition published by Barnes & Noble, Inc. by arrangement with Helicon Publishing

Satellite images: PP ©WorldSat International Inc, Ontario, Canada

Photograph credits: p8/9 R Stephey/Helicon

ISBN 0-7607-7841-8

05 06 07 08 09 9 8 7 6 5 4 3 2 1

Printed in Thailand

CONTENTS

Page		Scale
6	**KEY MAP**	
8-11	**THE WORLD**	
9	Key to map symbols	
10	World	

Page		Scale
12-39	**EUROPE**	
14	Europe	1:20 200 000
16	Scandinavia	1:5 800 000
18	Central Europe	1:3 450 000
20	Germany	1:2 600 000
22	Benelux	1:2 300 000
24	British Isles	1:3 450 000
26	France	1:3 450 000
28	Spain and Portugal	1:3 450 000
30	The Alpine States	1:2 600 000
32	Italy	1:3 450 000
34	The Balkans	1:3 450 000
36	Greece and Western Turkey	1:3 450 000
38	European Russia	1:10 400 000

Page		Scale
40-63	**ASIA**	
42	Asia	1:32 900 000
44	Northwest Asia	1:13 800 000
46	Northeast Asia	1:13 800 000
48	Eastern China	1:11 600 000
50	Japan and Korea	1:5 800 000
52	Southeast Asia	1:11 600 000
54	Malaysia and Indonesia	1:11 600 000
56	Southern Asia	1:11 600 000
58	The Middle East	1:12 700 000
60	Turkey	1:5 800 000
62	Israel and the Gulf States	1:2 850 000

Page		Scale
64-77	**AFRICA**	
66	Africa	1:30 000 000
68	Northeast Africa	1:11 600 000
70	Northwest Africa	1:11 600 000
72	West Africa	1:11 600 000

Page		Scale
74	Central Africa	1:11 600 000
76	Southern Africa	1:11 600 000

Page		Scale
78-85	**OCEANIA**	
80	Oceania	1:40 500 000
82	Australia	1:13 800 000
84	New Zealand	1:4 650 000

Page		Scale
86-103	**NORTH AMERICA**	
88	North America	1:34 700 000
90	Canada	1:13 800 000
92	United States	1:15 500 000
94	Northwest United States	1:7 200 000
96	Northeast United States	1:7 200 000
98	Southeast United States	1:7 200 000
100	Southwest United States	1:7 200 000
102	Central America and the Caribbean	1:16 100 000

Page		Scale
104-111	**SOUTH AMERICA**	
106	South America	1:28 000 000
108	Northern South America	1:16 100 000
110	Southern South America	1:16 100 000

Page		
112	**POLAR REGIONS**	

Page		
113-144	**NATIONS OF THE WORLD**	

Page		
145-192	**INDEX**	
145	How to use the index	
146	Glossary	
147	Index	

Key map

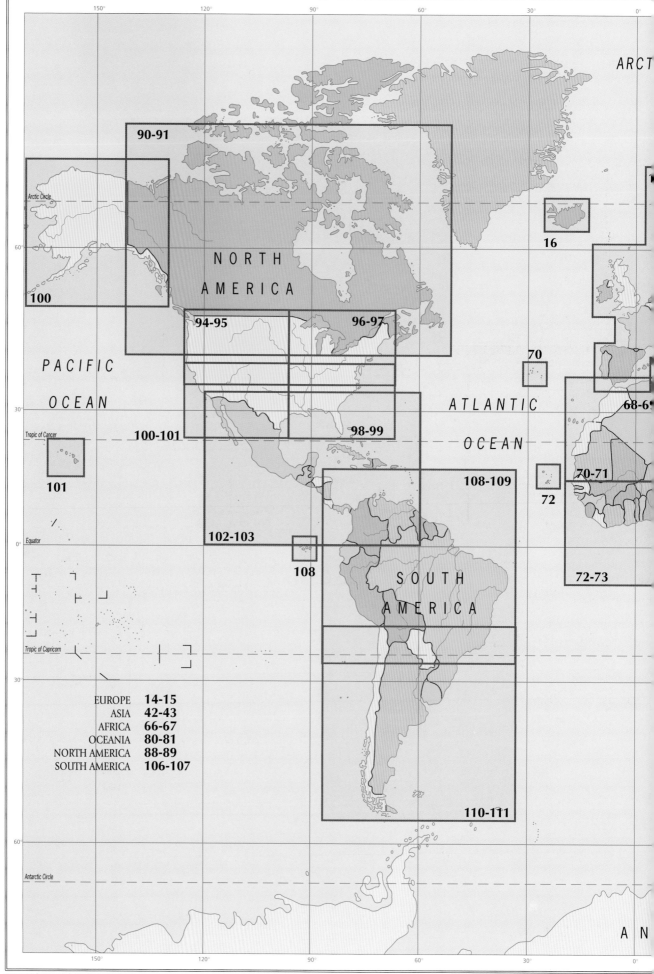

150° 120° 90° 60° 30° 0°

ARCT

90-91

Arctic Circle

NORTH
AMERICA

PACIFIC

OCEAN

100

60°

94-95

96-97

16

70

ATLANTIC

30°

Tropic of Cancer

100-101

OCEAN

68-6

70-71

98-99

101

72

102-103

108-109

Equator 0°

108

SOUTH

AMERICA

72-73

Tropic of Capricorn

30°

EUROPE **14-15**
ASIA **42-43**
AFRICA **66-67**
OCEANIA **80-81**
NORTH AMERICA **88-89**
SOUTH AMERICA **106-107**

110-111

60°

Antarctic Circle

A N

150° 120° 90° 60° 30° 0°

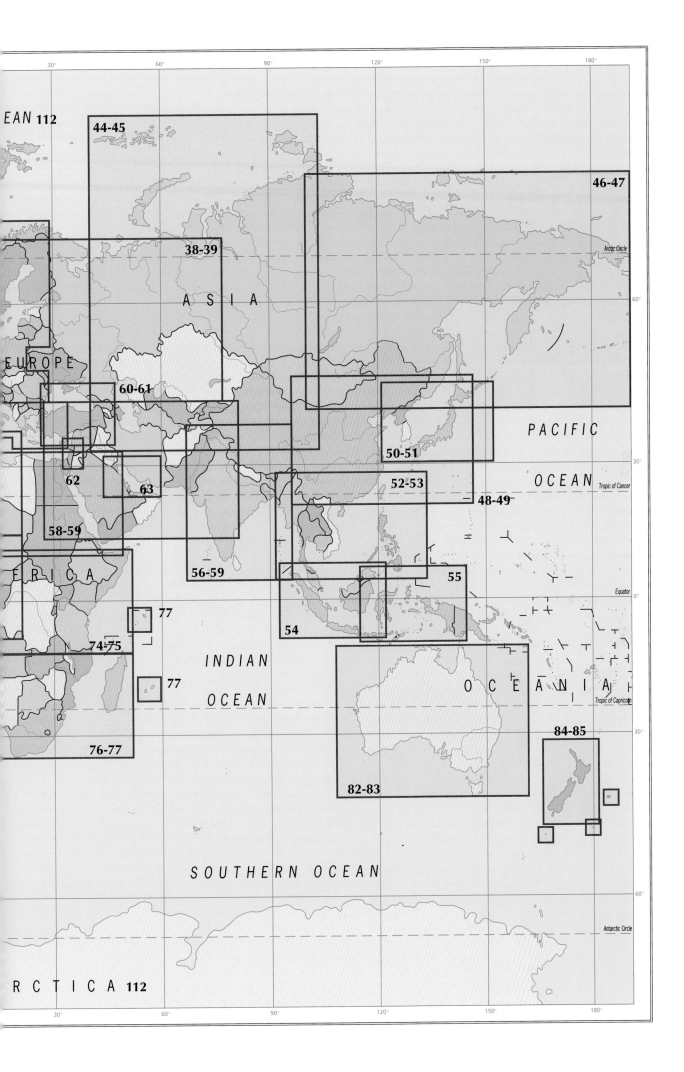

EAN **112**

44-45

46-47

Arctic Circle

38-39

A S I A

60°

EUROPE

60-61

PACIFIC

62

63

OCEAN Tropic of Cancer

30°

50-51

52-53

48-49

58-59

56-59

55

FRICA

54

Equator 0°

77

INDIAN

74-75

77

OCEAN

O C E A N I A

Tropic of Capricorn

84-85

30°

76-77

82-83

SOUTHERN OCEAN

60°

Antarctic Circle

RCTICA **112**

7

THE WORLD

KEY TO MAP SYMBOLS

Political regions

CANADA	country
ONTARIO	state or province
---------------	international boundary (physical regional maps)
———————	international boundary (political continental maps)
———————	state or province boundary
·—·—·—·—·—·	undefined/disputed boundary or ceasefire/demarcation line

Communications

———————	motorway
———————	main road
———————	other road
– – – – – –	track
———————	railway
✈	international airport

Hydrographic features

～～～	river, canal
······	seasonal river
Niagara Falls Kariba Dam	waterfall, dam
⬭	lake, seasonal lake
⬭	salt lake, seasonal salt lake
⬭	ice cap or glacier

Cities, towns & capitals

▣ **CHICAGO**	over 3 million
▢ **HAMBURG**	1–3 million
○ **Bulawayo**	250 000–1 million
● Antofogasta	100 000–250 000
○ Ajaccio	25 000–100 000
· Indian Springs	under 25 000
LONDON	country capital
Columbia	state or province capital
⬯	urban area

Cultural features

∴ Persepolis	ancient site or ruin
▪▪▪▪▪▪▪▪▪▪▪▪▪	ancient wall

Topographic features

▲ **Mount Ziel** 1510	elevation above sea level (in metres)
▾ 133	elevation of land below sea level (in metres)
)(**Khyber Pass** 1080	mountain pass (height in metres)

Each page also features a guide to relief colours

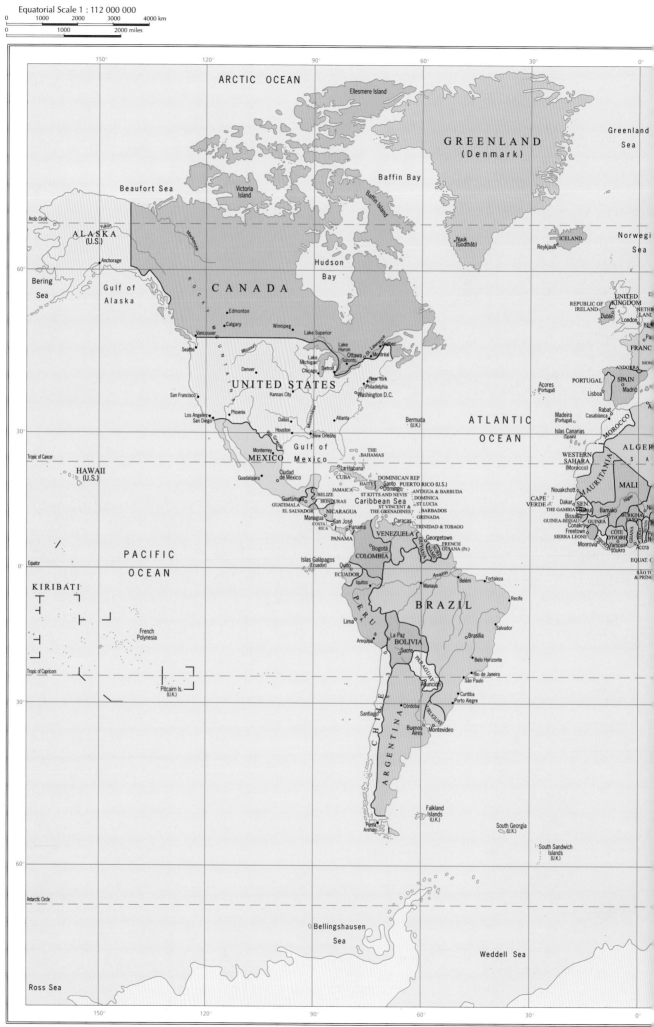

Equatorial Scale 1 : 112 000 000

0   1000   2000   3000   4000 km
0   1000   2000 miles

© Copyright Research Machines plc 2005

ARCTIC OCEAN

Ellesmere Island

GREENLAND
(Denmark)

Greenland
Sea

Baffin Bay

Baffin Island

Beaufort Sea

Victoria
Island

Nuuk
(Godthåb)

ICELAND

Norwegi

Arctic Circle

ALASKA
(U.S.)

Yukon

Reykjavik

Anchorage

Mackenzie

Hudson

Bay

UNITED
KINGDOM

NETH
LAN

60°

Bering
Sea

Gulf of
Alaska

CANADA

REPUBLIC OF
IRELAND

Dublin

London

BE

Edmonton

Calgary

Winnipeg

Lake Superior

FRANC

Vancouver

R
O
C
K
Y

Lake
Huron

St. Lawrence

Québec

MON

Seattle

Missouri

Lake
Michigan

Ottawa
Toronto

Montréal

ANDORRA

Açores
(Portugal)

PORTUGAL

SPAIN

M
O
U
N
T
A
I
N

Denver

Chicago

Detroit

New York

Madrid

Philadelphia

Lisboa

San Francisco

UNITED STATES

Kansas City

Washington D.C.

30°

Los Angeles
San Diego

Phoenix

Dallas

Mississippi

Atlanta

Bermuda
(U.K.)

ATLANTIC

Madeira
(Portugal)

Rabat
Casablanca

MOROCCO

Houston

OCEAN

Islas Canarias
(Spain)

ALGE

Tropic of Cancer

New Orleans

Gulf of

Monterrey

Rio Grande

Mexico

WESTERN
SAHARA
(Morocco)

S   A

HAWAII
(U.S.)

MEXICO

THE
BAHAMAS

Ciudad
de México

La Habana

CUBA

Guadalajara

DOMINICAN REP

CAPE
VERDE

Nouakchott

M
A
U
R
I
T
A
N
I
A

MALI

HAITI

Santo
Domingo

PUERTO RICO (U.S.)

Dakar

SEN

BELIZE

JAMAICA

ST KITTS AND NEVIS

ANTIGUA & BARBUDA

THE GAMBIA

Banjul

Bamako

BURKINA
FASO

GUATEMALA

Guatemala

HONDURAS

DOMINICA

Caribbean Sea

ST LUCIA

Bissau

GUINEA-BISSAU

Conakry

GUINEA

CÔTE

EL SALVADOR

NICARAGUA

ST VINCENT &
THE GRENADINES

BARBADOS

Freetown

D'IVOIRE

GHANA

Managua

GRENADA

SIERRA LEONE

Yamous-
soukro

Monrovia

Accra

San José

Panamá

TRINIDAD & TOBAGO

COSTA
RICA

EQUAT. G

PANAMA

Caracas

Georgetown

VENEZUELA

FRENCH
GUIANA (Fr.)

SÃO TO
& PRÍN

Bogotá

COLOMBIA

GUYANA

SURINAME

Islas Galápagos
(Ecuador)

Quito

0°

Equator

ECUADOR

Iquitos

Amazon

Belém

Fortaleza

Manaus

KIRIBATI

P
E
R
U

Recife

BRAZIL

French
Polynesia

Lima

Salvador

Arequipa

La Paz

Brasília

BOLIVIA

Belo Horizonte

Sucre

Tropic of Capricorn

PARAGUAY

Rio de Janeiro

São Paulo

Pitcairn Is.
(U.K.)

Asunción

Curitiba

Porto Alegre

C
H
I
L
E

Córdoba

U
R
U
G
U
A
Y

30°

Santiago

A
R
G
E
N
T
I
N
A

Buenos
Aires

Montevideo

PACIFIC

OCEAN

Falkland
Islands
(U.K.)

Punta
Arenas

South Georgia
(U.K.)

South Sandwich
Islands
(U.K.)

60°

Antarctic Circle

Bellingshausen
Sea

Weddell Sea

Ross Sea

150°   120°   90°   60°   30°   0°

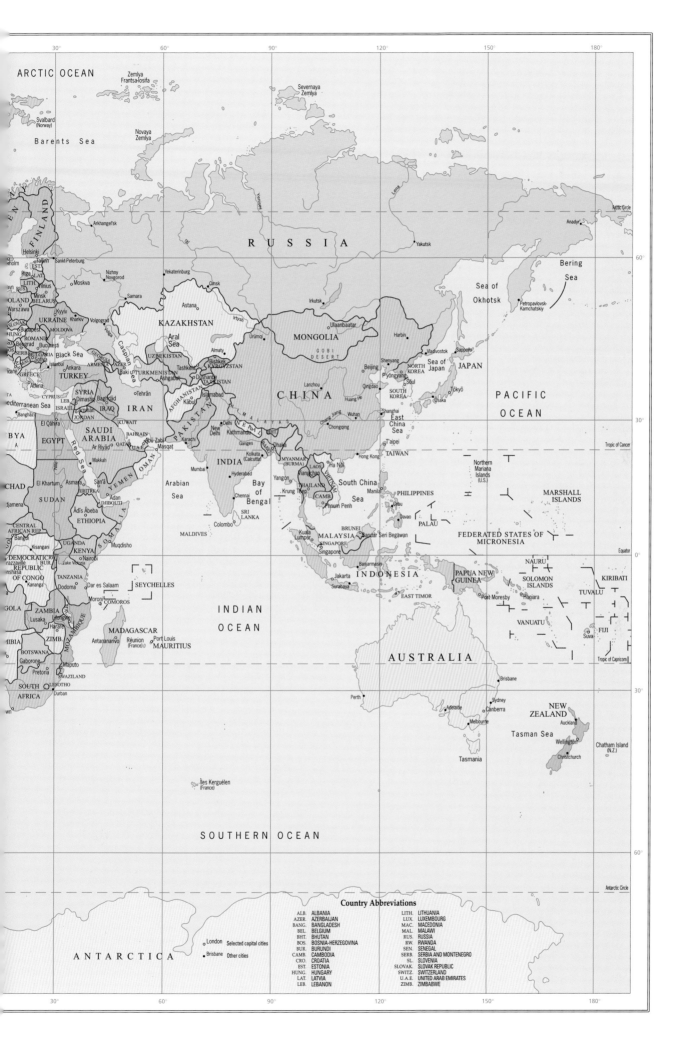

ARCTIC OCEAN

Zemlya
Frantsa-Iosifa

Severnaya
Zemlya

Svalbard
(Norway)

Barents Sea

Novaya
Zemlya

Arctic Circle

Anadyr

Arkhangel'sk

RUSSIA

Yakutsk

Bering
Sea

60°

FINLAND

Helsinki

Sea of
Okhotsk

Petropavlovsk-
Kamchatskiy

tholm
Tallinn
Sankt-Peterburg

Nizhny
Novgorod

Yekaterinburg

Riga
EST.
LAT.

Irkutsk

LITH.
Vilnius
Moskva

Vladivostok
Sapporo

Sea of
Japan

JAPAN

BVN RUS.
Minsk
Samara

Astana

Harbin

OLAND
BELARUS
Warszawa

Kyiv
Volgograd

KAZAKHSTAN

Irtysh

Ürümqi

Ulaanbaatar

Shenyang

NORTH
KOREA

P'yŏngyang

Tōkyō

SLOVAK
Budapest
UKRAINE
Kharkiv

Aral
Sea

Almaty

Bishkek

MONGOLIA

Beijing

SOUTH
KOREA

Sŏul

Ōsaka

HUNG.
MOLDOVA

ROMANIA
Belgrad
Bucuresti

UZBEKISTAN

Tashkent

KYRGYZSTAN

GOBI
DESERT

Lanzhou

Qingdao

PACIFIC

SERBIA
Sofiya

Black Sea

GEORGIA
ARMENIA

Baki TURKMENISTAN

Dushanbe
TAJIKISTAN

Huang He

Shanghai

OCEAN

GREECE
Ankara
Athina
TURKEY
CYPRUS

Ashgabat

AFGHANISTAN

Islamabad

CHINA

Chang Jiang
Wuhan

Chongqing

East
China
Sea

CAMB.
Beirut

SYRIA
Dimashq
Baghdād

Tehrān

Kābul

T'aipei

Tropic of Cancer

Mediterranean Sea
LEB.
ISRAEL
Amman
JORDAN

IRAQ

IRAN

New
Delhi

Delhi

Kathmandu

NEPAL

BHUTAN

Dhaka

Hong Kong

TAIWAN

El Qāhira
KUWAIT

BAHRAIN

Abu Zabi
QATAR

U.A.E.

Masqat

Karachi

Ganges

Kolkata
(Calcutta)

MYANMAR
(BURMA)

Ha Nôi

LAOS

BYA

EGYPT

SAUDI
ARABIA

Ar Riyād

Makkah

INDIA

Mumbai

Hyderabad

Vientiane

VIETNAM

South China
Sea

PHILIPPINES

Northern
Mariana
Islands
(U.S.)

MARSHALL
ISLANDS

A

CHAD

El Khartum

Asmara

San'ā

OMAN

Arabian
Sea

Yangon

THAILAND

Krung Thep

Chennai

Manila

CAMB.

Phnum Penh

Cebu

Davao

PALAU

FEDERATED STATES OF
MICRONESIA

djamena

SUDAN

ERITREA

YEMEN

Adan
DJIBOUTI

Bay
of
Bengal

SRI
LANKA

MALDIVES

Colombo

BRUNEI

Bandar Seri Begawan

Equator

CENTRAL
AFRICAN REP.

Bangui

Ādis Ābeba

ETHIOPIA

Kuala
Lumpur

MALAYSIA

SINGAPORE
Singapore

NAURU

Kisangani

UGANDA
BUR.

SOMALIA

Banjarmasin

KIRIBATI

DEMOCRATIC
razzaville
REPUBLIC
OF CONGO

KENYA

Nairobi

Lake Victoria

Jakarta

INDONESIA

Surabaya

PAPUA NEW
GUINEA

SOLOMON
ISLANDS

Honiara

inshasa
Kananga

TANZANIA

Dodoma

Dar es Salaam

SEYCHELLES

EAST TIMOR

Port Moresby

TUVALU

GOLA

ZAMBIA

Lilongwe
Lusaka

Moroni

COMOROS

INDIAN

VANUATU

FIJI

Suva

Harare

OCEAN

MIBIA
ZIMB.

MADAGASCAR

Antananarivo

Réunion
(France)

Port Louis

MAURITIUS

Tropic of Capricorn

BOTSWANA
Gaborone

Maputo

MOZAMBIQUE

AUSTRALIA

Brisbane

30°

Pretoria
SWAZILAND

SOUTH
AFRICA

LESOTHO

Durban

Perth

Sydney

Adelaide
Canberra

NEW
ZEALAND

Auckland

wn

Melbourne

Tasman Sea

Wellington

Chatham Island
(N.Z.)

Tasmania

Christchurch

Îles Kerguélen
(France)

SOUTHERN OCEAN

60°

Antarctic Circle

ANTARCTICA

London

Brisbane

Selected capital cities

Other cities

Country Abbreviations

ALB.	ALBANIA	LITH.	LITHUANIA
AZER.	AZERBAIJAN	LUX.	LUXEMBOURG
BANG.	BANGLADESH	MAC.	MACEDONIA
BEL.	BELGIUM	MAL.	MALAWI
BHT.	BHUTAN	RUS.	RUSSIA
BOS.	BOSNIA-HERZEGOVINA	RW.	RWANDA
BUR.	BURUNDI	SEN.	SENEGAL
CAMB.	CAMBODIA	SERB.	SERBIA AND MONTENEGRO
CRO.	CROATIA	SL.	SLOVENIA
EST.	ESTONIA	SLOVAK.	SLOVAK REPUBLIC
HUNG.	HUNGARY	SWITZ.	SWITZERLAND
LAT.	LATVIA	U.A.E.	UNITED ARAB EMIRATES
LEB.	LEBANON	ZIMB.	ZIMBABWE

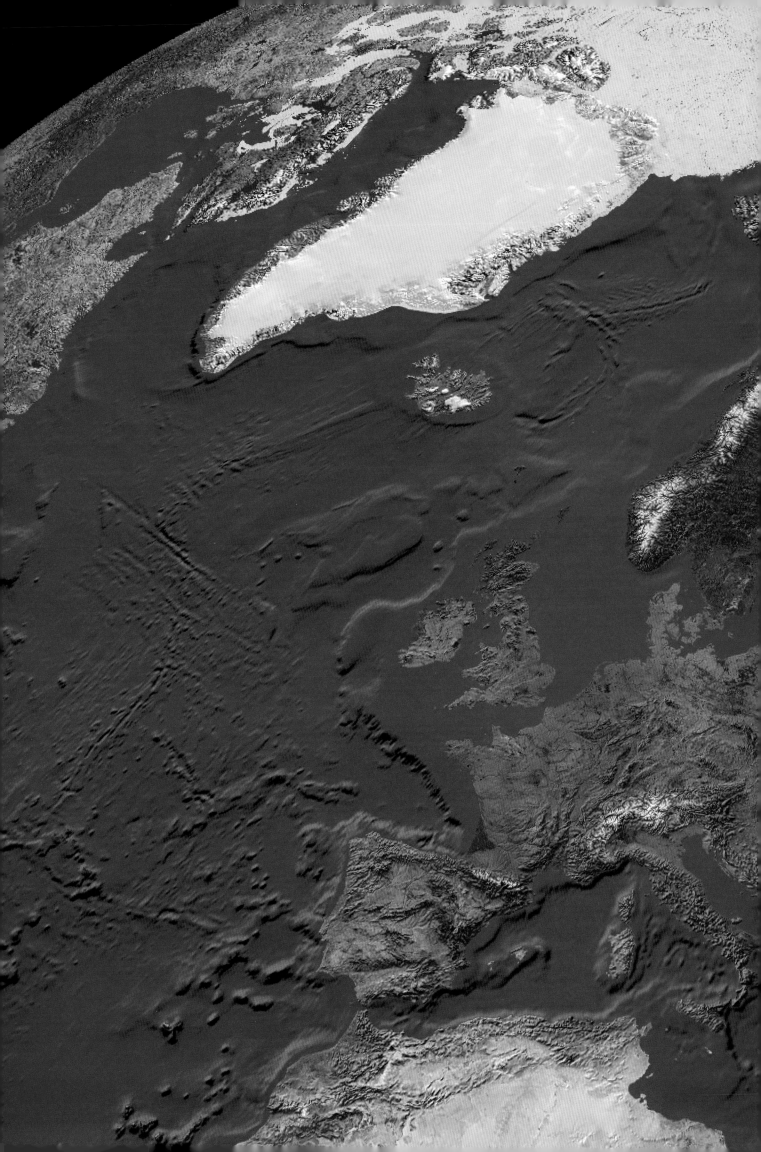

EUROPE

Europe   14

Scandinavia   16

Central Europe   18

Germany   20

Benelux   22

British Isles   24

France   26

Spain and Portugal   28

The Alpine States   30

Italy   32

The Balkans   34

Greece and Western Turkey   36

European Russia   38

0 250 500 750 km
0 100 200 300 miles

60° N A 1 30° W B 20° C 70° 10° D 0° E 10° F 20°

Arctic Circle

Tromsø

Reykjavik **ICELAND**

N o r w e g i a n
S e a

Faeroes
(Denmark)

Kir

Trondheim

N
O
R
W
A
Y

S
W
E
D
E
N

Gulf of Both

Rockall

Shetland Is.
(U.K.)

Bergen

Stavanger

Oslo

Sundsvall

Tampe

Outer
Hebrides

Orkney Is.

Göteborg

Stockholm

Vänern

Ta

SCOTLAND

Glasgow

Edinburgh

N o r t h
S e a

Gotland

NORTHERN
IRELAND

Belfast

DENMARK

Århus

R

REP. OF
IRELAND

DUBLIN
(BAILE ÁTHA CLIATH)

UNITED

København
(Copenhagen)

Bornholm

Baltic Sea

LIT

Gdansk

RUSSIA

Ka

WALES

KINGDOM

BIRMINGHAM

Kalinin

ATLANTIC

Cardiff

ENGLAND

Elbe

HAMBURG

Hannover

Wisla

Hrod

Plymouth

LONDON

s-Gravenhage
(The Hague)

NETHER-
LANDS

BERLIN

Channel
Islands

English Channel

Bruxelles
(Brussels)

Rhine

WARSZAWA
(WARSAW)

Vistula

OCEAN

Seine

BELGIUM

Luxembourg

Bonn

GERMANY

Frankfurt

Odra (Oder)

POLAND

L

PARIS

LUXEMBOURG

PRAHA
(PRAGUE)

Loire

Strasbourg

MÜNCHEN
(MUNICH)

Danube

CZECH REP.

Bay
of
Biscay

FRANCE

Bern Vaduz

SWITZERLAND

LIECHTENSTEIN

WIEN
(VIENNA)

SLOVAK REP.

Bratislava

Cabo Fisterra

Bordeaux

Lyon

4808
Mt.
Blanc

A l p s

AUSTRIA

BUDAPEST

Cluj
Napoca

Massif

Central

Rhône

MILANO
(MILAN)

Ljubljana

SLOVENIA

HUNGARY

P y r e n e e s

Andorra
la Vella

Genova
(Genoa)

Zagreb

RO

PORTUGAL

Tagus

Ebro

ANDORRA

Marseille

SAN
MARINO

CROATIA

Lisboa
(Lisbon)

MADRID

MONACO

Apennines

BOSNIA-
HERZEGOVINA

BEOGRAD
(BELGRAD

Cabo de
São Vicente

SPAIN

BARCELONA

Corse
(Corsica)
(France)

Ajaccio

VATICAN
CITY

I
T
A
L
Y

Adriatic Sea

Sarajevo

SERBIA AND
MONTENEGRO

Valencia

Islas Baleares
(Balearic Islands)

Menorca

Sardegna
(Sardinia)
(Italy)

ROMA
(ROME)

SOFIYA
(SOFIA)

Strait of Gibraltar

Gibraltar (U.K.)

Eivissa

Mallorca

NAPOLI
(NAPLES)

Tirane
(Tirana)

Skopje

MACEDON

Ceuta
(Spain)

M e d i t e r r a n e a n

ALBANIA

RABAT

Melilla
(Spain)

Cagliari

Taranto

Kerkyra
(Corfu)

GRE

ALGER
(ALGIERS)

Tyrrhenian
Sea

Palermo

Mte. Etna
3340

Ath
(Ath

Tunis

S e a

Sicilia
(Sicily)

I o n i a n
S e a

Valletta

MALTA

AFRICA

Tarābulus
(Tripoli)

Banghāzī

D 0° E 10° F 20°

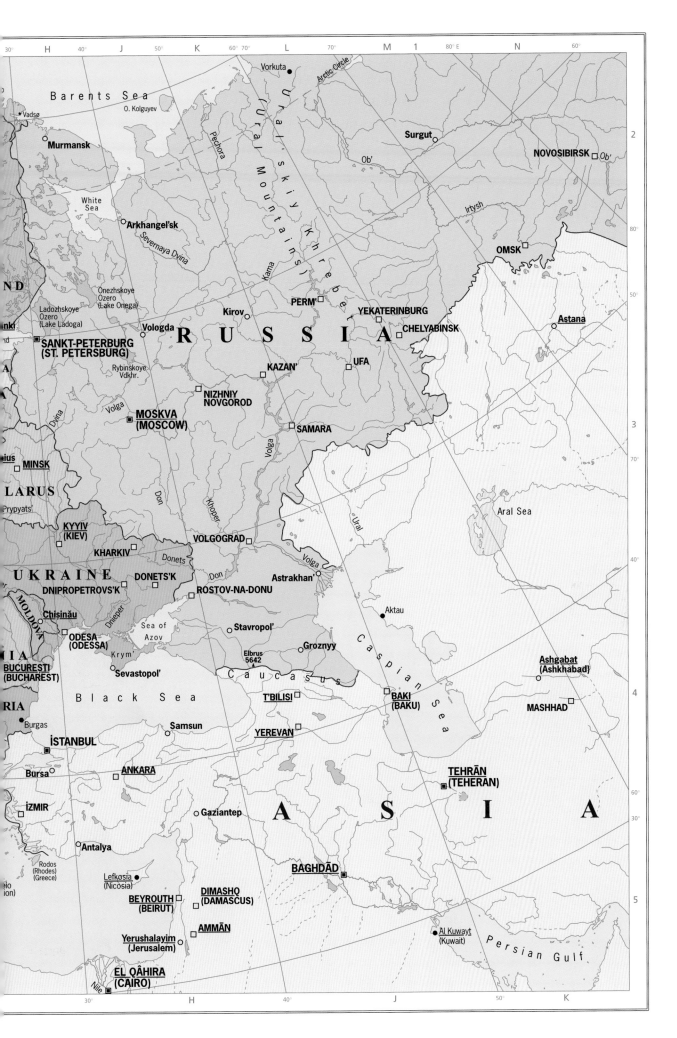

Barents Sea

Vadsø

O. Kolguyev

Murmansk

White
Sea

Arkhangel'sk

Severnaya Dvina

Vorkuta

Arctic Circle

Pechora

Surgut

Ob'

NOVOSIBIRSK   Ob'

Irtysh

OMSK

Onezhskoye
Ozero
(Lake Onega)

Ladozhskoye
Ozero
(Lake Ladoga)

Kirov

PERM'

YEKATERINBURG

CHELYABINSK

Astana

Vologda

R U S S I A

SANKT-PETERBURG
(ST. PETERSBURG)

Rybinskoye
Vdkhr.

KAZAN'

UFA

Dvina

NIZHNIY
NOVGOROD

Volga

MOSKVA
(MOSCOW)

SAMARA

MINSK

Don

Volga

LARUS

Prypyats'

Khoper

Aral Sea

KYYIV
(KIEV)

VOLGOGRAD

Ural

KHARKIV

Donets

U K R A I N E

DONETS'K

Don

Astrakhan'

DNIPROPETROVS'K

ROSTOV-NA-DONU

Volga

Aktau

MOLDOVA

Chişinău

Dnieper

Sea of
Azov

Stavropol'

ODESA
(ODESSA)

Krym'

Groznyy

Caspian Sea

Ashgabat
(Ashkhabad)

BUCUREŞTI
(BUCHAREST)

Sevastopol'

Elbrus
5642

C a u c a s u s

IA

B l a c k   S e a

T'BILISI

BAKI
(BAKU)

MASHHAD

RIA

Burgas

Samsun

YEREVAN

İSTANBUL

Bursa

ANKARA

TEHRĀN
(TEHERAN)

İZMIR

Gaziantep

A S I A

Antalya

Rodos
(Rhodes)
(Greece)

ion)

Lefkosia
(Nicosia)

BAGHDĀD

BEYROUTH
(BEIRUT)

DIMASHQ
(DAMASCUS)

AMMĀN

Al Kuwayt
(Kuwait)

P e r s i a n   G u l f

Yerushalayim
(Jerusalem)

EL QĀHIRA
(CAIRO)

Nile

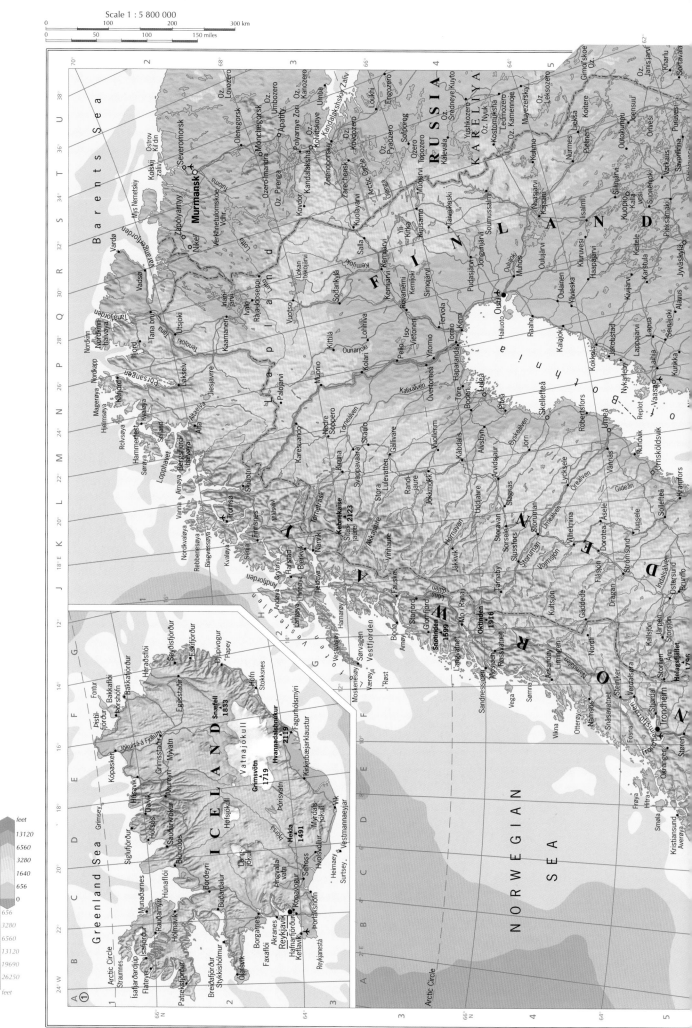

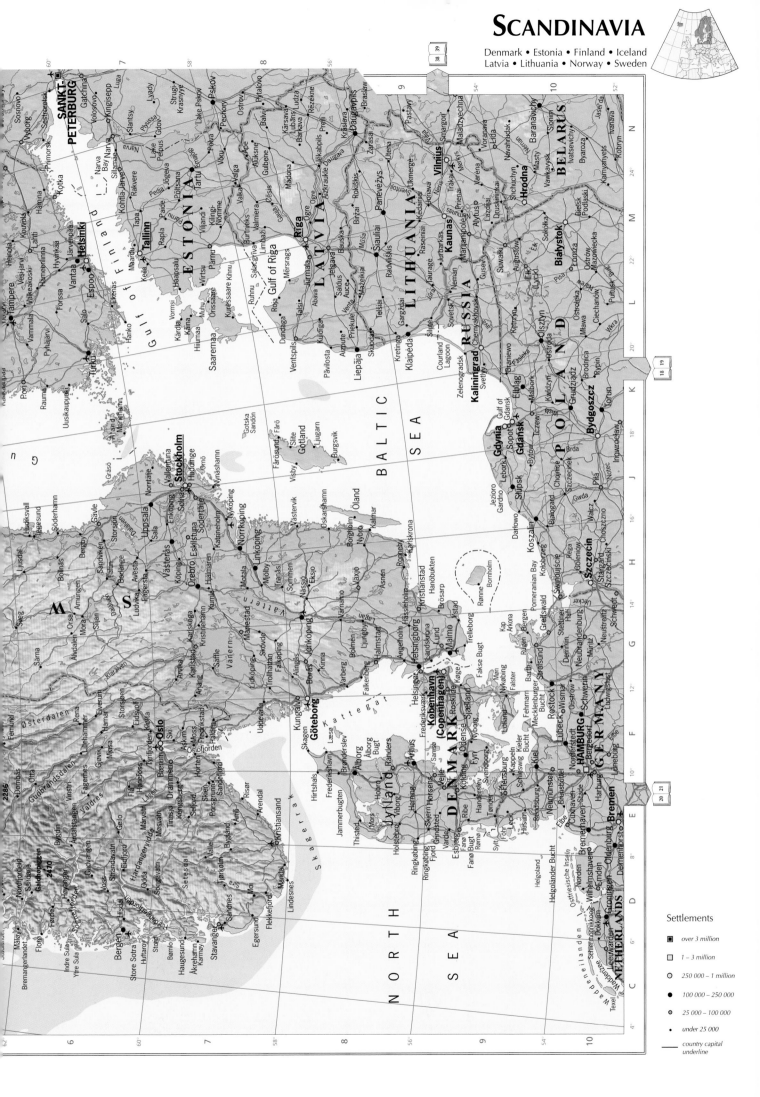

Settlements

- ■ over 3 million
- □ 1 – 3 million
- ◎ 250 000 – 1 million
- ● 100 000 – 250 000
- ◉ 25 000 – 100 000
- • under 25 000
- — country capital underline

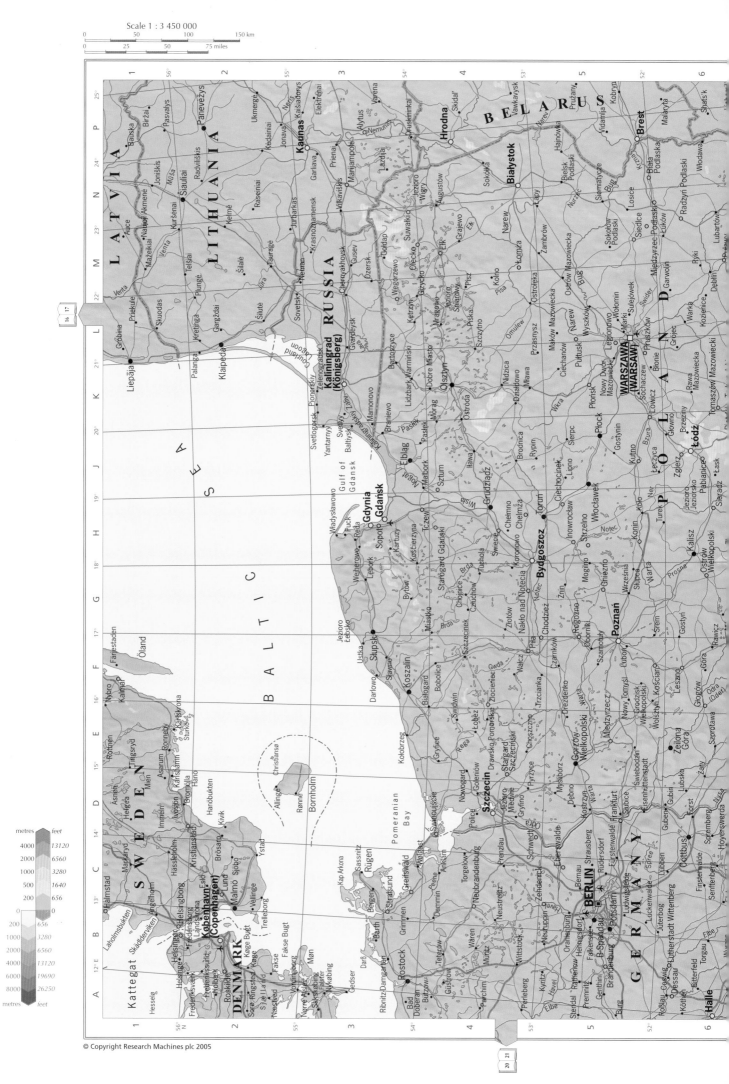

0   50   100   150 km
0 25 50 75 miles

metres   feet
4000   13120
2000   6560
1000   3280
500   1640
200   656
0   0
200   656
1000   3280
2000   6560
4000   13120
6000   19690
8000   26250
metres   feet

LATVIA

LITHUANIA

RUSSIA

BELARUS

Kaliningrad (Königsberg)

BALTIC SEA

Gulf of Gdansk

Pomeranian Bay

SWEDEN

DENMARK

København (Copenhagen)

Bornholm

Rügen

Gdańsk
Gdynia
Sopot

Hrodna

Białystok

Brest

WARSZAWA (WARSAW)

POLAND

Łódź

Poznań

Bydgoszcz

Szczecin

BERLIN

GERMANY

Halle

Kaunas

Liepāja

Klaipėda

Panevėžys
Šiauliai

Słupsk
Koszalin

16 17

20 21

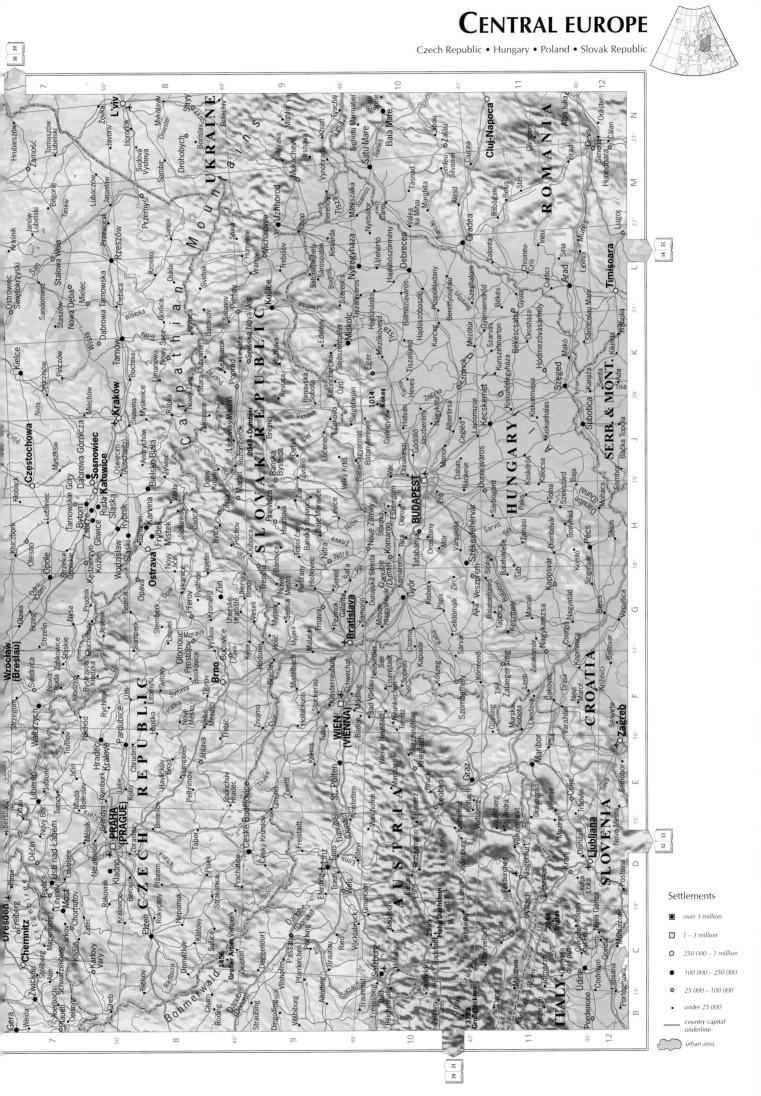

Settlements

■	over 3 million
☐	1 – 3 million
○	250 000 – 1 million
●	100 000 – 250 000
◉	25 000 – 100 000
•	under 25 000
—	country capital underline
	urban area

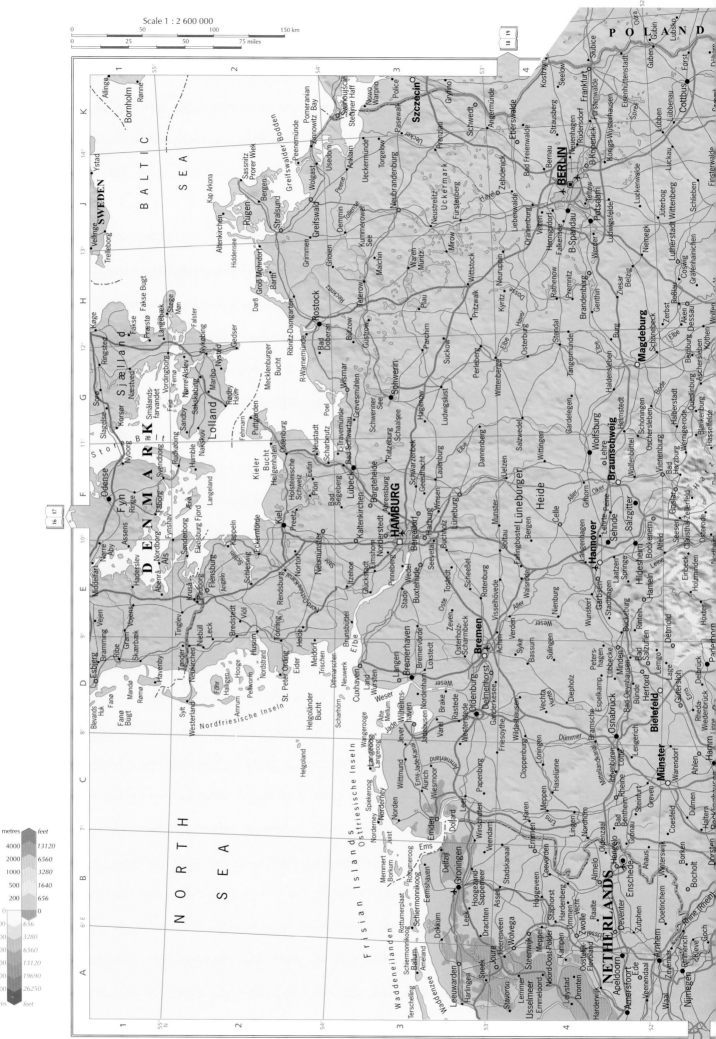

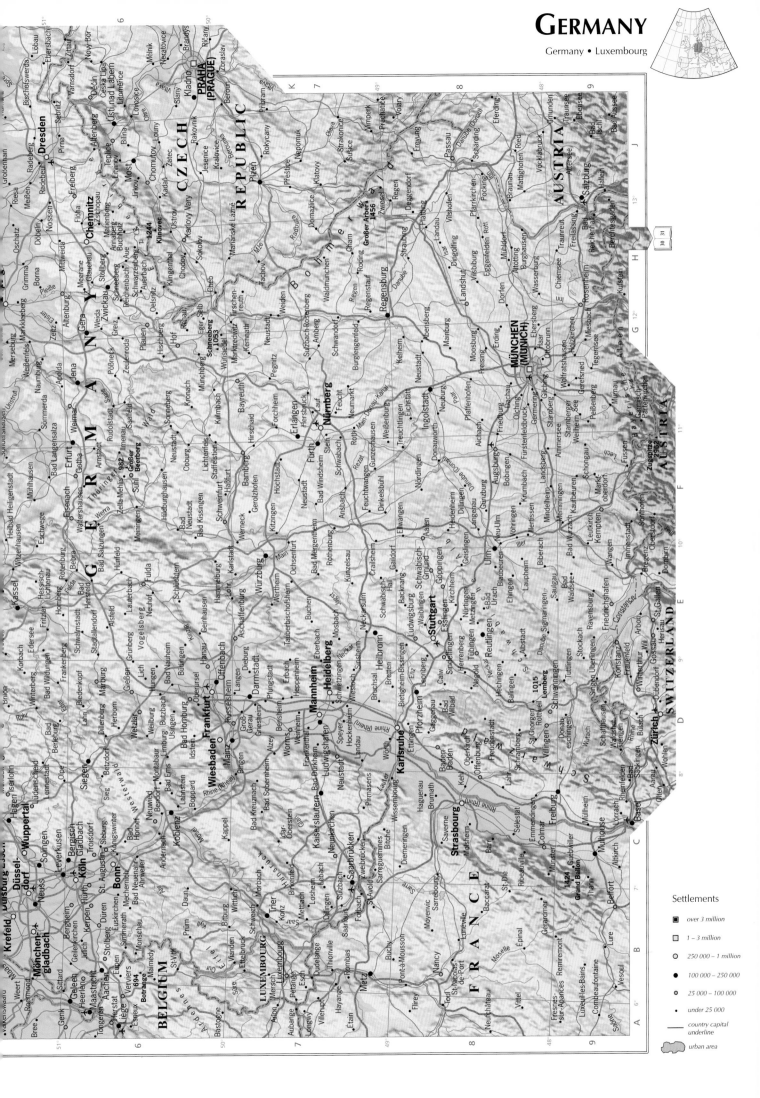

Settlements

▣	over 3 million
▢	1 – 3 million
○	250 000 – 1 million
●	100 000 – 250 000
◦	25 000 – 100 000
·	under 25 000
—	country capital underline
⬡	urban area

Scale 1 : 2 300 000

metres	feet
4000	13120
2000	6560
1000	3280
500	1640
200	656
0	0
200	656
1000	3280
2000	6560
4000	13120
6000	19690
8000	26250
metres	feet

UNITED KINGDOM

NORTH SEA

ENGLAND

Buxton
Chesterfield
Worksop
East Retford
Louth
Mablethorpe
Leek
Matlock
Bolsover
Mansfield
Lincoln
Horncastle
Alfreton
Newark-on-Trent
Skegness
Derby
Nottingham
Sleaford
Long Eaton
Grantham
Boston
The Wash
Hunstanton
Cromer
Burton-upon-Trent
Loughborough
Cannock
Melton Mowbray
Oakham
Spalding
King's Lynn
East Dereham
The Broads
Norwich
Leicester
Tamworth
Nuneaton
Walsall
BIRMINGHAM
Bedworth
Market Harborough
Corby
March
Peterborough
Wisbech
Great Yarmouth
Coventry
Rugby
Kettering
The Fens
Ely
Lowestoft
Warwick
Redditch
Royal Leamington Spa
Wellingborough
Huntingdon
Great Ouse
Thetford
Little Ouse
Diss
Southwold
Stratford-upon-Avon
Daventry
Northampton
Newmarket
Bury St Edmunds
Stowmarket
Aldeburgh
Evesham
Avon
Towcester
Bedford
Cambridge
Woodbridge
Orford Ness
Banbury
Chipping Norton
Milton Keynes
Letchworth
Royston
Stour
Sudbury
Ipswich
Bicester
Leighton Buzzard
Stevenage
Bishop's Stortford
Braintree
Felixstowe
Harwich
Woodstock
Aylesbury
Hemel Hempstead
Welwyn Garden City
Harlow
Colchester
The Naze
Witney
Oxford
High Wycombe
St. Albans
Chelmsford
Clacton-on-Sea
Thames
Abingdon
Didcot
Watford
Cheshunt
Enfield
Foulness
Swindon
Maidenhead
Slough
Brentwood
Hungerford
Reading
Windsor
LONDON
Basildon
Southend-on-Sea
Newbury
Bracknell
Camberley
Staines
Kingston upon Thames
Grays
Gravesend
Rochester
Thames
Margate
North Foreland
Ramsgate
Basingstoke
Farnborough
Woking
Epsom
Gillingham
Whitstable
Herne Bay
Andover
Aldershot
Guildford
Faversham
Canterbury
Deal
Salisbury
Alton
Reigate
Sevenoaks
Maidstone
Winchester
Haslemere
Crawley
Ashford
Dover
Romsey
Petersfield
Horsham
East Grinstead
Royal Tunbridge Wells
Folkestone
Southampton
Eastleigh
The Weald
Strait of Dover
Fareham
Havant
South Downs
Uckfield
Rye
Dungeness
Calais
Portsmouth
Chichester
Worthing
Brighton
Lewes
Bexhill
Hastings
Cap Gris-Nez
Gosport
Bognor Regis
Shoreham-by-Sea
Newhaven
Eastbourne
Lymington
The Solent
Cowes
Newport
Ryde
Beachy Head
Isle of Wight

English Channel

FRANCE (borders)

Zeebrugge
Knokke-Heist
Blankenberge
Oostende
Middelkerke
Bru
De Panne
Nieuwpoort
Torhout
Dunkerque
Diksmuide
Tielt
Roeselare
Gravelines
Veurne
Poperinge
Ieper
Kortrijk
Menen
St-Omer
Bailleul
Armentières
Tourcoing
Boulogne-sur-Mer
Hazebrouck
Lille
Roub
Desvres
Lys
Étaples
Fruges
Béthune
Lens
Berck
Montreuil
Hénin-Beaumont
Avion
Douai
Dena
Rue
Hesdin
St-Pol-sur-Ternoise
Arras
Baie de la Somme
Le Crotoy
St-Valéry-sur-Somme
Doullens
Bapaume
Péronne
Abbeville
Le Tréport
Somme
Albert
Fauville-en-Caux
Dieppe
Blangy-sur-Bresle
Amiens
Roye
Cherbourg
Fécamp
Cap d'Antifer
Étretat
Tôtes
Neufchâtel-en-Bray
Forges-les-Eaux
Breteuil
Montdidier
Tergnier
Valognes
Bolbec
Yvetôt
Marseille-en-Beauvaisis
Chaun
Baie de la Seine
Gonfreville-Orcher
Lillebonne
Barentin
Gournay-en-Bray
Beauvais
Noyon
Le Havre
Seine
Carentan
La Haye-du-Puits
Isigny-sur-Mer
Honfleur
Rouen
Clermont
Compiègne
Aisne
Bayeux
Ouistreham
St-Étienne-du-Rouvray
Creil
Soiss
Périers
Elbeuf
Louviers
Les Andelys
Méru
St-Lô
Hérouville-St-Clair
Senlis
Coutances
Caen
Lisieux
Chambly
Chantilly
Crépy-en-Valois
Villers-Bocage
Bernay
Vernon
Pontoise
Granville
Orbec
Évreux
Falaise
Vimoutiers
Conches-en-Ouche
Mantes-la-Jolie
Hertlay
St-Denis
Meaux
Jullouville
Vire
Gacé
Eure
PARIS
Bobigny
Marne-la-Vallée
Villedieu-les-Poêles
Condé-sur-Noireau
Flers
St-Germain-en-Laye
Coulommi
Tinchebray
Argentan
L'Aigle
Houdan
Versailles
Créteil
Avranches
Mortain
Rânes
Dreux
Verneuil
Trappes
Pontorson
Orsay
Orly
Courtacon

© Copyright Research Machines plc 2005

Frisian Islands

Memmert Juist
Borkum Norden
Borkum
Rottumerplaat Rottumeroog
Schiermonnikoog Schiermonnikoog Eemshaven
Terschelling Ballum Delfzijl Emden
West-Terschelling Ameland Dokkum Dollard Leer Westerstede
Oost-Vlieland Vlieland Harlingen Leeuwarden Groningen Hoogezand-Sappemeer Winschoten Papenburg Friesoythe Oldenburg Delmenhorst Ganderkesee Achim Bremen
De Cocksdorp Franeker Leek Roden Veendam Cloppenburg Vechta Wildeshausen
Texel Sneek Joure Drachten Assen Haren Löningen Bassum
Den Helder Heerenveen Stadskanaal Haselünne Sulingen
Den Burg Stavoren Lemmer Wolvega Hoogeveen Emmen Meppen Lingen Diepholz
Wieringermeer IJsselmeer Steenwijk Coevorden Nordhorn Bramsche Espelkamp Peters-hagen
Polder Markermeer Emmeloord Meppel Staphorst Lübbecke Minden
Schagen Noord-Oost-Polder Hardenberg Mittellandkanal Ibbenbüren Osnabrück Bad Oeynhausen Bünde Herford
Bergen Enkhuizen Kampen Ommen Lotte Lengerich Bad Salzuflen Lemgo
Alkmaar Hoorn Lelystad Zwolle Almelo Oldenzaal Rheine Greven Bielefeld Lage Detmold
Castricum Purmerend Oostelijk-Flevoland Raalte Borne Bad Bentheim Steinfurt 52°
IJmuiden Zaandam Edam Dronten Hengelo Gronau Gütersloh
Haarlem Marken NETHERLANDS Deventer Enschede Münster Warendorf Rheda- Delbrück
Zandvoort Bussum Apeldoorn Lochem Ahaus Wiedenbrück Paderborn
Lisse Hilversum Zutphen Coesfeld Ahlen Beckum
Katwijk Noordwijk aan Zee Amersfoort Ede Arnhem Winterswijk Dülmen Selm Lippe Lippstadt
Leiden Wassenaar Zeist Veenendaal Doetinchem Borken Bocholt Haltern Lünen Werl Soest Büren
Scheveningen Alphen Utrecht Westervoort Zevenaar Rhine (Rhein) Wesel Dorsten Recklinghausen Unna Warstein
's-Gravenhage Delft Gouda Lek Nijmegen Emmerich Kleve Xanten Gelsenkirchen Herne Dortmund Menden Brilon
(The Hague) hoek van Holland Waal Goch Oberhausen Bottrop Bochum Arnsberg Meschede
Europoort Rotterdam Gorinchem Maas Oss 's Hertogenbosch Venray Moers Duisburg Mülheim Essen Witten Iserlohn Korbach
Schiedam Putten Waalwijk Geldern Venlo Krefeld Hagen Winterberg
Voorne Dordrecht Tilburg Helmond Deurne Mönchengladbach Düssel- Wuppertal Lüdenscheid Frankenberg
Goeree Oosterhout Eindhoven dorf Neuss Solingen Remscheid Lennestadt Bad Berleburg
Zierikzee Breda Valkenswaard Roermond Grevenbroich Dormagen Gummersbach Ölpe
Duiveland Roosendaal Weert Leverkusen Bergisch Biedenkopf
Oosterschelde Bergen op Zoom Essen Lommel Bree Bergheim Gladbach Siegen Marburg
Tholen Oudenbosch Turnhout Mol Geel Sittard Geilenkirchen Jülich Köln Hürth Troisdorf Siegburg (Sieg) GERMANY Dillenburg
bord- Terneuzen Herentals Diest Genk Geleen Heerlen Kerpen Bonn St. Augustin Betzdorf Herborn
Hulst St. Niklaas Mechelen Aarschot Hasselt Maastricht Aachen Düren Euskirchen Königswinter Gießen
Lokeren Lier Leuven St. Kerkrade Eschweiler Stolberg Brühl Eupen Simmerath Rheinbach Bad Weilburg Wetzlar Lich
Gent Scheldt Tienen Truiden Tongeren Herstal Verviers Mechernich Honnef Westerwald Butzbach
Aalst Vilvoorde Liège Esneux Sprimont Monschau Bad Neuenahr- Remagen Neuwied Montabaur Limburg Bad Nauheim
Mere Asse Bruxelles Waremme Amay Seraing 694 Spa Schleiden Ahrweiler Andernach Bendorf Bad Usingen Bad Homburg
(Brussels) Halle Gembloux Huy Botrange Blankenheim Koblenz Ems Idstein Oberursel
Enghien Waterloo Nivelles Andenne Ciney Malmédy Taunus Bad Frankfurt
Ath Soignies La Louvière Namur Dinant St-Vith Lahnstein Homburg
Mons Binche Thuin Mettet Marche Prüm Daun Boppard Wiesbaden
Boussu Florennes Rochefort Eifel Kyll Mosel Rüssels- Mainz Groß-
Maubeuge Philippeville Givet St-Hubert Bitburg Wittlich Rhine (Rhein) heim Bingen Ingelheim Gerau
Avesnes- Couvin Bastogne ARDENNES Bad Kreuznach Darmstadt
Fourmies sur-Helpe Revin Our Clervaux Schweich Griesheim
Rumigny Neufchâteau Bad Pfungstadt
Charleville- Ettelbruck Morbach Sobernheim Bensheim
Marle Mézières Sedan Vianden LUXEMBOURG Mersch Trier Idar-Oberstein Heppenheim Weinheim
aon Florenville Konz Birkenfeld Glan Kirchheimbolanden Frankenthal
Reims Semois Arlon Luxembourg Saarburg Losheim Worms Mannheim
Rethel Aubange Saar Mettlach Merzig Landstuhl Neunkirchen Kaiserslautern Ludwigshafen
Montmédy Virton Longwy Esch Dudelange Dillingen Saarlouis Sulzbach Neustadt Schwetzingen Speyer Hockenheim
Tanney Stenay Villerupt Thionville Saarbrücken Zweibrücken Pirmasens Dahn Germersheim
Mazagran Hayange Völklingen Forbach Dillingen Bad Dürkheim
Fismes Rombas Diemeringen Landau Worth Karlsruhe
Epernay Verdun Étain Metz St-Avold Sarreguemines Bitche Wissembourg Bruchsal
Châlons- Souilly Pont-à-Mousson Buchy Haguenau Ettlingen
Champaubert sur-Marne St-Mihiel Flirey Sarre Rastatt
Sézanne Moyenvic Sarrebourg Brumath Baden- Gaggenau
Vitry-le-François Bar-le-Duc Toul Nancy Saverne Baden Bad Wildbad Forbach
Commercy

694
Botrange

FRANCE

ARDENNES Eifel Westerwald Taunus

Rhine (Rhein)

53°

52°

51°

50°

49°

20 21

Settlements

■	over 3 million
□	1 – 3 million
○	250 000 – 1 million
●	100 000 – 250 000
◎	25 000 – 100 000
•	under 25 000
—	country capital underline
⬭	urban area

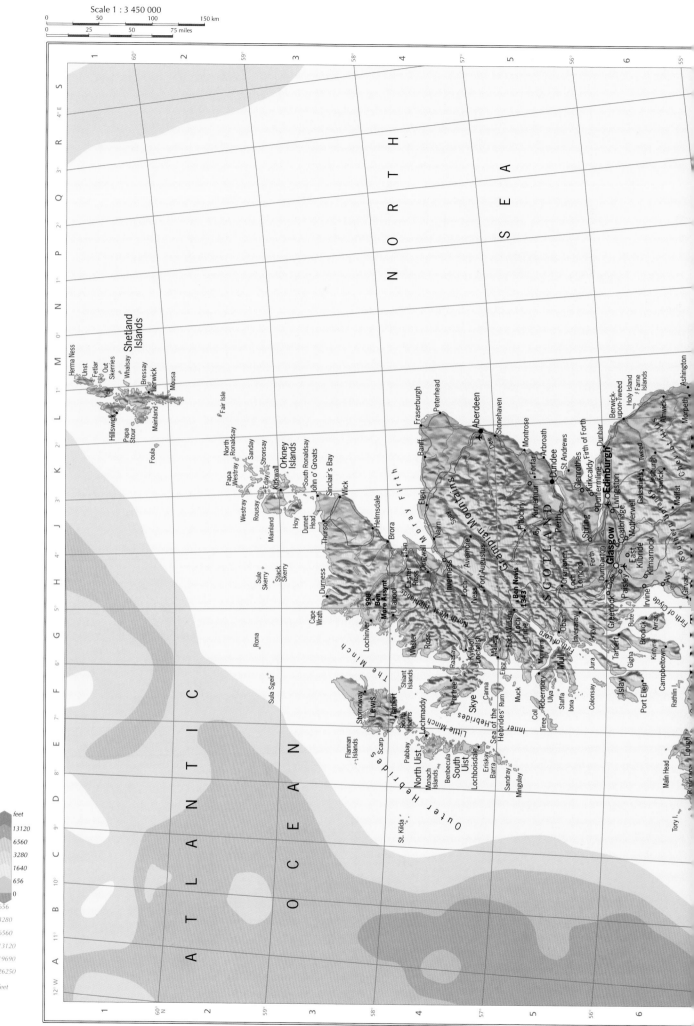

Scale 1 : 3 450 000

| 0 | 50 | 100 | 150 km |
| 0 | 25 | 50 | 75 miles |

NORTH SEA

ATLANTIC OCEAN

Shetland Islands

Herma Ness
Unst
Fetlar
Yell
Out Skerries
Whalsay
Bressay
Lerwick
Mousa
Hillswick
Papa Stour
Mainland
Foula
Fair Isle

Orkney Islands

North Ronaldsay
Papa Westray
Westray
Sanday
Stronsay
Rousay
Mainland
Eday
Kirkwall
South Ronaldsay
Hoy
John o' Groats
Dunnet Head
Sinclair's Bay
Wick
Sule Skerry
Stack Skerry
Thurso
Helmsdale
Durness
Cape Wrath
Brora
Rona
Lochinver
Ben More Assynt 998
Ulapool
Tain
Dornoch
Easter Ross
Dingwall
Nairn
Elgin
Banff
Fraserburgh
Peterhead
Aberdeen
Stonehaven
Montrose
Arbroath
Dundee
St Andrews
Kirkcaldy
Dunfermline
Glenrothes
Dunbar
Berwick-upon-Tweed
Holy Island
Farne Islands
Bamburgh
Alnwick
Morpeth
Ashington

Sula Sgeir

Wester Ross
Inverness
Loch Ness
Fort Augustus
Aviemore
Grampian Mountains
Kingussie
Pitlochry
Forfar
Kirriemuir
Perth
Stirling
Edinburgh
Livingston
Motherwell
Coatbridge
Galashiels
Jedburgh
Hawick
Moffat
Cheviot Hills
Southern Uplands

The Minch

Stornoway
Lewis
Tarbert
Harris
Scarp
Pabbay
North Uist
Benbecula
South Uist
Lochboisdale
Barra
Sandray
Mingulay
Eriskay
Monach Islands
Lochmaddy

Flannan Islands

St. Kilda

Shiant Islands
Portree
Raasay
Skye
Canna
Rum
Eigg
Muck
Coll
Tiree
Staffa
Iona
Ulva
Mull
Tobermory
Colonsay
Jura
Islay
Port Ellen
Gigha
Rathlin I.
Campbeltown
Kintyre

Sea of the Hebrides
Inner Hebrides
Little Minch
Outer Hebrides

North West Highlands
Kyle of Lochalsh
Mallaig
Loch Linnhe
Fort William
Ben Nevis 1343
Loch Lomond
Morvern
Oban
Inveraray
Argyll
Bute
Brodick
Arran
Tarbert
Greenock
Paisley
Glasgow
East Kilbride
Kilmarnock
Irvine
Ayr
Girvan
Firth of Clyde
Dumbarton
Clyde

Malin Head
Tory I.
Lough
Mull of

SCOTLAND

Moray Firth
Spey
Dee

© Copyright Research Machines plc 2005

metres	feet
4000	13120
2000	6560
1000	3280
500	1640
200	656
0	0
200	656
1000	3280
2000	6560
4000	13120
6000	19690
8000	26250
metres	feet

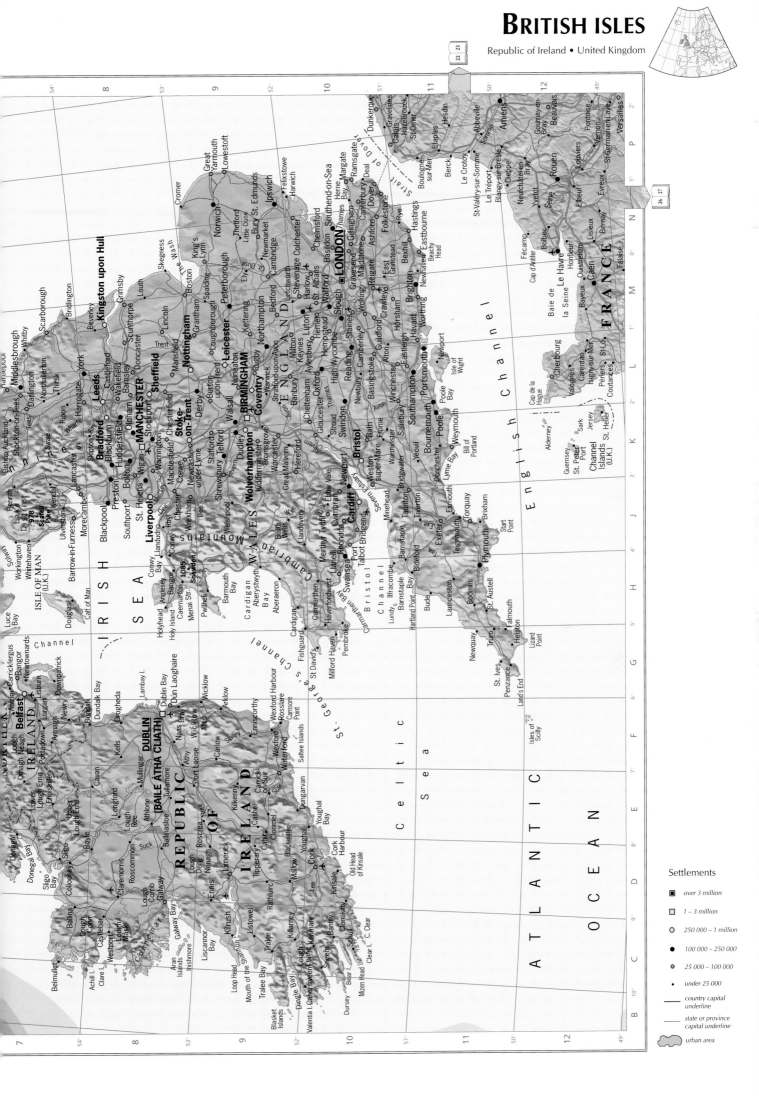

Settlements

■	over 3 million
□	1 – 3 million
○	250 000 – 1 million
●	100 000 – 250 000
◉	25 000 – 100 000
•	under 25 000
—	country capital underline
—	state or province capital underline
⬡	urban area

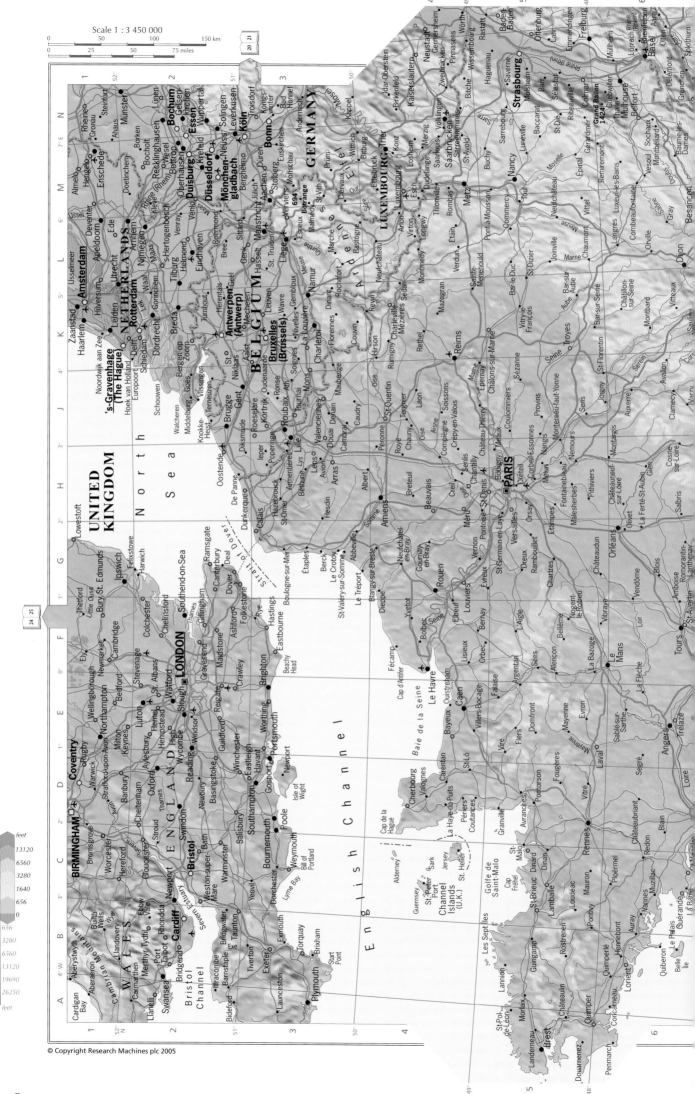

Scale 1 : 3 450 000

| 0 | 50 | 100 | 150 km |

| 0 | 25 | 50 | 75 miles |

metres feet
4000 13120
2000 6560
1000 3280
500 1640
200 656
0 0
200 656
1000 3280
2000 6560
4000 13120
6000 19690
8000 26250
metres feet

UNITED KINGDOM

ENGLAND

WALES

NETHERLANDS

Amsterdam

Rotterdam

's-Gravenhage (The Hague)

NORTH SEA

North Sea

English Channel

Strait of Dover

Bristol Channel

BELGIUM

Bruxelles (Brussels)

Antwerpen (Antwerp)

GERMANY

Köln

Bonn

Essen

Duisburg

Düsseldorf

Mönchen-gladbach

LUXEMBOURG

Luxembourg

Strasbourg

PARIS

LONDON

BIRMINGHAM

Coventry

Bristol

Cardiff

Swansea

Newport

© Copyright Research Machines plc 2005

FRANCE

Andorra • Channel Islands
France • Monaco

Settlements

- ◼ over 3 million
- ◻ 1 – 3 million
- ◯ 250 000 – 1 million
- ● 100 000 – 250 000
- ◉ 25 000 – 100 000
- · under 25 000
- ▬ country capital underline
- ▬ state or province capital underline
- urban area

Scale 1 : 3 450 000

0   50   100 km
0   25   50 miles

ATLANTIC OCEAN

Costa Verde

Bay of Biscay

Cabo Ortegal
Pta da Estaca de Bares
Ortigueira
Cervo
Cabo Peñas
Aviles
Gijón
Viveiro
Foz
Ribadeo
Luarca
Villaviciosa
Ferrol
As Pontes de García Rodríguez
Tineo
Pola de Siero
Llanes
Santander
Santoña
Getxo
A Coruña
Betanzos
Villalba
A Fonsagrada
Oviedo
Mieres
Laviana
Laredo
Barakaldo
Portugalete
Cambre
Carballo
Guitiriz
Lugo
Cangas de Narcea
Cabañaquinta (Aller)
Bilbao
Camariñas
Ordes Sta. Comba
Ordes
Melide
Becerreá
Villablino
Cordillera Cantábrica
Embalse del Ebro
Trespaderne
Cabo Fisterra (Cape Finisterre)
Santiago
Teo
Sarria
Bembibre
León
Cistierna
Reinosa
Ebro
Sedano
Nava
Muros
Noia
Padrón
Lalín
Monforte de Lemos
Ponferrada
Astorga
Sahagún
Guardo
Briviesca
Porto do Son
A Estrada
Sil
O Barco (Barco de Valdeorras)
La Bañeza
Burgos
Hortigüela
Cabo Corrubedo
Sta. Eugenia (Ribeira)
Villagarcía
O Grove
Pontevedra
Carballiño
Ourense
Miño
Benavente
Palencia
Lerma
Navalero
Marín
Cangas
Redondela
Ponteareas
Xinzo de Limia
A Gudiña
Esla
Venta de Baños
El P. de D.
Vigo
Porriño
Verín
Villalpando
Aranda de Duero
Peñafiel
Tui
O Seixo
Caminha
Ponte da Barca
Chaves
Bragança
Miranda do Douro
Emb. de Ricobayo
Valladolid
Duero
Duero
Cerezo de Abajo
Viana do Castelo
Venda Nova
Mirandela
Zamora
Toro
Tordesillas
Segovia
Barcelos
Braga
Guimarães
Vila Real
Tua
Sabor
Alaejos
Medina del Campo
Puerto de Navacerrada
Guada
Póvoa de Varzim
Vila do Conde
Douro
Meda
Lumbrales
Salamanca
Peñaranda de Bracamonte
Arévalo
Sistema Central
Colmenar Viejo
S. Sebastián de los Reyes
Matosinhos
Porto
Gondomar
Trancoso
Pinhel
Emb. de Almendra
Fuentesauco
Alba
Ávila
Collado-Villalba
Alcobendas
Alcalá de H
Vila Nova de Gaia
Espinho
São João da Madeira
Viseu
Vilar Formoso
Ciudad Rodrigo
Guijuelo
Emb. de Sta. Teresa
MADRID
Torrejón de Ard
Murtosa
Santa Comba Dão
Guarda
Sierra de Gata
Béjar
2592 Pico Almanzor
Alcorcón
Móstoles
Getafe
Alcalá de H
Aveiro
Sierra da Estrela
Covilhã
Emb. de Gabriel y Galán
Parla
Valdemoro
Cabo Mondego
Figueira da Foz
Estrela 1993
Fundão
Coria
Plasencia
Tiétar
Talavera de la Reina
Maqueda
Aranjuez
Tagus (Ta
Coimbra
Soure
Pombal
Navalmoral de la Mata
Toledo
Ocaña
Tarancó
Merinha Grande
Leiria
Sertã
Castelo Branco
Emb. de Alcántara Uno
SPAIN
Nazaré
Tomar
Bgem. do Castelo de Bode
Cáceres
Trujillo
Navahermosa
Madridejos
Campo de Criptar
Peniche
Cabo Carvoeiro
Caldas da Rainha
Entroncamento
Abrantes
Nisa
Valencia de Alcántara
Emb. de García Sola
Alcázar de S. Juan
Socuélla
Torres Vedras
Santarém
PORTUGAL
Portalegre
Alburquerque
Miajadas
Navalvillar de Pela
Puebla de Don Rodrigo
Guadiana
Daimiel
Tomelloso
Vila Franca de Xira
Tagus (Tejo)
Coruche
Môra
Bgem. do Maranhão
Monforte
Montijo
Mérida
Don Benito
Abenójar
Ciudad Real
Manzanares
Amadora
Lisboa (Lisbon)
Estoril
Cascais
Almada
Barreiro
Setúbal
Évora
Elvas
Badajoz
Almendralejo
Castuera
Emb. de la Serena
Cabeza del Buey
Puertollano
Valdepeñas
Costa do Sol
Cabo de Espichel
Alcácer do Sal
Sado
Portel
Santa Marta
Villafranca de los Barros
Zafra
Sierra Morena
Emb. del Guadalmena
Be
Grândola
Ferreira do Alentejo
Beja
Amareleja
Jerez de los Caballeros
Llerena
Azuaga
Pozoblanco
Villanueva de Córdoba
La Carolina
Sines
Aljustrel
R. Ardila
Moura
Fregenal de la Sierra
Emb. del Bembézar
Montoro
Andújar
Bailén
Linares
Baeza
Úbeda
Castro Verde
Serpa
Cortegana
Guadalquivir
Córdoba
Martos
Jaén
Jódar
Emb. d Negrat
Odemira
Bgem. de Sta. Clara
Alcoutim
Valverde del Camino
Lora del Río
Palma del Río
La Carlota
Écija
Montilla
Baena
Alcaudete
Alcalá la Real
Priego de Córdoba
Emb. de Guadalhorce
Monchique
Gibraleón
Sevilla
Carmona
Marchena
Puente-Genil
Lucena
Rute
Cordillera Per
Bordeira
Aljezur
Portimão
Lepe
Huelva
Almonte
Alcalá de Guadaira
Dos Hermanas
Osuna
Archidona
Genil
Granada
Guadi
Sagres
Lagos
Albufeira
Loulé
Tavira
Ayamonte
Morón de la Frontera
Utrera
Antequera
Vélez-Málaga
Sierra Nevada
3482 Mulhacén
Cabo de S. Vicente
Faro
Olhão
Golfo de Cádiz
Las Cabezas de San Juan
Olvera
Alhaurín el Grande
Nerja
Almuñécar
Motril
Adra
Playa de Castilla
Lebrija
Villamartín
Ronda
Málaga
Torremolinos
Fuengirola
ATLANTIC OCEAN
Sanlúcar de Barrameda
Arcos de la Frontera
Emb. de Guadalhorce
Marbella
Estepona
Costa del Sol
Jerez de la Frontera
El Puerto de Sta. María
Puerto Real
Medina Sidonia
San Roque
La Línea
Cádiz
San Fernando
Chiclana de la Frontera
Vejer de la Frontera
Barbate
Algeciras
Gibraltar (U.K.)
Cabo de Trafalgar
Tarifa
Costa del Sol
Isla de Alborán (Spain)
Cap Spartel
Strait of Gibraltar
Ceuta (Spain)
Tanger
Cap Negro
El Borj
Tétouan
Cap des Fourch
Asilah
Dar Ben Karricha el Behri
Oued Laou
MOROCCO
Bou Ahmed

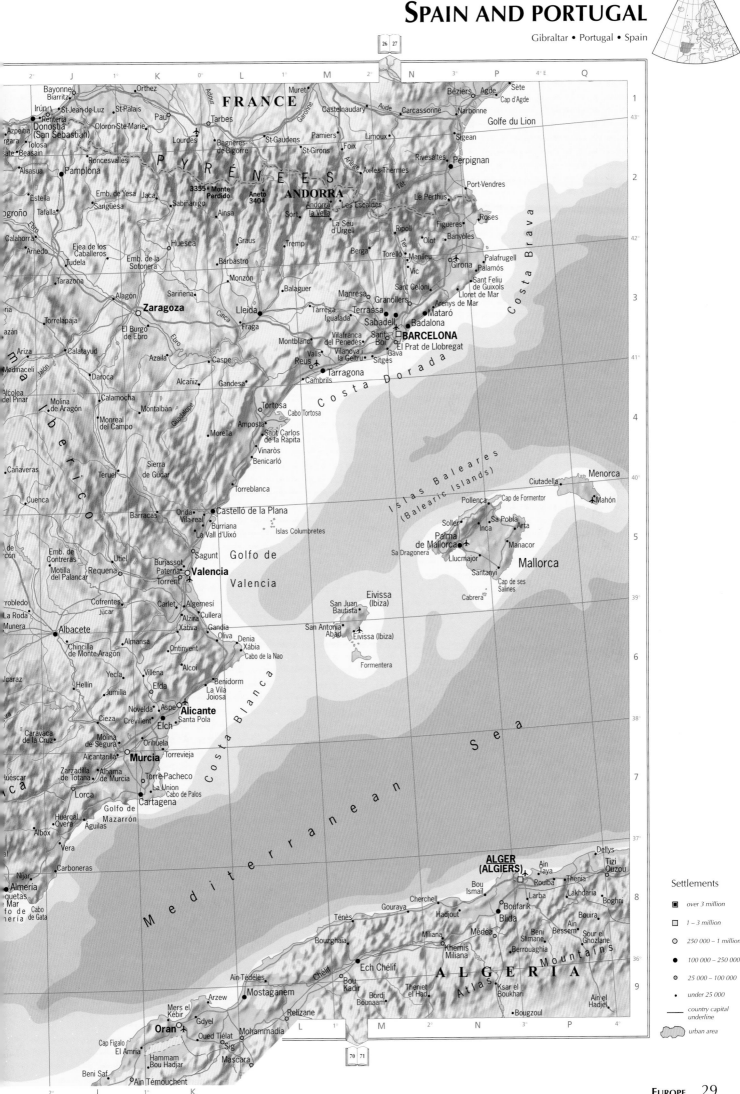

Settlements

■	over 3 million
□	1 – 3 million
○	250 000 – 1 million
●	100 000 – 250 000
◌	25 000 – 100 000
•	under 25 000
—	country capital underline
	urban area

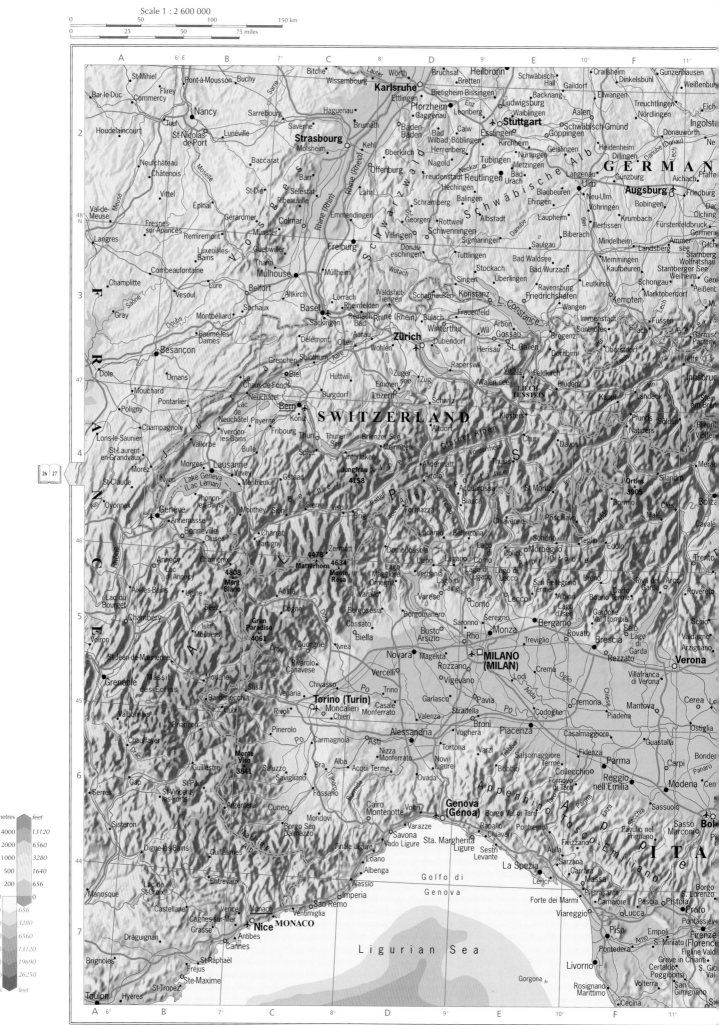

20 | 21

32 | 33

34 | 35

CZECH REPUBLIC

SLOVAK REP.

AUSTRIA

HUNGARY

SLOVENIA

CROATIA

BOSNIA-
HERZEGOVINA

Regensburg
Zwiesel
Vimperk
Prachatice
Moravské Budějovice
Kyjov
Uhérský Brod
Veselí

Regensdauf
Danube (Donau)
Straubing
Regen
Trebon
Lužnice
České Budějovice
Znojmo
Mikulov
Břeclav
Holíč
Myjava
Senica
Nové Město

Abensberg
Deggendorf
Český Krumlov
Gmünd
Schrems
Thaya
Dyje
Drasenhofen
Myjava
Piešťany
Hlohovec

Neustadt
Plattling
Kaplice
Horn
Mistelbach
Zistersdorf
Malacky
Trnava
Seréd

Mainburg
Dingolfing
Landau
Rohrbach
Freistadt
Zwettl
Krems
Hollabrunn
Stockerau
Angern
Pezinok
Senec
Galanta

Landshut
Isar
Vilshofen
Schärding
Danube (Donau)
St. Pölten
WIEN (VIENNA)
Klosterneuburg
Tulln
Bratislava
Malý Dunaj
Šamorín

Moosburg
Vilsbiburg
Pfarrkirchen
Pocking
Linz
Melk
Mödling
Schwechat
Danube
Dunajská Streda

Erding
Dorfen
Altötting
Braunau
Grieskirchen
Traun
Enns
Amstetten
Baden
Traiskirchen
Bruck
Danube (Dunaj)

MÜNCHEN (MUNICH)
Mühldorf
Burghausen
Ried
Wels
Steyr
Scheibbs
Bad Vöslau
Neusiedler See
Mosonmagyaróvár
Győr

Haar
Ebersberg
Wasserburg
Maffighofen
Vöcklabruck
Kremsmünster
Waidhofen
Lilienfeld
Wiener Neustadt
Eisenstadt
Pamhagen
Jánossomorja

Chiemsee
Traunreut
Oberndorf
Atter see
Gmunden
Klaus
Mariazell
Ternitz
Neunkirchen
Sopron
Rabca
Csorna

Miesbach
Rosenheim
Freilassing
Salzburg
Bad Ischl
Traunsee
Ebensee
Windischgarsten
Murzzuschlag
Aspang Markt
Kapuvar
Köszeg
Hegyfalu
Rába
Pápa

Reichenhall
Hallein
Bad Ausee
AUSTRIA
Liezen
Rottenmann
Eisenerz
Krieglach
Hartberg
Oberwart
Sárvár
Celldömölk

Berchtesgaden
Bischofshofen
Gröbming
Erns
Bruck
Kapfenberg
Güssing
Szombathely

Kufstein
Saalfelden
Niedere Tauern
Föhnsdorf
Knittelfeld
Leoben
Raab
Feistritz
Lafnitz
Vasvár
Zalaszentgrót
Tapolca

Wörgl
Schwaz
Mittersill
Zell am See
Badgastein
Tamsweg
Judenburg
Köflach
Graz
Gleisdorf
Zala
Zalaegerszeg
Keszthely
Balaton
Fonyod

Mayrhofen
Großglockner 3798
Hohe Tauern
Lungau
Friesach
Voitsberg
Feldbach
Körmend
Marcali

Brunico
Matrei
Lienz
Gmünd
Wolfsberg
St. Andrä
Leibnitz
Murska Sobota
Lendava
Lenti
Zalakomár
Marcali

Dobbiaco
Oberdrauburg
Spittal
Feldkirchen
St. Veit
Völkermarkt
Pesnica
Letenye
Nagykanizsa

Cortina d'Ampezzo
Mauthen
Hermagor
Villach
Klagenfurt
Dravograd
Maribor
Ptuj
Čakovec
Csurgó
Nagyatád

Vigo di Cadore
Ampezzo
Tolmezzo
Tarvisio
Ferlach
Sloveni Gradec
Slovenská Bistrica
Varaždin
Koprivnica
Drava
Barcs

Pieve di Cadore
Gemona del Friuli
Triglav 2864
Ješenice
Mozirje
Velenje
Novi Marof
Krapinske Toplice
Grubišno Polje

Longarone
Spilimbergo
Cividale del Friuli
Bled
Tržić
Celje
Trbovlje
Zabok
Bjelovar
Virovitica

Belluno
Sedico
Udine
Tolmin
Kranj
Škofja Loka
Domžale
Ljubljana
Sava
Zelina
Casma

Vittorio Veneto
Pordenone
Nova Gorica
SLOVENIA
Logatec
Krško
Brežice
Zapresić
Zagreb
Velika Gorica
CROATIA
Grubišno Polje

Conegliano
Sacile
Oderzo
Codroipo
Palmanova
Gorizia
Vipava
Cerknica
Trebnje
Novo Mesto
Samobor
Popovača
Daruvar

Montebelluna
Treviso
Latisana
Monfalcone
Postojna
Ribnica
Metlika
Jastrebarsko
Kutina
Pakrac

Bassano del Grappa
Cittadella
Preganziol
San Donà di Piave
Caorle
Portogruaro
Golfo di Trieste
Trieste
Pivka
Snežnik 1796
Kočevje
Karlovac
Sisak
Cesma

Mestre
Lido di Jesolo
Izola
Koper
Umag
Buje
Rupa
Rijeka
Vrbovsko
Petrinja
Glina
Kostajnica
Nova Gradiška

Venezia (Venice)
Piove di Sacco
Golfo di Venezia
Novigrad
Istra
Pazin
Lovran
Kraljevica
Delnice
Ogulin
Slunj
Velita Kladuša
Bosanski Novi
Bosanska Kostajnica
Bosanska Dubica
Bosanska Gradiška

Chioggia
Cavarzere
Poreč
Baderna
Labin
Porozina
Novi Vinodolski
Rakovica
Bosanska Krupa
Bosanski Novi
Prijedor

Abano Terme
Monselice
Adria
Rovinj
Vodnjan
Cres
Krk
Plavnik
Prvic
Senj
Otočac
Bihać
Banja Luka

Rovigo
Po
Porto Tolle
Fažana
Pula
Krk
Cres
Rab
Titova Korenica
Bosanska Krupa
Sanski Most
Kotor Varoš

Codigoro
Comacchio
Osor
Rab
Gospić
Bosanski Petrovac
Ključ

Portomaggiore
Argenta
Valli di Comacchio
Unije
Lošinj
Pag
Vaganski Vrh 1758
Drvar
Mrkonjić Grad
Jajce

Lugo
Ravenna
Susak
Pag
Gračac
Bosansko Grahovo
Donji Vakuf

Faenza
Cervia
Silba
Maun
Nin
Knin
Glamoč

Forlì
Cesena
Cesenatico
Rimini
Premuda
Olib
Molat
Sestrunj
Vir
Zadar
Benkovac
Livno
Duvno

Mercato Saraceno
Riccione
Cattolica
Pesaro
Fano
Dugi Otok
Pašman
Biograd
Drniš
Trilj

Bagno di Romagna
San Marino
SAN MARINO
Urbino
Fossombrone
Senigallia
Žut
Murter
Vodice
Šibenik
Sinj
Posušje

Bibbiena
Urbania
Sansepolcro
Falconara Marittima
Ancona
Kornat
Žirje
Trogir
Split
Omiš
Imotski
Makarska

Arezzo
Città di Castello
Cagli
Jesi
Osimo
Castelfidardo
Šolta
Supetar
Brač

Castiglion Fiorentino
Gubbio
Fabriano
Macerata
Potenza
Civitanova Marche
Hvar

Adriatic Sea

Golfo di Venezia

Dinaric Alps

Settlements

Symbol	Population
□	1 – 3 million
○	250 000 – 1 million
●	100 000 – 250 000
◉	25 000 – 100 000
•	under 25 000
—	country capital underline
	urban area

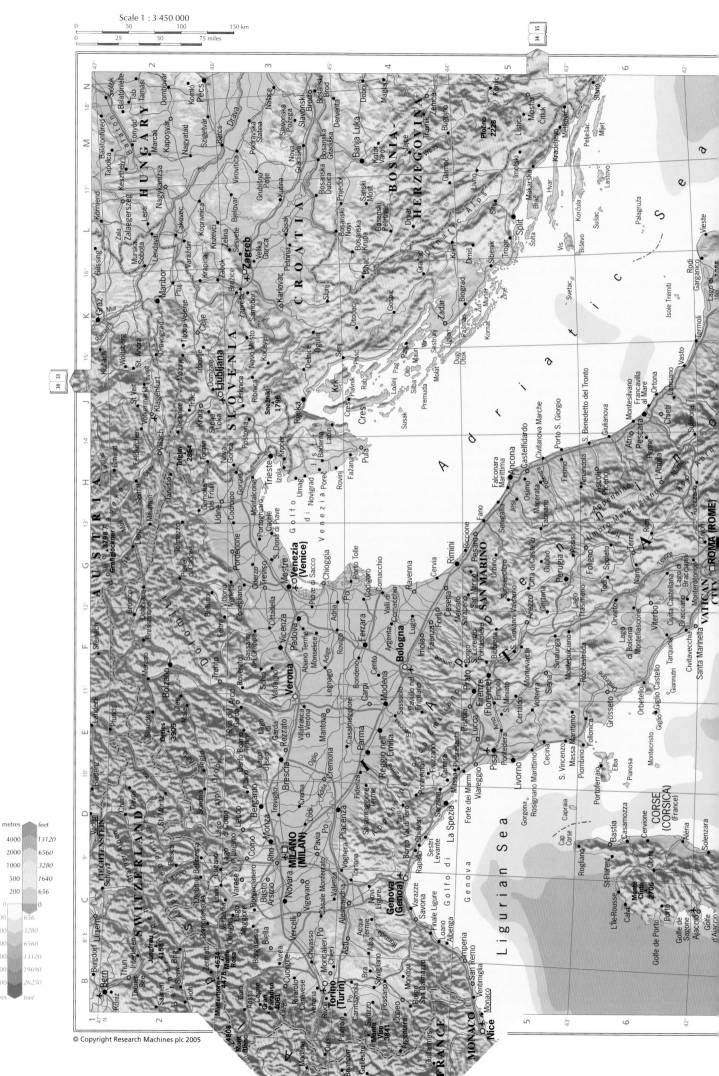

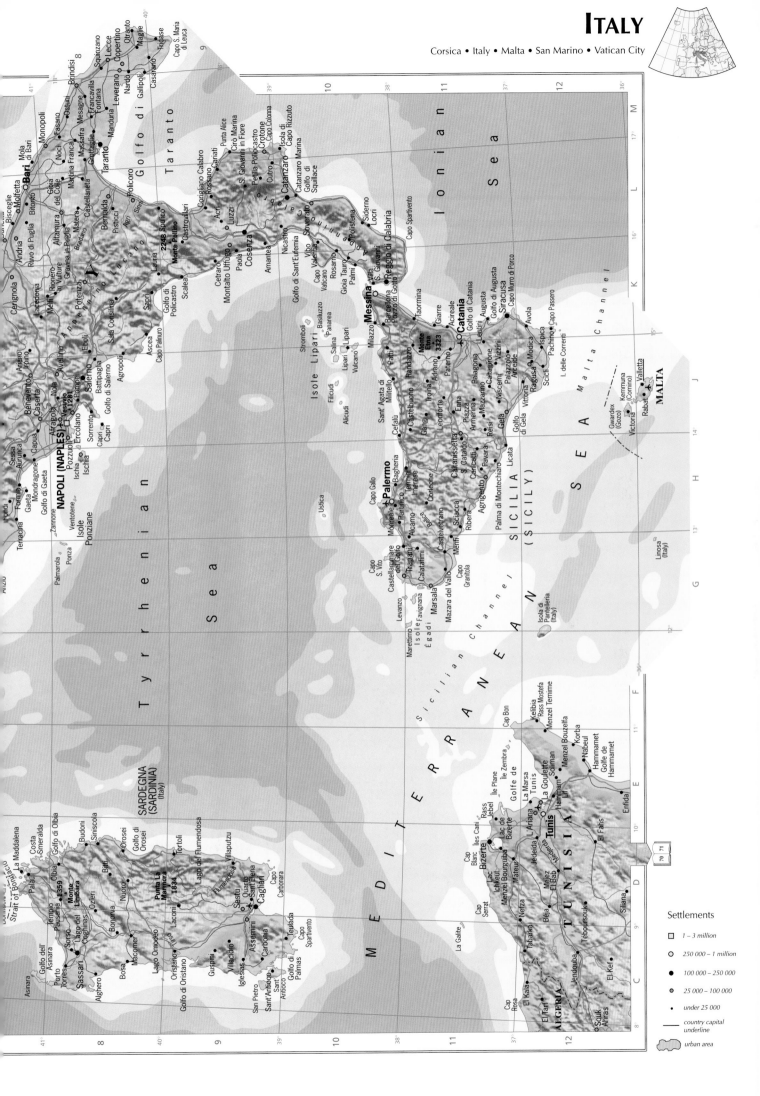

UKRAINE

MOLDOVA

Chişinău

ODESA
(ODESSA)

UKRAINE

ROMANIA

Cluj-Napoca

2544
Vârful
Moldoveanu

BUCUREŞTI
(BUCHAREST)

Constanţa

Drobeta-
Turnu Severin

Craiova

Mouths of
the Danube

Danube
(Dunărea)

Midzor
2169

Varna

BLACK

Pleven

SEA

Stara Planina

SOFIJA
(SOFIA)

BULGARIA

Stara Zagora

Burgas

Musala
2925

Plovdiv

Edirne

TURKEY

İSTANBUL

Kartal

GREECE

Pendik

Marmara Denizi
(Sea of Marmara)

Settlements

■	over 3 million
□	1 – 3 million
○	250 000 – 1 million
●	100 000 – 250 000
◉	25 000 – 100 000
•	under 25 000
——	country capital underline
——	state or province capital underline
⬡	urban area

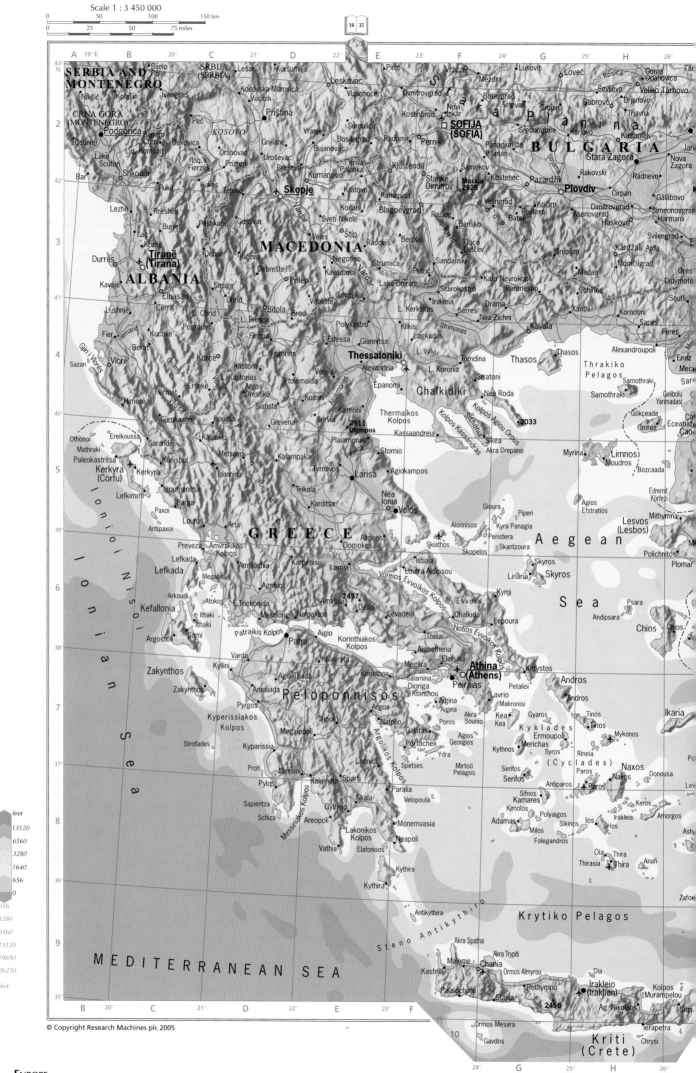

0   50   100   150 km

0   25   50   75 miles

SERBIA AND
MONTENEGRO

CRNA GORA
(MONTENEGRO)
Podgorica

Niksić   Kolašin   Ivangrad

Bijelo
Polje

SRBIJA
(SERBIA)   Lešak   Kuršumlija

Kosovska Mitrovica   Leskovac   Pirot
Vucitrh   Vlasotince   Dimitrovgrad
Pristina   Vraca
Peć   KOSOVO   Surdulica   Kostinbrod   Mezdra
Orahovac   Vranje   Radomir   Pernik   SOFIJA
Dakovica   Gnjilane   Bosilegrad   (SOFIA)
Prizren   Bujanovac   Kjustendil   Panagjuriste
Kumanovo   Kriva   Stanke   Samokov   Ihtiman
Tetovo   Palanka   Dimitrov   Kostenec
Skopje   Kratovo   Kamenica   Blagoevgrad   Velingrad

Cetinje
Bar
Shkodër
Lake
Scutari
Lia. i Komanit
Puke
Lezhë   Rreshen
Burrel
Peshkopi
Tiranë
(Tirana)
Durrës
ALBANIA
Kavaje
Lushnjë   Elbasan
Cerrik
Fier   Pogradec
Berat
Vlorë
Himarë

Kukës
Debar   Gostivar
Debreste
Kicevo
Prilep
Struga
Ohrid
L. Ohrid
Bitola
L. Prespa
Florina

MACEDONIA
Veles
Stip
Radovis
Negotino
Kavadarci
Brod
Vitoliste
Polykastro
Edessa
Giannitsa

Sveti Nikole
Kocani
Berovo
Strumica
Lake Dojran
Gevgelija
Kilkis
Lagkadas

Samokov
Pazardzik
Goce
Delcev
Smoljan
Petric
Sidirokastro
Serres
Nea Zichni
Drama

BULGARIA
SOFIJA
(SOFIA)
Stara Zagora
Plovdiv
Kricim
Asenovgrad
Haskovo
Kardzali   Arda
Momcilgrad
Madan
Echinos
Xanthi
Komotini

Mediterranean Sea

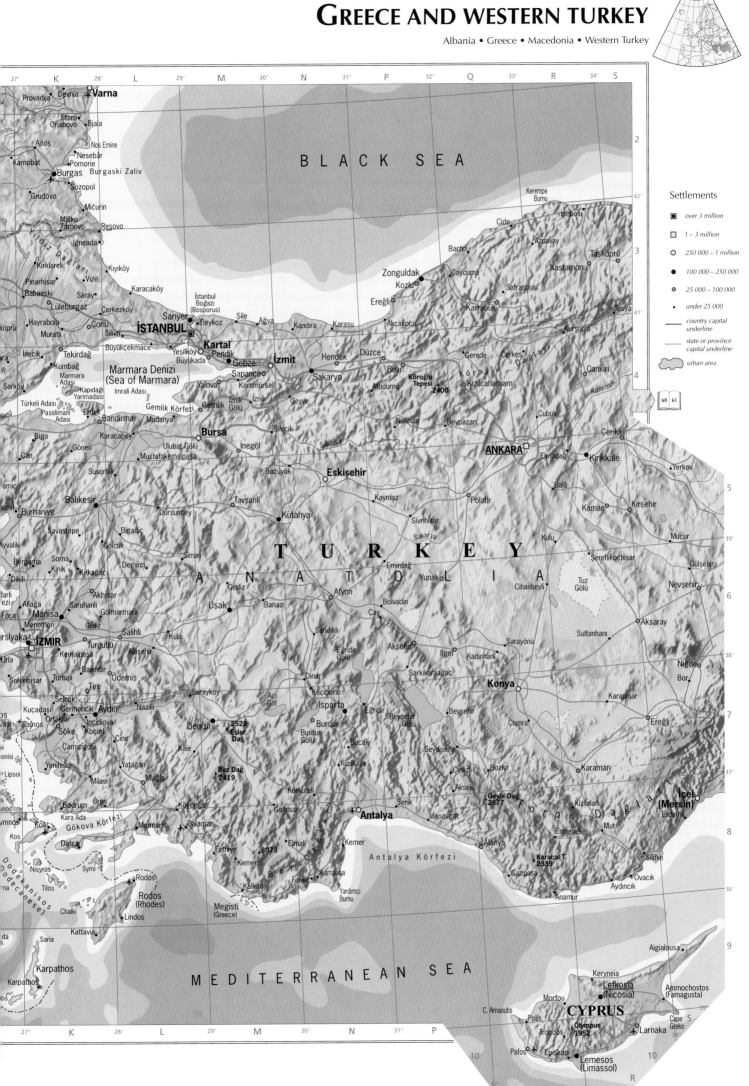

GREECE AND WESTERN TURKEY

Albania • Greece • Macedonia • Western Turkey

BLACK SEA

MEDITERRANEAN SEA

TURKEY

ANATOLIA

İSTANBUL

ANKARA

İZMİR

Bursa

Konya

Antalya

CYPRUS

Marmara Denizi
(Sea of Marmara)

Settlements

■ over 3 million

□ 1 – 3 million

○ 250 000 – 1 million

● 100 000 – 250 000

◉ 25 000 – 100 000

• under 25 000

country capital underline

state or province capital underline

urban area

EUROPE 37

Scale 1 : 10 400 000

© Copyright Research Machines plc 2005

J   50°   K   55°   L   60°   M   65°   N   70°   P   75°   Q   80°   R   85°

O. Kolguyev

Bugrino
Indiga
Oksino
Nar'yan Mar
Shapkina
Tobseda
Nosevaya
Severnyy
Vorkuta
Chum
1499
Aksarka
Yar Sale
Nyda
Obskaya Guba
Arctic Circle
Krasnosel'kup

Volonga
Vizhas
Safonovo
oma
eshukonskoye
Sula
Sula
Yermitsa
Krestovka
Trusovo
Khoseda Khard
Khoreyver
Adz'vavom
Abez'
Petrun
Ust'-Usa
Shuryshkary
Khashgort
Inta
Salekhard
Pitlyar
Ob'
Nadym
Tarko Sale
Tanlovo
Khe'Byakha
Leyva Khetta
Nadym
Novyy
Urengoy
Urengoy
Tol'ka
Tol'ka
Kharampur

Vozhgora
Bol. Pyssa
Vazhgort
lyukhcha
Koslan
Loptyuga
Koynas
Shegmas
Kartayel'
Kadzherom
Synya
Kos'yu
1883
Mutnyy
Materik
Ust'-Tsil'ma
Izhma
Pechora
Ustrem
Saranpul
Berezovo
Vanzevat
Sos'vinskaya
Beloyarskiy
Gorki
Numto
Noyabr'sk
Raduzhnyy
Lar'yak
Vakh

KOMI
Yarensk
Irta
Mikun'
Aykino
Storozhevsk
Ust'-Kulom
Yaksha
Pechora
Ust'
Un'ya
Ust' Tapsuy
Lyapin
Sartyn'ya
Igrim
Peregrebnoye
Sherkaly
Nyagan'
Nov. Karymkary
Bol. Atlym
Nizhnevartovsk
Lokosovo
Strezhevoy
Aleksandrovskoye

yaya
na
rasnoborsk
Kotlas
Luza
Ust'-Alekseyevo
chmengskiy
orodok
Oparino
Vozhgora
Koygorodok
Gayny
Kosa
Kerchevskiy
Cherdyn
Krasnovishersk
Severoural'sk
Krasnotur'insk
Serov
Sos'va
Pelym
Pionerskiy
Ivdel'
Los'ya
Uray
Kondinskoye
Yagodnyy
Dem'yanskoye
Nefedovo
Charymovo

Vychegda
Syktyvkar
Vizinga
Nagorsk
Murashi
Loyno
Yurla
Kudymkar
Chermoz
Kizel
Gubakha
Chusovoy
Verh.
Tura
Nov. Lyalya
Turinsk
Tavda
Yarkovo
Salym
Khanty-Mansiysk
Bol. Yugan
Konda
Demyanka
Irtysh
Uvat
Turtas
Znamenskoye
Tara
Tara

Kirov
Kirovo-Chepetsk
Kotel'nich
Kumeny
Glazov
Dobryanka
Lys'va
Nizhniy Tagil
Irbit
Nitsa
Talitsa
Tyumen'
Golyshmanovo
Ishim
Ozero
Saltaim
Tobol'sk
Sumkino
Ust'-Ishim
Tevriz
Ozero
Ishim
Kolosovka
Bol'sherech'ye
Ust'-Tarka

uga
eninskoye
iga
Shakhun'ya
Yaransk
Sovetsk
Nolinsk
Igra
Votkinsk
PERM'
Okhansk
Chastyye
Kungur
Achit
Pervoural'sk
Revda
Asbest
Isetskoye
Vinzili
Yalutorovsk
Ozero
Chernoye
Belozerskoye
Nazyvayevsk
Kalachinsk

rsk
Yoshkar Ola
UDMURTIYA
Urzhum
Kil'mez
Izhevsk
Krasnoufimsk
Chernushka
YEKATERINBURG
Kamensk-Ural'skiy
Kasli
Techa
Petukhovo
Petropavlovsk
OMSK

MARIY EL
Novocheboksarsk
oksary
KAZAN'
HUVASHIYA
Mamadysh
Nizhnekamsk
Agryz
Mozhga
Sarapul
Nizhnekamskoye
Vodokhranilishche
Neftekamsk
Kambarka
Belaya
Birsk
Asha
Min'yar
Miass
Kopeysk
Korkino
Yuzhnoural'sk
Shumikha
Kurgan
Tobol
Presnogorkovka
Kzyltu
OZ.
Seletyteniz
Kokshetau

Alatyr'
ye
nnost'
Buinsk
Ul'yanovsk
Dimitrovgrad
TATARIYA
Al'met'yevsk
Tuymazy
Bugul'ma
UFA
NABEREZHNYYE
Chelny
CHELYABINSK
Zlatoust
Plast
Troitsk
Yuzhnoural'sk
Borovskoy
Uritskiy
Fedorovka
Sergeyevka
Ishim
Volodarskoye
Makinsk
Aksu
Alekseyevka
44   45

Tol'yatti
SAMARA
Syzran'
Novokuybyshevsk
Buzuluk
Sorochinsk
Bugand
BASHKIRIYA
Sterlitamak
1638
Beloretsk
Verkhneural'sk
Magnitogorsk
Kartaly
Sibay
Kizil'skoye
Ural
Kostanay
Rudnyy
Tobol
Dzhetygara
Semiozernoye
Ozero
Kushmurun
Kushmurun
Zhaksy
Yesil'
Atbasar
Zhaltyr
Ishim
Koluton
Lomonosovka
Astana
Zholymbet
Vishnevka
Nura

Kuznetsk
tov
el's
Balakovo
Yershov
Novokuybyshevsk
Ozinki
Krasnyy Kut
Saraktash
Ilek
Burlin
Ural'sk
Ilek
Orenburg
Novotroitsk
Mednogorsk
Orsk
Svetlyy
Yasnyy
Energetik
Zhailma
Turgayskaya
Stolovaya
Strana
Amengel'dy
Arkalyk
Ozero
Tengiz
Ladyzhenka
Kurgal'dzhinskiy

Nov.
Kasanka
Furmanovo
Mergenevo
Chapayev
Dzhambeyty
Novoalekseyevka
Aktyubinsk
Karabutak
Turgay
Turgay
Ulytau
Gory Ulutau
Kzyl-Dzhar
Karazhal

iy
chak
Ozero
Aralsor
Malyy Uzen
Mosteksay
Kalmykovo
Uil
Oktyabr'sk
Mugodzhary
Shubarkuduk
Emba
Uil
264
Irgiz
Ozero
Zhamanakkol'
Dzhezkazgan
Zhezkazgan
Karsakpay
Baykonur
Sarysu

Kharabali
-24
Atyrau
Balykshi
Kul'sary
Kulagino
Makat
Emba
Sagiz
Sagiz
Zharkamys 408
249
Aral'sk
KAZAKHSTAN
Peski Priaral'skiye
Karakumy
Betpak-Dala

akhan'
Krasnyy Yar
Kamyzyak
-13
Ryn-
Peski
Prikaspiyskaya Nizmennost'
Ozero
Zhaltyr
Karaton
Oparnoy
Zal.
Paskevicha
Novokazalinsk
Dzhusaly
Syrdar'ya
Kyzylorda
Tasbuget
Suzak
Chili

Lagan'
hubey
Caspian
Sea
Aral Sea

50°   K   55°   L   60°   M   65°   N

Settlements

■	over 3 million
□	1 – 3 million
○	250 000 – 1 million
●	100 000 – 250 000
◉	25 000 – 100 000
•	under 25 000
——	country capital underline
—	state or province capital underline

RUSSIA

Zapadno-Sibirskaya Ravnina

(West Siberian Plain)

URAL'SKIY KHREBET (URAL MOUNTAINS)

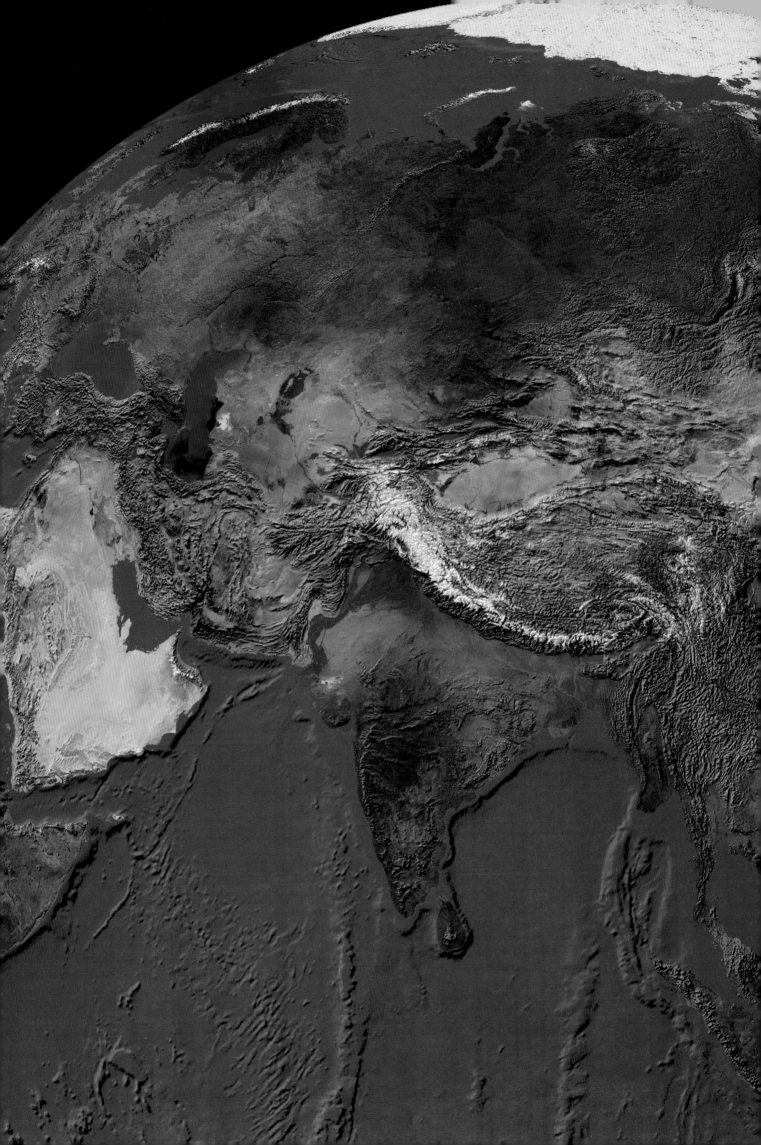

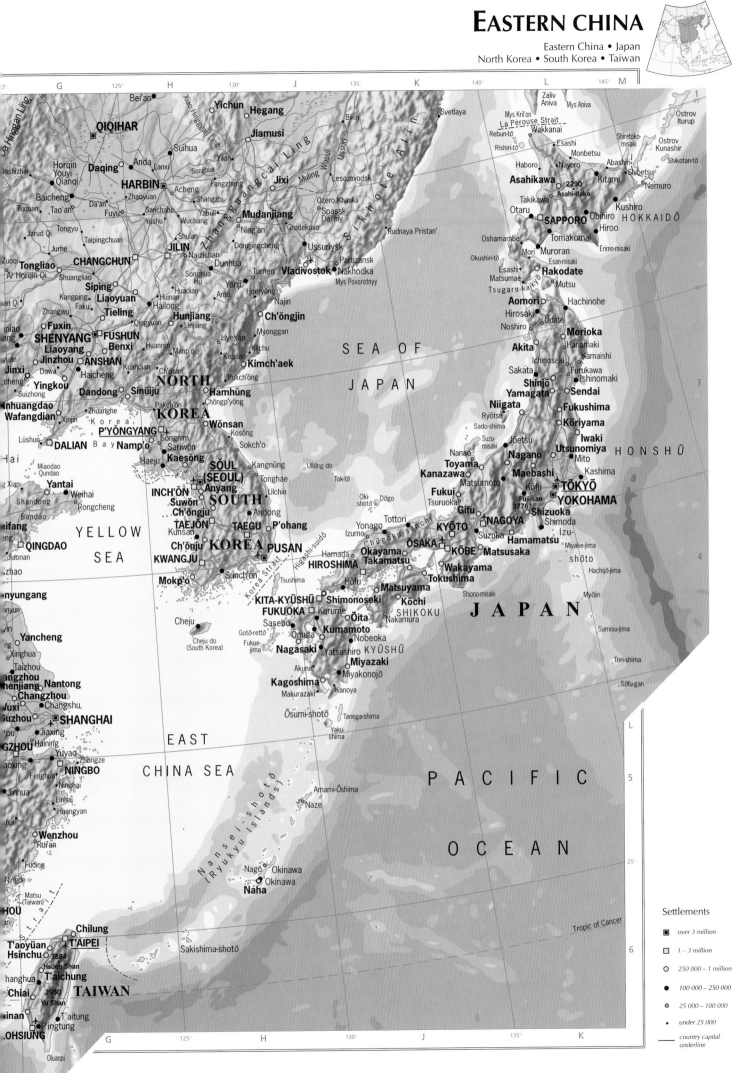

Scale 1 : 5 800 000

48 49

48 49

© Copyright Research Machines plc 2005

Krasnodar
Slavyánsk-na-Kubáni
Ust'-Labinsk
Armavir
Svetlograd
Stavropol'
Blagodarnyy
Neftekumsk
Yuzhno-Sukhokumsk
Kutan
KALMYKIYA

Krymsk
Adygeysk
Labinsk
Nevinnomyssk
Budennovsk
Kizlyarskiy Zaliv

Goryachiy Klyuch
vorossiysk
Belorechensk
Psebay
Cherkessk
Pyatigorsk
Mineral'nyye Vody
Zelenokumsk
Kochubey

ndztlik
Khadyzhensk
Maykop
RUSSIA
Kislovodsk Prokhladnyy
Mozdok
Kargalinskaya
Babayurt
Os. Chechen'

Tuapse
KARACHAYEVO-
Teberda
Nal'chik
Terek
Nazran'
Gudermes
Khasavyurt
Agrakhanskiy Poluostrov

mikhaylovskiy
Sochi
Adler
Karachayevsk
CHERKESIYA
KABARDINO-
BALKARIYA
5642
Elbrus
5203
Vladikavkaz
INGUSHETIYA
Groznyy
Urus Martan
DAGESTAN
Makhachkala
Kaspiysk

Gagra
Gudauťa
Sokhumi
SEVERNAYA
Sadon
OSETIYA
CHECHNYA
Buynaksk
Izberbash
CASPIAN

Och'amch'ire
Tqvaroh'eli
Lajanurpekhi
Oni
Tś'khinvali
5047
Kazbek
4494
4276
Diklosmta
Gunib
Levashi
Kumukh
Derbent
SEA

Zugdidi
K'uťaisi
Samtredia
Khashuri
Gori
Kaspi
T'elavi
Qvareli
4131
Kasumkent
Qusar
Xaçmaz

P'oťi
Ozurgeťi
GEORGIA
Borjomi
Arkhalts'ikhe
Bolnisi
Akhalk'alak'i
T'BILISI
Rusťavi
Dedoplis
Zaqatala
Qax
Şäki
Göra
Bazärdyuzü
4466
Quba
Däväçi
Siyäzän
Gilazi

Bať umi
Hopa
Pazar
Anadolu
Artvin
Ardahan
Tashir
Alaverdi
Qazax
Tovuz
Mingäçevir Su Anbarı
Mingäçevir
Ismayıllı
Samaxı
Sumqayıt

Trabzon
Rize
Dağları
3937
Yusufeli
Göle
Kars
Vanadzor
Dilijan
Gäncä
AZERBAIJAN
Bärdä
Kürdämir
Ağsu
BAKI
(BAKU)

Giresun
Gümüşhane
Bayburt
Oltu
Sarıkamış
Gyumri
4090
Hrazdan
Sevana Lich
3724
Ağcabädi
İmişli
Saatlı
Ali Bayramlı
Sanqaçal

Şuşehri
Erzincan
Aşkale
Pasinler
Horasan
Ağri
ARMENIA
YEREVAN
Ejmiadzin
Vedi
Vardenis
Xankändi
Susa
Horadiz
Tazeh Kand
Biläsuvar
Qazımämmäd

Divriği
Kemaliye
Pülümür
Varto
Vedi
Ararat
Mt. Ararat
5165
Särur
Şahbuz
AZER.
Naxçıvan
Goris
Sisian
Minċivan
Xudā Āfarīn
Āvärsin
Salyan
Neftçala

Ağın
Tunceli
Keban Baraji
Karakoçan
Bingöl
Solhan
4434
Süphan Dağı
Muradiye
Dogubeyazıt
Maku
Pareh
Jolfa
3829
Qazangöldag
Culfa
Khīyāv
4810
Ardabīl
Länkäran
Astara

Elazığ
Maden
Fırat (Euphrates)
Muş
Tätvan
Van Gölü
Erciş
Ercek
Qotur
Van
Marand
Ahar
Lerik
Tälesh

Malatya
Ergani
Silvan
Bitlis
Gevas
Başkale
Marägheh
Bandar-e Anzali
Rasht

nşehir
Diyarbakır
Batman
Sîirt
Çatak
Lūra Shīrīn
Daryācheh-ye Ūrūmīyeh
Salmās
Bastānābād
3710
Kuh-e Sahand
Āzarān
Mīāneh
Qezel Owżan
Nik Pey

Kâhta
Siverek
Mardin
Cizre
Şınak
Hakkari
Yüksekova
TABRĪZ
Sarāb
Zanjān

yaman
Hilva
Viranşehir
Kızıltepe
Nusaybin
Zākhō
Amādīyah
Zēbār
Haydarābād
Miāndowāb
Bonāb
Orūmīyeh
Kırk Bulāğ D.
3107
Abhar

Bozova
Şanlıurfa
Akçakale
Al Qāmishlī
Dahūk
Tall 'Uwaynāt
Ränya
Saqqez
Yangi Kand

Jarābulus
'Ayn 'Īsā
Al Hasakah
Tall 'Afar
Rawāndiz
Sar Dasht
Bowkan
IRAN

anbij
Buhayrat al Asad
Ar Raqqah
Sinjār
Ash Shadādah
Koi Sanjaq
Bānehi
Dīvāndarreh
Zāgheh-ye Bālā
Bijār
Abhar

Ar Rušāfah
Al Mawşil
Arbīl
As Sulaymānīyah
Marīvān
Sanandaj
Qorveh

MESOPOTAMIA
Ash Sharqāţ
Kirkūk
Halabja
Pāveh
Ravānsar

Dayr az Zawr
Mayādīn
Bājī
IRAQ
Tuz Khurmātū
Kifrī
Karand
Eslāmābād e Gharb
Kermānshāh
Harsin

RIA
As Sukhnah
Tikrīt
Sämarrā
Jalūlā
Gilan Garb
Kūhdasht

Tadmur
Āl Bū Kamāl
'Anāh
Rāwah
Buhayrat ath Tharthār
Al Khālis
Al Muqdādīyah
Ba'qūbah
Mehrān
Īlām
Mālavī

ādiyat ash Shām
(Syrian Desert)
Ar Ruţba
Khān al Baghdādī
Hīt
Euphrates
Habbānīyah
BAGHDĀD
Ar Ramādī
Bar al Milh
Dehlorān

Settlements

■ over 3 million

□ 1 – 3 million

○ 250 000 – 1 million

● 100 000 – 250 000

◉ 25 000 – 100 000

• under 25 000

—— country capital
underline

—— state or province
capital underline

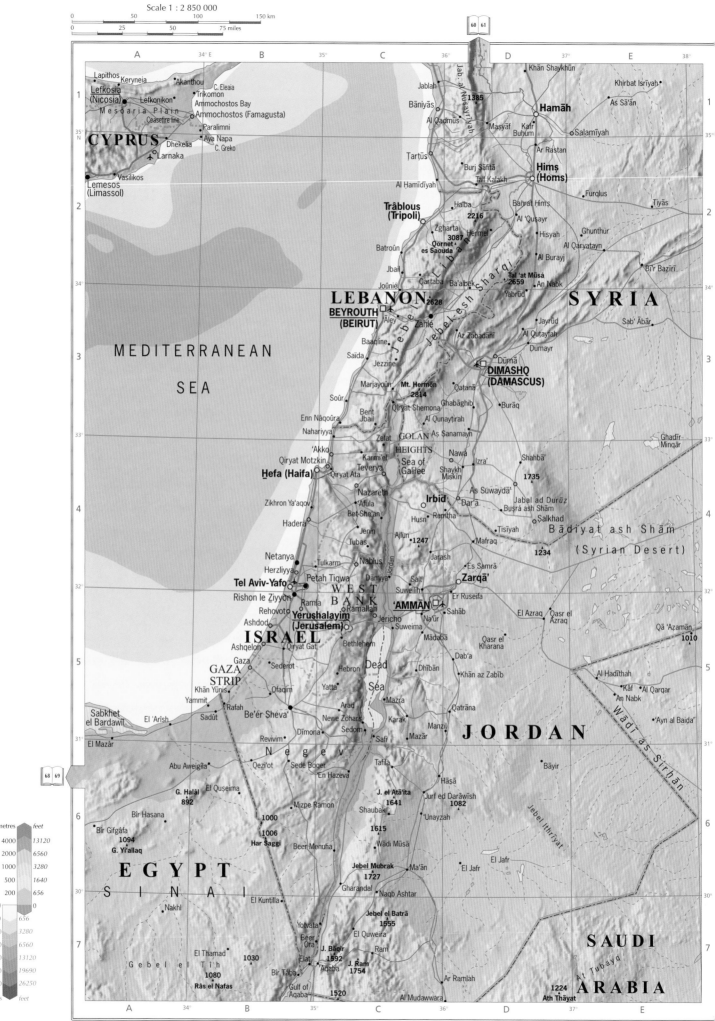

Scale 1 : 2 850 000

| 0 | 50 | 100 | 150 km |
| 0 | 25 | 50 | 75 miles |

60 61

A   34° E   B   35°   C   36°   D   37°   E   38°

CYPRUS

Lapithos · Keryneia · Akanthou
Lefkosia (Nicosia) · Trikomon · Lefkonikon · C. Eleaia
Ammochostos Bay
Mesoaria Plain · Ammochostos (Famagusta)
Ceasefire line · Paralimni
Dhekelia · Aya Napa
Larnaka · C. Greko

Vasilikos
Lemesos (Limassol)

Khirbat Isrīyah
Khān Shaykhūn
As Sā'an
Jablah
Bāniyās
Al Qadmūs
Masyāf · Kafr Buhum · **Hamāh** · Salamīyah
Ar Rastan
Tartūs
Burj Sāfītā · Al Hamīdīyah · Tall Kalakh
Halba · Bahrat Hims · **Hims (Homs)**
Furqlus · Tiyās
Trâblous (Tripoli) · 2216 · Al 'Qusayr
Zgharta · Hermel · Hisyah · Ghunthūr · Al Qaryatayn · Bīr Bazīrī
Batroûn · 3087 Qornet es Saouda · Ba'albek · Al Burayj
Jbaïl · Qartaba · Tal 'at Mūsá 2659 · An Nabk
Joûnié · Yabrūd
LEBANON 2628 · **SYRIA**
BEYROUTH (BEIRUT) · Âley · Zahlé · Jayrūd · Sab' Ābār
Baaqline · Az Zabadānī · Al Qutayfah · Dumayr
Saïda · Jezzine · Dūmā · **DIMASHQ (DAMASCUS)**
Marjayoûn · Mt. Hermon 2814 · Qatanā · Burāq
Soûr · Qiryat Shemona · Al Qunaytirah · Ghabāghib
Bent Jbail · GOLAN · As Sanamayn · Ghadîr Minqâr
Enn Nâqoûra · Zefat · HEIGHTS · Nawā · Shahbā
Nahariyya · Karmi'el · Sea of Galilee · Shaykh Miskīn · Izra' · 1735
'Akko · Teverya · As Suwaydā' · Jabal ad Durūz
Qiryat Motzkin · Qiryat Ata · Dar'a · Busrá ash Shām
Hefa (Haifa) · Nazareth · **Irbid** · Ramtha · Salkhad
Zikhron Ya'aqov · 'Afula · Husn · Tisīyah · 1234 · **Bādiyat ash Shām (Syrian Desert)**
Bet-She'an · Ajlūn · 1247 · Mafraq
Hadera · Jenin · Jarash · Es Samrā
Tubas · Na'ur · 1010 · Qā 'Azaman
Netanya · Tulkarm · Nablus · Salt · **Zarqā'** · El Azraq · Qasr el Azraq
Herzliyya · Petah Tiqwa · Damiya · Suweilih · Er Ruseifa
Tel Aviv-Yafo · **WEST** · **'AMMĀN** · Sahāb
Rishon le Ziyyon · Ramla · Ramallah · BANK · Jericho · Suweima · Qasr el Kharana
Rehovot · **Yerushalayim (Jerusalem)** · Na'ur · Mādabā · Dab'a
Ashdod · **ISRAEL** · Bethlehem · Khān az Zabīb · Al Hadīthah
Ashqelon · Qiryat Gat · Dead · Dhībān
GAZA STRIP · Hebron · Sea · Qatrāna · Kāf · Al Qarqar
Gaza · Sederot · Yatta · Mazra · An Nabk
Khān Yūnis · Ofaqim · Arad · Karak · Manzil · **JORDAN** · 'Ayn al Baida
Yammit · Rafah · Newe Zohars · Mazār
Sabkhet el Bardawil · Be'ér Shéva' · Sedom · Safi
El Mazār · Dimona · Revivim · Tafila · Bāyir
Negev · Qezi'ot · Sede Boqer · 'En Hazeva · Hāsā
Abu Aweigila · **J. el Atā'ita** 1641 · Jurf ed Darāwīsh 1082
G. Halāl 892 · El Quseima · Mizpe Ramon · Shaubak · 'Unayzah
Bîr Hasana · 1000 · 1615 · Wādī Mūsā · El Jafr
Bîr Gifgâfa 1094 · 1006 Har Saggi · Beer Menuha · El Jafr
G. Yi'allaq · **Jebel Mubrak** 1727 · Ma'ān
EGYPT · Gharandal · Naqb Ashtar
SINAI · El Kuntilla · Nakhl · **Jebel el Batrā** 1555
El Thamad · 1030 · Yotvata · El Quweira
Gebel el Tîh · 1080 Râs el Nafas · Beer Ora · J. Bâqir 1592 · Ram
Bîr Tâba · Elat · **J. Ram** 1754
Gulf of Aqaba · 'Aqaba · Ar Ramlah
1520 · Al Mudawwara · 1224 Ath Thāyat · **ARABIA**
SAUDI

MEDITERRANEAN SEA

35° N · 35° · 34° · 33° · 32° · 31° · 30°

68 69

metres	feet
4000	13120
2000	6560
1000	3280
500	1640
200	656
0	0
200	656
1000	3280
2000	6560
4000	13120
6000	19690
8000	26250
metres	feet

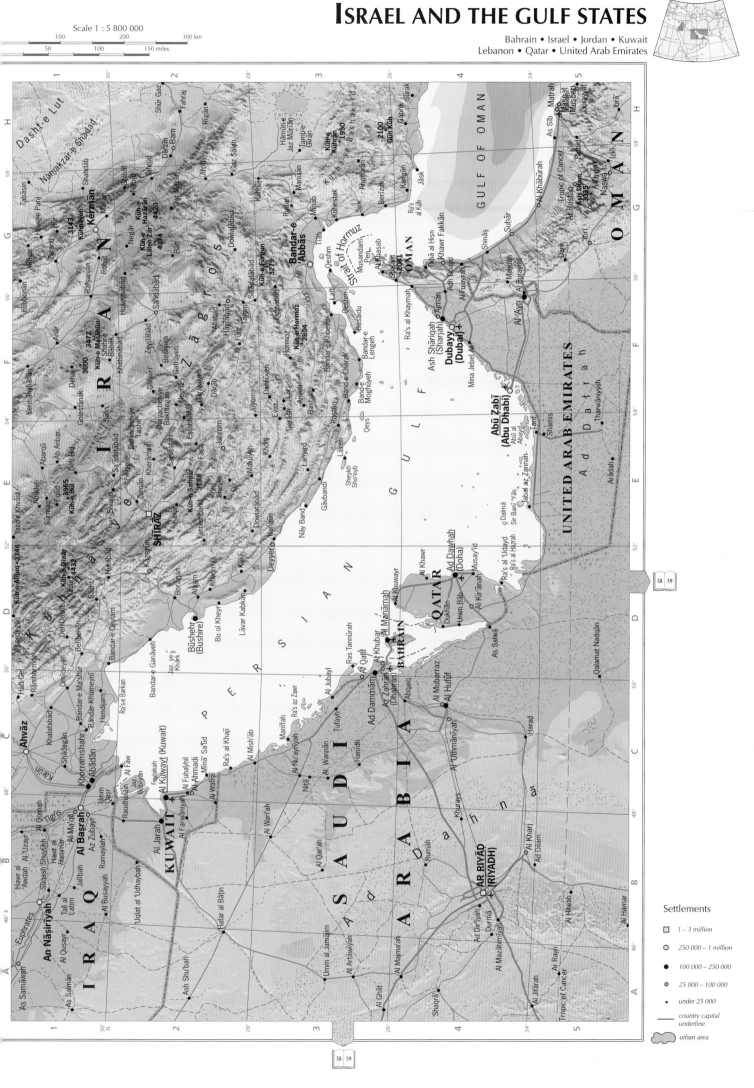

ISRAEL AND THE GULF STATES

Bahrain • Israel • Jordan • Kuwait
Lebanon • Qatar • United Arab Emirates

Scale 1 : 5 800 000

Settlements

☐ 1 – 3 million

◯ 250 000 – 1 million

● 100 000 – 250 000

◉ 25 000 – 100 000

• under 25 000

— country capital
underline

urban area

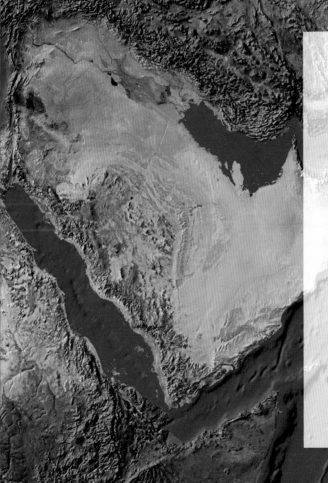

AFRICA

Africa   66

Northeast Africa   68

Northwest Africa   70

West Africa   72

Central Africa   74

Southern Africa   76

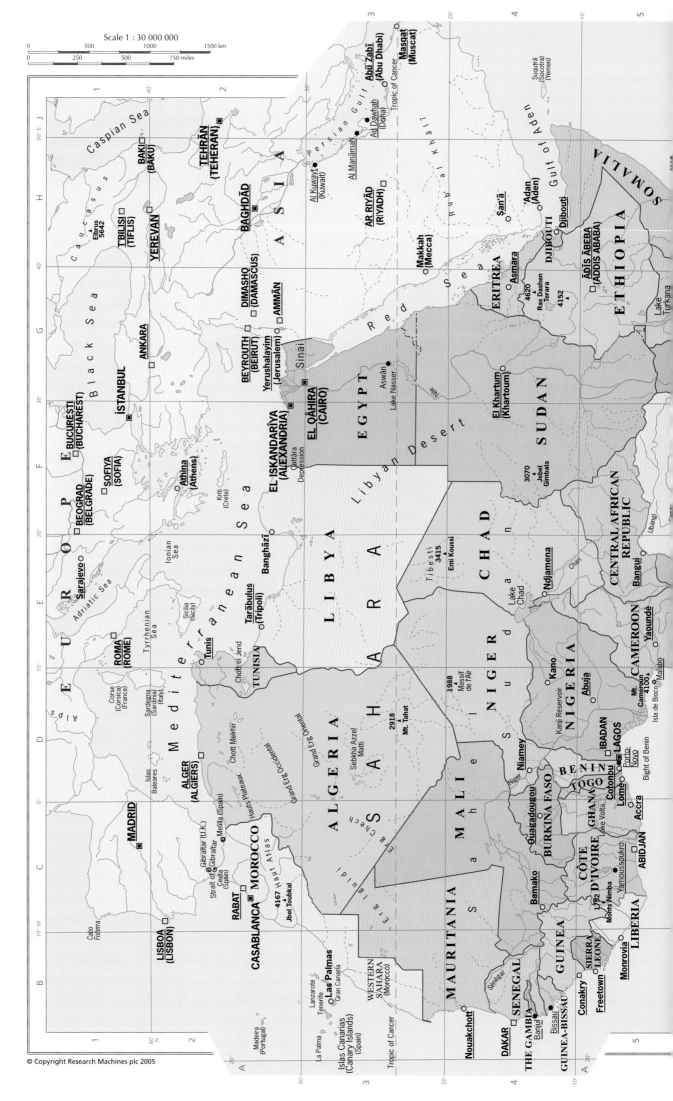

Scale 1 : 30 000 000

0   500   1000   1500 km
0   250   500   750 miles

EUROPE

Caspian Sea

BAKI (BAKU)

TEHRĀN (TEHERAN)

Elbrus 5642

Caucasus

T'BILISI (TIFLIS)

YEREVAN

BAGHDĀD

AR RIYĀD (RIYADH)

Abū Ẓabī (Abu Dhabi)

Al Manāmah (Doha)

Ad Dawḥah (Doha)

Tropic of Cancer

Masqaṭ (Muscat)

Suquṭrā (Socotra) (Yemen)

Al Kuwayt (Kuwait)

Persian Gulf

Rub' al Khālī

Gulf of Aden

Black Sea

ANKARA

İSTANBUL

BUCUREŞTI (BUCHAREST)

BEOGRAD (BELGRADE)

SOFIYA (SOFIA)

Sarajevo

BEYROUTH (BEIRUT)

DIMASHO (DAMASCUS)

AMMĀN

Yerushalayim (Jerusalem)

Sinai

EGYPT

Aswān

Lake Nasser

Red Sea

Nile

SUDAN

El Khartum (Khartoum)

3070 Jebel Gimbala

ERITREA

Asmara

4620 Ras Dashen Terara

4152

San'ā

Adan (Aden)

DJIBOUTI

Djibouti

ĀDĪS ĀBEBA (ADDIS ABABA)

ETHIOPIA

SOMALIA

Lake Turkana

Makkah (Mecca)

Athina (Athens)

Kríti (Crete)

Ionian Sea

Adriatic Sea

Mediterranean Sea

EL ISKANDARÎYA (ALEXANDRIA)

EL QÂHIRA (CAIRO)

Qattâra Depression

LIBYA

Libyan Desert

S A H A R A

Banghāzī

Ţarābulus (Tripoli)

Tunis

TUNISIA

Chott el Jerid

Sicilia (Sicily)

Tyrrhenian Sea

ROMA (ROME)

Corse (Corsica) (France)

Sardegna (Sardinia) (Italy)

ALGER (ALGIERS)

Chott Melrhir

Grand Erg Oriental

Sebkha Azzel Matti

2918 Mt. Tahat

Tibesti 3415 Emi Koussi

CHAD

Ndjamena

Lake Chad

Charí

CENTRAL AFRICAN REPUBLIC

Bangui

Ubangi

CAMEROON

Yaoundé

Mt. Cameroun 4100

Isla de Bioco (Malabo)

Bight of Benin

NIGER

1988 Massif de l'Aïr

Kano

Kanji Reservoir

Abuja

NIGERIA

IBADAN

LAGOS

Porto Novo

BENIN

TOGO

Lomé

Cotonou

Niamey

Ouagadougou

BURKINA FASO

Lake Volta

GHANA

Accra

CÔTE D'IVOIRE

Yamoussoukro

ABIDJAN

1752 Monts Nimba

LIBERIA

Monrovia

GUINEA

Conakry

SIERRA LEONE

Freetown

GUINEA-BISSAU

Bissau

THE GAMBIA

Banjul

SENEGAL

DAKAR

Nouakchott

MAURITANIA

MALI

Bamako

Sénégal

A z a o u a d

Ségou

El Djouf

Erg Chech

I g u i d i

Adrar des Iforas

Niger

MADRID

LISBOA (LISBON)

Cabo Fisterra

Islas Baleares

Melilla (Spain)

Gibraltar (U.K.)

Strait of Gibraltar

Ceuta (Spain)

RABAT

CASABLANCA

MOROCCO

4167 Haut Atlas

Jbel Toubkal

WESTERN SAHARA (Morocco)

Las Palmas

Lanzarote

Tenerife

Gran Canaria

La Palma

Islas Canarias (Canary Islands) (Spain)

Madeira (Portugal)

Tropic of Cancer

ALGERIA

Hauts Plateaux

Grand Erg Occidental

A S I A

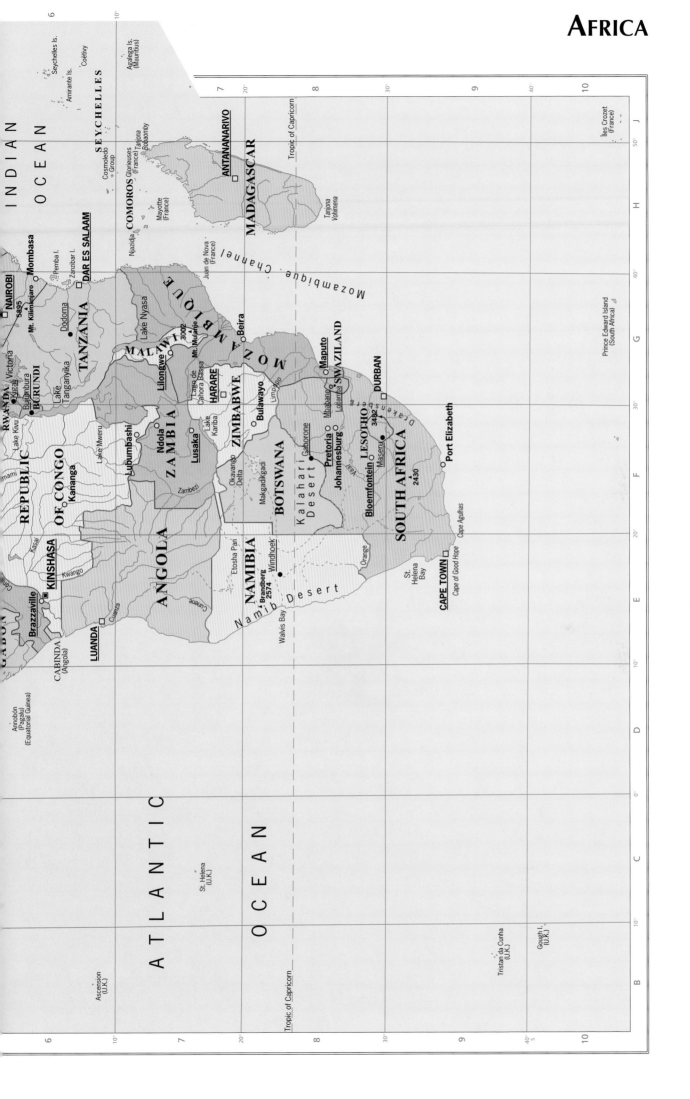

AFRICA

INDIAN OCEAN

Seychelles Is.
Coëtivy
Amirante Is.
Agalega Is. (Mauritius)
SEYCHELLES
Cosmoledo Group
COMOROS Glorieuses (France) Tanjona Bobaomby
Njazidja
Mayotte (France)

ANTANANARIVO

MADAGASCAR

Tanjona Vohimena

Tropic of Capricorn

Mombasa
Pemba I.
Zanzibar I.
NAIROBI
DAR ES SALAAM
Mt. Kilimanjaro 5895
Dodoma
TANZANIA
Beira
Lake Nyasa
MALAWI
Lilongwe Mt. Mulanje 3002
RWANDA Kigali
BURUNDI Bujumbura
Lake Victoria
Lake Tanganyika
Lake Kivu
MOZAMBIQUE
Mozambique Channel
Juan de Nova (France)

Maputo
SWAZILAND
Mbabane Lobamba
DURBAN
Lago de Cahora Bassa
HARARE
ZIMBABWE
Bulawayo
Limpopo
LESOTHO
Maseru 3482
Drakensberg

Lake Mweru
mami
REPUBLIC OF CONGO
Kananga
Lubumbashi
ZAMBIA
Ndola
Lusaka
Lake Kariba
Zambezi
Okavango Delta
Makgadikgadi
Gaborone
Kalahari Desert
BOTSWANA
Pretoria
Johannesburg
Vaal
Bloemfontein 2430
SOUTH AFRICA
Port Elizabeth
Cape Agulhas

KINSHASA
Kwango
ANGOLA
Cuanza
Kasai
Etosha Pan
NAMIBIA
Brandberg 2574
Windhoek
Cunene
Namib Desert
Orange
Walvis Bay
St. Helena Bay
CAPE TOWN
Cape of Good Hope

Brazzaville
GABON
CABINDA (Angola)
LUANDA
Kwanza
Congo

Annobón (Pagalu) (Equatorial Guinea)

ATLANTIC OCEAN

St. Helena (U.K.)
Ascension (U.K.)

Tropic of Capricorn

Tristan da Cunha (U.K.)
Gough I. (U.K.)

Prince Edward Island (South Africa)
Îles Crozet (France)

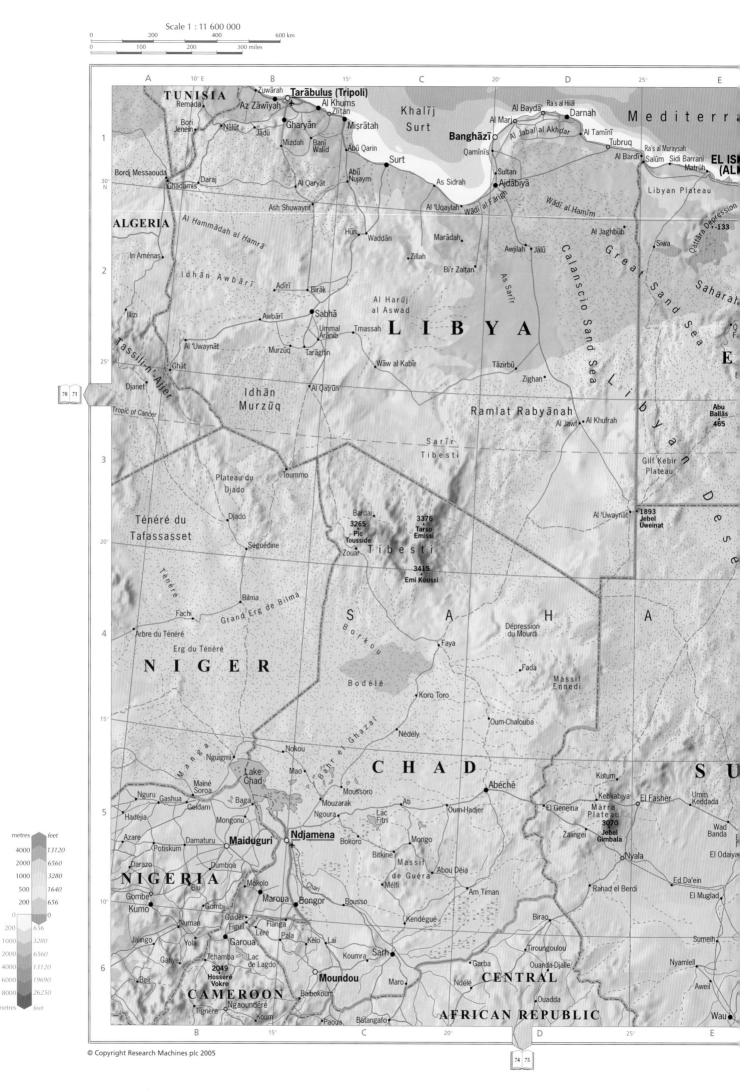

Scale 1 : 11 600 000

| 0 | 200 | 400 | 600 km |
| 0 | 100 | 200 | 300 miles |

TUNISIA

Zuwārah · **Tarābulus (Tripoli)**
Remada · Az Zāwiyah · Al Khums
Borj · Nālūt · Jādū · **Gharyān** · Misrātah · Zlītan
Jenien · Mizdah · Banī · Abū Qarin
Bordj Messaouda · Daraj · Walīd
Ghadamis · Al Qaryāt · Surt · Abū Nujaym

Khalīj Surt

Al Bayḍā' · Ra's al Hilāl
Al Marj · Darnah
Banghāzī · Al Jabal al Akhḍar · Al Tamīnī
Qāmīnis · Tubruq
Sultan · Ra's al Muraysah
As Sidrah · **Ajdābiyā** · Al Bardī · Salūm · Sidi Barrani
Al 'Uqaylah · Matrūh
EL IS (AL

Mediterra

30° N

ALGERIA

Ash Shuwayrif
Wādī al Fārigh · Wādī al Hamīm
Libyan Plateau

In Aménas · Hūn · Waddān · Marādah · Al Jaghbūb
Zillah · Awjilah · Jālū · Siwa
Bi'r Zaltan · Qattāra Depression · -133

Idhān Awbārī · Adīrī · Birāk
Al Harūj al Aswad · As Sarīr
Sabhā · Ummal · Tmassah
Illizi · Awbārī · Arānib

Great Sand Sea
Saharat

L I B Y A

Calanscio Sand Sea

Al 'Uwaynāt · Murzūq · Tarāghin
Ghāt · Wāw al Kabīr · Tāzirbū
Tassili-n'Ajjer · Tāzirbū · Zighan

25°

Djanet · Al Qaṭrūn
Idhān Murzūq · Ramlat Rabyānah
Abu Ballās · 465

Tropic of Cancer · Al Jawf · Al Khufrah

Gilf Kebir Plateau

Sarīr Tibesti

Plateau du Djado · Toummo
Al 'Uwaynāt · 1893 Jebel Uweinat

Ténéré du Tafassasset · Djado
Bardai · 3376 Tarso Emissi
3265 Pic Tousside · Libyan Dese
Séguédine · Zouar · Tibesti

20°

Ténéré · Zouar
3415 Emi Koussi

Bilma
Grand Erg de Bilma
S A H A R A
Fachi · Borkou
Arbre du Ténéré · Dépression du Mourdi
Erg du Ténéré · Faya
Bodélé · Fada
Massif Ennedi

N I G E R
Koro Toro
Oum-Chalouba

15°

Nédély
Nokou
Manga · Nguigmi

C H A D
Kutum
SU
Maïné · Mao · Moussoro · Abéché · Kebkabiya · El Fasher · Umm Keddada
Soroa · Mouzarak · Ati · Oum-Hadjer · El Geneina · Marra Plateau
Nguru · Gashua · Baga · Ngoura · Lac Fitri · Mongo · Zalingei · 3070 Jebel Gimbala · Wad Banda
Hadéjia · Geidam · Mongonu · **Ndjamena** · Bokoro · Nyala
Azare · Damaturu · **Maiduguri** · Bitkine · Mongo · El Odaiya
Darazo · Dumboa · Bongor · Bousso · Massif de Guéra · Abou Déia · Am Timan · Rahad el Berdi · Ed Da'ein · El Muglad
Kumo · Biu · Mokolo · Mélfi
NIGERIA · Gombi · Maroua · Bongor · Birao
Gombe · Guider · Fianga · Kendégué · Tiroungoulou · Sumeih
Jalingo · Numan · Figuil · Lèrè · Pala · Koumra · Garba
Yola · Garoua · Kélo · Laï · Sarh · Ouanda-Djallé · Nyamlell
Ganye · Tchamba · Lac de Lagdo · Koumra · Ndélé · Aweil
Beli · 2049 Hosséré Vokre · Maro · **CENTRAL** · Ouadda · Wau
CAMEROON · **Moundou** · Baïbokoum · Ouadda
Tignère · Ngaoundéré · Koum · Paoua · Bátangafo · **AFRICAN REPUBLIC**

Lake Chad

metres	feet
4000	13120
2000	6560
1000	3280
500	1640
200	656
0	0
200	656
1000	3280
2000	6560
4000	13120
6000	19690
8000	26250
metres	feet

60 61

58 59

LEBANON
Saïda
Sour
SYRIA
As Suwaydā'
Ar Ruṭba
Karbalā' **Al Ḥillah** Al Kūt
Dezfūl
Masjed
Soleymān

Ḥefa (Haifa)
Badiyat ash Shām
(Syrian Desert)
An Nukhayb
An Najaf
Al 'Amārah
Aḥvāz
IRAQ
IRAN

ISRAEL
Tel Aviv-Yafo
Irbid
Zarqā'
AMMĀN
As Samāwah
An Nāsirīyah
Khorramshahr
Bandar-e Ma'shur

Kafr el
Sheikh
Dumyât
Yerushalayim
(Jerusalem)
Gaza
Ma'ān
'Ar'ar
As Salmān
Al Baṣrah
Abādān

Bûr Sa'îd (Port Said)
JORDAN
Turayf
Al 'Ashurīyah
As Busayyah

El Mansûra
Benha
Tanta
Ismâ'ilîya
Al Jālamīd
Al 'Uwayqilah
Al Jawf
Rafḥā
Hafar al Bāṭin
Al Kuwayt (Kuwait)
KUWAIT

EL QÂHIRA (CAIRO)
Suez Canal
Al Qurayyāt
Ash Shu'bah
Al Wafrā'
Persian
Gulf

EL GIZA
Giza Pyramids
El Suweis (Suez)
Sharmah
Ḥā'il
Al Artāwīyah
Rumāḥ

El Faiyûm
Helwan
S i n a i
Elat
Aqaba
Tabūk
Taymā'
Buraydah
Al Majma'ah

Beni Suef
Beni Mazâr
2637
Gebel
Katherina
Al Humaydah
An Nafud
AR RIYĀD (RIYADH)
Al Kharj
Tropic of Cancer

El Minya
Mallawi
Ras
Ghārib
Sharm el Sheikh
Jabal Shammar
'Unayzah
Al Mazāhimīyah
Harad

Abnûb
Hurghada
Dubā
Ash Shurayf
Ad Dawādimī
Zalim
S A U D I
A d D a h

Asyût
Akhmîm
Bûr Safâga
Hanalc
Afīf
Ḥalabān
Ālayl ā

Sohâg
Qena
Quseir
Ash Shurayf
Lāyl ā

Girga
Qus
Al Wajh
Marsa Alam
Qadīmah
A R A B I A

El Khârga
Valley of the Kings
Luxor
Umm Lajj
Yanbu'al
Baḥr
Al Madīnah (Medina)

Bûlâq
Isna
Idfu
Badr
Hunayn
Qal'at
Bīshah
As Sulayyil

Bâris
Kom Ombo
Aswân
Aswân Dam
Râs Banâs
Rābigh
Usfān
Makkah (Mecca)
Dawqah
Al Qunfudhah

Abu Simbel
Lake
Nasser
Qadīmah
Dahabān
At Tā'if
Abhā
Khamis Mushayt
Sharūrah

Hamīd
Akasha
Wadi Halfa
ADMINISTERED
BY SUDAN
Halaib
JIDDAH (JEDDA)
Zahrān
Najrān
Wuday'ah
Zamakh

Tagab
Delgo
Nubian Desert
Ras Abu
Shagara
Dungunab
Muhammad Qol
Al Lith
Jīzān
Ṣa'dah
Ḥūth
Mīdī

Dongola
El Khandaq
Kerma
Keheili
Abu Hamed
Suakin
Sinkat
Dahlak
Archipelago
Jaza'ir
Farasān
Harad
As Zaydīyah
Mar'ib
Shabwah

Ed Debba
Korti
Merowe
Berber
Musmar
Haiya
2780
Algena
Ras Kasar
Dehalak Deset
Massawa
San'ā
3760
Jabal an
Nabī Shu'ayb
2514
Jabal
Thamar
Lawdar
Habbān

Atbara
Shendi
Derudeb
'Amm Adam
Tokar
ERITREA
Akordat
Keren
Al Ḥudaydah
Bayt al
Faqīh
Ibb
Ta'izz

Umm Durman (Omdurman)
El Khartum Bahri
Aroma
Kassala
Teseney
Barentu
Asmara
T'i'o
Ed
Dhamār
Zinjibār

El Khartum (Khartoum)
Khashm
el Girba
Adi Ugri
Om Hajer
Subcule
1280
Al Mukha
At Turbah
'Adan (Aden)

Wad Medani
Gedaref
Himora
Āksum
Adīgrat
Āsale
Aṣṣab
Bāb al Mandab
Gulf of Aden

El Obeid
Kosti
Rabak
Singa
Sennar
Gallabat
Metema
Dabat
4620
Ras
Dashen
Terara
Mek'ele
Maych'ew
DJIBOUTI
Ras Bir
At Turbah

Er Rahad
Umm Ruwaba
Ed Dueim
Gonder
T'ana
Hāyk'
Debre
Tabor
4193
Abune
Yosef
Téndaho
Yoboki
Djibouti
Maydh

Bahir Dar
4231
Guna
Terara
Mot'a
Desē
Dikhil
Sāylac
Berbera
Ceerigaabo

Ed Damazin
Er Renk
Guba
Burē
4152
Birhan
Debre Markos
4000
Abuye
Meda
Gewanē
Cabdul Qaadir

Kadugli
Melut
Āsosa
Fichē
Mī'eso
Hargeysa
SOMALIA

Tonga
Malakal
Gīmbī
Nek'emtē
Debre Markos
ĀDĪS ĀBEBA (ADDIS ABABA)
Nazrēt
Dirē Dawa
Hārer
Degeh Bur
Caynabo

Kan
Tulu
Weiel
3302
Gorē
Gambēla
3357
Dendi
Giyon
ETHIOPIA
Werdēr
Geladī

Duk Faiwil
Āgaro
3359
Mai Gudo
Negēle
4193
K'ebrī Dehar

Nasir
Mendī
K'ech'a
Terara
Goba
Gīnīr

Settlements

- ■ over 3 million
- □ 1 – 3 million
- ◎ 250 000 – 1 million
- ● 100 000 – 250 000
- ◉ 25 000 – 100 000
- • under 25 000
- ___ country capital underline

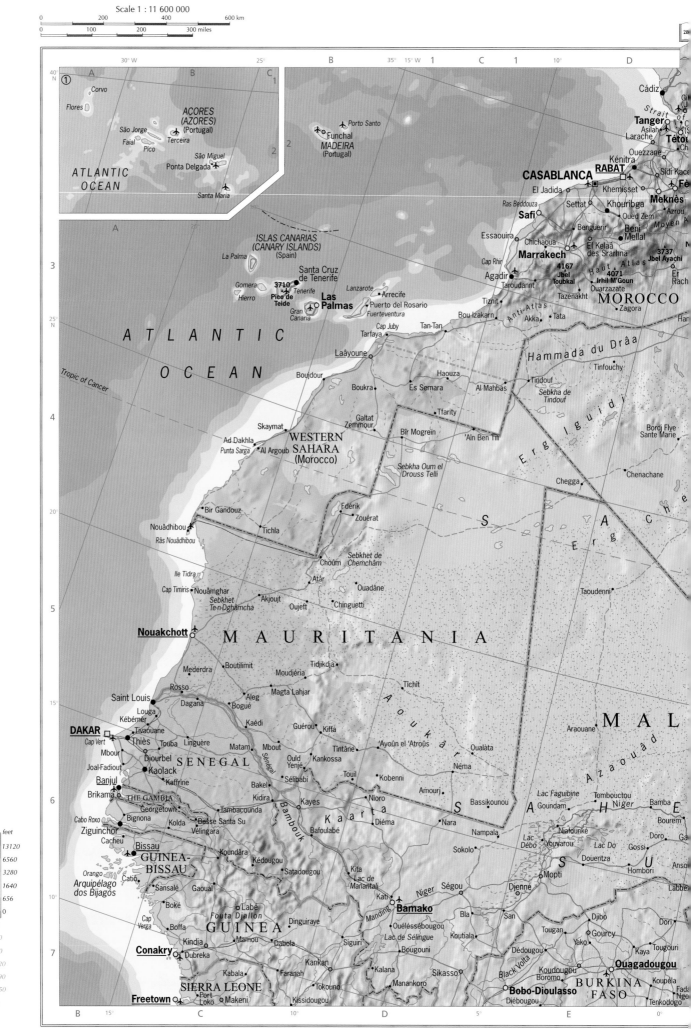

Scale 1 : 11 600 000

| 0 | 200 | 400 | 600 km |
| 0 | 100 | 200 | 300 miles |

ATLANTIC OCEAN

① Corvo
Flores

AÇORES
(AZORES)
(Portugal)

São Jorge
Faial • Pico
Terceira

São Miguel
Ponta Delgada

Santa Maria

Cádiz
Strait
Tanger
Asilah
Larache
Tétou
Ouezzane
Kénitra
Sidi Kace
RABAT
Khemisset
Fè
Meknès
Arrou
Moyen

Porto Santo
Funchal
MADEIRA
(Portugal)

CASABLANCA
El Jadida
Ras Beddouza
Settat
Khouribga
Oued Zem
**Beni
Mellal**
Safi
Essaouira
Chichaoua
El Kelaâ
des Srarhna
3737
Jbel Ayachi

ISLAS CANARIAS
(CANARY ISLANDS)
(Spain)
La Palma
Santa Cruz
de Tenerife
Cap Rhir
Marrakech
4167
**Jbel
Toubkal**
Haut
Atlas
4071
Irhil M'Goun
Er
Rach

Gomera
3710
**Pico de
Teide**
Tenerife
Hierro
Gran
Canaria
**Las
Palmas**
Lanzarote
Arrecife
Puerto del Rosario
Fuerteventura

Agadir
Taroudannt
Anti-Atlas
Tiznit
Bou Izakarn
Akka
Tazenakht
Ouarzazate
Tata
Zagora
MOROCCO
Han

Cap Juby
Tarfaya
Tan-Tan

Hammada du Drâa
Tinfouchy

25°N

Laâyoune
Haouza
Tindouf
Sebkha de
Tindouf

ATLANTIC

Boujdour
Boukra
Es Semara
Al Mahbâs

OCEAN

Tropic of Cancer

Skaymat
Galtat
Zemmour
Tfarity
'Aïn Ben Tili

Erg Iguidi

Bordj Flye
Sante Marie

Ad Dakhla
**WESTERN
SAHARA
(Morocco)**
Bîr Mogrein

Punta Sarga
Al Argoub
Sebkha Oum el
Drouss Telli
Chegga
Chenachane

Bir Gandouz
Edérik
Zouérat
S
A
Erg Che

Nouâdhibou
Ràs Nouâdhibou
Tichla
Choûm
Sebkhet de
Chemchâm
Taoudenni

Ile Tidra
Atâr
Ouadâne

Cap Timiris
Nouâmghar
Akjoujt
Chinguetti
Sebkhet
Te-n-Dghâmcha
Oujeft

Nouakchott
M A U R I T A N I A

Mederdra
Boutilimit
Tidjikdja
Tîchît

Rosso
Aleg
Moudjéria
Magta Lahjar

Saint Louis
Dagana
Bogué
Guérou
Kiffa
Aoukâr
Araouane
M A L

Louga
Kébémer
Kaédi
'Ayoûn el 'Atroûs
Oualàta
Tombouctou
Niger
Bamba

DAKAR
Tivaouane
Thiès
Touba
Linguère
Matam
Mbout
Ould
Yenje
Kankossa
Tintâne
Néma
Goundam
Niger
Doro
Ga

Cap Vert
Mbour
Djourbel
S E N E G A L
Bakel
Sélibâbi
Touil
Kobenni
Bassikounou
Lac Faguibine
Niafounké
Gossi

Joal-Fadiout
Kaolack
Kaffrine
Kidira
Nioro
Amourj
Nampala
Lac
Débo
Youvarou
Lac Do
Douentza
Hombori

Banjul
Brikama
THE GAMBIA
Georgetown
Tambacounda
Kayes
Diéma
Nara
Sokolo
S U

Cabo Roxo
Bignona
Kolda
Bafoulabé
Kaarta
Ziguinchor
Cacheu
Basse Santa Su
Vélingara
Kidira
Mopti

Bissau
**GUINEA-
BISSAU**
Koundâra
Kédougou
Kita
Lac de
Manantali
Ségou
Djenné

Orango
Catió
Sansalé
Gaoual
Satadougou
Kati
Niger
Bla
San
Djibo
Dori

Arquipélago
dos Bijagós
Boké
Labé
Fouta Djallon
Dinguiraye
Lac de Sélingue
Bamako
Ouéléssébougou
Tougan
Gourcy

Cap
Verga
Boffa
G U I N E A
Mamou
Siguiri
Kangaba
Koutiala
Dédougou
Yako
Kaya
Tougouri

Conakry
Dubreka
Kindia
Dabola
Kankan
Kalana
Sikasso
Boromo
Koudougou
Ouagadougou
Fada

Kabala
Faranah
Kalana
Manankoro
Tokouno
Diébougou
Bobo-Dioulasso
**BURKINA
FASO**
Koupéla
Tenkodogo

SIERRA LEONE
Port
Loko
Makeni
Kissidougou
Black Volta

Freetown

metres	feet
4000	13120
2000	6560
1000	3280
500	1640
200	656
0	0
200	656
1000	3280
2000	6560
4000	13120
6000	19690
8000	26250
metres	feet

MEDITERRANEAN SEA

ITALY
Cosenza
Catanzaro
SARDEGNA
(SARDINIA)
(Italy)
Cagliari
Isole Lipari
Palermo
Messina
Reggio di
Calabria
SICILIA
(SICILY)
Mte. Etna
3323
Catánia
Siracusa
Pantelleria
(Italy)
Lampedusa
(Italy)
MALTA

ALGER
(ALGIERS)
Tizi
Ouzou
Khemis
Miliana
Ténès
Blida
Bouira
Bejaïa
Cap de Fer
Bizerte
Mostaganem
Oran
Skikda
Mila
Guelma
Annaba
Béja
Jendouba
Tunis
Cap Bon
Ech
Chélif
Bordj Bou Arréridj
Sétif
Constantine
Hammam Lif
Nabeul
Relizane
Mascara
Ain Oussera
M'Sila
Aïn Beïda
Kasserine
Sousse
Golfe de Hammamet
Sidi Bel Abbès
Tiaret
Frenda
Bou
Saâda
Chott el
Hodna
Batna
Khenchela
Tébessa
Kairouan
Ksour Essaf
Saïda
Djelfa
Biskra
Négrine
Gafsa
TUNISIA
Sfax
Îles Kerkenah
Oujda
Tlemcen
Ghazaouet
Melilla (Spain)
Almería
Jerada
ceima
aga
AIN
Tendrara
Aïn Sefra
Brézina
Messaad
Laghouat
Chott
Melrhir
Tozeur
Chott
el Jerid
Nefta
Gabès
Golfe de Gabès
Houmt Souk
Île de Jerba
Figuig
Benoud
Ghardaïa
Djamâa
El Oued
Matmata
Medenine
uârfa
Touggourt
Tataouine
Rass Ajdir
Sbaa
Adrar
Sebkha de
Timimoun
Timimoun
El Homr
Ouargla
Hassi Messaoud
Rebaa
Dehiba
Remada
Az
Zāwīyah
Tarābulus
(Tripoli)
Al Khums
Zlītan
El Goléa
Bordj Jenein
Nālūt
Tarhūnah
Gharyān
Mişrātah
and Erg Occidental
Grand Erg Oriental
Bordj Messaouda
Ghadāmis
Daraj
Jādū
Mizdah
Banī
Walid
Abū Qarin
Khalīj
Surt
Plateau du Tademaït
Hassi Bel
Guebbour
Ohanet
Al Hammādah al Hamrā'
Al Qaryāt
Abū
Nujaym
Surt
As
Sidrah
ALGERIA
Reggane
In Salah
Bordj
Omar Driss
In Aménas
Ash
Shuwayrif
Hūn
Waddān
Sebkha Mekerrhane
A
Sebkha Azzel
Matti
LIBYA
Birāk
Zillah
Amguid
Illizi
Idhān Awbārī
Adīrī
R
Tassili-n'-Ajjer
A
Awbārī
Sabhā
Tmassah
Al Harūj
al Aswad
Arak
Meniet
Al 'Uwaynāt
Ummal Arānib
Murzūq
Tarāghin
Wāw
al Kabīr
Post Weygand
nezrouft
In Ekker
Zaouatallaz
Ghāt
Idhān
Murzūq
Djanet
Tin
Alkoum
Al Qaţrūn
Hoggar
2918
Mont
Tahat
2306
Mont
Serkout
Tamanrasset
Sarīr
Tropic of Cancer
Tibesti
Bordj Mokhtar
Plateau du
Djado
Toummo
Tassili du Hoggar
Ténéré du
Tafassasset
Djado
Bardaï
Adrar des
Aguelhok
Ifôghas
In-Guezzam
Assamakka
Séguédine
Zouar
3265
Pic
Toussidé
3376
Tarso
Émissi
Tibesti
essalit
Kidal
Talak
1988
Adrar
Tamgak
Massif
de l'Aïr
Arlit
Ténéré
3415
Emi Koussi
Vallée de Azaouagh
2022
Monts
Bagzane
Arbre du
Ténéré
Bilma
Grand Erg de Bilma
Borkou
L
Ménaka
Agadez
Fachi
Faya
D
A
N
Andéramboukane
Falaise de Tiguidit
Erg du Ténéré
Bani-Bangou
Tchin Tabaradene
Tahoua
Aderbissinat
NIGER
Bodélé
CHAD
Tillabéri
Bagaroua
Laba
Tanout
Manga
Dogondoutchi
Birnin
Konni
Dakoro
Gangara
Nguigmi
Nokou
Nédély
mey
Dosso
Argungu
Sokoto
Maradi
Zinder
Katsina
Nguimi
Lake
Chad
Mao
hari
ye
Baléyara
Madaoua
Sokoto
NIGERIA

68 69
72 73

Settlements

■	over 3 million
□	1 – 3 million
○	250 000 – 1 million
●	100 000 – 250 000
◉	25 000 – 100 000
•	under 25 000
—	country capital underline
—	state or province capital underline

Scale 1 : 11 600 000

| 0 | 200 | 400 | 600 km |
| 0 | 100 | 200 | 300 miles |

MAURITANIA

Moudjéria
Boutilimit
Médedra
Aleg
Rosso
Bogué
Kiffa
Dagana
Kaédi
Mbout
Saint Louis
Louga
Linguère
Matam
Kébémer
Tivaouane
Touba
DAKAR
Cap Vert
Thiès
Diourbel
Mbour
SENEGAL
Joal-Fadiout
Kaolack
Kaffrine
Banjul
THE
Brikama
GAMBIA
Ziguinchor
Bignona
Cabo Roxo
Cacheu
GUINEA-
Bissau
BISSAU
Orango
Arquipélago
dos Bijagós
Catió

Ayoûn el
'Atroûs
Kobenni
Amourj
Kankossa
Nara
Ould
Yenjé
Sélibabi
Nioro du Sahel
Bakel
Kidira
Kayes
Bafoulabé
Tambacounda
Georgetown
Kolda
Vélingara
Kédougou
Satadougou
Koundára
Gaoual
Fouta
Labé
Djallon
Sansalé
Dinguiraye
Boké
Dabola
Boffa
Kindia
Mamou
Cap
Verga
Dubreka
Conakry
Kabala

Néma
Oualàta
Bassikounou
Bamba
Tombouctou
Lac Faguibine
Niger
Bourem
Goundam
Doro
Niafounke
Gossi
Gao
Youvarou
Lac Do
Hombori
Lac Débo
Douentza
Sokolo
MALI
Mopti
Djibo
Tougouri
Ségou
Tougan
Yako
Gourcy
Kaya
Bamako
Bla
Koutiala
BURKINA
Ouéléssébougou
Dédougou
Koudougou
Ouagadougou
Bougouni
Boromo
FASO
Lac de
Sikasso
Bobo-
Léo
Navrongo
Sélingue
Diébougou
Dioulasso
Bawku
Kalana
Lawra
Bolgatanga
Mango
Manankoro
Quangolodougou
Wa
Tamale

Kankan
Boundiali
Korhogo
Bouna
Bole
GHANA
Odienné
Ferkessédougou
Faranah
Tokounou
Kissidougou
Guéckédou
Beyla
Katiola
Tanda
Techiman
SIERRA
Makeni
Koïdu
Niakaramandougou
Bondoukou
Kintampo
Port Loko
Voinjama
Nzérékoré
Touba
CÔTE
Bouaké
Sunyani
LEONE
Bo
Kenema
Man
Bouaké
Agnibilekrou
Kumasi
Freetown
1752
Lac de Kossou
Bonthe
Gbarnga
Monts
Daloa
Yamoussoukro
Abengourou
Obuasi
Sherbro Island
Zimmi
Ganta
Nimba
Issia
Adzopé
Oda
Mano River
Touleplêu
D'IVOIRE
LIBERIA
Kakata
Guiglo
Gagnoa
Divo
Dunkwa
Accra
Monrovia
Zwedru
Soubré
Aboisso
Sekondi
Buchanan
Abidjan
Cape Coast
Tema
River Cess
Gbaaka
Sassandra
Takoradi
Greenville
Cape Three
Barclayville
Tabou
San-Pédro
Points
Cape
Palmas

Gulf   of

Equator

ATLANTIC

OCEAN

CAPE VERDE

Ascension
(U.K.)

© Copyright Research Machines plc 2005

WEST AFRICA

Benin • Burkina Faso • Cameroon • Cape Verde • Congo • Côte d'Ivoire •Equatorial Guinea • Gabon • The Gambia
Ghana • Guinea • Guinea-Bissau • Liberia • Nigeria • São Tomé & Príncipe • Senegal • Sierra Leone • Togo

70 71

74 75

Settlements

■	over 3 million
▫	1 – 3 million
○	250 000 – 1 million
●	100 000 – 250 000
◉	25 000 – 100 000
•	under 25 000
——	country capital underline
——	state or province capital underline

Scale 1 : 11 600 000

0   200   400   600 km
0 100 200 300 miles

NIGERIA

Mokolo
Maroua
Guider
Fianga
Figuil Léré Pala
Moundou Doba
Gore

Ngaoundéré
Koum
Bocaranga
Bozoum
Bouar
Garoua
Boulaï
Baoro

CAMEROON

Dja
Sembé
Mékambo

GABON

Equator
Makoua
Ewo
Okoyo
Gamboma
Djambala

Plateaux Batéké

CONGO

Owando
Obouya

Ngo

Brazzaville

72 73

Bongor
Bousso
Kendégué
Koumra
Sarh
Maro
Baïbokoum
Paoua
Batangafo
Bossangoa
Bossembélé
Damara
Carnot
Berbérati
Gamboula
Yokadouma
Nola
Mbaïki
Zongo
Libenge
Bomassa
Quésso
Dongou
Impfondo
Epéna
Makanza

Bangui

Dongo
Imese
Bolomba

Mbandaka

Bokatola
Lac Tumba
Inongo

Lac Mai-Ndombe

Bolobo
Kutu
Kasai
Bandundu

C H A D

Massif
Abou Déia
Mélfi du Guéra
Am Timan
Garba
Tiroungoulou
Ouanda-
Djallé
Ndélé
Ouadda

Birao

**CENTRAL
AFRICAN REPUBLIC**

Kaga Bandoro
Ippy Bria
Sibut Bambari
Kouango Alindao
Bangassou
Mobaye
Mobayi-
Mbongo Yakoma
Gemena Abumombazi
Businga
Kungu
Akula Lisala
Bumba
Congo
Bongandanga
Basankusu
Wenga
Boende Djolu
Tshuapa Bokungu
Busira Anzi
Boende Ikela

Monkoto

**DEMOCRATIC
REPUBLIC OF CONGO**

Mobomou
Rafaï Zémio
Obo
Bondo
Ango
Niangara
Poko
Bambesa
Banalia
Bomili
Yohuma Basoko
Yangambi

Kisangani

Opala
Lomela
Punia

Lubutu
Lomela
Lomami

Kibombo
Kama

Kindu
Kalima
Shabunda
Ulindi
Kasongo

Kongolo

S U D A

Rahad el Berdi Babanusa
Ed Da'ein El Muglad Kadugli
Sumeih
Nyamlell
Aweil
Wau
Tonj
Rumbek

Bahr el Ghazal

Tonga

Sudd

Amadi
Maridi Lanya
Doruma Yambio Yeï
Dungu
Faradjé Arua Nebbi
Watsa
Isiro Mungbere Mahagi
Aburo 2437
Wamba
Nia-Nia Irumu Lake Albert
Mambasa Bunia
Bafwasende Fort Portal
Bem 5110
Mount
Stanley
Lubero Lake
Butembo Edward Mbarara
Masak
Kamande
Muhulu Lowa Mount
Karisimbi
4510 Kabale
Goma Buka
Lake Kivu Gisenyi **Kigali**
Bukavu **RWANDA**
Butare
Ngozi
Bujumbura Gitega
Kamituga **BURUNDI**
3303 Buru
Fizi Rutana
Makamba
Uvira
Uvinza

Great Rift Valley

Lake Tanganyika

Kalemie
Nyunzu
Kabalo
Moba
Manono
Pweto

Djema

Obo

Am Timan

Katonga
Masaka

Ngara
Muyinga
Nyar
Kibondo
Kasulu
Kigoma
Ujiji

Mpa

Milolo
Mbala
Lake
Mweru Wantipa
Kiwa
Lake Mweru
Mporokoso
Lubudi
Kawambwa
Kasenga
Mwenda Nsombo
Lac de Retenue
de la Lufira
Minga Mansa
Lake
Bangweulu
Mukuku

KINSHASA
Mayamba Kenge
Mabanza-Ngungu Masi-Manimba
Inkisi-Kisantu
Popokabaka
Kikwit Idiofa
Luozi
Matadi Gungu
Banana Songololo
Boma Lukuni
M'banza Congo
Maquela
do Zombo
Quimbele

N'zeto

LUANDA

Caxito

Barra do
Cuanza
Lucala
Malanje

Porto Amboim

Sumbe

Luremo

Quibala
Musseride
Waku-Kungo
Andulo

Lobito
Benguela
Cubal
Huambo
Cuito
Caconda

Lucira
Caluquembe
Chitembo

Ilebo
Kole
Dekese
Lodja
Bena Dibele
Mweka
Lusambo
Lubefu
Kananga
Mbuji-Mayi
Tshikapa Gandajika
Mwene-Ditu
Kahemba Luiza
Chitato
Luremo
Cuilo
Chicapa
Kapanga
Cuango
Capenda-
Camulemba
Saurimo
Cacola
Muconda
Dala
Luau Dilolo
Lóvua
Luena
Camacupa
Sachanga
Lucusse
Lumbala
Kaquengue

A N G O L A

Chitembo
Cangamba
Lutembo

Kaniama
Kamina
Kinda
Sandoa
Kasaji
Lac Nzilo
Kolwezi
Caianda
Mwinilunga
Solwezi
Chavuma
Zambezi
Manyinga
Kabompo
Kasempa

Kabongo

Lubilash
Lubudi

Kasenga

ZAMBIA

Tenke Guba
Likasi
Lubumbashi
Chingola
Mufulira
Ndola
Kitwe
Luanshya

Serenje

Luangwa

West Lunga

76 77

© Copyright Research Machines plc 2005

metres feet
4000 13120
2000 6560
1000 3280
500 1640
200 656
0 0
200 656
1000 3280
2000 6560
4000 13120
6000 19690
8000 26250
metres feet

ATLANTIC OCEAN

15° E 20° 25° 30°

1

2

3

4

5

6

A B C D

10° N

5°

0°

5°

10° S

CENTRAL AFRICA

Angola • Burundi • Central African Republic • Democratic Republic of Congo
Djibouti • Ethiopia • Kenya • Rwanda • Somalia • Tanzania • Uganda

Scale 1 : 11 600 000

| 0 | 200 | 400 | 600 km |
| 0 | 100 | 200 | 300 miles |

A   15° E   B   20°   C   25°   D   30°

1

10° S

DEMOCRATIC REPUBLIC
OF CONGO

Barra do Cuanza
Lucala
Capenda-Camulemba
Chicapa
Saurimo
Sandoa
Kitwa
Lake Mweru
Mp

Porto Amboim
Quibala
Malanje
Cacola
Muconda
Dilolo
Kasaji
Lubudi
Kawamb

Sumbe
Waku-Kungo
Mussende
Dala
Luau
Caianda
Kolwezi
Tenke
Lac de Retenue de la Lufira
Mansa
La

2

Lobito
Benguela
Andulo
Camacupa
Luena
Lucusse
Lôvua
Mwinilunga
Minga
Likasi
Lubumbashi
Mwend

Cuio
Cubali
Bailundo
Huambo
Kuito
Cuemba
Sachanga
Lumbala Kaquengue
Solwezi
Chingola
Mufulira

Lucira
Caluquembe
Caconda
Chitembo
A N G O L A
Lutembo
Zambezi
Manyinga
Kasempa
Kitwe
Luanshya
Ndola

Cuvango
Menongue
Cangamba
Chiume
Lukulu
Kaoma
Mumbwa
Kapiri Mposhi
Z A M B I

15°
Lubango
Namibe
Huila Plateau
Cuito Cuanavale
Mongu
Luampa
Lusaka
Luang

Tombua
Punta Albina
Gahama
Caiundo
Mavinga
Senanga
Kafue
Namwala
Zambezi

Foz do Cunene
Humbe
Chitado
Ondjiva
Nkurenkuru
Cuangar
Mulobezi
Kariba Dam
Kariba
Chinho

3

Cape Fria
Ruacana
Ondangwa
Rundu
Bagani
Kongola
Sesheke
Kazungula
Livingstone
Lake Kariba
Chegut

Opuwo
Etosha Pan
Tsumeb
Tsumkwe
Mohembo
Seronga
Okavango Delta
Victoria Falls
Hwange
Shangani
Kwekwe

Sesfontein
Grootfontein
Maun
Ntwetwe Pan
Z I M B

20°
Outjo
Eiseb
Sehithwa
Nata
Plumtree
Zvishavane

2574
Brandberg
Otjiwarongo
Bulawayo
Gwa

Omaruru
Steinhausen
Ghanzi
Lake Xau
Orapa
Francistown
Gwanda

Karibib
Okahandja
Mamuno
B O T S W A N A
Serowe
Selebi-Phikwe
Alldays

Swakopmund
Windhoek
Gobabis
K a l a h a r i
Mahalapye
Palapye
Limpopo
LIMPO
PROVIN

4
Walvis Bay
N A M I B I A
Ncojane
Kang
Molepolole
Mochudi
Thabazimbi
Piete

Tropic of Capricorn
Rehoboth
Leonardville
Tshane
Gaborone
Kanye
Potgietersrus
Nylstroom

Nauchas
Narib
Aranos
D e s e r t
Lobatse
Sun City
Pretoria
Mamelodi
Ly

Narib
Mariental
Gochas
Tshabong
Vorstershoop
Mmabatho
GAUTENG
MPUMAL

Maltahöhe
Johannesburg
Soweto
Springs

Lüderitz
Keetmanshoop
Bokspits
NORTH WEST
Vanderbijlpark
Vereeniging

Aus
Seeheim
Aroab
Vryburg
Klerksdorp

5
Grünau
Karasburg
Kuruman
Bloemhof
Kroonstad

Orangemund
Karasburg
Upington
Postmasburg
Warrenton
Welkom
Bethlehem
FREE STATE

Alexander Bay
Vioolsdrift
Orange
Douglas
Kimberley
Mont aux Sources 3299
Maseru

Port Nolloth
Pofadder
Kenhardt
Bloemfontein
LESOTHO
Pietermaritzbu

Springbok
Prieska
Jagersfontein
3095
Thaba Putsoa
Mafeteng
Under

30°
Garies
NORTHERN
CAPE
Brandvlei
Britstown
Colesberg
Aliwal North
Kokstad
CAPE

Kraai
Port Shepst

A T L A N T I C
Calvinia
Williston
Carnarvon
Dé Aar
Middelburg
Elliot
Gama

O C E A N
Vanrhynsdorp
Victoria West
Fraserburg
SOUTH AFRICA
Cradock
Queenstown
Unitata

Lambert's Bay
St. Helena Bay
Sutherland
G r e a t   K a r o o
Beaufort West
Graaff-Reinet
Aberdeen
EASTERN CAPE
Port S

Cape Columbine
Vrendenburg
Piketberg
Doring
Touws River
Laingsburg
Willowmore
Fort Beaufort
King William's Town

6
Malmesbury
WESTERN
CAPE
Little
Karoo
Oudtshoorn
Uitenhage
East London

CAPE TOWN
Worcester
Paarl
Strand
Riversdale
George
Knysna
Port Elizabeth

Khayelitsha
Mosselbaai
Cape St. Francis

Cape of Good Hope
Bredasdorp
Cape Agulhas

35°
A   15°   B   20°   C   25°   D   30

metres	feet
4000	13120
2000	6560
1000	3280
500	1640
200	656
0	0
200	656
1000	3280
2000	6560
4000	13120
6000	19690
8000	26250
metres	feet

© Copyright Research Machines plc 2005

SOUTHERN AFRICA

Botswana • Comoros • Lesotho • Madagascar • Malawi • Mauritius
Mozambique • Namibia • Seychelles • South Africa • Swaziland • Zambia • Zimbabwe

Nakonde • Njombe
Lukumburu
Chitipa • Liwale
Karonga
Isoka
Livingstonia
Lindi
Chama
Songea
Nyamtumbo
Mbamba Bay
Masasi
Newala
Mtwara
Chikwa
Mzuzu
Tunduru
Masuguru
Quionga
Cabo Delgado
ika
Mzimba
Ruvuma
Negomane
Mocímboa da Praia
Diaca

TANZANIA

Lundazi
Nkhotakota
Metangula
Maniamba
Lichinga
Mecula
Lugenda
Marrupa
Montepuez
Pemba

Mfuwe
Salima

MALAWI
Lilongwe
Dedza
Mandimba
Namapa
Memba

Chipata
Zomba
Lake Chilwa
2419
Nacaroa
Nacala

AEARE
Songo
Ulongue
Guamba
Monte
Namuli
Alto Molócuè
Moçambique
Bene
Blantyre
3002
Nampula
ugwiza
Lago de
Cahora Bassa
Tete
Chiromo
Mount
Mulanje
Lugela

MOZAMBIQUE
Changara
Mocuba
Moma
Caia
Mopeia
Angoche
Catandica
Quelimane

Mutare
Chimoio
Inhaminga
Chinde
Cashel

Espungabera
Beira

angle
Nova Mambone

Save
Save

Chicualacuala
Ilha do Bazaruto
Mapinhane
Chigubo
Nhachengue

Mabalane
Massinga
Inhambane
Chibuto
Ponta Zavora

Chókwè
Macia
Xai-Xai

Maputo
Ponta Khehuene
Bela Vista

ILAND
Mkuze
Lake St. Lucia
Empangeni

BAN

MADAGASCAR

Aldabra
Islands
SEYCHELLES
Assumption
Cosmoledo
Group
Astove
Farquhar
Group

Mitsamiouli
COMOROS
Moroni
Njazidja
Íles Glorieuses
(France)
Tanjona
Bobaomby
Fomboni
Mwali
Mutsamudu
Nzwami
Antsirañana
Mamoudzou
Mayotte
(France)
Nosy Bé
Ambilobe
Nosy Mitsio
Iharaña
Ambanja
Nosy Radama
Massif du
Bealanana
2876
Sambava
Analalava
Andapa
Antalaha
Mahajanga
Mandritsara
Maroansetra
Mitsinjo
Mananara
Avaratra
Tanjona
Masoala
Soalala
Ambato Boeny
Soanierana-Ivongo
Tanjona Vilanandro
Maevatanana
Andilamena
Nosy
Besalampy
Farihy Alaotra
Boraha
Morafenobe
Ambatondrazaka
Maintirano
Beravina
Ambatolampy
Toamasina
Nosy Barren
Antsalova
ANTANANARIVO
Tsiroanomandidy
Moramanga
Miandrivazo
2643
Tsiafajavona
Vatomandry
Belo Tsiribihina
Antsirabe
Mahanoro
Morondava
Mania
Marolambo
Mandabe
Fandriana
Nosy-
Varika
Matsiatra
Ambositra
Ambohimahasoa
Manja
Fianarantsoa
Mananjary
Morombe
Mangoky
Ifanadiana
Tanjona
Ankaboa
Ankazoabo
Zazafotsy
Manakara
Ihosy
Ivohibe
Vohipeno
Mahaboboka
Farafangana
Sakaraha
Betroka
Vangaindrano
Toliara
Onilahy
Betioky
Bekily
Manantenina
Ampanihy
Tôlañaro
Beloha
Ambovombe
Tanjona
Vohimena

Tropic of Capricorn

Mozambique Channel

Juan de
Nova
(France)

Bassas da
India
(France)

Île Europa
(France)

INDIAN

OCEAN

①
A   B
Port Louis
Phoenix
St-Denis
MAURITIUS
St-Pierre
Réunion
(France)
INDIAN
OCEAN

②
A
Aldabra
Islands
Assumption
Cosmoledo Group
Astove
St. Pierre I.
Providence I.
Farquhar Group
Agalega Islands
(Mauritius)

SEYCHELLES
Praslin
Silhouette I.
Victoria
Mahé
Amirante Is.
Coëtivy

INDIAN OCEAN

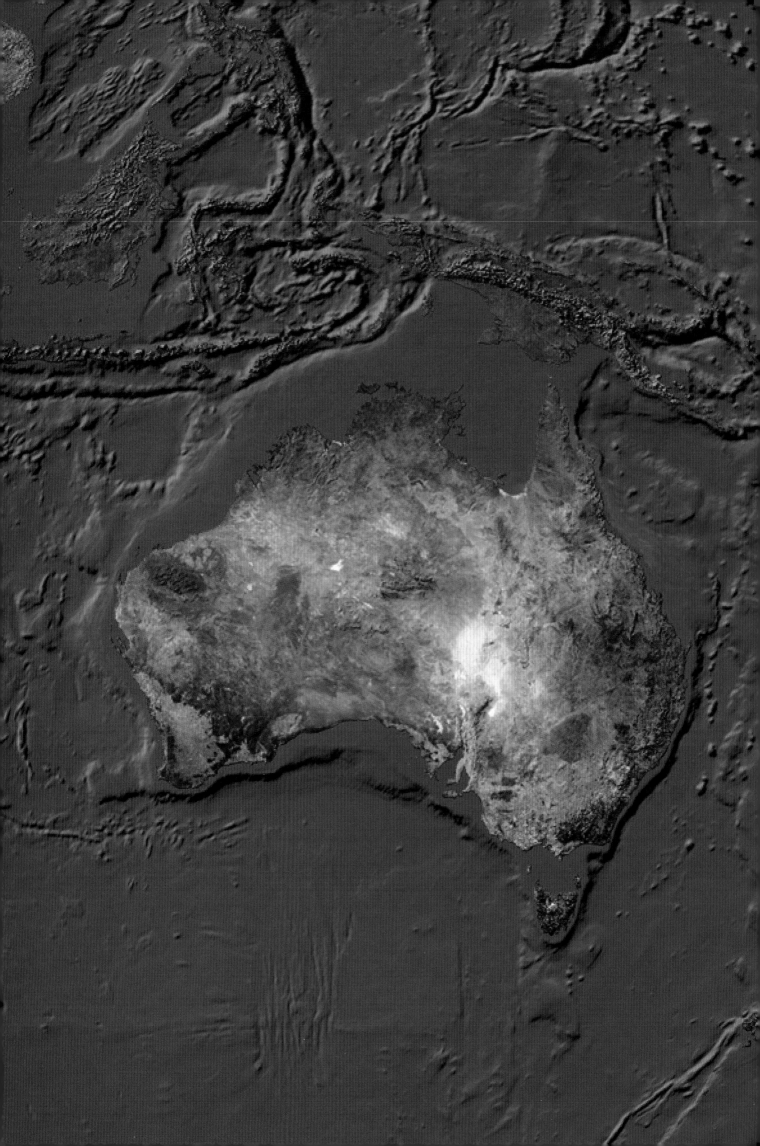

OCEANIA

Oceania   80

Australia   82

New Zealand   84

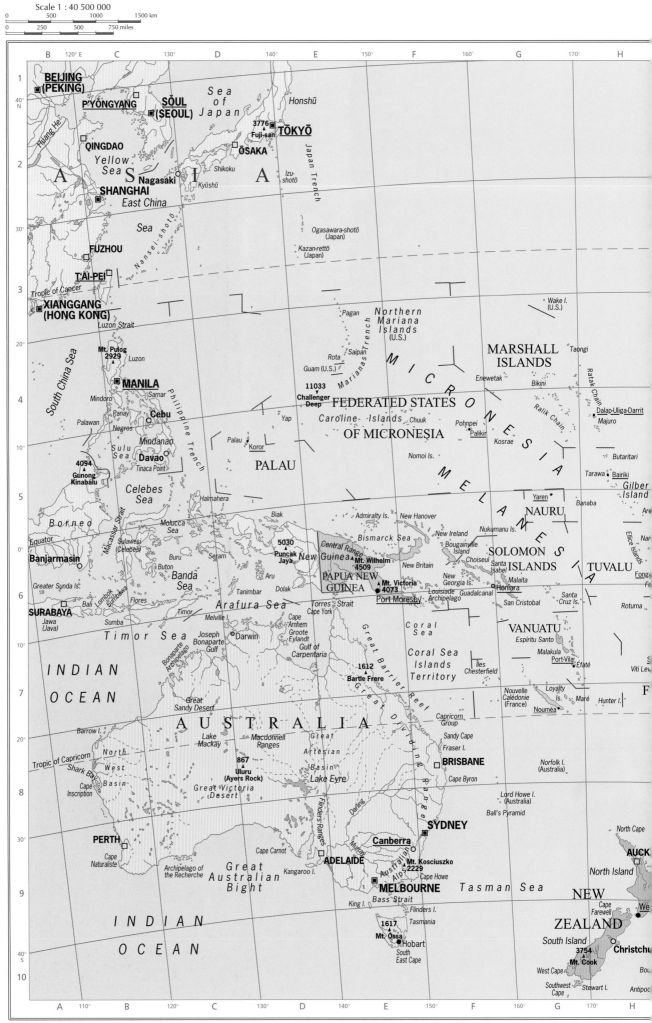

Scale 1 : 40 500 000

0   500   1000   1500 km
0   250   500   750 miles

B   120° E   C   130°   D   140°   E   150°   F   160°   G   170°   H

BEIJING (PEKING)

P'YŎNGYANG   **SŎUL (SEOUL)**   Honshū

Sea of Japan

QINGDAO   3776 Fuji-san   **TŌKYŌ**

Yellow Sea   **ŌSAKA**

A   S   Shikoku   Japan Trench   I   A

Nagasaki   Kyūshū   Izu-shotō

SHANGHAI   East China

Sea

Ogasawara-shotō (Japan)

FUZHOU   Kazan-rettō (Japan)

T'AI-PEI

Tropic of Cancer

XIANGGANG (HONG KONG)   Wake I. (U.S.)

Luzon Strait   Pagan   Northern Mariana Islands (U.S.)

Mt. Pulog 2929   Luzon   MARSHALL ISLANDS   Taongi

South China Sea   Rota   Saipan   M   I   C   R   O   N   E   S   I   A

Guam (U.S.)   Enewetak   Bikini   Ratak Chain

MANILA   Mindoro   Samar   11033 Challenger Deep   FEDERATED STATES   Dalap-Uliga-Darrit

Cebu   Panay   Yap   Caroline Islands   Chuuk   OF MICRONESIA   Majuro

Palawan   Negros   Palau   Koror   Pohnpei   Kosrae   Nomoi Is.   Butaritari

4094 Gunong Kinabalu   Mindanao   Tinaca Point   PALAU   Tarawa   Bairiki

Davao   Gilber Island

Sulu Sea   Celebes Sea   Halmahera   M   E   L   A   N   E   S   I   A   Yaren   Banaba

Borneo   Molucca Sea   Biak   Admiralty Is.   New Hanover   NAURU

Equator   Sulawesi (Celebes)   Seram   5030 Puncak Jaya   Central Range   New   New Ireland   Nukumanu Is.   SOLOMON   TUVALU   Fong

Banjarmasin   Buru   Guinea   Mt. Wilhelm 4509   Bougainville Island   ISLANDS

Greater Sunda Is.   Buton   Aru   PAPUA NEW   New Britain   Choiseul   Santa Isabel   Malaita   Honiara   Rotuma

Bali   Lombok   Banda Sea   Tanimbar   Dolak   GUINEA   Mt. Victoria 4073   New Georgia Is.   Guadalcanal   Santa Cruz Is.

SURABAYA   Sumbawa   Flores   Port Moresby   Louisiade Archipelago   San Cristobal

Jawa (Java)   Sumba   Timor   Arafura Sea   Torres Strait   Cape York   VANUATU

Melville I.   Cape Arnhem   Coral Sea   Espiritu Santo   Malakula

Timor Sea   Joseph Bonaparte Gulf   Groote Eylandt   Port-Vila   Éfaté

Bonaparte Archipelago   Darwin   Gulf of Carpentaria   Coral Sea Islands Territory   Îles Chesterfield

INDIA N   1612 Bartle Frere   Nouvelle Calédonie (France)   Loyalty Is.   Maré   Hunter I.

OCEAN   Great Sandy Desert   A   U   S   T   R   A   L   I   A   Capricorn Group   Nouméa

Barrow I.   Lake Mackay   Macdonnell Ranges   Great   Sandy Cape   Norfolk I. (Australia)

Tropic of Capricorn   North   Artesian   Fraser I.   **BRISBANE**

Shark Bay   West   867   Basin   Cape Byron

Cape Inscription   Basin   Uluru (Ayers Rock)   Lake Eyre   Lord Howe I. (Australia)

Great Victoria Desert   Flinders Ranges   Ball's Pyramid

PERTH   Murray   **SYDNEY**   North Cape

Cape Naturaliste   Darling   **Canberra**   Mt. Kosciuszko 2229   **AUCK**

Archipelago of the Recherche   Great Australian Bight   Kangaroo I.   **ADELAIDE**   Australian   Cape Howe   North Island

Cape Carnot   Alps   **MELBOURNE**   Tasman Sea   **NEW**

King I.   Bass Strait   **ZEALAND**

INDIA N   Flinders I.   Cape Farewell   We

1617   Tasmania   South Island

OCEAN   Mt. Ossa   **Hobart**   3754 Mt. Cook   **Christchu**

South East Cape   West Cape   Bou

Southwest Cape   Stewart I.   Antipo

1   2   3   4   5   6   7   8   9   10

A   110°   B   120°   C   130°   D   140°   E   150°   F   160°   G   170°   H

80   Oceania

J   170°   K   160°   L   150°   M   140°   N   130°   P   120° W   Q

NORTH AMERICA

LOS ANGELES

SAN DIEGO

P A C I F I C

Guadalupe (Mexico)

Tropic of Cancer

HAWAII (U.S.)

Hawaiian Islands

Necker I.

Kauai
Oahu
Honolulu Maui
Hawaii

Is. Revillagigedo (Mexico)

Johnston I. (U.S.)

N. W. Christmas Island Ridge

O C E A N

Palmyra I. (U.S.)

Tabuaeran Kiritimati

Howland (U.S.)
Baker (U.S.)

Jarvis (U.S.)

Line Islands

Phoenix Islands
Birnie Rawaki
Orona Manra
KIRIBATI Malden I.

Starbuck I.

Equator

P O L Y N E S I A

Atafu Tokelau
Nukunonu (New Zealand) Tongareva

Swains I. Danger Is. Vostok I. Caroline I. Nuku Hiva Marquesas Islands
Nassau Manihiki Hiva Oa

SAMOA American
Savaii Apia Samoa Flint I. Îles de
Is. Upolu Tutuila Désappointement
ce) Suvorov I. Pukapuka
Tafahi Rose I. Îles Palliser Raroia
Cook Islands Motu One
(New Zealand)

TONGA Niue Palmerston I. Aitutaki Arch. Tahiti
(New Zealand) de la Société Hao
lofa French Îles Duc de
Ata Rarotonga Polynesia Gloucester Groupe Actéon

**Horizon Depth
10882** Mangaia Îles Rurutu Morane Gambier
Maria Mururoa Is.
Tubuai Mangareva

Tonga Trench Tubuai Islands Raevavae
Oeno Tropic of Capricorn
Rapa Henderson I.
Marotiri **Pitcairn Is.** Ducie I.
(U.K.)

Archipel des Tuamotu

Easter I. (Chile)

S o u t h   W e s t

P a c i f i c

B a s i n

ec Islands
Zealand)

dec Trench

Is.
and)

J   170°   K   160°   L   150°   M   140°   N   130°   P   120°   Q   110°   R

Scale 1 : 13 800 000

| 0 | 200 | 400 | 600 km |
| 0 | 100 | 200 | 300 miles |

INDONESIA

Sawu
Sea

Savu
Rote

Timor

Kupang

Timor
Sea

Ara*f*

Cobo
Croker *Penins*
Island *Cape*

Melville
Island
Van
Bathurst *Diemen*
Island *Gulf*
Clarence Strait
Beagle Gulf Darwin Jabiru
Rum Jungle Batchelor
Adelaide River
Pine Creek 366
Mou
Evely
Katheri

INDIAN OCEAN

Cape
Londonderry

Seringapatam
Reef
Cape Scott
Sandy I. Scott
Reef
Bonaparte
Port
Warrender
Archipelago
Joseph
Bonaparte
Gulf
Wingate Mountains
Matarank

Wyndham
Drysdale
River
Timber Creek
Kununurra
Victoria
River
Larrima

Collier Bay
Lake
Argyle
Daly Wate

Sunday Strait
Cape Lévêque
Lombadina
King
Sound
Mount
Ord
936
Kimberley
Halls
Creek
Newcas
Wate

Derby
Plateau
Inverway
Kalkaring
La
Woo

Broome
Fitzroy Crossing

Lagrange

Rowley
Shoals

Gregory
Lake
N O R
Sandfire Flat Roadhouse
Tanami
T E R

Port Hedland
Great Sandy Desert
Lake
White
Lake
Wills
Ba
Cre

Goldsworthy
Percival Lakes

Monte Bello Is. Karratha
Marble Bar
A U S T R
Barrow I. Roebourne
Lake
Mackay
Yuendumu
Mount
Ziel
1510

North West Cape
Exmouth
Hamersley Range
Nullagine
Lake
Dora
Mount
Liebig 1524
Mount
Alice S

Mount
Bruce
1235
Wittenoom
Tom Price
Gibson Desert
Lake
Macdonald
Macdonnell Rang

Nanutarra
Roadhouse
1251
Mount Meharry
Newman
Lake Disappointment
Lake
Hopkins
Lake
Neale
Lake Amadeus

Cardabia
North
Uluru (Ayers Rock)
867

Minilya Roadhouse
1106
Mount
Augustus
910
Mount
Essendon
WESTERN
Mount
Aloysius
1085
Musgrave Ranges

Lake
Macleod
West
Lake
Carnegie
AUSTRALIA
1440
Mount
Woodroffe

Carnarvon
Landor

Cape Inscription
Shark Bay
Denham
Wiluna
Great Victoria Deser
S O
AUS

Dirk Hartog I.
Overlander
Useless Loop
Roadhouse
Meekatharra
Nannine
Yeo Lake

Basin
Lake
Austin
Leinster
Rason
Lake
Lake
Maurice

Kalbarri
Mount
Magnet
Leonora
Lake
Carey

Northampton
Lake Barlee
Menzies
Kookynie

Geraldton
Mullewa
Payne's Find
Nullarbor Plain
Deakin

Dongara
Lake
Moore
Coolgardie
Kalgoorlie
Rawlinna
Eucla

Wubin
Pithara
Bonnie
Rock
Lake Lefroy
Mundrabilla
Head of
Bight
Coorat

Badgingarra
Bindi Bindi
Southern
Cross
Merredin
Norseman
Balladonia
Point
Culver
Twilight
Cove

Goomalling
Northam
Cunderdin
Hyden
Lake Dundas
Israelite
Bay

PERTH
Fremantle
Mandurah
Williams
Lake Grace
Ravensthorpe
Esperance
Cape Arid

Bunbury
Geographe Bay
Cape
Naturaliste
Jerramungup
Boxwood Hill
Cheyne
Bay
Esperance Bay
Archipelago
of the
Recherche
Great

Manjimup
Cranbrook
Albany
Australian Bigh

Cape Leeuwin
Augusta
Walpole
Denmark
INDIAN OC

Point d'Entrecasteaux

Tropic of Capricorn

metres	feet
4000	13120
2000	6560
1000	3280
500	1640
200	656
0	0
200	656
1000	3280
2000	6560
4000	13120
6000	19690
8000	26250
metres	feet

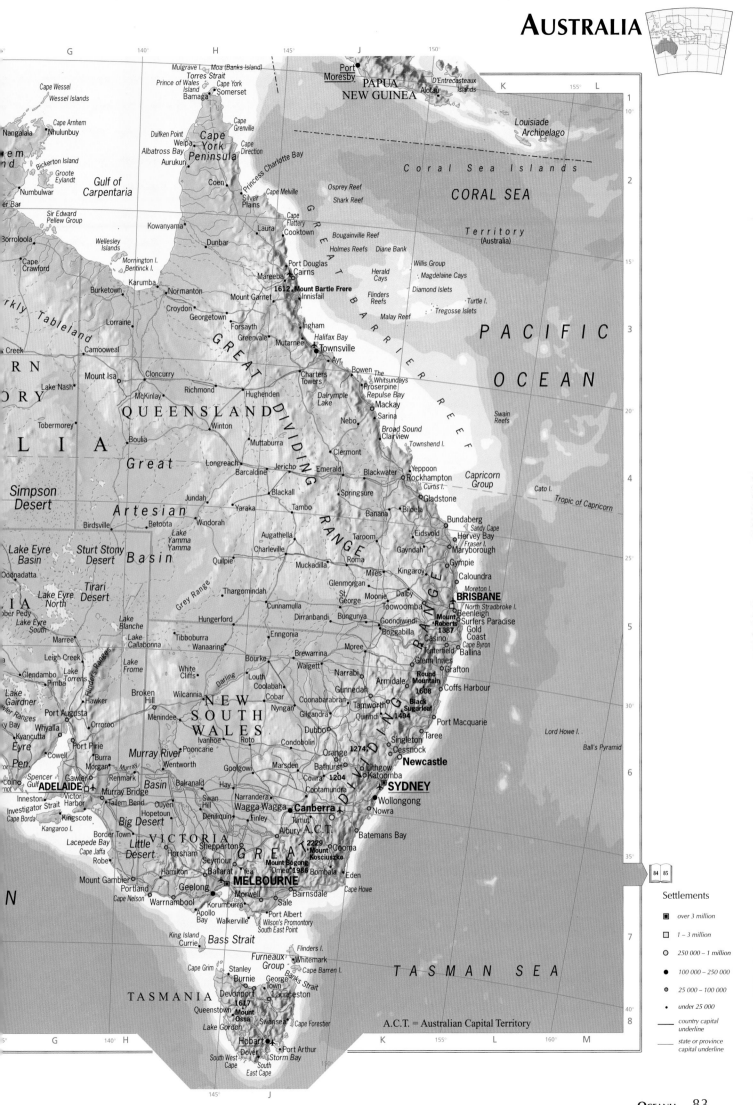

AUSTRALIA

Nangalala • **Nhulunbuy**

Cape Wessel
Wessel Islands
Cape Arnhem

Numbulwar

er Bar

Bickerton Island
Groote
Eylandt

Borroloola

Sir Edward
Pellew Group

Cape
Crawford

Gulf of
Carpentaria

Mulgrave I. Moa (Banks Island)
Torres Strait
Prince of Wales
Island Cape York
Bamaga Somerset

Cape York
Peninsula

Duifken Point Cape
Weipa Grenville
Albatross Bay Cape
Aurukun Direction

Wellesley
Islands

Mornington I.
Bentinck I.

Coen

Kowanyama

Princess Charlotte Bay
Cape Melville

Laura

Cape
Flattery
Cooktown

Port
Moresby
PAPUA
NEW GUINEA

D'Entrecasteaux
Alotau Islands

Louisiade
Archipelago

Coral Sea Islands
CORAL SEA

Osprey Reef
Shark Reef

Territory
(Australia)

Bougainville Reef
Holmes Reefs Diane Bank

Willis Group
Magdelaine Cays

Herald
Cays Diamond Islets

Flinders
Reefs Turtle I.
Tregosse Islets

Malay Reef

PACIFIC

OCEAN

Burketown

Karumba

Normanton

Croydon

Georgetown

Forsayth

Greenvale

Port Douglas
Cairns
Mareeba
1612 Mount Bartle Frere
Innisfail
Mount Garnet

Ingham

Halifax Bay
Mutarnee
Townsville
Ayr

rkly Tableland

Creek

Camooweal

Mount Isa

Lake Nash

Tobermorey

Cloncurry

McKinlay

Richmond

Hughenden

Winton

Muttaburra

QUEENSLAND

Great

Artesian

Basin

Simpson
Desert

LIA

Boulia

Longreach

Barcaldine

Jericho

Blackall

Charters
Towers
Bowen
The
Proserpine Whitsundays
Repulse Bay

Dalrymple
Lake
Mackay
Nebo
Sarina

Broad Sound
Clairview
Townshend I.

Swain
Reefs

GREAT DIVIDING RANGE

Emerald

Blackwater

Yeppoon
Rockhampton

Capricorn
Group

Cato I.

Tropic of Capricorn

Birdsville

Betoota

Windorah

Yaraka

Tambo

Clermont

Springsure

Banana
Biloela

Curtis I.
Gladstone

Lake
Yamma
Yamma

Oodnadatta

Lake Eyre
Basin

Sturt Stony
Desert

IA

ber Pedy

Tirari
Desert

Lake Eyre
North

Lake Eyre
South

Marree

Thargomindah

Grey Range

Augathella

Charleville

Quilpie

Muckadilla
Roma

Taroom

St
George
Glenmorgan **Miles**
Moonie **Dalby**
Toowoomba

Gayndah

Bundaberg
Sandy Cape
Hervey Bay
Fraser I.
Maryborough
Gympie

Caloundra

Moreton I.
BRISBANE
North Stradbroke I.

Leigh Creek
Lake
Blanche

Tibooburra

Wanaaring

Hungerford

Cunnamulla

Dirranbandi
Bungunya

Goondiwindi
Boggabilla

Beenleigh
Surfers Paradise
Gold
Coast

Glendambo
Lake
Torrens

Lake
Callabonna

Marree

Lake
Frome

Bourke

White
Cliffs

Brewarrina

Walgett

Moree

Mount
Roberts
1387

Casino
Tenterfield Ballina
Cape Byron

Pimba

Hawker

Broken
Hill

Wilcannia

Darling

Louth
Coolabah

NEW
SOUTH
WALES

Narrabri

Gunnedah

Glenn Innes
Grafton

Round
Mountain
1608

Coffs Harbour

Lake
Gairdner

Flinders Ranges

Lake
Eyre
Pen.

er Ranges

Orroroo

Menindee

Cobar
Nyngan

Coonabarabran

Armidale

Tamworth
Black
Sugarloaf
1494
Quirindi

Port Macquarie

Lord Howe I.

Ball's Pyramid

Port Augusta

Whyalla

Kyancutta

Cowell

Port Pirie

Burra
Morgan

Murray River
Murray

Ivanhoe
Roto

Gilgandra

Dubbo

Singleton
Cessnock

Taree

Eyre

Cowra

Port

Spencer
Gulf

Renmark

Basin

Balranald

Hay

Condobolin

Orange 1274

Bathurst

1204

Newcastle

mo

Inneston

Gawler

ADELAIDE

Murray Bridge
Victor
Harbor

Tailem Bend

Ouyen

Swan
Hill

Narrandera

Wagga Wagga
Finley

Cootamundra

Lithgow
Katoomba

SYDNEY

Wollongong

Nowra

Kingscote

Kangaroo I.

Big Desert

Border
Town

Lacepede Bay
Cape Jaffa
Robe

Hopetoun

Deniliquin

VICTORIA

Little
Desert

Horsham

Seymour

Shepparton

Albury

Tumut

A.C.T.

GREAT

2229
Mount
Kosciuszko
Mount Bogong
1986 Bombala
Omeo

Canberra

Cooma

Batemans Bay

Hamilton

Mount Gambier

Portland

Cape Nelson

Ballarat

Geelong

Yea

MELBOURNE

Morwell

Bairnsdale

Eden

Cape Howe

Warrnambool

Apollo
Bay

Korumburra
Port Albert
Wilson's Promontory
South East Point

Sale

Walkerville

King Island
Currie

Bass Strait

Furneaux
Group

Flinders I.

Whitemark

Cape Barren I.

Banks Strait

TASMAN SEA

Cape Grim

Stanley

Burnie
Devonport

George
Town
Launceston

TASMANIA

1617
Mount
Queenstown Ossa

Swansea

Cape Forestier

A.C.T. = Australian Capital Territory

Lake Gordon

Hobart

South West
Cape
Dover
Storm Bay
South
East Cape

Port Arthur

84 | 85

Settlements

■ over 3 million

□ 1 – 3 million

◎ 250 000 – 1 million

● 100 000 – 250 000

◉ 25 000 – 100 000

• under 25 000

___ country capital
underline

___ state or province
capital underline

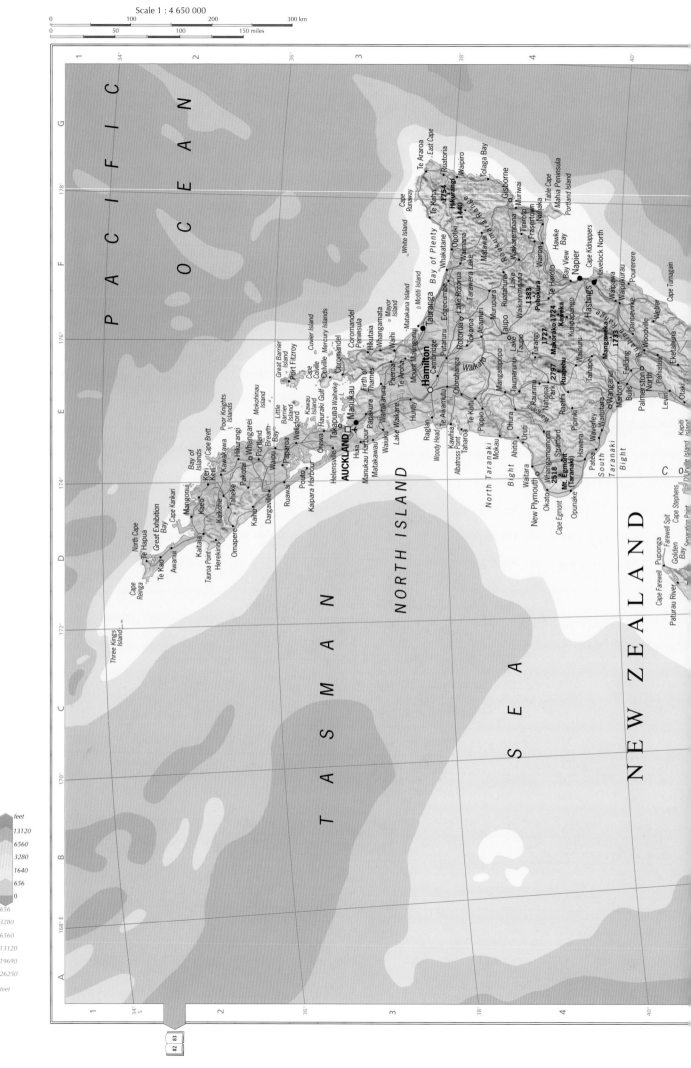

Scale 1 : 4 650 000

metres	feet
4000	13120
2000	6560
1000	3280
500	1640
200	656
0	0
1000	3280
2000	6560
4000	13120
6000	19690
8000	26250
metres	feet

PACIFIC OCEAN

TASMAN SEA

NORTH ISLAND

NEW ZEALAND

Cape Reinga
North Cape
Te Kao
Te Hapua
Awanui
Great Exhibition Bay
Cape Karikari
Kaitaia
Mangonui
Tauroa Point
Kaeo
Cape Brett
Herekino
Kaikohe
Bay of Islands
Kerikeri
Keri
Omapere
Taheke
Hikurangi
Whangarei
Dargaville
Kaihu
Poor Knights Islands
Ruawai
Paparoa
Portland
Waipu
Bream Bay
Pouto
Kaipara Harbour
Little Barrier Island
Mokohinau Island
Great Barrier Island
Port Fitzroy
Kawau Island
Helensville
Orewa
Waiheke I.
Takapuna
AUCKLAND
Manukau
Cuvier Island
Mercury Islands
Hua
Manukau Harbour
Papakura
Waiuku
Matakawau
Thames
Coromandel
Colville
Cape Colville
Coromandel Peninsula
Hikutaia
Firth of Thames
Te Aroha
Waihi
Whangamata
Mayor Island
Matakana Island
Motiti Island
Tauranga
Bay of Plenty
White Island
Whakatane
Opotiki
Te Kaha
Te Araroa
East Cape
Ruatoria
Hikurangi 1754
Waipiro
Tolaga Bay
Gisborne
Murewai
Wairoa
Matawai
Lake
Taupo
Waikato
Hamilton
Cambridge
Putaruru
Raglan
Woody Head
Kawhia
Kawhia Harbour
Lake Waikare
Huntly
Te Awamutu
Otorohanga
Rotorua
Lake Rotorua
Mamaku
Lake Tarawera
Rotorua
Taupo
Lake Taupo
Mangakino
Mangatupopo
Taumarunui
National Park
2797
Ruapehu
1727
Raetihi
Ohakune
Taihape
1383
Pohokura
Te Haroto
Makorako 1724
Kaweka
Mangaweka 1733
Ruahine Range
Napier
Hastings
Hawke Bay
Cape Kidnappers
Bay View
Havelock North
Waipawa
Waipukurau
Pourerere
Dannevirke
Woodville
Weber
Cape Turnagain
Eketahuna
Feilding
Palmerston North
Bulls
Marton
Wanganui
Waitotara
Waverley
Patea
Hawera
Stratford
2518
Mt. Egmont (Taranaki)
Opunake
Cape Egmont
New Plymouth
North Taranaki Bight
South Taranaki Bight
Urenui
Motunui
Ahititi
Ohura
Piriaka
Levin
Otaki
Kapiti Island
Cape Farewell
Puponga
Farewell Spit
Golden Bay
Cape Stephens
Separation Point
D'Urville Island

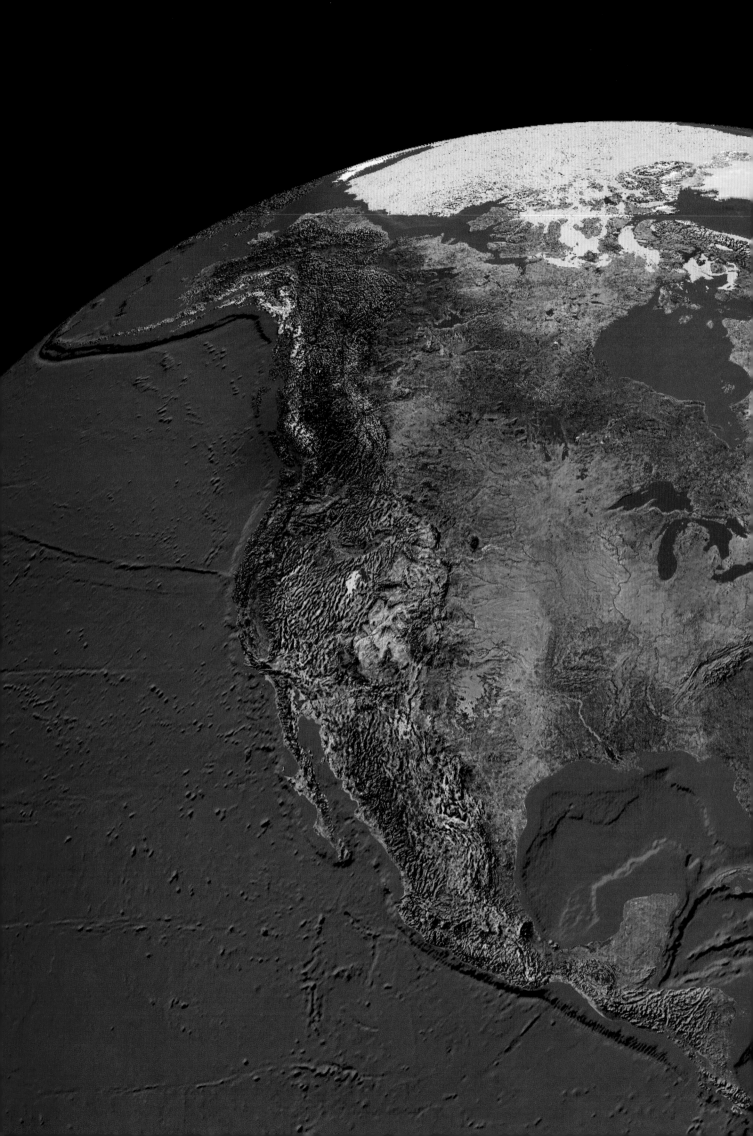

SOUTH AMERICA

South America   106

Northern South America   108

Southern South America   110

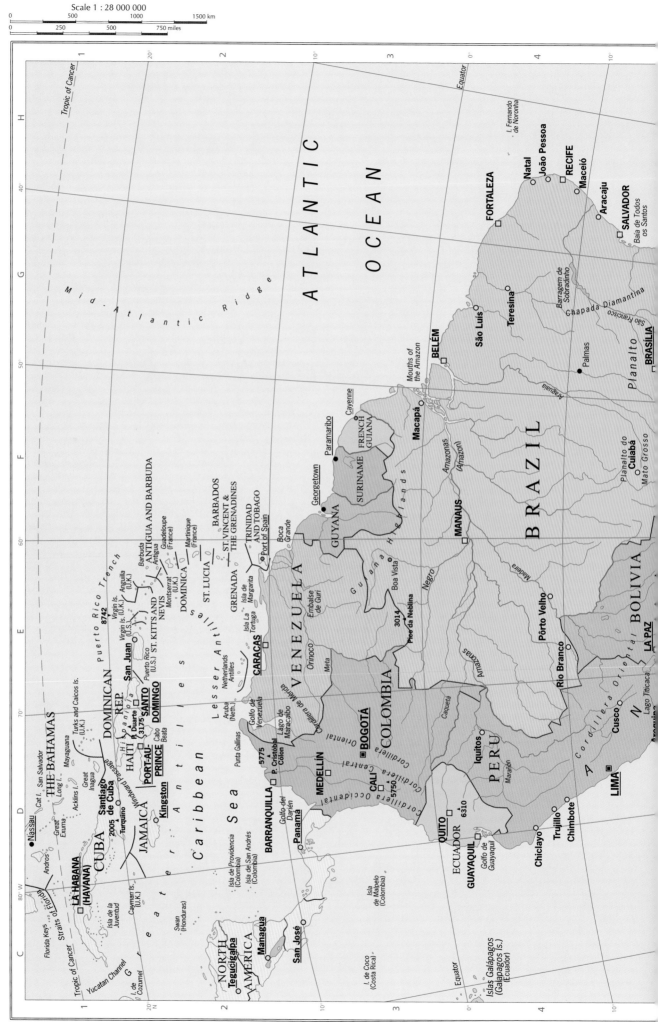

Scale 1 : 28 000 000

| 0 | 500 | 1000 | 1500 km |
| 0 | 250 | 500 | 750 miles |

Tropic of Cancer

H

Mid-Atlantic Ridge

A T L A N T I C

O C E A N

I. Fernando
de Noronha

Natal
João Pessoa
RECIFE
FORTALEZA
Maceió
Aracaju
SALVADOR
Baía de Todos
os Santos

G

Teresina
Barragem de
Sobradinho
Chapada Diamantina

São Luís

BELÉM
Mouths of
the Amazon
Palmas
BRASÍLIA
Planalto

F

Cayenne
FRENCH
GUIANA
Paramaribo
SURINAME
Macapá
Amazonas
(Amazon)
Planalto do
Mato Grosso
Cuiabá

Georgetown
GUYANA
Boca
Grande
Guiana Highlands
Boa Vista
Negro
Madeira
MANAUS

Pôrto Velho

E

Puerto Rico Trench
8742
DOMINICAN
REP.
San Juan
Virgin Is. (U.K.)
Virgin Is. (U.S.)
Puerto Rico
(U.S.)
ST. KITTS AND
NEVIS
Montserrat
(U.K.)
Barbuda
Antigua
ANTIGUA AND BARBUDA
Guadeloupe
(France)
DOMINICA
Martinique
(France)
ST. LUCIA
BARBADOS
ST. VINCENT &
THE GRENADINES
GRENADA
Isla de
Margarita
TRINIDAD
AND TOBAGO
Port of Spain
CARACAS
Orinoco
Embalse
de Guri
Meta
V E N E Z U E L A
3014
Pico da Neblina
Rio Branco
BOLIVIA
LA PAZ
Lago Titicaca

D

THE BAHAMAS
Cat I., San Salvador
Long I.
Mayaguana
Great
Inagua
Turks and Caicos Is.
(U.K.)
HAITI
Hispaniola
3175
P. Duarte
Cabo
Beata
SANTO
DOMINGO
PORT-AU-
PRINCE
Isla La
Tortuga
Punta Gallinas
Golfo de
Venezuela
Lago de
Maracaibo
Cordillera de Mérida
5775
P. Cristóbal
Colón
BARRANQUILLA
Golfo del
Darién
MEDELLÍN
BOGOTÁ
COLOMBIA
Cordillera Oriental
Cordillera Central
5750
CALI
Caquetá
Iquitos
PERU
Marañón
Cusco
Cordillera Oriental

C

Florida Keys
Straits of Florida
Andros
CUBA
Santiago
de Cuba
2005
Turquino
JAMAICA
Kingston
LA HABANA
(HAVANA)
Isla de la
Juventud
Cayman Is.
(U.K.)
Swan
(Honduras)
Isla de Providencia
(Colombia)
Isla de San Andrés
(Colombia)
Greater Antilles
Lesser Antilles
Netherlands
Antilles
Aruba
(Neth.)
Caribbean Sea
NORTH
AMERICA
Tegucigalpa
Managua
San José
PANAMÁ
Panamá
Golfo de
Panamá
Isla de Malpelo
(Colombia)
I. de Coco
(Costa Rica)
ECUADOR
QUITO
6310
GUAYAQUIL
Golfo de
Guayaquil
Chiclayo
Trujillo
Chimbote
LIMA
Islas Galápagos
(Galápagos Is.)
(Ecuador)
Equator
I. de
Cozumel
Yucatan Channel
Tropic of Cancer
Nassau

Nassau

Windward Passage

B R A Z I L

São Francisco
Araguaia
Cordillera Occidental

Equator

ATLANTIC

OCEAN

PACIFIC

OCEAN

SCOTIA SEA

Scotia Ridge

Drake Passage

ARGENTINA

PARAGUAY

URUGUAY

CHILE

Paraguay

Tropic of Capricorn

South Sandwich Trench

Meteor Depth
8325

Traversay Is.

Candlemas I.
Saunders I.
Montague I.

South Sandwich Is.
(U.K.)

South Georgia
(U.K.)

Shag Rocks
(U.K.)

South Orkney Is.
(U.K.)

South Shetland Is.
(U.K.)

Falkland Is.
(U.K.)

Stanley

East Falkland

West Falkland

Isla de los
Estados

Isla Grande
de
Tierra del Fuego

Cabo de Hornos
(Cape Horn)

Archipiélago
de la Reina
Adelaida

Punta
Arenas

Estrecho de Magallanes

Río Gallegos

Bahía
Grande

Comodoro Rivadavia

Golfo de
San Jorge

Golfo San
Matías

Bahía
Blanca

Neuquén

Patagonia

Isla de Chiloé

Archipiélago
de los
Chonos

Valdivia

Concepción

SANTIAGO

Valparaíso

Aconcagua
6960

Ojos del
Salado
6908

Mendoza

CÓRDOBA

San Miguel de
Tucumán

Sierra de Catalasteo

Tarija

Central

Occidental

Poopó

Laguna
Mar Chiquita

Santa Fé

Rosario

Paraná

BUENOS AIRES

La Plata

Río de la Plata

MONTEVIDEO

Lago de
Rincón del
Bonete

Laguna
dos
Patos

Río Grande

PORTO ALEGRE

Florianópolis

CURITIBA

SÃO PAULO

Asunción

Resistencia

Campo Grande

Paraná

Serra

Ribeirão Prêto

HORIZONTE

Niterói

RIO DE JANEIRO

Santos

Vitória

Ilhas
Martin Vaz
(Brazil)

Ilha da
Trindade
(Brazil)

Tropic of Capricorn

Islas Juan Fernández
(Chile)

Islas de los Desventurados
(Chile)

Chile Trench

Nazca

Pampas

Scale 1 : 16 100 000

| 0 | 200 | 400 | 600 km |
| 0 | 100 | 200 | 300 miles |

102 103

CARIBBEAN SEA

Lesser Antilles

Kingstown

ST. VINCENT & THE GRENADIN

St. George's GREN

Punta
Gallinas
Aruba
(Neth.) Netherlands
Antilles
Islas Los
Roques
Willemstad

Por
SP

NICARAGUA

Isla de San Andrés
(Colombia)

Lago de
Nicaragua

COSTA
RICA

San José
Chirripó
3820
Volcán Barú
3475

PANAMA

Golfo de los
Mosquitos

Canal de Panamá
(Panama Canal)

Golfo de
Chiriquí
Chitré
Isla de
Coiba
Punta
Mala
Golfo de
Panamá
Punta Mariato

Panamá

La Palma

Golfo del
Darién

Turbo
Caucasia

Golfo de
Morrosquillo
Sincelejo
El Banco

Plato

Riohacha
P. Cristóbal
Colón
5775

Santa Marta
BARRANQUILLA
Cartagena
Valledupar

Maicao

MARACAIBO
Cabimas

CARACAS
Petare
Los Teques

Cumaná
Carúpano
Güiria

TRINIDAD AN
TOBAGO
Porlamar

Coro
San Juan de
los Cayos
Isla La
Tortuga
Isla de
Margarita

Machiques Lago de
Maracaibo
San Carlos
del Zulia
Valera

Maracay
VALENCIA

Barquisimeto

Acarigua
Guanare
San Juan de
los Morros
Zaraza

Barcelona
Guanta

Maturín
Tucupita
Delta del
Orinoco
(Delta)

Monteria

Sierra

Bucaramanga
5493

Bello
MEDELLÍN
Quibdó
La Dorada Tunja
Manizales
5399

Cúcuta
Pamplona

San Cristóbal

Mérida
Barinas

San Fernando
de Apure

El Baúl
Calabozo

Achaguas

Apure

Arauca

El Tigre

Ciudad Bolívar
Ciudad
Guayana
Matt

Puerto
Nuevo
Puerto
Carreño

Puerto Páez

Maripa

Embalse
de Guri

El Callao
La Paragua
Salto
Angel
La Gran
Sabana

Golfo de
Cupica

Nuquí

Cabo Corrientes

Pereira
Armenia
Ibagué
BOGOTÁ
4560
Villavicencio

Sogamoso

Orocué

Meta

Puerto Ayacucho

Cerro Yavi
2441

El Dorado

4083

Buenaventura

CALI
5750
Popayán
4686
Neiva

Palmira

Isla de Malpelo
(Colombia)

Isla Gorgona

Tumaco
Patia

Pasto
4764
N. de
Cumbal
Ipiales
Puerto Limón
Florencia

Tres Esquinas

COLOMBIA

Mesa de
Yambi

Miraflores

San José
de Ocuné

San Fernando
de Atabapo

San Carlos

Calamar

Guaviare

Inírida

La Esmeralda

Cerro
Marahuaca
2579

ROR AI

Serra Pacaraima

Mt. Roraim
2810
Sta Elena

Uraricoera

Esmeraldas

Santo Domingo
de los Colorados

Bahía
de Manta
Manta
Chone
Portoviejo
Bahía de
Santa Elena

Volcán
Cayambe
5790
QUITO
5896 Volcán
Cotopaxi
Ambato
6310 Chimborazo

Mitú

Iutica

Cucui
Icaña

Pico da
Neblina
3014

Uaupés

Negro

Boiaçu

Serra Curupira

Caquetá

Puerto Leguízamo

La Chorrera

El Encanto

Ilha Grande

Tomar
Barcelos

Maraã

Airão

MAN

Equator

GUAYAQUIL

ECUADOR
5230
Macas
Azogues

Salinas
Playas
Isla
Puná
Golfo de
Guayaquil

Cuenca

Machala

Loja

Río Tigre

Andoas

Napo

Putumayo

Japurá

Iquitos

Nauta

Caballococha

Pebas
Santa Clara

Santo Antônio
do Içá
Uarini

Leticia

São Paulo
de Olivença

Fonte
Boa

Alvarães
Codajás

Amazonas
(Amazon)

Manacapuru
Coari

AMAZONAS

Aruma

Talara
Sullana
Paita
Punta Pariñas
Bahía de Sechura
Piura
Sechura

Chulucanas

Olmos

Jaén
Chachapoyas

Cahuapanas

Yurimaguas
Tarapoto

Marañón

Barranca
Requena

Iberia
Yavari

Elvira

Marari

Atalaia
do Norte
Benjamin
Constant

Caruari

Juruá

Jutaí

Eirunepé

Itui

Canutama

Tapauá

Lábrea

Humaitá

B R

Punta Negra

Chiclayo

Cajamarca
Pacasmayo

Contamana

Trujillo

Nevado de
Huascarán
6768

Chimbote

Huaraz
6634 Huánuco
Yerupaja

Tingo
María

Pucallpa

Cruzeiro
do Sul
Tarauacá
Feijó

Santa Rosa
Sena Madureira
Esperanza

ACRE

Bolognesi

Río Branco

Xapuri
Brasileia

Purus

Bôca do Acre

Madeira

Represa
de Samuel

Pôrto Velho

Aripuanã

Ariquemes

Guajará

RONDÔNIA

Pimenta Bueno

Huarmey
Barranca
Huacho

Cerro de
Pasco
La Oroya

Manu

Iñapari

Cobija
Puerto Rico

Guayaramerín
Riberalta

Rondônia

Callao
LIMA
Huancayo
Chincha Alta
Huancavelica
Bahía de Pisco
Pisco

Ayacucho

Cusco
6394
Nevado
Auzángate

Abancay

Madre de Dios

Puerto
Maldonado

Puerto
Heath

Cavinas

Lago
Rogaguado

Magdalena

Exaltación

Puerto
Alegre

Ica
Chalhuanca

Nazca

Ayaviri

Juliaca

Puerto
Acosta

San Borja

Trinidad

Blanco

Cerros de Bala

Beni

Yacuma

Serra

PERU

Nudo
Coropuna
6425

Arequipa

Atico
Camana
Mollendo

Lomas

Puno
Lago
Titicaca
6485
Nevado de
Illampu
Guaqui
LA PAZ
Corocoro
Nevado
Sajama
6542

Santa Ana

Sécure

San Miguel

Ascensión

Concepc

B O L I V I A

Cochabamba

Oruro
Poopó
Challapata

SANTA CRUZ

Montero

Samaipata

Totora

Sucre

El
San Jos
de Chiquito

Bañados
del Izozo

Ilo

Tacna

Arica

Cuya

CHILE

Lago de
Poopó

Challapata

Potosí

Río Mulatos
Uyuni

Lagunillas

Cabezas

Iquique

Salar
de Uyuni

Boyuibe

Fortín Co
Eugenio C

PACIFIC
OCEAN

Nazca Ridge

Peru–Chile Trench

Tocopilla
María Elena

Calama

Punta Angamos

6159
Volcán
San Pedro

La
Quiaca

Tupiza

Tarija

Pilcomayo

Villa Montes

Tartagal

ARGENTINA

PA

Mariscal
Estigarribi

PAz

metres		feet
4000		13120
2000		6560
1000		3280
500		1640
200		656
	0	0
200		656
1000		3280
2000		6560
4000		13120
6000		19690
8000		26250
metres		feet

① A   90° W   B

Islas Galápagos
(Galápagos Islands)
(Ecuador)

I. Culpepper

1 I. Wenman
Isla
Pinta
Isla
Marchena

Equator

Isla San Salvador
Isla
Fernandina
Isla Santa Cruz

2 Isla Isabela
Isla
San Cristóbal

Isla Santa
María
Isla
Española

ATLANTIC OCEAN

Settlements

■	over 3 million
☐	1 – 3 million
○	250 000 – 1 million
●	100 000 – 250 000
◉	25 000 – 100 000
•	under 25 000
—	country capital underline
—	state or province capital underline

Georgetown
New Amsterdam
Corriverton
Nieuw Nickerie
Albina
St. Laurent
Kourou
Apoera
Brokopondo
Embalse Toekomstig
Blommesteinmeer
Paramaribo
Nieuw Amsterdam
Iracoubo
Cayenne

SURINAME
FRENCH GUIANA

1230 Juliana Top

Serra Acari
Maloca
Meriruma
Azauri
Serra Tumucumaque
Oyapock
Regina

Cabo Orange
Oiapoque
Vila Velha
Camopi

AMAPÁ
Pôrto Grande
Cabo Norte
Amapá
Calçoene

Trombetas
Pôrto Santana
Mazagão
Afuá
Macapá
Chaves

Mouths of the Amazon

Faro
Óbidos
Monte Alegre
Prainha
Almeirim
Breves
Portel
Ilha Grande de Gurupá

Baía de Marajó
Salinópolis
Vigia
BELÉM
Castanhal
Bragança
Viseu

Santarém
Altamira
Belo Monte
Cametá
Acará
Camiranga

São Luís
Ilha de São Luís

Parnaíba
Camocim

Parintins
Itacoatiara

AMAZONAS (Amazon)

PARÁ

Jacareacanga
Barra do São Manuel
Manuelzinho

Araras
São Félix

Conceição do Araguaia
Santa Maria das Barreiras

Rosário
Itapicuru Mirim

Sobral
Itapipoca
Caucaia
FORTALEZA
Aracati

Pindaré Mirim
Luzilândia
Piripiri

MARANHÃO
Imperatriz
Barra do Corda
Grajaú
Bacabal
Codó
Caxias
Timon
Teresina
Campo Maior
Canindé

CEARÁ
Mossoró
Areia Branca
Macau
Cabo de São Roque

Araguatins
Pôrto Franco
Carolina
Balsas
Pastos Bons
Floriano
Oeiras
Amarante
Picos
Juàzeiro do Norte
Crato
RIO GRANDE DO NORTE
Currais Novos
Natal
Sousa
Iguatu
Tauá

PIAUÍ
Uruçuí
Canto do Buriti
São Raimundo Nonato
Alto Parnaíba
Gilbués

Ouricuri
Juàzeiro
Petrolina
PERNAMBUCO
PARAÍBA
Guarabira
João Pessoa
Campina Grande
Jaboatão
Olinda
RECIFE
Caruaru
Palmares

TOCANTINS
Macaúba
Palmas
Pôrto Nacional
Dianópolis
Peixe
Paranã

Serra do Cachimbo
Pedro Afonso

Barragem de Sobradinho
Barra
Grande

Barreiras
Ibotirama
Bom Jesus da Lapa

Xique Xique
Irecê
Jacobina
Mundo Novo
Serrinha

BAHIA
Feira de Santana
Santa Antônio de Jesus
Alagoinhas
Camaçari
SALVADOR
Baía de Todos os Santos

Senhor do Bonfim
Tucano

ALAGOAS
Maceió
Jeremoabo
Arapiraca

SERGIPE
Aracaju
Estância

Itaberaba
Jequié
Gandu
Ubaitaba

MATO GROSSO
Lucas
Diamantino
Nova Xavantina

Niquelândia
GOIÁS
Ceres
Goiás
BRASÍLIA
DISTRITO FEDERAL
Anápolis
GOIÂNIA
Cristalina

Porangatu
Uruaçu
Posse

Guanambi
Brumado
Ipiaú
Vitória da Conquista
Itabuna
Ilhéus
Manga
Itapetinga

Planalto

Monte Azul
Jánuária
Janaúba
Salinas

Pedra Azul
Itapebi
Belmonte
Pôrto Seguro
Prado
Caravelas

Rosário Oeste
Barra do Bugres
Cáceres
Rondonópolis

Barra do Garças
Aragarças
Iporá
Piers do Rio
Ipameri

Central
Paracatu

MINAS GERAIS
Bocaiúva
Montes Claros
Minas Novas
Diamantina
Corinto
Curvelo

Teófilo Otoni
Nanuque
Governador Valadares

MATO GROSSO
Corumbá

Jataí
Rio Verde
Itumbiara

Rio Verde de Mato Grosso
Alto Garças

Araguari
Uberlândia
Uberaba
Araxá
Patos de Minas

2033 Pico de Itambé
Itabira
Ipatinga
Governador Valadares

ESPÍRITO SANTO
Linhares

MATO GROSSO DO SUL
Campo Grande
Aquidauana
Miranda

São José do Rio Prêto
Barretos
França

Sete Lagoas
Pará de Minas
Divinópolis
BELO HORIZONTE
Manhuaçu
Cariacica
Vitória
Cachoeiro de Itapemirim

2890 Pico da Bandeira

Jardim
Pôrto Murtinho
Andradina
Araçatuba

SÃO PAULO
Ribeirão Prêto
São Carlos
Lavras
Juiz de Fora
Campos

Douradas
Presidente Prudente
Marília
Assis
Bauru
Limeira
Piracicaba

2797
Agulhas Negras
Volta Redonda
Nova Iguaçu
RIO DE JANEIRO
Niterói

Pedro Juan Caballero
Ponta Porã
Paranavaí

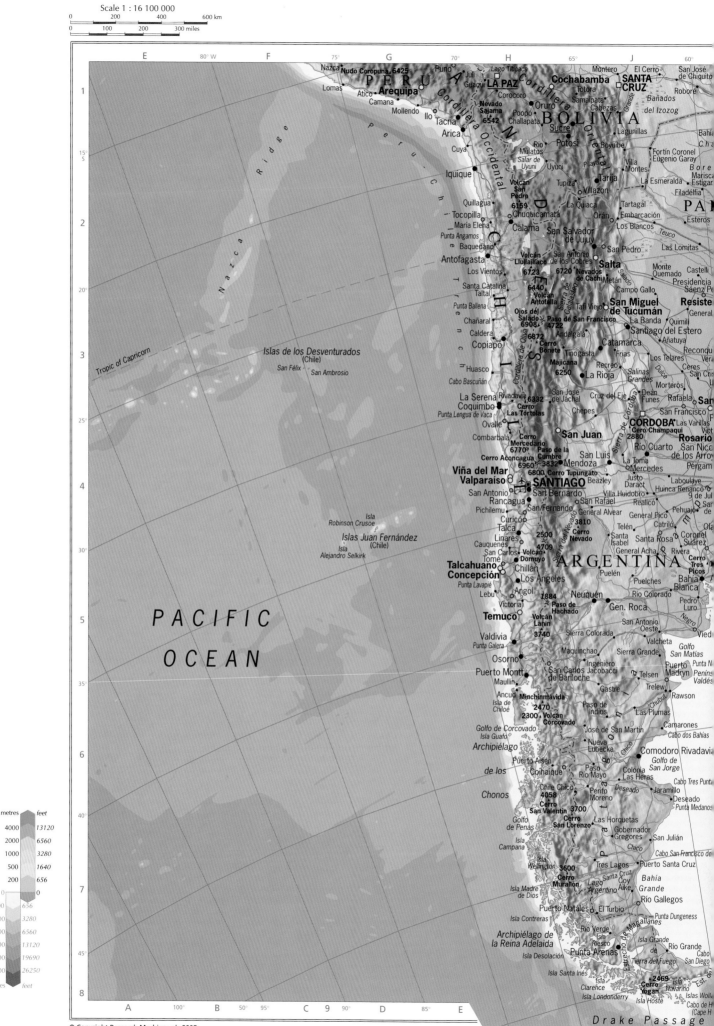

Scale 1 : 16 100 000

| 0 | 200 | 400 | 600 km |

| 0 | 100 | 200 | 300 miles |

PERU

Nazca
Nudo Coropuna 6425
Lomas
Arequipa
Atico
Camana
Mollendo Ilo
Tacna
Arica
Cuya

Iquique

Tocopilla
Maria Elena
Punta Angamos
Baquedano
Antofagasta
Los Vientos
Santa Catalina
Taltal
Punta Ballena
Chañaral
Caldera
Copiapó
Huasco
Cabo Bascuñán

La Serena
Coquimbo
Punta Lengua de Vaca
Ovalle
Combarbalá

Viña del Mar
Valparaíso
San Antonio
Rancagua
Pichilemu
Curicó
Talca
Linares
Cauquenes
San Carlos
Tomé
Talcahuano
Concepción
Punta Lavapié
Lebu
Victoria
Angol

Temuco

Valdivia
Punta Galera
Osorno
Puerto Montt
Maullín
Ancud
Isla de
Chiloé

Golfo de Corcovado
Isla Guafo
Archipiélago

de los

Chonos

Golfo
de Penas
Isla
Campana

Isla
Wellington
Isla Madre
de Dios

Archipiélago de
la Reina Adelaida
Isla Desolación
Isla Santa Inés

Islas de los Desventurados
(Chile)
San Félix   San Ambrosio

Tropic of Capricorn

Isla
Robinson Crusoe
Islas Juan Fernández
(Chile)
Isla
Alejandro Selkirk

PACIFIC

OCEAN

Nazca Ridge

Peru-Ch

Tre

c

BOLIVIA

Puno
Juli
Guaqui Lago Titicaca
LA PAZ
Corocoro
Nevado   Oruro
Sajama   Poopó
6542   Challapata
Río
Mulatos   Potosí
Salar de
Uyuni   Uyuni
Volcán   Pulacayo
San
Pedro   La Quiaca
6159
Chuquicamata
Calama   San Salvador
de Jujuy
Volcán   San Antonio
Llullaillaco de los Cobres   Salta
6723   6720   Nevados
6440   de Cachi   Metán
Volcán
Antofalla
Ojos del
Salado   Paso de San Francisco
6908   4722
6872
Cerro   Tinogasta
Bonete
Majícana
6250   La Rioja
6332
Cerro   San José
Las Tórtolas   de Jáchal   Chepes
Cerro
Mercedario
6770   Paso de la
Cerro Aconcagua   Cumbre   San Luis
6960   3832   Mendoza
6800 Cerro Tupungato
SANTIAGO   Beazley
San Bernardo
San Fernando   San Rafael
General Alvear
3810
Cerro   Santa
2500   Nevado   Isabel
4709
Volcán
Chillán   Domuyo   General Acha
Los Ángeles
1884   Neuquén
Paso de   Gen. Roca
Hachado   San Antonio
Volcán   Oeste
Lanín   Sierra Colorada
3740
Valcheta
Maquinchao
Ingeniero
San Carlos Jacobacci
de Bariloche   Telsen
Paso de
Indios
2470   Gastre
2300 Volcán   José de San Martín   Rawson
Corcovado
Nueva
Lubecka
Puerto Aisén   Chico
Coihaique   Río Mayo   Colonia
Las Heras
Chile Chico   Perito
4058   Moreno
Cerro   Jaramillo
San Valentín 3700   Deseado
Cerro
San Lorenzo   Las Horquetas
Gobernador
Gregores   San Julián
3600
Cerro   Tres Lagos   Puerto Santa Cruz
Murallón
Santa Cruz
Lago   Coy   Bahía
Argentino   Aike   Grande
Puerto Natales   Río Gallegos
El Turbio
Río Verde   Punta Dungeness
Isla
Isla   Riesco   Isla Grande
Punta Arenas   de
Tierra del Fuego
San Diego
2469
Cerro   Isla   Cabo
Isla   Yogan   Navarino   Cabo H
Clarence   Islas Woll
Isla Londonderry   Cabo de H
Isla Hoste   (Cape H

Cochabamba   Montero   El Cerro   San José
Totora   de Chiquito
Samaipata   SANTA
Sucre   CRUZ   Robore
Bañados
del Izozog
Lagunillas   Bahía
Boyuibe
Fortín Coronel
Villa   Eugenio Garay
Montes
Tarija   La Esmeralda   Estigar
Villazón   Filadélfia
Orán   Tartagal   Embarcación   Esteros
Los Blancos   Teuco
San Pedro   Las Lomitas
Monte
Quemado   Castelli
Campo Gallo   Presidencia
Sáenz Pe
San Miguel   Resiste
de Tucumán   General
La Banda   Quimili
Santiago del Estero   Añatuya
Andalgalá   Reconqu
Catamarca   Frías   San Cris
Recreo   Salinas
Grandes   Ceres
Morteros
CÓRDOBA
Cerro Champaquí   Las Varillas   Vict
2880   Rosario
Río Cuarto   San Nicc
La Toma   de los Arro
Mercedes   Pergam
Justo   Laboulaye
Daract   Huinca Renancó
Realicó   9 de
Villa Huidobro   Pehuai
Telén   General Pico   Catrilo
Santa Rosa   Coronel
Rivera   Suárez
Cerro
Puelén   Tres
Puelches   Picos
Río Colorado   Bahía
Pedro   Blanca
Luro
Vied
Golfo
San Matías
Punta N
Puerto   Penín
Madryn   Valdés
Trelew
Las Plumas   Camarones
Cabo dos Bahías
Comodoro Rivadavi
Golfo de
San Jorge
Cabo Tres Punt
Deseado
Punta Medanos
Cabo San Francisco de

PARA

PA

Drake Passage

Cordillera Occidental
Cordillera Oriental
Cordillera de Oliva
Sierra de Calchaquí
Cordillera de Córdoba
Estrecho de Magallanes

ARGENTINA

© Copyright Research Machines plc 2005

metres	feet
4000	13120
2000	6560
1000	3280
500	1640
200	656
0	0
200	656
1000	3280
2000	6560
4000	13120
6000	19690
8000	26250
metres	feet

SOUTHERN SOUTH AMERICA

Argentina • Chile • Falkland Islands • Paraguay • Uruguay

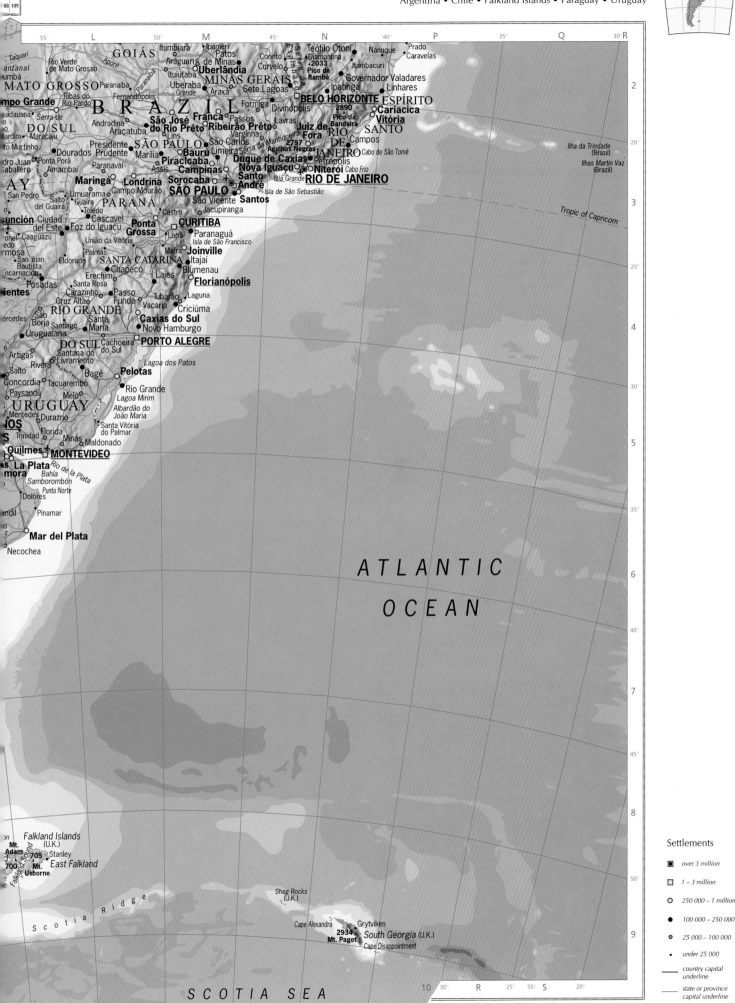

ATLANTIC

OCEAN

Tropic of Capricorn

Ilha da Trindade
(Brazil)

Ilhas Martin Vaz
(Brazil)

GOIÁS
MATO GROSSO
umbá
mpo Grande
DO SUL
B R A Z I L
MINAS GERAIS
BELO HORIZONTE
ESPÍRITO
SANTO
SÃO PAULO
RIO DE
JANEIRO
RIO DE JANEIRO
PARANÁ
CURITIBA
SANTA CATARINA
Florianópolis
RIO GRANDE
DO SUL
PORTO ALEGRE
Lagoa dos Patos
Pelotas
URUGUAY
MONTEVIDEO
La Plata
Mar del Plata
Necochea

Scotia Ridge

Shag Rocks
(U.K.)

Falkland Islands
(U.K.)
Mt.
Adam 705
700 Mt. Stanley
Usborne East Falkland

Scotia Sea

Cape Alexandra Grytviken
2934 South Georgia (U.K.)
Mt. Paget Cape Disappointment

S C O T I A   S E A

Settlements

■	over 3 million
□	1 – 3 million
◎	250 000 – 1 million
●	100 000 – 250 000
◦	25 000 – 100 000
•	under 25 000
___	country capital underline
___	state or province capital underline

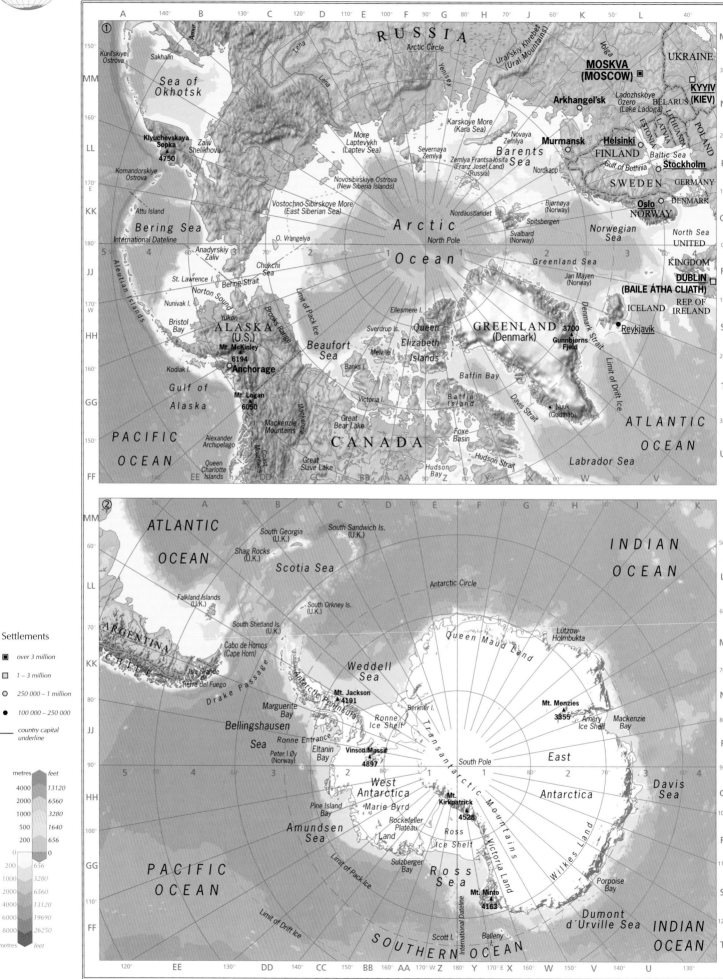

Settlements

■ over 3 million

□ 1 – 3 million

○ 250 000 – 1 million

● 100 000 – 250 000

— country capital underline

metres	feet
4000	13120
2000	6560
1000	3280
500	1640
200	656
0	0
200	656
1000	3280
2000	6560
4000	13120
6000	19690
8000	26250
metres	feet

Map ①

RUSSIA
Arctic Circle
UKRAINE
MOSKVA (MOSCOW)
KYYIV (KIEV)
BELARUS
LITHUANIA
LATVIA
Arkhangel'sk
Ladozhskoye Ozero (Lake Ladoga)
ESTONIA
POLAND
Karskoye More (Kara Sea)
Novaya Zemlya
Murmansk
Helsinki
FINLAND
Stockholm
Kuril'skiye Ostrova
Sakhalin
Sea of Okhotsk
Lena
Yenisey
Volga
Severnaya Zemlya
Zemlya Frantsa-Iosifa (Franz Josef Land) (Russia)
Nordkapp
Gulf of Bothnia
SWEDEN
GERMANY
Klyuchevskaya Sopka 4750
Zaliv Shelikhova
More Laptevykh (Laptev Sea)
Barents Sea
Nordaustlandet
Spitsbergen
Svalbard (Norway)
Bjørnøya (Norway)
Oslo
NORWAY
DENMARK
Komandorskiye Ostrova
Vostochno-Sibirskoye More (East Siberian Sea)
Arctic
Ocean
North Pole
Norwegian Sea
North Sea
UNITED KINGDOM
Attu Island
Bering Sea
International Dateline
O. Vrangelya
Greenland Sea
Jan Mayen (Norway)
DUBLIN (BAILE ÁTHA CLIATH)
Anadyrskiy Zaliv
Chukchi Sea
Denmark Strait
ICELAND
REP. OF IRELAND
St. Lawrence I.
Bering Strait
Ellesmere I.
Queen Elizabeth Islands
GREENLAND (Denmark) 3700
Gunnbjørns Fjeld
Reykjavík
Nunivak I.
Norton Sound
Sverdrup Is.
Bristol Bay
Yukon
ALASKA (U.S.)
Mt. McKinley 6194
Anchorage
Brooks Range
Beaufort Sea
Melville I.
Banks I.
Baffin Bay
Limit of Drift Ice
ATLANTIC OCEAN
Kodiak I.
Mt. Logan 6050
Victoria I.
Baffin Island
Nuuk (Godthåb)
PACIFIC OCEAN
Gulf of Alaska
Alexander Archipelago
Mackenzie Mountains
Mackenzie
Great Bear Lake
Foxe Basin
Queen Charlotte Islands
Coast Mountains
CANADA
Great Slave Lake
Hudson Bay
Hudson Strait
Labrador Sea

Map ②

ATLANTIC OCEAN
South Georgia (U.K.)
South Sandwich Is. (U.K.)
INDIAN OCEAN
Shag Rocks (U.K.)
Scotia Sea
Antarctic Circle
Falkland Islands (U.K.)
South Orkney Is. (U.K.)
Lützow-Holmbukta
ARGENTINA
CHILE
South Shetland Is. (U.K.)
Cabo de Hornos (Cape Horn)
Queen Maud Land
Isla Grande de Tierra del Fuego
Weddell Sea
Mt. Menzies 3355
Drake Passage
Antarctic Peninsula
Mt. Jackson 4191
Berkner I.
Amery Ice Shelf
Mackenzie Bay
Marguerite Bay
Ronne Ice Shelf
Bellingshausen Sea
Ronne Entrance
Peter I Øy (Norway)
Eltanin Bay
Vinson Massif 4897
South Pole
East Antarctica
Davis Sea
West Antarctica
Marie Byrd
Mt. Kirkpatrick 4528
Transantarctic Mountains
Pine Island Bay
Rockefeller Plateau
Amundsen Sea
Land
Ross Ice Shelf
Victoria Land
Wilkes Land
PACIFIC OCEAN
Sulzberger Bay
Ross Sea
Porpoise Bay
Limit of Pack Ice
Mt. Minto 4163
Dumont d'Urville Sea
INDIAN OCEAN
Limit of Drift Ice
Scott I.
Balleny Is.
International Dateline
SOUTHERN OCEAN

Nations of the World

T HIS IS AN ALPHABETICAL LISTING of all the 192 sovereign nations of the world. A map page reference is included for each country. The statistics used are the latest available at the time of going to press. Place names are given in English where a popular form exists and otherwise are shown in their local form.

There is a list of useful web site links for each country denoted by the following symbol:

Sites for each country are listed below with the web address and a brief description on the site content. Certain sites cover many or all of the countries of the world. These are indicated by the abbreviations alongside the web site symbol. An explanation of these abbreviations together with the details of each site are given opposite:

■ CIA
World Factbook 2000
http://www.odci.gov/cia/publications/factbook/
Official Central Intelligence Agency Web site for The World Factbook. This site offers detailed and accurate statistics for all the countries of the world, including sections on geography, population, government, and economy. Although the site contains few graphics, a map of each country and an image of its flag are also included.

■ LC
Library of Congress: Country Studies
http://lcweb2.loc.gov/frd/cs/
Online version of a series of books published by the Federal Research Division of the US Library of Congress. Studies of over 100 countries are featured, covering such subjects as geography, economy, and government. There are also informative articles on each country's historical and social background, together with maps and timelines.

■ AN
Arabnet
http://www.arab.net/
Features detailed country data on all the major Arab nations, including sections on history, government, business, and culture. The site contains the latest Arab-related news worldwide, as well as a collection of articles written by leading journalists and editors from the Middle East. Although the site lacks graphics, this is compensated for by the large amount of information available.

■ LP
Lonely Planet Online
http://www.lonelyplanet.com/
From the makers of the Lonely Planet series comes a comprehensive resource for travellers. The 'World guide' section offers detailed

information on each country, with pages for attractions, health risks, and visa requirements. There is also regularly updated news, as well as a bulletin board for travellers to share advice.

■ RG
Rough Guides to Travel
http://travel.roughguides.com/
Well-designed resource from the makers of the Rough Guide travel series. The 'Travel talk' section allows users to share advice on travelling the world, with sections including 'First-time travel', and 'Travel partners'. The site features regular articles on selected destinations around the world, and the opportunity to sign up for weekly travel updates.

■ WTG
World Travel Guide
http://www.wtgonline.com
Informative travel guide to the countries of the world. There are sections on history and government for every featured country, as well as advice aimed more specifically at the traveller. It will keep you up-to-date on visa and currency requirements, accommodation options, travel, and highlights not to be missed.

■ NA
New Africa
http://www.allafrica.com/
Extensive resource that features detailed information on each country in Africa, with subjects including health, economy, and population. The site also features the latest news events affecting Africa, as well as information on investment opportunities. Although the site's emphasis is primarily on statistical data, it also provides a useful insight into the continent's national parks and tourist attractions, as well as a travel guide for each country.

AFGHANISTAN
Map page 58

National name Dowlat-e Eslāmi-ye Afghānestān/Islamic State of Afghanistan
Area 652,225 sq km/ 251,825 sq mi
Capital Kābul
Major towns/cities Kandahār, Herāt, Mazār-e Sharīf, Jalālābād, Konduz, Qal'eh-ye Now
Physical features mountainous in centre and northeast (Hindu Kush mountain range; Khyber and Salang passes, Wakhan salient, and Panjshir Valley), plains in north and southwest, Amu Darya (Oxus) River, Helmand River, Lake Saberi
Currency afgháni
GNP per capita (PPP) (US$) 800 (2000 est)
Resources natural gas, coal, iron ore, barytes, lapis lazuli, salt, talc, copper, chrome, gold, silver, asbestos, small petroleum reserves
Population 23,897,000 (2003 est)
Population density (per sq km) 37 (2003 est)
Language Pashto, Dari (both official), Uzbek, Turkmen, Balochi, Pashai
Religion Muslim (84% Sunni, 15% Shiite), other 1%
Time difference GMT+4.5

 ■ CIA ■ LP ■ WTG

ALBANIA
Map page 36

National name Republika e Shqipërisë/Republic of Albania
Area 28,748 sq km/11,099 sq mi
Capital Tirana
Major towns/cities Durrës, Shkodër, Elbasan, Vlorë, Korçë
Major ports Durrës

Physical features mainly mountainous, with rivers flowing east–west, and a narrow coastal plain
Currency lek
GNP per capita (PPP) (US$) 4,040 (2002)
Resources chromite (one of world's largest producers), copper, coal, nickel, petroleum and natural gas
Population 3,166,000 (2003 est)
Population density (per sq km) 110 (2003 est)
Language Albanian (official), Greek
Religion Muslim, Albanian Orthodox, Roman Catholic
Time difference GMT +1

 ■ CIA ■ LC ■ LP ■ WTG

■ Tirana
http://www.albania.co.uk/cityguide/tirana.html
Good introduction to the Albanian capital. There are descriptions of the city, its history, public buildings, and cultural and artistic institutions. There are a number of photographs to accompany the descriptions.

ALGERIA
Map page 70

National name Al-Jumhuriyyat al-Jaza'iriyya ad-Dimuqratiyya ash-Sha'biyya/Democratic People's Republic of Algeria
Area 2,381,741 sq km/ 919,590 sq mi
Capital Algiers (Arabic al-Jaza'ir)
Major towns/cities Oran, Annaba, Blida, Sétif, Constantine
Major ports Oran (Ouahran), Annaba (Bône)
Physical features coastal plains backed by mountains in north, Sahara desert in south; Atlas mountains, Barbary Coast, Chott Melrhir depression, Hoggar mountains
Currency Algerian dinar
GNP per capita (PPP) (US$) 5,330 (2002)
Resources natural gas and petroleum, iron ore, phosphates, lead, zinc, mercury, silver, salt, antimony, copper

Population 31,800,000 (2003 est)
Population density (per sq km) 13 (2003 est)
Language Arabic (official), Berber, French
Religion Sunni Muslim (state religion) 99%, Christian and Jewish 1%
Time difference GMT +/–0

 ■ CIA ■ LC ■ AN ■ LP ■ NA ■ WTG

■ Algeria
http://i-cias.com/m.s/algeria/index.htm
Colourful travelling guide to Algeria and some of its major cities. It includes sections on 'Getting there', 'Visas and passports', 'Climate', 'Health', 'What to buy', as well as a long, illustrated list of places to go.

ANDORRA
Map page 28

National name Principat d'Andorra/ Principality of Andorra
Area 468 sq km/181 sq mi
Capital Andorra la Vella
Major towns/cities Les Escaldes
Physical features mountainous, with narrow valleys; the eastern Pyrenees, Valira River
Currency euro
GNP per capita (PPP) (US$) 19,370 (2000 est)
Resources iron, lead, aluminium, hydroelectric power
Population 71,000 (2003 est)
Population density (per sq km) 157 (2003 est)
Language Catalan (official), Spanish, French
Religion Roman Catholic (92%)
Time difference GMT +1

 ■ CIA ■ LP ■ WTG

ANGOLA

Map page 66

National name República de Angolo/Republic of Angola

Area 1,246,700 sq km/ 481,350 sq mi

Capital Luanda (and chief port)

Major towns/cities Lobito, Benguela, Huambo, Lubango, Malanje, Namibe, Kuito

Major ports Huambo, Lubango, Malanje

Physical features narrow coastal plain rises to vast interior plateau with rainforest in northwest; desert in south; Cuanza, Cuito, Cubango, and Cunene rivers

Currency kwanza

GNP per capita (PPP) (US$) 1730 (2002)

Resources petroleum, diamonds, granite, iron ore, marble, salt, phosphates, manganese, copper

Population 13,625,000 (2003 est)

Population density (per sq km) 11 (2003 est)

Language Portuguese (official), Bantu, other native dialects

Religion Roman Catholic 38%, Protestant 15%, animist 47%

Time difference GMT +1

 ■ CIA ■ LC ■ LP ■ NA ■ WTG

■ **Angola**
http://www.angola.org/
Angola's official Web site has a noticeable pro-government stance, but is well worth looking up for travel information; notes on the country's economy, geography, population, and history; and a virtual tour of Angola's historic buildings.

ANTIGUA AND BARBUDA

Map page 102

Area 440 sq km/169 sq mi (Antigua 280 sq km/108 sq mi, Barbuda 161 sq km/62 sq mi, plus Redonda 1 sq km/0.4 sq mi)

Capital St. John's (on Antigua) (and chief port)

Major towns/cities Codrington (on Barbuda)

Physical features low-lying tropical islands of limestone and coral with some higher volcanic outcrops; no rivers and low rainfall result in frequent droughts and deforestation. Antigua is the largest of the Leeward Islands; Redonda is an uninhabited island of volcanic rock rising to 305 m/1,000 ft

Currency East Caribbean dollar

GNP per capita (PPP) (US$) 9,960 (2002 est)

Population 73,000 (2003 est)

Population density (per sq km) 166 (2003 est)

Language English (official), local dialects

Religion Christian (mostly Anglican)

Time difference GMT –4

 ■ CIA ■ LP ■ RG ■ WTG

■ **Official Guide to Antigua and Barbuda**
http://www.interknowledge.com/antigua-barbuda/
Official Web site of Antigua and Barbuda's Department of Tourism aimed, naturally enough, at the prospective tourist, with sections on travel tips, activities, and accommodation.

ARGENTINA

Map page 110

National name República Argentina/Argentine Republic

Area 2,780,400 sq km/1,073,518 sq mi

Capital Buenos Aires

Major towns/cities Rosario, Córdoba, San Miguel de Tucumán, Mendoza, Santa Fé, La Plata

Major ports La Plata and Bahía Blanca

Physical features mountains in west, forest and savannah in north, pampas (treeless plains) in east-central area, Patagonian plateau in south; rivers Colorado, Salado, Paraná, Uruguay, Río de La Plata estuary; Andes mountains, with Aconcagua the highest peak in western hemisphere; Iguaçu Falls

Territories disputed claim to the Falkland Islands (Islas Malvinas), and part of Antarctica

Currency peso (= 10,000 australs, which it replaced in 1992)

GNP per capita (PPP) (US$) 9,930 (2002)

Resources coal, crude oil, natural gas, iron ore, lead ore, zinc ore, tin, gold, silver, uranium ore, marble, borates, granite

Population 38,428,000 (2003 est)

Population density (per sq km) 14 (2003 est)

Language Spanish (official) (95%), Italian (3%), English, German, French

Religion predominantly Roman Catholic (state-supported), 2% protestant, 2% Jewish

Time difference GMT –3

 ■ CIA ■ LP ■ WTG

■ **Introduction to Argentina**
http://www.interknowledge.com/argentina/index.html
Lively, illustrated guide to the six major regions which make up this country, and sections on such things as 'History & culture', 'Calendar of events', and 'Travel tips'.

■ **Buenos Aires, Argentina**
http://travel.lycos.com/destinations/location.asp?pid=28474
Profile of Argentina's multi-ethnic capital, Buenos Aires. There is a general introduction to the city's main features, and four sections – 'Visitors' guide', 'Culture and history', 'News and weather', and 'Entertainment' – with links to photographs, and to further useful information in English and Spanish about the city and the country.

■ **Tierra del Fuego, Argentina**
http://www.tierradelfuego.org.ar/
General introduction to the 'land of fire', Tierra del Fuego, and its capital Ushuaia. This official site also includes photographs, and information on the activities available in the surrounding area, such as fishing and skiing.

ARMENIA

Map page 60

National name Hayastani Hanrapetoutioun/Republic of Armenia

Area 29,800 sq km/11,505 sq mi

Capital Yerevan

Major towns/cities Gyumri (formerly Leninakan), Vanadzor (formerly Kirovakan), Hrazdan, Aboyvan

Physical features mainly mountainous (including Mount Ararat), wooded

Currency dram (replaced Russian rouble in 1993)

GNP per capita (PPP) (US$) 2,880 (2001)

Resources copper, zinc, molybdenum, iron, silver, marble, granite

Population 3,061,000 (2003 est)

Population density (per sq km) 103 (2003 est)

Language Armenian (official)

Religion Armenian Orthodox

Time difference GMT +4

 ■ CIA ■ LC ■ LP ■ WTG

■ **Armenian Land and Culture Organization**
http://www.lcousa.org/
Armenian international organization intent on preserving their monuments and history. As well as providing an Armenian perspective on the history, culture, and sovereignty of this region of Azerbaijan, this site gives information about the organization's campaigns and how the organization operates.

AUSTRALIA

Map page 82

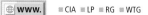

National name Commonwealth of Australia

Area 7,682,850 sq km/ 2,966,136 sq mi

Capital Canberra

Major towns/cities Adelaide, Alice Springs, Brisbane, Darwin, Melbourne, Perth, Sydney, Hobart, Newcastle, Wollongong

Physical features Ayers Rock; Arnhem Land; Gulf of Carpentaria; Cape York Peninsula; Great Australian Bight; Great Sandy Desert; Gibson Desert; Great Victoria Desert; Simpson Desert; the Great Barrier Reef; Great Dividing Range and Australian Alps in the east (Mount Kosciusko, 2,229 m/7,136 ft, Australia's highest peak). The fertile southeast region is watered by the Darling, Lachlan, Murrumbridgee, and Murray rivers. Lake Eyre basin and Nullarbor Plain in the south

Territories Norfolk Island, Christmas Island, Cocos (Keeling) Islands, Ashmore and Cartier Islands, Coral Sea Islands, Heard Island and McDonald Islands, Australian Antarctic Territory

Currency Australian dollar

GNP per capita (PPP) (US$) 26,960 (2002 est)

Resources coal, iron ore (world's third-largest producer), bauxite, copper, zinc (world's second-largest producer), nickel (world's fifth-largest producer), uranium, gold, diamonds

Population 19,731,000 (2003 est)

Population density (per sq km) 3 (2003 est)

Language English (official), Aboriginal languages

Religion Anglican 26%, Roman Catholic 26%, other Christian 24%

Time difference GMT +8/10

 ■ CIA ■ LP ■ RG ■ WTG

■ **Sydney Interactive Visitors Guide**
http://www.visitorsguide.aust.com/~tourism/sydney/index.html
Interactive guide to Sydney, Australia. The guide features the 'museums, art galleries, history, maps, attractions, tours, festivals, hotels, and fine dining for both visitors and residents of Sydney.'

■ **Melbourne City Search**
http://www.melbourne.vic.gov.au//
Searchable source of information on Australia's second city. Primarily designed for residents, this site is updated on a daily basis with news of local events, community groups, local government, cultural life, sport, and weather. For visitors there is information on accommodation and tourist attractions.

■ **Great Barrier Reef Marine Park Authority**
http://www.gbrmpa.gov.au/
Comprehensive official information on all aspects of the Great Barrier Reef and efforts to preserve this World Heritage Area. The online edition of the authority's quarterly Reef Research gives detail of current related scientific work.

■ **Destination Queensland**
http://www.qttc.com.au/
Large source of well-organized official tourist information on Australia's fastest growing state. The attractions of all regions of the vast state are described and easily accessible. Practical information is provided together with links to further sources. There is extensive information on the state's commitment to ecotourism and environmental protection.

■ **Tasmania – Discover Your Natural State**
http://www.tourism.tas.gov.au/nu_index.html
Official guide to Australia's island state. The quiet charms of 'Tassie' and local pride in its heritage, culture, and cuisine are evoked by informative text and a series of photographs. The history of the state is presented by means of quotes from famous visitors. All the regions of the state are covered.

■ **Australian Capital Territory**
http://www.act.gov.au/
Official guide to Australia's federal territory. There is information on government services, business life, local amenities, and the environment. This site also includes a guide to tourist attractions in Canberra and elsewhere in the territory.

AUSTRIA

Map page 30

National name Republik Österreich/
Republic of Austria
Area 83,859 sq km/32,367 sq mi
Capital Vienna
Major towns/cities Graz, Linz,
Salzburg, Innsbruck, Klagenfurt
Physical features landlocked mountainous state, with Alps in
west and south (Austrian Alps, including Grossglockner and
Brenner and Semmering passes, Lechtaler and Allgauer Alps
north of River Inn, Carnic Alps on Italian border) and low relief in
east where most of the population is concentrated; River Danube
Currency euro (schilling until 2002)
GNP per capita (PPP) (US$) 28,240 (2002 est)
Resources lignite, iron, kaolin, gypsum, talcum, magnesite, lead,
zinc, forests
Population 8,116,000 (2003 est)
Population density (per sq km) 97 (2003 est)
Language German (official)
Religion Roman Catholic 78%, Protestant 5%
Time difference GMT +1

 ■ CIA ■ LC ■ LP ■ RG ■ WTG

■ **Vienna**
http://www.info-austria.net
Guide to Vienna. Aimed at the tourist, this site details what to do
before you go, and what to do when you get there. History,
geography, and travel information, as well as features on festivals,
make up the majority of the remaining information on this site,
but there are also details of local transport and a list of useful
telephone numbers.

■ **Information from Austria**
http://www.austria.gv.at/e/
Easily navigable official guide to Austria from the office of the
Chancellor. There is comprehensive information on Austrian
foreign policy, as well as education, electoral, parliamentary, and
social security systems. There is regularly updated news and
foreign ministry press releases. This is an essential first stop for
anybody wanting to know about Austria.

■ **City of Graz**
http://www.gcongress.com/graz.htm
Informative guide to Austria's second city. An aerial photo on the
home page leads to comprehensive information on history,
museums, business, and the city's universities. There is also
practical information on hotels, restaurants, and transport.

■ **Innsbruck, Austria**
http://travel.lycos.com/destinations/location.asp?pid=11369
Guide to the Tirolean capital. There is a good description of this
city and its attractions. There are also links to a number of local
institutions and the media.

AZERBAIJAN
Map page 60

National name Azärbaycan
Respublikasi/Republic of Azerbaijan
Area 86,600 sq km/33,436 sq mi
Capital Baku
Major towns/cities Gäncä,
Sumqayit, Naxçivan, Xankändi,
Mingäçevir
Physical features Caspian Sea with rich oil reserves; the
country ranges from semidesert to the Caucasus Mountains
Currency manat (replaced Russian rouble in 1993)
GNP per capita (PPP) (US$) 2,920 (2002 est)
Resources petroleum, natural gas, iron ore, aluminium, copper,
barytes, cobalt, precious metals, limestone, salt
Population 8,370,000 (2003 est)
Population density (per sq km) 97 (2003 est)
Language Azeri (official), Russian
Religion Shiite Muslim 68%, Sunni Muslim 27%, Russian
Orthodox 3%, Armenian Orthodox 2%
Time difference GMT +4

 ■ CIA ■ LC ■ LP ■ WTG

THE BAHAMAS
Map page 102

National name Commonwealth
of the Bahamas
Area 13,880 sq km/5,383 sq mi
Capital Nassau (on New
Providence island)
Major towns/cities Freeport (on Grand Bahama)
Physical features comprises 700 tropical coral islands and
about 1,000 cays; the Exumas are a narrow spine of 365 islands;
only 30 of the desert islands are inhabited; Blue Holes of Andros,
the world's longest and deepest submarine caves
Currency Bahamian dollar
GNP per capita (PPP) (US$) 16,500 (2001 est)
Resources aragonite (extracted from seabed), chalk, salt
Population 314,000 (2003 est)
Population density (per sq km) 23 (2003 est)
Language English (official), Creole
Religion Christian 94% (Baptist 32%, Roman Catholic 19%,
Anglican 20%, other Protestant 23%)
Time difference GMT –5

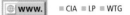 ■ CIA ■ LP ■ WTG

■ **Bahamas Online**
http://www.bahamas-on-line.com/
One-stop information service for anyone planning to visit the
Bahamas, with sections on such topics as Bahamian history,
shops and services, places to stay, and things to do.

BAHRAIN
Map page 63

National name Dawlat
al-Bahrayn/State of Bahrain
Area 688 sq km/266 sq mi
Capital Al Manāmah (on Bahrain
island)
Major towns/cities Sitra, Al
Muharraq, Jidd Ḥafş, Madinat 'Īsá
Physical features archipelago of 35 islands in Arabian Gulf,
composed largely of sand-covered limestone; generally poor and
infertile soil; flat and hot; causeway linking Bahrain to mainland
Saudi Arabia
Currency Bahraini dinar
GNP per capita (PPP) (US$) 15,900 (2002 est)
Resources petroleum and natural gas
Population 724,000 (2003 est)
Population density (per sq km) 1,068 (2003 est)
Language Arabic (official), Farsi, English, Urdu
Religion 85% Muslim (Shiite 60%, Sunni 40%), Christian; Islam
is the state religion
Time difference GMT +3

 ■ CIA ■ LC ■ AN ■ LP ■ WTG

BANGLADESH
Map page 56

National name Gana Prajatantri
Bangladesh/People's Republic of
Bangladesh
Area 144,000 sq km/55,598 sq mi
Capital Dhaka
Major towns/cities Rajshahi,
Khulna, Chittagong, Sylhet,
Rangpur, Narayanganj
Major ports Chittagong, Khulna
Physical features flat delta of rivers Ganges (Padma) and
Brahmaputra (Jamuna), the largest estuarine delta in the world;
annual rainfall of 2,540 mm/100 in; some 75% of the land is less

---

than 3 m/10 ft above sea level; hilly in extreme southeast and
northeast
Currency taka
GNP per capita (PPP) (US$) 1,720 (1999)
Resources natural gas, coal, limestone, china clay, glass sand
Population 146,736,000 (2003 est)
Population density (per sq km) 1,019 (2003 est)
Language Bengali (official), English
Religion Muslim 88%, Hindu 11%; Islam is the state religion
Time difference GMT +6

 ■ CIA ■ LC ■ LP ■ WTG

■ **Bangladesh**
http://www.bangladesh.net/
Online guide to Bangladesh. The site includes information on all
aspects of life and culture in Bangladesh, including the
architecture and history of the country.

BARBADOS

Map page 102

Area 430 sq km/166 sq mi
Capital Bridgetown
Major towns/cities
Speightstown, Holetown, Oistins
Physical features most easterly
island of the West Indies; surrounded by coral reefs; subject to
hurricanes June–November; highest point Mount Hillaby 340 m/
1,115 ft
Currency Barbados dollar
GNP per capita (PPP) (US$) 15,560 (2002 est)
Resources petroleum and natural gas
Population 270,000 (2003 est)
Population density (per sq km) 629 (2003 est)
Language English (official), Bajan (a Barbadian English dialect)
Religion 40% Anglican, 8% Pentecostal, 6% Methodist, 4%
Roman Catholic
Time difference GMT –4

 ■ CIA ■ LP ■ RG ■ WTG

■ **Barbados – Isle of Dreams**
http://www.barbados.org/
Here are facts and figures about Barbados, weather reports, an
illustrated history and chronology, a feature on Barbados rum,
and links to associated sites.

BELARUS

Map page 38

National name Respublika Belarus/
Republic of Belarus
Area 207,600 sq km/80,154 sq mi
Capital Minsk (Belorussian
Mensk)
Major towns/cities Homyel',
Vitsyebsk, Mahilyow, Babruysk, Hrodna, Brest
Physical features more than 25% forested; rivers Dvina,
Dnieper and its tributaries, including the Pripet and Beresina; the
Pripet Marshes in the east; mild and damp climate
Currency Belarus rouble, or zaichik
GNP per capita (PPP) (US$) 5,330 (2002 est)
Resources petroleum, natural gas, peat, salt, coal, lignite
Population 9,895,000 (2003 est)
Population density (per sq km) 48 (2003 est)
Language Belorussian (official), Russian, Polish
Religion 80% Eastern Orthodox; Baptist, Roman Catholic
Muslim, and Jewish minorities
Time difference GMT +2

 ■ CIA ■ LC ■ LP ■ WTG

■ **Minsk in Your Pocket Home Page**
http://www.inyourpocket.com/Belarus/Minsk_home.shtml
Guide to everything you ever wanted to know about this
Belarusian capital city. This is an electronic form of a published

guide book and includes sections on such topics as language, media, what to see, getting there, and where to stay.

BELGIUM
Map page 22

National name Royaume de Belgique (French), Koninkrijk België (Flemish)/ Kingdom of Belgium
Area 30,510 sq km/11,779 sq mi
Capital Brussels
Major towns/cities Antwerp, Ghent, Liège, Charleroi, Brugge, Mons, Namur, Louvain
Major ports Antwerp, Oostende, Zeebrugge
Physical features fertile coastal plain in northwest, central rolling hills rise eastwards, hills and forest in southeast; Ardennes Forest; rivers Schelde and Meuse
Currency euro (Belgian franc until 2002)
GNP per capita (PPP) (US$) 27,350 (2002 est)
Resources coal, coke, natural gas, iron
Population 10,318,000 (2003 est)
Population density (per sq km) 338 (2003 est)
Language Flemish (a Dutch dialect, known as Vlaams; official) (spoken by 56%, mainly in Flanders, in the north), French (especially the dialect Walloon; official) (spoken by 32%, mainly in Wallonia, in the south), German (0.6%; mainly near the eastern border)
Religion Roman Catholic 75%, various Protestant denominations
Time difference GMT +1

 ■ CIA ■ LP ■ RG ■ WTG

■ **Antwerp**
http://users.pandora.be/eric.kumiko/
General introduction to the city, including history, art, and culture, with links to more specific sites.

■ **Things to see in Brussels**
http://pespmc1.vub.ac.be/BRUSSEL.html
Guide to places of interest to visit in this city, from medieval houses to futuristic buildings, provided by the Free University of Brussels.

■ **Belgium: Overview**
http://pespmc1.vub.ac.be/Belgcul.html
General information about Belgium, its cities and regions, plus a special focus on its culture, with features on 'typically Belgian things', such as the Belgian character and Hergé's Tintin.

■ **Tourist Office for Flanders**
http://www.toervl.be
Good official source of information on the history, geography, and culture of the Dutch-speaking region of Belgium. There are sections on gastronomy, accommodation, attractions, festivals and celebrations, in addition to profiles of the main cities and towns of Flanders.

■ **Belgian Federal Government Online**
http://belgium.fgov.be/pa/ena_frame.htm
Official Belgium site that includes a history of the country and its organs of state. Visitors can read governmental press releases and find a wealth of information in the databases of the 'Federal information service', from photographs of the Belgian royal family, to electoral results for the last decade.

BELIZE
Map page 102

Area 22,963 sq km/8,866 sq mi
Capital Belmopan
Major towns/cities Belize, Dangriga, Orange Walk, Corozal, San Ignacio
Major ports Belize, Dangriga, Punta Gorda
Physical features tropical swampy coastal plain, Maya Mountains in south; over 90% forested
Currency Belize dollar
GNP per capita (PPP) (US$) 5,340 (2002 est)

Population 256,000 (2003 est)
Population density (per sq km) 11 (2003 est)
Language English (official), Spanish (widely spoken), Creole dialects
Religion Roman Catholic 62%, Protestant 30%
Time difference GMT –6

 ■ CIA ■ LC ■ LP ■ WTG

■ **Belize Online Tourism and Investment Guide**
http://www.belize.com/
Designed to attract tourists and commerce to the country, with information grouped under headings such as culture, music, ancient treasures, and news and information.

BENIN
Map page 72

National name République du Bénin/Republic of Benin
Area 112,622 sq km/ 43,483 sq mi
Capital Porto-Novo (official), Cotonou (de facto)
Major towns/cities Abomey, Natitingou, Parakou, Kandi, Ouidah, Djougou, Bohicon, Cotonou
Major ports Cotonou
Physical features flat to undulating terrain; hot and humid in south; semiarid in north; coastal lagoons with fishing villages on stilts; Niger River in northeast
Currency franc CFA
GNP per capita (PPP) (US$) 1,020 (2002 est)
Resources petroleum, limestone, marble
Population 6,736,000 (2003 est)
Population density (per sq km) 60 (2003 est)
Language French (official), Fon (47%), Yoruba (9%) (both in the south), six major tribal languages in the north
Religion animist 70%, Muslim 15%, Christian 15%
Time difference GMT +1

 ■ CIA ■ LP ■ NA ■ WTG

BHUTAN
Map page 56

National name Druk-yul/Kingdom of Bhutan
Area 47,500 sq km/18,147 sq mi
Capital Thimphu
Major towns/cities Paro, Punakha, Mongar, Phuntsholing, Tashigang
Physical features occupies southern slopes of the Himalayas; Gangkar Punsum (7,529 m/24,700 ft) is one of the world's highest unclimbed peaks; cut by valleys formed by tributaries of the Brahmaputra; thick forests in south
Currency ngultrum, although the Indian rupee is also accepted
GNP per capita (PPP) (US$) 1,530 (2002 est)
Resources limestone, gypsum, coal, slate, dolomite, lead, talc, copper
Population 2,257,000 (2003 est)
Population density (per sq km) 48 (2003 est)
Language Dzongkha (a Tibetan dialect; official), Tibetan, Sharchop, Bumthap, Nepali, English
Religion 70% Mahayana Buddhist (state religion), 25% Hindu
Time difference GMT +6

 ■ CIA ■ LC ■ LP ■ WTG

BOLIVIA
Map page 108

National name República de Bolivia/Republic of Bolivia
Area 1,098,581 sq km/ 424,162 sq mi

Capital La Paz (seat of government), Sucre (legal capital and seat of the judiciary)
Major towns/cities Santa Cruz, Cochabamba, Oruro, El Alto, Potosí, Tarija
Physical features high plateau (Altiplano) between mountain ridges (cordilleras); forest and lowlands (llano) in east; Andes; lakes Titicaca (the world's highest navigable lake, 3,800 m/ 12,500 ft) and Poopó
Currency boliviano
GNP per capita (PPP) (US$) 2,300 (2002 est)
Resources petroleum, natural gas, tin (world's fifth-largest producer), zinc, silver, gold, lead, antimony, tungsten, copper
Population 8,808,000 (2003 est)
Population density (per sq km) 8 (2003 est)
Language Spanish (official) (4%), Aymara, Quechua
Religion Roman Catholic 90% (state-recognized)
Time difference GMT –4

 ■ CIA ■ LC ■ LP ■ WTG

■ **Bolivia Web**
http://www.boliviaweb.com/
Whether it's Bolivian history, music and arts, tourism, or sport, this site should have the answer. There are plenty of photographs, music to listen to, and links to Bolivian newspapers and radio stations. Most of it is in English, but some information is only available in Spanish.

■ **La Paz, Bolivia**
http://travel.lycos.com/destinations/location.asp?pid=334819
Profile of La Paz, Bolivia, the highest capital city in the world. There is a general introduction to the city's main features, and four sections – 'Visitors' guide', 'Culture and history', 'News and weather', and 'Entertainment and photos' – with links to photographs, and to useful information in English and Spanish about both the city and the country.

■ **Potosí, Bolivia**
http://travel.lycos.com/destinations/location.asp?pid=334820
Profile of Potosí, Bolivia, once one of South America's wealthiest cities. There is a general introduction to its main features, and four sections – 'Visitors' guide', 'Culture and history', 'News and weather', and 'Entertainment and photos' – with links to photographs, and to further useful information in English and Spanish about both the city and the country.

BOSNIA-HERZEGOVINA
Map page 34

National name Bosna i Hercegovina/ Bosnia-Herzegovina
Area 51,129 sq km/19,740 sq mi
Capital Sarajevo
Major towns/cities Banja Luka, Mostar, Prijedor, Tuzla, Zenica, Bihac, Gorazde
Physical features barren, mountainous country, part of the Dinaric Alps; limestone gorges; 20 km/12 mi of coastline with no harbour
Currency konvertable mark
GNP per capita (PPP) (US$) 5,800 (2002 est)
Resources copper, lead, zinc, iron ore, coal, bauxite, manganese
Population 4,161,000 (2003 est)
Population density (per sq km) 81 (2003 est)
Language Serbian, Croat, Bosnian
Religion 40% Muslim, 31% Serbian Orthodox, 15% Roman Catholic
Time difference GMT +1

 ■ CIA ■ LP ■ WTG

■ **Bosnia Home Page**
http://www.cco.caltech.edu/~bosnia/bosnia.html
Political and social news about this troubled country, with photo-essays, a timeline of the conflict, maps of ethnic occupation and military front lines, features on its culture and daily life, and links to other Bosnian sites.

BOTSWANA
Map page 76

National name Republic of
Botswana
Area 582,000 sq km/
224,710 sq mi
Capital Gaborone
Major towns/cities Mahalapye,
Serowe, Francistown,
Selebi-Phikwe, Molepolole, Maun
Physical features Kalahari Desert in southwest (70–80% of
national territory is desert), plains (Makgadikgadi salt pans) in
east, fertile lands and Okavango Delta in north
Currency pula
GNP per capita (PPP) (US$) 7,770 (2002 est)
Resources diamonds (world's third-largest producer), copper-
nickel ore, coal, soda ash, gold, cobalt, salt, plutonium, asbestos,
chromite, iron, silver, manganese, talc, uranium
Population 1,785,000 (2003 est)
Population density (per sq km) 3 (2003 est)
Language English (official), Setswana (national)
Religion Christian 50%, animist 50%
Time difference GMT +2

 www. ■ CIA ■ LP ■ NA ■ WTG

BRAZIL
Map page 106

National name República
Federativa do Brasil/Federative
Republic of Brazil
Area 8,511,965 sq km/
3,286,469 sq mi
Capital Brasília
Major towns/cities São Paulo, Belo
Horizonte, Nova Iguaçu,
Rio de Janeiro, Belém, Recife,
Porto Alegre, Salvador, Curitiba,
Manaus, Fortaleza
Major ports Rio de Janeiro, Belém, Recife, Porto Alegre,
Salvador
Physical features the densely forested Amazon basin covers the
northern half of the country with a network of rivers; south is
fertile; enormous energy resources, both hydroelectric (Itaipú
Reservoir on the Paraná, and Tucuruí on the Tocantins) and
nuclear (uranium ores); mostly tropical climate
Currency real
GNP per capita (PPP) (US$) 7,250 (2002)
Resources iron ore (world's second-largest producer), tin
(world's fourth-largest producer), aluminium (world's fourth-
largest producer), gold, phosphates, platinum, bauxite, uranium,
manganese, coal, copper, petroleum, natural gas, hydroelectric
power, forests
Population 178,470,000 (2003 est)
Population density (per sq km) 21 (2003 est)
Language Portuguese (official), Spanish, English, French, 120
Indian languages
Religion Roman Catholic 70%; Indian faiths
Time difference GMT –2/5

 www. ■ CIA ■ LC ■ LP ■ RG ■ WTG

■ **Brasilia's Home Page**
http://www.geocities.com/TheTropics/3416/
Good introduction to the Brazilian capital. There is a history of the
construction of the city, a description of its attractions, and a
frank listing of its problems. There are a large number of photos.

■ **Belem, Brazil**
http://www.belem.com/
Profile of Brazil's port city of Belém. There is a general
introduction to its main features, and four sections – 'visitors'
guide', 'culture and history', 'news and weather', and
'entertainment and photos' – with links to photographs, and to
further useful information about both the city and the country.

■ **Rio de Janeiro, Brazil**
http://www.if.ufrj.br/general/tourist.html
Profile of the colourful Brazilian city of Rio de Janeiro. There is a
general introduction to the its main features, and four sections –
'visitors' guide', 'culture and history', 'news and weather', and
'entertainment' – with links to photographs, and to further useful
information in English and Portuguese about both the city and the
country.

BRUNEI
Map page 54

National name Negara Brunei
Darussalam/State of Brunei
Area 5,765 sq km/2,225 sq mi
Capital Bandar Seri Begawan
(and chief port)
Major towns/cities Seria,
Kuala Belait
Physical features flat coastal plain with hilly lowland in west
and mountains in east (Mount Pagon 1,850 m/6,070 ft); 75% of
the area is forested; the Limbang valley splits Brunei in two, and
its cession to Sarawak in 1890 is disputed by Brunei; tropical
climate; Temburong, Tutong, and Belait rivers
Currency Bruneian dollar, although the Singapore dollar is also
accepted
GNP per capita (PPP) (US$) 25,320 (2000 est)
Resources petroleum, natural gas
Population 358,000 (2003 est)
Population density (per sq km) 62 (2003 est)
Language Malay (official), Chinese (Hokkien), English
Religion Muslim 66%, Buddhist 14%, Christian 10%
Time difference GMT +8

www. ■ CIA ■ LP ■ RG ■ WTG

BULGARIA
Map page 34

National name Republika Bulgaria/
Republic of Bulgaria
Area 110,912 sq km/42,823 sq mi
Capital Sofia
Major towns/cities Plovdiv,
Varna, Ruse, Burgas, Stara
Zagora, Pleven
Major ports Burgas, Varna
Physical features lowland plains in north and southeast
separated by mountains (Balkan and Rhodope) that cover three-
quarters of the country; River Danube in north
Currency lev
GNP per capita (PPP) (US$) 6,840 (2002)
Resources coal, iron ore, manganese, lead, zinc, petroleum
Population 7,897,000 (2003 est)
Population density (per sq km) 71 (2003 est)
Language Bulgarian (official), Turkish
Religion Eastern Orthodox Christian, Muslim, Jewish, Roman
Catholic, Protestant
Time difference GMT +2

 www. ■ CIA ■ LC ■ LP ■ RG ■ WTG

■ **All About Bulgaria**
http://www.cs.columbia.edu/~radev/bulginfo.html
Links to more than 700 Bulgarian-related sites, answers to
'Frequently Asked Questions', and an archive of 200 poems make
this an impressive page.

■ **Welcome to Sofia**
http://www.sofia.com
Large source of information on past and present life in the
Bulgarian capital. The contents include shopping, sightseeing, a
good history, a guide to cultural events, accommodation,
restaurants, media, and sports. There is also a map and many
photographs of the city.

■ **Welcome to Plovdiv!**
http://www.plovdiv.org/

Guide to the second-largest Bulgarian city. A good history of the
city and guide to its attractions are illustrated with photographs.
There is also information on famous residents, as well as cultural
and commercial events.

BURKINA FASO
Map page 72

Area 274,122 sq km/105,838 sq mi
Capital Ouagadougou
Major towns/cities Bobo-
Dioulasso, Koudougou, Banfora,
Ouahigouya, Tenkodogo
Physical features landlocked
plateau with hills in west and
southeast; headwaters of the River Volta; semiarid in north, forest
and farmland in south; linked by rail to Abidjan in Côte d'Ivoire,
Burkina Faso's only outlet to the sea
Currency franc CFA
GNP per capita (PPP) (US$) 1,010 (2002 est)
Resources manganese, zinc, limestone, phosphates, diamonds,
gold, antimony, marble, silver, lead
Population 13,002,000 (2003 est)
Population density (per sq km) 47 (2003 est)
Language French (official), 50 Sudanic languages (90%)
Religion animist 40%, Sunni Muslim 50%, Christian (mainly
Roman Catholic) 10%
Time difference GMT+/–0

 www. ■ CIA ■ LP ■ NA ■ WTG

BURUNDI
Map page 74

National name Republika
y'Uburundi/République du Burundi/
Republic of Burundi
Area 27,834 sq km/10,746 sq mi
Capital Bujumbura
Major towns/cities Gitega, Bururi,
Ngozi, Muyinga, Ruyigi, Kayanaza
Physical features landlocked grassy highland straddling
watershed of Nile and Congo; Lake Tanganyika, Great Rift Valley
Currency Burundi franc
GNP per capita (PPP) (US$) 610 (2002 est)
Resources nickel, gold, tungsten, phosphates, vanadium,
uranium, peat, petroleum deposits have been detected
Population 6,825,000 (2003 est)
Population density (per sq km) 245 (2003 est)
Language Kirundi, French (both official), Kiswahili
Religion Roman Catholic 62%, Pentecostalist 5%, Anglican 1%,
Muslim 1%, animist
Time difference GMT +2

 www. ■ CIA ■ LP ■ WTG

CAMBODIA
Map page 52

National name Preah
Réaché'anachâkr Kâmpuchéa/
Kingdom of Cambodia
Area 181,035 sq km/69,897 sq
mi
Capital Phnum Penh
Major towns/cities
Bâtdâmbâng, Kâmpóng Cham, Siĕmréab, Prey Vêng
Major ports Kâmpóng Cham
Physical features mostly flat, forested plains with mountains in
southwest and north; Mekong River runs north–south; Lake Tonle
Sap
Currency Cambodian riel
GNP per capita (PPP) (US$) 1,590 (2002 est)

Resources phosphates, iron ore, gemstones, bauxite, silicon, manganese

Population 14,144,000 (2003 est)

Population density (per sq km) 78 (2003 est)

Language Khmer (official), French

Religion Theravada Buddhist 95%, Muslim, Roman Catholic

Time difference GMT +7

 ■ CIA ■ LC ■ LP ■ WTG

■ **Cambodia Mega Attraction – Angkor**
http://www.asiatour.com/cambodia/e-04angk/ec-ang10.htm
Guide to Cambodia's most impressive attraction. Good photographs accompany a history of the vast complex and details of Angkor Thom, Angkor Wat, and other sites.

CAMEROON
Map page 72

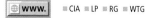

National name République du Cameroun/Republic of Cameroon

Area 475,440 sq km/ 183,567 sq mi

Capital Yaoundé

Major towns/cities Garoua, Douala, Nkongsamba, Maroua, Bamenda, Bafoussam, Ngaoundéré

Major ports Douala

Physical features desert in far north in the Lake Chad basin, mountains in west, dry savannah plateau in the intermediate area, and dense tropical rainforest in south; Mount Cameroon 4,070 m/ 13,358 ft, an active volcano on the coast, west of the Adamawa Mountains

Currency franc CFA

GNP per capita (PPP) (US$) 1,640 (2002 est)

Resources petroleum, natural gas, tin ore, limestone, bauxite, iron ore, uranium, gold

Population 16,018,000 (2003 est)

Population density (per sq km) 34 (2003 est)

Language French, English (both official; often spoken in pidgin), Sudanic languages (in the north), Bantu languages (elsewhere); there has been some discontent with the emphasis on French – there are 163 indigenous peoples with their own African languages

Religion animist 50%, Christian 33%, Muslim 16%

Time difference GMT +1

 ■ CIA ■ LP ■ NA ■ WTG

■ **Home Page of the Republic of Cameroon**
http://www.compufix.demon.co.uk/camweb/
Factual data about the country of Cameroon, plus links to a number of associated sites. This site includes a map, an audio clip of the national anthem, and a brief text-only section on tourism in this African country.

CANADA
Map page 90

Area 9,970,610 sq km/3,849,652 sq mi

Capital Ottawa

Major towns/cities Toronto, Montréal, Vancouver, Edmonton, Calgary, Winnipeg, Québec, Hamilton, Saskatoon, Halifax, London, Kitchener, Mississauga, Laval, Surrey

Physical features mountains in west, with low-lying plains in interior and rolling hills in east; St. Lawrence Seaway, Mackenzie River; Great Lakes; Arctic Archipelago; Rocky Mountains; Great Plains or Prairies; Canadian Shield; Niagara Falls; climate varies from temperate in south to arctic in north; 45% of country forested

Currency Canadian dollar

GNP per capita (PPP) (US$) 28,070 (2002 est)

Resources petroleum, natural gas, coal, copper (world's third-largest producer), nickel (world's second-largest producer), lead (world's fifth-largest producer), zinc (world's largest producer), iron, gold, uranium, timber

---

Population 31,510,000 (2003 est)

Population density (per sq km) 3 (2003 est)

Language English (60%), French (24%) (both official), American Indian languages, Inuktitut (Inuit)

Religion Roman Catholic 45%, various Protestant denominations

Time difference GMT –3.5/9

 ■ CIA ■ LP ■ RG ■ WTG

■ **Oh Canada!**
http://www.ualberta.ca/~bleeck/canada/
Aims to define, by means of selected annotated links, what it is to be Canadian. It includes information on Canadian history, the constitution, national anthem, and more.

■ **Montreal**
http://www.tourism-montreal.org/
Both historical and contemporary information on Montreal. Visitors can choose from a general presentation of the city and its development, tourist information, specialized overviews of arts, architecture, and business in the city.

■ **Toronto Star City Search**
http://www.starcitysearch.com/
Huge source of information on Canada's largest city. Primarily designed for residents, this site is constantly updated with news of local events, community groups, local government, cultural life, sport, and weather. For visitors there is information on accommodation and tourist attractions. There is also a good search engine.

■ **Welcome to Whitehorse Online**
http://www.city.whitehorse.yk.ca
Official guide to Canada's most westerly city. There are details of local government services, business activities, and community groups. Information for visitors includes local attractions, suggested drives and hikes, and a guide to the Klondike Bathtub Race and other events.

■ **Québec History at a Glance**
http://www.tourisme.gouv.qc.ca/anglais/menu_a/histoire_a.html
Introduction to the history, culture, and economy of Quebec. It is accompanied by photos of the province and a video. This is part of the official site of the Quebec government which contains a wealth of information on the provincial government, economic opportunities, tourist information, and local news stories.

CAPE VERDE
Map page 72

National name República de Cabo Verde/Republic of Cape Verde

Area 4,033 sq km/1,557 sq mi

Capital Praia

Major towns/cities Mindelo, Santa Maria

Major ports Mindelo

Physical features archipelago of ten volcanic islands 565 km/ 350 mi west of Senegal; the windward (Barlavento) group includes Santo Antão, São Vicente, Santa Luzia, São Nicolau, Sal, and Boa Vista; the leeward (Sotovento) group comprises Maio, São Tiago, Fogo, and Brava; all but Santa Luzia are inhabited

Currency Cape Verde escudo

GNP per capita (PPP) (US$) 4,720 (2002 est)

Resources salt, pozzolana (volcanic rock), limestone, basalt, kaolin

Population 463,000 (2003 est)

Population density (per sq km) 115 (2003 est)

Language Portuguese (official), Creole

Religion Roman Catholic 93%, Protestant (Nazarene Church)

Time difference GMT –1

 ■ CIA ■ LP ■ NA ■ WTG

■ **Republic of Cape Verde Home Page**
http://www.umassd.edu/SpecialPrograms/caboverde/capeverdean .html

Information about Cape Verde – its islands, geography and environment, history, culture, and news, plus food aid updates and a 'Did you know...?' section.

CENTRAL AFRICAN REPUBLIC
Map page 74

National name République Centrafricaine/Central African Republic

Area 622,436 sq km/ 240,322 sq mi

Capital Bangui

Major towns/cities Berbérati, Bouar, Bambari, Bossangoa, Carnot, Kaga Bandoro

Physical features landlocked flat plateau, with rivers flowing north and south, and hills in northeast and southwest; dry in north, rainforest in southwest; mostly wooded; Kotto and Mbali river falls; the Oubangui River rises 6 m/20 ft at Bangui during the wet season (June–November)

Currency franc CFA

GNP per capita (PPP) (US$) 1,190 (2002 est)

Resources gem diamonds and industrial diamonds, gold, uranium, iron ore, manganese, copper

Population 3,865,000 (2003 est)

Population density (per sq km) 6 (2003 est)

Language French (official), Sangho (national), Arabic, Hunsa, Swahili

Religion Protestant 25%, Roman Catholic 25%, animist 24%, Muslim 15%

Time difference GMT +1

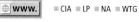 ■ CIA ■ LP ■ NA ■ WTG

CHAD
Map page 68

National name République du Tchad/Republic of Chad

Area 1,284,000 sq km/ 495,752 sq mi

Capital Ndjamena (formerly Fort Lamy)

Major towns/cities Sarh, Moundou, Abéché, Bongor, Doba, Kélo, Koumra

Physical features landlocked state with mountains (Tibetsi) and part of Sahara Desert in north; moist savannah in south; rivers in south flow northwest to Lake Chad

Currency franc CFA

GNP per capita (PPP) (US$) 1,000 (2002 est)

Resources petroleum, tungsten, tin ore, bauxite, iron ore, gold, uranium, limestone, kaolin, titanium

Population 8,598,000 (2003 est)

Population density (per sq km) 7 (2003 est)

Language French, Arabic (both official), over 100 African languages

Religion Muslim 50%, Christian 25%, animist 25%

Time difference GMT +1

 ■ CIA ■ LC ■ LP ■ NA ■ WTG

CHILE
Map page 110

National name República de Chile/Republic of Chile

Area 756,950 sq km/ 292,258 sq mi

Capital Santiago

Major towns/cities Concepción, Viña del Mar, Valparaíso, Talcahuano, Puente Alto, Temuco, Antofagasta

Major ports Valparaíso, Antofagasta, Arica, Iquique, Punta Arenas

Physical features Andes mountains along eastern border, Atacama Desert in north, fertile central valley, grazing land and forest in south

Territories Easter Island, Juan Fernández Islands, part of Tierra del Fuego, claim to part of Antarctica

Currency Chilean peso

GNP per capita (PPP) (US$) 9,810 (2002 est)

Resources copper (world's largest producer), gold, silver, iron ore, molybdenum, cobalt, iodine, saltpetre, coal, natural gas, petroleum, hydroelectric power

Population 15,805,000 (2003 est)

Population density (per sq km) 21 (2003 est)

Language Spanish (official)

Religion Roman Catholic 80%, Protestant 13%, atheist and nonreligious 6%

Time difference GMT −4

 ■ CIA ■ LC ■ LP ■ WTG

■ Santiago
http://sunsite.dcc.uchile.cl/chile/turismo/santiago.html
Comprehensive introduction to Chile's capital city, Santiago. The page includes information about historical landmarks, cultural and artistic life, its natural environment, shopping, restaurants, conference centres, and its suburbs, as well as general information about population, climate, language, and transport. There is also a list of useful addresses in the city.

■ Snapshot of Chile
http://www.gobiernodechile.cl/nuestro_pais/snapshot.htm
This government site, aiming to promote Chile for both investment and tourism purposes, contains a range of detailed information including a thorough explanation of the governmental structure and social policy, and information for visitors.

CHINA

Map page 42

National name Zhonghua Renmin Gongheguo (Zhongguo)/People's Republic of China

Area 9,572,900 sq km/ 3,696,000 sq mi

Capital Beijing (or Peking)

Major towns/cities Shanghai, Hong Kong, Chongqing, Tianjin, Guangzhou (English Canton), Shenyang (formerly Mukden), Wuhan, Nanjing, Harbin, Chengdu, Xi'an

Major ports Tianjin, Shanghai, Hong Kong, Qingdao, Guangzhou

Physical features two-thirds of China is mountains or desert (north and west); the low-lying east is irrigated by rivers Huang He (Yellow River), Chang Jiang (Yangtze-Kiang), Xi Jiang (Si Kiang)

Territories Paracel Islands

Currency yuan

GNP per capita (PPP) (US$) 4.390 (2002 est)

Resources coal, graphite, tungsten, molybdenum, antimony, tin (world's largest producer), lead (world's fifth-largest producer), mercury, bauxite, phosphate rock, iron ore (world's largest producer), diamonds, gold, manganese, zinc (world's third-largest producer), petroleum, natural gas, fish

Population 1,304,196,000 (2003 est)

Population density (per sq km) 136 (2003 est)

Language Chinese (dialects include Mandarin (official), Yue (Cantonese), Wu (Shanghaiese), Minbai, Minnah, Xiang, Gan, and Hakka)

Religion Taoist, Confucianist, and Buddhist; Muslim 2–3%; Christian about 1% (divided between the 'patriotic' church established in 1958 and the 'loyal' church subject to Rome); Protestant 3 million

Time difference GMT +8

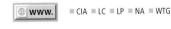 ■ CIA ■ LC ■ LP ■ RG ■ WTG

■ Beijing Pages
http://www.flashpaper.com/beijing/
Everything about the Chinese capital, from its location and population to its culture, economy, and government. The site also includes detailed tourism links as well as information about industrial development in the city.

■ China Today
http://www.chinatoday.com/

Complete guide to China, including culture and ethnology, art and entertainment, education, political organizations, and travel. There is also a section on current events and a basic introduction to this country.

■ Discover Hong Kong
http://www.discoverhongkong.com/eng/gateway/index.jhtml
Jumping-off point for sources of political, social, and cultural news about Hong Kong. This site is directed at the tourist and includes practical information on such topics as sightseeing, shopping, transportation, where to stay, and local culture, as well as a more practical hotel and restaurant guide.

■ Tibet in the 20th Century
http://www.tibetinfo.net/tibet-file/chronol.htm
Brief chronology of significant events in Tibet's history over the past century – 1902–90 – prepared by the Tibet Information Network, an independent organization based in the UK and the USA. Click on links at the bottom of the page to access news updates, reports, and basic information.

■ Shanghai
http://english.sh.com/directory.jsp?dirId=44&rootId=44
Guide to Shanghai. History, geography, and travel information as well as features on festivals make up the majority of the tourist-oriented information on this site, in addition to local transport information and a list of useful telephone numbers.

COLOMBIA

Map page 108

National name República de Colombia/Republic of Colombia

Area 1,141,748 sq km/ 440,828 sq mi

Capital Bogotá

Major towns/cities Medellín, Cali, Barranquilla, Cartagena, Bucaramanga, Cúcuta, Ibagué

Major ports Barranquilla, Cartagena, Buenaventura

Physical features the Andes mountains run north–south; flat coastland in west and plains (llanos) in east; Magdalena River runs north to Caribbean Sea; includes islands of Providencia, San Andrés, and Mapelo; almost half the country is forested

Currency Colombian peso

GNP per capita (PPP) (US$) 5,870 (2002 est)

Resources petroleum, natural gas, coal, nickel, emeralds (accounts for about half of world production), gold, manganese, copper, lead, mercury, platinum, limestone, phosphates

Population 44,222,000 (2003 est)

Population density (per sq km) 39 (2003 est)

Language Spanish (official) (95%)

Religion Roman Catholic

Time difference GMT −5

 ■ CIA ■ LC ■ LP ■ WTG

■ Colombia
http://www.ddg.com/LIS/aurelia/colombi.htm
General resource on Colombia, with plenty of information on topics such as history, geography, the economy, and politics. There are also two maps to accompany the text.

■ Bogotá, Colombia
http://travel.lycos.com/destinations/location.asp?pid=334833
Page devoted to Colombia's largest city Bogotá. There is a general introduction to the city's attractions, and four sections – 'Visitor's guide', 'Culture and history', 'News and weather', and 'Entertainment' – each with links to further useful information in both English and Spanish about both the city and the country.

■ Medellín, Colombia
http://travel.lycos.com/destinations/location.asp?pid=334836
Page devoted to the Colombian city of Medellín, a busy industrial and commercial centre. There is a general introduction to the city's attractions, and four sections – 'Visitors' guide', 'Culture and history', 'News and weather', and 'Entertainment' – each with links to further useful information in English and Spanish about both the city and the country.

COMOROS

Map page 76

National name Jumhuriyyat al-Qumur al-Itthadiyah al-Islamiyah (Arabic), République fédérale islamique des Comores (French)/ Federal Islamic Republic of the Comoros

Area 1,862 sq km/718 sq mi

Capital Moroni

Major towns/cities Mutsamudu, Domoni, Fomboni, Mitsamiouli

Physical features comprises the volcanic islands of Njazídja, Nzwani, and Mwali (formerly Grande Comore, Anjouan, Moheli); at northern end of Mozambique Channel in Indian Ocean between Madagascar and coast of Africa

Currency Comorian franc

GNP per capita (PPP) (US$) 1,640 (2002 est)

Population 768,000 (2003 est)

Population density (per sq km) 344 (2003 est)

Language Arabic, French (both official), Comorian (a Swahili and Arabic dialect), Makua

Religion Muslim; Islam is the state religion

Time difference GMT +3

 ■ CIA ■ LC ■ AN ■ LP ■ WTG

CONGO, DEMOCRATIC REPUBLIC OF

Map page 74

National name République Démocratique du Congo/ Democratic Republic of Congo

Area 2,344,900 sq km/ 905,366 sq mi

Capital Kinshasa

Major towns/cities Lubumbashi, Kananga, Mbuji-Mayi, Kisangani, Kolwezi, Likasi, Boma

Major ports Matadi, Kalemie

Physical features Congo River basin has tropical rainforest (second-largest remaining in world) and savannah; mountains in east and west; lakes Tanganyika, Albert, Edward; Ruwenzori Range

Currency congolese franc

GNP per capita (PPP) (US$) 580 (2002 est)

Resources petroleum, copper, cobalt (65% of world's reserves), manganese, zinc, tin, uranium, silver, gold, diamonds (one of the world's largest producers of industrial diamonds)

Population 52,771,000 (2003 est)

Population density (per sq km) 23 (2003 est)

Language French (official), Swahili, Lingala, Kikongo, Tshiluba (all national languages), over 200 other languages

Religion Roman Catholic 41%, Protestant 32%, Kimbanguist 13%, animist 10%, Muslim 1–5%

Time difference GMT +1/2

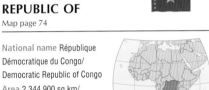 ■ CIA ■ LC ■ LP ■ NA ■ WTG

CONGO

Map page 72

National name République du Congo/Republic of Congo

Area 342,000 sq km/ 132,046 sq mi

Capital Brazzaville

Major towns/cities Pointe-Noire, Nkayi, Loubomo, Bouenza, Mossendjo, Ouésso, Owando

Major ports Pointe-Noire

Physical features narrow coastal plain rises to central plateau, then falls into northern basin; Congo River on the border with the Democratic Republic of Congo; half the country is rainforest

Currency franc CFA

GNP per capita (PPP) (US$) 700 (2002 est)

Resources petroleum, natural gas, lead, zinc, gold, copper, phosphate, iron ore, potash, bauxite

Population 3,724,000 (2003 est)

Population density (per sq km) 11 (2003 est)

Language French (official), Kongo, Monokutuba and Lingala (both patois), and other dialects

Religion Christian 50%, animist 48%, Muslim 2%

Time difference GMT +1

  ▪ CIA ▪ LP ▪ NA ▪ WTG

COSTA RICA
Map page 102

National name República de Costa Rica/Republic of Costa Rica

Area 51,100 sq km/19,729 sq mi

Capital San José

Major towns/cities Alajuela, Cartago, Limón, Puntarenas, San Isidro, Desamparados

Major ports Limón, Puntarenas

Physical features high central plateau and tropical coasts; Costa Rica was once entirely forested, containing an estimated 5% of the Earth's flora and fauna

Currency colón

GNP per capita (PPP) (US$) 8,260 (2002 est)

Resources gold, salt, hydro power

Population 4,173,000 (2003 est)

Population density (per sq km) 82 (2003 est)

Language Spanish (official)

Religion Roman Catholic 95% (state religion)

Time difference GMT –6

▪ www. ▪ CIA ▪ LP ▪ WTG

▪ **Costa Rica: Facts**

http://www.centralamerica.com/

Costa Rica for tourists. The site provides a summary of Costa Rican history, geography, and politics, as well as information about the activities you can enjoy in the country.

▪ **Costa Rica TravelWeb**

http://www.crica.com/info/info_intro.html

Information for the traveller and prospective business investor, with details of Costa Rica's government and political parties, healthcare and medical system, plus an overview of its history and culture.

CÔTE D'IVOIRE
Map page 72

National name République de la Côte d'Ivoire/Republic of the Ivory Coast

Area 322,463 sq km/ 124,502 sq mi

Capital Yamoussoukro

Major towns/cities Abidjan, Bouaké, Daloa, Man, Korhogo, Gagnoa

Major ports Abidjan, San Pedro

Physical features tropical rainforest (diminishing as exploited) in south; savannah and low mountains in north; coastal plain; Vridi canal, Kossou dam, Monts du Toura

Currency franc CFA

GNP per capita (PPP) (US$) 1,430 (2002 est)

Resources petroleum, natural gas, diamonds, gold, nickel, reserves of manganese, iron ore, bauxite

Population 16,631,000 (2003 est)

Population density (per sq km) 52 (2003 est)

Language French (official), over 60 ethnic languages

Religion animist 17%, Muslim 39% (mainly in north), Christian 26% (mainly Roman Catholic in south)

Time difference GMT +/–0

  ▪ CIA ▪ LC ▪ LP ▪ NA ▪ WTG

CROATIA
Map page 34

National name Republika Hrvatska/Republic of Croatia

Area 56,538 sq km/21,829 sq mi

Capital Zagreb

Major towns/cities Osijek, Split, Dubrovnik, Rijeka, Zadar, Pula

Major ports chief port: Rijeka (Fiume); other ports: Zadar, Šibenik, Split, Dubrovnik

Physical features Adriatic coastline with large islands; very mountainous, with part of the Karst region and the Julian and Styrian Alps; some marshland

Currency kuna

GNP per capita (PPP) (US$) 9,760 (2002 est)

Resources petroleum, natural gas, coal, lignite, bauxite, iron ore, salt

Population 4,428,000 (2003 est)

Population density (per sq km) 78 (2003 est)

Language Croat (official), Serbian

Religion Roman Catholic (Croats) 76.5%; Orthodox Christian (Serbs) 11%, Protestant 1.4%, Muslim 1.2%

Time difference GMT +1

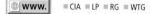 ▪ CIA ▪ LP ▪ RG ▪ WTG

▪ **Facts about Croatia**

http://www.hr/index_en.shtml

Presentation of Croatia with a variety of focuses on history, culture and media, financial aspects, political issues and government structure, sections on educational institutions, social and health care, a science fact-sheet, and gastronomic guidance. An extra bonus of the site is its extensive list of Web links on contemporary Croatia, including Web sites of ministries, educational and cultural organizations and networks, tourist associations, and media enterprises.

▪ **Government of the Republic of Croatia**

http://www.vlada.hr/default.asp?ru=2

Full information about the Croatian government, including biographies and pictures of all the political leaders, documents including the Croatian constitution, and links to other related sites.

▪ **Celebrating 17 Centuries of the City of Split**

http://www.st.carnet.hr/split/

Good source of information on this Croatian port. There are many photos of the city and descriptions of Diocletian's palace and other noted buildings. This site was prepared to mark the 1,700th anniversary of the founding of the city.

▪ **Welcome to Zagreb**

http://www.tel.fer.hr/hrvatska/HRgradovi/Zagreb/Zagreb.html

Guide to the Croatian capital that includes a description and outline of Zagreb's history. This site also includes maps, photos, a Webcam trained on the city centre, and a restaurant guide.

CUBA
Map page 102

National name República de Cuba/Republic of Cuba

Area 110,860 sq km/ 42,803 sq mi

Capital Havana

Major towns/cities Santiago de Cuba, Camagüey, Holguín, Guantánamo, Santa Clara, Bayamo, Cienfuegos

Physical features comprises Cuba and smaller islands including Isle of Youth; low hills; Sierra Maestra mountains in southeast; Cuba has 3,380 km/2,100 mi of coastline, with deep bays, sandy beaches, coral islands and reefs

Currency Cuban peso

GNP per capita (PPP) (US$) 2,300 (2002 est)

Resources iron ore, copper, chromite, gold, manganese, nickel, cobalt, silver, salt

Population 11,300,000 (2003 est)

Population density (per sq km) 102 (2003 est)

Language Spanish (official)

Religion Roman Catholic; also Episcopalians and Methodists

Time difference GMT –5

 ▪ CIA ▪ LP ▪ RG ▪ WTG

▪ **CubaWeb**

http://www.cubaweb.com/

Business library, with background information about Cuba for the prospective business investor, and a culture library, covering Cuban history, art, music, literature, food, sport, and collections of photographs.

CYPRUS
Map page 36

National name Kipriakí Dimokratía/ Greek Republic of Cyprus (south); Kibris Cumhuriyeti/Turkish Republic of Northern Cyprus (north)

Area 9,251 sq km/3,571 sq mi (3,335 sq km/1,287 sq mi is Turkish-occupied)

Capital Nicosia (divided between Greek and Turkish Cypriots)

Major towns/cities Limassol, Larnaka, Pafos, Lefkosia, Famagusta

Major ports Limassol, Larnaka, and Pafos (Greek); Keryneia and Famagusta (Turkish)

Physical features central plain between two east–west mountain ranges

Currency Cyprus pound and Turkish lira

GNP per capita (PPP) (US$) 18,040 (2002 est)

Resources copper precipitates, beutonite, umber and other ochres

Population 802,000 (2003 est)

Population density (per sq km) 87 (2003 est)

Language Greek, Turkish (both official), English

Religion Greek Orthodox 78%, Sunni Muslim 18%, Maronite, Armenian Apostolic

Time difference GMT +2

▪ www. ▪ CIA ▪ LC ▪ LP ▪ WTG

▪ **Cyprus**

http://www.stwing.upenn.edu/~durduran/cyprus2.shtml

Devoted to Cyprus – its news, geography, and culture. Included are picture galleries, Cypriot jokes, and guides to Cypriot and Turkish Cypriot dances.

▪ **Republic of Cyprus**

http://www.pio.gov.cy/

This official Web site contains detailed information about the Cyprus government system (including a full copy of the Cypriot constitution), Cypriot international relations, and documents relating to the 'Cyprus issue'. This site also includes a history of the island and the culture of the people.

CZECH REPUBLIC
Map page 18

National name Česká Republika/Czech Republic

Area 78,864 sq km/30,449 sq mi

Capital Prague

Major towns/cities Brno, Ostrava, Olomouc, Liberec, Plzen, Hradec Králové, České Budějovice

Physical features mountainous; rivers: Morava, Labe (Elbe), Vltava (Moldau)

Currency koruna (based on the Czechoslovak koruna)

GNP per capita (PPP) (US$) 14,500 (2002 est)

Resources coal, lignite

Population 10,236,000 (2003 est)

Population density (per sq km) 130 (2003 est)

Language Czech (official), Slovak

Religion Roman Catholic 39%, atheist 30%, Protestant 5%, Orthodox 3%

Time difference GMT +1

 ■ CIA ■ LC ■ LP ■ RG ■ WTG

■ Czech Info Centre

http://www.muselik.com/czech/

Updated daily and aimed primarily at the traveller. However, this site also has information on how to trace a Czech ancestor, traditional recipes, and Czech fonts to download.

■ Czech Republic

http://www.czech.cz/

Root page for the official Czech Republic site, with information on history, geography, and politics. It contains a daily news section, photographs, and Czech music, as well as practical information for tourists.

DENMARK
Map page 16

National name Kongeriget Danmark/ Kingdom of Denmark

Area 43,075 sq km/16,631 sq mi

Capital Copenhagen

Major towns/cities Århus, Odense, Ålborg, Esbjerg, Randers, Kolding, Horsens

Major ports Århus, Odense, Ålborg, Esbjerg

Physical features comprises the Jutland peninsula and about 500 islands (100 inhabited) including Bornholm in the Baltic Sea; the land is flat and cultivated; sand dunes and lagoons on the west coast and long inlets on the east; the main island is Sjælland (Zealand), where most of Copenhagen is located (the rest is on the island of Amager)

Territories the dependencies of Faroe Islands and Greenland

Currency Danish krone

GNP per capita (PPP) (US$) 29,450 (2002 est)

Resources crude petroleum, natural gas, salt, limestone

Population 5,384,000 (2003 est)

Population density (per sq km) 125 (2003 est)

Language Danish (official), German

Religion Evangelical Lutheran 87% (national church), other Protestant and Roman Catholic 3%

Time difference GMT +1

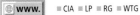 ■ CIA ■ LP ■ RG ■ WTG

■ Aarhus Webben

http://www.aarhuswebben.dk/index.uk.html

Guide to the Danish city of Aarhus. There is information on the city's culture, entertainment, restaurants, and hotels. A street map is also provided and there are links to local Web sites.

■ Copenhagen, Denmark

http://travel.excite.com/show/?loc=13648

Comprehensive guide around Copenhagen that offers all the essential facts plus useful directions concerning hotels, eating out, transportation, and sightseeing. Its travel tools include searchable maps, message boards and a 'Yellow pages' section on things to see and do. The site also features selected links to useful pages on all aspects of life in Copenhagen.

■ Greenland Guide

http://www.greenland-guide.dk/

Official guide to Greenland. The site is highly informative about all regions of the country and is filled with practical information. There are also links to several other sites on Greenland.

■ Faroe Islands Tourist Board

http://www.tourist.fo/

Comprehensive official source of information on the Faroe Islands. There are sections on the Faroese language, geography, history, economy, tourism, and current political controversies in this autonomous region of Norway.

DJIBOUTI
Map page 68

National name Jumhouriyya Djibouti/Republic of Djibouti

Area 23,200 sq km/8,957 sq mi

Capital Djibouti (and chief port)

Major towns/cities Tadjoura, Obock, Dikhil, Ali-Sabieh

Physical features mountains divide an inland plateau from a coastal plain; hot and arid

Currency Djibouti franc

GNP per capita (PPP) (US$) 2,070 (2002 est)

Population 703,000 (2003 est)

Population density (per sq km) 30 (2003 est)

Language French (official), Issa (Somali), Afar, Arabic

Religion Sunni Muslim

Time difference GMT +3

 ■ CIA ■ AN ■ LP ■ NA ■ WTG

DOMINICA
Map page 102

National name Commonwealth of Dominica

Area 751 sq km/290 sq mi

Capital Roseau

Major towns/cities Portsmouth, Marigot, Mahaut, Atkinson, Grand Bay

Major ports Roseau, Portsmouth, Berekua, Marigot

Physical features second-largest of the Windward Islands, mountainous central ridge with tropical rainforest

Currency East Caribbean dollar, although the pound sterling is also accepted

GNP per capita (PPP) (US$) 4,840 (2002 est)

Resources pumice, limestone, clay

Population 79,000 (2003 est)

Population density (per sq km) 105 (2003 est)

Language English (official), a Dominican patois (which reflects earlier periods of French rule)

Religion Roman Catholic 80%

Time difference GMT –4

 ■ CIA ■ LP ■ WTG

DOMINICAN REPUBLIC
Map page 102

National name República Dominicana/Dominican Republic

Area 48,442 sq km/18,703 sq mi

Capital Santo Domingo

Major towns/cities Santiago, La Romana, San Pedro de Macoris, La Vega, San Juan, San Cristóbal

Physical features comprises eastern two-thirds of island of Hispaniola; central mountain range with fertile valleys; Pico Duarte 3,174 m/10,417 ft, highest point in Caribbean islands

Currency Dominican Republic peso

GNP per capita (PPP) (US$) 5,870 (1999 est)

Resources ferro-nickel, gold, silver

Population 8,745,000 (2003 est)

Population density (per sq km) 179 (2003 est)

Language Spanish (official)

Religion Roman Catholic

Time difference GMT –4

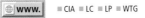 ■ CIA ■ LC ■ LP ■ WTG

■ Dominican Republic on the Internet

http://www.latinworld.com/caribe/rdominicana/index.html

Resources about the Dominican Republic – its news, culture, government, sport, travel opportunities, and economy, plus links

to other sites. Please note that some of the information is only available in Spanish.

EAST TIMOR
Map page 55

National name Democratic Republic of East Timor

Area 14,874 sq km/ 5,743 sq mi

Capital Dili

Major towns/cities Ainaro, Bacau, Maliana, Suai, Viqueque

Physical features comprises the largely mountinous eastern half of the island of Timor in the Malay Archilapelago, together with two islands, Atauro and Jaco, and an enclave around Ocusse on the northwest coast

Currency US dollar

GNP per capita (PPP) (US$) 520 (2002 est)

Resources coffee, rice, maize, livestock, fishing, offshore oil and gas fields due to be exploited from 2004.

Population 778,000 (2003 est)

Population density (per sq km) 52 (2003 est)

Language Potugese (official), Tetum (national)

Religion 86% Roman Catholic, Islam, Animism

Time difference GMT +9

 ■ CIA ■ LP ■ RG ■ WTG

ECUADOR
Map page 108

National name República del Ecuador/Republic of Ecuador

Area 270,670 sq km/ 104,505 sq mi

Capital Quito

Major towns/cities Guayaquil, Cuenca, Machala, Portoviejo, Manta, Ambato, Santo Domingo

Major ports Guayaquil

Physical features coastal plain rises sharply to Andes Mountains, which are divided into a series of cultivated valleys; flat, low-lying rainforest in the east; Galapagos Islands; Cotopaxi, the world's highest active volcano. Ecuador is crossed by the Equator, from which it derives its name

Currency US dollar

GNP per capita (PPP) (US$) 3,130 (2002 est)

Resources petroleum, natural gas, gold, silver, copper, zinc, antimony, iron, uranium, lead, coal

Population 13,003,000 (2003 est)

Population density (per sq km) 48 (2003 est)

Language Spanish (official), Quechua, Jivaro, other indigenous languages

Religion Roman Catholic

Time difference GMT –5

■ CIA ■ LC ■ LP ■ WTG

■ Guayaquil, Ecuador

http://travel.lycos.com/destinations/location.asp?pid=334844

Profile of the city of Guayaquil, Ecuador's busiest port. There is a general introduction to the city's main features, and four sections – 'Visitors' guide', 'Culture and history', 'News and weather', and 'Entertainment' – each with links to photographs, and further information in English and Spanish about both the city and the country.

■ Quito, Ecuador

http://travel.lycos.com/destinations/location.asp?pid=334845

Profile of the Ecuadorian capital, the beautiful city of Quito. There is a general introduction to the city's attractions, and four sections – 'Visitors' guide', 'Culture and history', 'News and weather', and 'Entertainment' – each with links to further useful information in English and Spanish about both the city and the country.

EGYPT

Map page 68

National name Jumhuriyyat Misr al-'Arabiyya/Arab Republic of Egypt

Area 1,001,450 sq km/ 386,659 sq mi

Capital Cairo

Major towns/cities El Giza, Shubrâ el Kheima, Alexandria, Port Said, El-Mahalla el-Koubra, El Mansûra, Suez

Major ports Alexandria, Port Said, Suez, Dumyât, Shubra Al Khayma

Physical features mostly desert; hills in east; fertile land along Nile valley and delta; cultivated and settled area is about 35,500 sq km/13,700 sq mi; Aswan High Dam and Lake Nasser; Sinai

Currency Egyptian pound

GNP per capita (PPP) (US$) 3,710 (2002)

Resources petroleum, natural gas, phosphates, manganese, uranium, coal, iron ore, gold

Population 71,931,000 (2003 est)

Population density (per sq km) 72 (2003 est)

Language Arabic (official), Coptic (derived from ancient Egyptian), English, French

Religion Sunni Muslim 90%, Coptic Christian and other Christian 6%

Time difference GMT +2

www. ■ CIA ■ LC ■ AN ■ LP ■ NA ■ WTG

■ Cairo, the Jewel of the Orient

http://ce.eng.usf.edu/pharos/cairo/

Comprehensive guide to the city's history with a gallery of maps and pictures. It includes detailed information for visitors – places to visit (both ancient and modern), where to stay, where to eat, and details of transportation.

■ Alexandria, Egypt

http://ce.eng.usf.edu/pharos/alexandria/

Information about the Egyptian city of Alexandria including an historical guide, a visitor guide, a picture gallery, maps, and links to related Web sites.

■ Aswan

http://touregypt.net/aswan/

Tourist guide to this relatively undiscovered Egyptian resort. It contains practical information including maps, weather forecasts, and hotel listings. Perhaps unsurprisingly, the bulk of the site is devoted to the museums and monuments, for which there is plenty of historical information. Part of a collection of guides to all major and less popular destinations in Egypt.

EL SALVADOR

Map page 102

National name República de El Salvador/Republic of El Salvador

Area 21,393 sq km/8,259 sq mi

Capital San Salvador

Major towns/cities Santa Ana, San Miguel, Nueva San Salvador, Apopa, Delgado

Physical features narrow coastal plain, rising to mountains in north with central plateau

Currency US dollar (replaced Salvadorean colón in 2001)

GNP per capita (PPP) (US$) 4,570 (2002 est)

Resources salt, limestone, gypsum

Population 6,515,000 (2003 est)

Population density (per sq km) 310 (2003 est)

Language Spanish (official), Nahuatl

Religion about 75% Roman Catholic, Protestant

Time difference GMT –6

www. ■ CIA ■ LC ■ LP ■ WTG

EQUATORIAL GUINEA

Map page 72

National name República de Guinea Ecuatorial/Republic of Equatorial Guinea

Area 28,051 sq km/10,830 sq mi

Capital Malabo

Major towns/cities Bata, Mongomo, Ela Nguema, Mbini, Campo Yaunde, Los Angeles

Physical features comprises mainland Río Muni, plus the small islands of Corisco, Elobey Grande and Elobey Chico, and Bioko (formerly Fernando Po) together with Annobón (formerly Pagalu); nearly half the land is forested; volcanic mountains on Bioko

Currency franc CFA

GNP per capita (PPP) (US$) 5,590 (2002 est)

Resources petroleum, natural gas, gold, uranium, iron ore, tantalum, manganese

Population 494,000 (2003 est)

Population density (per sq km) 18 (2003 est)

Language Spanish (official), pidgin English, a Portuguese patois (on Annobón, whose people were formerly slaves of the Portuguese), Fang and other African patois (on Río Muni)

Religion Roman Catholic, Protestant, animist

Time difference GMT +1

www. ■ CIA ■ LP ■ NA ■ WTG

ERITREA

Map page 68

National name Hagere Eretra al-Dawla al-Iritra/State of Eritrea

Area 125,000 sq km/48,262 sq mi

Capital Asmara

Major towns/cities Assab, Keren, Massawa, Adi Ugri, Ed

Major ports Assab, Massawa

Physical features coastline along the Red Sea 1,000 km/620 mi; narrow coastal plain that rises to an inland plateau; Dahlak Islands

Currency nakfa

GNP per capita (PPP) (US$) 950 (2002 est)

Resources gold, silver, copper, zinc, sulphur, nickel, chrome, potash, basalt, limestone, marble, sand, silicates

Population 4,141,000 (2003 est)

Population density (per sq km) 35 (2003 est)

Language Tigre, Tigrinya, Arabic, English, Afar, Amharic, Kunama, Italian

Religion mainly Sunni Muslim and Coptic Christian, some Roman Catholic, Protestant, and animist

Time difference GMT +3

www. ■ CIA ■ LP ■ NA ■ WTG

ESTONIA

Map page 16

National name Eesti Vabariik/Republic of Estonia

Area 45,000 sq km/17,374 sq mi

Capital Tallinn

Major towns/cities Tartu, Narva, Kohtla-Järve, Pärnu

Physical features lakes and marshes in a partly forested plain; 774 km/481 mi of coastline; mild climate; Lake Peipus and Narva River forming boundary with Russian Federation; Baltic islands, the largest of which is Saaremaa

Currency kroon

GNP per capita (PPP) (US$) 11,120 (2002 est)

Resources oilshale, peat, phosphorite ore, superphosphates

Population 1,323,000 (2003 est)

Population density (per sq km) 29 (2003 est)

Language Estonian (official), Russian

Religion Eastern Orthodox, Evangelical Lutheran, Russian Orthodox, Muslim, Judaism

Time difference GMT +2

www. ■ CIA ■ LC ■ LP ■ RG ■ WTG

■ Estonia Country Guide

http://www.ciesin.ee/ESTCG/

General information and news about Estonia, plus sections on its history, political system, economy, and culture. There is, however, little information of direct use to people wishing to visit the country, except for pages on upcoming events and public transport.

■ Tallinn

http://www.tallinn.ee/english/index.html

Good official guide to the Estonian capital. There is good coverage of the city's rich history, culture, economy, educational and scientific institutions, and transport services. In addition there is a demographic profile of its inhabitants.

ETHIOPIA

Map page 66

National name Ya'Ityopya Federalawi Dimokrasiyawi Repeblik/ Federal Democratic Republic of Ethiopia

Area 1,096,900 sq km/ 423,513 sq mi

Capital Addis Ababa

Major towns/cities Dirē Dawa, Harar, Nazrēt, Desē, Gonder, Mek'ele, Bahir Dar

Physical features a high plateau with central mountain range divided by Rift Valley; plains in east; source of Blue Nile River; Danakil and Ogaden deserts

Currency Ethiopian birr

GNP per capita (PPP) (US$) 720 (2002 est)

Resources gold, salt, platinum, copper, potash. Reserves of petroleum have not been exploited

Population 70,678,000 (2003 est)

Population density (per sq km) 64 (2003 est)

Language Amharic (official), Arabic, Tigrinya, Orominga, about 100 other local languages

Religion Muslim 45%, Ethiopian Orthodox Church (which has had its own patriarch since 1976) 35%, animist 12%, other Christian 8%

Time difference GMT +3

www. ■ CIA ■ LC ■ LP ■ NA ■ WTG

FIJI

Map page 80

National name Matanitu Ko Viti/Republic of the Fiji Islands

Area 18,333 sq km/7,078 sq mi

Capital Suva

Major towns/cities Lautoka, Nadi, Ba, Labasa, Nausori

Major ports Lautoka, Levuka

Physical features comprises about 844 Melanesian and Polynesian islands and islets (about 100 inhabited), the largest being Viti Levu (10,429 sq km/4,028 sq mi) and Vanua Levu (5,556 sq km/2,146 sq mi); mountainous, volcanic, with tropical rainforest and grasslands; almost all islands surrounded by coral reefs; high volcanic peaks

Currency Fiji dollar

GNP per capita (PPP) (US$) 5,310 (2002 est)

Resources gold, silver, copper

Population 839,000 (2003 est)

Population density (per sq km) 46 (2003 est)

Language English (official), Fijian, Hindi

Religion Roman Catholic 92%, Church of Ireland, other Protestant denominations 3%

Time difference GMT +/–0

 www. ■ CIA ■ LP ■ RG ■ WTG

■ **Complete Guide to Ireland**

http://members.tripod.com/~AndrewGallagher/ireland/

Guide to the geography, history, and politics of Ireland. The site can be viewed with or without frames and also includes sections on sport, tourism, culture, and the Celts.

■ **Cork Guide Online**

http://www.cork-guide.ie/corkcity.htm

Good source of information on Ireland's third-largest city. A description of the city, its heritage, and attractions is accompanied by some fine photographs. There is also information on accommodation, entertainment, transport, and restaurants

■ **Complete Guide to Galway**

http://www.wombat.ie/galwayguide/

Thorough and well-arranged source of information on this western Irish county. The needs of residents, tourists, and investors are fully met with sections on attractions, transport, entertainment, accommodation, things to do with children, community groups, and local government services. In addition to a good summary of Galway's history, there are online versions of several detailed history books of the county.

■ **Kerry Insight**

http://www.kerry-insight.com/

Guide to the Irish county. This site includes sections on fishing, sports, entertainment, accommodation, places of historical interest, events and festivals, an extensive commercial directory, community organizations, guides to towns in the county, maps, and a weather report.

■ **Government of Ireland**

http://www.irlgov.ie/gov.htm

Complete guide to all the departments of the Irish government, including contact details. The 'Department of the taoiseach' includes a virtual tour of the parliament building, complete with the history of the position of taoiseach, or prime minister.

ISRAEL
Map page 62

National name Medinat Israel/State of Israel

Area 20,800 sq km/8,030 sq mi (as at 1949 armistice)

Capital Jerusalem (not recognized by the United Nations)

Major towns/cities Tel Aviv-Yafo, Haifa, Bat-Yam, Holon, Ramat Gan, Petah Tiqwa, Rishon le Ziyyon, Be'ér Sheva'

Major ports Tel Aviv-Yafo, Haifa, 'Akko (formerly Acre), Elat

Physical features coastal plain of Sharon between Haifa and Tel Aviv noted since ancient times for its fertility; central mountains of Galilee, Samaria, and Judea; Dead Sea, Lake Tiberias, and River Jordan Rift Valley along the east are below sea level; Negev Desert in the south; Israel occupies Golan Heights, West Bank, East Jerusalem, and Gaza Strip (the last was awarded limited autonomy, with West Bank town of Jericho, in 1993)

Currency shekel

GNP per capita (PPP) (US$) 19,920 (2002 est)

Resources potash, bromides, magnesium, sulphur, copper ore, gold, salt, petroleum, natural gas

Population 6,433,000 (2003 est)

Population density (per sq km) 291 (2003 est)

Language Hebrew, Arabic (both official), English, Yiddish, other European and west Asian languages

Religion Israel is a secular state, but the predominant faith is Judaism 80%; also Sunni Muslim (about 15%), Christian, and Druze

Time difference GMT +2

 www. ■ CIA ■ LC ■ LP ■ WTG

■ **Bethlehem University**

http://www.bethlehem.edu/

History of the town, guide to churches and religious institutions. This is site is part of the Web site of Bethlehem University.

■ **Applied Resource Institute – Jerusalem**

http://www.arij.org/

Comprehensive Palestinian source of up-to-date information on geography, climate, water, agriculture, land use, and settlement activities in the West Bank. This site is indispensable for understanding the Israeli-Palestinian conflict over natural resources.

ITALY
Map page 32

National name Repubblica Italiana/ Italian Republic

Area 301,300 sq km/ 116,331 sq mi

Capital Rome

Major towns/cities Milan, Naples, Turin, Palermo, Genoa, Bologna, Florence

Major ports Naples, Genoa, Palermo, Bari, Catania, Trieste

Physical features mountainous (Maritime Alps, Dolomites, Apennines) with narrow coastal lowlands; continental Europe's only active volcanoes: Vesuvius, Etna, Stromboli; rivers Po, Adige, Arno, Tiber, Rubicon; islands of Sicily, Sardinia, Elba, Capri, Ischia, Lipari, Pantelleria; lakes Como, Maggiore, Garda

Currency euro (lira until 2002)

GNP per capita (PPP) (US$) 25,320 (2002 est)

Resources lignite, lead, zinc, mercury, potash, sulphur, fluorspar, bauxite, marble, petroleum, natural gas, fish

Population 57,423,000 (2003 est)

Population density (per sq km) 191 (2003 est)

Language Italian (official), German and Ladin (in the north), French (in the Valle d'Aosta region), Greek and Albanian (in the south)

Religion Roman Catholic 98% (state religion)

Time difference GMT +1

 www. ■ CIA ■ LP ■ RG ■ WTG

■ **Windows on Italy – History**

http://www.mi.cnr.it/WOI/

Packed with information about the history and culture of Italy's regions and towns. This index leads to pages of information dealing with every major period from prehistoric times to the present day.

■ **History of Venice**

http://www.doge.it/storia/storiai.htm

From the first inhabitants to the present day, this is a look at the origins and historical development of the Italian city of Venice. It includes numerous pictures and photographs of the city, and a map of the surrounding area.

■ **Rome, Italy**

http://www.geocities.com/Athens/Forum/2680/

Huge source of information on 'the eternal city'. An offbeat introduction to the 'home of popes and pickpockets' leads to detailed information on the history, monuments, and modern attractions of the Italian capital. There is a weather report, links to local media, and access to a large number of guides to Rome.

JAMAICA
Map page 102

Area 10,957 sq km/4,230 sq mi

Capital Kingston

Major towns/cities Montego Bay, Spanish Town, Portmore, May Pen

Physical features mountainous tropical island; Blue Mountains (so called because of the haze over them)

Currency Jamaican dollar

GNP per capita (PPP) (US$) 3,550 (2002 est)

Resources bauxite (one of world's major producers), marble, gypsum, silica, clay

Population 2,651,000 (2003 est)

Population density (per sq km) 241 (2003 est)

Language English (official), Jamaican Creole

Religion Protestant 70%, Rastafarian

Time difference GMT –5

 www. ■ CIA ■ LP ■ RG ■ WTG

■ **JamaicaTravel.com**

http://www.jamaicatravel.com/

Official site of the Jamaica Tourist Board. A colourful site, this guide covers everything the visitor needs to know, such as where to stay, what to do, and what to see. There is also a calendar to keep you abreast of events in Jamaica, and a visitor's forum to share questions and advice with other visitors.

JAPAN
Map page 50

National name Nihon-koku/State of Japan

Area 377,535 sq km/145,766 sq mi

Capital Tōkyō

Major towns/cities Yokohama, Ōsaka, Nagoya, Fukuoka, Kita-Kyūshū, Kyōto, Sapporo, Kobe, Kawasaki, Hiroshima

Major ports Ōsaka, Nagoya, Yokohama, Kobe

Physical features mountainous, volcanic (Mount Fuji, volcanic Mount Aso, Japan Alps); comprises over 1,000 islands, the largest of which are Hokkaido, Honshu, Kyushu, and Shikoku

Currency yen

GNP per capita (PPP) (US$) 26,070 (2002 est)

Resources coal, iron, zinc, copper, natural gas, fish

Population 127,654,000 (2003 est)

Population density (per sq km) 338 (2003 est)

Language Japanese (official), Ainu

Religion Shinto, Buddhist (often combined), Christian (less than 1%)

Time difference GMT +9

 www. ■ CIA ■ LC ■ LP ■ RG ■ WTG

■ **Japan Information Network**

http://www.jinjapan.org/index.html

Searchable set of links to resources about Japan – its regions, society, culture, current events, and other aspects of Japanese life.

■ **Tokyo**

http://www.pandemic.com/tokyo/

City guide to the Japanese capital Tokyo. There are also details of the city's history, geography, and features on festivals. The section on tourist information is supplemented with maps and photographs and contains a list of useful phone numbers.

JORDAN
Map page 58

National name Al-Mamlaka al-Urduniyya al-Hashemiyyah/ Hashemite Kingdom of Jordan

Area 89,206 sq km/34,442 sq mi (excluding the West Bank 5,879 sq km/2,269 sq mi)

Capital Ammān

Major towns/cities Zarqā', Irbid, Ma'ān

Major ports Aqaba

Physical features desert plateau in east; Rift Valley separates east and west banks of River Jordan

Currency Jordanian dinar

GNP per capita (PPP) (US$) 4,070 (2002 est)

Resources phosphates, potash, shale

Population 5,473,000 (2003 est)

Population density (per sq km) 61 (2003 est)

Language Arabic (official), English

Religion over 90% Sunni Muslim (official religion), small communities of Christians and Shiite Muslims

Time difference GMT +2

■ **Pictures of Jordan**

http://www.geocities.com/TheTropics/Cabana/2973/Jordan.html

Impressive collection of photographs from Jordan. This site includes photographs of some of Jordan's most interesting places such as Petra, Mount Nebo, Wadi Rum, The Dead Sea, and Aquaba, as well as an 'Impressions' section.

KAZAKHSTAN
Map page 44

National name Kazak Respublikasy/Republic of Kazakhstan

Area 2,717,300 sq km/ 1,049,150 sq mi

Capital Astana (formerly Akmola)

Major towns/cities Qaraghandy, Pavlodar, Semey, Petropavl, Shymkent

Physical features Caspian and Aral seas, Lake Balkhash; Steppe region; natural gas and oil deposits in the Caspian Sea

Currency tenge

GNP per capita (PPP) (US$) 5,480 (2002 est)

Resources petroleum, natural gas, coal, bauxite, chromium, copper, iron ore, lead, titanium, magnesium, tungsten, molybdenum, gold, silver, manganese

Population 15,433,000 (2003 est)

Population density (per sq km) 6 (2003 est)

Language Kazakh (related to Turkish; official), Russian

Religion Sunni Muslim 50–60%, Russian Orthodox 30–35%

Time difference GMT +6

KENYA
Map page 74

National name Jamhuri ya Kenya/ Republic of Kenya

Area 582,600 sq km/ 224,941 sq mi

Capital Nairobi

Major towns/cities Mombasa, Kisumu, Nakuru, Eldoret, Nyeri

Major ports Mombasa

Physical features mountains and highlands in west and centre; coastal plain in south; arid interior and tropical coast; semi-desert in north; Great Rift Valley, Mount Kenya, Lake Nakuru (salt lake with world's largest colony of flamingos), Lake Turkana (Rudolf)

Currency Kenyan shilling

GNP per capita (PPP) (US$) 990 (2002 est)

Resources soda ash, fluorspar, salt, limestone, rubies, gold, vermiculite, diatonite, garnets

Population 31,987,000 (2003 est)

Population density (per sq km) 55 (2003 est)

Language English, Kiswahili (both official), many local dialects

Religion Roman Catholic 28%, Protestant 8%, Muslim 6%, traditional tribal religions

Time difference GMT +3

■ **Kenyaweb**

http://www.kenyaweb.com/

Social, cultural, and political information about Kenya. This site includes travel-oriented information about this African country, including sections on safaris, national parks, key facts, and even a bus route guide.

KIRIBATI
Map page 80

National name Ribaberikan Kiribati/Republic of Kiribati

Area 717 sq km/277 sq mi

Capital Bairiki (on Tarawa atoll)

Major towns/cities principal islands are the Gilbert Islands, the Phoenix Islands, the Line Islands, Banaba

Major ports Bairiki, Betio (on Tarawa)

Physical features comprises 33 Pacific coral islands: the Kiribati (Gilbert), Rawaki (Phoenix), Banaba (Ocean Island), and three of the Line Islands including Kiritimati (Christmas Island); island groups crossed by Equator and International Date Line

Currency Australian dollar

GNP per capita (PPP) (US$) 2,070 (2002 est)

Resources phosphate, salt

Population 88,000 (2003 est)

Population density (per sq km) 121 (2003 est)

Language English (official), Gilbertese

Religion Roman Catholic, Protestant (Congregationalist)

Time difference GMT –10/–11

KUWAIT
Map page 63

National name Dowlat al-Kuwayt/ State of Kuwait

Area 17,819 sq km/6,879 sq mi

Capital Kuwait (and chief port)

Major towns/cities as-Salimiya, Ḥawallī, Al Farwānīyah, Abraq Kheetan, Al Jahrah, Al Aḥmadī, Al Fuḥayḥil

Physical features hot desert; islands of Faylakah, Bubiyan, and Warbah at northeast corner of Arabian Peninsula

Currency Kuwaiti dinar

GNP per capita (PPP) (US$) 18,800 (2002 est)

Resources petroleum, natural gas, mineral water

Population 2,521,000 (2003 est)

Population density (per sq km) 142 (2003 est)

Language Arabic (78%) (official), English, Kurdish (10%), Farsi (4%)

Religion Sunni Muslim 45%, Shiite Muslim 40%; Christian, Hindu, and Parsi about 5%

Time difference GMT +3

KYRGYZSTAN
Map page 44

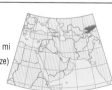

National name Kyrgyz Respublikasy/Kyrgyz Republic

Area 198,500 sq km/76,640 sq mi

Capital Bishkek (formerly Frunze)

Major towns/cities Osh, Karakol, Kyzyl-Kiya, Tokmak, Djalal-Abad

Physical features mountainous, an extension of the Tien Shan range

Currency som

GNP per capita (PPP) (US$) 1,520 (2002 est)

Resources petroleum, natural gas, coal, gold, tin, mercury, antimony, zinc, tungsten, uranium

Population 5,138,000 (2003 est)

Population density (per sq km) 26 (2003 est)

Language Kyrgyz (a Turkic language; official), Russian

Religion Sunni Muslim 70%, Russian Orthodox 20%

Time difference GMT +5

■ **Destination Kyrgyzstan**

http://www.peacecorps.gov/wws/guides/kyrgyzstan/

Peace Corps guide, for schoolchildren, to this tiny Central Asian state. There are classroom activities divided by age group and teachers' notes, as well as plentiful maps, illustrations, and guides to other Internet resources.

LAOS
Map page 52

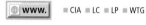

National name Sathalanalat Praxathipatai Paxaxôn Lao/ Democratic People's Republic of Laos

Area 236,790 sq km/ 91,424 sq mi

Capital Vientiane

Major towns/cities Louangphrabang (the former royal capital), Pakxé, Savannakhet

Physical features landlocked state with high mountains in east; Mekong River in west; rainforest covers nearly 60% of land

Currency new kip

GNP per capita (PPP) (US$) 1,610 (2002 est)

Resources coal, tin, gypsum, baryte, lead, zinc, nickel, potash, iron ore; small quantities of gold, silver, precious stones

Population 5,657,000 (2003 est)

Population density (per sq km) 24 (2003 est)

Language Lao (official), French, English, ethnic languages

Religion Theravada Buddhist 85%, animist beliefs among mountain dwellers

Time difference GMT +7

■ **Laos – The Internet Travel Guide**

http://www.pmgeiser.ch/laos/

Written by a traveller for travellers, this is a useful resource for anyone visiting Laos in Southeast Asia. The guide is divided into a number of sections, offering advice on 'Climate', 'Events', 'Border crossing', and so on. A large part of the guide is devoted to the country's numerous attractions, ranging from the Ho Chi Minh trail to the Plain of Jars.

LATVIA
Map page 16

National name Latvijas Republika/ Republic of Latvia

Area 63,700 sq km/24,594 sq mi

Capital Rīga

Major towns/cities Daugavpils, Liepāja, Jūrmala, Jelgava, Ventspils

Major ports Ventspils, Liepāja

Physical features wooded lowland (highest point 312 m/ 1,024 ft), marshes, lakes; 472 km/293 mi of coastline; mild climate

Currency lat

GNP per capita (PPP) (US$) 8,940 (2002 est)

Resources peat, gypsum, dolomite, limestone, amber, gravel, sand

Population 2,307,000 (2003 est)

Population density (per sq km) 36 (2003 est)

Language Latvian (official)

Religion Lutheran, Roman Catholic, Russian Orthodox

Time difference GMT +2

■ **LatviaNet**

http://www.tvnet.lv/en/

Bilingual guide to this Eastern European country, including an overview of the Baltic region, as well as plenty of country-specific information on such topics as the environment, communications, government, tourism, and society.

■ **Riga in Your Pocket Home Page**
http://www.inyourpocket.com/Latvia/Riga_home.shtml
Guide to everything you ever wanted to know about this Baltic capital city. This is an electronic form of a published guide book and includes sections on such topics as language, media, what to see, getting there, and where to stay.

LEBANON

Map page 62

National name Jumhouria al-Lubnaniya/Republic of Lebanon
Area 10,452 sq km/4,035 sq mi
Capital Beirut (and chief port)
Major towns/cities Tripoli, Zahlé, Baabda, Ba'albek, Jezzine
Major ports Tripoli, Soûr, Saïda, Joûnié
Physical features narrow coastal plain; fertile Bekka valley running north–south between Lebanon and Anti-Lebanon mountain ranges
Currency Lebanese pound
GNP per capita (PPP) (US$) 4,470 (2002 est)
Resources there are no commercially viable mineral deposits; small reserves of lignite and iron ore
Population 3,653,000 (2003 est)
Population density (per sq km) 351 (2003 est)
Language Arabic (official), French, Armenian, English
Religion Muslim 70% (Shiite 35%, Sunni 23%, Druze 7%, other 5%); Christian 30% (mainly Maronite 19%), Druze 3%; other Christian denominations including Greek Orthodox, Armenian, and Roman Catholic
Time difference GMT +2

 www. ■ CIA ■ LC ■ AN ■ LP ■ WTG

LESOTHO
Map page 76

National name Mmuso oa Lesotho/ Kingdom of Lesotho
Area 30,355 sq km/11,720 sq mi
Capital Maseru
Major towns/cities Qacha's Nek, Teyateyaneng, Mafeteng, Hlotse, Roma, Quthing
Physical features mountainous with plateaux, forming part of South Africa's chief watershed
Currency loti
GNP per capita (PPP) (US$) 2,710 (2002 est)
Resources diamonds, uranium, lead, iron ore; believed to have petroleum deposits
Population 1,802,000 (2003 est)
Population density (per sq km) 59 (2003 est)
Language English (official), Sesotho, Zulu, Xhosa
Religion Protestant 42%, Roman Catholic 38%, indigenous beliefs
Time difference GMT +2

www. ■ CIA ■ LP ■ RG ■ NA ■ WTG

■ **Lesotho Page**
http://www.sas.upenn.edu/African_Studies/Country_Specific/Lesotho.html
Concise set of resources, including a map, US travel advisories, a database of its languages, and links to further sources of information.

LIBERIA

Map page 72

National name Republic of Liberia
Area 111,370 sq km/42,999 sq mi
Capital Monrovia (and chief port)
Major towns/cities Bensonville, Gbarnga, Voinjama, Buchanan
Major ports Buchanan, Greenville

Physical features forested highlands; swampy tropical coast where six rivers enter the sea
Currency Liberian dollar
GNP per capita (PPP) (US$) N/A
Resources iron ore, diamonds, gold, barytes, kyanite
Population 3,367,000 (2003 est)
Population density (per sq km) 30 (2003 est)
Language English (official), over 20 Niger-Congo languages
Religion animist 70%, Sunni Muslim 20%, Christian 10%
Time difference GMT +/–0

www. ■ CIA ■ LP ■ NA ■ WTG

LIBYA

Map page 68

National name Al-Jamahiriyya al-'Arabiyya al-Libiyya ash-Sha'biyya al-Ishtirakiyya al-'Uzma/Great Libyan Arab Socialist People's State of the Masses
Area 1,759,540 sq km/679,358 sq mi
Capital Tripoli
Major towns/cities Banghāzī, Mişrātah, Az Zāwīyah, Tubruq, Ajdābiyā, Darnah
Major ports Banghāzī, Mişrāta, Az Zāwīyah, Tubruq, Ajdābiyā, Darnah
Physical features flat to undulating plains with plateaux and depressions stretch southwards from the Mediterranean coast to an extremely dry desert interior
Currency Libyan dinar
GNP per capita (PPP) (US$) N/A
Resources petroleum, natural gas, iron ore, potassium, magnesium, sulphur, gypsum
Population 5,551,000 (2003 est)
Population density (per sq km) 3 (2003 est)
Language Arabic (official), Italian, English
Religion Sunni Muslim 97%
Time difference GMT +1

www. ■ CIA ■ LC ■ AN ■ LP ■ NA ■ WTG

LIECHTENSTEIN

Map page 30

National name Fürstentum Liechtenstein/Principality of Liechtenstein
Area 160 sq km/62 sq mi
Capital Vaduz
Major towns/cities Balzers, Schaan, Eschen
Physical features landlocked Alpine; includes part of Rhine Valley in west
Currency Swiss franc
GNP per capita (PPP) (US$) 24,000 (1998 est)
Resources hydro power
Population 34,000 (2003 est)
Population density (per sq km) 216 (2003 est)
Language German (official), an Alemannic dialect
Religion Roman Catholic 80%, Protestant 7%
Time difference GMT +1

www. ■ CIA ■ LP ■ WTG

■ **Liechtenstein National Tourist Guide**
http://www.news.li/
Official guide to the tiny principality. There is comprehensive information on history, attractions, sporting and recreational pursuits, entertainment, accommodation, and transport. There is a commercial directory, a listing of events, and a guide for philatelists.

LITHUANIA

Map page 16

National name Lietuvos Respublika/ Republic of Lithuania
Area 65,200 sq km/25,173 sq mi
Capital Vilnius
Major towns/cities Kaunas, Klaipėda, Šiauliai, Panevėžys
Physical features central lowlands with gentle hills in west and higher terrain in southeast; 25% forested; some 3,000 small lakes, marshes, and complex sandy coastline; River Nenumas
Currency litas
GNP per capita (PPP) (US$) 9,880 (2002 est)
Resources small deposits of petroleum, natural gas, peat, limestone, gravel, clay, sand
Population 3,444,000 (2003 est)
Population density (per sq km) 53 (2003 est)
Language Lithuanian (official)
Religion predominantly Roman Catholic; Evangelical Lutheran, also Russian Orthodox, Evangelical Reformist, and Baptist
Time difference GMT +2

www. ■ CIA ■ LC ■ LP ■ RG ■ WTG

■ **Vilnius in Your Pocket Home Page**
http://www.inyourpocket.com/Lithuania/Vilnius_home.shtml
Guide to everything you ever wanted to know about this Baltic capital city. This is an electronic form of a published guide book and includes sections on such topics as language, media, what to see, getting there, and where to stay.

LUXEMBOURG

Map page 22

National name Grand-Duché de Luxembourg/Grand Duchy of Luxembourg
Area 2,586 sq km/998 sq mi
Capital Luxembourg
Major towns/cities Esch, Differdange, Dudelange, Pétange
Physical features on the River Moselle; part of the Ardennes (Oesling) forest in north
Currency euro (Luxembourg franc until 2002)
GNP per capita (PPP) (US$) 51,060 (2002 est)
Resources iron ore
Population 453,000 (2003 est)
Population density (per sq km) 175 (2003 est)
Language Letzeburgisch (a German-Moselle-Frankish dialect; official), English
Religion Roman Catholic about 95%, Protestant and Jewish 4%
Time difference GMT +1

www. ■ CIA ■ LP ■ RG ■ WTG

■ **Luxembourg Tourist Office in London**
http://www.luxembourg.co.uk/
Detailed guide to Luxembourg that is aimed primarily at the tourist. The site comprises a number of articles, covering topics such as the country's museums, activities, and culture. Also featured is a directory of hotels, guesthouses, and youth hostels.

MACEDONIA

Map page 36

National name Republika Makedonija/Republic of Macedonia (official internal name); Poranesna Jugoslovenska Republika Makedonija/Former Yugoslav Republic of Macedonia (official international name)
Area 25,700 sq km/9,922 sq mi
Capital Skopje

Major towns/cities Bitola, Prilep, Kumanovo, Tetovo
Physical features mountainous; rivers: Struma, Vardar; lakes: Ohrid, Prespa, Scutari; partly Mediterranean climate with hot summers
Currency Macedonian denar
GNP per capita (PPP) (US$) 6,210 (2002 est)
Resources coal, iron, zinc, chromium, manganese, lead, copper, nickel, silver, gold
Population 2,056,000 (2003 est)
Population density (per sq km) 80 (2003 est)
Language Macedonian (related to Bulgarian; official), Albanian
Religion Christian, mainly Orthodox 67%; Muslim 30%
Time difference GMT +1

 ■ CIA ■ LP ■ WTG

■ **Macedonia – Frequently Asked Questions**
http://faq.rmacedonia.org/
Large source of well-presented information on the Balkan state. There is comprehensive information about the Macedonian language, literary heritage, history, cuisine, arts, economy, sports, and religion. This site also has regularly updated news of internal and external affairs.

■ **Skopje, Republic of Macedonia**
http://www.skopje.com.mk/angliski/prva.asp
Guide to the Macedonian capital. The economic basis and cultural life of Skopje are described prior to a summary of the city's long history. There are also a number of photographs.

MADAGASCAR
Map page 76

National name Repoblikan'i Madagasikara/République de Madagascar/Republic of Madagascar
Area 587,041 sq km/ 226,656 sq mi
Capital Antananarivo
Major towns/cities Antsirabe, Mahajanga, Fianarantsoa, Toamasina, Ambatondrazaka
Major ports Toamasina, Antsiranana, Mahajanga
Physical features temperate central highlands; humid valleys and tropical coastal plains; arid in south
Currency Malagasy franc
GNP per capita (PPP) (US$) 720 (2002 est)
Resources graphite, chromite, mica, titanium ore, small quantities of precious stones, bauxite and coal deposits, petroleum reserves
Population 17,404,000 (2003 est)
Population density (per sq km) 30 (2003 est)
Language Malagasy, French (both official), local dialects
Religion over 50% traditional beliefs, Roman Catholic, Protestant about 40%, Muslim 7%
Time difference GMT +3

 ■ CIA ■ LC ■ LP ■ NA ■ WTG

■ **Madagascar**
http://www.geocities.com/SoHo/Atrium/5431/mad/Index.html
Virtual tour of the island of Madagascar that is aimed at the independent traveller. The tour consists of a series of photographs that follow a trail across the island. There is also a map of the island, as well as an article and fact sheet on Madagascar.

MALAWI
Map page 76

National name Republic of Malawi
Area 118,484 sq km/45,735 sq mi
Capital Lilongwe
Major towns/cities Blantyre, Mzuzu, Zomba
Physical features landlocked narrow plateau with rolling plains; mountainous west of Lake Nyasa

Currency Malawi kwacha
GNP per capita (PPP) (US$) 570 (2002 est)
Resources marble, coal, gemstones, bauxite and graphite deposits, reserves of phosphates, uranium, glass sands, asbestos, vermiculite
Population 12,105,000 (2003 est)
Population density (per sq km) 102 (2003 est)
Language English, Chichewa (both official), other Bantu languages
Religion Protestant 50%, Roman Catholic 20%, Muslim 2%, animist
Time difference GMT +2

 ■ CIA ■ LP ■ NA ■ WTG

■ **Malawi – The Warm Heart of Africa**
http://members.tripod.com/~malawi/
Well-illustrated guide to Malawi. Aimed at the traveller, this site offers advice on the country's attractions and accommodation. Visitors can also learn a few words of Chichewa and sample some of the country's music.

MALAYSIA
Map page 54

National name Persekutuan Tanah Malaysia/Federation of Malaysia
Area 329,759 sq km/127,319 sq mi
Capital Kuala Lumpur
Major towns/cities Johor Bahru, Ipoh, George Town (on Penang island), Kuala Terengganu, Kuala Bahru, Petaling Jaya, Kelang, Kuching (on Sarawak), Kota Kinabalu (on Sabah)
Major ports Kelang
Physical features comprises peninsular Malaysia (the nine Malay states – Johore, Kedah, Kelantan, Negri Sembilan, Pahang, Perak, Perlis, Selangor, Terengganu – plus Malacca and Penang); states of Sabah and Sarawak on the island of Borneo; and the federal territory of Kuala Lumpur; 75% tropical rainforest; central mountain range; Mount Kinabalu, the highest peak in southeast Asia, is in Sabah; swamps in east; Niah caves (Sarawak)
Currency ringgit
GNP per capita (PPP) (US$) 8,260 (2002 est)
Resources tin, bauxite, copper, iron ore, petroleum, natural gas, forests
Population 24,425,000 (2003 est)
Population density (per sq km) 74 (2003 est)
Language Bahasa Malaysia (Malay; official), English, Chinese, Tamil, Iban, many local dialects
Religion Muslim (official) about 53%, Buddhist 19%, Hindu, Christian, local beliefs
Time difference GMT +8

 ■ CIA ■ LP ■ RG ■ WTG

■ **Malaysia Home Page**
http://www.sesrtcic.org/members/mly/mlyhome.shtml
Information about Malaysian history, events, education, economy, politics, tourism, and laws, as well as hyperlinks to other relevant sites.

MALDIVES
Map page 56

National name Divehi Raajjeyge Jumhuriyya/Republic of the Maldives
Area 298 sq km/115 sq mi
Capital Malé
Physical features comprises 1,196 coral islands, grouped into 12 clusters of atolls, largely flat, none bigger than 13 sq km/5 sq mi, average elevation 1.8 m/6 ft; 203 are inhabited
Currency rufiya
GNP per capita (PPP) (US$) 2,740 (2002 est)

Resources coral (mining was banned as a measure against the encroachment of the sea)
Population 318,000 (2003 est)
Population density (per sq km) 1,068 (2003 est)
Language Divehi (a Sinhalese dialect; official), English, Arabic
Religion Sunni Muslim
Time difference GMT +5

 ■ CIA ■ LP ■ WTG

■ **Visit Maldives**
http://www.visitmaldives.com/intro.html
Well-designed guide to the Maldives from their Ministry of Tourism. The site features a 'Travel advisor', offering practical information on health and resorts. There is also a photo gallery, as well as sections devoted to sailing and diving in the Maldives.

MALI
Map page 70

National name République du Mali/ Republic of Mali
Area 1,240,142 sq km/ 478,818 sq mi
Capital Bamako
Major towns/cities Mopti, Kayes, Ségou, Tombouctou, Sikasso
Physical features landlocked state with River Niger and savannah in south; part of the Sahara in north; hills in northeast; Senegal River and its branches irrigate the southwest
Currency franc CFA
GNP per capita (PPP) (US$) 840 (2002 est)
Resources iron ore, uranium, diamonds, bauxite, manganese, copper, lithium, gold
Population 13,007,000 (2003 est)
Population density (per sq km) 10 (2003 est)
Language French (official), Bambara, other African languages
Religion Sunni Muslim 80%, animist, Christian
Time difference GMT +/–0

 ■ CIA ■ LP ■ NA ■ WTG

MALTA
Map page 32

National name Repubblika ta'Malta/ Republic of Malta
Area 320 sq km/124 sq mi
Capital Valletta (and chief port)
Major towns/cities Rabat, Birkirkara, Qormi, Sliema
Major ports Marsaxlokk, Valletta
Physical features includes islands of Gozo 67 sq km/26 sq mi and Comino 3 sq km/1 sq mi
Currency Maltese lira
GNP per capita (PPP) (US$) 16,790 (2002 est)
Resources stone, sand; offshore petroleum reserves were under exploration 1988–95
Population 394,000 (2003 est)
Population density (per sq km) 1,248 (2003 est)
Language Maltese, English (both official)
Religion Roman Catholic 98%
Time difference GMT +1

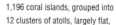 ■ CIA ■ LP ■ WTG

MARSHALL ISLANDS
Map page 80

National name Majol/Republic of the Marshall Islands
Area 181 sq km/70 sq mi
Capital Dalap-Uliga-Darrit (on Majuro atoll)
Major towns/cities Ebeye (the only other town)
Physical features comprises the Ratak and Ralik island chains in the West Pacific, which together form an archipelago of 31

coral atolls, 5 islands, and
1,152 islets

Currency US dollar

GNP per capita (PPP) (US$)
4,820 (2002 est)

Resources phosphates

Population 53,000 (2003 est)

Population density (per sq km) 293 (2003 est)

Language Marshallese, English (both official)

Religion Christian (mainly Protestant) and Baha'i

Time difference GMT +12

 ■ CIA ■ LP

■ **Internet Guide to the Republic of the Marshall Islands**
http://www.rmiembassyus.org/
Comprehensive official guide to the Micronesian state. The
history, culture, cuisine, economy, government services, and
democratic system of the Marshall Islands are fully explained with
the help of maps and photos. RMI concerns about global
warming, from a state whose highest elevation is a mere six
metres, are set out.

MAURITANIA
Map page 70

National name Al-Jumhuriyya
al-Islamiyya al-Mawritaniyya/
République Islamique Arabe et
Africaine de Mauritanie/Islamic
Republic of Mauritania

Area 1,030,700 sq km/
397,953 sq mi

Capital Nouakchott (and chief port)

Major towns/cities Nouâdhibou, Kaédi, Zouérat, Kiffa, Rosso,
Atâr

Major ports Nouâdhibou

Physical features valley of River Senegal in south; remainder
arid and flat

Currency ouguiya

GNP per capita (PPP) (US$) 1,740 (2002 est)

Resources copper, gold, iron ore, gypsum, phosphates, sulphur,
peat

Population 2,893,000 (2003 est)

Population density (per sq km) 3 (2003 est)

Language Hasaniya Arabic (official), Pulaar, Soninke, Wolof (all
national languages), French (particularly in the south)

Religion Sunni Muslim (state religion)

Time difference GMT +/–0

 ■ CIA ■ LC ■ AN ■ LP ■ NA ■ WTG

MAURITIUS
Map page 76

National name Republic of
Mauritius

Area 1,865 sq km/720 sq mi

Capital Port Louis (and chief port)

Major towns/cities Beau Bassin,
Rose Hill, Curepipe, Quatre Bornes,
Vacoas-Phoenix

Physical features mountainous, volcanic island surrounded by
coral reefs; the island of Rodrigues is part of Mauritius; there are
several small island dependencies

Currency Mauritian rupee

GNP per capita (PPP) (US$) 10,530 (2002 est)

Population 1,221,000 (2003 est)

Population density (per sq km) 599 (2003 est)

Language English (official), French, Creole (36%), Bhojpuri
(32%), other Indian languages

Religion Hindu over 50%, Christian (mainly Roman Catholic)
about 30%, Muslim 17%

Time difference GMT +4

 ■ CIA ■ LC ■ LP ■ WTG

MEXICO
Map page 102

National name Estados Unidos
Mexicanos/United States of Mexico

Area 1,958,201 sq km/
756,061 sq mi

Capital Mexico City

Major towns/cities Guadalajara,
Monterrey, Puebla, Ciudad Juárez, Tijuana

Major ports 49 ocean ports

Physical features partly arid central highlands; Sierra Madre
mountain ranges east and west; tropical coastal plains;
volcanoes, including Popocatepetl; Rio Grande

Currency Mexican peso

GNP per capita (PPP) (US$) 8,540 (2002 est)

Resources petroleum, natural gas, zinc, salt, silver, copper, coal,
mercury, manganese, phosphates, uranium, strontium sulphide

Population 103,457,000 (2003 est)

Population density (per sq km) 53 (2003 est)

Language Spanish (official), Nahuatl, Maya, Zapoteco, Mixteco,
Otomi

Religion Roman Catholic about 90%

Time difference GMT –6/8

 ■ CIA ■ LC ■ LP ■ RG ■ WTG

■ **Amigo! Mexico Online**
http://www.mexonline.com/
Although a membership-based service, this page also offers lots
of free information for the casual browser – with sections on
activities, arts and culture, pre-Columbian history, and help for
prospective travellers.

■ **Mexico**
http://www.trace-sc.com/index1.htm
Wide variety of fully-searchable information on Mexico. It
includes pages about the ancient Aztec culture, including
examples of some historical documents. On a more
contemporary note, there is a current news section, as well as
information on places for the tourist to visit.

■ **Acapulco Today**
http://accessmexico.com/acapulco/
Cornucopia of images, maps, news, and general information on
this Mexican seaside resort – its culture, nightlife, food, and
events. This site also includes details of local archaeological digs
and an exploration of the Mayan world, with many links to other
Mexican sites.

MICRONESIA, FEDERATED STATES OF
Map page 80

National name Federated
States of Micronesia (FSM)

Area 700 sq km/270 sq mi

Capital Palikir (in Pohnpei island
state)

Major towns/cities Kolonia (in
Pohnpei), Weno (in Truk), Lelu (in
Kosrae)

Physical features an archipelago of 607 equatorial, volcanic
islands in the West Pacific

Currency US dollar

GNP per capita (PPP) (US$) 4,760 (2002 est)

Population 109,000 (2003 est)

Population density (per sq km) 156 (2003 est)

Language English (official), eight officially recognized local
languages (including Trukese, Pohnpeian, Yapese, and Kosrean),
a number of other dialects

Religion Christianity (mainly Roman Catholic in Yap state,
Protestant elsewhere)

Time difference GMT +10 (Chuuk and Yap); +11 (Kosrae and
Pohnpei)

 ■ CIA ■ LP ■ WTG

■ **Welcome to the Federated States of Micronesia**
http://www.fsmgov.org/
Official site of the four Pacific islands comprising the Federated
States of Micronesia. The contents include a good history,
information on culture, language, natural resources, and
government structures. The tourist attractions of the four states
of Micronesia are listed, together with practical information for
visitors.

MOLDOVA
Map page 34

National name Republica Moldova/
Republic of Moldova

Area 33,700 sq km/13,011 sq mi

Capital Chişinău (Russian
Kishinev)

Major towns/cities Tiraspol,
Bălţi, Tighina

Physical features hilly land lying largely between the rivers Prut
and Dniester; northern Moldova comprises the level plain of the
Bălţi Steppe and uplands; the climate is warm and moderately
continental

Currency leu

GNP per capita (PPP) (US$) 1,560 (2002)

Resources lignite, phosphorites, gypsum, building materials;
petroleum and natural gas deposits discovered in the early 1990s
were not yet exploited in 1996

Population 4,267,000 (2003 est)

Population density (per sq km) 127 (2003 est)

Language Moldovan (official), Russian, Gaganz (a Turkish
dialect)

Religion Eastern Orthodox 98.5%; remainder Jewish

Time difference GMT +2

■ www. ■ CIA ■ LC ■ LP ■ WTG

■ **Chisinau, Moldova**
http://www.beebware.com/directory/Regional/Europe/Moldova/
Localities/Chisinau/
Good introduction to the Moldovan capital. There is a description
of the city, its economy, and history. Among the useful links are
those to the Moldovan government site and one describing the
revival of the Jewish community in Chisinau.

MONACO
Map page 26

National name Principauté de Monaco/
Principality of Monaco

Area 1.95 sq km/0.75 sq mi

Physical features steep and
rugged; surrounded landwards
by French territory; being
expanded by filling in the sea

Currency euro

GNP per capita (PPP) (US$) 27,500 (2001)

Population 34,000 (2003 est)

Population density (per sq km) 23,090 (2003 est)

Language French (official), Monégasgne (a mixture of the
French Provençal and Italian Ligurian dialects), Italian

Religion Roman Catholic about 90%

Time difference GMT +1

■ www. ■ CIA ■ LP ■ WTG

■ **Monaco Online**
http://www.monaco.mc
Colourful site on the Principality of Monaco. There are sections
on all major aspects of life in the principality including the history
of Monaco, the Grand Prix, financial advice, a business directory,
the annual television festival, and a panorama of impressive shots
of the cliffs and shores of Monaco.

MONGOLIA
Map page 46

National name Mongol Uls/
State of Mongolia
Area 1,565,000 sq km/
604,246 sq mi
Capital Ulaanbaatar
Major towns/cities Darhan,
Choybalsan, Erdenet
Physical features high plateau with desert and steppe
(grasslands); Altai Mountains in southwest; salt lakes; part of
Gobi desert in southeast; contains both the world's southernmost
permafrost and northernmost desert
Currency tugrik
GNP per capita (PPP) (US$) 1,650 (2002 est)
Resources copper, nickel, zinc, molybdenum, phosphorites,
tungsten, tin, fluorospar, gold, lead; reserves of petroleum
discovered in 1994
Population 2,594,000 (2003 est)
Population density (per sq km) 2 (2003 est)
Language Khalkha Mongolian (official), Kazakh (in the province
of Bagan-Ölgiy), Chinese, Russian, Turkic languages
Religion there is no state religion, but traditional lamaism
(Mahayana Buddhism) is gaining new strength; the Sunni Muslim
Kazakhs of Western Mongolia have also begun the renewal of
their religious life, and Christian missionary activity has increased
Time difference GMT +8

 ▪ CIA ▪ LC ▪ LP ▪ WTG

▪ **Mongolia Page**
http://www.ozemail.com.au/~mongolei/ENGLISH/engindex.html
Account of the geography, history, politics, and culture of
Mongolia. It includes an overview of the country's art, music, and
festivals, and a collection of images. This site also has
information on travel and even some useful contacts in this
country.

MOROCCO
Map page 70

National name Al-Mamlaka
al-Maghribyya/Kingdom of
Morocco
Area 458,730 sq km/
177,115 sq mi (excluding Western
Sahara)
Capital Rabat
Major towns/cities Casablanca, Marrakech, Fès, Oujda, Kénitra,
Tétouan, Meknès
Major ports Casablanca, Tanger, Agadir
Physical features mountain ranges, including the Atlas
Mountains northeast–southwest; fertile coastal plains in west
Currency dirham
GNP per capita (PPP) (US$) 3,690 (2002 est)
Resources phosphate rock and phosphoric acid, coal, iron ore,
barytes, lead, copper, manganese, zinc, petroleum, natural gas,
fish
Population 30,566,000 (2003 est)
Population density (per sq km) 68 (2003 est)
Language Arabic (75%) (official), Berber dialects (25%), French,
Spanish
Religion Sunni Muslim; Christian and Jewish minorities
Time difference GMT +/–0

 ▪ CIA ▪ AN ▪ LP ▪ RG ▪ WTG

▪ **Kingdom of Morocco**
http://www.mincom.gov.ma/
Morocco's official bilingual window on the World Wide Web. It
offers articles on Moroccan identity, lifestyle, and culture,
overviews of the different regions of the country, a fauna and flora
section, a financial and investment guide, and information on the
government.

MOZAMBIQUE
Map page 76

National name República de
Moçambique/Republic of
Mozambique
Area 799,380 sq km/
308,640 sq mi
Capital Maputo (and chief port)
Major towns/cities Beira,
Nampula, Nacala, Chimoio
Major ports Beira, Nacala, Quelimane
Physical features mostly flat tropical lowland; mountains in
west; rivers Zambezi and Limpopo
Currency metical
GNP per capita (PPP) (US$) 1,180 (2002 est)
Resources coal, salt, bauxite, graphite; reserves of iron ore,
gold, precious and semi-precious stones, marble, natural gas (all
largely unexploited in 1996)
Population 18,863,000 (2003 est)
Population density (per sq km) 24 (2003 est)
Language Portuguese (official), 16 African languages
Religion animist 48%, Muslim 20%, Roman Catholic 16%,
Protestant 16%
Time difference GMT +2

 ▪ CIA ▪ LP ▪ NA ▪ WTG

MYANMAR (BURMA)
Map page 52

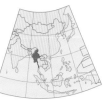

National name Pyedawngsu
Myanma Naingngan/Union of
Myanmar
Area 676,577 sq km/
261,226 sq mi
Capital Yangon (formerly
Rangoon) (and chief port)
Major towns/cities Mandalay, Moulmein, Bago, Bassein,
Taung-gyi, Sittwe,
Physical features over half is rainforest; rivers Irrawaddy and
Chindwin in central lowlands ringed by mountains in north, west,
and east
Currency kyat
GNP per capita (PPP) (US$) 1,570 (2002 est)
Resources natural gas, petroleum, zinc, tin, copper, tungsten,
coal, lead, gems, silver, gold
Population 49,485,000 (2003 est)
Population density (per sq km) 73 (2003 est)
Language Burmese (official), English, tribal dialects
Religion Hinayana Buddhist 89%, Christian 5%, Muslim 4%,
animist 1.5%
Time difference GMT +6.5

 ▪ CIA ▪ LP ▪ WTG

▪ **Shan People of Burma**
http://pw2.netcom.com/~burma/tai/pride.html
Pages devoted to the history, language, culture, and present
situation of the Shan, or Tai, people of Burma. There is also a link
to the Panglong Agreement that led to Burma's independence in
1948.

NAMIBIA
Map page 76

National name Republic of Namibia
Area 824,300 sq km/318,262 sq mi
Capital Windhoek
Major towns/cities Swakopmund,
Rehoboth, Rundu
Major ports Walvis Bay
Physical features mainly desert
(Namib and Kalahari); Orange River; Caprivi Strip links Namibia to
Zambezi River; includes the enclave of Walvis Bay (area 1,120 sq
km/432 sq mi)

Currency Namibian dollar
GNP per capita (PPP) (US$) 6,650 (2002 est)
Resources uranium, copper, lead, zinc, silver, tin, gold, salt,
semi-precious stones, diamonds (one of the world's leading
producers of gem diamonds), hydrocarbons, lithium, manganese,
tungsten, cadmium, vanadium
Population 1,987,000 (2003 est)
Population density (per sq km) 2 (2003 est)
Language English (official), Afrikaans, German, Ovambo (51%),
Nama (12%), Kavango (10%), other indigenous languages
Religion about 90% Christian (Lutheran, Roman Catholic, Dutch
Reformed Church, Anglican)
Time difference GMT +1

 ▪ CIA ▪ LP ▪ NA ▪ WTG

▪ **Namibia Online Travel Guide**
http://www.southafrica-travel.net/namibia/enamib.htm
Colourful and informative guide to Namibia. Not only are there
descriptions of the country's history and government, but the site
also covers Namibia's climate and vegetation as well as its many
popular attractions.

NAURU
Map page 80

National name Republic of
Nauru
Area 21 sq km/8.1 sq mi
Capital Yaren District (seat of
government)
Physical features tropical coral
island in southwest Pacific; plateau
encircled by coral cliffs and sandy beaches
Currency Australian dollar
GNP per capita (PPP) (US$) 5,120 (2002 est)
Resources phosphates
Population 13,000 (2003 est)
Population density (per sq km) 622 (2003 est)
Language Nauruan, English (both official)
Religion majority Protestant, Roman Catholic
Time difference GMT +12

 ▪ CIA ▪ LP ▪ WTG

NEPAL
Map page 56

National name Nepál Adhirajya/
Kingdom of Nepal
Area 147,181 sq km/56,826 sq mi
Capital Kathmandu
Major towns/cities Biratnagar,
Lalitpur, Bhadgaon, Pokhara,
Birganj, Dahran Bazar
Physical features descends from the Himalayas in the north
through foothills to the River Ganges plain in the south; Mount
Everest, Mount Kanchenjunga
Currency Nepalese rupee
GNP per capita (PPP) (US$) 1,350 (2002 est)
Resources lignite, talcum, magnesite, limestone, copper, cobalt
Population 25,164,000 (2003 est)
Population density (per sq km) 179 (2003 est)
Language Nepali (official), Tibetan, numerous local languages
Religion Hindu 90%; Buddhist 5%, Muslim 3%, Christian
Time difference GMT +5.5

 ▪ CIA ▪ LC ▪ LP ▪ RG ▪ WTG

NETHERLANDS
Map page 22

National name Koninkrijk der Nederlanden/Kingdom of the
Netherlands

Area 41,863 sq km/16,163 sq mi

Capital Amsterdam (official), The Hague (legislative and judicial)

Major towns/cities Rotterdam, Utrecht, Eindhoven, Groningen, Tilburg, Maastricht, Apeldoorn, Nijmegen, Breda

Major ports Rotterdam

Physical features flat coastal lowland; rivers Rhine, Schelde, Maas; Frisian Islands

Territories Aruba, Netherlands Antilles (Caribbean)

Currency euro (guilder until 2002)

GNP per capita (PPP) (US$) 27,470 (2002 est)

Resources petroleum, natural gas

Population 16,149,000 (2003 est)

Population density (per sq km) 395 (2003 est)

Language Dutch (official)

Religion atheist 39%, Roman Catholic 31%, Dutch Reformed Church 14%, Calvinist 8%

Time difference GMT +1

 ■ CIA ■ LP ■ RG ■ WTG

■ **Amsterdam Channel Home Page**
http://www.channels.nl/adam.html

Provides an innovative 'tour' through Amsterdam through a wealth of images of the city – select the direction you wish to follow next and a view of that area is called up. There are links to details of some sites and a street map is also available.

■ **General Information on the Netherlands**
http://www.netherlands-embassy.org/

Well-organized official introduction to Holland from the Dutch embassy in Washington DC. The easily accessed sections include information on the country's history, economy, industry, defence, political structure, social policy, tourism, health, education, environment, and the media. There are a large number of useful links making this site a starting point for finding further information on Holland.

NEW ZEALAND

Map page 84

National name Aotearoa/New Zealand

Area 268,680 sq km/103,737 sq mi

Capital Wellington

Major towns/cities Auckland, Hamilton, Christchurch, Manukau

Major ports Auckland, Wellington

Physical features comprises North Island, South Island, Stewart Island, Chatham Islands, and minor islands; mainly mountainous; Ruapehu in North Island, 2,797 m/9,180 ft, highest of three active volcanoes; geysers and hot springs of Rotorua district; Lake Taupo (616 sq km/238 sq mi), source of Waikato River; Kaingaroa state forest. In South Island are the Southern Alps and Canterbury Plains

Territories Tokelau (three atolls transferred in 1926 from former Gilbert and Ellice Islands colony); Niue Island (one of the Cook Islands, separately administered from 1903: chief town Alafi); Cook Islands are internally self-governing but share common citizenship with New Zealand; Ross Dependency in Antarctica

Currency New Zealand dollar

GNP per capita (PPP) (US$) 20,070 (2002 est)

Resources coal, clay, limestone, dolomite, natural gas, hydroelectric power, pumice, iron ore, gold, forests

Population 3,875,000 (2003 est)

Population density (per sq km) 14 (2003 est)

Language English (official), Maori

Religion Christian (Anglican 18%, Roman Catholic 14%, Presbyterian 13%)

Time difference GMT +12

 ■ CIA ■ LP ■ WTG

■ **New Zealand on the Web**
http://nz.com/

Aimed at the prospective visitor, this site includes a virtual tour of New Zealand, a guidebook, and background information on its history and culture. There is also some information about trade and commerce.

■ **Welcome to Paradise – the Cook Islands**
http://www.ck/index.html

Very thorough guide to the Cook Islands in English and French. The many pages are packed with information on the geography, culture, economy, and government of the fifteen far-flung islands. The differing needs of tourists and investors are both met by this well-organized site.

■ **Bay of Plenty**
http://www.bayofplenty.co.nz/

Guide to the towns, beaches, and other natural attractions of this New Zealand region. There is practical information for visitors and a suggested itinerary. There are also a number of links to other sites about towns and places around the inlet.

■ **NZHistory.net.nz**
http://www.nzhistory.net.nz/index.html

Site for anyone interested in the recent history of New Zealand, with illustrated extracts from history books and biographies spanning the 19th and 20th centuries, and exhibitions on military, social, and government history. There are also links to other relevant sites and a discussion group.

NICARAGUA
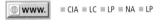
Map page 102

National name República de Nicaragua/Republic of Nicaragua

Area 127,849 sq km/49,362 sq mi

Capital Managua

Major towns/cities León, Chinandega, Masaya, Granada, Estelí

Major ports Corinto, Puerto Cabezas, El Bluff

Physical features narrow Pacific coastal plain separated from broad Atlantic coastal plain by volcanic mountains and lakes Managua and Nicaragua; one of the world's most active earthquake regions

Currency cordoba

GNP per capita (PPP) (US$) 1,970 (2002 est)

Resources gold, silver, copper, lead, antimony, zinc, iron, limestone, gypsum, marble, bentonite

Population 5,466,000 (2003 est)

Population density (per sq km) 42 (2003 est)

Language Spanish (official), English, American Indian languages

Religion Roman Catholic 95%

Time difference GMT −6

 ■ CIA ■ LC ■ LP ■ WTG

■ **Experience Nicaragua**
http://library.thinkquest.org/17749/

Well-designed and in-depth resource for the study of Nicaragua. The site is divided into three main sections – 'History', 'Economy', and 'Culture' – with numerous articles and graphics in each. Travel advice is also included, as well as a number of video and audio clips that offer a sample of Nicaraguan society and culture.

NIGER

Map page 70

National name République du Niger/Republic of Niger

Area 1,186,408 sq km/458,072 sq mi

Capital Niamey

Major towns/cities Zinder, Maradi, Tahoua, Agadez, Birnin Konni, Arlit

Physical features desert plains between hills in north and savannah in south; River Niger in southwest, Lake Chad in southeast

Currency franc CFA

GNP per capita (PPP) (US$) 770 (2002 est)

Resources uranium (one of world's leading producers), phosphates, gypsum, coal, cassiterite, tin, salt, gold; deposits of other minerals (including petroleum, iron ore, copper, lead, diamonds, and tungsten) have been confirmed

Population 11,972,000 (2003 est)

Population density (per sq km) 9 (2003 est)

Language French (official), Hausa (70%), Djerma, other ethnic languages

Religion Sunni Muslim 95%; also Christian, and traditional animist beliefs

Time difference GMT +1

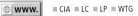 ■ CIA ■ LP ■ NA ■ WTG

NIGERIA

Map page 72

National name Federal Republic of Nigeria

Area 923,773 sq km/356,668 sq mi

Capital Abuja

Major towns/cities Ibadan, Lagos, Ogbomosho, Kano, Oshogbo, Ilorin, Abeokuta, Zaria, Port Harcourt

Major ports Lagos, Port Harcourt, Warri, Calabar

Physical features arid savannah in north; tropical rainforest in south, with mangrove swamps along coast; River Niger forms wide delta; mountains in southeast

Currency naira

GNP per capita (PPP) (US$) 780 (2002 est)

Resources petroleum, natural gas, coal, tin, iron ore, uranium, limestone, marble, forest

Population 124,009,000 (2003 est)

Population density (per sq km) 134 (2003 est)

Language English, French (both official), Hausa, Ibo, Yoruba

Religion Sunni Muslim 50% (in north), Christian 35% (in south), local religions 15%

Time difference GMT +1

 ■ CIA ■ LC ■ LP ■ NA ■ LP

NORTH KOREA

Map page 50

National name Chosun Minchu-chui Inmin Konghwa-guk/Democratic People's Republic of Korea

Area 120,538 sq km/46,539 sq mi

Capital P'yŏngyang

Major towns/cities Hamhŭng, Ch'ŏngjin, Namp'o, Wŏnsan, Sinŭiji

Physical features wide coastal plain in west rising to mountains cut by deep valleys in interior

Currency won

GNP per capita (PPP) (US$) 820 (2001)

Resources coal, iron, lead, copper, zinc, tin, silver, gold, magnesite (has 40–50% of world's deposits of magnesite)

Population 22,664,000 (2003 est)

Population density (per sq km) 188 (2003 est)

Language Korean (official)

Religion Buddhist (predominant religion), Chondoist, Christian, traditional beliefs

Time difference GMT +9

 ■ CIA ■ LC ■ LP ■ WTG

■ **Korea Central News Agency**
http://www.kcna.co.jp/

Site of the Korea Central News Agency. This online propaganda from the North Korean regime provides a fascinating insight into the outlook of one of the world's most isolated regimes.

NORWAY

Map page 16

National name Kongeriket Norge/
Kingdom of Norway

Area 387,000 sq km/149,420 sq
mi (including Svalbard and Jan
Mayen)

Capital Oslo

Major towns/cities Bergen, Trondheim,
Stavanger, Kristiansand, Drammen

Physical features mountainous with fertile valleys and deeply
indented coast; forests cover 25%; extends north of Arctic Circle

Territories dependencies in the Arctic (Svalbard and Jan Mayen)
and in Antarctica (Bouvet and Peter I Island, and Queen Maud
Land)

Currency Norwegian krone

GNP per capita (PPP) (US$) 35,840 (2002 est)

Resources petroleum, natural gas, iron ore, iron pyrites, copper,
lead, zinc, forests

Population 4,533,000 (2003 est)

Population density (per sq km) 14 (2003 est)

Language Norwegian (official), Saami (Lapp), Finnish

Religion Evangelical Lutheran (endowed by state) 88%; other
Protestant and Roman Catholic 4%

Time difference GMT +1

 ▪ CIA ▪ LP ▪ RG ▪ WTG

▪ **Welcome to Bergen – The Gateway to the Fjords of
Norway**
http://www.uib.no/Bergen/reiseliv/tourist/index.html
Well-arranged guide to the Norwegian city. This site includes a
history, a guide to local attractions, and information about cultural
life. There are also details of how to visit nearby fjords.

▪ **Stavanger**
http://www.stavanger-web.com/
Good introduction to the Norwegian seaport. There are over 1,800
links to sites about Stavanger, including information on history,
accommodation, transport, cultural events, and entertainment.

▪ **Official Documentation and Information from Norway**
http://odin.dep.no/odin/engelsk/index-b-n-a.html
Well-presented official introduction to all aspects of Norwegian
life. There are sections on geography, economy, foreign policy,
the political system, the royal family, culture, education, health,
sport, and Norway's position within the European Union.
Assistance is provided for those wishing to trace their Norwegian
ancestry. The site is frequently updated with official Foreign
Ministry information and news articles on Norwegian life.

▪ **Tromsø, Norway**
http://www.destinasjontromso.no/english/index.html
Information on the northern Norwegian 'gateway to the Arctic'. An
introduction to the city includes a weather report. A large number
of photos are included of Tromso in all seasons including the
midnight sun and northern lights.

OMAN

Map page 58

National name Saltanat `Uman/
Sultanate of Oman

Area 272,000 sq km/
105,019 sq mi

Capital Muscat

Major towns/cities Sallālah,
Ibrī, Suḩār, Al Buraymī, Nazwā, Sūr, Maṭraḩ

Physical features mountains to the north and south of a high
arid plateau; fertile coastal strip; Jebel Akhdar highlands; Kuria
Muria Islands

Currency Omani rial

GNP per capita (PPP) (US$) 12,910 (2002 est)

Resources petroleum, natural gas, copper, chromite, gold, salt,
marble, gypsum, limestone

Population 2,851,000 (2003 est)

Population density (per sq km) 13 (2003 est)

Language Arabic (official), English, Urdu, other Indian languages

Religion Muslim 75% (predominantly Ibadhi Muslim), about
25% Hindu

Time difference GMT +4

 ▪ CIA ▪ LC ▪ AN ▪ LP ▪ WTG

PAKISTAN

Map page 58

National name Islami Jamhuriyya e
Pakistan/Islamic Republic of
Pakistan

Area 803,940 sq km/
310,321 sq mi

Capital Islamabad

Major towns/cities Lahore, Rawalpindi, Faisalabad, Karachi,
Hyderabad, Multan, Peshawar, Gujranwala, Quetta

Major ports Karachi

Physical features fertile Indus plain in east, Baluchistan plateau
in west, mountains in north and northwest; the 'five rivers'
(Indus, Jhelum, Chenab, Ravi, and Sutlej) feed the world's largest
irrigation system; K2 mountain; Khyber Pass

Currency Pakistan rupee

GNP per capita (PPP) (US$) 1,940 (2002 est)

Resources iron ore, natural gas, limestone, rock salt, gypsum,
silica, coal, petroleum, graphite, copper, manganese, chromite

Population 153,578,000 (2003 est)

Population density (per sq km) 193 (2003 est)

Language Urdu (official), English, Punjabi, Sindhi, Pashto,
Baluchi, other local dialects

Religion Sunni Muslim 90%, Shiite Muslim 5%; also Hindu,
Christian, Parsee, Buddhist

Time difference GMT +5

 ▪ CIA ▪ LC ▪ LP ▪ WTG

PALAU

Map page 80

National name Belu'u era
Belau/Republic of Palau

Area 508 sq km/196 sq mi

Capital Koror (on Koror island)

Physical features more than
350 (mostly uninhabited) islands,
islets, and atolls in the west Pacific;
warm, humid climate, susceptible to typhoons

Currency US dollar

GNP per capita (PPP) (US$) 7,460 (2002 est)

Population 20,003 (2000 est)

Population density (per sq km) 45 (2003 est)

Language Palauan, English (both official in most states)

Religion Christian, principally Roman Catholic; Modekngei
(indigenous religion)

Time difference GMT +9

 ▪ CIA ▪ LP ▪ WTG

▪ **Welcome to Palau**
http://visit-palau.com/
Guide to the Pacific state. Information on local history and Palaun
culture is supported by good photographs. There is practical
information for tourists and for those interested in fishing and
diving.

PANAMA

Map page 102

National name República de
Panamá/Republic of Panama

Area 77,100 sq km/29,768 sq mi

Capital Panamá

Major towns/cities San
Miguelito, Colón, David, La Chorrera, Santiago, Chitré,
Changuinola

Major ports Colón, Cristóbal, Balboa

Physical features coastal plains and mountainous interior;
tropical rainforest in east and northwest; Archipelago de las
Perlas in Gulf of Panama; Panama Canal

Currency balboa

GNP per capita (PPP) (US$) 5,870 (2002 est)

Resources limestone, clay, salt; deposits of coal, copper, and
molybdenum have been discovered

Population 3,120,000 (2003 est)

Population density (per sq km) 41 (2003 est)

Language Spanish (official), English

Religion Roman Catholic 93%

Time difference GMT –5

 ▪ CIA ▪ LC ▪ LP ▪ WTG

▪ **Welcome to the Panama Canal**
http://www.pancanal.com/
Good source of information on the organization, operation, and
history of the Panama Canal from its operating authority.
Photographs and diagrams help explain the workings of the canal
and its system of locks.

PAPUA NEW GUINEA

Map page 80

National name Gau Hedinarai
ai Papua-Matamata Guinea/
Independent State of Papua New
Guinea

Area 462,840 sq km/178,702 sq
mi

Capital Port Moresby (on East New
Guinea)

Major towns/cities Lae, Madang, Arawa, Wewak, Goroka,
Rabaul

Major ports Port Moresby, Rabaul

Physical features mountainous; swamps and plains; monsoon
climate; tropical islands of New Ireland, New Britain, and
Bougainville; Admiralty Islands, D'Entrecasteaux Islands, and
Louisiade Archipelago; active volcanoes Vulcan and Tavurvur

Currency kina

GNP per capita (PPP) (US$) 2,080 (2002 est)

Resources copper, gold, silver; deposits of chromite, cobalt,
nickel, quartz; substantial reserves of petroleum and natural gas
(petroleum production began in 1992)

Population 5,711,000 (2003 est)

Population density (per sq km) 12 (2003 est)

Language English (official), pidgin English, over 700 local
languages

Religion Christian 97%, of which 3% Roman Catholic; local
pantheistic beliefs

Time difference GMT +10

▪ CIA ▪ LP ▪ WTG

▪ **Papua New Guinea Information Site**
http://www.niugini.com/
Guide to Papua New Guinea. The ethnic and linguistic diversity of
the country and its complex history are well presented. A
'clickable' map accesses information on each of the country's
twenty provinces.

PARAGUAY

Map page 110

National name República del
Paraguay/Republic of Paraguay

Area 406,752 sq km/
157,046 sq mi

Capital Asunción (and chief port)

Major towns/cities Ciudad del
Este, Pedro Juan Caballero, San
Lorenzo, Fernando de la Mora,
Lambare, Luque, Capiatá

Major ports Concepción

Physical features low marshy plain and marshlands; divided by Paraguay River; Paraná River forms southeast boundary

Currency guaraní

GNP per capita (PPP) (US$) 4,450 (2002 est)

Resources gypsum, kaolin, limestone, salt; deposits (not commercially exploited) of bauxite, iron ore, copper, manganese, uranium; deposits of natural gas discovered in 1994; exploration for petroleum deposits ongoing mid-1990s

Population 5,878,000 (2003 est)

Population density (per sq km) 14 (2003 est)

Language Spanish (official), Guaraní (an indigenous Indian language)

Religion Roman Catholic (official religion) 85%; Mennonite, Anglican

Time difference GMT –3/4

 ■ CIA ■ LC ■ LP ■ WTG

■ **Asuncion, Paraguay**

http://travel.lycos.com/destinations/location.asp?pid=334832

Profile of Asunción, capital of Paraguay. There is a general introduction to its main features, and four sections – 'Visitors' guide', 'Culture and history', 'News and weather', and 'Entertainment' – with links to photographs, and to further useful information in English and Spanish about the city and the country.

PERU

Map page 108

National name República del Perú/Republic of Peru

Area 1,285,200 sq km/ 496,216 sq mi

Capital Lima

Major towns/cities Arequipa, Iquitos, Chiclayo, Trujillo, Huancayo, Piura, Chimbote

Major ports Callao, Chimbote, Salaverry

Physical features Andes mountains running northwest–southeast cover 27% of Peru, separating Amazon river-basin jungle in northeast from coastal plain in west; desert along coast north–south (Atacama Desert); Lake Titicaca

Currency nuevo sol

GNP per capita (PPP) (US$) 4,800 (2002 est)

Resources lead, copper, iron, silver, zinc (world's fourth-largest producer), petroleum

Population 27,167,000 (2003 est)

Population density (per sq km) 21 (2003 est)

Language Spanish, Quechua (both official), Aymara, many indigenous dialects

Religion Roman Catholic (state religion) 95%

Time difference GMT –5

[⊕ **www.**] ■ CIA ■ LC ■ LP ■ WTG

■ **Peru Home Page**

http://www.rcp.net.pe/peru/peru_ingles.html

Basic information about Peru, including links to audio clips of Peruvian music and a section on ecotourism.

■ **Arequipa, Peru**

http://travel.lycos.com/destinations/location.asp?pid=334848

Profile of the 'white city' of Arequipa in southern Peru. There is a general introduction to the city's main features, and four sections – 'Visitors' guide', 'Culture and history', 'News and weather', and 'Entertainment' – each with links to further useful information in English and Spanish about both the city and the country.

■ **Cuzco, Peru**

http://travel.lycos.com/destinations/location.asp?pid=334849

Page devoted to the ancient Peruvian city of Cuzco. There is a general introduction to the city's main features, and four sections – 'Visitors' guide', 'Culture and history', 'News and weather', and 'Entertainment' – each with links to further useful information in English and Spanish about both the city and the country.

■ **Lima, Peru**

http://travel.lycos.com/destinations/location.asp?pid=334850

Profile of the historic city of Lima, capital of Peru. There is a general introduction to the city's main features, and four sections – 'Visitors' guide', 'Culture and history', 'News and weather', and

'Entertainment' – each with links to further useful information in English and Spanish about both the city and the country.

PHILIPPINES

Map page 52

National name Republika Ñg Pilipinas/Republic of the Philippines

Area 300,000 sq km/115,830 sq mi

Capital Manila (on Luzon island) (and chief port)

Major towns/cities Quezon City, Davao, Caloocan, Cebu, Bacolod, Cagayan de Oro, Iloilo

Major ports Cebu, Davao (on Mindanao), Iloilo, Zamboanga (on Mindanao)

Physical features comprises over 7,000 islands; volcanic mountain ranges traverse main chain north–south; 50% still forested. The largest islands are Luzon 108,172 sq km/ 41,754 sq mi and Mindanao 94,227 sq km/36,372 sq mi; others include Samar, Negros, Palawan, Panay, Mindoro, Leyte, Cebu, and the Sulu group; Pinatubo volcano (1,759 m/5,770 ft); Mindanao has active volcano Apo (2,954 m/9,690 ft) and mountainous rainforest

Currency peso

GNP per capita (PPP) (US$) 4,280 (2002 est)

Resources copper ore, gold, silver, chromium, nickel, coal, crude petroleum, natural gas, forests

Population 79,999,000 (2003 est)

Population density (per sq km) 267 (2003 est)

Language Filipino, English (both official), Spanish, Cebuano, Ilocano, more than 70 other indigenous languages

Religion Christian 94%, mainly Roman Catholic (84%), Protestant; Muslim 4%, local religions

Time difference GMT +8

[⊕ **www.**] ■ CIA ■ LC ■ LP ■ WTG

■ **Philippine History**

http://www.tribo.org/history/index.html

Well organized source of information about Philippine history, with sections on such topics as the islands' ancient past, the colonial period, the Spanish and US occupations, and the Philippine republic.

POLAND

Map page 20

National name Rzeczpospolita Polska/ Republic of Poland

Area 312,683 sq km/120,726 sq mi

Capital Warsaw

Major towns/cities Łódź, Kraków, Wroclaw, Poznan, Gdansk, Szczecin, Katowice, Bydgoszcz, Lublin

Major ports Gdansk (Danzig), Szczecin (Stettin), Gdynia (Gdingen)

Physical features part of the great plain of Europe; Vistula, Oder, and Neisse rivers; Sudeten, Tatra, and Carpathian mountains on southern frontier

Currency zloty

GNP per capita (PPP) (US$) 10,130 (2002 est)

Resources coal (world's fifth-largest producer), copper, sulphur, silver, petroleum and natural gas reserves

Population 38,587,000 (2003 est)

Population density (per sq km) 119 (2003 est)

Language Polish (official)

Religion Roman Catholic 95%

Time difference GMT +1

[⊕ **www.**] ■ CIA ■ LC ■ LP ■ RG ■ WTG

■ **Cracow**

http://www.krakow.pl/en/

Official guide to the Polish World Heritage city. There are sections

on the government structure, local economy, cultural life, and local attractions. There is practical information for visitors.

■ **Polish National Tourist Office**

http://www.polandtour.org/

Well-designed guide to Poland that is available in English, French, and German. Choose from five different sections – 'About Poland', 'Travel information', 'Regions and cities', 'Recreation and sports', and 'Culture and arts' – each of which offers a number of in-depth articles about the country.

PORTUGAL

Map page 20

National name República Portuguesa/Republic of Portugal

Area 92,000 sq km/35,521 sq mi (including the Azores and Madeira)

Capital Lisbon

Major towns/cities Porto, Coimbra, Amadora, Setúbal, Funchal, Braga, Vila Nova de Gaia

Major ports Porto, Setúbal

Physical features mountainous in the north (Serra da Estrêla mountains); plains in the south; rivers Minho, Douro, Tagus (Tejo), Guadiana

Currency euro (escudo until 2002)

GNP per capita (PPP) (US$) 17,350 (2002 est)

Resources limestone, granite, marble, iron, tungsten, copper, pyrites, gold, uranium, coal, forests

Population 10,062,000 (2003 est)

Population density (per sq km) 109 (2003 est)

Language Portuguese (official)

Religion Roman Catholic 97%

Time difference GMT +/–0

[⊕ **www.**] ■ CIA ■ LC ■ LP ■ RG ■ WTG

■ **Lisbon**

http://lisboa.kpnqwest.pt/i/lisboa.html

Bilingual site with information about the 'city of the seven hills' including its history, a town map, and information on museums, restaurants, bars, and hotels. It also includes plenty of pictures and some audio clips from Portuguese artists.

■ **Porto, Portugal**

http://travel.lycos.com/destinations/location.asp?pid=334625

Good source of practical, historical, and cultural information on Portugal's second city. The attractions of the city are well-presented. There is also information on the celebrated 'vinho do Porto' – port – which takes it name from the city.

■ **Welcome to the Algarve**

http://www.nexus-pt.com/algarve.htm

Comprehensive source of information on the region of southern Portugal. A 'clickable' map gives access to information on the history, culture, and facilities of all the communities of the Algarve. There is a weather report and links to local newspapers, as well as more practical information for tourists and residents.

■ **Madeira Web**

http://www.madeira-web.com/PagesUK/index.html

Guide to the Portuguese island group. There are sections on history, culture, food, and government services, in addition to practical information for visitors to Madeira and Porto Santo. There is also a bibliography giving links to further sources of information.

■ **Portugal's National Tourism Service**

http://www.portugal-live.net/

Travel guide dedicated to those planning a holiday or business trip to Portugal. The site features a directory of hotels and resorts, together with information on the country's attractions and a number of maps to help you locate them! The site is kept up to date, especially the useful sections on current events and weather.

QATAR

Map page 63

National name Dawlat Qatar/ State of Qatar

Area 11,400 sq km/4,401 sq mi

Capital Doha (and chief port)

Major towns/cities Dukhān, ad Dawhah, ar-Rayyan, Umm Salal, Musay'īd, aš-Šahniyah

Physical features mostly flat desert with salt flats in south

Currency Qatari riyal

GNP per capita (PPP) (US$) N/A

Resources petroleum, natural gas, water resources

Population 610,000 (2003 est)

Population density (per sq km) 55 (2003 est)

Language Arabic (official), English

Religion Sunni Muslim 95%

Time difference GMT +3

 ▪ CIA ▪ LC ▪ AN ▪ LP ▪ WTG

ROMANIA
Map page 34

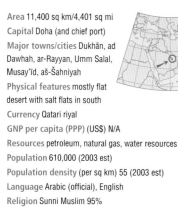

National name România/Romania

Area 237,500 sq km/91,698 sq mi

Capital Bucharest

Major towns/cities Brasov, Timisoara, Cluj-Napoca, Iaşi, Constanta, Galati, Craiova

Major ports Galati, Constanta, Brăila

Physical features mountains surrounding a plateau, with river plains in south and east. Carpathian Mountains, Transylvanian Alps; River Danube; Black Sea coast; mineral springs

Currency leu

GNP per capita (PPP) (US$) 6,290 (2002 est)

Resources brown coal, hard coal, iron ore, salt, bauxite, copper, lead, zinc, methane gas, petroleum (reserves expected to be exhausted by mid- to late 1990s)

Population 22,334,000 (2003 est)

Population density (per sq km) 94 (2003 est)

Language Romanian (official), Hungarian, German

Religion Romanian Orthodox 87%; Roman Catholic and Uniate 5%, Reformed/Lutheran 3%, Unitarian 1%

Time difference GMT +2

 ▪ CIA ▪ LC ▪ LP ▪ RG ▪ WTG

▪ Romania & Constitutional Monarchy
http://www.geocities.com/CapitolHill/Lobby/8957/

Historical information, facts, and stories about Romania. The history of the Romanian Monarchy and, in particular, His Majesty, King Michael I, are described here. The Web site features interviews with the king and many photographs of members of the Romanian royal family.

▪ Cluj-Napoca
http://travel.lycos.com/destinations/location.asp?pid=334499

Good guide to the Transylvanian capital. There is a description and history of the city in addition to information on museums, accommodation, and entertainment. There are a large number of useful links to other sources of information.

RUSSIA
Map page 42

National name Rossiiskaya Federatsiya/Russian Federation

Area 17,075,400 sq km/ 6,592,811 sq mi

Capital Moscow

Major towns/cities St. Petersburg, Nizhniy Novgorod, Samara, Yekaterinburg, Novosibirsk, Chelyabinsk, Kazan, Omsk, Perm', Ufa

Physical features fertile Black Earth district; extensive forests; the Ural Mountains with large mineral resources; Lake Baikal, world's deepest lake

Currency rouble

GNP per capita (PPP) (US$) 7,820 (2002 est)

Resources petroleum, natural gas, coal, peat, copper (world's

fourth-largest producer), iron ore, lead, aluminium, phosphate rock, nickel, manganese, gold, diamonds, platinum, zinc, tin

Population 143,246,000 (2003 est)

Population density (per sq km) 8 (2003 est)

Language Russian (official) and many East Slavic, Altaic, Uralic, Caucasian languages

Religion traditionally Russian Orthodox; significant Muslim and Buddhist communities

Time difference GMT +2–12

 ▪ CIA ▪ LC ▪ LP ▪ RG ▪ WTG

▪ Saint Petersburg, Russia
http://www.geocities.com/TheTropics/Shores/6751/

Introduction to the city of St Petersburg, including a walking tour and a map, a guide to the city's museums, a history, and a regularly updated 'What's new' section.

▪ Russia Alive!
http://www.alincom.com/russ/index.htm

Guide to the new Russia, with links to related sites and a virtual tour of Moscow.

▪ SovInform Bureau
http://www.siber.com/sib/index.html

Dedicated to all things Russian, including information about Russian art, culture, humour, politics, communication and technology, travel, and visas. Advice and tools are also offered which enable you to 'Russify' your PC.

▪ Russia Today
http://www.russiatoday.com/

Extensive general information magazine on Russia. As well as daily press reviews and business news, the site provides sections on the government, the constitution, and coverage of hot current issues. Russia Today has a reputation for being on top of the news and getting its readers involved: it even offered them a chance to select the next Russian president in a mock election. A must for everyone wanting to make sense of the bewildering developments in the region.

▪ Exploring Moscow
http://www.interknowledge.com/russia/moscow01.htm

Walk about Moscow with stops at the Kremlin, Red Square, Lenin's Mausoleum, St Basil's cathedral, old Moscow, and other highlights of the Russian capital. The site also offers separate sections on fine art and theatrical life in the city, a calendar of events, and advice on accommodation.

▪ Kalingrad in Your Pocket Home Page
http://www.inyourpocket.com/Kaliningrad/index.shtml

Guide to everything you ever wanted to know about this Russian enclave. This is an electronic form of a published guide book and includes sections on such topics as language, media, what to see, getting there, and where to stay.

▪ Novgorod the Great
http://www.adm.nov.ru/web.nsf/pages/englishhome

Good guide to the culture and history of the Russian World Heritage city. There are descriptions and photos of the many historical buildings in Novgorod. This site includes sections on Novgorodian artistic and musical traditions.

RWANDA
Map page 74

National name Republika y'u Rwanda/Republic of Rwanda

Area 26,338 sq km/10,169 sq mi

Capital Kigali

Major towns/cities Butare, Ruhengeri, Gisenyi, Kibungo, Cyangugu

Physical features high savannah and hills, with volcanic mountains in northwest; part of lake Kivu; highest peak Mount Karisimbi 4,507 m/14,792 ft; Kagera River (whose headwaters are the source of the Nile)

Currency Rwandan franc

GNP per capita (PPP) (US$) 1,210 (2002 est)

Resources cassiterite (a tin-bearing ore), wolframite (a tungsten-bearing ore), natural gas, gold, columbo-tantalite, beryl

Population 8,387,000 (2003 est)

Population density (per sq km) 318 (2003 est)

Language Kinyarwanda, French (both official), Kiswahili

Religion about 50% animist; about 40% Christian, mainly Roman Catholic; 9% Muslim

Time difference GMT +2

 ▪ CIA ▪ LP ▪ NA ▪ WTG

ST. KITTS AND NEVIS
Map page 102

National name Federation of St. Christopher and St. Nevis

Area 262 sq km/101 sq mi (St. Kitts 168 sq km/65 sq mi, Nevis 93 sq km/36 sq mi)

Capital Basseterre (on St. Kitts) (and chief port)

Major towns/cities Charlestown (Nevis), Newcastle, Sandy Point Town, Dieppe Bay Town

Physical features both islands are volcanic; fertile plains on coast; black beaches

Currency East Caribbean dollar

GNP per capita (PPP) (US$) 9,780 (2002 est)

Population 42,000 (2003 est)

Population density (per sq km) 160 (2003 est)

Language English (official)

Religion Anglican 36%, Methodist 32%, other Protestant 8%, Roman Catholic 10%

Time difference GMT –4

 ▪ CIA ▪ LP ▪ WTG

▪ St Kitts and Nevis Government
http://www.stkittsnevis.net/index.html

The 'How we are governed' section provides a detailed explanation of the structure of this twin-island nation. There is also regularly updated information about the hurricanes that may affect the islands, as well as a biography of the 'Hero of the nation', Robert L Bradshaw, who was instrumental in securing their independence.

ST. LUCIA
Map page 102

Area 617 sq km/238 sq mi

Capital Castries

Major towns/cities Soufrière, Vieux Fort, Choiseul, Gros Islet

Major ports Vieux-Fort

Physical features mountainous island with fertile valleys; mainly tropical forest; volcanic peaks; Gros and Petit Pitons

Currency East Caribbean dollar

GNP per capita (PPP) (US$) 5,000 (2002 est)

Resources geothermal energy

Population 149,000 (2003 est)

Population density (per sq km) 240 (2003 est)

Language English (official), French patois

Religion Roman Catholic 85%; Anglican, Protestant

Time difference GMT –4

 ▪ CIA ▪ LP ▪ RG ▪ WTG

▪ St Lucia Travel Guide
http://www.stluciaguide.com/

Guide offering information on and reservations for accommodation and car rental in the Caribbean island of St Lucia. The site also includes advice on the country's many attractions, which include the national rainforest, sulphur springs, and scuba-diving.

ST. VINCENT AND THE GRENADINES
Map page 102

Area 388 sq km/150 sq mi (including islets of the Northern Grenadines 43 sq km/17 sq mi)

Capital Kingstown

Major towns/cities Georgetown, Châteaubelair, Dovers

Physical features volcanic mountains, thickly forested; La Soufrière volcano

Currency East Caribbean dollar

GNP per capita (PPP) (US$) 5,100 (2002 est)

Population 120,000 (2003 est)

Population density (per sq km) 309 (2003 est)

Language English (official), French patois

Religion Anglican, Methodist, Roman Catholic

Time difference GMT −4

 ▪ CIA ▪ LP ▪ WTG

▪ **St Vincent and the Grenadines – Jewels of the Caribbean**
http://www.svgtourism.com/

From the Department of Tourism, this guide offers detailed information on St Vincent and the Grenadines. It includes advice on travel information and accommodation, as well as sections on the islands' attractions, sports, and current events. Be sure to visit the site's photo album, which highlights the beauty of the islands.

SAMOA
Map page 80

National name 'O la Malo Tu To'atasi o Samoa/Independent State of Samoa

Area 2,830 sq km/1,092 sq mi

Capital Apia (on Upolu island) (and chief port)

Major towns/cities Lalomanu, Tuasivi, Falealupo, Falelatai, Taga

Physical features comprises South Pacific islands of Savai'i and Upolu, with two smaller tropical islands and uninhabited islets; mountain ranges on main islands; coral reefs; over half forested

Currency tala, or Samoan dollar

GNP per capita (PPP) (US$) 5,350 (2002 est)

Population 178,000 (2003 est)

Population density (per sq km) 63 (2003 est)

Language English, Samoan (both official)

Religion Congregationalist; also Roman Catholic, Methodist

Time difference GMT −11

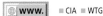 ▪ CIA ▪ LP ▪ WTG

SAN MARINO
Map page 32

National name Serenissima Repubblica di San Marino/Most Serene Republic of San Marino

Area 61 sq km/24 sq mi

Capital San Marino

Major towns/cities Serravalle, Faetano, Fiorentino, Borgo Maggiore, Domagnano

Physical features the slope of Mount Titano

Currency euro

GNP per capita (PPP) (US$) 26,960 (2001)

Resources limestone and other building stone

Population 28,000 (2003 est)

Population density (per sq km) 452 (2003 est)

Language Italian (official)

Religion Roman Catholic 95%

Time difference GMT +1

▪ CIA ▪ WTG

▪ **Welcome to the Republic of San Marino**
http://inthenet.sm/rsm/intro.htm

Good official guide to the world's smallest and oldest nation state. The history of San Marino is interestingly presented. There is a wealth of practical information on attractions, accommodation, and restaurants, as well as coverage of all aspects of political, economic, and cultural life. The pride of the 25,000 Sammarinese shines through this well-organized site.

SÃO TOMÉ AND PRÍNCIPE
Map page 72

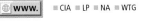

National name República Democrática de São Tomé e Príncipe/ Democratic Republic of São Tomé and Príncipe

Area 1,000 sq km/386 sq mi

Capital São Tomé

Major towns/cities Santo António, Sant Ana, Porto Alegre, Neves, Santo Amaro

Physical features comprises two main islands and several smaller ones, all volcanic; thickly forested and fertile

Currency dobra

GNP per capita (PPP) (US$) 1,310 (2002 est)

Population 161,000 (2003 est)

Population density (per sq km) 167 (2003 est)

Language Portuguese (official), Fang (a Bantu language), Lungwa São Tomé (a Portuguese Creole)

Religion Roman Catholic 80%, animist

Time difference GMT +/−0

 ▪ CIA ▪ LP ▪ NA ▪ WTG

SAUDI ARABIA
Map page 58

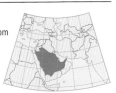

National name Al-Mamlaka al-'Arabiyya as-Sa'udiyya/Kingdom of Saudi Arabia

Area 2,200,518 sq km/ 849,620 sq mi

Capital Riyadh

Major towns/cities Jedda, Mecca, Medina, Ad Dammām, Tabūk, Buraydah

Major ports Jedda, Ad Dammām, Jīzān, Yanbu

Physical features features desert, sloping to The Gulf from a height of 2,750 m/9,000 ft in the west

Currency riyal

GNP per capita (PPP) (US$) 11,480 (2002 est)

Resources petroleum, natural gas, iron ore, limestone, gypsum, marble, clay, salt, gold, uranium, copper, fish

Population 24,217,000 (2003 est)

Population density (per sq km) 11 (2003 est)

Language Arabic (official), English

Religion Sunni Muslim 85%; there is a Shiite minority

Time difference GMT +3

▪ CIA ▪ LC ▪ AN ▪ LP ▪ WTG

▪ **All Saudi**
http://www.all-saudi.com

A dedicated search engine for all things related to Saudi Arabia, with maps, recipes, a travel guide, and useful Arabic phrases.

SENEGAL
Map page 72

National name République du Sénégal/Republic of Senegal

Area 196,200 sq km/75,752 sq mi

Capital Dakar (and chief port)

Major towns/cities Thiès, Kaolack, Saint-Louis, Ziguinchor, Diourbel, Mbour

Physical features plains rising to hills in southeast; swamp and tropical forest in southwest; River Senegal; The Gambia forms an enclave within Senegal

Currency franc CFA

GNP per capita (PPP) (US$) 1,510 (2002 est)

Resources calcium phosphates, aluminium phosphates, salt, natural gas; offshore deposits of petroleum to be developed

Population 10,095,000 (2003 est)

Population density (per sq km) 51 (2003 est)

Language French (official), Wolof, other ethnic languages

Religion mainly Sunni Muslim; Christian 4%, animist 1%

Time difference GMT +/−0

 ▪ CIA ▪ LP ▪ NA ▪ WTG

SERBIA AND MONTENEGRO
Map page 34

National name Srbija i Crna Gora/ Serbia and Montenegro

Area 58,300 sq km/22,509 sq mi

Capital Belgrade

Major towns/cities Priština, Novi Sad, Niš, Kragujevac, Podgorica (formerly Titograd), Subotica

Physical features federation of republics of Serbia and Montenegro and two former autonomous provinces, Kosovo and Vojvodina

Currency new Yugoslav dinar

GNP per capita (PPP) (US$) 2,500 (2002 est)

Resources petroleum, natural gas, coal, copper ore, bauxite, iron ore, lead, zinc

Population 10,527,000 (2003 est)

Population density (per sq km) 103 (2003 est)

Language Serbo-Croat (official), Albanian (in Kosovo)

Religion Serbian and Montenegrin Orthodox; Muslim in southern Serbia

Time difference GMT +1

▪ CIA ▪ LC ▪ LP ▪ WTG

SEYCHELLES
Map page 76

National name Republic of Seychelles

Area 453 sq km/174 sq mi

Capital Victoria (on Mahé island) (and chief port)

Major towns/cities Cascade, Anse Boileau, Takamaka

Physical features comprises two distinct island groups: one, the Granitic group, concentrated, the other, the Outer or Coralline group, widely scattered; totals over 100 islands and islets

Currency Seychelles rupee

GNP per capita (PPP) (US$) 11,150 (2001)

Resources guano; natural gas and metal deposits were being explored mid-1990s

Population 81,000 (2003 est)

Population density (per sq km) 178 (2003 est)

Language Creole (an Asian, African, European mixture) (95%), English, French (all official)

Religion Roman Catholic 90%

Time difference GMT +4

 ▪ CIA ▪ LC ▪ LP ▪ NA ▪ WTG

▪ **Seychelles Super Site**
http://www.sey.net/

Immodestly-named guide to the Seychelles that lives up to its title. The site contains a wealth of information about the islands, including sections on 'Accommodation', 'What to see & do', and 'Activities'. The 'Travellers' information' section is particularly useful for locating advice about visas, money, and health.

SIERRA LEONE
Map page 72

National name Republic of Sierra Leone

Area 71,740 sq km/27,698 sq mi

Capital Freetown

Major towns/cities Koidu, Bo, Kenema, Makeni

Major ports Bonthe

Physical features mountains in
east; hills and forest; coastal
mangrove swamps
Currency leone
GNP per capita (PPP) (US$)
490 (2002 est)
Resources gold, diamonds,
bauxite, rutile (titanium dioxide)
Population 4,971,000 (2003 est)
Population density (per sq km) 69 (2003 est)
Language English (official), Krio (a Creole language), Mende,
Limba, Temne
Religion animist 45%, Muslim 44%, Protestant 8%, Roman
Catholic 3%
Time difference GMT +/–0

 ■ CIA ■ LP ■ NA ■ WTG

SINGAPORE
Map page 54

National name Repablik
Singapura/ Republic of Singapore
Area 622 sq km/240 sq mi
Capital Singapore
Physical features comprises
Singapore Island, low and flat,
and 57 small islands;
Singapore Island is joined to the mainland by causeway across
Strait of Johore
Currency Singapore dollar
GNP per capita (PPP) (US$) 23,090 (2002 est)
Resources granite
Population 4,253,000 (2003 est)
Population density (per sq km) 6,882 (2003 est)
Language Malay, Mandarin Chinese, Tamil, English (all official),
other Indian languages, Chinese dialects
Religion Buddhist, Taoist, Muslim, Hindu, Christian
Time difference GMT +8

www. ■ CIA ■ LC ■ LP ■ RG ■ WTG

■ **Singapore**
http://www.stb.com.sg/
Guide to Singapore. History, geography, and travel information,
as well as features on festivals, make up the majority of the
tourist- and business-oriented information on this site. However,
there is also a useful 'Tourist news' features with regularly
updated information on events in and around Singapore.

■ **Singapore – The People**
http://www.sg
Comprehensive page devoted to the people of Singapore, their
origins, religion, and customs. Scroll through the information, or
click on headings, to find out about early immigration; birth,
marriage and death; language and literacy; religions; and
numerous local festivals.

■ **Singapore Government**
http://www.gov.sg/
Official Web site of the Singapore government that includes an
overview of the government departments, and a section dedicated
to recent government campaigns. There is also the opportunity to
send the government your comments and suggestions.

SLOVAK REPUBLIC
Map page 20

National name Slovenská Republika/
Slovak Republic
Area 49,035 sq km/18,932 sq mi
Capital Bratislava
Major towns/cities Košice,
Nitra, Prešov, Banská Bystrica,
Zilina, Trnava, Martin
Physical features Western range of Carpathian Mountains,
including Tatra and Beskids in north; Danube plain in south;
numerous lakes and mineral springs

Currency Slovak koruna (based on Czechoslovak koruna)
GNP per capita (PPP) (US$) 12,190 (2002 est)
Resources brown coal, lignite, copper, zinc, lead, iron ore,
magnesite
Population 5,402,000 (2003 est)
Population density (per sq km) 110 (2003 est)
Language Slovak (official), Hungarian, Czech, other ethnic
languages
Religion Roman Catholic (over 50%), Lutheran, Reformist,
Orthodox, atheist 10%
Time difference GMT +1

www. ■ CIA ■ LP ■ RG ■ WTG

■ **Slovakia Document Store**
http://slovakia.eunet.sk/
Collection of resources in Slovak and English, including a
traveller's guide and information about the country's geography,
natural resources, history, culture, and religion.

SLOVENIA
Map page 30

National name Republika Slovenija/ Republic of Slovenia
Area 20,251 sq km/7,818 sq mi
Capital Ljubljana
Major towns/cities Maribor, Kranj,
Celje, Velenje, Koper, Novo Mesto
Major ports Koper
Physical features
mountainous; Sava and Drava
rivers
Currency tolar
GNP per capita (PPP) (US$) 17,690 (2002 est)
Resources coal, lead, zinc; small reserves/deposits of natural
gas, petroleum, salt, uranium
Population 1,984,000 (2003 est)
Population density (per sq km) 98 (2003 est)
Language Slovene (related to Serbo-Croat; official), Hungarian,
Italian
Religion Roman Catholic 70%; Eastern Orthodox, Lutheran,
Muslim
Time difference GMT +1

www. ■ CIA ■ LP ■ RG ■ WTG

■ **Slovenia – Country Information**
http://www.matkurja.com/eng/country-info/
Index of pages covering Slovenia. There is information about
history, culture, food and drink, and places to visit, as well as
Slovenia's economy and government.

■ **Ljubljana**
http://www.ijs.si/slo/ljubljana/
Well-presented guide to the Slovenian capital. A 'clickable' map
highlights points of interest in the city. There is history and a
large number of photographs in addition to practical information
for visitors.

SOLOMON ISLANDS
Map page 80

Area 27,600 sq km/
10,656 sq mi
Capital Honiara (on
Guadalcanal island) (and chief
port)
Major towns/cities Gizo,
Auki, Kirakira, Buala
Major ports Yandina
Physical features comprises all but the northernmost islands
(which belong to Papua New Guinea) of a Melanesian archipelago
stretching nearly 1,500 km/900 mi. The largest is Guadalcanal
(area 6,500 sq km/2,510 sq mi); others are Malaita, San
Cristobal, New Georgia, Santa Isabel, Choiseul; mainly
mountainous and forested
Currency Solomon Island dollar
GNP per capita (PPP) (US$) 1,520 (2002 est)

Resources bauxite, phosphates, gold, silver, copper, lead, zinc,
cobalt, asbestos, nickel
Population 477,000 (2003 est)
Population density (per sq km) 17 (2003 est)
Language English (official), pidgin English, more than 80
Melanesian dialects (85%), Papuan and Polynesian languages
Religion more than 80% Christian; Anglican 34%, Roman
Catholic 19%, South Sea Evangelical, other Protestant, animist
5%
Time difference GMT +11

www. ■ CIA ■ LP ■ WTG

■ **Solomon Islands – Pearl of the Pacific**
http://www.solomons.com/
Good source of information on the far-flung islands, atolls, and
reefs comprising the state of the Solomon Islands. The contents
include a good history, map, and information on the culture,
investment opportunities, and government structures. There is
also practical information for tourists.

SOMALIA
Map page 74

National name
Jamhuuriyadda
Soomaaliya/Republic of
Somalia
Area 637,700 sq km/
246,215 sq mi
Capital Mogadishu (and chief
port)
Major towns/cities Hargeysa, Berbera, Kismaayo, Marka
Major ports Berbera, Marka, Kismaayo
Physical features mainly flat, with hills in north
Currency Somali shilling
GNP per capita (PPP) (US$) N/A
Resources chromium, coal, salt, tin, zinc, copper, gypsum,
manganese, iron ore, uranium, gold, silver; deposits of petroleum
and natural gas have been discovered but remain unexploited
Population 9,890,000 (2003 est)
Population density (per sq km) 16 (2003 est)
Language Somali, Arabic (both official), Italian, English
Religion Sunni Muslim; small Christian community, mainly
Roman Catholic
Time difference GMT +3

www. ■ CIA ■ LC ■ AN ■ LP ■ NA ■ WTG

SOUTH AFRICA
Map page 76

National name Republiek
van
Suid-Afrika/Republic of
South Africa
Area 1,222,081 sq km/
471,845 sq mi
Capital Cape Town
(legislative), Pretoria (administrative), Bloemfontein (judicial)
Major towns/cities Johannesburg, Durban, Port Elizabeth,
Vereeniging, Pietermaritzburg, Kimberley, Soweto, Tembisa
Major ports Cape Town, Durban, Port Elizabeth, East London
Physical features southern end of large plateau, fringed by
mountains and lowland coastal margin; Drakensberg Mountains,
Table Mountain; Limpopo and Orange rivers
Territories Marion Island and Prince Edward Island in the
Antarctic
Currency rand
GNP per capita (PPP) (US$) 9,870 (2002 est)
Resources gold (world's largest producer), coal, platinum, iron
ore, diamonds, chromium, manganese, limestone, asbestos,
fluorspar, uranium, copper, lead, zinc, petroleum, natural gas
Population 45,026,000 (2003 est)
Population density (per sq km) 37 (2003 est)

Language English, Afrikaans, Xhosa, Zulu, Sesotho (all official), other African languages

Religion Dutch Reformed Church and other Christian denominations 77%, Hindu 2%, Muslim 1%

Time difference GMT +2

 ■ CIA ■ LC ■ LP ■ RG ■ NA ■ WTG

■ **South Africa.com – News & Information**

http://www.southafrica.com/

South African site with general information about, and maps of, the country and links to over ten different newspapers, related organizations, and the South African yellow pages. You can also get hourly weather reports from various weather stations across the country. There are also links back to large sections on 'Travel & tourism', 'Business & finance', and 'Society & culture'.

■ **Cape Town**

http://www.toptentravel.com/capetown.html

City guide to Cape Town, South Africa. Aimed at the tourist, this site details what to do before you go, and what to do when you get there. History, geography, and travel information, as well as features on festivals, make up the majority of the remaining information on this site, but there are also details of local transport and a list of useful telephone numbers. It also includes images of Cape Town, and maps of the city area.

SOUTH KOREA
Map page 50

National name Daehan Minguk/ Republic of Korea

Area 98,799 sq km/38,146 sq mi

Capital Seoul

Major towns/cities Pusan, Taegu, Inch'ŏn, Kwangju, Taejŏn, Songnam

Major ports Pusan, Inch'ŏn

Physical features southern end of a mountainous peninsula separating the Sea of Japan from the Yellow Sea

Currency won

GNP per capita (PPP) (US$) 16,480 (2002 est)

Resources coal, iron ore, tungsten, gold, molybdenum, graphite, fluorite, natural gas, hydroelectric power, fish

Population 47,700,000 (2003 est)

Population density (per sq km) 482 (2003 est)

Language Korean (official)

Religion Buddhist 48%, Confucian 3%, Christian 47%, mainly Protestant; Chund Kyo (peculiar to Korea, combining elements of Shaman, Buddhist, and Christian doctrines)

Time difference GMT +9

 ■ CIA ■ LC ■ LP ■ WTG

■ **Welcome to Pusan**

http://pusanweb.com/

Comprehensive guide to Korea's main port. There is useful information on Pusan's history, culture, cuisine, transport, and facilities for visitors.

SPAIN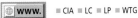
Map page 28

National name España/Spain

Area 504,750 sq km/194,883 sq mi (including the Balearic and Canary islands)

Capital Madrid

Major towns/cities Barcelona, Valencia, Zaragoza, Sevilla, Málaga, Bilbao, Las Palmas (on Gran Canarias island), Murcia, Palma (on Mallorca)

Major ports Barcelona, Valencia, Cartagena, Málaga, Cádiz, Vigo, Santander, Bilbao

Physical features central plateau with mountain ranges, lowlands in south; rivers Ebro, Douro, Tagus, Guadiana, Guadalquivir; Iberian Plateau (Meseta); Pyrenees, Cantabrian Mountains, Andalusian Mountains, Sierra Nevada

Territories Balearic and Canary Islands; in North Africa: Ceuta, Melilla, Alhucemas, Chafarinas Islands, Peñón de Vélez

Currency euro (peseta until 2002)

GNP per capita (PPP) (US$) 20,460 (2002 est)

Resources coal, lignite, anthracite, copper, iron, zinc, uranium, potassium salts

Population 41,060,000 (2003 est)

Population density (per sq km) 81 (2003 est)

Language Spanish (Castilian; official), Basque, Catalan, Galician

Religion Roman Catholic 98%

Time difference GMT +1

 ■ CIA ■ LC ■ LP ■ RG ■ WTG

■ **Barcelona, Spain**

http://travel.lycos.com/Destinations/Europe/Spain/Barcelona/

Guide to the Catalan capital. Information on the history, culture, traditions, churches, museums, architectural sites, cafes, transport system, and restaurants of Barcelona is well-presented. There is also a weather report, maps, and links to local media.

■ **Seville, Spain**

http://www.sol.com/

Substantial source of information on the Andalusian capital. The history, culture, and cuisine of Seville are well-presented. There is a wealth of practical information about accommodation, restaurants, the Alcazar and other local attractions, the famous fiesta, and cultural events.

■ **Costa del Sol, Spain**

http://travel.lycos.com/destinations/location.asp?pid=334652

Comprehensive source of information on the 300 km long Spanish coastal region. There is information on all the main resorts as well as the history and culture of the region. The needs of tourists, residents, and investors are all catered for. This site also includes a weather report and links to local media.

■ **Balearic Islands, Spain**

http://travel.lycos.com/destinations/location.asp?pid=334645

Source of information on all of the Balearic Islands. The history, culture, and political status of this Mediterranean island chain are well-presented and there is a wealth of practical information for visitors and residents. This site also includes a weather report and links to local media and other sources of local information.

■ **Turespaña**

http://www.tourspain.es/

Official site of the Spanish National Tourist Office, available in English, Spanish, French, and German. The site features articles on the country's cities and islands, arts and culture, and landscapes and beaches. There is also an accommodation directory containing listings of hotels, apartments, and campsites.

SRI LANKA
Map page 56

National name Sri Lanka Prajatantrika Samajavadi Janarajaya/Democratic Socialist Republic of Sri Lanka

Area 65,610 sq km/25,332 sq mi

Capital Sri Jayewardenapura Kotte

Major towns/cities Colombo, Kandy, Dehiwala-Mount Lavinia, Moratuwa, Jaffna, Galle

Major ports Colombo, Jaffna, Galle, Negombo, Trincomalee

Physical features flat in north and around coast; hills and mountains in south and central interior

Currency Sri Lankan rupee

GNP per capita (PPP) (US$) 3,390 (2002 est)

Resources gemstones, graphite, iron ore, monazite, rutile, uranium, iemenite sands, limestone, salt, clay

Population 19,065,000 (2003 est)

Population density (per sq km) 291 (2003 est)

Language Sinhala, Tamil (both official), English

Religion Buddhist 69%, Hindu 15%, Muslim 8%, Christian 8%

Time difference GMT +5.5

 ■ CIA ■ LC ■ LP ■ WTG

■ **Sri Lanka Info Page**

http://www.lacnet.org/srilanka/

Host of links grouped under headings such as news, issues, culture, nature, food and cooking, and travel and tourism.

SUDAN
Map page 68

National name Al-Jumhuryyat es-Sudan/Republic of Sudan

Area 2,505,800 sq km/967,489 sq mi

Capital Khartoum

Major towns/cities Omdurman, Port Sudan, Juba, Wad Medani, El Obeid, Kassala, Gedaref, Nyala

Major ports Port Sudan

Physical features fertile Nile valley separates Libyan Desert in west from high rocky Nubian Desert in east

Currency Sudanese dinar

GNP per capita (PPP) (US$) 1,690 (2002 est)

Resources petroleum, marble, mica, chromite, gypsum, gold, graphite, sulphur, iron, manganese, zinc, fluorspar, talc, limestone, dolomite, pumice

Population 33,610,000 (2003 est)

Population density (per sq km) 13 (2003 est)

Language Arabic (51%) (official), 100 local languages

Religion Sunni Muslim 70%; also animist 25%, and Christian 5%

Time difference GMT +2

 ■ CIA ■ LC ■ AN ■ LP ■ NA ■ WTG

SURINAME
Map page 108

National name Republiek Suriname/Republic of Suriname

Area 163,820 sq km/63,250 sq mi

Capital Paramaribo

Major towns/cities Nieuw Nickerie, Moengo, Brokopondo, Nieuw Amsterdam, Albina, Groningen

Physical features hilly and forested, with flat and narrow coastal plain; Suriname River

Currency Suriname guilder

GNP per capita (PPP) (US$) 3,420 (2002 est)

Resources petroleum, bauxite (one of the world's leading producers), iron ore, copper, manganese, nickel, platinum, gold, kaolin

Population 436,000 (2003 est)

Population density (per sq km) 3 (2003 est)

Language Dutch (official), Spanish, Sranan (Creole), English, Hindi, Javanese, Chinese, various tribal languages

Religion Christian 47%, Hindu 28%, Muslim 20%

Time difference GMT −3.5

 ■ CIA ■ LP ■ WTG

■ **Paramaribo, Suriname**

http://travel.lycos.com/destinations/location.asp?pid=334839

Profile of Surinam's historic capital, Paramaribo. There is a general introduction to the city's main features, and four sections – 'Visitors' guide', 'Culture and history', 'News and weather', and 'Entertainment' – each with links to further information in English and Dutch about both the city and the country.

SWAZILAND
Map page 76

National name Umbuso wakaNgwane/Kingdom of Swaziland

Area 17,400 sq km/6,718 sq mi

Capital Mbabane, Lobamba

Major towns/cities Manzini, Big Bend, Mhlume, Nhlangano
Physical features central valley; mountains in west (Highveld); plateau in east (Lowveld and Lubombo plateau)
Currency lilangeni
GNP per capita (PPP) (US$) 4,530 (2002 est)
Resources coal, asbestos, diamonds, gold, tin, kaolin, iron ore, talc, pyrophyllite, silica
Population 1,077,000 (2003 est)
Population density (per sq km) 62 (2003 est)
Language Swazi, English (both official)
Religion about 60% Christian, animist
Time difference GMT +2

www ▪ CIA ▪ LP ▪ RG ▪ NA ▪ WTG

SWEDEN
Map page 16

National name Konungariket Sverige/Kingdom of Sweden
Area 450,000 sq km/173,745 sq mi
Capital Stockholm
Major towns/cities Göteborg, Malmö, Uppsala, Norrköping, Västerås, Linköping, Örebro, Helsingborg
Major ports Helsingborg, Malmö, Göteborg, Stockholm
Physical features mountains in west; plains in south; thickly forested; more than 20,000 islands off the Stockholm coast; lakes, including Vänern, Vättern, Mälaren, and Hjälmaren
Currency Swedish krona
GNP per capita (PPP) (US$) 25,080 (2002 est)
Resources iron ore, uranium, copper, lead, zinc, silver, hydroelectric power, forests
Population 8,876,000 (2003 est)
Population density (per sq km) 20 (2003 est)
Language Swedish (official), Finnish, Saami (Lapp)
Religion Evangelical Lutheran, Church of Sweden (established national church) 90%; Muslim, Jewish
Time difference GMT +1

www ▪ CIA ▪ LP ▪ RG ▪ WTG

▪ **Stockholm**
http://travel.excite.com/show/?loc=2693
Guide to the city of Stockholm. This site includes local news and weather, as well as details of places to visit, hotels, transportation, and maps of the area.

▪ **Sweden – Provincial Information**
http://www.sverigeturism.se/smorgasbord/
Guide to all 27 regions of Sweden from an active map on the home page. Each region contains sections of useful tourist information, such as 'History', 'Culture', 'Events and festivities', 'Family', and 'Major cities'. There is also a separate section called 'Swedish image gallery'.

▪ **Visby – World Heritage City**
http://www.ovpm.org/ville.asp?v=88
Information about the capital of Gotland and World Heritage site. There is a history of the Hanseatic League city and a description of its sights. There is also a link to information about UNESCO's criteria for World Heritage status.

SWITZERLAND
Map page 30

National name Schweizerische Eidgenossenschaft (German)/Confédération Suisse (French)/Confederazione Svizzera (Italian)/Confederaziun Svizra (Romansch)/Swiss Confederation
Area 41,300 sq km/15,945 sq mi
Capital Bern
Major towns/cities Zürich, Geneva, Basel, Lausanne, Luzern, St. Gallen, Winterthur
Major ports river port Basel (on the Rhine)
Physical features most mountainous country in Europe (Alps and Jura mountains); highest peak Dufourspitze 4,634 m/15,203 ft in Apennines
Currency Swiss franc
GNP per capita (PPP) (US$) 31,250 (2002 est)
Resources salt, hydroelectric power, forest
Population 7,169,000 (2003 est)
Population density (per sq km) 174 (2003 est)
Language German (65%), French (18%), Italian (10%), Romansch (1%) (all official)
Religion Roman Catholic 46%, Protestant 40%
Time difference GMT +1

www ▪ CIA ▪ LP ▪ RG ▪ WTG

▪ **Welcome to Berne**
http://www.berntourismus.ch/
Large source of well-arranged official information on the Swiss federal capital. There are sections on the city's history, attractions, accommodation, as well as some lesser known facts. This site also offers maps, a guide to the local cuisine, and a listing of restaurants.

SYRIA
Map page 58

National name al-Jumhuriyya al-Arabiyya as-Suriyya/Syrian Arab Republic
Area 185,200 sq km/71,505 sq mi
Capital Damascus
Major towns/cities Aleppo, Homs, Al Lādhiqīyah, Hamāh, Ar Raqqah, Dayr az Zawr
Major ports Al Lādhiqīyah
Physical features mountains alternate with fertile plains and desert areas; Euphrates River
Currency Syrian pound
GNP per capita (PPP) (US$) 3,250 (2002 est)
Resources petroleum, natural gas, iron ore, phosphates, salt, gypsum, sodium chloride, bitumen
Population 17,800,000 (2003 est)
Population density (per sq km) 96 (2003 est)
Language Arabic (89%) (official), Kurdish (6%), Armenian (3%), French, English, Aramaic, Circassian
Religion Sunni Muslim 74%; other Islamic sects 16%, Christian 10%
Time difference GMT +2

www ▪ CIA ▪ LC ▪ AN ▪ LP ▪ WTG

▪ **Cafe Syria**
http://www.cafe-syria.com/
Portal dedicated to promoting all things to do with Syria. Included here is descriptions of all major cities, facts and information for the tourist, and an overview of the history and government of the country.

TAIWAN
Map page 72

National name Chung-hua Min-kuo/Republic of China
Area 36,179 sq km/13,968 sq mi
Capital T'aipei
Major towns/cities Kaohsiung, T'aichung, T'ainan, Panch'iao, Chungho, Sanch'ung
Major ports Kaohsiung, Chilung
Physical features island (formerly Formosa) off People's Republic of China; mountainous, with lowlands in west; Penghu (Pescadores), Jinmen (Quemoy), Mazu (Matsu) islands
Currency New Taiwan dollar
GNP per capita (PPP) (US$) 22,650 (2002 est)
Resources coal, copper, marble, dolomite; small reserves of petroleum and natural gas
Population 22,500,000 (2002 est)
Population density (per sq km) 620 (2002 est)
Language Chinese (dialects include Mandarin (official), Min, and Hakka)
Religion officially atheist; Buddhist 23%, Taoist 18%, I-Kuan Tao 4%, Christian 3%, Confucian and other 3%
Time difference GMT +8

www ▪ CIA ▪ LP ▪ WTG

TAJIKISTAN
Map page 68

National name Jumhurii Tojikiston/Republic of Tajikistan
Area 143,100 sq km/55,250 sq mi
Capital Dushanbe
Major towns/cities Khŭjand, Qŭrghonteppa, Kŭlob, Ŭroteppa, Kofarnihon

Physical features mountainous, more than half of its territory lying above 3,000 m/10,000 ft; huge mountain glaciers, which are the source of many rapid rivers
Currency Tajik rouble
GNP per capita (PPP) (US$) 900 (2002 est)
Resources coal, aluminium, lead, zinc, iron, tin, uranium, radium, arsenic, bismuth, gold, mica, asbestos, lapis lazuli; small reserves of petroleum and natural gas
Population 6,245,000 (2003 est)
Population density (per sq km) 44 (2003 est)
Language Tajik (related to Farsi; official), Russian
Religion Sunni Muslim; small Russian Orthodox and Jewish communities
Time difference GMT +5

www ▪ CIA ▪ LC ▪ LP ▪ WTG

TANZANIA
Map page 74

National name Jamhuri ya Muungano wa Tanzania/United Republic of Tanzania
Area 945,000 sq km/364,864 sq mi
Capital Dodoma (official), Dar es Salaam (administrative)
Major towns/cities Zanzibar, Mwanza, Mbeya, Tanga, Morogoro
Major ports Dar es Salaam
Physical features central plateau; lakes in north and west; coastal plains; lakes Victoria, Tanganyika, and Nyasa; half the country is forested; comprises islands of Zanzibar and Pemba; Mount Kilimanjaro, 5,895 m/19,340 ft, the highest peak in Africa; Olduvai Gorge; Ngorongoro Crater, 14.5 km/9 mi across, 762 m/2,500 ft deep
Currency Tanzanian shilling
GNP per capita (PPP) (US$) 550 (2002 est)
Resources diamonds, other gemstones, gold, salt, phosphates, coal, gypsum, tin, kaolin (exploration for petroleum in progress)
Population 36,977,000 (2003 est)
Population density (per sq km) 39 (2003 est)
Language Kiswahili, English (both official), Arabic (in Zanzibar), many local languages
Religion Muslim, Christian, traditional religions
Time difference GMT +3

www ▪ CIA ▪ LP ▪ NA ▪ WTG

▪ **Tanzania**
http://www.tanzania-online.gov.uk/tourism/tourism.html
Official Web site of the Tanzania High Commission in London, England. The site features articles on Tanzania's national parks,

game reserves, and mountains, and also includes more general information on visa requirements, currency, and the best time of year to visit.

THAILAND

Map page 52

National name Ratcha Anachak Thai/Kingdom of Thailand
Area 513,115 sq km/198,113 sq mi
Capital Bangkok (and chief port)
Major towns/cities Chiang Mai, Hat Yai, Khon Kaen, Songkhla, Nakhon Ratchasima, Nonthaburi, Udon Thani
Major ports Nakhon Sawan
Physical features mountainous, semi-arid plateau in northeast, fertile central region, tropical isthmus in south; rivers Chao Phraya, Mekong, and Salween
Currency baht
GNP per capita (PPP) (US$) 6,680 (2002 est)
Resources tin ore, lignite, gypsum, antimony, manganese, copper, tungsten, lead, gold, zinc, silver, rubies, sapphires, natural gas, petroleum, fish
Population 62,833,000 (2003 est)
Population density (per sq km) 122 (2003 est)
Language Thai, Chinese (both official), English, Lao, Malay, Khmer
Religion Buddhist 95%; Muslim 5%
Time difference GMT +7

WWW. ▪ CIA ▪ LC ▪ LP ▪ RG ▪ WTG

▪ Thailand Information
http://www.bu.ac.th/english/visitor/thailand/thailand.php
Cultural background and tourist information combine with beautiful photographs to make this site the best starting point for a virtual tour of the 'Land of Smiles'. From Thai boxing to road distances, this Bangkok University run site has a whole range of facts about the country.

TOGO

Map page 72

National name République Togolaise/Togolese Republic
Area 56,800 sq km/21,930 sq mi
Capital Lomé
Major towns/cities Sokodé, Kpalimé, Kara, Atakpamé, Bassar, Tsévié
Physical features two savannah plains, divided by range of hills northeast–southwest; coastal lagoons and marsh; Mono Tableland, Oti Plateau, Oti River
Currency franc CFA
GNP per capita (PPP) (US$) 1,430 (2002 est)
Resources phosphates, limestone, marble, deposits of iron ore, manganese, chromite, peat; exploration for petroleum and uranium was under way in the early 1990s
Population 4,909,000 (2003 est)
Population density (per sq km) 86 (2003 est)
Language French (official), Ewe, Kabre, Gurma, other local languages
Religion animist about 50%, Catholic and Protestant 35%, Muslim 15%
Time difference GMT +/–0

WWW. ▪ CIA ▪ LP ▪ NA ▪ WTG

TONGA

Map page 80

National name Pule'anga Fakatu'i 'o Tonga/Kingdom of Tonga
Area 750 sq km/290 sq mi

Capital Nuku'alofa (on Tongatapu island)
Major towns/cities Neiafu, Vaini

Physical features three groups of islands in southwest Pacific, mostly coral formations, but actively volcanic in west; of the 170 islands in the Tonga group, 36 are inhabited
Currency pa'anga, or Tongan dollar
GNP per capita (PPP) (US$) 6,340 (2002 est)
Population 104,000 (2003 est)
Population density (per sq km) 139 (2003 est)
Language Tongan (official), English
Religion mainly Free Wesleyan Church; Roman Catholic, Anglican
Time difference GMT +13

WWW. ▪ CIA ▪ LP ▪ WTG

▪ Welcome to the Royal Kingdom of Tonga
http://www.tongaholiday.com/
Well-presented official guide to the Polynesian monarchy. There is a map, history, and guide to local culture and investment opportunities. The needs of tourists are met with practical information on attractions and accommodation. This site also includes an audio welcome message from Tonga's Crown Prince.

TRINIDAD AND TOBAGO

Map page 102

National name Republic of Trinidad and Tobago
Area 5,130 sq km/1,980 sq mi (Trinidad 4,828 sq km/1,864 sq mi and Tobago 300 sq km/115 sq mi)
Capital Port of Spain (and chief port)
Major towns/cities San Fernando, Arima, Point Fortin
Major ports Scarborough
Physical features comprises two main islands and some smaller ones in Caribbean Sea; coastal swamps and hills east–west
Currency Trinidad and Tobago dollar
GNP per capita (PPP) (US$) 8,680 (2002 est)
Resources petroleum, natural gas, asphalt (world's largest deposits of natural asphalt)
Population 1,303,000 (2003 est)
Population density (per sq km) 254 (2003 est)
Language English (official), Hindi, French, Spanish
Religion Roman Catholic 33%, Hindu 25%, Anglican 15%, Muslim 6%, Presbyterian 4%
Time difference GMT –4

WWW. ▪ CIA ▪ LP ▪ RG ▪ WTG

▪ Welcome to Trinidad and Tobago!
http://www.visittnt.com/
Official Web site of Trinidad and Tobago tourism. This site provides information on the 'cool, serene, and green' country, divided into four main sections: 'General information', 'How to get here?', 'Where to stay?', and 'What to do here?'. Particularly worth a visit is the section on the annual carnival, which includes photographs and audio clips from previous years.

TUNISIA

Map page 70

National name Al-Jumhuriyya at-Tunisiyya/Tunisian Republic
Area 164,150 sq km/63,378 sq mi
Capital Tunis (and chief port)
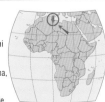
Major towns/cities Sfax, L'Ariana, Bizerte, Gabès, Sousse, Kairouan
Major ports Sfax, Sousse, Bizerte
Physical features arable and forested land in north graduates towards desert in south; fertile island of Jerba, linked to mainland

---

by causeway (identified with island of lotus-eaters); Shott el Jerid salt lakes
Currency Tunisian dinar
GNP per capita (PPP) (US$) 6,280 (2002 est)
Resources petroleum, natural gas, phosphates, iron, zinc, lead, aluminium fluoride, fluorspar, sea salt
Population 9,832,000 (2003 est)
Population density (per sq km) 60 (2003 est)
Language Arabic (official), French
Religion Sunni Muslim (state religion); Jewish and Christian minorities
Time difference GMT +1

WWW. ▪ CIA ▪ AN ▪ LP ▪ NA ▪ WTG

TURKEY

Map page 60

National name Türkiye Cumhuriyeti/Republic of Turkey
Area 779,500 sq km/300,964 sq mi
Capital Ankara
Major towns/cities İstanbul, İzmir, Adana, Bursa, Gaziantep, Konya, Mersin, Antalya, Diyarbakduringr
Major ports İstanbul and İzmir
Physical features central plateau surrounded by mountains, partly in Europe (Thrace) and partly in Asia (Anatolia); Bosporus and Dardanelles; Mount Ararat (highest peak Great Ararat, 5,137 m/16,854 ft); Taurus Mountains in southwest (highest peak Kaldi Dag, 3,734 m/12,255 ft); sources of rivers Euphrates and Tigris in east
Currency Turkish lira
GNP per capita (PPP) (US$) 6,120 (2002 est)
Resources chromium, copper, mercury, antimony, borax, coal, petroleum, natural gas, iron ore, salt
Population 71,325,000 (2003 est)
Population density (per sq km) 92 (2003 est)
Language Turkish (official), Kurdish, Arabic
Religion Sunni Muslim 99%; Orthodox, Armenian churches
Time difference GMT +3

WWW. ▪ CIA ▪ LC ▪ LP ▪ RG ▪ WTG ▪ Discover Turkey

http://www.turkishnews.com/DiscoverTurkey/
Collection of pages on Turkey, its culture, and people. There is a country map, as well as sections on tourism, business, poetry, politics, and even carpets.

▪ Pamukkale
http://www.exploreturkey.com/pamukkal.htm
Good guide to the history of Turkey's 'Holy City' and the current attractions of Pamukkale. Information on recent archaeological discoveries is presented here and there are also good pictures of the ruins and the spectacular geological formations in the area.

▪ Ankara
http://www.hitit.co.uk/regions/Ankara/About.html
Tourist guide to the Turkish capital. The history of the city is summarized and its public buildings, institutions, and attractions described. There is also a section outlining places of interest outside the capital.

▪ Izmir
http://www.turkey.org/tourism/izmir/izmir.htm
Good guide to Turkey's third biggest city – 'the pearl of the Aegean'. There is an outline of the city's history and heritage, and a guide to hotels, museums, and other places of interest. Information on nearby recreational areas is supported by photographs.

▪ NatureKey Online Travel Magazine
http://www.naturekey.com/
Devoted, not to the towns and cities of Turkey, but to the country's natural areas. The monthly issues of this online magazine include regular features such as 'news' and links to related outdoor pursuits sites. It also contains an image gallery, a

TURKMENISTAN
Map page 44

National name Türkmenistan/ Turkmenistan

Area 488,100 sq km/ 188,455 sq mi

Capital Ashkhabad

Major towns/cities Chardzhev, Mary, Nebitdag, Dashkhovuz, Turkmenbashi

Major ports Turkmenbashi

Physical features about 90% of land is desert including the Kara Kum 'Black Sands' desert (area 310,800 sq km/120,000 sq mi)

Currency manat

GNP per capita (PPP) (US$) 4,570 (2002 est)

Resources petroleum, natural gas, coal, sulphur, magnesium, iodine-bromine, sodium sulphate and different types of salt

Population 4,867,000 (2003 est)

Population density (per sq km) 10 (2003 est)

Language Turkmen (a Turkic language; official), Russian, Uzbek, other regional languages

Religion Sunni Muslim

Time difference GMT +5

 ■ CIA ■ LC ■ LP ■ WTG

TUVALU
Map page 80

National name Fakavae Aliki-Malo i Tuvalu/ Constitutional Monarchy of Tuvalu

Area 25 sq km/9.6 sq mi

Capital Fongafale (on Funafuti atoll)

Physical features nine low coral atolls forming a chain of 579 km/650 mi in the Southwest Pacific

Currency Australian dollar

GNP per capita (PPP) (US$) 1,300 (2001)

Population 11,000 (2003 est)

Population density (per sq km) 408 (2003 est)

Language Tuvaluan, English (both official), a Gilbertese dialect (on Nui)

Religion Protestant 96% (Church of Tuvalu)

Time difference GMT +12

 ■ CIA ■ LP ■ WTG

■ **Tuvalu Travel Guide**

http://www.pi-travel.co.nz/search.cfm?regionid=32&list_type=main

Travel guide to the islands of Tuvalu, one of the world's smallest and most isolated countries. The guide is divided into a number of sections, offering information on the country's attractions, a directory of accommodation, and practical advice on topics such as entry requirements and health risks.

UGANDA
Map page 74

National name Republic of Uganda

Area 236,600 sq km/ 91,351 sq mi

Capital Kampala

Major towns/cities Jinja, Mbale, Entebbe, Masaka, Mbarara, Soroti

Physical features plateau with mountains in west (Ruwenzori Range, with Mount Margherita, 5,110 m/16,765 ft); forest and grassland; 18% is lakes, rivers,

and wetlands (Owen Falls on White Nile where it leaves Lake Victoria; Lake Albert in west); arid in northwest

Currency Ugandan new shilling

GNP per capita (PPP) (US$) 1,320 (2002 est)

Resources copper, apatite, limestone; believed to possess the world's second-largest deposit of gold (hitherto unexploited); also reserves of magnetite, tin, tungsten, beryllium, bismuth, asbestos, graphite

Population 25,827,000 (2003 est)

Population density (per sq km) 109 (2003 est)

Language English (official), Kiswahili, other Bantu and Nilotic languages

Religion Christian 65%, animist 20%, Muslim 15%

Time difference GMT +3

 ■ CIA ■ LC ■ LP ■ NA ■ WTG

UKRAINE
Map page 38

National name Ukrayina/ Ukraine

Area 603,700 sq km/ 233,088 sq mi

Capital Kiev

Major towns/cities Kharkiv, Donets'k, Dnipropetrovs'k, L'viv, Kryvyy Rih, Zaporizhzhya, Odessa

Physical features Russian plain; Carpathian and Crimean Mountains; rivers: Dnieper (with the Dnieper dam 1932), Donetz, Bug

Currency hryvna

GNP per capita (PPP) (US$) 4,650 (2002 est)

Resources coal, iron ore (world's fifth-largest producer), crude oil, natural gas, salt, chemicals, brown coal, alabaster, gypsum

Population 48,523,000 (2003 est)

Population density (per sq km) 80 (2003 est)

Language Ukrainian (a Slavonic language; official), Russian (also official in Crimea), other regional languages

Religion traditionally Ukrainian Orthodox; also Ukrainian Catholic; small Protestant, Jewish, and Muslim communities

Time difference GMT +2

 ■ CIA ■ LP ■ WTG

■ **EuroScope: Ukraine**

http://pages.prodigy.net/euroscope/guidetoc.html

Tourist guide to Ukraine. This in-depth site features profiles of Ukraine's major towns and cities, with information on hotels and restaurants in each. Make sure you visit the photo galleries, which offer an insight into Hutsul folk art and Ukrainian Jewry.

■ **Kiev, Ukraine**

http://travel.lycos.com/destinations/location.asp?pid=334503

Large source of information on the Ukrainian capital. There are descriptions of the city, its history, attractions, entertainment, and cultural events. There are also links to a number of sources of information on Ukraine.

■ **Odessa Web**

http://www.odessit.com/tours/tours/english/overview.htm

Guide to this Ukrainian seaport. Dealing with both the old and the new, this site has sections on the history and cultural traditions and also the night life. There are also a number of photographs of notable buildings.

UNITED ARAB EMIRATES
Map page 63

National name Dawlat Imarat al-'Arabiyya al Muttahida/State of the Arab Emirates (UAE)

Area 83,657 sq km/32,299 sq mi

Capital Abu Dhabi

Major towns/cities Dubai, Sharjah, Ra's al Khaymah, Ajmān, Al 'Ayn

Major ports Dubai

Physical features desert and flat coastal plain; mountains in east

Currency UAE dirham

GNP per capita (PPP) (US$) 20,620 (2001)

Resources petroleum and natural gas

Population 2,995,000 (2003 est)

Population density (per sq km) 36 (2003 est)

Language Arabic (official), Farsi, Hindi, Urdu, English

Religion Muslim 96% (of which 80% Sunni); Christian, Hindu

Time difference GMT +4

■ CIA ■ LC ■ AN ■ LP ■ WTG

■ **Ras al Khaimah**

http://www.uaeforever.com/RasAlKhaimah/

Guide to the most traditional of the United Arab Emirates. There is a good description of the history and attractions of the small strategically placed emirate. There are also good photos of Ras al Khaimah and its leader.

■ **Abu Dhabi**

http://www.uaeforever.com/AbuDhabi/

Well-presented guide to the largest and richest of the United Arab Emirates. There is a good description of the history, cultural heritage, attractions, and local economy. There are a number of good photos of Abu Dhabi and its ruler, the UAE president.

■ **Dubai**

http://www.uaeforever.com/Dubai/

Well-presented guide to the second-largest of the United Arab Emirates. There is a good description of the history of the trading entrepot, the role of the Makhtoum family, as well as details of it's cultural heritage, attractions, and the local economy. There are a number of good photos of Dubai and its ruler.

UNITED KINGDOM
Map page 24

National name United Kingdom of Great Britain and Northern Ireland (UK)

Area 244,100 sq km/94,247 sq mi

Capital London

Major towns/cities Birmingham, Glasgow, Leeds, Sheffield, Liverpool, Manchester, Edinburgh, Bradford, Bristol, Coventry, Belfast, Cardiff

Major ports London, Grimsby, Southampton, Liverpool

Physical features became separated from European continent in about 6000 BC; rolling landscape, increasingly mountainous towards the north, with Grampian Mountains in Scotland, Pennines in northern England, Cambrian Mountains in Wales; rivers include Thames, Severn, and Spey

Territories Anguilla, Bermuda, British Antarctic Territory, British Indian Ocean Territory, British Virgin Islands, Cayman Islands, Falkland Islands, Gibraltar, Montserrat, Pitcairn Islands, St. Helena and Dependencies (Ascension, Tristan da Cunha), South Georgia, South Sandwich Islands, Turks and Caicos Islands; the Channel Islands and the Isle of Man are not part of the UK but are direct dependencies of the crown

Currency pound sterling

GNP per capita (PPP) (US$) 25,870 (2002 est)

Resources coal, limestone, crude petroleum, natural gas, tin, iron, salt, sand and gravel

Population 59,251,000 (2003 est)

Population density (per sq km) 243 (2003 est)

Language English (official), Welsh (also official in Wales), Gaelic

Religion about 46% Church of England (established church); other Protestant denominations, Roman Catholic, Muslim, Jewish, Hindu, Sikh

Time difference GMT +/–0

■ CIA ■ LP ■ RG ■ WTG

■ **Gateway to Scotland**

http://www.geo.ed.ac.uk/home/scotland/scotland.html

Guide to all things Scottish, including an 'active map', a guide to the major cities, and information on the language, as well as sections on famous residents and history.

UK Travel Guide
http://www.uktravel.com/index.html

Essential resource for anyone planning to travel in the UK. It includes an A–Z of practical information from accommodation to the weather. The site also includes a 'clickable' map with features on towns and cities as well as several images.

Lake District National Park Authority
http://www.lake-district.gov.uk/index.htm

Official guide to the attractions of Britain's largest national park. There are sections on geology, history, conservation activities, and exhibitions in the Park's visitor's centre. There is a daily weather report for keen walkers. There are also some fabulous photographs of Lakeland beauty spots.

Cardiff, Capital City of Wales
http://www.cardiff.gov.uk/

Official guide to the Welsh capital. Local government functions are fully explained and investment opportunities outlined. There are many photos of the city and a listing of local amenities and historic sites.

States of Jersey
http://www.jersey.com/

Official information about the largest of the Channel Islands. This well organized site caters for the needs of residents and visitors. There is good coverage of the history and cultural heritage of Jersey. Information for visitors is first-rate with details of local attractions, events, and even the weather.

LondonNet – The Net Magazine Guide to London
http://www.londonnet.co.uk/

Informative guide to London, suitable for both tourists and residents alike. There are notes on accommodation in London, covering hotels, apartments, and even places for the 'cost conscious'. Other areas covered here include the museums to visit, the best ways to travel, and the pick of the London nightlife. In addition, there are also notes on the places to shop and eat.

Northern Ireland Tourist Board
http://www.ni-tourism.com/index.asp

This site covers the needs of anyone planning to visit Northern Ireland, from accommodation to events and attractions. It also features a virtual tour covering history, activities, food and drink, and places to stay.

UNITED STATES OF AMERICA

Map page 92

National name United States of America (USA)

Area 9,372,615 sq km/ 3,618,766 sq mi

Capital Washington D.C.

Major towns/cities New York, Los Angeles, Chicago, Philadelphia, Detroit, San Francisco, Dallas, San Diego, San Antonio, Houston, Boston, Phoenix, Indianapolis, Honolulu, San José

Physical features topography and vegetation from tropical (Hawaii) to arctic (Alaska); mountain ranges parallel with east and west coasts; the Rocky Mountains separate rivers emptying into the Pacific from those flowing into the Gulf of Mexico; Great Lakes in north; rivers include Hudson, Mississippi, Missouri, Colorado, Columbia, Snake, Rio Grande, Ohio

Territories the commonwealths of Puerto Rico and Northern Marianas; Guam, the US Virgin Islands, American Samoa, Wake Island, Midway Islands, Johnston Atoll, Baker Island, Howland Island, Jarvis Island, Kingman Reef, Navassa Island, Palmyra Island

Currency US dollar

GNP per capita (PPP) (US$) 35,060 (2002 est)

Resources coal, copper (world's second-largest producer), iron, bauxite, mercury, silver, gold, nickel, zinc (world's fifth-largest producer), tungsten, uranium, phosphate, petroleum, natural gas, timber

Population 294,043,000 (2003 est)

Population density (per sq km) 31 (2003 est)

Language English, Spanish

Religion Protestant 58%; Roman Catholic 28%; atheist 10%; Jewish 2%; other 4% (1998)

Time difference GMT –5–11

■ CIA ■ LP ■ RG ■ WTG

Best of Hawaii
http://www.bestofhawaii.com/

Jumping-off point for visitors seeking information about the best of Hawaii. This site includes a wealth of information aimed at the tourist – including maps, food, weather, accommodation, and even an online version of the Hawaiian phone directory.

Grand Canyon
http://www.kaibab.org/

Visitors to this site will find an outline of the geological and human history tracing the gradual conquest of the Canyon, and a spectacular photo gallery with close-ups and panoramas. There are also details of recommended hikes and trails, and you can discover valuable tips on hiking and backpacking.

New York
http://newyork.citysearch.com/

Impressive, user-friendly guide to New York City, filled with practical information. There are interesting feature articles and constant updates on what's on in the Big Apple. If the pace of life gets too hectic, the search engine can even provide a comprehensive listing of mind and body healing centres.

Washington DC
http://www.washington.org/

Site of the Washington DC Convention and Visitors' Association. This is a helpful guide filled with practical information for tourists and details of the attractions in the Washington area. There is also a useful set of maps.

Prehistory of Alaska
http://www.nps.gov/akso/akarc/

Alaska's prehistory divided into five sections: 'early prehistory', 'tundra and Arctic Alaska', 'southeast Alaska', 'southwest Alaska and Pacific coast', and 'interior Alaska'. there are also links to Alaska's 15 national parks and preserves – click on the acronym to access a general description of each park's cultural resources.

URUGUAY

Map page 110

National name República Oriental del Uruguay/Eastern Republic of Uruguay

Area 176,200 sq km/68,030 sq mi

Capital Montevideo

Major towns/cities Salto, Paysandú, Las Piedras, Rivera, Tacuarembó

Physical features grassy plains (pampas) and low hills; rivers Negro, Uruguay, Río de la Plata

Currency Uruguayan peso

GNP per capita (PPP) (US$) 12,010 (2002 est)

Resources small-scale extraction of building materials, industrial minerals, semi-precious stones; gold deposits are being developed

Population 3,415,000 (2003 est)

Population density (per sq km) 19 (2003 est)

Language Spanish (official), Brazilero (a mixture of Spanish and Portuguese)

Religion mainly Roman Catholic

Time difference GMT –3

■ CIA ■ LP ■ WTG

Uruguay – General Information
http://www.embassy.org/uruguay/

Comprehensive information about Uruguay. There are links to a profile of the country detailing its main features, as well as to its history, geography and climate, culture, cuisine, and wine. The site includes a map and a list of new Uruguay telephone numbers.

UZBEKISTAN

Map page 44

National name Özbekiston Respublikasi/Republic of Uzbekistan

Area 447,400 sq km/ 172,741 sq mi

Capital Tashkent

Major towns/cities Samarkand, Bukhara, Namangan, Andijon, Nukus, Karshi

Physical features oases in deserts; rivers: Amu Darya, Syr Darya; Fergana Valley; rich in mineral deposits

Currency som

GNP per capita (PPP) (US$) 1,590 (2002 est)

Resources petroleum, natural gas, coal, gold (world's seventh-largest producer), silver, uranium (world's fourth-largest producer), copper, lead, zinc, tungsten

Population 26,093,000 (2003 est)

Population density (per sq km) 58 (2003 est)

Language Uzbek (a Turkic language; official), Russian, Tajik

Religion predominantly Sunni Muslim; small Wahhabi, Sufi, and Orthodox Christian communities

Time difference GMT +5

■ CIA ■ LC ■ LP ■ WTG

VANUATU

Map page 80

National name Ripablik blong Vanuatu/République de Vanuatu/Republic of Vanuatu

Area 14,800 sq km/5,714 sq mi

Capital Port-Vila (on Efate island) (and chief port)

Major towns/cities Luganville (on Espíritu Santo)

Physical features comprises around 70 inhabited islands, including Espíritu Santo, Malekula, and Efate; densely forested, mountainous; three active volcanoes; cyclones on average twice a year

Currency vatu

GNP per capita (PPP) (US$) 2,770 (2002 est)

Resources manganese; gold, copper, and large deposits of petroleum have been discovered but have hitherto remained unexploited

Population 212,000 (2003 est)

Population density (per sq km) 17 (2003 est)

Language Bislama (82%), English, French (all official)

Religion Christian 80%, animist about 8%

Time difference GMT +11

■ CIA ■ LP ■ WTG

Vanuatu Online
http://www.vanuatu.net.vu/VanuatuOnlineDirectory.html

Source of information on the Melanesian state. There is a history of the islands, information on government services, the local economy, and attractions. This is in addition to practical information for tourists which includes a special section for philatelists.

Port-Vila, Vanuatu
http://travel.lycos.com/destinations/location.asp?pid=332748

Guide to the capital of Vanuatu. There is coverage of local attractions, culture, and history. The site also has practical information for visitors and those planning to reside in the city, and the text is improved by the inclusion of several photographs of Port-Vila.

VATICAN CITY

Map page 32

National name Stato della Città del Vaticano/Vatican City State

Area 0.4 sq km/0.2 sq mi

Physical features forms an enclave in the heart of Rome, Italy

Currency euro

GNP per capita (PPP) see Italy

Population 1,000 (2003 est)

Population density (per sq km) 1,784 (2003 est)

Language Latin (official), Italian

Religion Roman Catholic

Time difference GMT +1

 ▪ CIA ▪ LP ▪ WTG

▪ Holy See (Vatican City)

http://www.vatican.va/

Multilingual, searchable page, with recent news reports and press releases from the Vatican Information Service. As well as the latest news from the Vatican City State, it also includes information about the Vatican museums and their plans for celebrating the year 2000.

VENEZUELA
Map page 108

National name República de Venezuela/Republic of Venezuala

Area 912,100 sq km/352,161 sq mi

Capital Caracas

Major towns/cities Maracaibo, Maracay, Barquisimeto, Valencia, Ciudad Guayana, Petare

Major ports Maracaibo

Physical features Andes Mountains and Lake Maracaibo in northwest; central plains (llanos); delta of River Orinoco in east; Guiana Highlands in southeast

Currency bolívar

GNP per capita (PPP) (US$) 5,080 (2002 est)

Resources petroleum, natural gas, aluminium, iron ore, coal, diamonds, gold, zinc, copper, silver, lead, phosphates, manganese, titanium

Population 25,699,000 (2003 est)

Population density (per sq km) 28 (2003 est)

Language Spanish (official), Indian languages (2%)

Religion Roman Catholic 92%

Time difference GMT –4

 ▪ CIA ▪ LC ▪ LP ▪ WTG

▪ Fodor's Trip Planner – Caracas

http://www.fodors.com/miniguides/mgresults.cfm?destination=caracas@46

Create your own personal mini-guide to the Venezuelan capital with this handy on-line tourist guide. By choosing price ranges of accommodation and restaurants, and selecting options such as transport, currency and languages, a detailed pamphlet can be quickly compiled. If you select the language option, a link will appear to a site that provides useful phrases.

▪ Venezuela Yours

http://www.venezuelatuya.com/eng.htm

Guide to Venezuela that is available in six languages, including English. The site features profiles of a number of the country's attractions, including the Andes, Caracas, and La Gran Sabana. There is also a selection of beautifully-illustrated articles on Venezuela's history and wildlife.

VIETNAM
Map page 52

National name Công-hòa xâ-hôi chu-nghia Viêt Nam/Socialist Republic of Vietnam

Area 329,600 sq km/127,258 sq mi

Capital Hanoi

Major towns/cities Ho Chi Minh (formerly Saigon), Hai Phong, Da Nãng, Cân Tho, Nha Trang, Biên Hoa, Huê

Major ports Ho Chi Minh (formerly Saigon), Da Nãng, Hai Phong

Physical features Red River and Mekong deltas, centre of cultivation and population; tropical rainforest; mountainous in north and northwest

Currency dong

GNP per capita (PPP) (US$) 2,240 (2002 est)

Resources petroleum, coal, tin, zinc, iron, antimony, chromium, phosphate, apatite, bauxite

Population 81,377,000 (2003 est)

Population density (per sq km) 245 (2003 est)

Language Vietnamese (official), French, English, Khmer, Chinese, local languages

Religion mainly Buddhist; Christian, mainly Roman Catholic (8–10%); Taoist, Confucian, Hos Hoa, and Cao Dai sects

Time difference GMT +7

 ▪ CIA ▪ LC ▪ LP ▪ WTG

▪ Administrative Structure Of Vietnam

http://www.batin.com.vn/vninfo/asv.htm

Fascinating insight into Vietnamese government and politics: at times it almost feels as if you are privy to state secrets! There are few multimedia frills on this site, but the colourful propaganda easily makes up for that.

▪ Vietnam Pictures

http://sunsite.unc.edu/vietnam/

Multimedia archive of Vietnam, including photographs, audio clips, video footage, and text articles covering many aspects of Vietnamese life. The many hypertext links included on this page can take you on a virtual tour of this Southeast Asian country.

YEMEN
Map page 58

National name Al-Jumhuriyya al Yamaniyya/Republic of Yemen

Area 531,900 sq km/ 205,366 sq mi

Capital Şan'ā

Major towns/cities Aden, Ta'izz, Al Mukallā, Al Ḥudaydah, Ibb, Dhamār

Major ports Aden

Physical features hot, moist coastal plain, rising to plateau and desert

Currency riyal

GNP per capita (PPP) (US$) 750 (2002 est)

Resources petroleum, natural gas, gypsum, salt; deposits of copper, gold, lead, zinc, molybdenum

Population 20,010,000 (2003 est)

Population density (per sq km) 38 (2003 est)

Language Arabic (official)

Religion Sunni Muslim 63%, Shiite Muslim 37%

Time difference GMT +3

▪ CIA ▪ AN ▪ LP ▪ WTG

▪ Yemen

http://www.al-bab.com/yemen/

Impressive source of comprehensive information on Yemen. There is coverage of history, culture, archaeology, tourism, economics, the political scene, international relations, and the local media. A large number of photographs include some stunning satellite images.

ZAMBIA
Map page 76

National name Republic of Zambia

Area 752,600 sq km/ 290,578 sq mi

Capital Lusaka

Major towns/cities Kitwe, Ndola, Kabwe, Mufulira, Chingola, Luanshya, Livingstone

Physical features forested plateau cut through by rivers; Zambezi River, Victoria Falls, Kariba Dam

Currency Zambian kwacha

GNP per capita (PPP) (US$) 770 (2002 est)

Resources copper (world's fourth-largest producer), cobalt, zinc, lead, coal, gold, emeralds, amethysts and other gemstones, limestone, selenium

Population 10,812,000 (2003 est)

Population density (per sq km) 14 (2003 est)

Language English (official), Bantu languages

Religion about 64% Christian, animist, Hindu, Muslim

Time difference GMT +2

 ▪ CIA ▪ LP ▪ NA ▪ WTG

ZIMBABWE
Map page 76

National name Republic of Zimbabwe

Area 390,300 sq km/ 150,694 sq mi

Capital Harare

Major towns/cities Bulawayo, Gweru, Kwekwe, Mutare, Kadoma, Chitungwiza

Physical features high plateau with central high veld and mountains in east; rivers Zambezi, Limpopo; Victoria Falls

Currency Zimbabwe dollar

GNP per capita (PPP) (US$) 2,120 (2002 est)

Resources gold, nickel, asbestos, coal, chromium, copper, silver, emeralds, lithium, tin, iron ore, cobalt

Population 12,891,000 (2003 est)

Population density (per sq km) 33 (2003 est)

Language English, Shona, Ndebele (all official)

Religion 50% follow a syncretic (part Christian, part indigenous beliefs) type of religion, Christian 25%, animist 24%, small Muslim minority

Time difference GMT +2

▪ CIA ▪ LP ▪ NA ▪ WTG

INDEX

HOW TO USE THE INDEX

This is an alphabetically arranged index of the places and features that can be found on the maps in this atlas. Each name is generally indexed to the largest scale map on which it appears. If that map covers a double page, the name will always be indexed by the left-hand page number.

Names composed of two or more words are alphabetized as if they were one word.

All names appear in full in the index, except for 'St.' and 'Ste.', which, although abbreviated, are indexed as though spelled in full.

Where two or more places have the same name, they can be distinguished from each other by the country or province name that immediately follows the entry. These names are indexed in the alphabetical order of the country or province.

Alternative names, such as English translations, can also be found in the index and are cross-referenced to the map form by the '=' sign. In these cases the names also appear in brackets on the maps.

Settlements are indexed to the position of the symbol; all other features are indexed to the position of the name on the map.

Abbreviations and symbols used in this index are explained in the list opposite.

FINDING A NAME ON THE MAP

Each index entry contains the name, followed by a symbol indicating the feature type (for example, settlement, river), a page reference and a grid reference:

Name —————— Owosso	⊙ 128	D2
Owyhee	⊙ 126	C2
Owyhee	⟋ 126	C2
Symbol —————— Oxford, *New Zealand*	● 116	D6
Oxford, *United Kingdom*	⊙ 38	G4
Oxnard	⊙ 132	C2
Page reference ———— Oxted	⊙ **38**	J4
Oyama	⊙ 82	K5
Oyapock	⟋ 140	G3
Grid reference ———— Oyem	⊙ 104	G4

The grid reference locates a place or feature within a rectangle formed by the network of lines of longitude and latitude. A name can be found by referring to the red letters and numbers placed around the maps. First find the letter, which appears along the top and bottom of the map, and then the number, down the sides. The name will be found within the rectangle uniquely defined by that letter and number. A number in brackets preceding the grid reference indicates that the name is to be found within an inset map.

ABBREVIATIONS

Ak.	Alaska	N.D.	North Dakota
Al.	Alabama	Nebr.	Nebraska
Ariz.	Arizona	Nev.	Nevada
Ark.	Arkansas	Nfld.	Newfoundland
B.C.	British Columbia	N.H.	New Hampshire
Calif.	California	N. Ire.	Northern Ireland
Colo.	Colorado	N.J.	New Jersey
Conn.	Connecticut	N. Mex.	New Mexico
Del.	Delaware	N.W.T.	Northwest Territories
Dem. Rep. of Congo		N.Y.	New York
	Democratic Republic of Congo	Oh.	Ohio
Eng.	England	Okla.	Oklahoma
Fla.	Florida	Ont.	Ontario
Ga.	Georgia	Oreg.	Oregon
Ia.	Iowa	Orkney Is.	Orkney Islands
Id.	Idaho	Pa.	Pennsylvania
Ill.	Illinois	R.G.S.	Rio Grande do Sul
Ind.	Indiana	R.I.	Rhode Island
Kans.	Kansas	S.C.	South Carolina
Ky.	Kentucky	Scot.	Scotland
La.	Louisiana	S.D.	South Dakota
Man.	Manitoba	Shetland Is.	Shetland Islands
Mass.	Massachusetts	Tenn.	Tennessee
Md.	Maryland	Tex.	Texas
Me.	Maine	Ut.	Utah
M.G.	Mato Grosso	Va.	Virginia
Mich.	Michigan	Vt.	Vermont
Minn.	Minnesota	Wash.	Washington
Miss.	Mississippi	Wis.	Wisconsin
Mo.	Missouri	W. Va.	West Virginia
Mont.	Montana	Wyo.	Wyoming
N.B.	New Brunswick	Y.T.	Yukon Territory
N.C.	North Carolina		

SYMBOLS

🗙	Continent name	🝔	Lake, salt lake
🅰	Country name	🝕	Gulf, strait, bay
ⓐ	State or province name	🝖	Sea, ocean
■	Country capital	⯆	Cape, point
▣	State or province capital	🝗	Island or island group, rocky or coral reef
●	Settlement		
▲	Mountain, volcano, peak	✳	Place of interest
🝘	Mountain range	🝙	National park or other protected area
🝚	Physical region or feature		
⟋	River, canal	🝛	Historical or cultural region

GLOSSARY

This is an alphabetically arranged glossary of the geographical terms used on the maps and in this index. The first column shows the map form, the second the language of origin and the third the English translation.

A

açude	Portuguese	reservoir
adası	Turkish	island
akra	Greek	peninsula
alpen	German	mountains
alpes	French	mountains
alpi	Italian	mountains
älven	Swedish	river
archipiélago	Spanish	archipelago
arquipélago	Portuguese	archipelago

B

bab	Arabic	strait
bahía	Spanish	bay
bahir, bahr	Arabic	bay, lake, river
baía	Portuguese	bay
baie	French	bay
baja	Spanish	lower
bandar	Arabic, Somalian, Malay, Persian	harbour, port
baraji	Turkish	dam
barragem	Portuguese	reservoir
ben	Gaelic	mountain
Berg(e)	German	mountain(s)
boğazı	Turkish	strait
Bucht	German	bay
buḥayrat	Arabic	lake
burnu, burun	Turkish	cape

C

cabo	Spanish	cape
canal	French, Spanish	canal, channel
canale	Italian	canal, channel
cerro	Spanish	mountain
chott	Arabic	marsh, salt lake
co	Tibetan	lake
collines	French	hills
cordillera	Spanish	range

D

dağ(ı)	Turkish	mountain
dağlar(ı)	Turkish	mountains
danau	Indonesian	lake
daryacheh	Persian	lake
dasht	Persian	desert
djebel	Arabic	mountain(s)
-do	Korean	island

E

embalse	Spanish	reservoir
erg	Arabic	sandy desert
estrecho	Spanish	strait

F

feng	Chinese	mountain
-fjördur	Icelandic	fjord
-flói	Icelandic	bay

G

Gebirge	German	range
golfe	French	bay, gulf
golfo	Italian, Portuguese, Spanish	bay, gulf
göl, gölü	Turkish	lake
gora	Russian	mountain
gory	Russian	mountains
gunong	Malay	mountain
gunung	Indonesian	mountain

H

hai	Chinese	lake, sea
hāmūn	Persian	lake, marsh
hawr	Arabic	lake
hu	Chinese	lake, reservoir

I

île(s)	French	island(s)
ilha(s)	Portuguese	island(s)
isla(s)	Spanish	island(s)

J

jabal	Arabic	mountain(s)
-järvi	Finnish	lake
jaza'īr	Arabic	islands
jazīrat	Arabic	island
jbel	Arabic	mountain
jebel	Arabic	mountain
jezero	Serbo-Croatian	lake
jezioro	Polish	lake
jiang	Chinese	river
-jima	Japanese	island
-joki	Finnish	river
-jökull	Icelandic	glacier

K

kepulauan	Indonesian	islands
khrebet	Russian	mountain range
-ko	Japanese	lake
kolpos	Greek	bay, gulf
körfezi	Turkish	bay, gulf
kryazh	Russian	ridge
kūh(ha)	Persian	mountain(s)

L

lac	French	lake
lacul	Romanian	lake
lago	Italian, Portuguese, Spanish	lake
lagoa	Portuguese	lagoon
laguna	Spanish	lagoon, lake
limni	Greek	lake
ling	Chinese	mountain(s), peak
liqeni	Albanian	lake
loch, lough	Gaelic	lake

M

massif	French	mountains
-meer	Dutch	lake, sea
mont	French	mount
monte	Italian, Portuguese, Spanish	mount
montes	Portuguese, Spanish	mountains
monts	French	mountains
muntii	Romanian	mountains
mys	Russian	cape

N

nafud	Arabic	desert
nevado	Spanish	snow-capped mountain
nuruu	Mongolian	mountains

O

nuur	Mongolian	lake

ostrov(a)	Russian	island(s)
ozero	Russian	lake

P

pegunungan	Indonesian	mountains
pelagos	Greek	sea
pendi	Chinese	basin
pesky	Russian	sandy desert
pic	French	peak
pico	Portuguese, Spanish	peak
planalto	Portuguese	plateau
planina	Bulgarian	mountains
poluostrov	Russian	peninsula
puerto	Spanish	harbour, port
puncak	Indonesian	peak
punta	Italian, Spanish	point
puy	French	peak

Q

qundao	Chinese	archipelago

R

ras, râs, ra's	Arabic	cape
represa	Portuguese	dam, reservoir
-rettō	Japanese	archipelago
rio	Portuguese	river
río	Spanish	river

S

sahra	Arabic	desert
salar	Spanish	salt flat
-san	Japanese, Korean	mountain
-sanmaek	Korean	mountains
sebkha	Arabic	salt flat
sebkhet	Arabic	salt marsh
See	German	lake
serra	Portuguese	range
severnaya, severo-	Russian	northern
shan	Chinese	mountain(s)
-shima	Japanese	island
-shotō	Japanese	islands
sierra	Spanish	range

T

tanjona	Malagasy	cape
tanjung	Indonesian	cape
teluk	Indonesian	bay, gulf
ténéré	Berber	desert
-tō	Japanese	island

V

vârful	Romanian	mountain
-vesi	Finnish	lake
vodokhranilishche	Russian	reservoir
volcán	Spanish	volcano

W

wādī	Arabic	watercourse
Wald	German	forest

Z

-zaki	Japanese	cape
zaliv	Russian	bay, gulf

A

Place	Page	Grid
Aachen	22	J4
Aalen	20	F8
Aalst	22	G4
Aarau	30	D3
Aare	30	C3
Aarschot	22	G4
Aba	72	F3
Ābādān	63	C1
Ābādeh	63	E1
Abadla	70	E2
Abaji	72	F3
Abakaliki	72	F3
Abakan	44	S7
Āb Anbar	63	E1
Abancay	108	C6
Abano Terme	30	G5
Abarqū	63	E1
Abashiri	50	N1
Abava	16	M8
Ābaya Hāyk'	74	F2
Abay Wenz	68	G5
Abbeville, France	22	D4
Abbeville, United States	98	C4
Abd al Kūrī	58	F7
Abéché	68	D5
Abengourou	72	D3
Abenójar	28	F6
Åbenrå	20	E1
Abensberg	20	G8
Abeokuta	72	E3
Aberaeron	24	H9
Aberdeen, South Africa	76	C6
Aberdeen, United Kingdom	24	K4
Aberdeen, Miss., United States	98	D3
Aberdeen, S.D., United States	94	G1
Aberdeen, Wash., United States	94	B1
Aberdeen Lake	90	M4
Aberystwyth	24	H9
Abez'	38	M1
Abhā	68	H4
Abhar	60	N5
Abidjan	72	D3
Abilene	100	G2
Abingdon, United Kingdom	22	A3
Abingdon, United States	98	E2
Abnūb	68	F2
Aboisso	72	D3
Abomey	72	E3
Abong Mbang	72	G4
Abou Déia	68	C5
Abqaiq	63	C4
Abrantes	28	B5
Abrud	34	L3
Absaroka Range	94	E1
Abū al Abayḍ	63	E4
Abu Aweigila	62	B6
Abu Ballās	68	E3
Abu Dhabi = Abū Ẓabī	63	F4
Abu Hamed	68	F4
Abuja	72	F3
Abumombazi	74	C3
Ābune Yosēf	68	G5
Abū Nujaym	68	C1
Abū Qarin	68	C1
Aburo	74	E3
Abu Simbel	68	F3
Abut Head	84	B6
Abuye Meda	74	F1
Abū Ẓabī	63	F4
Acaponeta	92	E7
Acapulco	102	E5
Acará	108	H4
Acarigua	108	D2
Accra	72	D3
Achaguas	102	L7
Achayvayam	46	W4
Acheng	48	H1
Achenkirch	30	G3
Achen See	30	G3
Achill Island	24	B8
Achim	20	E3
Achinsk	44	S6
Achit	38	L3
Aci Göl	36	M7
A Cihanbeyli	36	Q6
Acireale	32	K11
Acklins Island	102	K4
Aconcagua	106	D7
Açores	70	(1)B2
A Coruña	28	B1
Acquarossa	30	D4
Acqui Terme	30	D6
Acre	108	C5
Acri	32	L9
Ada, United States	98	B3
Ada, Serbia and Montenegro	18	K12
Adak Island	100	(3)C1
Adam	58	G5
Adamas	36	G8
Adams Island	84	(2)B1
Adana	60	E7
Adana	60	F5
Adda	30	E5
Ad Dafrah	63	E5
Ad Dahnā	63	B3
Ad Dakhla	70	B4
Ad Dammām	63	D3
Ad Dawādimī	58	D5
Ad Dawḥah	63	D4
Ad Dilam	63	B5
Ad Dir'īyah	63	B4
Addis Ababa = Ādīs Ābeba	74	F2
Ad Dīwānīyah	58	D3
Adel	96	B2
Adelaide	82	G6
Adelaide Peninsula	90	M3
Adelaide River	82	F2
Aden = Adan	58	E7
Aderbissinat	72	F1
Adh Dhayd	63	F4
Adi	55	D3
Adige	30	G5
Adīgrat	56	G5
Adilabad	56	C5
Adin	94	B2
Adīrī	68	B2
Ādīs Ābeba	74	F2
Adi Ugri	68	G5
Adiyaman	60	H5
Adjud	34	Q3
Adler	60	H2
Admiralty Island	90	E5
Admiralty Islands	80	E6
Adoni	56	C5
Adour	26	H8
Adra	28	H8
Adrano	32	J11
Adrar	70	E3
Adrar des Ifôghas	70	F5
Adrar Tamgak	70	G5
Adria	30	H5
Adriatic Sea	32	H4
Adycha	46	P3
Adygeya	60	J1
Adygeysk	60	H1
Adzopé	72	D3
Adz'vavom	38	L1
Aegean Sea	36	H5
A Estrada	28	B2
Afghanistan	58	H3
Afgooye	74	H3
'Afīf	68	H3
Afikpo	72	F3
Afmadow	74	G3
Afognak Island	100	(1)G4
A Fonsagrada	28	C1
Afragola	32	J8
Africa	66	F5
'Afrīn	60	G5
Afuá	108	G4
'Afula	62	C4
Afyon	36	N6
Agadez	70	G5
Agadir	70	D2
Agadyr'	44	N8
Agalega Islands	66	J7
Agan	46	B4
Āgaro	74	F2
Agartala	56	F4
Agathonisi	36	J7
Agattu Island	46	W6
Ağcabädi	60	M3
Agde	26	J10
Agen	26	F9
Agia Triada	36	D7
Aginskoye	44	S6
Agiokampos	36	E5
Agios Efstratios	36	H5
Agios Georgios	36	F7
Agios Nikolaos	36	H9
Agnibilekrou	72	D3
Agnita	34	M4
Agra	56	C3
Agrakhanskiy Poluostrov	60	M2
Ağri	60	K4
Agri	32	L8
Agrigento	32	H11
Agrinio	36	D6
Agropoli	32	K8
Agryz	38	K3
Ağsu	60	N3
Agua Prieta	100	E2
Aguascalientes	102	D4
A Gudiña	28	C2
Aguelhok	70	F5
Águilas	28	J7
Agulhas Negras	108	H8
Ağva	36	M3
Ahar	60	M4
Ahaura	84	C6
Ahaus	22	K2
Ahititi	84	E4
Ahlen	22	K3
Ahmadabad	56	B4
Ahmadnagar	56	B5
Ahmadpur East	56	B3
Ahr	20	B6
Ahram	63	D2
Ahrensburg	20	F3
Ahvāz	58	E3
Aichach	20	G8
Aigialousa	60	F6
Aigina	36	F7
Aigio	36	E6
Aigosthena	36	F6
Aiguillon	26	F9
Aihui	46	M6
Aim	46	N5
Ain	26	L7
Aïn Beïda	70	G1
'Aïn Ben Tili	70	D3
Aïn Bessem	28	P8
Aïn el Hadjel	28	P9
Aïn Oussera	70	F1
Ainsa	28	L2
Aïn Sefra	70	E2
Ain Taya	28	P8
Aïn-Tédélès	28	L8
Aïn Témouchent	28	J9
Airão	108	E4
Aire	24	L8
Air Force Island	90	S3
Airolo	30	D4
Airpanas	55	C4
Aisne	22	F5
Aitape	55	F3
Aitkin	96	B1
Aitutaki	80	K7
Aiud	34	L3
Aix-en-Provence	26	L10
Aix-les-Bains	26	L8
Aizawl	56	F4
Aizkraukle	16	N8
Aizpute	16	L8
Aizu-wakamatsu	50	K5
Ajaccio	32	C7
Aj Bogd Uul	48	B2
Ajdābiyā	68	D1
Ajigasawa	50	L3
Ajka	18	G10
Ajlun	62	C4
Ajmān	63	F4
Ajmer	56	B3
Ajo	100	D2
Ajtos	34	Q7
Akanthou	62	A1
Akaroa	84	D6
Akasha	68	F3
Akashi	50	H6
Akbalyk	44	P8
Akçakale	60	H5
Akçakoca	36	P3
Akdağmadeni	60	F4
Aken	20	H5
Aketi	74	C3
Akhalk'alak'i	60	K3
Akhisar	36	K6
Akhmīm	68	F2
Akhty	60	M3
Akimiski Island	90	Q6
Akita	50	L4
Akjoujt	70	C5
Akka	70	D3
Akkajaure	16	J3
Akkeshi	50	N2
'Akko	62	C4
Akmeqit	58	L2
Akobo	74	E2
Akola	56	C4
Akonolinga	72	G4
Akordat	68	G4
Akpatok Island	90	T4
Akqi	58	P9
Akra Drepano	36	G5
Akranes	16	(1)B2
Akra Sounio	36	F7
Akra Spatha	36	F9
Akra Trypiti	36	G9
Akrehamn	16	C7
Akron	96	D2
Aksaray	60	E4
Aksarka	38	N4
Akşehir	36	P6
Akseki	36	P7
Aksha	46	J6
Akshiy	44	P9
Aksu	44	Q9
Aksuat	44	Q8
Āksum	68	G5
Aktau, Kazakhstan	14	K3
Aktau, Kazakhstan	44	N7
Aktogay, Kazakhstan	44	N8
Aktogay, Kazakhstan	44	P8
Aktuma	44	M8
Aktyubinsk	38	L4
Akula	74	C3
Akulivik	90	R4
Akune	50	F8
Akure	72	F3
Akwanga	72	F3
Alabama	98	D3
Alaçam	60	F3
Alaejos	28	E3
Alagoas	108	K5
Alagoinhas	108	K6
Alagón	28	J3
Al Ahmadi	63	C2
Al 'Amārah	58	E3
Alaminos	52	F3
Alamo	94	C3
Alamogordo	100	E2
Alamo Lake	100	D2
Åland	16	K6
Alanya	60	E3
Alappuzha	56	C7
Al Argoub	70	B4
Al Arṭāwīyah	58	E4
Alaşehir	36	L6
Al 'Ashūriyah	58	D3
Alaska	100	(1)F2
Alaska Peninsula	100	(1)E4
Alaska Range	100	(1)G3
Alassio	30	D6
Alatri	32	H7
Alatyr'	38	J4
Alaverdi	60	L3
Alavus	16	M5
Al 'Ayn	63	F4
Alazeya	46	S2
Alba, Italy	30	D6
Alba, Spain	28	E4
Albacete	28	J5
Alba Iulia	34	L3
Albania	36	B3
Albany	36	Q6
Albany, Australia	82	C6
Albany, Ga., United States	98	E3
Albany, Ky., United States	98	E2
Albany, N.Y., United States	96	F2
Albany, Oreg., United States	94	B2
Albardão do João Maria	110	L4
Al Bardī	68	D1
Al Başrah	58	E3
Albatross Bay	82	H2
Albatross Point	84	E4
Al Baydā	68	D1
Albenga	30	D6
Albert	22	E4
Alberta	90	H6
Albertirsa	18	J10
Albert Kanaal	22	G3
Albert Lea	96	B2
Albert Nile	74	E3
Albertville	26	M8
Albi	26	H10
Albina	108	G2
Albino	30	E5
Albino	94	F1
Ålborg	16	E8
Ålborg Bugt	16	F8
Albox	28	H7
Albstadt	20	E8
Albufeira	28	B7
Ål Bū Kamāl	60	J6
Albuquerque	100	E1
Al Burayj	62	D2
Al Buraymī	58	G5
Alburquerque	28	D5
Albury	82	J7
Al Buşayyah	63	B1
Alcácer do Sal	28	B6
Alcalá de Guadaira	28	E7
Alcalá de Henares	28	G4
Alcalá la Real	28	G7
Alcamo	32	G11
Alcañiz	28	K3
Alcantarilla	28	J7
Alcaraz	28	H6
Alcaudete	28	F7
Alcázar de San Juan	28	G5
Alcobendas	28	G4
Alcoi	28	K6
Alcolea del Pinar	28	H3
Alcorcón	28	G4
Alcoutim	28	C7
Aldabra Islands	76	(2)A2
Aldan	46	M5
Aldan	46	N5
Aldeburgh	22	D2
Alderney	26	C4
Aldershot	22	B3
Aleg	70	C5
Aleksandrov-Sakhalinskiy	46	Q6
Aleksandrovskiy Zavod	46	K6
Aleksandrovskoye	38	Q2
Alekseyevka	44	N7
Aleksin	34	J6
Alençon	26	F5
Aleppo = Ḥalab	60	G5
Aléria	32	D6
Alès	26	K9
Aleşd	18	M10
Alessandria	30	D6
Ålesund	16	D5
Aleutian Islands	100	(3)B1
Aleutian Range	100	(1)F4
Aleutian Trench	42	W5
Alexander Archipelago	100	(1)K4
Alexander Bay	76	B5
Alexander City	98	D3
Alexandra	84	B7
Alexandreia	36	E4
Alexandria = El Iskandarīya, Egypt	68	E1
Alexandria, Romania	34	N6
Alexandria, La., United States	98	C3
Alexandria, Minn., United States	96	A1
Alexandria, Va., United States	96	E3
Alexandroupoli	36	H4
Alexis Creek	90	G6
'Aley	62	C3
Aley	44	Q7
Aleysk	44	Q7
Al Farwāniyah	63	B2
Al Fāw	63	C2
Alfeld	20	E5
Alföld	34	H2
Alfonsine	30	H6
Alfreton	22	A1
Al Fuḥayyil	63	C2
Al-Fujayrah	63	G4
Algeciras	28	E8
Algemesí	28	K5
Algena	68	G4
Alger	70	F1
Algeria	70	E3
Al Ghāt	63	A3
Al Ghaydah	58	F6
Alghero	32	C8
Algiers = Alger	70	F1
Algona	96	B2
Al Hadīthah	62	E5
Alhama de Murcia	28	J7
Al Hamar	63	B5
Al Hamīdīyah	62	C2
Al Hammādah al Hamrā'	70	G3
Al Harūj al Aswad	68	C2
Al Hasakah	60	J5
Alhaurmín el Grande	28	F8
Al Hijāz	68	G2
Al Hillah	58	D3
Al Hilwah	63	B5
Al Hoceima	70	E1
Al Hudaydah	56	H5
Al Hufūf	63	C4
Al Humaydah	58	C4
Aliabad	63	F2
Aliağa	36	J6
Aliakmonas	36	E4
Äli Bayramlı	60	N4
Alicante	28	K6
Alice	98	B4
Alice Springs	82	F4
Alicudi	32	J10
Aligarh	56	C3
Alindao	74	C2
Alingås	16	G8

147

Name	Page	Grid
Alisos	100	D2
Aliwal North	76	D6
Al Jabal al Akhḍar	68	D1
Al Jaghbūb	68	D2
Al Jālamīd	68	G1
Al Jarah	63	B2
Al Jawf, *Libya*	68	D3
Al Jawf, *Saudi Arabia*	68	G2
Aljezur	28	B7
Al Jīfārah	63	A5
Al Jubayl	63	C3
Aljustrel	28	B7
Al Kāmil	58	G5
Al Khābūrah	63	G5
Al Khālis	60	L7
Al Kharj	63	B4
Al Khaṣab	63	G3
Al Khawr	63	D4
Al Khubar	63	D3
Al Khufrah	68	D3
Al Khums	70	H2
Al Khuwayr	63	D3
Al Kir'ānah	63	D4
Alkmaar	22	G2
Al Kūt	58	E3
Al Kuwayt	63	C2
Al Lādhiqīyah	60	F6
Allahabad	56	D4
Allakh-Yun'	46	P4
Alldays	76	D4
Allen	52	G4
Allendale	98	E3
Allentown	96	E2
Aller = Cabañaquinta	28	E1
Aller	20	E4
Alliance	94	F2
Allier	26	J8
Allinge	18	D2
Al Lith	68	G3
Alma, *Canada*	96	F1
Alma, *Nebr., United States*	94	G2
Alma, *Wis., United States*	96	B2
Almada	28	A6
Almadén	28	F6
Al Madīnah	68	G3
Al Mahbas	70	D3
Al Majma'ah	58	E4
Almalyk	44	M9
Al Manāmah	63	D3
Almansa	28	J6
Al Ma'qil	63	B1
Al Marj	68	G2
Almaty	44	P9
Al Mawṣil	60	K5
Al Mazāḥimīyah	63	B4
Almazán	28	H3
Almeirim	108	G4
Almelo	22	J2
Almendralejo	28	D6
Almería	28	H8
Al'met'yevsk	44	J7
Almiros	36	E5
Al Mish'āb	63	C2
Almonte	28	D7
Almora	56	C3
Almosa	94	E3
Al Mubarraz	63	C4
Al Mudawwara	62	D7
Al Mukallā	58	E7
Al Mukhā	68	H5
Almuñécar	28	G8
Al Muqdādīyah	60	L7
Al Nu'ayrīyah	63	C3
Alnwick	24	L6
Alonnisos	36	F5
Alor	55	B4
Alor Setar	52	C5
Alotau	82	K2
Alpena	96	D1
Alphen	22	G2
Alpi Lepontine	30	C4
Alpine	100	E2
Alpi Orobie	30	E4
Alps	30	B5
Al Qadmūs	62	D1
Al Qalībah	68	G3
Al Qāmishlī	60	J5
Al Qar'ah	63	B3
Al Qarqar	62	E5
Al Qaryāt	68	B1
Al Qaryatayn	62	E2
Al Qaṭif	63	C3
Al Qaṭrūn	68	B3
Al Qunayṭirah	62	C3
Al Qunfudhah	68	H4
Al Qurayyāt	68	G1
Al Qurnah	63	B3
Al 'Quṣayr, *Iraq*	63	A1
Al 'Quṣayr, *Syria*	62	D2
Al Quṭayfah	62	D2
Als	20	E1
Alsask	90	K6
Alsasua	28	H2
Alsfeld	20	E6
Alta	16	M2
Altaelva	16	M2
Altai Mountains	48	A1
Al Tamīnī	68	D1
Altamira	108	G4
Altamura	32	L8
Altanbulag	46	H6
Altay	44	R7
Altay, *China*	44	R8
Altay, *Mongolia*	48	B1
Altdorf	30	D4
Alte Mellum	20	D3
Altenberg	20	J6
Altenburg	20	H6
Altenkirchen	20	J2
Altkirch	30	C3
Alto Garças	108	G7
Alto Molócuè	76	F3
Alton, *United Kingdom*	22	B3
Alton, *United States*	96	B3
Altoona	96	E2
Alto Parnaíba	108	H5
Altötting	30	H2
Altun Shan	44	S10
Alturas	94	B2
Altus	98	B3
Al 'Ubaylah	58	F5
Alūksne	16	P8
Alupka	60	E1
Al 'Uqaylah	68	C1
Alushta	60	F1
Al 'Uthmānīyah	63	C4
Al 'Uwaynāt, *Libya*	68	B2
Al 'Uwaynāt, *Libya*	68	D3
Al 'Uwayqīlah	68	H1
Al 'Uzayr	63	B1
Alva	98	B2
Alvarães	108	E4
Älvdalen	16	H6
Älvsbyn	16	L4
Al Wafrā'	63	B2
Al Wajh	68	G2
Al Wannān	63	C3
Alwar	56	C3
Al Wari'ah	63	B3
Alxa Zouqi	48	D3
Alytus	18	P3
Alzey	20	D7
Alzira	28	K5
Amadi	74	E2
Amādīyah	60	K5
Amadjuak Lake	90	S4
Amahai	55	C3
Amakusa-Shimo-shima	50	E7
Amaliada	36	D7
Amalner	56	C4
Amamapare	55	E3
Amambaí	110	K3
Amami-Ōshima	42	S7
Amanab	55	F3
Amandola	32	H6
Amantea	32	L9
Amapá	108	G3
Amapá	108	G3
Amarante	108	J5
Amarapura	52	B2
Amareleja	28	C6
Amarillo	100	F1
Amasya	60	F3
Amay	22	H4
Amazar	46	L6
Amazon = Amazonas	106	F4
Amazonas	108	D4
Amazonas	108	E4
Ambala	56	C2
Ambanjä	76	H2
Ambarchik	46	U3
Ambato	108	B4
Ambato Boeny	76	H3
Ambatondrazaka	76	H3
Amberg	20	G7
Ambikapur	56	D4
Ambilobe	76	H2
Ambohimahasoa	76	H4
Amboise	26	G6
Ambon	55	C3
Ambositra	76	H4
Ambovombe	76	H5
Amchitka Island	100	(3)B1
Amderma	44	L4
Amdo	56	F2
Ameland	22	H1
Amengel'dy	44	M7
American Falls	94	D2
American Samoa	80	J7
Americus	98	E3
Amersfoort	22	H2
Amery	90	N5
Amery Ice Shelf	112	(2)M2
Ames	96	B2
Amfilochia	36	D6
Amfissa	36	E6
Amga	46	N4
Amga	46	L5
Amguid	70	G3
Amgun'	46	P6
Amherst	90	U7
Amiens	22	E5
Amirante Islands	76	(2)B2
Amistad Reservoir	100	F3
Amlekhganj	56	D3
Åmli	16	E7
'Amm Adam	68	G4
'Ammān	62	C5
Ammassalik	90	Z3
Ammerland	22	K1
Ammersee	30	F2
Ammochostos	60	E6
Ammochostos Bay	62	C2
Amo	52	C2
Amol	58	F2
Amorgos	36	H8
Amos	96	E1
Amourj	70	D5
Ampana	55	B3
Ampanihy	76	G4
Amparai	56	D7
Ampezzo	30	H4
Amposta	28	L4
Amrān	58	D6
Amravati	56	C4
Amritsar	56	B2
Amroha	56	C3
Amrum	20	D2
Amsterdam, *Netherlands*	22	G2
Amsterdam, *United States*	96	F2
Amstetten	30	K2
Am Timan	68	D5
Amudar'ya	44	L9
Amundsen Gulf	90	G2
Amundsen Sea	112	(2)GG3
Amungen	16	H6
Amuntai	54	F3
Amur	46	P6
Amursk	46	P6
Amvrakikos Kolpos	36	C6
Anabanua	55	B3
Anabar	46	J2
Anaconda	94	D1
Anacortes	94	B1
Anadarko	94	G3
Anadolu Dağları	60	H3
Anadyr'	46	X4
Anadyrskaya Nizmennost'	46	X3
Anadyrskiy Zaliv	46	Y3
Anafi	36	H8
'Ānah	60	J6
Anaheim	100	C2
Anáhuac	100	F3
Analalava	76	H2
Anamur	60	E5
Anan	50	H7
Anantapur	56	C6
Anan'yiv	34	T2
Anapa	60	G1
Anápolis	108	H7
Anār	63	F1
Anārak	58	F3
Anardara	58	H3
Anatolia	36	M6
Añatuya	110	J4
Anchorage	100	(1)H3
Ancona	32	H5
Ancud	110	G7
Anda	48	H1
Andalgalá	110	H4
Åndalsnes	16	D5
Andalusia	98	D3
Andaman Islands	52	A4
Andaman Sea	52	A4
Andapa	76	H2
Andarāb	58	J2
Andenne	22	H4
Andéramboukane	72	E1
Andermatt	30	D4
Andernach	22	K4
Anderson	98	E3
Anderson	90	F3
Andes	106	D5
Andfjorden	16	J2
Andilamena	76	H3
Andipsara	36	H6
Andizhan	44	N9
Andkhvoy	58	J2
Andoas	108	B4
Andong	50	E5
Andorra	28	L2
Andorra la Vella	28	M2
Andover	22	A3
Andøya	16	H2
Andradina	110	L3
Andreanof Islands	100	(3)C1
Andrews	100	F2
Andria	32	L7
Andriamena	76	H3
Andros	36	G7
Andros, *Greece*	36	G7
Andros, *The Bahamas*	98	F5
Andros Town	98	F5
Andrott	56	B6
Andrychów	18	J8
Andújar	28	F6
Andulo	76	B2
Aneto	28	L2
Angara	46	G5
Angarsk	46	G6
Ånge	16	H5
Angel de la Guarda	100	D3
Angeles	52	G3
Ängelholm	16	G8
Angeln	20	E2
Angermünde	20	K4
Angern	30	M2
Angers	26	E6
Anglesey	24	H8
Angmagssalik = Ammassalik	90	Z3
Ango	74	D3
Angoche	76	F3
Angohrān	63	G3
Angol	110	G6
Angola	66	E7
Angostura Reservoir	94	F2
Angoulême	26	F8
Angren	44	M9
Anguilla	102	M5
Aniak	100	(1)F3
Anina	34	J4
Ankang	48	D4
Ankara	60	E4
Ankazoabo	76	G4
Anklam	20	J3
Ankpa	72	F3
Ånn	16	G5
Anna	38	H4
Annaba	70	G1
Annaberg-Buchholz	20	H6
An Nabk, *Saudi Arabia*	62	E5
An Nabk, *Syria*	62	D2
An Nafud	68	G2
An Nā'irīyah	58	E3
An Najaf	58	D3
Annapolis	96	E3
Annapurna	56	D3
Ann Arbor	96	D2
An Nāṣirīyah	68	J1
Annecy	30	B5
Annemasse	30	B4
Anniston	98	D3
Annobón	72	F5
Annonay	26	K8
An Nukhayb	58	D3
Anqing	48	F4
Ansbach	20	F7
Anshan	50	B3
Anshun	48	D5
Ansley	94	G2
Anson	98	B3
Ansongo	70	F5
Antakya	60	G5
Antalaha	76	J2
Antalya	36	N8
Antalya Körfezi	36	N8
Antananarivo	76	H3
Antarctic Peninsula	112	(2)LL3
Antequera	28	F7
Anti-Atlas	70	D3
Antibes	30	C7
Antigo	96	C1
Antigua	102	M5
Antigua and Barbuda	102	M5
Antikythira	36	F9
Antiparos	36	G7
Antipaxoi	36	C5
Antipayuta	44	P4
Antipodes Islands	84	(3)A1
Antlers	98	B3
Antofagasta	110	G3
Antonito	94	E3
Antrim	24	F7
Antropovo	38	H3
Antsalova	76	G3
Antsirabe	76	H3
Antsirañana	76	H2
Antu	50	E2
Antwerp = Antwerpen	22	G3
Antwerpen	22	G3
Anuradhapura	56	D7
Anveh	63	F3
Anxi	48	B2
Anyang, *China*	48	E3
Anyang, *South Korea*	50	D5
Anyuysk	46	V3
Anzhero-Sudzhensk	44	R6
Anzi	74	C4
Anzio	32	G7
Aoga-shima	50	K7
Aomori	50	L3
Aosta	30	C5
Aoukâr	70	C5
Aoukoukar	72	C1
Apalachee Bay	98	E4
Apalachicola	98	D4
Aparri	52	G3
Apatin	34	F4
Apatity	38	F1
Ape	16	P8
Apeldoorn	22	H2
Api	56	D2
Apia	80	J7
Apoera	108	F2
Apolda	20	G5
Apollo Bay	82	H7
Aporé	108	G7
Apostle Islands	96	B1
Apoteri	108	F3
Appalachian Mountains	98	E3
Appennino	32	G5
Appennino Abruzzese	32	H6
Appennino Calabro	32	K10
Appennino Lucano	32	K8
Appennino Tosco-Emiliano	30	E6
Appennino Umbro-Marchigiano	32	H6
Appleton	96	C2
Aprilia	32	G7
Apure	108	D2
Apurimac	108	C6
Āqā	58	H3
'Aqaba	62	C7
Aquidauana	108	F8
Ara	56	D3
Arabian Sea	58	H6
Aracaju	108	K6
Aracati	108	K4
Araçatuba	108	G8
Aracuca	102	L7
Arad	34	J3
Arādah	58	F5
Arafura Sea	55	D5
Aragarças	108	G7
Araguaia	106	F4
Araguaína	108	H5
Araguari	108	H7
Araguatins	108	H5
Arāk	58	E3
Arak	70	F3
Aral Sea	44	K8
Aral'sk	38	M5
Aranda de Duero	28	G3
Aranđelovac	34	H5
Aran Island	24	D6
Aran Islands	24	B8
Aranjuez	28	G4
Aranos	76	B4
Aranyaprathet	52	C4
Araouane	70	E5
Arapahoe	94	G2
Arapiraca	108	K5
'Ar'ar	58	D3
Araras	108	G5
Ararat	60	L4
Arauca	108	D2
Araxá	108	H7
Araz	60	L4
Arbīl	60	K5
Arbon	30	E3
Arbre du Ténéré	70	G5
Arbroath	24	K5

Esbjerg 16 E9
Escanaba 96 C1
Escárcega 102 F5
Esch 22 J5
Eschwege 20 F5
Eschweiler 22 J4
Escondido 100 C2
Eséka 72 G4
Eşfahān 58 F3
Eskifjörđhur 16 (1)G2
Eskilstuna 16 J7
Eskimo Lakes 100 (1)L2
Eskişehir 60 D4
Esla 28 E3
Eslāmābād e Gharb 60 M6
Eslamshahr 58 F2
Esler Dağ 36 M7
Eslö 18 C2
Esmeraldas 108 B3
Esneux 22 H4
Espalion 26 H9
Espanola, *Canada* 96 D1
Espanola, *United States* 94 E3
Espelkamp 20 D4
Esperance 82 D6
Esperance Bay 82 D6
Esperanza 108 C5
Espinho 28 B4
Espírito Santo 108 J7
Espiritu Santo 80 G7
Esplanada 108 K6
Espoo 16 N6
Espungebera 76 E4
Es Samrā 62 D4
Essaouira 70 D2
Es Semara 70 C3
Essen, *Belgium* 22 G3
Essen, *Germany* 22 K3
Essequibo 108 F2
Esslingen 30 E2
Eşţahbānāt 63 F2
Este 30 G5
Esteila 28 H2
Estepona 28 E8
Esteros 110 J3
Estevan 92 F2
Estonia 16 M7
Estoril 28 A6
Estrecho de Le Maire 110 H10
Estrecho de Magallanes 110 G9
Estrela 28 C4
Estremoz 28 C6
Estuário do Rio Amazonaz 108 H3
Esztergom 34 F2
Étain 22 H5
Étampes 26 H5
Étang de Berre 26 L10
Étaples 22 D4
Etawah 56 C3
Ethiopia 66 G5
Etolin Strait 100 (1)D3
Etosha Pan 76 B3
Étretat 22 C5
Ettelbruck 20 B7
Ettlingen 20 D8
Eucla 82 E6
Euclid 96 D2
Eufaula 98 D3
Eufaula Lake 98 B2
Eugene 94 B2
Eupen 20 B6
Euphrates = Firat 60 H4
Eure 22 D6
Eureka, *Calif., United States* 94 B2
Eureka, *Mont., United States* 94 C1
Eureka, *Nev., United States* 100 C1
Eureka, *Ut., United States* 94 D3
Europe 16 G2
Europoort 22 F3
Euskirchen 20 B6
Eutin 20 F2
Eutsuk Lake 90 F6
Evans Strait 90 Q4
Evanston, *Ill., United States* 96 C2
Evanston, *Wyo., United States* 94 D2
Evansville 98 D2
Evaz 63 F3
Everett 94 B1
Everglades City 98 E4
Evergreen 98 D3
Evesham 22 A2
Évora 28 C6
Évreux 22 D5
Evron 26 E5
Evvoia 36 F6
Ewo 72 G5
Exaltación 108 D6
Exe 24 J11
Exeter 24 J11
Exmouth, *Australia* 82 B4
Exmouth, *United Kingdom* 24 J11
Exuma Sound 92 L7
Eyl 74 H2
Eyre Peninsula 82 G2
Ezine 36 J5

F

Faadippolu Atoll 56 B8
Fåborg 20 F1
Fabriano 30 H7
Fachi 70 H5
Fada 68 D4
Fada Ngourma 72 E2
Faenza 30 G6
Færingehavn = Kangerluarsoruseq 90 W4
Faeroes 14 D1
Fafanlap 55 D3
Făgăraş 34 M4
Fagernes 16 E6
Fagersta 16 H6
Făget 34 K4
Fagurhólsmýri 16 (1)E3
Fahraj 63 H2
Faial 70 (1)B2
Fairbanks 100 (1)H3
Fair Isle 24 L2
Fairlie 84 C7
Fairmont 96 B2
Faisalabad 56 B2
Faith 94 F1
Faizabad 56 D3
Fakfak 55 D3
Fakse 20 H1
Fakse Bugt 16 G9
Faku 48 G2
Falaise 22 B6
Falaise de Tiguidit 70 G5
Falconara Marittima 30 J7
Falcon Lake 98 B4
Fălesţi 34 Q2
Falfurrias 98 B4
Falkenberg 16 G8
Falkensee 20 J4
Falkland Islands 110 K9
Falkland Sound 110 J9
Falköping 16 G7
Fallingbostel 20 E4
Fallon 94 C3
Fall River 96 F2
Falls City 92 G3
Falmouth, *United Kingdom* 24 G11
Falmouth, *United States* 96 F2
Falster 20 H2
Fălticeni 34 P2
Falun 16 H6
Famagusta = Ammochostos 62 A1
Fanchang 48 F4
Fandriana 76 H4
Fangzheng 48 H1
Fannūj 58 G4
Fano 30 J7
Fanø 20 D1
Fanø Bugt 20 D1
Faradje 74 D3
Farafangana 76 H4
Farāh 58 H3
Farah Rud 58 H3
Faranah 72 B2
Fareham 22 A4
Farewell Spit 84 D5
Fargo 92 G2
Faribault 96 B2
Faridabad 56 C3
Farihy Alaotra 76 H3
Färjestaden 18 F1
Farmington, *Me., United States* 96 F2
Farmington, *N. Mex., United States* 100 E1
Farnborough 22 B3
Farne Islands 24 L6
Fårö 16 K8
Faro, *Brazil* 108 F4
Faro, *Portugal* 28 C7
Fårösund 16 K8
Farquhar Group 76 (2)B3
Farrāshband 63 E2
Farson 94 E2
Fasā 63 E2
Fasano 32 M8
Fatehgarh 56 C3
Fatehpur 56 D3
Făurei 34 Q4
Fauske 16 H3
Fauville-en-Caux 22 C5
Favara 32 H11
Faversham 22 C3
Favignana 32 G11
Faxaflói 16 (1)B2
Faya 68 C4
Fayette 98 D3
Fayetteville, *Ark., United States* 98 C2
Fayetteville, *N.C., United States* 96 E3
Fayetteville, *Tenn., United States* 98 D2
Faylakah 63 C2
Fažana 32 H4
Fdérik 70 C4
Featherston 84 E5
Fécamp 22 C5
Federated States of Micronesia 80 E5
Fedorovka 38 M4
Fehmarn 20 G2
Feijó 108 C5
Feilding 84 E5
Feira de Santana 108 K6
Feistritz 30 L3
Fejø 20 G2
Feldbach 30 L4
Feldkirch 30 E3
Feldkirchen 30 K4
Felidu Atoll 56 B8
Felixstowe 22 D3
Feltre 30 G4
Femø 20 G2
Femund 16 F5
Fengcheng 50 C3
Fenghua 48 G5
Fengning 48 F2
Feng Xian 48 D4
Feni 56 F4
Fenyang 48 E3
Feodosiya 60 F1
Feres 36 J4
Fergana 58 K1
Fergus Falls 92 G2
Ferkessédougou 72 C3
Ferlach 30 K4
Fermo 32 H5
Fernandina Beach 98 E3
Fernandópolis 110 L3
Ferrara 30 G6
Ferreira do Alentejo 28 B7
Ferrol 28 B1
Ferry Lake 98 C2
Fès 70 E2
Festus 96 B3
Feteşti 34 Q5
Fethiye 36 M8
Fetisovo 58 F1
Fetlar 24 M1
Feucht 20 G7
Feuchtwangen 20 F7
Feyzābād 58 K2
Fianarantsoa 76 H4
Fianga 74 B2
Fichē 74 F2
Fidenza 30 F6
Fieni 34 N4
Fier 36 B4
Figari 32 D7
Figeac 26 G9
Figline Valdarno 30 G7
Figueira da Foz 28 B4
Figueres 28 N2
Figuig 70 E2
Figuil 72 G3
Fiji 80 H8
Filadélfia 110 J3
Fil'akovo 18 J9
Filiaşi 34 L5
Filicudi 32 J10
Filtu 74 G2
Finale Ligure 30 D6
Findlay 96 D2
Fingoè 76 E3
Finike 36 N8
Finland 16 P3
Finlay 90 F5
Finley 82 J7
Finnsnes 16 K2
Finsterwalde 20 J5
Firat 60 H4
Firenze 30 G7
Firminy 26 K8
Firozabad 56 C3
Firozpur 56 B2
Firth of Clyde 24 G6
Firth of Forth 24 K5
Firth of Lorn 24 G5
Firth of Thames 84 E3
Fish 76 B5
Fisher Strait 90 Q4
Fishguard 24 H9
Fiskenæsset = Qeqertarsuatsiaat 90 W4
Fismes 22 F5
Fitzroy Crossing 82 E3
Fivizzano 30 F6
Fizi 74 D4
Flå 16 E6
Flaming Gorge Reservoir 94 E2
Flamingo 98 E4
Flannan Islands 24 E3
Flåsjön 16 H4
Flateyri 16 (1)B1
Flathead Lake 94 D1
Flat Point 84 E5
Flekkefjord 16 D7
Flensburg 20 E2
Flensburg Fjord 20 E2
Flers 22 B6
Flinders Island 82 J7
Flinders Ranges 82 G6
Flinders Reefs 82 J3
Flin Flon 90 L6
Flint, *United States* 96 D2
Flint Island 80 L7
Flirey 30 A2
Flöha 20 J6
Florac 26 J9
Florence = Firenze, *Italy* 30 G7
Florence, *Al., United States* 98 D3
Florence, *S.C., United States* 98 F3
Florencia 108 B3
Florennes 22 G4
Florenville 22 H5
Flores, *Azores* 70 (1)A2
Flores, *Indonesia* 55 B4
Flores Sea 55 A4
Floreşti 34 R2
Floriano 108 J5
Florianópolis 110 M4
Florida 98 E4
Florida 110 K5
Florida Keys 88 K7
Florina 36 D4
Florissant 96 B3
Florø 16 C6
Floydada 100 F2
Flumendosa 32 D9
Fly 55 F4
Foča 34 F6
Foça 36 J6
Focşani 34 Q4
Foggia 32 K7
Fogo 72 (1)B1
Fogo Island 90 W7
Fohnsdorf 30 K3
Föhr 20 D2
Foix 26 G11
Folegandros 36 G8
Foleyet 96 D1
Foligno 32 G6
Folkestone 22 D3
Folkston 98 E3
Follonica 32 E6
Fomboni 76 G2
Fond du Lac 96 C2
Fondi 32 H7
Fongafale 80 H6
Fontainebleau 26 H5
Fontana 32 M8
Fonte Boa 108 D4
Fontenay-le-Comte 26 E7
Fontur 16 (1)F1
Fonyód 32 M2
Forbach, *France* 22 J5
Forbach, *Germany* 22 L6
Forchheim 20 G7
Førde 16 C6
Fordyce 98 C3
Forest, *Canada* 96 D2
Forest, *United States* 98 D3
Forestville 96 G1
Forfar 24 K5
Forges-les-Eaux 22 D5
Forks 94 B1
Forlì 30 H6
Formazza 30 D4
Formentera 28 M6
Formia 32 H7
Formiga 110 M3
Formosa, *Brazil* 108 H7
Formosa, *Paraguay* 110 K4
Fornovo di Taro 30 F6
Forsayth 82 H3
Forssa 16 M6
Forst 20 K5
Forsyth 94 E1
Fort Abbas 56 B3
Fortaleza 108 K4
Fort Augustus 24 H4
Fort Bayne 96 C4
Fort Beaufort 76 D6
Fort Benton 94 D1
Fort Bragg 100 B1
Fort Chipewyan 90 J5
Fort Cobb Reservoir 98 B2
Fort Collins 94 E2
Fort-de-France 102 M6
Fort Dodge 96 B2
Forte dei Marmi 30 F7
Fortezza 30 G4
Fort Frances 96 B1
Fort George 90 R6
Fort Gibson Lake 98 B2
Fort Good Hope 90 F3
Forth 24 H5
Fort Hope 90 P6
Fortín Coronel Eugenio Garay 110 J3
Fort Kent 96 G1
Fort Lauderdale 98 E4
Fort Liard 90 G4
Fort Mackay 90 J5
Fort Macleod 94 D1
Fort McMurray 90 J5
Fort McPherson 100 (1)L2
Fort Munro 58 J4
Fort Myers 98 E4
Fort Nelson 90 G5
Fort Norman 100 (1)M3
Fort Payne 98 D3
Fort Peck Reservoir 94 E1
Fort Pierce 98 E4
Fort Pierre 94 F2
Fort Portal 74 E3
Fort Providence 90 H4
Fortrose 84 B8
Fort Rupert 90 R6
Fort St. John 90 G5
Fort Saint Lucie 98 E4
Fort Scott 98 C2
Fort Severn 90 P5
Fort Shevchenko 44 J9
Fort Simpson 90 G4
Fort Smith, *Canada* 90 J4
Fort Smith, *United States* 98 C2
Fort Stockton 100 F2
Fort Summer 100 F2
Fortuna 94 F1
Fortune Bay 90 V7
Fort Vermilion 90 H5
Fort Wayne 98 D1
Fort William 24 G5
Fort Worth 98 B3
Fort Yates 94 F1
Foshan 52 E2
Fosna 16 F5
Fossano 30 C6
Fossombrone 30 H7
Fougamou 72 G5
Fougères 26 D5
Foula 24 K1
Foulness 22 C3
Foumban 72 G3
Fourmies 22 G4
Fournoi 36 J7
Fouta Djallon 72 B2
Foveaux Strait 84 A8
Foxe Basin 90 R3
Foxe Channel 90 R4
Foxe Peninsula 90 R4
Fox Glacier 84 B6
Fox Islands 100 (1)D5
Foz 28 C1
Foz do Cunene 76 A3
Foz do Iguaçu 110 L4
Fraga 28 L3
Franca 110 M3
Francavilla al Mare 32 J6
France 26 G7
Franceville 72 G5
Francisco I. Madero 100 F4
Francistown 76 D4
Francs Peak 94 E2
Franeker 22 H1
Frankenberg 20 D5
Frankenthal 20 D7
Frankfort, *Ind., United States* 98 D1
Frankfort, *Ky., United States* 98 E2
Frankfurt, *Germany* 20 K4
Frankfurt, *Germany* 20 D6
Franklin, *N.C., United States* 96 D3
Franklin, *Tenn., United States* 96 C3

Franklin Bay 90 F2
Franklin D. Roosevelt Lake 94 C1
Franklin Mountains 90 F3
Franklin Strait 90 M2
Franz Josef Glacier 84 C6
Franz Josef Land = Zemlya Frantsa-Iosifa 44 J2
Fraser 90 G6
Fraserburg 76 C6
Fraserburgh 24 L4
Fraser Island 82 K5
Frasertown 84 F4
Frater 96 D1
Frauenfeld 30 D3
Fredensborg 18 B2
Frederick, *Md., United States* 96 E3
Frederick, *Okla., United States* 98 B3
Fredericksburg, *Tex., United States* 98 B3
Fredericksburg, *Va., United States* 96 E3
Fredericktown 96 B3
Fredericton 90 T7
Frederikshåb = Paamiut 90 X4
Frederikshavn 16 F8
Frederikssund 18 B2
Frederiksværk 16 G9
Fredrikstad 16 F7
Freeport, *Ill., United States* 96 C2
Freeport, *Tex., United States* 98 B4
Freeport City 98 F4
Freer 98 B4
Free State 76 D5
Freetown 72 B3
Fregenal de la Sierra 28 D6
Freiberg 20 J6
Freiburg 30 C3
Freilassing 30 H3
Freising 30 G2
Freistadt 30 K2
Fréjus 26 M10
Fremantle 82 C6
Fremont, *Calif., United States* 100 B1
Fremont, *Nebr., United States* 92 G3
Frenchglen 94 C2
French Guiana 108 G3
French Pass 84 D5
French Polynesia 80 L7
Frenda 70 F1
Fresnes-sur-Apances 30 A3
Fresnillo 102 D4
Fresno 100 C1
Fresno Reservoir 94 E1
Freudenstadt 30 D2
Freyung 20 J8
Frias 110 H4
Fribourg 30 C4
Friedburg 30 G2
Friedrichshafen 30 E3
Friesach 30 K4
Friesoythe 20 C3
Frisian Islands 22 H1
Fritzlar 20 E5
Frobisher Bay 90 T4
Frolovo 38 H5
Frome 24 K10
Frontera 102 F5
Frontignan 26 J10
Frosinone 32 H7
Frøya 16 D5
Fruges 22 E4
Frýdek Místek 18 H8
Fudai 50 L4
Fuding 48 G5
Fuengirola 28 F8
Fuentesauco 28 E3
Fuerte Olimpo 110 K3
Fuerteventura 70 C3
Fugu 48 E3
Fuhai 44 R8
Fujieda 50 K6
Fujin 46 N7
Fuji-san 50 K6
Fukuchiyama 50 H6
Fukue 50 E7
Fukue-jima 50 E7
Fukui 50 J5
Fukuoka 50 F7
Fukushima 50 L5
Fukuyama 50 G6
Fulda 20 E6
Fulda 20 E6
Fuling 48 D5
Fulton 98 D2
Funabashi 50 L6
Funafuti 80 H6
Funchal 70 B2
Fundão 28 C4
Funing 52 D2
Funtua 72 F2
Furano 50 M2
Fürg 63 F2
Furmanovka 44 N9
Furmanovo 38 J5
Furneaux Group 82 J8
Furqlus 62 E2
Fürstenberg 20 J3
Fürstenfeldbruck 30 G2
Fürstenwalde 20 K4
Fürth 20 F7
Furukawa 50 L4
Fushun 50 B3
Fusong 50 D2
Füssen 30 F3
Futog 34 G4
Fuxhou 48 F5
Fu Xian 48 D3
Fuxin 48 G2
Fuyang 48 F4
Fuyu 48 G1
Fuyun 44 R8
Fuzhou 52 F1
Fyn 20 F1
Fynshav 20 F2

G

Gaalkacyo 74 H2
Gabès 70 H2
Gabon 72 G5
Gaborone 76 D4
Gābrik 63 H4
Gabrovo 34 N7
Gacé 22 C6
Gacko 34 F6
Gäddede 16 H4
Gadsden 98 D3
Găeşti 34 N5
Gaeta 32 H7
Gafsa 70 G2
Gaggenau 30 D2
Gagnoa 72 C3
Gagra 60 J2
Gaildorf 30 E2
Gaillac 26 G10
Gainesville, *Fla., United States* 98 E4
Gainesville, *Ga., United States* 98 E3
Gainesville, *Mo., United States* 98 C2
Gainesville, *Tex., United States* 98 B3
Gai Xian 50 B3
Gala 56 E3
Galana 74 F4
Galanta 30 N2
Galapagos Islands = Islas Galápagos 108 (1)B1
Galashiels 24 K6
Galatas 36 F7
Galaţi 34 R4
Galdhøpiggen 16 D6
Galena 100 (1)F3
Galesburg 96 B2
Galich 38 H3
Gallabat 68 G5
Galle 56 D7
Gallipoli 32 N8
Gallipolis 98 E2
Gällivare 16 L3
Gallup 100 E1
Galtat Zemmour 70 C3
Galveston Bay 92 G6
Galway 24 C8
Galway Bay 24 C8
Gamalakhe 76 E6
Gambēla 74 E2
Gambell 46 Z4
Gambier Islands 80 N8
Gamboma 74 B4
Gamboula 74 B3
Gan 46 L7
Ganado 100 E1
Gäncä 60 M3
Gandajika 74 C5
Gander 90 W7
Ganderkesee 20 D3
Gandesa 28 L3
Gāndhīdhām 56 B4
Gandhinagar 56 B4
Gandía 28 K6
Gandu 108 K6
Ganganagar 56 B3
Gangara 72 F2
Gangdise Shan 56 D2
Ganges 26 J10
Ganges 56 E3
Gangi 32 J11
Gangtok 56 E3
Gannett Peak 94 E2
Ganta 72 C3
Ganye 72 G3
Ganzhou 48 E5
Gao 70 E5
Gaoual 70 C6
Gap 30 B6
Gapan 52 G3
Garanhuns 108 K5
Garba 72 J3
Garbsen 20 E4
Gardelegen 20 G4
Garden City 94 F3
Gardēz 58 J3
Gardone Val Trompia 30 F5
Gargždai 18 L2
Gariau 55 D3
Garies 76 B6
Garissa 74 F4
Garland 98 B3
Garlasco 30 D5
Garliava 18 N3
Garmisch-Partenkirchen 30 G3
Garnett 98 B2
Garonne 26 E9
Garoowe 74 H2
Garoua 72 G3
Garoua Boulaï 72 G3
Garry Lake 90 L3
Garsen 74 G4
Garut 54 D4
Garwa 56 D4
Garwolin 18 L6
Gary 92 J3
Garyarsa 56 D2
Garzê 48 B4
Gasan Kuli 58 F2
Gasht 58 H4
Gashua 72 G2
Gastonia 98 E2
Gastre 110 H7
Gatchina 38 F3
Gateshead 24 L7
Gatesville 98 B3
Gatineau 96 E1
Gatrūyeh 63 F2
Gauja 16 N8
Gaula 16 F5
Gaurella 56 D4
Gauteng 76 D5
Gava 28 N3
Gāvbandī 63 E3
Gavdos 36 G10
Gävle 16 J6
Gawler 82 G6
Gawler Ranges 82 G6
Gaxun Nur 48 C2
Gaya, *India* 56 E4
Gaya, *Niger* 72 E2
Gaylord 96 D1
Gayndah 82 K5
Gayny 38 K2
Gaza 62 B5
Gaz-Achak 44 L9
Gazandzhyk 44 K10
Gaza Strip 62 B5
Gaziantep 60 G5
Gazipaşa 36 Q8
Gazli 44 L9
Gaz Şāleḩ 63 G2
Gbaaka 72 C3
Gbarnga 72 C3
Gdańsk 18 H3
Gdov 16 P7
Gdyel 28 K9
Gdynia 18 H3
Gebel el Tîh 62 A7
Gebel Halâl 62 A6
Gebel Katherina 68 F2
Gebel Yi'allaq 62 A6
Gebze 36 M4
Gedaref 68 G5
Gediz 36 M6
Gediz 36 K6
Gedser 20 G2
Geel 22 H3
Geelong 82 H7
Geesthacht 20 F3
Gê'gyai 56 D2
Geidam 72 G2
Geilenkirchen 22 J4
Geilo 16 E6
Geinhausen 20 E6
Geislingen 30 E2
Geita 74 E4
Gejiu 52 C2
Gela 32 J11
Geladī 74 H2
Geldern 22 J3
Geleen 22 H4
Gelendzhik 60 H1
Gelibolu 36 J4
Gelibolu Yarimadasi 36 J4
Gelsenkirchen 22 K3
Gembloux 22 G4
Gembu 72 G3
Gemena 74 B3
Gemlik 36 M4
Gemlik Körfezi 36 L4
Gemona del Friuli 30 J4
Genalē Wenz 74 G2
General Acha 110 J6
General Alvear 110 H6
General Pico 110 J6
General Pinedo 110 J4
General Roca 110 H6
General Santos 52 H5
Geneva 96 E2
Genève 30 B4
Gengma 52 B2
Genil 28 F7
Genk 22 H4
Genoa = Genova 30 D6
Genova 30 D6
Gent 22 F3
Genteng 54 D4
Genthin 20 H4
Geographe Bay 82 B6
George 76 C6
George 90 T5
George Town, *Australia* 82 J8
George Town, *Malaysia* 54 C1
George Town, *The Bahamas* 98 F5
Georgetown, *Australia* 82 H3
Georgetown, *Guyana* 108 F2
Georgetown, *The Gambia* 72 B2
Georgetown, *Ky., United States* 98 E2
Georgetown, *S.C., United States* 98 F3
Georgetown, *Tex., United States* 98 B3
George West 98 B4
Georgia 60 K2
Georgia 98 E3
Georgian Bay 96 D1
Gera 20 H6
Geraldine 84 C7
Geraldton, *Australia* 82 B5
Geraldton, *Canada* 92 J2
Gérardmer 30 B2
Gerāsh 63 F3
Gerede 60 E3
Gerefsried 30 G3
Gereshk 58 H3
Gérgal 28 H7
Gerik 52 C5
Gerlach 94 C2
Germantown 96 C3
Germany 20 E6
Germencik 36 K7
Germering 30 G2
Germersheim 22 L5
Gernika 28 H1
Gerolzhofen 20 F7
Gêrzê 56 D2
Geser 55 D3
Getafe 28 G4
Gettysburg 94 F2
Getxo 28 H1
Geugnon 26 K7
Gevaş 60 K4
Gevgelija 36 E3
Gewanē 68 H5
Geyik Dağ 36 Q8
Geyser 94 D1
Geyve 36 N4
Ghabāghib 62 D3
Ghadāmis 70 G2
Ghadīr Minqār 62 E3
Ghana 72 D3
Ghanzi 76 C4
Gharandal 62 C6
Ghardaïa 70 F2
Gharo 58 J5
Gharyān 70 H2
Ghāt 68 B2
Ghazaouet 70 E1
Ghaziabad 56 C3
Ghazipur 56 D3
Ghazn 58 J3
Gheorgheni 34 N3
Gherla 34 L2
Ghizar 56 B1
Ghotāru 56 B3
Ghōwrī 63 F2
Ghunthur 62 E2
Giannitsa 36 E4
Giannutri 32 F6
Giarre 32 K11
Gibraleón 28 D7
Gibraltar 28 E8
Gibson Desert 82 D4
Gideån 16 K5
Gien 26 H6
Gießen 20 D6
Gifhorn 20 F4
Gifu 50 J6
Gigha 24 G6
Giglio 32 E6
Giglio Castello 32 E6
Gijón 28 E1
Gila 100 E2
Gila Bend 100 D2
Gilan Garb 60 L6
Gilău 34 L3
Gilazi 60 N3
Gilbert Islands 80 H5
Gilbués 108 H5
Gilching 30 G2
Gilf Kebir Plateau 68 E3
Gilgandra 82 J6
Gilgit 56 B1
Gilimanuk 54 E4
Gillam 90 N5
Gillette 94 E2
Gillingham 22 C3
Gills Rock 96 C1
Gilroy 94 B3
Gîmbi 74 F2
Gimli 90 M6
Gimol'skoe Ozero 16 R5
Gīnīr 74 G2
Gioia del Colle 32 L8
Gioia Tauro 32 K10
Gioura 36 F5
Giresun 60 H3
Girga 68 F2
Girona 28 N3
Gironde 26 E8
Girvan 24 H6
Gisborne 84 G4
Gisenyi 74 D4
Gitega 74 D4
Giurgiu 34 N6
Givet 22 G4
Givors 26 K8
Giyon 74 F2
Gizhiga 46 U4
Gizhiginskaya Guba 46 T4
Giżycko 18 L3
Gjiri i Vlorës 36 B4
Gjirokaster 36 C4
Gjoa Haven 90 M3
Gjøvik 16 F6
Glacier Peak 94 B1
Gladstone 82 K4
Glamoč 34 D5
Glan 55 C1
Glan 20 C7
Glarner Alpen 30 D4
Glasgow, *United Kingdom* 24 H6
Glasgow, *Ky., United States* 96 C3
Glasgow, *Mont., United States* 94 E1
Glauchau 20 H6
Glazov 44 J6
Gleisdorf 30 L3
Glendale, *Ariz., United States* 100 D2
Glendale, *Calif., United States* 100 C2
Glendambo 82 G6
Glendive 94 F1
Glenmorgan 82 J5
Glennallen 100 (1)H3
Glenn Innes 82 K5
Glenrothes 24 J5
Glens Falls 96 F2
Glenwood, *Ark., United States* 96 B4
Glenwood, *Minn., United States* 96 A1
Glenwood, *N. Mex., United States* 100 E2
Glenwood Springs 94 E3
Glidden 96 B1
Glina 30 M5
Gliwice 18 H7
Glodeni 34 Q2
Głogów 18 F6
Glomfjord 16 H3
Glomma 16 F5
Glorieuses 66 H7
Gloucester, *United Kingdom* 24 K10
Gloucester, *United States* 96 F2

Głowno 18 J6
Głuchołazy 18 G7
Glückstadt 20 E3
Gmünd, *Austria* 30 J4
Gmünd, *Austria* 30 L2
Gmunden 30 J3
Gniezno 18 G5
Gnjilane 36 D2
Gnoien 20 H3
Goalpara 56 F3
Goba 74 F2
Gobabis 76 B4
Gobernador Gregores 110 G8
Gobi Desert 48 C2
Gobo 50 H7
Gobustan 58 E1
Goce Delčev 36 F3
Goch 22 J3
Gochas 76 B4
Godbout 96 G1
Godé 74 G2
Goderich 96 D2
Godhra 56 B4
Gödöllő 34 G2
Gods Lake 90 N6
Godthåb = Nuuk 90 W4
Goeree 22 F3
Goes 22 F3
Gogama 96 D1
Goiânia 108 H7
Goiás 108 G6
Goiás 108 G7
Gökçeada 36 H4
Gökova Körfezi 36 K8
Göksun 60 G5
Golaghat 56 F3
Golan Heights 62 C3
Golbāf 63 G2
Gölbasi 60 G5
Gol'chikha 44 Q3
Gölcük 36 K5
Gołdap 18 M3
Gold Coast 82 K5
Golden Bay 84 D5
Goldendale 94 B1
Golden Gate 100 B1
Goldfield 94 C3
Goldsboro 96 E3
Goldsworthy 82 C4
Göle 60 K3
Goleniów 18 D4
Golestānak 63 F1
Golfe d'Ajaccio 32 C7
Golfe de Gabès 70 H2
Golfe de Hammamet 70 H1
Golfe de Porto 32 C6
Golfe de Sagone 32 C6
Golfe de Saint-Malo 26 C5
Golfe de Tunis 32 E11
Golfe de Valinco 32 C7
Golfe du Lion 26 J10
Golfo de Almería 28 H8
Golfo de Batabanó 102 H4
Golfo de Cádiz 28 C7
Golfo de California 102 B3
Golfo de Chiriquí 102 H7
Golfo de Corcovado 110 F7
Golfo de Cupica 108 B2
Golfo de Fonseca 102 G6
Golfo de Guayaquil 108 A4
Golfo de Honduras 102 G5
Golfo del Darién 108 B2
Golfo dell' Asinara 32 C7
Golfo de los Mosquitos 108 A2
Golfo de Mazarrón 28 J7
Golfo de Morrosquillo 108 B1
Golfo de Panamá 102 J7
Golfo de Penas 110 F8
Golfo de San Jorge 110 H8
Golfo de Santa Clara 100 D2
Golfo de Tehuantepec 102 E5
Golfo de València 28 L5
Golfo de Venezuela 108 C1
Golfo di Augusta 32 K11
Golfo di Catania 32 K11
Golfo di Gaeta 32 H7
Golfo di Gela 32 J11
Golfo di Genova 32 C4
Golfo di Manfredonia 32 L7
Golfo di Olbia 32 D8
Golfo di Oristano 32 C9
Golfo di Orosei 32 D8
Golfo di Palmas 32 C10
Golfo di Policastro 32 K9
Golfo di Salerno 32 J8
Golfo di Sant'Eufemia 32 K10
Golfo di Squillace 32 L10
Golfo di Taranto 32 L8
Golfo di Trieste 30 J5
Golfo di Venezia 30 H5
Golfo San Matías 110 J6
Gölhisar 36 M8
Golin Baixing 50 A1
Gölköy 60 G3
Gölmarmara 36 K6
Golyshmanovo 44 M6
Goma 74 D4
Gombe 72 G2
Gombi 72 G2
Gomera 70 B3
Gómez Palacio 100 F3
Gonam 46 M5
Gonbad-e Kavus 58 G2
Gonda 56 D3
Gonder 68 G5
Gondia 56 D4
Gondomar 28 B3
Gönen 36 K4
Gonfreville-Orcher 22 C5
Gongga Shan 48 C5
Gonghe 48 C3
Gongliu 44 Q9
Gongpoquan 48 B2
Gongshan 52 B1
Gonzáles 92 G7
Gonzales 98 B4
González 100 G4
Goodland 94 F3
Goolgowi 82 J6
Goomalling 82 C6
Goondiwindi 82 K5
Goose Lake 94 B2
Göppingen 30 E2
Góra 18 F6
Gora Bazardyuzi 60 M3
Gora Kamen 44 S4
Gorakhpur 56 D3
Gora Ledyanaya 46 W4
Gora Pobeda 46 R4
Gora Yenashimskiy Polkan 44 S6
Goražde 34 F6
Gorbitsa 46 K6
Goré 72 H3
Gorē 74 F2
Gore 84 B8
Gorgān 58 F2
Gorgona 30 E7
Gori 60 L2
Gorinchem 22 H3
Goris 60 M4
Gorizia 30 J5
Gorki 38 N1
Gorlice 18 L8
Görlitz 18 D6
Gorna Orjakhovica 34 N6
Gornji Milanovac 34 H5
Gorno-Altaysk 44 R7
Gorodets 38 H3
Gorontalo 55 B2
Goryachiy Klyuch 58 H1
Gory Belukha 44 R8
Gory Ulutau 38 N5
Gorzów Wielkopolski 18 E5
Goslar 20 F5
Gospić 32 K4
Gosport 26 D3
Gossau 30 E3
Gossi 72 D1
Gostivar 36 C3
Gostyń 18 G6
Gostynin 18 J5
Göteborg 16 F8
Gotha 20 F6
Gothèye 72 E2
Gotland 16 K8
Gotō-rettō 50 E7
Gotska Sandön 16 K7
Göttingen 20 E5
Gouda 22 G2
Gough Island 66 B10
Goundam 70 E5
Gouraya 28 M8
Gourcy 72 D2
Gourdon 26 G9
Gournay-en-Bray 22 D5
Governador Valadares 108 J7
Governor's Harbour 98 F4
Govorovo 46 M3
Gowārān 58 J4
Goya 110 K4
Gozha Co 56 D1
Gozo = Gwardex 32 J12
Graaff-Reinet 76 C6
Grabovica 34 K5
Gračac 30 L6
Gračanica 34 F5
Gradačac 34 F5
Gräfenhainichen 20 H5
Grafton, *Australia* 82 K5
Grafton, *United States* 94 G1
Graham Island 100 (1)L5
Grajaú 108 H5
Grajewo 18 M4
Gram 20 E1
Gramat 26 G9
Grampian Mountains 24 H5
Granada, *Nicaragua* 102 G6
Granada, *Spain* 28 G7
Granby 96 F1
Gran Canaria 70 B3
Grand Bahama 98 F4
Grand Ballon 26 N6
Grand Bank 90 V7
Grand Canyon 94 D3
Grande, *Bolivia* 108 E7
Grande, *Brazil* 108 J6
Grande Cache 90 H6
Grande Prairie 90 H5
Grand Erg de Bilma 70 H5
Grand Erg Occidental 70 E3
Grand Erg Oriental 70 F3
Grand Falls, *N.B., Canada* 96 G1
Grand Falls, *Nfld., Canada* 90 V7
Grand Forks, *Canada* 92 C2
Grand Forks, *United States* 94 G1
Grand Haven 96 C2
Grand Island 94 G2
Grand Junction 94 E3
Grand Marais, *Mich., United States* 96 C1
Grand Marais, *Minn., United States* 96 B1
Grand-Mère 96 F1
Grândola 28 B6
Grand Portage 96 C1
Grand Rapids, *Canada* 90 M6
Grand Rapids, *Mich., United States* 96 C2
Grand Rapids, *Minn., United States* 96 B1
Grand Teton 94 D2
Grangeville 94 C1
Granite Falls 96 A2
Granollers 28 N3
Gran Paradiso 30 C5
Grantham 24 M9
Grants 100 E1
Grants Pass 94 B2
Granville 26 D5
Granville Lake 90 M5
Gräsö 16 K6
Grasse 30 B7
Grassrange 94 E1
Grass Valley 94 B3
Graulhet 26 G10
Graus 28 L2
Gravelines 22 E3
Gravenhurst 96 E2
Gravesend 22 C3
Gravina in Puglia 32 L8
Gray 26 L6
Grayling 96 D2
Grays 22 C3
Grays Lake 94 D2
Grayville 96 C3
Graz 30 L3
Great Abaco 98 F4
Great Artesian Basin 82 H4
Great Australian Bight 82 E6
Great Bahama Bank 102 J4
Great Barrier Island 84 E3
Great Barrier Reef 82 J2
Great Basin 94 C3
Great Bear Lake 100 (1)M2
Great Bend 100 G1
Great Dividing Range 82 J4
Greater Antilles 102 J5
Greater Sunda Islands 80 B6
Great Exhibition Bay 84 D2
Great Exuma 92 L7
Great Falls 94 D1
Great Inagua 102 K4
Great Karoo 76 C6
Great Malvern 24 K9
Great Nicobar 56 F7
Great Ouse 24 N9
Great Plains 94 F2
Great Rift Valley 74 E5
Great Salt Lake 94 D2
Great Salt Lake Desert 94 D2
Great Sand Sea 68 D2
Great Sandy Desert 82 D4
Great Slave Lake 88 N3
Great Victoria Desert 82 E5
Great Wall 48 C3
Great Yarmouth 24 P9
Greece 36 D5
Greeley 94 F2
Green 94 D3
Green Bay 96 C2
Greenfield 98 D2
Greenland 88 G2
Greenland Sea 88 B2
Greenock 24 H6
Green River, *Wyo., United States* 94 E2
Green River, *Ut., United States* 94 D3
Greensboro 98 F2
Greensburg, *Ind., United States* 98 D2
Greensburg, *Pa., United States* 96 E2
Greenvale 82 J3
Green Valley 102 B2
Greenville, *Liberia* 72 C3
Greenville, *Al., United States* 98 D3
Greenville, *Fla., United States* 98 E3
Greenville, *Miss., United States* 98 C3
Greenville, *N.C., United States* 96 E3
Greenville, *S.C., United States* 98 E3
Greenwood, *Miss., United States* 98 C3
Greenwood, *S.C., United States* 98 E3
Gregory 94 G2
Gregory Lake 82 E4
Greifswald 20 J2
Greifswalder Bodden 20 J2
Greiz 20 H6
Grenada 108 E1
Grenada 92 J5
Grenchen 30 C3
Grenoble 26 L8
Gretna 98 C4
Greve in Chianti 30 G7
Greven 22 K2
Grevena 36 D4
Grevenbroich 22 J3
Grevesmühlen 20 G3
Greybull 94 E2
Greymouth 84 C6
Grey Range 82 H5
Griesheim 20 D7
Grieskirchen 30 J2
Grigoriopol 34 S2
Grimma 20 H5
Grimmen 20 J2
Grimsby 24 M8
Grímsey 16 (1)D1
Grímsstaðir 16 (1)E2
Grímsvötn 16 (1)E2
Grindsted 16 E9
Grobina 18 L1
Gröbming 30 J3
Grodekovo 48 J2
Grodzisk Wielkopolski 18 F5
Grójec 18 K6
Gronau 20 C4
Groningen 20 B3
Groote Eylandt 82 G2
Grootfontein 76 B3
Großenhain 20 J5
Großer Arber 20 J7
Großer Beerberg 20 F6
Grosseto 32 F6
Groß-Gerau 20 D7
Großglockner 30 H3
Groß Mohrdorf 20 H2
Groswater Bay 90 V6
Grottaglie 32 M8
Groupe Actéon 80 N8
Grove Hill 98 D3
Groznyy 60 L2
Grubišno Polje 34 E4
Grudovo 36 K2
Grudziądz 18 H4
Grünau 76 B5
Grünberg 20 D6
Gryazi 38 G4
Gryazovets 38 H3
Gryfice 18 E4
Gryfino 20 K3
Grytøya 16 J2
Grytviken 110 P9
Gstaad 30 C4
Guadalajara, *Mexico* 102 D4
Guadalajara, *Spain* 28 G4
Guadalcanal 80 F7
Guadalope 28 K4
Guadalquivir 28 E7
Guadalupe 102 E3
Guadalupe 102 A3
Guadeloupe 106 E2
Guadiana 28 C7
Guadix 28 G7
Guaíra 110 L3
Guajará Mirim 108 D6
Guajarraã 108 D5
Guam 80 E4
Guanambi 108 J6
Guanare 108 D2
Guane 102 H4
Guangshui 48 E4
Guangyuan 48 D4
Guangzhou 52 E2
Guanipa 108 E2
Guanling 48 D5
Guantánamo 102 J4
Guanyun 48 F4
Guaporé 108 E6
Guaqui 108 D7
Guarabira 108 K5
Guarda 28 C4
Guardo 28 F2
Guasave 92 E6
Guastalla 30 F6
Guatemala 102 F5
Guatemala 102 F6
Guaviare 108 D3
Guayaquil 108 B4
Guayaramerín 108 D6
Guaymas 100 D3
Guba, *Demcratic Republic of Congo* 74 D6
Guba, *Ethiopia* 68 G5
Guba Buorkhaya 46 N2
Gubakha 38 L3
Guban 74 G2
Gubbi 56 C6
Gubbio 30 H7
Guben 20 K5
Gubin 18 D6
Gudaut'a 60 J2
Gudbransdalen 16 E6
Gudermes 60 M2
Gudvangen 16 D6
Guebwiller 20 C9
Guéckédou 72 B3
Guelma 70 G1
Guelph 96 D2
Guérande 26 C6
Guéret 26 B7
Guernsey 94 F2
Guernsey 26 C4
Guérou 70 C5
Guerrero Negro 100 D3
Gugē 74 F2
Güh Küh 58 G4
Guiana 102 L7
Guiana Highlands 108 F3
Guider 72 G3
Guiglo 72 C3
Guijuelo 28 E4
Guildford 24 M10
Guilianova 32 H6
Guilin 52 E1
Guillaumes 30 B6
Guillestre 30 B6
Guimarães 28 B3
Guinea 72 B2
Guinea-Bissau 72 A2
Güines 102 H4
Guingamp 26 B5
Güiria 108 E1
Guise 22 F5
Guitiriz 28 C1
Guiyang 48 D5
Gujranwala 56 B2
Gujrat 56 B2
Gulang 48 C3
Gulbarga 56 C5
Gulbene 16 P8
Gulf of Aden 58 E7
Gulf of Alaska 100 (1)H4
Gulf of Aqaba 58 B4
Gulf of Boothia 90 N2
Gulf of Bothnia 16 K6
Gulf of Carpentaria 82 G2
Gulf of Finland 16 M7
Gulf of Gdansk 18 J3
Gulf of Guinea 72 D4
Gulf of Mannar 56 C7
Gulf of Martaban 52 B3
Gulf of Mexico 102 F3
Gulf of Oman 63 G4
Gulf of Riga 16 M8
Gulf of St. Lawrence 90 U7
Gulf of Santa Catalina 100 C2
Gulf of Thailand 52 C4
Gulf of Tongking 52 D3
Gulfport 98 D3
Gulistan 44 M9
Gülşehir 36 S6
Gulu 74 E3

Gülübovo 36 H2
Gumdag 58 F2
Gumel 72 F2
Gumla 56 D4
Gummersbach 22 K3
Gummi 72 F2
Gümüşhane 60 H3
Guna 56 C4
Guna Terara 68 G5
Gungu 74 B5
Gunib 60 M2
Gunnbjørns Fjeld 112 (1)U2
Gunnedah 82 K6
Gunnison, *Colo., United States* 94 E3
Gunnison, *Ut., United States* 94 D3
Gunong Kinabalu 54 F1
Guntakal 56 C5
Guntur 56 D5
Gunung Kerinci 54 C3
Gunung Korbu 54 C2
Gunung Kwoka 55 D3
Gunung Leuser 54 B2
Gunung Mekongga 55 B3
Gunung Mulu 54 E2
Gunung Pangrango 54 D4
Gunungsitoli 54 B2
Gunung Togwomeri 55 D3
Günzburg 30 F2
Gunzenhausen 20 F7
Guoyang 48 F4
Gura Humorului 34 N2
Gurk 30 K4
Gurskoye 46 P6
Gürün 60 G4
Gurupi 108 H4
Gusau 72 F2
Gusev 18 M3
Gushgy 58 H2
Gusinoozersk 46 H6
Guspini 32 C9
Güssing 30 M3
Güstrow 18 B4
Gütersloh 20 D5
Guthrie, *Okla., United States* 94 G3
Guthrie, *Tex., United States* 100 F2
Gutsuo 56 E3
Guttenberg 96 B2
Guwahati 56 F3
Guyana 108 F2
Guyang 48 E2
Guymon 100 F1
Guyuan 48 D3
Guzar 58 J2
Gvardeysk 18 L3
Gwadar 58 H4
Gwalior 56 C3
Gwanda 76 D4
Gwardex 32 J12
Gwda 18 F4
Gweebarra Bay 24 C7
Gweru 76 D3
Gyangzê 56 E3
Gyaring Hu 48 B4
Gyaros 36 G7
Gyda 44 P3
Gydanskiy Poluostrov 44 P3
Gyirong 56 E3
Gyldenløves Fjord 90 Y4
Gympie 82 K5
Gyomaendrőd 34 H3
Gyöngyös 34 G2
Győr 34 E2
Gypsumville 90 M6
Gytheio 36 E8
Gyula 34 J3
Gyumri 60 K3
Gyzylarbat 58 G2

H

Haapajärvi 16 N5
Haapsalu 16 M7
Haar 30 G2
Haarlem 22 G2
Haast 84 B6
Habahe 44 R8
Habarūt 58 F6
Habaswein 74 F3
Habbān 58 E7
Habbānīyah 60 K7
Habirag 48 F2
Habomai-Shoto 46 R8
Haboro 50 L1
Hachijō-jima 50 K7
Hachinohe 50 L3
Hachiōji 50 K6
Hadadong 44 Q9
Hadejia 72 G2
Hadejia 72 F2
Hadera 62 B4
Haderslev 20 E1
Ḩaḑramaut 58 E6
Hadhunmathi Atoll 56 B8
Hadilik 44 R10
Hadjout 28 N8
Haeju 50 C4
Haenam 50 D6
Ḩafar al Bāţin 63 A2
Hafik 60 G4
Hafnarfjörđhur 16 (1)C2
Haft Gel 63 C1
Hagen 22 K3
Hagenow 20 G3
Hāgere Hiywet 74 F2
Hagerstown 96 E3
Ha Giang 48 C6
Haguenau 22 K6
Haicheng 50 B3
Haifa = Ḩefa 62 B4
Haikou 52 E3
Hā'il 58 D4
Hailar 46 K7
Hailey 94 D2
Hailong 50 C2
Hailuoto 16 N4
Hainan 52 D3
Haines Junction 100 (1)K3
Haining 48 G4
Hai Phong 52 D2
Haiti 102 K5
Haiya 68 G4
Hajdúböszörmény 34 J2
Hajdúhadház 18 L10
Hajdúnánás 18 L10
Hajdúszoboszló 18 L10
Hajipur 56 E3
Ḩājjīābād 63 F2
Hajmah 58 G6
Hajnówka 18 N5
Haka 56 F4
Hakkâri 60 K5
Hakodate 50 L3
Ḩalab 60 G5
Ḩalabān 68 H3
Ḩalabja 60 L6
Halaib 68 G3
Halba 62 D2
Halberstadt 20 G5
Halden 16 F7
Haldensleben 20 G4
Halifax 90 U8
Halifax Bay 82 J3
Hall 30 G3
Hall Beach 90 Q3
Halle 22 G4
Hallein 30 J3
Halligen 20 D2
Hallock 94 G1
Hall Peninsula 90 T4
Halls Creek 82 E3
Halmahera 55 C2
Halmahera Sea 55 C3
Halmstad 18 B1
Haltern 22 K3
Hamada 50 G6
Hamadān 58 E3
Hamaguir 70 E2
Hamāh 60 G6
Hamamatsu 50 J6
Hamar 16 F6
Hamarøy 16 H2
Hamatonbetsu 50 M1
Hambantota 56 D7
Hamburg, *Germany* 20 E3
Hamburg, *Ark., United States* 98 C3
Hamburg, *N.Y., United States* 96 E2
Hämeenlinna 16 N6
Hameln 20 E4
Hamersley Range 82 C4
Hamhŭng 50 D3
Hami 44 S9
Hamīd 68 F3
Hamilton, *Australia* 82 H7
Hamilton, *Bermuda* 102 M2
Hamilton, *Canada* 96 E2
Hamilton, *New Zealand* 84 E3
Hamilton, *Al., United States* 98 D3
Hamilton, *Mont., United States* 94 D1
Hamilton, *Oh., United States* 96 D3
Hamina 16 P6
Hamirpur 56 D3
Hamm 20 C5
Hammada du Drâa 70 D3
Hammam Bou Hadjar 28 K9
Hammamet 32 E12
Hammam Lif 70 H1
Hammelburg 20 E6
Hammerfest 16 M1
Hammer Springs 84 D6
Hampden 84 C7
Hāmūn-e Jaz Mūrīān 63 H3
Ḩanalc 68 G2
Hanamaki 50 L4
Hanau 20 D6
Hancheng 48 E3
Hancock 96 C1
Handan 48 E3
Handeni 74 F5
Handerslev 16 E9
Handlová 18 H9
Hanford 100 C1
Hangayn Nuruu 44 T8
Hangu 48 F3
Hangzhou 48 F4
Hanīdh 63 C3
Hanko 16 M7
Hanksville 94 D3
Hanna 90 K6
Hannibal 98 C2
Hannover 20 E4
Hanö 18 D2
Hanöbukten 18 D2
Ha Nôi 52 D2
Hanoi = Ha Nôi 52 D2
Hanover 96 F2
Han Shui 48 D4
Hanson Bay 84 (1)B1
Hanumangarh 56 B3
Hanzhong 48 D4
Hao 80 M7
Häora 56 E4
Haouza 70 C3
Haparanda 16 N4
Hāpoli 56 F3
Hapur 56 C3
Ḩaraḑ, *Saudi Arabia* 58 E5
Ḩaraḑ, *Yemen* 68 H4
Haramachi 50 L5
Harare 76 E3
Harbin 48 H1
Harbour Breton 90 V7
Harburg 20 F3
Hardangerfjorden 16 C7
Hardangervidda 16 D6
Hardenberg 22 J2
Harderwijk 22 H2
Hardin 94 E1
Hardy 98 C2
Haren 22 K2
Härer 74 G2
Hargeysa 74 G2
Har Hu 48 B3
Haridwar 56 C3
Harihari 84 C6
Harima-nada 50 H6
Hari Rud 58 H3
Harlan 96 A2
Hârlău 34 P2
Harlem 94 E1
Harlingen, *Netherlands* 22 H1
Harlingen, *United States* 98 B4
Harlow 24 N10
Harlowtown 94 E1
Harmanli 36 H3
Harney Basin 92 B3
Harney Lake 94 C2
Härnösand 16 J5
Har Nur 46 K7
Har Nuur 44 S8
Haro 28 H2
Harricanaw 90 R6
Harrisburg, *Ill., United States* 96 C3
Harrisburg, *Pa., United States* 98 F1
Harrison 96 B3
Harrison Bay 100 (1)G1
Harrisville 96 D2
Harrogate 24 L8
Har Saggi 62 B6
Harsin 60 M6
Hârşova 34 Q5
Harstad 16 J2
Hartberg 30 L3
Hartford 96 F2
Hartland Point 24 H10
Hartlepool 24 L7
Har Us Nuur 44 S8
Harvey 94 G1
Harwich 22 D3
Harz 20 F5
Hāsā 62 C6
Haselünne 20 C4
Hashtpar 60 N5
Hāsik 58 G6
Haskell 98 B3
Haskovo 36 H3
Haslemere 22 B3
Hassan 56 C6
Hasselfelde 20 F5
Hasselt 22 H4
Haßfurt 20 F6
Hassi Bel Guebbour 70 G3
Hassi Messaoud 70 G2
Hässleholm 16 G8
Hastings, *New Zealand* 84 F4
Hastings, *United Kingdom* 22 C4
Hastings, *Minn., United States* 96 B2
Hastings, *Nebr., United States* 94 G2
Haţeg 34 K4
Hatgal 46 G6
Ha Tinh 52 D3
Hatteras 98 F2
Hattiesburg 98 D3
Hatvan 34 G2
Hat Yai 52 C5
Haud 68 H6
Haud Ogadēn 74 G2
Haugesund 16 C7
Hauraki Gulf 84 E3
Haut Atlas 70 D2
Hauts Plateaux 70 E2
Havana = La Habana 102 H4
Havana 98 C1
Havant 24 M11
Havel 18 C5
Havelock, *New Zealand* 84 D5
Havelock, *United States* 98 F3
Havelock North 84 F4
Havenby 20 D1
Haverfordwest 24 H10
Havlíčkův Brod 18 E8
Havre 94 E1
Havre-St-Pierre 90 U6
Havrylivtsi 34 P1
Havza 60 F3
Hawaii 100 (2)E2
Hawaii 100 (2)E4
Hawaiian Islands 80 J3
Hawera 84 E4
Hawi 100 (2)F3
Hawick 24 K6
Hawke Bay 84 F4
Hawker 82 G6
Hawr al'Awdah 63 B1
Hawr al Ḩammar 63 B1
Hawthorne 94 C3
Hay 82 H6
Hay 90 H5
Hayange 22 J5
Haydarābad 60 L5
Hayden 100 D2
Hayrabolu 36 K3
Hay River 90 H4
Hays 98 B2
Hazard 96 D3
Hazārībāg 56 E4
Hazebrouck 22 E4
Hazelton, *Canada* 90 F5
Hazelton, *United States* 96 E2
Head of Bight 82 F6
Hearne 98 B3
Hearst 96 D1
Hebbronville 100 G3
Hebgen Lake 94 D2
Hebi 48 E3
Hebron, *Canada* 90 U5
Hebron, *Israel* 62 C5
Hebron, *Nebr., United States* 94 G2
Hebron, *N.D., United States* 94 F1
Hecate Strait 90 E6
Hechi 52 D2
Hechingen 30 D2
Hede 16 G5
Heerenveen 22 H2
Heerlen 22 J4
Ḩefa 62 B4
Hefei 48 F4
Hegang 48 J1
Hegura-jima 50 J5
Hegyfalu 30 M3
Heide 20 E2
Heidelberg 20 D7
Heidenheim 30 F2
Heilbad Heiligenstadt 20 F5
Heilbronn 20 E7
Heilgenhafen 20 F2
Heimaey 16 (1)C3
Heinola 16 N6
Hejing 44 R9
Hekla 16 (1)D3
Helagsfjället 16 G5
Helena, *Ark., United States* 98 C3
Helena, *Mont., United States* 94 D1
Helen Reef 55 D2
Helensville 84 E3
Helgea 18 D1
Helgoland 20 C2
Helgoländer Bucht 20 D2
Hellín 28 J6
Helmand 58 H3
Helmond 22 H3
Helmsdale 24 J3
Helmstedt 20 G4
Helodrano Antongila 76 H3
Helong 50 E2
Helsingborg 16 G8
Helsinge 18 B1
Helsingør 16 G8
Helsinki 16 N6
Helston 24 G11
Helwan 68 F2
Hemel Hempstead 24 M10
Henashi-zaki 50 K3
Hendek 36 N4
Henderson, *Ky., United States* 96 C3
Henderson, *Nev., United States* 94 D3
Henderson, *N.C. United States* 98 F2
Henderson Island 80 P8
Hendersonville 96 C3
Hendījān 63 C1
Hengelo 22 J2
Hengyang 48 E5
Henichesk 38 F5
Hénin-Beaumont 22 E4
Hennebont 26 B6
Hennigsdorf 20 J4
Henryetta 96 A3
Henzada 52 B3
Heppenheim 20 D7
Heppner 94 C1
Hepu 52 D2
Herald Cays 82 J3
Herāt 58 H3
Hérađhsflói 16 (1)F2
Herbert 84 C7
Herborn 20 D6
Herceg-Novi 34 F7
Hereford, *United Kingdom* 24 K9
Hereford, *United States* 102 D2
Herekino 84 D2
Herentals 22 G3
Herford 20 D4
Herisau 30 E3
Herlen Gol 48 E1
Hermagor 30 J4
Herma Ness 24 M1
Hermel 62 D2
Hermiston 94 C1
Hermosillo 92 D6
Hernád 18 L9
Herne 20 C5
Herne Bay 22 D3
Herning 16 E8
Hérouville-St-Clair 22 B5
Herrenberg 30 D2
Hersbruck 20 G7
Herstat 22 H4
Hertlay 22 E6
Hervey Bay 82 K5
Herzberg 20 F5
Herzliyya 62 B4
Hesdin 22 E4
Heshan 52 D2
Hesselø 18 A1
Hessisch-Lichtenau 20 E5
Hettstedt Lutherstadt 20 G5
Heves 18 K10
He Xian 52 E2
Hexigten Qi 48 F2
Heze 48 F3
Hezuozhen 48 C3
Hialeah 98 E4
Hiawatha 98 B2
Hibbing 96 B1
Hickory 96 D3
Hidaka-sammyaku 50 M2
Hidalgo del Parral 102 C3
Hiddensee 20 H2
Hierro 70 B3
Higashi-suidō 50 E7
High Point 96 E3
High Wycombe 22 B3
Hiiumaa 16 M7

Name	Page	Grid
Hikurangi	84	E2
Hikurangi	84	G3
Hikutaia	84	E3
Hildburghausen	20	F6
Hildesheim	20	E4
Hillsboro, Oh., United States	98	E2
Hillsboro, Oreg., United States	94	B1
Hillsboro, Tex., United States	100	G2
Hillsville	96	D3
Hillswick	24	L1
Hilo	100	(2)F4
Hilton Head Island	98	E3
Hilva	60	H5
Hilversum	22	H2
Himalayas	42	L6
Himarë	36	B4
Himatnagar	56	B4
Himeji	50	H6
Himi	50	J5
Himora	68	G5
Ḥimṣ	62	D2
Hîncești	34	R3
Hindu Kush	56	A1
Hindupur	56	C6
Hinesville	98	E3
Hingoli	56	C5
Hinnøya	16	H2
Hiroo	50	M2
Hirosaki	50	L3
Hiroshima	50	G6
Hirschaid	20	F7
Hirson	22	G5
Hirtshals	16	E8
Hisar	56	C3
Hischberg	20	G6
Hisdal	16	C6
Hispaniola	106	D2
Hisyah	62	D2
Hīt	60	K7
Hitachi	50	L5
Hitoyoshi	50	F7
Hitra	16	D5
Hiuchi-nada	50	G6
Hiva Oa	80	M6
Hjälmaren	16	H7
Hjalmar Lake	90	K4
Hjelmsøya	16	M1
Hlinsko	18	E8
Hlohovec	30	N2
Hlyboka	34	N1
Hlybokaye	38	E3
Ho	72	E3
Hobart, Australia	82	J8
Hobart, United States	100	G1
Hobbs	100	F2
Hobro	16	E8
Hobyo	74	H3
Hô Chi Minh	52	D4
Höchstadt	20	F7
Hockenheim	20	D7
Hódmezővásárhely	34	H3
Hodonin	18	G9
Hoek van Holland	22	G3
Hoeryŏng	50	E2
Hoeyang	50	D4
Hof	20	G6
Hofgeismar	20	E5
Höfn	16	(1)F2
Hofsjökull	16	(1)D2
Hofsós	16	(1)D2
Höfu	50	F6
Hohe	30	H3
Hohe Dachstein	20	C10
Hohe Tauern	32	G1
Hohhot	48	E2
Hoh Xil Shan	56	E1
Hôi An	52	D3
Hoima	74	E3
Hokitika	84	C6
Hokkaidō	50	N2
Holbæk	18	A2
Holbrook	100	D2
Holdrege	94	G2
Holguín	102	J4
Holíč	30	N2
Hollabrunn	30	M2
Holland	96	C2
Hollis	100	G2
Hollywood	98	E4
Holman	90	H2
Hólmavík	16	(1)C2
Holmes Reefs	82	J3
Holstebro	16	E8
Holsteinische Schweiz	20	F2
Holsteinsborg = Sisimiut	90	W3
Holton	98	B2
Holyhead	24	H8
Holy Island, Eng., United Kingdom	24	L6
Holy Island, Wales, United Kingdom	24	H8
Holyoke	94	F2
Holzkirchen	30	G3
Holzminden	20	E5
Homa Bay	74	E4
Homberg	20	E5
Hombori	72	E5
Home Bay	90	T3
Homestead	98	E4
Homewood	98	D3
Homs = Ḥimṣ	62	D2
Homyel'	38	F4
Hondo, N. Mex., United States	100	E2
Hondo, Tex., United States	100	G3
Honduras	102	G6
Hønefoss	16	F6
Honey Lake	94	B2
Honfleur	28	C5
Hon Gai	52	D2
Hong Kong = Xianggang	52	E2
Hongliuyuan	48	B2
Hongor	48	E1
Honiara	80	F6
Honjō	50	K4
Honokaa	100	(2)F3
Honolulu	100	(2)D2
Honshū	50	L5
Hooge	20	D2
Hoogeveen	22	J2
Hoogezand-Sappemeer	22	J1
Hooper Bay	100	(1)D3
Hoorn	22	H2
Hoorn Islands	80	H7
Hopa	60	J3
Hope, Canada	94	B1
Hope, Ak., United States	90	B4
Hope, Ark., United States	98	C3
Hopedale	90	U5
Hopetoun	82	H7
Hopin	56	G4
Hopkinsville	96	C3
Hoquiam	94	B1
Horadiz	60	M4
Horasan	60	K3
Horgo	46	F7
Horizon Depth	80	D8
Hormak	58	H4
Hormoz	63	F3
Horn	30	L2
Hornavan	16	J3
Horncastle	22	B1
Horodenka	34	N1
Horodok	18	N8
Horqin Youyi Qianqi	46	L7
Horsens	16	E9
Horsham, Australia	82	H7
Horsham, United Kingdom	22	B3
Horten	16	F7
Hortiguela	28	G2
Horton	100	(1)N2
Ḥoseynābād	63	G2
Hoshab	58	H4
Hoshangabad	56	C4
Hospet	56	C5
Hosséré Vokre	72	G3
Hotan	44	Q10
Hotan	44	Q10
Hot Springs, Ark., United States	96	B4
Hot Springs, N.C., United States	96	D3
Hottah Lake	90	H3
Houdan	22	D6
Houdelaincourt	30	A2
Houghton	96	C1
Houlton	96	G1
Houma, China	48	C1
Houma, United States	92	H6
Houmt Souk	70	H2
Houston	92	G6
Hovd	44	S8
Hövsgöl Nuur	46	F6
Hövüün	48	C2
Howard Junction	84	D5
Howland	80	J5
Howz-e Panj	63	G1
Hoxie	98	C2
Höxter	20	E5
Hoxud	44	R9
Hoy	24	J3
Høyanger	16	D6
Hoyerswerda	20	K5
Hradec Králové	18	E7
Hranice	18	G8
Hrazdan	60	L3
Hrodna	38	N4
Hron	18	H9
Hrubieszów	18	N7
Hsinchu	52	G2
Hsüeh Shan	52	G2
Hsweni	52	B2
Huacho	108	B6
Huade	48	E2
Huadian	50	D2
Huaibei	48	F4
Huaibin	48	F4
Huaihua	48	D5
Huainan	48	F4
Huaiyin	48	F4
Huaki	55	C4
Huallaga	108	B5
Huambo	76	B2
Huancavelica	108	B6
Huancayo	108	B6
Huang	48	F3
Huangchuan	48	F4
Huangshan	48	F5
Huangshi	48	F4
Huang Xian	48	G3
Huangyan, China	48	C3
Huangyan, China	48	G5
Huanren	50	C2
Huanuco	108	B5
Huaráz	108	B5
Huarmey	108	B6
Huasco	110	G4
Huashixia	48	B3
Huatabampo	92	C5
Hubli	56	C5
Huch'ang	50	D3
Huddersfield	24	L8
Huddinge	16	K7
Hudiksvall	16	J6
Hudson	96	F2
Hudson	96	F2
Hudson Bay	90	L6
Hudson Bay	90	P5
Hudson Strait	90	S4
Huê	52	D3
Huelva	28	D7
Huercal Overa	28	J7
Huesca	28	K2
Huéscar	28	H7
Huftaroy	16	C6
Hughenden	82	H4
Hugo	98	B3
Hugo Lake	98	B3
Huia	84	E3
Huich'ŏn	50	D3
Huila Plateau	76	A3
Huinan	50	C2
Huinca Renancó	110	J5
Huizhou	52	E2
Hulin	46	N7
Hull	96	E1
Hulst	22	G3
Hulun Nur	46	K7
Huma	46	M6
Huma	46	M6
Humaitá	108	E5
Humbe	76	A3
Humble	20	F2
Humboldt	90	L6
Humboldt	94	C2
Hümedän	58	G4
Humenné	18	L9
Humphrey	94	D2
Humpolec	18	E8
Hün	68	C2
Húnaflói	16	(1)C2
Hunchun	50	F2
Hunedoara	34	K4
Hünfeld	20	E6
Hungary	34	F3
Hungerford, Australia	82	H5
Hungerford, United Kingdom	22	A3
Hüngnam	50	D4
Hunjiang	50	D3
Hunsrück	20	B7
Hunstanton	22	C2
Hunter Island	80	H8
Huntingburg	98	D2
Huntingdon, United Kingdom	22	B2
Huntingdon, United States	98	E2
Huntington	98	D1
Huntington Beach	100	C2
Huntly, New Zealand	84	E3
Huntsville, Canada	96	E1
Huntsville, Al., United States	98	D3
Huntsville, Tex., United States	102	E2
Hunyuan	48	E3
Ḥūr	63	G1
Hurdiyo	74	J1
Hurghada	68	F2
Huron	94	G2
Hürth	22	J4
Húsavík	16	(1)E1
Huşi	34	R3
Huslia	100	(1)F2
Husn	62	C4
Husum	20	E2
Hutag	46	G7
Hutanopan	54	B2
Hutchinson	100	G1
Hūth	68	H4
Huttwil	30	C3
Huvadu Atoll	56	B8
Huy	22	H4
Huzou	48	G4
Hvannadalshnúkur	16	(1)E2
Hvar	34	D6
Hvar	34	D6
Hvolsvöllur	16	(1)C3
Hwange	76	D3
Hyak	94	B1
Hyannis	94	F2
Hyargas Nuur	44	S8
Hyden	82	C6
Hyderabad, India	56	C5
Hyderabad, Pakistan	58	J4
Hyères	26	M10
Hyesan	50	E3
Hyndam Peak	94	D2
Hyūga	50	F7
Hyvinkää	16	N6

I

Name	Page	Grid
Iaco	108	D6
Ialomița	34	P5
Ianca	34	Q4
Iași	34	Q2
Ibadan	72	E3
Ibagué	108	B3
Ibar	34	H6
Ibb	68	H5
Ibbenbüren	20	C4
Iberia	108	C5
Ibiza = Eivissa	28	M5
Ibiza = Eivissa	28	M6
Ibotirama	108	J6
Ibrä'	58	G5
'Ibrī	63	G5
Ica	108	B6
Içana	108	D3
Içel	60	F5
Iceland	34	C1
Ichalkaranji	56	B5
Ichinoseki	50	L4
Idabel	98	C3
Ida Grove	96	A2
Idah	72	F3
Idaho	94	D2
Idaho Falls	94	D2
Idar-Oberstein	20	C7
Idfu	68	F3
Idhän Awbäri	70	H3
Idhan Murzūq	70	H4
Idiofa	74	C4
Idlib	60	G6
Idstein	20	D6
Ieper	22	E4
Ierapetra	36	H9
Ifakara	74	F5
Ifanadiana	76	H4
Ife	72	E3
Ifjord	16	P1
Igarka	44	R4
Iggesund	16	J6
Igizyar	58	L2
Iglesias	32	C9
Igli	70	E2
Igloolik	90	Q3
Ignace	96	B1
Iğneada	36	K3
Igoumenitsa	36	C5
Igra	38	K3
Igrim	38	M2
Igualada	28	M3
Iguatu	108	K5
Ihosy	76	H4
Ihtiman	34	L7
Iida	50	J6
Iim	30	G2
Iiulissat	90	W3
Ijebu Ode	72	E3
IJmuiden	22	G2
IJssel	22	J2
IJsselmeer	22	H2
Ikaria	36	J7
Ikeda	50	M2
Ikela	74	C4
Iki	50	E7
Ikire	72	E3
Ikom	72	F3
Ikopa	76	H3
Ikorodu	72	E3
Ilagan	52	G3
Īlām	58	E3
Iława	18	J4
Ilbenge	46	L4
Ilebo	74	C4
Île d'Anticosti	90	U7
Île de Jerba	70	H2
Île de la Gonâve	102	K5
Île de Noirmoutier	26	C7
Île de Ré	26	D7
Île d'Oléron	26	D8
Île d'Yeu	26	C7
Île Europa	76	G4
Ilek	38	K4
Ilek	38	K4
Île Plane	32	E11
Îles Cani	32	D11
Îles Chesterfield	80	F7
Îles Crozet	66	J10
Îles de Désappointement	80	M7
Îles de la Madeleine	90	U7
Îles d'Hyères	26	M11
Îles du Duc de Gloucester	80	M7
Îles Glorieuses	76	H2
Ilesha	72	E3
Îles Kerkenah	70	H2
Îles Maria	80	L8
Îles Palliser	80	M7
Île Tidra	70	B5
Île Zembra	32	E11
Ilfracombe	24	H10
Ilgin	60	D4
Ilha da Trindade	106	H6
Ilha de Marajó	108	H4
Ilha de São Luís	108	J4
Ilha do Bazaruto	76	F4
Ilha Fernando de Noronha	108	L4
Ilha Grande	108	E4
Ilha Grande de Gurupa	108	G4
Ilharaña	76	H2
Ilhas Martin Vaz	110	Q3
Ilhéus	108	K6
Ili	44	P9
Iliamna Volcano	100	(1)G4
Iligan	52	G5
Ilkal	56	C5
Iller	30	F3
Illertissen	30	F2
Illichivs'k	34	T3
Illinois	92	H3
Illinois	96	C2
Illizi	70	G3
Illorsuit	90	W2
Ilmenau	20	F6
Ilo	108	C7
Iloilo	52	G4
Ilorin	72	E3
Ilovlya	38	H5
Il'pyrskiy	46	U4
Ilsalmi	16	P5
Ilwaco	94	B1
Ilych	38	L2
Imabari	50	G6
Imatra	16	Q6
Imeni-Babushkina	44	G6
Imeni Polinyosipenko	46	P6
Imese	74	B3
Imī	74	G2
İmişli	60	N4
Immeln	18	D1
Immenstadt	30	F3
Imola	30	G6
Imotski	34	E6
Imperatriz	108	H5
Imperia	30	D7
Imperial	94	F2
Impfondo	74	B3
Imphal	56	F4
Imrali Adası	36	L4
Imroz	36	H4
Ina	50	J6
Inambari	108	C6
In Aménas	70	G3
Inangahua	84	C5
Inanwatan	55	D3
Iñapari	108	D6
Inarijärvi	16	P2

163

Inca 28 N5
İnce Burun 60 F2
Inch'ŏn 50 D5
Incirliova 36 K7
Indalsälven 16 H5
Independence, *Kans., United States* 98 B2
Independence, *Mo., United States* 96 B3
India 56 C4
Indiana 92 J3
Indiana 96 E2
Indianapolis 98 D2
Indian Ocean 10 J4
Indianola 96 B2
Indian Springs 94 C3
Indiga 38 J1
Indio 100 C2
Indonesia 54 D3
Indore 56 C4
Indramayu 54 D4
Indre 26 G6
Indre Sula 16 C6
Indus 58 K3
İnebolu 60 E3
İnecik 36 K4
İnegöl 60 C3
In Ekker 70 G4
Ineu 34 J3
Ingelheim 22 L5
Ingeniero Jacobacci 110 H7
Ingham 82 J3
Ingoda 46 J6
Ingolstadt 30 G2
Ingrāj Bāzār 56 E3
I-n-Guezzam 70 G5
Ingushetiya 60 L2
Inhambane 76 F4
Inhaminga 76 E3
Inírida 108 D3
Inishmore 24 B8
Inkisi-Kisantu 72 H6
Inn 30 H2
Inner Hebrides 24 F5
Inner Mongolia = Nei Monggol 48 E2
Inneston 82 G7
Innisfail 82 J3
Innsbruck 30 G3
Inongo 74 B4
Inowrocław 18 H5
In Salah 70 F3
Insein 52 B3
Inta 44 K4
Interlaken 30 C4
International Falls 96 B1
Intsy 38 H1
Inubō-zaki 50 L6
Inukjuak 90 R5
Inuvik 100 (1)L2
Inveraray 24 G5
Invercargill 84 B8
Inverness 24 H4
Inverway 82 E3
Investigator Group 82 F6
Investigator Strait 82 G7
Inya 44 R7
Inya 46 R4
Ioannina 36 C5
Iokanga 44 F4
Iola 98 B2
Iona 24 F5
Ionești 34 M5
Ionian Sea 36 B6
Ionioi Nisoi 36 B5
Ios 36 H8
Ios 36 H8
Iowa 92 H3
Iowa City 96 B2
Iowa Falls 96 B2
Ipameri 108 H7
Ipatinga 110 N2
Ipatovo 38 H5
Ipiales 108 B3
Ipiaú 108 K6
Ipoh 54 C2
Iporá 108 G7
Ippy 74 C2
Ipsala 36 J4
Ipswich 24 P9
Iqaluit 90 T4
Iquique 110 G3
Iquitos 108 C4
Iracoubo 108 G2
Irakleia 36 F3
Irakleia 36 H8
Irakleio 36 H9
Iraklion = Irakleio 14 G4
Iran 58 F3
Irānshahr 58 H4
Irapuato 102 D4
Iraq 58 D3
Irbid 62 C4
Irbit 38 M3
Irecê 108 J6
Irgiz 38 M5
Irgiz 38 M5
Irhil M'Goun 70 D2
Irian Jaya 55 E3
Iringa 74 F5
Iriri 108 G4
Irish Sea 24 G8
Irkutsk 46 G6
Iron Mountain 96 C1
Ironton 98 E2
Ironwood 96 B1
Irrawaddy 56 F5
Irshava 34 L1
Irta 38 J2
Irtysh 38 P3
Irtyshsk 44 P7
Irumu 74 D3
Irún 28 J1
Irvine 24 H6
Irving 100 G2
Isabela 55 B1
Isabella 96 B1
Isabella Lake 100 C1
Ísafjarðhardjúp 16 (1)A1
Ísafjörðhur 16 (1)B1
Isahaya 50 F7
Isar 30 G3
Ischia 32 H8
Ischia 32 H8
Ise 50 J6
Isel 30 H4
Isère 30 B5
Iserlohn 22 K3
Isernia 32 J7
Isetskoye 38 N3
Iseyin 72 E3
Isfana 58 J2
Ishikari-wan 50 L2
Ishim 38 N3
Ishim 38 N4
Ishinomaki 50 L4
Ishkoshim 58 K2
Isigny-sur-Mer 22 A5
Isiolo 74 F3
Isiro 74 D3
Iskăr 34 M6
İskenderun 60 G5
Iskitim 44 Q7
Isla Alejandro Selkirk 110 E5
Isla Campana 110 F8
Isla Clarence 110 G9
Isla Clarión 102 B5
Isla Coiba 102 H7
Isla Contreras 110 F9
Isla de Alborán 28 G9
Isla de Bioco 72 F4
Isla de Chiloé 110 G7
Isla de Coco 102 G7
Isla de Cozumel 102 G4
Isla de la Juventud 102 H4
Isla de los Estados 110 J9
Isla de Malpelo 108 A3
Isla de Margarita 108 E1
Isla de Providencia 102 H6
Isla de San Andrés 102 H6
Isla de São Francisco 110 M4
Isla de São Sebastião 110 M3
Isla Desolación 110 F9
Isla Española 108 (1)B2
Isla Fernandina 108 (1)A2
Isla Gorgona 108 B3
Isla Grande 110 N3
Isla Grande de Tierra del Fuego 110 H9
Isla Guafo 110 F7
Isla Hoste 110 G10
Isla Isabela 108 (1)A2
Isla La Tortuga 108 D1
Isla Londonderry 110 G9
Islamabad 56 B2
Isla Madre de Dios 110 F9
Isla Marchena 108 (1)A1
Islamgarh 56 B3
Islamorada 98 E5
Isla Navarino 110 H10
Island Lake 90 M6
Islands of the Four Mountains 100 (1)C5
Isla Pinta 108 (1)A1
Isla Puná 108 A4
Isla Riesco 110 G9
Isla Robinson Crusoe 110 E5
Isla San Benedicto 102 B5
Isla San Cristóbal 108 (1)B2
Isla San Salvador 108 (1)A2
Isla Santa Cruz 108 (1)A2
Isla Santa Inés 110 F9
Isla Santa María 108 (1)A2
Islas Baleares 28 N5
Islas Canarias 70 B3
Islas Canarias 66 A3
Islas Columbretes 28 L5
Islas de la Bahía 102 G5
Islas de los Desventurados 110 E4
Islas Galápagos 108 (1)B1
Islas Juan Fernández 110 E5
Islas Los Roques 108 D1
Islas Marías 102 C4
Islas Socorro 102 B5
Islas Revillagigedo 102 B5
Islas Wollaston 110 H10
Isla Wellington 110 F8
Islay 24 F6
Isle 26 F8
Isle of Man 24 H7
Isle of Wight 24 L11
Isle Royale 96 C1
Isles of Scilly 24 F12
Ismâ'ilîya 68 F1
İsmayıllı 60 N3
Isna 68 F2
Isoka 76 E2
Isola delle Correnti 32 J12
Isola di Capo Rizzuto 32 M10
Isola di Pantelleria 32 G12
Isole Égadi 32 F11
Isole Lipari 32 J10
Isole Ponziane 32 H8
Isole Tremiti 32 K6
Iso-Vietonen 16 N3
Isparta 36 N7
Ispica 32 J12
Israel 62 B5
Israelite Bay 82 D6
Issia 72 C3
Issimu 55 B2
Issoire 26 J8
Issoudun 26 H7
Issyk-Kul' 44 P9
İstanbul 60 C3
İstanbul Boğazı 60 C3
Istiaia 36 F6
Istmo de Tehauntepec 102 F5
Istra 30 J5
Istres 26 K10
Itaberaba 108 J6
Itabira 108 J7
Itabuna 108 K6
Itacoatiara 108 F4
Itaituba 108 F4
Itajaí 110 M4
Italy 32 E4
Itambacuri 108 J7
Itanagar 56 F3
Itapebi 108 K7
Itapetinga 108 J7
Itapicuru 108 K6
Itapicuru Mirim 108 J4
Itapipoca 108 K4
Itarsi 56 C4
Ithaca 96 E2
Ithaki 36 C6
Ithaki 36 C6
Itiquira 108 G7
Ituí 108 C5
Ituiutaba 108 H7
Itumbiara 108 H7
Ituni 108 F2
Ituri 74 D3
Ituxi 108 D5
Itzehoe 20 E3
Iuaretê 108 D3
Iutica 108 D3
Ivalo 16 P2
Ivanava 16 N10
Ivangrad 34 G7
Ivanhoe, *Australia* 82 H6
Ivanhoe, *United States* 96 A2
Ivano-Frankivs'k 38 D5
Ivanovo 38 H3
Ivatsevichy 16 N10
Ivdel' 38 M2
Ivittuut 90 X4
Ivohibe 76 H4
Ivosjön 18 D1
Ivrea 30 C5
Ivujivik 90 R4
Iwaki 50 L5
Iwamizawa 50 L2
Iwo 72 E3
Iyo-nadā 50 G7
Izberbash 60 M2
Izegern 22 F4
Izhevsk 38 K3
Izhma 38 K1
Izhma 38 K2
Izk 58 G5
Izkī 63 G5
Izmayil 34 R4
İzmir 36 K6
İzmir Körfezi 36 J6
İzmit 60 C3
İznik 60 C3
İznik Gölü 60 C3
Izola 30 J5
Izra' 62 D4
Izuhara 50 E6
Izumo 50 G6
Izu-shotō 50 K6

J

Jabal ad Durūz 62 D4
Jabal Akhḑar 63 G5
Jabal al Nuşayrīyah 62 D1
Jabal an Nabī Shu'ayb 68 H4
Jabal Ash Sham 63 G5
Jabal az Zannah 63 E4
Jabalpur 56 C4
Jabal Shammar 68 G2
Jabal Thamar 68 J5
Jabiru 82 F2
Jablah 62 C1
Jablonec 18 E7
Jablunkov 18 H8
Jaboatão 108 K5
Jaca 28 K2
Jacareacanga 108 G5
Jackman 96 F1
Jacksboro 98 B3
Jackson, *Calif., United States* 94 B3
Jackson, *Minn., United States* 96 B2
Jackson, *Miss., United States* 98 C3
Jackson, *Oh., United States* 98 E2
Jackson, *Tenn., United States* 98 D2
Jackson Head 84 B6
Jackson Lake 94 D2
Jacksonville, *Fla., United States* 98 E3
Jacksonville, *Ill., United States* 96 B3
Jacksonville, *N.C., United States* 98 F3
Jacksonville, *Tex., United States* 98 B3
Jacmel 102 K5
Jacobabad 56 A3
Jacobina 108 J6
Jacunda 108 H4
Jacupiranga 110 M3
Jade 20 D3
Jadebusen 20 D3
Jādū 70 H2
Jaén 28 G7
Jaen 108 B5
Jaffna 56 D7
Jagdalpur 56 D5
Jagersfontein 76 D5
Jaggang 56 C2
Jagst 20 E7
Jahrom 63 E2
Jaipur 56 C3
Jaisalmer 56 B3
Jajce 34 E5
Jakarta 54 D4
Jäkkvik 16 J3
Jakobshavn = Ilulissat 90 W3
Jakobstad 16 M5
Jalālābād 56 B2
Jalandhar 56 C2
Jalapa Enriquez 102 E5
Jalgaon 56 C4
Jalībah 63 B1
Jalingo 72 G3
Jalna 56 C5
Jalón 28 J3
Jalpaiguri 56 E3
Jālū 68 D2
Jalūlā 60 L6
Jamaica 102 H5
Jamalpur 56 E3
Jambi 54 C3
Jambol 34 P7
James 94 G2
James Bay 90 Q6
Jamestown, *N.Y., United States* 96 E2
Jamestown, *N.D., United States* 94 G1
Jammerbugten 16 E8
Jammu 56 B2
Jammu and Kashmir 56 C2
Jamnagar 56 B4
Jämsä 16 N6
Jamshedpur 56 E4
Janakpur 56 E3
Janaúba 108 J7
Jandaq 58 F3
Jandongi 74 C3
Jane Peak 84 B7
Janesville 96 C2
Jan Mayen 88 C2
Jannatabad 44 L10
Janos 100 E2
Jánossomorja 30 N3
Janów Lubelski 18 M7
Januária 108 J7
Jaora 56 C4
Japan 50 L5
Japan Trench 80 E2
Japurá 108 D4
Jarābulus 60 H5
Jaramillo 110 H8
Jarash 62 C4
Jardim 110 K3
Jarosław 18 M7
Järpen 16 G5
Jarud Qi 48 G2
Järvenpää 16 N6
Jarvis 80 K6
Jasel'da 16 N10
Jäsk 63 G4
Jason Islands 110 J9
Jasper, *Al., United States* 98 D3
Jasper, *Fla., United States* 98 E3
Jasper, *Tex., United States* 98 C3
Jastrebarsko 30 L5
Jászberény 34 G2
Jataí 108 G7
Jatapu 108 F4
Jaunpur 56 D3
Java = Jawa 54 E4
Javarthushuu 46 J7
Java Sea 54 E4
Javoriv 18 N8
Jawa 54 E4
Jawhar 74 H3
Jayapura 55 F3
Jayrūd 62 D3
Jaza'īr Farasān 68 H4
Jazīrat Būbīyān 63 C2
Jazīrat-ye Khārk 63 D2
Jbail 62 C2
Jbel Ayachi 70 E2
Jbel Bou Naceur 70 E2
Jbel Toubkal 70 D2
Jean 94 C3
Jebba 72 E3
Jebel Bāqir 62 C7
Jebel el Atā'ita 62 C6
Jebel el Batrā 62 C7
Jebel-esh Sharqi 62 C3
Jebel Gimbala 68 D5
Jebel Ithrīyat 62 D6
Jebel Liban 62 C3
Jebel Mubrak 62 C6
Jebel Ram 62 C7
Jebel Uweinat 68 E3
Jedburgh 24 K6
Jedda = Jiddah 58 C5
Jedeida 32 D12
Jędrzejów 18 K7
Jefferson 96 B2
Jefferson City, *Mo., United States* 96 B3
Jefferson City, *Tenn., United States* 98 E2
Jeffersonville 96 C3
Jega 72 E2
Jēkabpils 16 N8
Jelgava 16 M8
Jemaja 54 D2
Jena 20 G6
Jendouba 70 G1
Jenin 62 C4
Jenkins 96 D3
Jequié 108 J6
Jequitinhonha 108 J7
Jerada 70 E2
Jeremoabo 108 K6
Jerez 100 F4
Jerez de la Frontera 28 D8
Jerez de los Caballeros 28 D6
Jericho, *Australia* 82 J4
Jericho, *Israel* 62 C5
Jerramungup 82 C6
Jersey 26 C4
Jersey City 98 G1
Jerusalem = Yerushalayim 62 C5
Jesenice 34 B3

Name	Page	Grid
Jesenik	18	G7
Jesi	30	J7
Jessore	56	E4
Jesup	98	E3
Jeumont	22	G4
Jever	20	C3
Jeypore	56	D5
Jezioro	18	D4
Jezioro Gardno	16	J9
Jezioro Jeziorsko	18	H6
Jezioro Łebsko	18	F3
Jezioro Śniardwy	18	L4
Jezioro Wigry	18	N2
Jezzine	62	C3
Jhang Maghiana	56	B2
Jhansi	56	C3
Jharsuguda	56	D4
Jhelum	56	B2
Jialing Jiang	48	D4
Jiamusi	48	J1
Ji'an	48	E5
Jiangle	48	F5
Jiangling	48	E4
Jiangmen	48	E6
Jiangyou	48	C4
Jianyang	48	F5
Jiaonan	48	F3
Jiaozou	48	E3
Jiaxing	48	G4
Jiayuguan	48	B3
Jibou	34	L2
Jičín	18	E7
Jiddah	58	C5
Jiesjavrre	16	N2
Jiexiu	48	E3
Jihlava	18	E8
Jijia	34	Q2
Jijiga	74	G2
Jilib	74	G3
Jilin	50	D2
Jima	74	F2
Jimbolia	34	H4
Jiménez	100	F3
Jimsar	44	R9
Jinan	48	F3
Jinapo Hu	50	E2
Jinchang	48	C3
Jincheng	48	E3
Jindřichův Hradec	18	E8
Jingdezhen	48	F5
Jinggu	48	C6
Jinghe	44	Q9
Jinghong	48	C6
Jingmen	48	E4
Jingning	48	D3
Jingxi	48	D6
Jingyuan	48	C3
Jinhua	48	F5
Jining, China	48	F3
Jining, China	48	E2
Jinja	74	E3
Jinka	74	F2
Jinsha	48	C5
Jinshi	48	E5
Jinta	48	B2
Jinxi	48	G2
Jinzhou	48	G2
Jirgatol	58	K2
Jirin Gol	48	F2
Jirkov	20	J6
Jīroft	63	G2
Jirriiban	74	H2
Jishou	48	D5
Jisr ash Shughūr	60	G6
Jiu	34	L4
Jiujiang	48	F5
Jiwani	58	H4
Jixi	50	F1
Jīzān	68	H4
Jizera	18	D7
J. J. Castelli	108	D4
Joal-Fadiout	70	B6
João Pessoa	108	L5
Jódar	28	G7
Jodhpur	56	B3
Joensuu	38	E2
Jōetsu	50	K5
Jõgeva	16	P7
Johannesburg, South Africa	76	D5
Johannesburg, United States	100	C1
John Day	94	C2
John o' Groats	24	J3
John Redmond Reservoir	98	B2
Johnson	98	A2
Johnson City	96	D3
Johnson's Crossing	100	(1)L3
Johnston Island	80	J4
Johnstown	96	E2
Johor Bahru	54	C2
Joigny	26	J5
Joinville, Brazil	110	M4
Joinville, France	26	L5
Jokkmokk	16	K3
Jökulsá-á Fjöllum	16	(1)E1
Jolfa	60	L4
Joliet	92	J3
Joliette	96	F1
Jolo	55	B1
Jolo	55	B1
Jonava	18	P2
Jonesboro	96	B3
Jones Sound	90	P1
Jonesville	98	C3
Jonglei Canal	74	E2
Jongunjärvi	16	P4
Joniškis	18	N1
Jönköping	16	H8
Jonquière	96	F1
Joplin	98	C2
Jordan	62	D5
Jordan	94	E1

Name	Page	Grid
Jordan Valley	94	C2
Jorhat	56	F3
Jörn	16	L4
Jos	72	F3
José de San Martin	110	G7
Joseph Bonaparte Gulf	82	E2
Joûnié	62	C2
Joure	22	H2
Juan de Nova	76	G3
Juàzeiro	108	J5
Juàzeiro do Norte	108	K5
Juba	74	E3
Jubba	74	G3
Júcar	28	J5
Juchitán	102	F5
Judenburg	30	K3
Juhre	46	L8
Juist	20	B4
Juiz de Fora	110	N3
Julesburg	94	F2
Juli	108	C7
Juliaca	108	C7
Juliana Top	108	F3
Jülich	22	J4
Jullouville	22	A6
Jumilla	28	J6
Jumla	56	D3
Junagadh	56	B4
Junction	98	B3
Junction City	98	B2
Jundah	82	H4
Juneau	100	(1)L4
Jungfrau	30	C4
Junggar Pendi	44	R8
Junsele	16	J5
Jun Xian	48	E4
Jura	30	B4
Jūra	18	M2
Jura	24	G5
Jurbarkas	18	M2
Jurf ed Darāwīsh	62	C6
Jurhe	48	G2
Jurilovca	34	R5
Jūrmala	16	M8
Juruá	108	D4
Juruena	108	F6
Juruena	108	F6
Justo Daract	110	H5
Jutaí	108	D5
Jüterbog	20	J5
Juwain	58	H3
Ju Xian	48	F3
Jūymand	58	G3
Jūyom	63	F2
Juzur al Halaniyat	58	G6
Jylland	16	E8
Jyvädskylä	38	E2
Jyväskylä	16	N5

K

Name	Page	Grid
K2	56	C1
Kaakhka	58	G2
Kaamanen	16	P2
Kaarta	70	C6
Kabaena	55	B4
Kabakly	58	H2
Kabala	72	B3
Kabale	74	E4
Kabalo	74	D5
Kabardino-Balkariya	60	K2
Kåbdalis	16	L3
Kabompo	76	C2
Kabongo	74	D5
Kabugao	52	G3
Kābul	58	J3
Kabwe	76	D2
Kachikattsy	46	M4
Kachug	46	H6
Kadama	56	B6
Kadañ	18	C7
Kadınhanı	36	Q6
Kadirli	60	G5
Kadoka	94	F2
Kadoma	76	D3
Kadugli	68	E5
Kaduna	72	F2
Kadzherom	38	L2
Kaédi	70	C5
Kaeo	84	D2
Kaesŏng	50	D5
Kâf	62	E5
Kafanchan	72	F3
Kaffrine	72	A2
Kafiau	55	C3
Kåfjord	16	N1
Kafr Buhum	62	D1
Kafr el Sheikh	68	F1
Kafue	76	D3
Kaga	50	J5
Kaga Bandoro	74	B2
Kagoshima	50	F8
Kahemba	74	B5
Kahnūj	63	G3
Kahraman Maraş	60	G5
Kahta	60	H5
Kahurangi Point	84	C5
Kaiama	72	E3
Kai Besar	55	D4
Kaifeng	48	E4
Kaihu	84	D2
Kaihua	48	F5
Kai Kecil	55	D4
Kaikohe	84	D2
Kaikoura	84	D6
Kaili	48	D5
Kailua	100	(2)D2
Kailua Kona	100	(2)E4
Kaimana	55	D3

Name	Page	Grid
Käina	16	M7
Kainji Reservoir	72	E2
Kaipara Harbour	84	D3
Kairouan	70	H1
Kaiserslautern	20	C7
Kaišiadorys	18	P3
Kaitaia	84	D2
Kaiwatu	55	C4
Kaiyuan	52	C2
Kajaani	16	P4
Kakamega	74	E3
Kakata	72	B3
Kakhovs'ke Vodoskhovyshche	38	F5
Kākī	63	D2
Kakinäda	56	D5
Kaktovik	100	(1)J1
Kalabagh	56	B2
Kalabahi	55	B4
Kalabakan	54	F2
Kalach	38	H4
Kalachinsk	38	P3
Kalach-na-Donu	38	H5
Kaladar	96	E2
Ka Lae	100	(2)F5
Kalahari Desert	76	C4
Kalajoki	16	M4
Kalakan	46	K5
Kalam	56	B1
Kalamata	36	E7
Kalamazoo	96	C2
Kalampaka	36	D5
Kalana	72	C2
Kalaotoa	55	B4
Kalapana	100	(2)G4
Kalaupapa	100	(2)E2
Kalavryta	36	E6
Kalbarri	82	B5
Kale	36	L7
Kalecik	60	E3
Kaledupa	55	B4
Kalemie	74	D5
Kalemyo	56	F4
Kalevala	16	R4
Kalewa	56	F4
Kalgoorlie	82	D6
Kalianda	54	D4
Kalibo	52	G4
Kalima	74	D4
Kalimantan	54	E2
Kaliningrad	18	K3
Kaliningradskiy Zaliv	18	J3
Kalispell	94	D1
Kalisz	18	H6
Kalixälven	16	M3
Kalkan	36	M8
Kalkaring	82	F3
Kalkaska	96	C2
Kallavesi	16	P5
Kallsjön	16	G5
Kalmar	16	J8
Kalmykiya	60	M1
Kalmykovo	38	K5
Kalocsa	34	F3
Kalol	56	B4
Kalpakio	36	C5
Kalpeni	56	B6
Kaltag	100	(1)F3
Kaltenkirchen	20	E3
Kaluga	38	G4
Kalyan	56	B5
Kalymnos	36	J8
Kalymnos	36	J7
Kama	74	D4
Kamaishi	50	L4
Kaman	60	E4
Kamande	74	D4
Kamango	44	U6
Kamares	36	G8
Kambarka	38	K3
Kambo Ho	56	E3
Kamchatskiy Zaliv	46	U5
Kamenica	36	E2
Kamenka, Russia	38	H1
Kamenka, Russia	38	H4
Kamen'-na-Obi	44	Q7
Kamen'-Rybolov	50	F1
Kamensk-Shakhtinskiy	38	H5
Kamensk-Ural'skiy	38	M3
Kamenz	18	D6
Kamet	56	C2
Kamiiso	50	L3
Kamina	74	C5
Kamitsushima	50	E6
Kamituga	74	D4
Kamiyaku	50	F8
Kamloops	90	G6
Kamoenai	50	L2
Kampala	74	E3
Kampen	22	H2
Kâmpóng Cham	52	D4
Kâmpóng Chhnăng	52	C4
Kâmpot	52	C4
Kamsuuma	74	G3
Kam"yanets'-Podil's'kyy	38	E5
Kam"yanets	16	M10
Kāmyārān	60	M6
Kamyshin	38	J4
Kamyzyak	38	J5
Kan	68	F6
Kanab	100	D1
Kananga	74	C5
Kanazawa	50	J5
Kanbalu	56	G4
Kanchipuram	56	C6
Kandahār	58	J3
Kandalaksha	16	S3
Kandalakshskiy Zaliv	38	F1
Kandi	72	E2
Kandira	36	N3

Name	Page	Grid
Kandy	56	D7
Kane	96	E2
Kaneohe	100	(2)D2
Kang	76	C4
Kangaatsiaq	90	W3
Kangal	60	G4
Kangân, Iran	63	E3
Kangân, Iran	63	G4
Kangar	54	C1
Kangaroo Island	82	G7
Kangchenjunga	56	E3
Kangding	48	C4
Kangeq	90	Y4
Kangerluarsoruseq	90	W4
Kangerlussuaq	90	Y4
Kangersuatsiaq	90	W2
Kangetet	74	F3
Kanggye	50	D3
Kangiqsualujjuaq	90	T5
Kangiqsujuaq	90	S4
Kangirsuk	90	S4
Kangmar	56	E3
Kangnŭng	50	E5
Kango	72	G4
Kangping	48	G2
Kaniama	74	C5
Kanin Nos	44	G4
Kanji Reservoir	66	D4
Kanjiža	34	H3
Kankaanpää	16	M6
Kankakee	96	C2
Kankan	72	C2
Kankossa	70	C5
Kannapolis	98	E2
Kano	72	F2
Kanoya	50	F8
Kanpur	56	D3
Kansas	98	A2
Kansas	98	B2
Kansas City, Kans., United States	98	C2
Kansas City, Mo., United States	98	C2
Kansk	44	T6
Kanta	74	F2
Kantchari	72	E2
Kantemirovka	38	G5
Kanye	76	C4
Kaohsiung	48	G6
Kaolack	70	B6
Kaoma	76	C2
Kapanga	74	C5
Kap Arkona	18	C3
Kapchagay	44	P9
Kap Cort Adelaer = Kangeq	90	Y4
Kap Farvel = Nunap Isua	90	Y5
Kapfenberg	30	L3
Kapidağı Yarimadası	36	K4
Kapiri Mposhi	76	D2
Kapit	54	E2
Kapiti Island	84	E5
Kaplice	30	K2
Kapoeta	74	E3
Kaposvár	34	E3
Kappel	20	C6
Kappeln	20	E2
Kappl	30	F3
Kapsan	50	E3
Kapuskasing	92	K2
Kapuvár	34	E2
Kara	44	M4
Kara, Russia	44	M4
Kara, Togo	72	E3
Kara Ada	36	K8
Kara-Balta	44	N9
Karabekaul	58	H2
Kara-Bogaz-Gol	58	F1
Karabutak	38	M5
Karacabey	36	L4
Karacaköy	36	L3
Karacal Tepe	36	Q8
Karachayevo-Cherkesiya	60	J2
Karachayevsk	60	J2
Karachi	58	J5
Karaganda	44	N8
Karaginskiy Zaliv	46	V5
Karaj	58	F2
Karak	62	C5
Kara-Kala	58	G2
Karakalpakiya	44	K9
Karakoçan	60	J4
Karakol	44	P9
Karakoram	42	L6
Karaksar	46	K6
Kara-Kul'	44	N9
Karam	46	H5
Karaman	60	E5
Karamay	44	R8
Karamea	84	D5
Karamea Bight	84	C5
Karamürsel	36	M4
Karand	60	M6
Karaoy	44	N8
Karapinar	36	R7
Kara-Say	44	P9
Karasburg	76	B5
Kara Sea = Karskoye More	44	L3
Karasu	36	D3
Karasuk	44	P7
Karasuk	44	P7
Karatal	44	P8
Karataş	60	F5
Karatobe	38	K5
Karaton	38	K5
Karatsu	50	E7
Karazhal	38	P5
Karbalā'	58	D3
Karcag	34	H2
Karditsa	36	D5
Kärdla	16	M7
Kârdžali	36	H3
Kareliya	16	R4
Karepino	38	L2

Name	Page	Grid
Karesuando	16	M2
Kargalinskaya	60	M2
Kargasok	44	Q6
Kargat	44	P6
Kargil	56	C2
Kargopol'	38	G2
Kariba	76	D3
Kariba Dam	76	D3
Karibib	76	B4
Karimata	54	D3
Karimnagar	56	C5
Karkaralinsk	44	P8
Karkinits'ka Zatoka	38	F5
Karlik Shan	48	A2
Karlovac	34	C4
Karlovasi	36	J7
Karlovo	36	G2
Karlovy Vary	20	H6
Karlshamn	18	D1
Karlskoga	16	H7
Karlskrona	16	H8
Karlsruhe	20	D8
Karlstad, *Norway*	16	G7
Karlstad, *United States*	96	A1
Karlstadt	20	E7
Karmala	56	C5
Karmi'el	62	C4
Karmøy	16	C7
Karnafuli Reservoir	56	F4
Karnal	56	C3
Karnische Alpen	30	H4
Karnobat	36	J2
Karodi	58	J4
Karonga	74	E5
Karpathos	36	K9
Karpathos	36	K9
Karpenisi	36	D6
Karpogory	38	H2
Karrabük	60	E3
Karratha	82	C4
Kars	60	K3
Karsakpay	38	N5
Kārsava	16	P8
Karshi	58	J2
Karskoye More	44	L3
Karslyaka	36	K6
Karstula	16	N5
Kartal	36	M4
Kartaly	38	M4
Kartayel'	38	K2
Kartuzy	18	H3
Karufa	55	D3
Karumba	82	H3
Karur	56	C6
Karvina	18	H8
Karwar	56	B6
Karystos	36	G6
Kasai	74	B4
Kasaji	76	C2
Kasama	76	E2
Kasansay	44	N9
Kasba Lake	90	L4
Kasempa	76	D2
Kasenga	76	D2
Kāshān	58	F3
Kashi	58	L2
Kashima	48	L3
Kashiwazaki	50	K5
Kāshmar	58	G2
Kashmor	58	J4
Kasimov	38	H4
Kasli	38	M3
Kasongo	74	D4
Kasos	36	K9
Kaspi	60	L3
Kaspiysk	60	M2
Kassala	68	G4
Kassandreia	36	F4
Kassel	20	E5
Kasserine	70	G1
Kastamonu	60	E3
Kastelli	36	F9
Kastoria	36	D4
Kasulu	74	E4
Kasumkent	60	N3
Kasur	56	B2
Kata	46	K9
Katchall	56	F7
Katerini	36	E4
Katete	76	E2
Katha	56	G4
Katherine	82	F2
Kathiawar	58	K5
Kathmandu	56	E3
Kati	72	C2
Katihar	56	E3
Katiola	72	C3
Kato Nevrokopi	36	F3
Katonga	74	E3
Katoomba	82	K6
Katowice	18	J7
Katrineholm	16	J7
Katsina	72	F2
Katsina-Ala	72	F3
Katsuta	50	L5
Katsuura	50	L6
Kattakurgan	58	J2
Kattavia	36	K9
Kattegat	16	F8
Katun'	44	R7
Katwijkaan Zee	22	D2
Kauai	100	(2)B1
Kaufbeuren	30	N5
Kauhajoki	16	M5
Kaunas	18	N3
Kauno	18	D3
Kaunus	14	G2
Kaura Namoda	72	F2
Kavadarci	36	D3
Kavajë	36	B3
Kavala	36	G4
Kavali	56	C5
Kavār	63	E2
Kavaratti	56	B6
Kavarna	34	R6
Kawabe	50	L4
Kawagoe	50	K6
Kawakawa	84	E2
Kawambwa	74	D5
Kawasaki	50	K6
Kawau Island	84	E3
Kaweka	84	F4
Kawhia	84	E4
Kawkareik	52	B3
Kawthaung	52	B4
Kaya	72	D2
Kayak	44	U3
Kaycee	94	E2
Kayenta	100	D1
Kayes	72	B2
Kaymaz	36	P5
Kaynar	44	P8
Kayseri	60	F4
Kayyerkan	44	R4
Kazachinskoye	46	E5
Kazach'ye	46	P2
Kazakdar'ya	44	K9
Kazakhstan	44	L8
Kazan'	38	J3
Kazan	90	M4
Kazanlāk	36	H2
Kazan-rettō	80	E3
Kazbek	60	L2
Kāzerūn	63	D2
Kazincbarcika	34	H1
Kazungula	76	D3
Kazuno	50	L3
Kazymskiy Mys	44	M5
Kea	36	G7
Kea	36	G7
Kearney	92	G3
Keban Barajı	60	H4
Kébémèr	70	B5
Kebkabiya	68	D5
Kebnekaise	16	K3
K'ebrī Dehar	74	G2
K'ech'a Terara	74	F2
Keçiborlu	36	N7
Kecskemet	34	G3
Kédainiai	18	N2
Kedgwick	96	G1
Kediri	54	E4
Kédougou	72	B2
Kędzierzyn-Koźle	18	H7
Keele	100	(1)M3
Keene	96	F2
Keetmanshoop	76	B5
Keewatin	96	B1
Kefallonia	36	C6
Kefamenanu	55	B4
Keflavík	16	(1)B2
Kegen'	44	P9
Keg River	90	H5
Keheili	68	F4
Kehl	30	C2
Keila	16	N7
Keitele	16	N5
Kekerengu	84	D5
Kékes	34	H2
Kelai Thiladhunmathee Atoll	56	B7
Kelheim	30	G2
Kelibia	32	F12
Kelkit	60	G3
Kelmė	18	M2
Kélo	72	H3
Kelowna	90	H7
Kelso, *United States*	94	B1
Keluang	54	C2
Kem'	38	F2
Kemaliye	60	H4
Kemalpaşa	36	K6
Kemasik	54	C2
Kemer, *Turkey*	36	M8
Kemer, *Turkey*	36	N8
Kemerovo	44	R6
Kemi	16	N4
Kemijärvi	16	P3
Kemijärvi	16	P3
Kemijoki	16	P3
Kemmerer	94	D3
Kemmuna	32	J12
Kemnath	20	G7
Kemp's Bay	98	F5
Kempten	30	F3
Kendal	24	K7
Kendall	98	E4
Kendari	55	B3
Kendawangan	54	E3
Kendégué	72	H2
Kendujhargarh	56	E4
Kenedy	98	B4
Kenema	72	B3
Keneurgench	58	G1
Kenge	74	B4
Kengtung	52	B2
Kenhardt	76	C5
Kénitra	70	D2
Kenmare	24	C10
Kennett	98	D2
Kennewick	94	C1
Keno Hill	100	(1)K3
Kenora	92	H2
Kenosha	96	C2
Kentau	44	M9
Kentucky	92	J4
Kentwood	98	C3
Kenya	74	G5
Keokuk	96	B2
Kępno	18	H6
Kepulauan Anambas	54	D2
Kepulauan Aru	55	E4
Kepulauan Ayu	55	D2
Kepulauan Balabalangan	54	F3
Kepulauan Banggai	55	B3
Kepulauan Barat Daya	55	C4
Kepulauan Batu	54	B3
Kepulauan Bonerate	55	A4
Kepulauan Kai	55	D4
Kepulauan Kangean	54	F4
Kepulauan Karimunjawa	54	D4
Kepulauan Karkaralong	55	B2
Kepulauan Laut Kecil	54	F3
Kepulauan Leti	55	C4
Kepulauan Lingga	54	C2
Kepulauan Lucipara	55	C4
Kepulauan Mentawai	54	B3
Kepulauan Nanusa	55	C2
Kepulauan Natuna	54	D2
Kepulauan Riau	54	C2
Kepulauan Sabalana	54	F4
Kepulauan Sangir	55	C2
Kepulauan Solor	55	B4
Kepulauan Sula	55	B3
Kepulauan Talaud	55	C2
Kepulauan Tanimbar	55	D4
Kepulauan Tengah	54	F4
Kepulauan Togian	55	B3
Kepulauan Tukangbesi	55	B4
Kepulauan Watubela	55	D3
Kerch	60	G1
Kerchevskiy	38	L3
Kerempe Burnu	36	R2
Keren	68	G4
Kericho	74	F4
Kerio	74	F3
Kerki	58	J2
Kerkrade	22	J4
Kerkyra	36	B5
Kerkyra	36	B5
Kerma	68	F4
Kermadec Islands	80	H8
Kermadec Trench	80	J9
Kermān	63	G1
Kermānshāh	58	E3
Kermānshāhān	63	F1
Keros	36	H8
Kerpen	22	J4
Kerrville	98	B3
Kerulen	46	J7
Keryneia	60	E6
Keşan	36	J4
Kesennuma	50	L4
Keşiş Dağları	60	C2
Keszthely	34	E3
Keta	72	E3
Ketapang	54	D3
Ketchikan	100	(1)L4
Kêtou	72	E3
Kętrzyn	18	L3
Kettering	24	M9
Kettle Falls	92	C2
Kewanee	96	C2
Keweenaw Peninsula	96	C1
Key Largo	98	E4
Keystone Lake	98	B2
Key West	98	E5
Kezhma	46	G5
Kežmarok	18	K8
Khabarovsk	46	P7
Khadyzhensk	60	H1
Khakasiya	44	R7
Khairwāra	56	B4
Khalafābād	63	C1
Khalīg el Suweis	68	F2
Khalīj Surt	68	C1
Khalūf	58	G5
Khambhat	56	B4
Khamis Mushay	58	D6
Khamis Mushayṭ	68	H4
Khamkkeut	52	C3
Khampa	46	L4
Khamrà	46	J4
Khān al Baghdād	60	K7
Khān az Zabīb	62	D5
Khandagayty	44	S7
Khandwa	56	C4
Khanewal	56	B2
Khannya	44	X4
Khanpur	56	B3
Khān Shaykhūn	62	D1
Khantau	44	N9
Khantayka	46	D3
Khanty-Mansiysk	38	N2
Khān Yūnis	62	B5
Khapalu	56	C1
Kharabali	38	J5
Kharagpur	56	E4
Kharampur	46	B4
Kharan	58	J4
Khargon	56	C4
Kharkiv	38	G5
Kharlu	16	R6
Kharnmam	56	D5
Kharovsk	38	H3
Khartoum = El Khartum	68	F4
Khasavyurt	60	M2
Khāsh	58	H4
Khashgort	38	N1
Khashm el Girba	68	G4
Khashuri	60	K3
Khatanga	46	G2
Khātūnābād	63	F1
Khatyrka	46	X4
Khavda	58	J5
Khawr Fakkān	58	G4
Khaydarkan	58	K2
Khayelitsha	76	B6
Khemis Miliana	70	F1
Khemisset	70	D2
Khenchela	70	G1
Kherämeh	63	E2
Kherson	38	F5
Kheta	44	T3
Kheta	44	T3
Kheygiyakha	38	P2
Khilok	46	J6
Khirbat Isrīyah	62	E1
Khīyāv	60	M4
Khmel'nyts'kyy	38	E5
Khodā Afarīn	60	M4
Kholmsk	46	Q7
Khonj	63	E3
Khon Kaen	52	C3
Khonuu	46	Q3
Khoper	38	H4
Khor	46	P7
Khor	46	P7
Khoreyver	38	L1
Khorinsk	46	H6
Khorramābād	58	E3
Khorramshahr	63	C1
Khorugh	58	K2
Khoseda Khard	38	L1
Khouribga	70	D2
Khrebet Cherskogo	46	P3
Khrebet Dzhagdy	46	N6
Khrebet Dzhugdzhur	46	N5
Khrebet Khamar Daban	46	G6
Khrebet Kolymskiy	42	U3
Khrebet Kopet Dag	58	G2
Khrebet Suntar Khayata	46	P4
Khrebet Tarbagatay	44	Q8
Khroma	46	Q2
Khudoseya	46	C3
Khudzhakh	46	R4
Khujand	58	J1
Khulna	56	E4
Khurayş	63	B4
Khushab	56	B2
Khust	34	L1
Khuwei	68	E5
Khuzdar	58	J4
Khvormūj	63	D2
Khvoy	60	L4
Khyber Pass	58	K3
Kibaya	74	F4
Kibombo	74	D4
Kibondo	74	E4
Kibre Mengist	74	F2
Kičevo	36	C3
Kichmengskiy Gorodok	38	J3
Kicking Horse Pass	90	H6
Kidal	70	F5
Kidderminster	24	K9
Kidira	72	B2
Kiel	20	F2
Kielce	18	K7
Kieler Bucht	20	F2
Kiev = Kyyiv	38	F4
Kiffa	70	C5
Kigali	74	E4
Kigoma	74	D4
Kihnu	16	M7
Kıkıköy	36	L3
Kikinda	34	H4
Kikonai	50	L3
Kikori	55	F4
Kikwit	74	B5
Kilchu	50	E3
Kilifi	74	F4
Kilindoni	74	F5
Kilingi-Nõmme	16	N7
Kilis	60	G5
Kiliya	34	S4
Kilkenny	24	E9
Kilkis	36	E4
Killarney, *Canada*	96	D1
Killarney, *Republic of Ireland*	24	C9
Kilmarnock	24	H6
Kil'mez	38	K3
Kilosa	74	F5
Kilrush	24	C9
Kilttan	56	B6
Kilwa	74	D5
Kilwa Masoko	74	F5
Kimberley	76	C5
Kimberley Plateau	82	E3
Kimch'aek	50	E3
Kimolos	36	G8
Kimongo	72	G5
Kimry	38	G3
Kinango	74	F4
Kincardine	96	D2
Kinda	74	C5
Kinder	98	C3
Kindia	72	B2
Kindu	74	D4
Kineshma	38	H3
Kingaroy	82	K5
King City	94	B3
King George Islands	90	R5
Kingisepp	16	Q7
King Island, *Australia*	82	H7
King Island, *Canada*	46	AA3
Kingman	100	D1
Kingri	58	J3
Kingscote	82	G7
Kingsland	98	E3
King's Lynn	24	N9
King Sound	82	D3
Kings Peak	94	D2
Kingsport	98	E2
Kingston, *Canada*	96	E2
Kingston, *Jamaica*	102	J5
Kingston, *United States*	96	F2
Kingston-upon-Hull	24	M8
Kingston upon Thames	22	B3
Kingstown	108	E11
Kingsville	98	B4
Kingville	102	E3
King William Island	90	M3
King William's Town	76	D6
Kinik	36	K5

Name	Page	Grid	Name	Page	Grid	Name	Page	Grid	Name	Page	Grid
Kinka-san	50	L4	Knokke-Heist	22	F3	Konya	60	E5	Kozloduy	34	L6
Kinna	16	G8	Knoxville	96	D3	Konz	20	B7	Kozlu	36	P3
Kinsale	24	D10	Knysna	76	C6	Kookynie	82	D5	Kōzu-shima	50	K6
Kinshasa	74	B4	Koba	54	D3	Kootenai	94	C1	Kpalimé	72	E3
Kinsley	98	B2	Kōbe	50	H6	Kootenay Lake	92	C2	Kraai	76	D6
Kinston	96	E3	Kobe	55	C2	Kópasker	16	(1)E1	Krabi	52	B5
Kintampo	72	D3	København	16	G9	Kópavogur	16	(1)C2	Kradeljevo	32	M5
Kintyre	24	G6	Kobenni	70	D5	Koper	30	J5	Kragujevac	34	H5
Kinyeti	74	E3	Koblenz	20	C6	Kopeysk	38	M3	Kraków	18	J7
Kinzig	20	E6	Kobo	56	G3	Köping	16	J7	Kraljeviča	30	K5
Kipini	74	G4	Kobroör	55	E4	Koplik	34	G7	Kraljevo	34	H6
Kipnuk	100	(1)E3	Kobryn	18	P5	Koprivnica	34	D3	Kralovice	18	C8
Kirchheim	30	E2	Kobuk	100	(1)F2	Korba, India	56	D4	Kramators'k	38	G5
Kirchheimbolanden	22	L5	Kobuk	100	(1)F2	Korba, Tunisia	32	E12	Kramfors	16	J5
Kirenga	46	H5	Kočani	36	E3	Korbach	20	D5	Kranj	34	B3
Kirensk	46	H5	Koçarli	36	K7	Korçë	36	C4	Krapina	32	K2
Kiribati	80	J6	Kočevje	34	B4	Korčula	34	D7	Krapinske Toplice	30	L4
Kırıkhan	60	G5	Ko Chang	52	C4	Kord Sheykh	63	E2	Krasino	44	J3
Kırıkkale	60	E4	Kŏch'ang	50	E6	Korea Bay	50	B4	Krāslava	16	P9
Kirillov	38	G3	Kochechum	46	F3	Korea Strait	50	B6	Krašnik	18	M7
Kirinyaga	74	F4	Kōchi	50	G7	Korf	46	V4	Krasnoarmeysk	38	N4
Kirishi	38	F3	Kochi	56	C7	Korhogo	72	C3	Krasnoborsk	38	J2
Kiritimati	80	L5	Kochki	44	Q7	Korinthiakos Kolpos	36	E6	Krasnodar	38	G5
Kirkağaç	36	K5	Kochkorka	44	P9	Korinthos	36	E7	Krasnohrad	38	G5
Kirk Bulāg Dāgh	58	E2	Kochubey	60	M1	Kōriyama	50	L5	Krasnokamensk	46	K6
Kirkcaldy	24	J5	Kodiak	100	(1)G4	Korkino	38	M4	Krasnosel'kup	46	C3
Kirkcudbright	24	H7	Kodiak Island	100	(1)G4	Korkuteli	60	D5	Krasnotur'insk	38	M3
Kirkjubæjarklaustur	16	(1)E3	Kodino	38	G2	Korla	44	R9	Krasnoufimsk	38	L3
Kirkland Lake	96	D1	Kodinsk	46	F5	Korliki	46	C4	Krasnovishersk	38	L2
Kirklareli	36	K3	Kodomari-misaki	50	L3	Körmend	34	D2	Krasnoyarsk	46	E5
Kirkūk	60	L6	Kodyma	34	S1	Kornat	34	C6	Krasnoyarskoye Vodokhranilishche	44	S6
Kirkwall	24	K3	Köflach	34	C2	Koroba	55	F4	Krasnoznamensk	18	M3
Kirov, Russia	38	J3	Kōfu	50	K6	Köroğlu Dağları	36	Q4	Krasnystaw	18	N7
Kirov, Russia	38	F4	Koge	18	B2	Köroğlu Tepesi	36	P4	Krasnyy Chikoy	46	H6
Kirovo-Chepetsk	38	K3	Køge Bugt	18	B2	Korogwe	74	F5	Krasnyy Kut	38	J4
Kirovohrad	38	F5	Kohat	56	B2	Koronowo	18	G4	Krasnyy Yar	38	J5
Kirriemuir	24	K5	Kohima	56	F3	Koror	80	D5	Kratovo	36	E2
Kirs	38	K3	Koh-i-Qaisir	58	H3	Korosten'	38	E4	Kraynovka	60	M2
Kirsanov	38	H4	Koh-i-Sangan	58	J3	Koro Toro	68	C4	Krefeld	22	J3
Kırşehir	60	F4	Kohtla-Järve	16	P7	Korsakov	46	Q7	Kremenchuk	38	F5
Kiruna	16	L3	Kohumadulu Atoll	56	B8	Korsør	20	G1	Kremmling	94	E2
Kiryū	50	K5	Koidu	72	B3	Korti	68	F4	Krems	30	L2
Kisangani	74	D3	Koi Sanjaq	60	L6	Kortrijk	22	F4	Kremsmünster	30	K2
Kisbér	34	E2	Koitere	16	R5	Korumburra	82	J7	Krestovka	38	K1
Kiselevsk	44	R7	Kokenau	55	E4	Koryakskiy Khrebet	46	V4	Krestyakh	46	K4
Kishanganj	56	E3	Kokkola	16	M5	Koryazhma	44	H5	Kretinga	18	L2
Kishangarh, India	56	B3	Kokomo	98	D1	Kos	36	K8	Kribi	72	F4
Kishangarh, India	56	B3	Kokpekty	44	Q8	Kos	36	K8	Kričim	36	G2
Kishi	72	E3	Kokshetau	38	N4	Kosa	38	L3	Krieglach	30	L3
Kishiwada	50	H6	Kokstad	76	D6	Ko Samui	52	C5	Krishna	56	C5
Kishtwar	56	C2	Kolaka	55	B3	Kościan	18	F5	Krishnagiri	56	C6
Kisii	74	E4	Kolar	56	C6	Kościerzyna	18	H3	Kristiansand	16	E7
Kiska Island	100	(3)B1	Kolari	16	M3	Kosciusko	98	D3	Kristianstad	16	H8
Kiskőrös	34	G3	Kolašin	34	G7	Kosh Agach	44	R8	Kristiansund	16	D5
Kiskunfélegyháza	34	G3	Kolda	72	B2	Koshoba	58	F1	Kristinehamn	16	H7
Kiskunhalas	34	G3	Kolding	16	E9	Košice	18	L9	Kristinestad	16	L5
Kiskunmajsa	34	G3	Kole	74	C4	Koslan	38	J2	Kriti	36	H10
Kislovodsk	60	K2	Kolhapur	56	B5	Kosŏng	50	E4	Kriva Palanka	36	E2
Kismaayo	74	G4	Kolin	18	E7	Kosovo	36	C2	Križevci	34	D3
Kissidougou	72	B3	Kolkata	56	E4	Kosovska Mitrovica	36	C2	Krk	30	K5
Kisumu	74	E4	Kollam	56	C7	Kosrae	80	G5	Krk	30	K5
Kisvárda	34	K1	Köln	20	B6	Kostajnica	30	M5	Kroměříž	18	G8
Kita	72	C2	Kolno	18	L4	Kostanay	38	M4	Kronach	20	G6
Kitakami	50	L4	Koło	18	H5	Kostenec	36	F2	Krŏng Kaôh Kŏng	52	C4
Kita-Kyūshū	50	F7	Kołobrzeg	18	E3	Kosti	68	F5	Kronotskiy Zaliv	46	U6
Kita-Kyūshū	48	H4	Kologriv	38	H3	Kostino	46	D3	Kroonstadt	76	D5
Kitami	50	M2	Kolomna	38	G3	Kostomuksha	16	R4	Kroper	32	H3
Kitchener	96	D2	Kolomyya	34	N1	Kostroma	38	H3	Kropotkin	38	H5
Kitgum	74	E3	Kolonedale	55	B3	Kostrzyn	18	D5	Krosno	18	L8
Kitimat	90	F6	Kolosovka	38	P3	Kos'yu	38	L1	Krško	30	L5
Kitilä	16	N3	Kolpashevo	44	Q6	Koszalin	18	F3	Krugë	36	B3
Kitunda	74	E5	Kolpos Agiou Orous	36	F4	Kőszeg	34	D2	Krui	54	C4
Kitwe	76	D2	Kolpos Kassandras	36	F4	Kota	56	C3	Krumbach	30	F2
Kitzingen	20	F7	Kolpos Murampelou	36	H9	Kotaagung	54	C4	Krung Thep	52	C4
Kiuruvesi	16	P5	Kolskijzaliv	38	S2	Kotabaru	54	F3	Kruså	20	E2
Kivijärvi	16	N5	Kolskiy Poluostrov	38	N4	Kota Belud	54	F1	Kruševac	34	J6
Kivik	18	D2	Koluton	38	N4	Kota Bharu	54	C1	Krychaw	38	F4
Kiya	46	D5	Kolva	38	L2	Kotabumi	54	C3	Krym'	60	E1
Kıyıköy	60	C3	Kolwezi	76	D2	Kota Kinabalu	54	F1	Krymsk	60	H1
Kizel	38	L3	Kolyma	46	R4	Kotamubagu	55	B2	Krynica	18	L8
Kizilalan	36	R8	Kolymskaya Nizmennost'	46	S3	Kotapinang	54	B2	Krytiko Pelagos	36	G9
Kızılcahamam	60	E3	Kolymskaye	46	T3	Kotel'nich	38	J3	Kryve Ozero	34	T2
Kızılırmak	60	F3	Komandorskiye Ostrova	46	V5	Kotel'nikovo	38	H5	Kryvyy Rih	38	F5
Kızılkaya	36	N7	Komárno	34	F2	Köthen	20	G5	Krzna	18	N5
Kizil'skoye	38	L4	Komárom	34	F2	Kotido	74	E3	Ksar el Boukhari	28	N9
Kızıltepe	60	J5	Komatsu	50	J5	Kotka	16	P6	Ksen'yevka	46	K6
Kizlyar	60	M2	Kombe	74	D4	Kotlas	38	J2	Ksour Essaf	70	H1
Kizlyarskiy Zaliv	60	M1	Komi	38	K2	Kotlik	100	(1)E3	Kuala Kerai	54	C1
Kizyl-Atrek	44	J10	Komló	34	F3	Kotor Varoš	34	E5	Kuala Lipis	54	C2
Kjustendil	36	E2	Kom Ombo	68	F3	Kotov'sk	38	E5	Kuala Lumpur	54	C2
Kladanj	34	F5	Komotini	36	H3	Kottagudem	56	D5	Kuala Terengganu	54	C1
Kladno	18	D7	Komsa	44	R5	Kotto	74	C2	Kuandian	50	C3
Klagenfurt	30	K4	Komsomol'skiy	38	J5	Kotuy	46	G2	Kuantan	54	C2
Klaipėda	16	L9	Komsomol'sk-na-Amure	46	P6	Kotzebue	100	(1)E2	Kuçadasi	36	K7
Klamath	94	B2	Konârka	56	E5	Kotzebue Sound	100	(1)D2	Kučevo	34	J5
Klamath	94	B2	Konda	38	N3	Kouango	74	H3	Kuching	54	E2
Klamath Falls	94	B2	Kondagaon	56	D5	Koudougou	72	D2	Kucovë	36	B4
Klarälven	16	G6	Kondinskoye	38	N3	Koulamoutou	72	G5	Kudat	54	F1
Klatovy	20	J7	Kondoa	74	F4	Koum	72	G3	Kudus	54	E4
Klaus	30	K3	Kondopoga	38	F2	Koumra	72	H3	Kudymkar	38	K3
Klerksdorp	76	D5	Kondrat'yeva	44	V5	Koundâra	72	B2	Kufstein	30	H3
Kleve	20	B5	Kondūz	58	J2	Koupéla	70	C6	Kugmallit Bay	90	E2
Klin	38	G3	Kong Frederik VI Kyst	90	Y4	Kourou	108	G2	Kühbonän	63	G1
Klingenthal	20	H6	Kongi	44	R9	Koutiala	72	C2	Kühdasht	60	M7
Klínovec	20	H6	Kongola	76	C3	Kouvola	16	P6	Küh-e Alijuq	63	D1
Klintsy	38	F4	Kongolo	74	D5	Kovdor	16	R3	Küh-e Bābā	58	J3
Ključ	30	M6	Kongsberg	16	E7	Kovel'	38	D4	Küh-e Bül	63	E1
Kłobuck	18	H7	Kongur Shan	44	N10	Kovin	34	H5	Küh-e Dīnār	63	D1
Kłodzko	18	F7	Königsberg = Kaliningrad	18	K3	Kovrov	38	H3	Küh-e Fürgun	63	G3
Klofta	16	F6	Königswinter	20	C6	Kowanyama	82	H3	Küh-e Hazārān	63	G2
Klosterneuburg	30	M2	Königs-Wusterhausen	20	J4	Köyceğiz	36	L8	Küh-e Hormoz	63	F3
Klosters	30	E4	Konin	18	H5	Koygorodok	38	K2	Küh-e Kalat	58	G3
Kluane	90	D4	Konispol	36	C5	Koykuk	100	(1)E3	Küh-e Kührān	63	H3
Kluane Lake	100	(1)J3	Konitsa	36	C4	Koynas	38	J2	Küh-e Lāleh Zār	63	G2
Kluczbork	18	H7	Köniz	30	C4	Koyukuk	100	(1)F2	Küh-e Masāhūn	63	F1
Klyuchevskaya Sopka	46	U5	Konjic	34	E6	Kozan	60	F5	Küh-e Safidār	63	E2
Klyuchi	46	U5	Konosha	38	H2	Kozani	36	D4	Kuh-e Sahand	60	M5
Kneža	34	M6	Konotop	38	F4	Kozheynikovo	44	W3	Kühestak	63	G3
Knin	34	D5	Konstanz	30	E3	Kozhikode	56	C6	Küh-e Taftān	58	H4
Knittelfeld	34	B2	Kontagora	72	F2	Kozienice	18	L6	Kühhā-ye Bashäkerd	63	G3
Knjaževac	34	K6	Kon Tum	52	D4				Kühhā-ye Zāgros	63	D1

167

Kuhmo 16 Q4
Kūhpāyeh 63 G1
Kuito 76 B2
Kuji 50 L3
Kukës 34 H7
Kukhtuy 46 Q4
Kukinaga 50 F8
Kula 34 K6
Kulagino 38 K5
Kulandy 44 K8
Kuldīga 16 L8
Kulgera 82 F5
Kulmbach 20 G6
Külob 58 J2
Kul'sary 38 K5
Kultsjön 16 H4
Kulu 60 E4
Kulunda 44 P7
Kulynigol 46 C4
Kuma 38 N3
Kumamoto 50 F7
Kumanovo 34 J7
Kumara, *New Zealand* 84 C6
Kumara, *Russia* 46 M6
Kumasi 72 D3
Kumba 72 F4
Kumbağ 36 K4
Kumbakonam 56 C6
Kumeny 38 K3
Kumertau 38 L4
Kumla 16 H7
Kumluca 36 N8
Kummerower See 20 H3
Kumo 72 G3
Kumta 56 B6
Kumukh 60 M2
Kunene 76 A3
Kungälv 16 F8
Kungrad 44 K9
Kungu 74 B3
Kungur 38 L3
Kunhing 52 B2
Kunlun Shan 56 D1
Kunming 48 C6
Kunsan 50 D6
Kunszetmarton 18 K11
Kununurra 82 E3
Künzelsau 20 E7
Kuolayarvi 16 Q3
Kuopio 38 E2
Kupang 82 B2
Kupino 44 P7
Kupreanof Point 100 (1)F4
Kup''yans'k 38 G5
Kuqa 44 Q9
Kür 60 M3
Kura 58 E2
Kuragino 46 E6
Kurashiki 50 G6
Kurasia 56 D4
Kurchum 44 Q8
Kürdämir 60 N3
Kurduvadi 56 C5
Kure 50 G6
Kure Island 80 J3
Kuressaare 16 M7
Kureyka 46 D3
Kureyka 46 E3
Kurgal'dzhinskiy 44 N7
Kurgan 38 N3
Kurikka 16 M5
Kuril Islands = Kuril'skiye Ostrova 46 S7
Kuril'sk 46 R7
Kuril'skiye Ostrova 46 S7
Kuril Trench 42 V5
Kuripapango 84 F4
Kurmuk 68 F5
Kurnool 56 C5
Kuroiso 50 K5
Kurow 84 C7
Kuršėnai 18 M1
Kursk 38 G4
Kuršumlija 34 J6
Kurşunlu 60 E3
Kuruman 76 C5
Kurume 50 F7
Kurumkan 46 J6
Kurunegala 56 D7
Kushikino 50 F8
Kushimoto 50 H7
Kushir 46 H6
Kushiro 50 N2
Kushmurun 38 M4
Kushum 38 K4
Kuskokwim Bay 100 (1)E4
Kuskokwim Mountains 100 (1)F3
Kussharo-ko 50 N2
Kütahya 60 C4
K'ut'aisi 60 K2
Kutan 60 M1
Kutchan 50 L2
Kutina 34 D4
Kutno 18 J5
Kutu 72 H5
Kutum 68 D5
Kuujjua 90 J2
Kuujjuaq 90 T5
Kuujjuarapik 90 R5
Kuusamo 38 E1
Kuvango 76 B2
Kuwait 63 B2
Kuwait = Al Kuwayt 63 C2
Kuya 38 H1
Kuybyshev 44 P6
Kuygan 44 N8
Kuytun 44 R9
Kuyumba 46 F4
Kuznetsk 38 J4
Kuzomen' 38 G1
Kvaløya, *Norway* 16 M1
Kvaløya, *Norway* 16 J2
Kvalynsk 44 H7
Kwale 74 F4
Kwangju 50 D6
Kwango 74 B5
Kwazulu Natal 76 E5
Kwekwe 76 D3
Kwidzyn 16 K10
Kwilu 72 H5
Kyakhta 46 H6
Kyancutta 82 G6
Kyaukpyu 52 A3
Kyaukse 56 G4
Kyeburn 84 C7
Kyeintali 56 F5
Kyjov 30 N2
Kyklades 36 G7
Kyle of Lochalsh 24 G4
Kyll 22 J4
Kyllini 36 D7
Kymi 36 G6
Kyŏngju 50 E6
Kyōto 50 H6
Kyparissia 36 D7
Kyperissiakos Kolpos 36 C7
Kyra Panagia 36 G5
Kyren 46 G6
Kyrgyzstan 44 N9
Kyritz 20 H4
Kyrta 38 L2
Kyshtovka 44 P6
Kystatyam 46 L3
Kytalyktakh 46 N3
Kythira 36 E8
Kythira 36 F8
Kythnos 36 G7
Kyushe 44 K8
Kyūshū 50 F7
Kyūshū-sanchi 50 F7
Kyusyur 46 M2
Kyyiv 38 F4
Kyzyl 44 S7
Kyzyl-Adyr 44 N9
Kyzylorda 38 N6
Kzyl-Dzhar 38 N5
Kzyltu 44 N7

L

Laascaanood 74 H2
Laatzen 20 E4
Laâyoune 70 C3
Laba 72 F2
La Banda 110 J4
La Bañeza 28 E2
La Baule 26 C6
La Bazoge 26 F5
Labbezenga 70 F5
Labé 72 B2
Labe 18 E7
Labin 30 K5
Labinsk 60 J1
Laboulaye 110 J5
Labrador 90 U6
Labrador City 90 T6
Labrador Sea 90 V4
Lábrea 108 E5
Labrieville 96 G1
Labuha 55 C3
Labuhan 54 D4
Labuhanbajo 55 A4
Labutta 52 A3
Labytnangi 44 M4
Laç 34 G8
Lac à l'Eau Claire 90 R5
Lacanau 26 D8
La Carlota 28 F7
La Carolina 28 G6
Lac Bienville 90 S5
Lac Brochet 90 L5
Laccadive Islands 56 B6
Lac d'Annecy 30 B5
Lac de Bizerte 32 D11
Lac Débo 70 E5
Lac de Kossou 72 C3
Lac de Lagdo 72 G3
Lac de Manantali 72 C2
Lac de Mbakaou 72 G3
Lac de Neuchâtel 30 B4
Lac de Retenue de la Lufira 74 D6
Lac de St-Croix 30 B7
Lac des Bois 90 G3
Lac de Sélingue 72 C2
Lac Do 70 E5
Lac du Bourget 30 A5
Lacedonia 32 K7
Lacepede Bay 82 G7
Lac Evans 90 R6
Lac Faguibine 70 E5
Lac Fitri 68 C5
La Charité-sur-Loire 26 J6
La Chaux-de-Fonds 30 B3
La Chorrera 108 C4
Lac Ichkeul 32 D11
La Ciotat 26 L10
Lac La Biche 90 J6
Lac la Martre 90 H4
Lac Léman = Lake Geneva 30 B4
Lac Mai-Ndombe 74 B4
Lac-Mégantic 96 F1
Lac Minto 90 R5
Lac Mistassini 90 S6
Lac Nzilo 74 D6
Lac Onangué 72 F5
Laconi 32 D9
Laconia 96 F2
Lac Payne 90 S5
La Crosse 96 B2
La Cruz 92 E7
Lac St-Jean 96 F1
Lac St. Joseph 90 N6
Lac Seul 90 N6
Lac Tumba 74 B4
Lacul Brateş 34 Q4
Lacul Razim 34 R5
Lacul Sinoie 34 R5
Lac Upemba 74 D5
La Dorada 108 C2
Ladozhskoye Ozero 38 F2
Ladysmith, *South Africa* 76 D5
Ladysmith, *United States* 96 B1
Ladyzhenka 38 N4
La Esmeralda, *Bolivia* 110 J3
La Esmeralda, *Venezuela* 108 D3
Læsø 16 F8
Lafayette, *Ind., United States* 96 C2
Lafayette, *La., United States* 98 C3
La Ferté-St-Aubin 26 G6
Lafia 72 F3
Lafiagi 72 F3
La Flèche 26 E6
Lafnitz 30 M3
Laft 63 F3
Lagan' 38 J5
Lagan 16 G8
Lage 22 L3
Lågen 16 E6
Lage's 94 D2
Laghouat 70 F2
Lagkadas 36 F4
Lagoa dos Patos 110 L5
Lagoa Mirim 110 L5
Lago Argentino 110 G9
Lago de Cahora Bassa 76 E3
Lago del Coghinas 32 C8
Lago del Flumendosa 32 D9
Lago de Maracaibo 108 C2
Lago de Nicaragua 102 G6
Lago de Poopó 108 D7
Lago di Bolsena 32 F6
Lago di Braciano 32 G6
Lago di Caine 30 D5
Lago di Como 30 E4
Lago di Garda 30 F5
Lago di Lecco 30 E5
Lago di Lugano 30 E5
Lago d'Iseo 30 E5
Lago di Varano 32 K7
Lago Maggiore 30 D5
Lago Omodeo 32 C8
Lago Rogaguado 108 D6
Lagos, *Nigeria* 72 E3
Lagos, *Portugal* 28 B7
Lago Titicaca 108 D7
Lago Trasimeno 32 G5
La Goulette 32 E12
La Grand-Combe 26 K9
La Grande 94 C1
La Grange 98 E3
Lagrange 82 D3
La Gran Sabana 108 E2
Laguna 110 M4
Laguna de Caratasca 102 H5
Laguna Madre 98 B4
Laguna Mar Chiquita 106 E7
Lagunillas 108 E7
La Habana 102 H4
Lahad Datu 52 F5
Lahat 54 C3
La Haye-du-Puits 22 A5
Lāhījān 58 F2
Lahn 22 L4
Lahnstein 22 K4
Laholmsbukten 18 B1
Lahore 56 B2
Lahr 30 C2
Lahti 16 N6
Laï 74 B2
Laiagam 55 F4
Lai Chau 52 C2
L'Aigle 22 C6
Laihia 16 M5
Laingsburg 76 C6
Laiwu 48 F3
Laiyuan 48 E3
Lajanurpekhi 60 K2
Lajes 110 L4
Lajosmizse 18 J10
La Junta 94 F3
Lake Abbe 74 G1
Lake Abitibi 96 E1
Lake Albert, *Democratic Republic of Congo/Uganda* 74 D3
Lake Albert, *United States* 94 B2
Lake Almanor 94 B2
Lake Amadeus 82 F4
Lake Andes 94 G2
Lake Argyle 82 E3
Lake Athabasca 90 K5
Lake Austin 82 C5
Lake Balkhash = Ozero Balkhash 42 L5
Lake Bangweulu 76 E2
Lake Barlee 82 C5
Lake Benmore 84 C7
Lake Blanche 82 H5
Lake Buchanan 100 G2
Lake Callabonna 82 H5
Lake Carey 82 D5
Lake Carnegie 82 D5
Lake Chad 68 B5
Lake Charles 98 C3
Lake Chelan 94 B1
Lake Chilwa 76 F3
Lake City 98 E3
Lake Claire 90 J5
Lake Coleridge 84 C6
Lake Constance 30 E3
Lake Crowley 94 C3
Lake C. W. McConaughy 94 F2
Lake Diefenbaker 90 K6
Lake Disappointment 82 D4
Lake District 24 J7
Lake Dojran 36 E3
Lake Dora 82 D4
Lake Dundas 82 B6
Lake Edward 74 D4
Lake Elwall 94 D1
Lake Erie 96 D2
Lake Eyasi 74 E4
Lake Eyre 80 D8
Lake Eyre Basin 82 G5
Lake Eyre North 82 G5
Lake Eyre South 82 G5
Lake Francis Case 94 G2
Lake Frome 82 H6
Lake Gairdner 82 G6
Lake Geneva 30 B4
Lake Gordon 82 H8
Lake Grace 82 C6
Lake Harbour 90 T4
Lake Hauroko 84 A7
Lake Havasu 100 C2
Lake Havasu City 100 D2
Lake Hopkins 82 E4
Lake Hudson 98 B2
Lake Huron 96 D1
Lake Jackson 98 B4
Lake Kariba 76 D3
Lake Kemp 98 B2
Lake Kerkinitis 34 L8
Lake Kivu 74 D4
Lake Kyoga 74 E3
Lake Ladoga = Ladozhskoye Ozero 38 F2
Lakeland 98 E4
Lake Lefroy 82 D6
Lake Louis 90 H6
Lake Macdonald 82 E4
Lake Mackay 82 E4
Lake Macleod 82 B4
Lake Manapouri 84 A7
Lake Manitoba 90 M6
Lake Manyara 74 F4
Lake Maurice 82 F5
Lake McDonald 94 D1
Lake McMillan 100 F2
Lake Mead 94 D3
Lake Melville 90 U6
Lake Michigan 96 C2
Lake Moore 82 C5
Lake Murray 55 F4
Lake Mweru 74 D5
Lake Mweru Wantipa 74 E5
Lake Nash 82 G4
Lake Nasser 68 F3
Lake Natron 74 F4
Lake Neale 82 E4
Lake Nipigon 90 P6
Lake Nipissing 96 E1
Lake Nyasa 76 E2
Lake Oahe 94 F2
Lake of the Woods 96 B1
Lake Ohau 84 B7
Lake Ohrid 36 C4
Lake Okeechobee 98 E4
Lake Onega = Onezhskoye Ozero 14 H1
Lake Ontario 96 E2
Lake O' The Cherokees 96 B3
Lake O' The Pines 98 C3
Lake Paringa 84 B6
Lake Peipus 16 P7
Lake Placid 98 E4
Lakeport 94 B3
Lake Poteriteri 84 A8
Lake Powell 94 D3
Lake Prespa 36 D4
Lake Providence 98 C3
Lake Pskov 16 P7
Lake Pukaki 84 C7
Lake Rotorua 84 F4
Lake Rukwa 74 E5
Lake St. Lucia 76 E5
Lake Sakakawea 94 F1
Lake Scutari 34 G7
Lake Simcoe 96 E2
Lake Superior 96 C1
Lake Tahoe 94 B3
Lake Tanganyika 74 D5
Lake Taupo 84 E4
Lake Te Anau 84 A7
Lake Tekapo 84 C6
Lake Tekapo 84 C6
Lake Texoma 98 B3
Lake Torrens 82 G6
Lake Travis 100 G2
Lake Tschida 94 F1
Lake Turkana 74 F3
Lake Victoria 74 E4
Lakeview 94 B2
Lake Volta 72 D3
Lake Waikare 84 E3
Lake Waikaremoana 84 F4
Lake Wakatipu 84 B7
Lake Wanaka 84 B7
Lake White 82 E4
Lake Wills 82 E4
Lake Winnipeg 90 M6
Lake Winnipegosis 90 L6
Lakewood 94 E3
Lake Woods 82 F3
Lake Xau 76 C4
Lake Yamma Yamma 82 H5
Lakhdaria 28 P8
Lakhimpur 56 D3
Lakhnadon 56 C4
Lakhpat 56 A4
Lakin 98 A2
Lakki 56 B2
Lakonikos Kolpos 36 E8
Lakota 94 G1
Lakselv 16 N1
Lalín 28 B2
La Línea 28 E8

Milton, *New Zealand*	84	B8
Milton, *United States*	98	D3
Milton Keynes	22	B2
Miluo	48	E5
Milwaukee	96	C2
Mily	44	L8
Mimizan-Plage	26	D9
Mīnāb	63	G3
Mina Jebel Ali	63	F4
Minas, *Indonesia*	54	C3
Minas, *Uruguay*	110	K5
Mīnā' Sa'ūd	63	C2
Minas Gerais	108	H7
Minas Novas	108	J7
Minatitián	102	F5
Minbu	52	A2
Minchinmávida	110	G7
Mincivan	60	M4
Mindanao	52	G5
Mindelheim	30	F2
Mindelo	72	(1)B1
Minden	22	L2
Mindoro	52	G4
Mindoro Strait	52	G4
Minehead	24	J10
Mineola	98	B3
Mineral'nyye Vody	60	K1
Minerva Reefs	80	J8
Minfeng	44	Q10
Minga	74	D6
Mingäçevir	60	M3
Mingäçevir Su Anbarı	60	M3
Mingulay	24	D5
Minhe	48	C3
Minicoy	56	B7
Minilya Roadhouse	82	B4
Minna	72	F3
Minneapolis	96	B2
Minnesota	96	A1
Minnesota	96	A2
Miño	28	C2
Minot	94	F1
Minsk	38	E4
Minturn	94	E3
Minusinsk	44	S7
Min Xian	48	C4
Min'yar	38	L3
Miquelon	96	E1
Miraflores	108	C3
Miramas	26	K10
Mirambeau	26	E8
Miranda	108	F8
Miranda de Ebro	28	H2
Miranda do Douro	28	D3
Mirandela	28	C3
Mirbāt	58	F6
Mīrjāveh	58	H4
Mirnyy	46	J4
Mirow	20	H3
Mirpur Khas	56	A3
Mirtoō Pelagos	36	F7
Mirzapur	56	D3
Miskolc	34	H1
Misoōl	55	D3
Mişrātah	68	C1
Missinaibi	90	Q6
Missinipe	90	L5
Mission	94	F2
Mississippi	98	C3
Mississippi	98	D2
Mississippi River Delta	98	D4
Missoula	94	D1
Missouri	96	B3
Missouri	94	F1
Missouri City	98	B4
Mistelbach	30	M2
Mitchell	94	G2
Mithankot	58	K4
Mithaylov	38	G4
Mithymna	36	J5
Mito	50	L5
Mitsamiouli	76	G2
Mitsinjo	76	H3
Mittellandkanal	22	K2
Mittersill	30	H3
Mittweida	20	H6
Mitú	108	C3
Mitzic	72	G4
Miyake-jima	50	K6
Miyako	50	L4
Miyakonojō	50	F8
Miyazaki	50	F8
Miyoshi	50	G6
Mīzan Teferī	74	F2
Mizdah	70	H2
Mizen Head	24	B10
Mizhhir"ya	34	L1
Mizil	34	P4
Mizpe Ramon	62	B6
Mjölby	16	H7
Mjøsa	16	F6
Mkuze	76	E5
Mladá Boleslav	18	D7
Mladenovac	34	H5
Mława	18	K4
Mljet	34	E7
Mmabatho	76	D5
Moa	82	H2
Moanda	72	G5
Moapa	94	D3
Moba	74	D5
Mobaye	74	C3
Mobayi-Mbongo	74	C3
Moberly	96	B3
Mobile	98	D3
Moçambique	76	G3
Môc Châu	52	C2
Mochudi	76	D4
Mocímboa da Praia	76	G2
Mocuba	76	F3
Modane	30	B5
Modena	30	F6
Modesto	94	B3
Modica	32	J12
Mödling	30	M2
Modowi	55	D3
Modriča	34	F5
Moenkopi	100	D1
Moers	22	J3
Moffat	24	J6
Moffat Peak	84	B7
Mogadishu = Muqdisho	74	H3
Mogaung	52	B1
Mogilno	18	G5
Mogocha	46	K6
Mogochin	44	Q6
Mogok	52	B2
Mohács	34	F4
Mohammadia	28	L9
Mohe	46	L6
Mohembo	76	C3
Mohoro	74	F5
Mohyliv-Podil's'kyy	34	Q1
Moi	16	D7
Moincêr	56	D2
Moinești	34	P3
Mo i Rana	16	H3
Moissac	26	G9
Mojave	100	C1
Mojave Desert	100	C2
Mokau	84	E4
Mokohinau Island	84	E2
Mokolo	72	G2
Mokoreta	84	B8
Mokp'o	50	D6
Mol	22	H3
Mola di Bari	32	M7
Molat	30	K6
Molde	16	D5
Moldova	34	R2
Moldova	34	P2
Moldova Nouă	34	J5
Molepolole	76	C4
Molfetta	32	L7
Molina de Aragón	28	J4
Molina de Segura	28	J6
Moline	96	B2
Möll	30	J4
Mollendo	108	C7
Molokai	100	(2)D2
Molopo	76	C5
Molsheim	30	C2
Molucca Sea	55	C2
Moma	76	F3
Mombasa	74	G4
Momčilgrad	34	N8
Møn	20	H2
Monach Islands	24	E4
Monaco	30	C7
Monaco	30	C7
Monahans	100	F2
Mona Passage	102	L5
Monbetsu, *Japan*	50	M1
Monbetsu, *Japan*	50	M2
Moncalieri	30	C5
Monchegorsk	16	S3
Mönchengladbach	22	J3
Monchique	28	B7
Monclova	100	F3
Moncton	90	U7
Mondovi	30	C6
Mondragone	32	H7
Mondy	46	G6
Monemvasia	36	F8
Monfalcone	30	J5
Monforte	28	C5
Monforte de Lemos	28	C2
Monfredónia	32	K7
Monga	74	C3
Mongkung	52	B2
Mongo	68	C5
Mongolia	48	B2
Mongonu	72	G2
Mongora	56	B2
Mongu	76	C3
Mong Yai	52	B2
Mong Yu	52	B2
Monkoto	74	C4
Monmouth, *United States*	96	B2
Mono	72	E3
Mono Lake	94	C3
Monopoli	32	M8
Monor	18	J10
Monowai	84	A7
Monreal del Campo	28	J4
Monreale	32	H10
Monroe, *La., United States*	98	C3
Monroe, *Mich., United States*	96	D2
Monroe, *N.C., United States*	98	E3
Monroe, *Wash., United States*	94	B1
Monroe City	98	C2
Monrovia	72	B3
Mons	22	F4
Monschau	22	J4
Monselice	30	G5
Montabaur	22	K4
Montague Island	106	J9
Montalbán	28	K4
Montalto Uffugo	32	L9
Montana	94	E1
Montana	34	L6
Montargis	26	H6
Montauban	26	G10
Montauk	96	F2
Mont aux Sources	76	D5
Montbard	26	K6
Montbéliard	30	B3
Montblanc	28	M3
Mont Blanc	30	B5
Montbrison	26	K8
Mont Cameroun	72	F4
Montceau-les-Mines	26	K7
Mont-de-Marsan	26	E10
Montdidier	22	E5
Monte Alegre	108	G4
Monte Azul	108	J7
Montebello	96	F1
Monte Bello Islands	82	B4
Montebelluna	30	H5
Monte Calvo	32	K7
Monte Cinto	32	C6
Montecristo	32	E6
Monte Etna	32	J11
Montefiascone	32	G6
Montego Bay	102	J5
Montélimar	26	K9
Monte Limbara	32	D8
Monte Lindo	110	K4
Montemorelos	98	B4
Monte Namuli	76	F3
Montenegro = Crna Gora	34	F7
Monte Perdido	28	L2
Monte Pollino	32	L9
Montepuez	76	F2
Montepulciano	32	F5
Monte Quemado	110	J4
Montereau-faut-Yonne	26	H5
Monterey	96	E3
Monterey Bay	94	B3
Montería	108	B2
Montero	108	E7
Monte Rosa	30	C5
Monterotondo	32	G6
Monterrey	100	F3
Monte Sant'Angelo	32	K7
Montes Claros	108	J7
Montesilvano	32	J6
Montevarchi	30	G7
Montevideo, *United States*	96	A1
Montevideo, *Uruguay*	110	K5
Monte Viso	30	C6
Monte Vista	100	E1
Montgomery	98	D3
Monthey	30	B4
Monticello	94	E3
Montijo	28	D6
Montilla	28	F7
Mont Joli	96	G1
Mont-Laurier	96	E1
Montluçon	26	H7
Montmagny	96	F1
Montmedy	22	H5
Mont Mézenc	26	K9
Montone	30	G6
Montoro	28	F6
Mont Pelat	26	M9
Montpelier, *Id., United States*	94	D2
Montpelier, *Vt., United States*	96	F2
Montpellier	26	J10
Montréal	96	F1
Montreuil	22	D4
Montreux	30	B4
Montrose, *United Kingdom*	24	K5
Montrose, *United States*	94	E3
Monts Bagzane	70	G5
Mont Serkout	70	G4
Montserrat	102	M5
Monts Nimba	72	C3
Monts Otish	90	S6
Mont Tahat	70	G4
Monywa	52	A2
Monza	30	E5
Monzón	28	L3
Moonie	82	K5
Moorcroft	94	F2
Moorhead	96	A1
Moosburg	30	G1
Moose Jaw	90	K6
Moose Lake	90	M6
Moosomin	90	L6
Moosonee	90	Q6
Mopeia	76	F3
Mopti	70	E6
Moqor	58	J3
Mór	34	F2
Mora	16	H6
Móra	28	B6
Moradabad	56	C3
Morafenobe	76	G3
Morag	18	J4
Moramanga	76	H3
Moran	94	D2
Morane	80	N8
Moratuwa	56	D7
Morava	18	G8
Moravské Budějovice	30	L1
Morawhanna	108	F2
Moray Firth	24	J4
Morbach	22	K5
Morbegno	30	E4
Morbi	56	B4
Morcenx	26	E9
Mordaga	46	L6
Mordoviya	38	H4
Moreau	94	F1
Morecambe	24	K7
Moree	82	J5
Morehead, *Papua New Guinea*	55	F4
Morehead, *United States*	96	D3
More Laptevykh	46	L1
Morelia	102	D5
Morella	28	K4
Moresby Island	100	(1)L5
Moreton Island	82	K5
Morez	26	M7
Morfou	36	Q9
Morgan	82	G6
Morgan City	98	C4
Morgantown	96	D3
Morges	30	B4
Mori	50	L2
Morioka	50	L4
Morkoka	46	J4
Morlaix	26	B5
Mornington Island	82	G3
Morocco	66	C2
Morogoro	74	F5
Moro Gulf	52	G5
Morombe	76	G4
Mörön	46	G7
Morondava	76	G4
Morón de la Frontera	28	E7
Moroni	76	G2
Moron Us He	56	F2
Morotai	55	C2
Moroto	74	E3
Morpeth	24	L6
Morris	94	G1
Morristown	98	E2
Mors	16	E8
Morshansk	38	H4
Mortain	22	B6
Morteros	110	J5
Morvern	24	G5
Morwell	82	J7
Mosbach	20	E7
Mosby	94	D1
Moscow = Moskva	38	G3
Mosel	22	K4
Moselle	22	G6
Moses Lake	94	C1
Mosgiel	84	C7
Moshi	74	F4
Mosjøen	16	G4
Moskenesøy	16	F3
Moskva	38	G3
Mosonmagyaróvár	30	N3
Mosquero	100	F1
Moss	16	F7
Mossburn	84	B7
Mosselbaai	76	C6
Mossoró	108	K5
Most	20	J6
Mostaganem	28	L9
Mostar	34	E6
Móstoles	28	G4
Møsvatn	16	E7
Mot'a	68	G5
Motala	16	H7
Motherwell	24	J6
Motihari	56	D3
Motilla del Palancar	28	J5
Motiti Island	84	F3
Motril	28	G8
Motru	34	K5
Motu One	80	L7
Motygino	44	S6
Mouchard	30	A4
Moudjéria	70	C5
Moudros	36	H5
Mouila	72	G5
Moulins	26	J7
Moulmein	52	B3
Moultrie	98	E3
Moundou	68	C6
Mount Adam	110	J9
Mount Adams	94	B1
Mountain Grove	96	B3
Mountain Home	96	B3
Mountain Nile = Bahr el Jebel	74	E2
Mount Alba	84	B7
Mount Aloysius	82	E5
Mount Anglem	84	A8
Mount Apo	52	H5
Mount Ararat	60	L4
Mount Arrowsmith	84	C6
Mount Aspiring	84	B7
Mount Assiniboine	90	H6
Mount Augustus	82	C4
Mount Baco	52	G3
Mount Baker	94	B1
Mount Bartle Frere	82	J3
Mount Bogong	82	J7
Mount Brewster	84	B7
Mount Bruce	82	C4
Mount Cameroun	66	D5
Mount Carmel	94	D3
Mount Columbia	90	H6
Mount Cook	84	C6
Mount Cook	84	C6
Mount Donald	84	A7
Mount Egmont	84	E4
Mount Elbert	94	E3
Mount Elgon	74	E3
Mount Essendon	82	D4
Mount Evelyn	82	F2
Mount Everest	56	E3
Mount Fairweather	90	D5
Mount Gambier	82	H7
Mount Garnet	82	J3
Mount Hermōn	62	C3
Mount Hood	94	B1
Mount Hutt	84	C6
Mount Huxley	84	B7
Mount Isa	82	G4
Mount Jackson	112	(2)MM2
Mount Karisimbi	74	D4
Mount Kendall	84	D5
Mount Kenya = Kirinyaga	74	F4
Mount Kilimanjaro	74	F4
Mount Kirkpatrick	112	(2)AA1
Mount Kosciuszko	82	J7
Mount Liebig	82	F4
Mount Lloyd George	90	G5
Mount Logan	90	C4
Mount Magnet	82	C5
Mount Maunganui	84	F3
Mount McKinley	100	(1)G3
Mount Meharry	82	C4
Mount Menzies	112	(2)L2
Mount Minto	112	(2)Y2
Mount Mulanje	76	F3
Mount Murchison	84	C6
Mount Nyiru	74	F3

Name	Page	Ref.
Mount Olympus	94	B1
Mount Ord	82	E3
Mount Ossa	82	J8
Mount Owen	84	D5
Mount Paget	110	P9
Mount Pleasant, *Ia., United States*	96	B2
Mount Pleasant, *Mich., United States*	96	D2
Mount Pleasant, *S.C., United States*	98	F3
Mount Pleasant, *Tex., United States*	98	B3
Mount Pleasant, *Ut., United States*	94	D3
Mount Pulog	52	G3
Mount Rainier	94	B1
Mount Ratz	90	E5
Mount Richmond	84	D5
Mount Roberts	82	K5
Mount Robson	90	H6
Mount Roosevelt	90	F5
Mount Roraima	108	E2
Mount Ross	84	E5
Mount Shasta	94	B2
Mount Somers	84	C6
Mount Stanley	74	D3
Mount Tahat	66	D3
Mount Travers	84	D6
Mount Tuun	50	D3
Mount Usborne	110	K9
Mount Vernon, *Al., United States*	98	D3
Mount Vernon, *Ill., United States*	96	C3
Mount Vernon, *Oh., United States*	96	D2
Mount Vernon, *Wash., United States*	94	B1
Mount Victoria, *Myanmar*	52	A2
Mount Victoria, *Papua New Guinea*	80	E6
Mount Waddington	90	F6
Mount Washington	90	S8
Mount Whitney	94	C3
Mount Wilson	94	E3
Mount Woodroffe	82	F5
Mount Ziel	82	F4
Moura	28	C6
Mousa	24	L2
Moussoro	68	C5
Moutamba	72	G5
Mouth of the Shannon	24	B9
Mouths of the Amazon	106	G3
Mouths of the Danube	34	S4
Mouths of the Ganges	56	E4
Mouths of the Indus	58	J5
Mouths of the Irrawaddy	52	A3
Mouths of the Krishna	56	D5
Mouths of the Mekong	52	D5
Mouths of the Niger	72	F4
Moûtiers	30	B5
Moutong	55	B2
Mouzarak	72	H2
Moyale	74	F3
Moyen Atlas	70	D2
Moyenvic	22	J6
Moyero	44	U4
Moyynty	44	N8
Mozambique	76	E3
Mozambique Channel	76	F4
Mozdok	60	L2
Mozhga	38	K3
Mozirje	30	K4
Mpanda	74	E5
Mpika	76	E2
Mporokoso	74	E5
Mpumalanga	76	D5
Mragowo	18	L4
Mrkonjić-Grad	30	N6
M'Sila	70	F1
Mtsensk	38	G4
Mtwara	74	G6
Muang Khammouan	52	C3
Muang Không	52	D4
Muang Khôngxédôn	52	D3
Muang Khoua	52	C2
Muang Pakxan	52	C3
Muang Phin	52	D3
Muang Sing	52	C2
Muang Xai	52	C2
Muar	54	C2
Muarabungo	54	C3
Muaradua	54	C3
Muarasiberut	54	B3
Muaratewen	54	E3
Muarawahau	54	F2
Mubarek	44	M10
Mubende	74	E3
Mubrani	55	D3
Muck	24	F5
Muckadilla	82	J5
Muconda	74	C6
Mucur	36	S5
Mudanjiang	50	F2
Mudanya	36	L4
Muddy Gap	94	E2
Mudurnu	36	P4
Mufulira	76	D2
Mughshin	58	F6
Muğla	36	L7
Mugodzhary	38	L5
Muhammad Qol	68	G3
Mühldorf	30	H2
Mühlhausen	20	F5
Muhos	16	N4
Muhu	16	M7
Muhulu	74	D4
Mukacheve	18	M9
Mukdahan	52	C3
Mukomuko	54	C3
Mukry	58	J2
Mukuku	76	D2
Mulaku Atoll	56	B8
Mulde	20	H5
Muleshoe	100	F2
Mulgrave Island	82	H2
Mulhacén	28	G7
Mülheim	22	J3
Mulhouse	30	C3
Muling	50	G1

Name	Page	Ref.
Mull	24	G5
Mullaittivu	56	D7
Mullewa	82	C5
Müllheim	30	C3
Mullingar	24	E8
Mulobezi	76	D3
Multan	58	K3
Mumbai	56	B5
Mumbwa	76	D2
Muna	55	B4
Munadarnes	16	(1)C1
Münchberg	20	G6
München	30	G2
Münden	20	E5
Mundo Novo	108	J6
Mundrabilla	82	E6
Munera	28	H5
Mungbere	74	D3
Munger	56	E3
Munich = München	30	G2
Munster, *France*	30	C2
Münster, *Germany*	22	K3
Munster, *Germany*	20	F4
Munte	55	A2
Muojärvi	16	Q4
Muonio	16	M3
Muqdisho	74	H3
Mur	30	L4
Muradiye	60	K4
Murang'a	74	F4
Murashi	38	J3
Murat	60	K4
Muratlı	36	K3
Murchison	84	D5
Murcia	28	J7
Murdo	94	F2
Mureş	34	J3
Muret	26	G10
Murfreesboro, *N.C., United States*	98	F2
Murfreesboro, *Tenn., United States*	98	D2
Murghob	58	K2
Muriaé	108	J8
Müritz	20	H3
Muriwai	84	F4
Murmansk	16	S2
Murnau	30	G3
Murom	38	H3
Muroran	50	L2
Muros	28	A2
Muroto	50	H7
Murphy	98	E2
Murray	96	C3
Murray	82	H6
Murray Bridge	82	G7
Murray River Basin	82	H6
Murska Sobota	30	M4
Murter	30	L7
Murtosa	28	B4
Murud	56	B5
Murupara	84	F4
Mururoa	80	M8
Murwara	56	D4
Mürzüq	70	H3
Mürzzuschlag	30	L3
Muş	60	J4
Müsa	18	N1
Musala	36	F2
Musandam Peninsula	63	G3
Musay'īd	63	D4
Muscat = Masqaţ	63	H5
Musgrave Ranges	82	E5
Mushin	72	E3
Muskegon	96	C2
Muskogee	98	B2
Musmar	68	G4
Musoma	74	E4
Mussende	74	B6
Mustafakemalpaşa	36	L4
Mut, *Egypt*	68	E2
Mut, *Turkey*	36	R8
Mutare	76	E3
Mutarnee	82	J3
Mutnyy Materik	38	L1
Mutoray	44	U5
Mutsamudu	76	G2
Mutsu	50	L3
Mutsu-wan	50	L3
Muttaburra	82	H4
Mutur	56	D7
Muyezerskiy	16	R5
Muyinga	74	E4
Muynak	44	K9
Muzaffarnagar	56	C3
Muzaffarpur	56	E3
Muzillac	26	C6
Múzquiz	100	F3
Muztagata	44	N10
Mwali	76	G2
Mwanza	74	E4
Mweka	74	C4
Mwenda	74	D6
Mwene-Ditu	74	C5
Mwenezi	76	E4
Mwenezi	76	E4
Mwinilunga	76	C2
Myanmar	52	B2
Myaungmya	52	A3
Myingyan	52	B2
Myitkyina	52	B1
Myjava	30	N2
Mykolayiv	18	N8
Mykonos	36	H7
Mymensingh	56	F3
Mynbulak	44	L9
Myndagayy	46	K9
Myŏjin	48	K4
Myonggan	50	E3
Mýrdalsjökull	16	(1)D3
Myrina	36	H5
Myrtle Beach	98	F3

Name	Page	Ref.
Mys Alevina	46	S5
Mys Aniva	48	L1
Mys Buorkhaya	46	N2
Mys Dezhneva	46	Z3
Mys Elizavety	46	Q6
Mys Enkan	46	P5
Mys Govena	46	V5
Mys Kanin Nos	38	H1
Mys Kril'on	48	L1
Myślenice	18	J8
Myślibórz	18	D5
Mys Lopatka, *Russia*	46	T6
Mys Lopatka, *Russia*	46	S2
Mys Navarin	46	X4
Mys Nemetskiy	16	S2
Mys Olyutorskiy	46	W5
Mysore	56	C6
Mys Peschanyy	44	J9
Mys Povorotnyy	50	G2
Mys Prubiynyy	38	F5
Mys Shelagskiy	46	V2
Mys Sivuchiy	46	U5
Mys Terpeniya	46	Q7
Mys Tolstoy	46	T5
Mys Yuzhnyy	46	T5
Mys Zhelaniya	44	M2
Myszksw	18	J7
My Tho	52	D4
Mytilini	36	J5
Mývatn	16	(1)E2
Mže	20	H7
Mzimba	76	E2
Mzuzu	76	E2

N

Name	Page	Ref.
Naalehu	100	(2)F4
Naas	24	F8
Nabas	52	G4
Naberezhnyye Chelny	38	K3
Nabeul	32	E12
Nabīd	63	G2
Nabire	55	E3
Nablus	62	C4
Nacala	76	G2
Nacaroa	76	F2
Náchod	18	F7
Nacogdoches	98	C3
Nadiad	56	B4
Nador	70	E2
Nadvirna	34	M1
Nadym	38	P1
Nadym	38	P2
Næstved	20	G1
Nafpaktos	36	D6
Nafplio	36	E7
Naga	52	G4
Nagano	50	K5
Nagaoka	50	K5
Nagaon	56	F3
Nagarzê	56	F3
Nagasaki	50	E7
Nagaur	56	B3
Nagercoil	56	C7
Nago	48	H5
Nagold	20	D8
Nagorsk	38	K3
Nagoya	50	J6
Nagpur	56	C4
Nagqu	56	F2
Nagyatád	30	N4
Nagykállš	34	J2
Nagykanizsa	30	N4
Nagykáta	18	J10
Nagykőrös	34	G2
Naha	48	H5
Nahanni	90	G4
Nahanni Butte	90	G4
Nahr en Nile = Nile	68	F2
Naiman Qi	48	G2
Nain	90	U5
Nairn	24	J4
Nairobi	74	F4
Naivasha	74	F4
Naizishan	50	D2
Najafābād	58	F3
Nájera	28	H2
Najibabad	56	C3
Najin	50	F2
Najrān	58	H4
Naju	50	D6
Nakamura	50	G7
Nakatsu	50	F7
Nakhl	62	A7
Nakhodka, *Russia*	50	G2
Nakhodka, *Russia*	44	P4
Nakhon Ratchasima	52	C3
Nakhon Sawan	52	B3
Nakhon Si Thammarat	52	B5
Nakina	90	P6
Nakło nad Notecią	18	G4
Naknek	100	(1)F4
Nakonde	74	E5
Nakskov	20	G2
Nakten	16	H5
Nakuru	74	F4
Nal'chik	60	K2
Nallihan	36	P4
Nālūt	70	H2
Namakzar-e Shadad	63	G1
Namanga	74	F4
Namangan	44	N9
Namapa	76	F2
Namasagali	74	E3
Nam Can	52	C5
Nam Co	56	F2
Namdalen	16	G4
Nam Dinh	52	D2
Namib Desert	76	A4

Name	Page	Ref.
Namibe	76	A3
Namibia	76	B4
Namidobe	76	F3
Namlea	55	C3
Namo	55	A3
Nampa	94	C2
Nampala	72	C1
Nam Ping	52	B3
Namp'o	50	C4
Nampula	76	F3
Namsos	16	F4
Namtsy	46	M4
Namur	22	G4
Namwala	76	D3
Namwŏn	50	D6
Nan	52	C3
Nanaimo	94	B1
Nanao	50	J5
Nanchang	48	F5
Nanchong	48	D4
Nancy	30	B2
Nanda Devi	56	C2
Nānded	56	C5
Nandurbar	56	B4
Nandyal	56	C5
Nanfeng	48	F5
Nangalala	82	G2
Nangapinoh	54	E3
Nangatayap	54	E3
Nangis	26	J5
Nangong	48	F3
Nang Xian	56	F3
Nanjing	48	F4
Nankoku	50	G7
Nanning	48	D2
Nanortalik	90	X4
Nanpan	52	D2
Nanping	48	F5
Nansei-shotō	48	G5
Nantes	26	D6
Nanton	92	D1
Nantong	48	G4
Nanumea	80	H6
Nanuque	108	J7
Nanutarra Roadhouse	82	C4
Nanyang	48	E4
Napa	94	B3
Napalkovo	44	N3
Napamute	100	(1)F3
Napas	46	C4
Napasoq	90	W3
Napier	84	F4
Naples = Napoli, *Italy*	32	J8
Naples, *United States*	98	E4
Napo	108	C4
Napoli	32	J8
Naqb Ashtar	62	C6
Nara, *Japan*	50	H6
Nara, *Mali*	70	D5
Narathiwat	52	C5
Narbonne	26	H10
Nardò	32	N8
Nares Strait	88	J2
Narev	18	N3
Narew	18	L5
Narib	76	B4
Narmada	56	C4
Narnaul	56	C3
Narni	32	G6
Narok	74	F4
Närpes	16	L5
Narrabri	82	J6
Narrandera	82	J6
Narsimhapur	56	C4
Nart	48	F2
Narva	16	Q7
Narva	16	P7
Narva Bay	16	P7
Narvik	16	J2
Nar'yan Mar	38	K1
Naryn	44	F6
Năsăud	34	M2
Nashua	96	F2
Nashville	98	D2
Našice	34	F4
Nasik	56	B4
Nasir	74	E2
Nassarawa	72	F3
Nassau	98	F4
Nässjö	16	H8
Nastapoka Islands	90	R5
Nasugbu	52	G4
Naswá	63	G5
Nata	76	D4
Natal	108	K5
Natara	46	L3
Natashquan	90	U6
Natchez	98	C3
Natchitoches	98	C3
National Park	84	E4
Natitingou	72	E2
Natori	50	L4
Natuna Besar	54	D2
Naucelle	26	H9
Nauchas	76	B4
Nauders	30	F4
Naujoji Akmenė	18	M1
Naumburg	20	G5
Na'ūr	62	C5
Nauru	80	G6
Nauta	108	C4
Nautonwa	56	D3
Navahermosa	28	F5
Navahrudak	16	N10
Navajo Reservoir	94	E3
Navalero	28	H3
Navalmoral de la Mata	28	E5
Navalvillar de Pela	28	E5
Navapolatsk	38	E3
Navlya	38	F4

Navoi	44	M9
Navojoa	92	E6
Navrongo	72	D2
Navsari	56	B4
Nawá	62	D4
Nawabshah	58	J4
Nāwah	58	J3
Naxçıvan	60	L4
Naxos	36	H7
Naxos	36	H7
Nayakhan	46	T4
Nāy Band, *Iran*	63	E3
Nāy Band, *Iran*	58	G3
Nayoro	50	M1
Nazaré	28	A5
Nazareth	62	C4
Nazarovo	44	S6
Nazca	108	C6
Nazca Ridge	110	E3
Naze	48	H5
Nazilli	36	L7
Nazino	44	P6
Nazran'	60	L2
Nazrēt	74	F2
Nazwá	58	G5
Nazyvayevsk	38	P3
Ncojane	76	C4
Ndélé	74	C2
Ndjamena	68	B5
Ndjolé	72	G5
Ndola	76	D2
Nea Ionia	36	E5
Neapoli	36	F8
Nea Roda	36	F4
Nea Zichni	36	F3
Nebbi	74	E3
Nebitdag	58	F2
Nebo	82	J4
Nebraska	94	G2
Neckar	20	D7
Neckar	20	D8
Neckarsulm	20	E7
Necker Island	80	K3
Necochea	110	K6
Nédély	68	C4
Nedre Soppero	16	L3
Needles	100	D2
Nefedovo	38	P3
Nefta	70	G2
Neftçala	60	N4
Neftekamsk	38	K3
Neftekumsk	60	L1
Nefteyugansk	38	P2
Nefza	32	D12
Negage	74	B5
Negār	63	G2
Negēlē	74	F2
Negele	74	F2
Negev	62	B6
Negomane	76	F2
Negombo	56	C7
Negotin	34	K5
Negotino	36	E3
Négrine	70	G2
Negro, *Argentina*	110	J7
Negro, *Brazil*	108	E4
Negros	52	G5
Negru Vodă	34	R6
Nehbandān	58	G3
Nehe	46	M7
Nehoiu	34	P4
Neijiang	48	C5
Nei Monggol	48	E2
Neiva	108	B3
Neixiang	48	E4
Nejanilini Lake	90	M5
Nek'emtē	74	F2
Nelidovo	38	F3
Neligh	94	G2
Nellore	56	C6
Nel'ma	46	P7
Nelson	90	N5
Nelson, *Canada*	94	C1
Nelson, *New Zealand*	84	D5
Nelspruit	76	E5
Nēma	70	D5
Neman	18	M2
Nēman	16	N10
Nemours	26	H5
Nemperola	55	B5
Nemunas	18	P3
Nemuro	50	N2
Nen	46	L7
Nenagh	24	D9
Nenana	100	(1)H3
Nene	22	B2
Nenjiang	46	M7
Neosho	96	B3
Nepa	46	H5
Nepal	56	D3
Nepalganj	56	D3
Nepean	96	E1
Nepomuk	20	J7
Ner	18	H5
Nera	32	G6
Neratovice	20	K6
Neris	18	P2
Nerja	28	G8
Neryungri	46	L5
Nesebăr	34	Q7
Ness City	98	B2
Netanya	62	B4
Netherlands	22	H2
Netherlands Antilles	102	L6
Nettilling Lake	90	S3
Neubrandenburg	20	J3
Neuburg	20	G8
Neuchâtel	30	B3
Neuenhagen	20	J4
Neufchâteau, *Belgium*	22	H5
Neufchâteau, *France*	26	L5
Neufchâtel-en-Bray	22	D5
Neuhof	20	E6
Neukirchen	20	D2
Neumarkt	20	G7
Neumünster	20	F2
Neunkirchen, *Austria*	30	M3
Neunkirchen, *Germany*	20	C7
Neuquén	110	H6
Neuruppin	20	H4
Neusiedler	18	F10
Neusiedler See	30	M3
Neuss	22	J3
Neustadt, *Germany*	22	L5
Neustadt, *Germany*	20	F2
Neustadt, *Germany*	20	F7
Neustadt, *Germany*	20	G6
Neustadt, *Germany*	20	G8
Neustadt, *Germany*	20	H7
Neustrelitz	20	J3
Neu-Ulm	20	F8
Neuwerk	20	D3
Neuwied	22	K4
Nevada	94	C3
Nevada	96	B3
Nevado Auzangate	108	C6
Nevado de Colima	102	D5
Nevado de Cumbal	108	B3
Nevado de Huascaran	108	B5
Nevado de Illampu	108	D7
Nevado Sajama	108	D7
Nevados de Cachi	110	H4
Never	46	L6
Nevers	26	J7
Nevesinje	34	F6
Nevėžis	16	M9
Nevinnomyssk	60	J1
Nevşehir	36	S6
Newala	74	F6
New Albany, *Ind., United States*	96	C3
New Albany, *Miss., United States*	98	D3
New Amsterdam	108	F2
Newark, *N.J., United States*	96	F2
Newark, *Oh., United States*	96	D3
Newark-on-Trent	22	B1
New Bedford	96	F2
Newberg	94	B1
New Bern	98	F2
Newberry	98	E3
New Braunfels	98	B4
New Britain	80	F6
New Brunswick	90	T7
Newburgh	96	F2
Newbury	22	A3
New Bussa	72	E3
Newcastle, *Australia*	82	K6
Newcastle, *United States*	94	F2
Newcastle-under-Lyme	24	K8
Newcastle upon Tyne	24	L6
Newcastle Waters	82	F3
New Delhi	56	C3
New England	94	F1
Newe Zohars	62	C5
Newfoundland	90	V7
Newfoundland	90	V7
New Georgia Islands	80	F6
New Glasgow	90	U7
New Guinea	42	S10
New Hampshire	96	F2
New Hampton	96	B2
New Hanover	80	F6
New Haven	96	F2
Newhaven	22	C4
New Iberia	98	C3
New Ireland	80	F6
New Jersey	96	F2
New Liskeard	96	E1
New London	96	F2
Newman	82	C4
Newmarket	22	C2
New Meadows	94	C2
New Mexico	100	E2
Newnan	98	E3
New Orleans	98	D4
New Plymouth	84	E4
Newport, *Eng., United Kingdom*	22	A4
Newport, *Wales, United Kingdom*	24	K10
Newport, *Ark., United States*	98	C2
Newport, *Oreg., United States*	94	B2
Newport, *R.I., United States*	96	F2
Newport, *Vt., United States*	96	F2
Newport, *Wash., United States*	94	C1
New Providence	98	F5
Newquay	24	G11
Newry	24	F7
New Siberia Islands = Novosibirskiye Ostrova	46	P1
New Smyrna Beach	98	E4
New South Wales	82	H6
Newton, *Ia., United States*	96	B2
Newton, *Kans., United States*	98	B2
Newtownards	24	G7
New Ulm	96	B2
New York	96	E2
New York	96	F2
New Zealand	84	B5
Neya	38	H3
Neyrīz	63	F2
Neyshābūr	58	G2
Ngabang	54	D2
Ngalu	55	B5
Ngamring	56	E3
Ngaoundéré	72	G3
Ngara	74	E4
Ngawihi	84	E5
Ngo	72	H5
Ngoura	68	C5
Ngozi	74	D4
Nguigmi	72	G2
Nguru	72	G2
Nhachengue	76	F4
Nha Trang	52	D4
Nhulunbuy	82	G2
Niafounké	70	E5
Niagara Falls	96	E2
Niakaramandougou	72	C3
Niamey	72	E2
Niangara	74	D3
Nia-Nia	74	D3
Nias	54	B2
Nicaragua	102	G6
Nicastro	32	L10
Nice	30	C7
Nicholl's Town	98	F4
Nicobar Islands	52	A5
Nicosia = Lefkosia	36	R9
Nida	18	K7
Nidym	46	F4
Nidzica	18	K4
Niebüll	20	D2
Niedere Tauern	30	J3
Niefang	72	G4
Niemegk	20	H4
Nienburg	20	E4
Niesky	20	K5
Nieuw Amsterdam	108	F2
Nieuw Nickerie	108	F2
Nieuwpoort	22	E3
Niğde	36	S7
Niger	70	G5
Niger	72	E2
Nigeria	72	F2
Nigoring Hu	48	B3
Niigata	50	K5
Niihau	100	(2)A2
Nii-jima	50	K6
Nijar	28	H8
Nijmegen	22	H3
Nikel'	16	R2
Nikolayevsk-na-Amure	46	Q6
Nikol'sk	38	J3
Nikol'skoye	46	V5
Nikopol'	38	F5
Nik Pey	60	N5
Nikšić	34	F7
Nilandhoo Atoll	56	B8
Nile	68	F3
Niles	96	C2
Nimach	56	B4
Nîmes	26	K10
Nimule	74	E3
Nin	30	L6
Nine Degree Channel	56	B7
9 de Julio	110	J6
Ning'an	50	E1
Ningbo	48	G5
Ningde	48	F5
Ninghai	48	G5
Ninh Binh	52	D2
Ninh Hoa	52	D4
Ninohoe	50	L3
Niobrara	94	G2
Niobrara	94	F2
Nioro	70	D5
Nioro du Sahel	72	C1
Niort	26	E7
Nipigon	96	C1
Niquelândia	108	H6
Nirmal	56	C5
Niš	34	J6
Nisa	28	C5
Niscemi	32	J11
Nishinoomote	50	F8
Nisporeni	34	R2
Nisyros	36	K8
Nițā	63	C3
Niterói	110	N3
Nitra	18	H9
Nitra	18	H9
Nitsa	38	M3
Niue	80	K7
Nivelles	22	G4
Nizamabad	56	C5
Nizhnekamsk	38	K3
Nizhnekamskoye Vodokhranilishche	38	K3
Nizhneudinsk	46	F5
Nizhnevartovsk	38	Q2
Nizhneyansk	46	P2
Nizhniy Lomov	38	H4
Nizhniy Novgorod	38	H3
Nizhniy Tagil	38	M3
Nizhnyaya Tunguska	46	H4
Nizhyn	38	F4
Nizip	60	G5
Nizza Monferrato	30	D6
Njazidja	76	G2
Njombe	74	E5
Njombe	74	E5
Nkambe	72	G3
Nkhotakota	76	E2
Nkongsamba	72	F4
Nkurenkuru	76	B3
Noatak	100	(1)F2
Nobeoka	50	F7
Noboribetsu	50	L2
Noci	32	M8
Nogales, *Mexico*	100	D2
Nogales, *United States*	100	D2
Nogat	18	J3
Nogent-le-Rotrou	26	F5
Noginsk	38	G3
Noginskiy	44	S5
Nogliki	46	Q6
Noheji	50	L3
Noia	28	B2
Noire	52	C2
Noirmoutier-en-l'Île	26	C6
Nojima-zaki	50	K6
Nok Kundi	58	H4
Nokou	70	H6
Nola, *Central African Republic*	74	B3
Nola, *Italy*	32	J8
Nolinsk	38	J3
Noma-misaki	50	F8
Nome	100	(1)D3
Nomoi Islands	80	F5
Nomo-saki	50	E7
Nong'an	50	C1
Nong Khai	52	C3
Noord-beveland	22	F3
Noord-Oost-Polder	22	H2
Noordwijk aan Zee	22	G2
Norak	58	J2
Noranda	96	E1
Nordaustlandet	112	(1)L1
Nordborg	20	E1
Norden	20	C3
Nordenham	20	D3
Norderney	20	C3
Norderney	20	C3
Norderstedt	20	F3
Nordfjordeid	16	D6
Nordfriesische Inseln	20	D2
Nordhausen	20	F5
Nordhorn	22	K2
Nordkapp	16	N1
Nordkinn	16	P1
Nordkinnhalvøya	16	P1
Nordkvaløya	16	J1
Nordli	16	G4
Nördlingen	20	F8
Nord-Ostsee-Kanal	20	E2
Nordstrand	20	D2
Nordvik	44	W3
Nore	24	E9
Norfolk, *Nebr., United States*	94	G2
Norfolk, *Va., United States*	96	E3
Norfolk Island	80	G8
Noril'sk	44	R4
Norman	98	B2
Normandia	108	F3
Normanton	82	H3
Norman Wells	90	F3
Nørre Åby	20	E1
Nørre Alslev	20	G2
Norristown	96	E2
Norrköping	16	J7
Norrtälje	16	K7
Norseman	82	D6
Norsk	46	N6
Northallerton	24	L7
Northam	82	C6
North America	88	L5
Northampton, *Australia*	82	B5
Northampton, *United Kingdom*	22	B2
North Andaman	52	A4
North Battleford	90	K6
North Bay	96	E1
North Cape	84	D2
North Carolina	98	F2
North Channel	24	G6
North Charleston	98	F3
North Dakota	94	F1
Northeast Providence Channel	98	F4
Northeim	20	F5
Northern Cape	76	C5
Northern Ireland	24	E7
Northern Mariana Islands	80	E4
Northern Territory	82	F4
North Foreland	22	D3
North Horr	74	F3
North Iberia	102	F2
North Island	84	D3
North Korea	50	C4
North Little Rock	98	C3
North Platte	94	F2
North Platte	92	F3
North Ronaldsay	24	K2
North Sea	24	N4
North Stradbroke Island	82	K5
North Taranaki Bight	84	D4
North Uist	24	E4
Northumberland Strait	90	U7
North Vancouver	94	B1
North West	76	C5
North West Basin	82	C4
North West Cape	82	B4
North West Christmas Island Ridge	80	K4
North West Highlands	24	G4
Northwest Territories	90	G4
Norton	98	B2
Norton Sound	100	(1)E3
Nortorf	20	E2
Norway	16	F5
Norwegian Sea	16	B4
Norwich, *United Kingdom*	22	D2
Norwich, *United States*	96	F2
Nos	38	H1
Nos Emine	34	Q7
Nosevaya	38	K1
Noshiro	50	K3
Nos Kaliakra	34	R6
Noşratābād	58	G4
Nos Šabla	34	R6
Nossen	20	J5
Nosy Barren	76	G3
Nosy Bé	76	H2
Nosy Boraha	76	J3
Nosy Mitsio	76	H2
Nosy Radama	76	H2
Nosy-Varika	76	H4
Notec	18	G4
Notios Evvoïkos Kolpos	36	F6
Notre Dame Bay	90	V7
Notsé	72	E3
Nottingham	22	A2
Nottingham Island	90	R4
Nouâdhibou	70	B4
Nouakchott	70	B5
Nouâmghar	70	B5
Nouméa	80	G8
Nouvelle Calédonie	80	G8
Nova Gorica	30	J5
Nova Gradiška	34	E4

Name	Page	Ref
Nova Iguaçu	110	N3
Nova Mambone	76	F4
Nova Pazova	34	H5
Novara	30	D5
Nova Scotia	90	T8
Nova Xavantina	108	G6
Novaya Igirma	46	G5
Novaya Karymkary	38	N2
Novaya Kasanka	38	J5
Novaya Lyalya	38	M3
Novaya Zemlya	44	J3
Nova Zagora	34	P7
Novelda	28	K6
Nové Město	18	F8
Nové Mesto	18	G9
Nové Zámky	18	H10
Novgorod	38	F3
Novi Bečej	34	H4
Novigrad	32	H3
Novi Iskăr	34	L7
Novi Ligure	30	D6
Novi Marof	30	M4
Novi Pazar, Bulgaria	34	Q6
Novi Pazar, Serbia and Montenegro	34	H6
Novi Sad	34	G4
Novi Vinodolski	30	K5
Novoaleksandrovsk	38	H5
Novoalekseyevka	38	L4
Novoanninsky	38	H4
Novocheboksarsk	38	J3
Novocherkassk	38	H5
Novodvinsk	38	H2
Novo Hamburgo	110	L4
Novohrad-Volyns'kyy	38	E4
Novokazalinsk	38	M5
Novokuybyshevsk	38	J4
Novokuznetsk	44	R7
Novoletov'ye	44	U3
Novo Mesto	30	L5
Novomikhaylovskiy	60	H1
Novomoskovsk	38	G4
Novonazimovo	46	E5
Novorossiysk	60	G1
Novorybnoye	46	H2
Novoselivka	34	S2
Novosergiyevka	38	K4
Novosibirsk	44	Q6
Novosibirskiye Ostrova	46	P1
Novosil'	38	G4
Novotroitsk	38	L4
Novouzensk	38	J4
Novozybkov	38	F4
Novvy	44	V3
Nový Bor	20	K6
Nový Jičín	18	H8
Novyy Port	44	N4
Novvy Uoyan	46	J5
Novyy Urengoy	44	P4
Novyy Urgal	46	N6
Novyy Uzen'	44	J9
Nowa Dęba	18	L7
Nowa Ruda	18	F7
Nowata	98	B2
Nowogard	18	E4
Nowo Warpno	20	K3
Nowra	82	K6
Now Shahr	58	F2
Nowy Dwór Mazowiecki	18	K5
Nowy Sącz	18	K8
Nowy Targ	18	K8
Nowy Tomyśl	18	F5
Noyabr'sk	44	P5
Noyon	22	E5
Nsombo	76	D2
Ntem	72	G4
Ntwetwe Pan	76	C4
Nu	56	G2
Nuasjärvi	16	Q7
Nubian Desert	68	F3
Nudo Coropuna	108	C7
Nueltin Lake	90	M4
Nueva Lubecka	110	G7
Nueva Rosita	100	F3
Nueva San Salvador	102	G6
Nuevo Casas Grandes	100	E2
Nuevo Laredo	100	G3
Nugget Point	84	B8
Nuhaka	84	F4
Nuku'alofa	80	J8
Nuku Hiva	80	M6
Nukumanu Islands	80	F6
Nukunonu	80	J5
Nukus	44	K9
Nullagine	82	D4
Nullarbor Plain	82	E6
Numan	72	G3
Numata	50	K5
Numazu	50	K6
Numbulwar	82	G2
Numfor	55	E4
Numto	38	P2
Nunap Isua	90	Y5
Nunarsuit	90	X4
Nunavik	90	W2
Nunavut	90	M3
Nuneaton	22	A2
Nungnain Sum	48	F1
Nunivak Island	100	(1)D3
Nunligram	46	Y3
Nuoro	32	D8
Nuqui	108	B2
Nura	38	P4
Nurābād	63	D1
Nurata	58	F2
Nurmes	16	Q5
Nürnberg	20	G7
Nürtingen	30	E2
Nurzec	18	M5
Nusaybin	60	J5
Nushki	58	J4
Nutak	90	U5
Nuuk	90	W4
Nuussuaq	90	W2
Nyagan'	38	N2
Nyahururu	74	F3
Nyala	68	D5
Nyalam	56	E3
Nyamlell	74	D2
Nyamtumbo	74	F6
Nyandoma	38	H2
Nyantakara	74	E4
Nyborg	20	F1
Nybro	16	H8
Nyda	44	N4
Nyima	56	E2
Nyingchi	54	F3
Nyírbátor	34	K2
Nyíregyháza	18	L10
Nykarleby	16	M5
Nykøbing	20	G2
Nyköping	16	J7
Nylstroom	76	D4
Nymburk	18	E7
Nynäshamn	16	J7
Nyngan	82	J6
Nyon	30	B4
Nysa	18	G7
Nysa	18	D6
Nysted	20	G2
Nyukhcha	38	J2
Nyunzu	74	D5
Nyurba	46	K4
Nyuya	46	K4
Nzega	74	E4
Nzérékoré	72	C3
N'zeto	74	A5
Nzwami	76	G2

O

Name	Page	Ref
Oaho	100	(2)D2
Oahu	80	L3
Oakdale	98	C3
Oakham	22	B2
Oak Lake	94	F1
Oakland	94	B3
Oak Lawn	96	C2
Oakley	98	A2
Oak Ridge	96	D3
Oamaru	84	C7
Oaxaca	102	E5
Ob'	38	N2
Obama	50	H6
Oban	24	G5
O Barco	28	D2
Oberdrauburg	30	H4
Oberhausen	22	J3
Oberkirch	20	D8
Oberlin	98	A2
Oberndorf	30	H3
Oberstdorf	30	F3
Oberursel	20	D7
Obervellach	18	C11
Oberwart	30	M3
Obi	55	C3
Obidos	108	F4
Obigarm	58	K2
Obihiro	50	M2
Obluch'ye	46	N7
Obninsk	38	G3
Obo, Central African Republic	74	D2
Obo, China	48	C3
Oborniki	18	F5
Obouya	72	H5
Oboyan'	38	G4
Obskaya Guba	44	N4
Obuasi	72	D3
Ob'yachevo	38	J2
Ocala	98	E4
Ocaña, Colombia	108	C2
Ocaña, Spain	28	G5
Ocean City	96	E3
Ocean Falls	90	F6
Oceania	80	G7
Oceanside	100	C2
Och'amch'ire	60	J2
Ochsenfurt	20	E7
Oconto	96	C2
Oda	72	D3
Ōda	50	G6
Ōdate	50	L3
Odda	16	D6
Odemira	28	B7
Ödemiş	36	L6
Odense	20	F1
Oder = Odra	18	F6
Oderzo	30	H5
Odesa	38	F5
Odessa = Odesa, Ukraine	38	F5
Odessa, United States	100	F2
Odienné	72	C3
Odorheiu Secuiesc	34	N3
Odra	18	F6
Odžaci	34	G4
Oeh	48	C2
Oeiras	108	J5
Oelrichs	94	F2
Oelsnitz	20	H6
Oeno	80	N8
Oestev	110	H7
Ofaqim	62	B5
Offenbach	20	D6
Offenburg	30	C2
Ōgaki	50	J6
Ogasawara-shotō	42	T7
Ogbomosho	72	E3
Ogden	94	D2
Ogdensburg	96	R8
Ogilvie Mountains	90	C4
Oglio	30	E5
Ogosta	34	L6
Ogre	16	N8
Ogre	16	N8
O Grove	28	B2
Ogulin	30	L5
Ohai	84	A7
Ohanet	70	G3
Ohio	96	D2
Ohio	96	C3
Ohre	20	J6
Ohrid	36	C3
Ohura	84	E4
Oia	36	H8
Oiapoque	108	G3
Oil City	96	D2
Oise	22	E5
Ōita	50	F7
Ojinaga	100	F3
Ojiya	50	K5
Ojos del Salado	110	H4
Oka	46	G6
Okaba	55	E4
Okahandja	76	B4
Okanagan Lake	92	C2
Okano	72	G4
Okanogan	94	C1
Okara	56	B2
Okarem	58	F2
Okato	84	D4
Okavango Delta	76	C3
Okaya	50	K5
Okayama	50	G6
Okene	72	F3
Oker	20	F4
Okha, India	58	J5
Okha, Russia	46	Q6
Okhansk	38	L3
Okhotsk	46	Q5
Okhtyrka	38	F4
Okinawa	48	H5
Okinawa	48	H5
Oki-shotō	50	G5
Okitipupa	72	E3
Oklahoma	98	B2
Oklahoma City	98	B2
Okoppe	50	M1
Okoyo	72	H5
Okranger	16	E5
Oksino	38	K1
Oktinden	16	H4
Oktyabr'sk	38	L5
Oktyabr'skiy	38	K4
Okurchan	46	S5
Okushiri-tō	50	K2
Ólafsvík	16	(1)B2
Olancha	94	C3
Öland	16	J8
Olanga	16	Q3
Olathe	98	C2
Olava	20	J7
Olavarría	110	J6
Otawa	18	G7
Olbia	32	D8
Olching	30	G2
Old Crow	100	(1)K2
Oldenburg, Germany	20	D3
Oldenburg, Germany	20	F2
Oldenzaal	22	J2
Oldham	24	L8
Old Head of Kinsale	24	D10
Olean	96	E2
Olecko	18	M3
Olekma	46	L5
Olekminsk	46	L4
Oleksandriya	38	F5
Olenegorsk	16	S2
Olenek	46	J3
Oleněk	46	L2
Oleněkskiy Zaliv	46	L2
Oleśnica	18	G6
Olesno	18	H7
Olhão	28	C7
Olib	30	K6
Olinda	108	L5
Oliva	28	K6
Olivet, France	26	G6
Olivet, United States	94	G2
Olivia	96	B2
Olmos	108	B5
Olney	98	B3
Olochi	46	K6
Olonets	38	F2
Olongapo	52	G4
Oloron-Ste-Marie	26	E10
Olot	28	N2
Olovyannaya	46	K6
Olpe	22	K3
Olsztyn	18	K4
Olt	34	M4
Olten	30	C3
Olteniţa	34	P5
Oltu	60	K3
Ouanpi	52	G8
Olvera	28	E8
Olympia	94	B1
Olympos	36	E4
Olympus	36	Q10
Olyutorskiy	46	W4
Olyutorskiy Zaliv	46	V4
Om'	44	N6
Oma	50	L3
Omae-saki	50	K6
Omagh	24	E7
Omaha	94	G2
Omak	94	C1
Omakau	84	B7
Oman	58	G5
Omapere	84	D2
Omarama	84	B7
Omaruru	76	B4
Omba, China	56	E2
Omba, Russia	44	E4
Omboué	72	F5
Ombrone	32	F6
Omdurman = Umm Durman	68	F4
Omegna	30	D5
Omeo	82	J7
Om Hajer	68	G5
Omīdeyeh	63	C1
Omis	30	M7
Ommen	22	J2
Omolon	46	T3
Omoloy	46	N3
Omo Wenz	74	F2
Omsk	44	N6
Omsukchan	46	S4
Omul	50	M1
Omulew	18	L4
Ōmura	50	F7
Ōmuta	50	F7
Onang	55	A3
Onda	28	K5
Ondangwa	76	B3
Ondjiva	76	B3
Ondo	72	E3
Ondörhaan	48	E1
One and a Half Degree Channel	56	B8
Onega	38	G2
O'Neill	94	G2
Oneonta	96	F2
Oneşti	34	P3
Onezhskoye Ozero	38	F2
Ongjin	50	C5
Ongole	56	D5
Onguday	44	R7
Oni	60	K2
Onilahy	76	G4
Onitsha	72	F3
Ono	50	J6
Onon	46	J7
Onon	46	J7
Onslow Bay	102	J2
Onsong	50	E2
Ontario	90	N6
Ontinyent	28	K6
Ontonagon	96	C1
Onyx	100	C1
Oodnadatta	82	G5
Oologah Lake	98	B2
Oostburg	22	F3
Oostelijk-Flevoland	22	H2
Oostende	22	E3
Oosterhout	22	G3
Oosterschelde	22	F3
Oost-Vlieland	22	H1
Ootsa Lake	90	F6
Opala	74	C4
Oparino	38	J3
Opava	18	G8
Opelika	98	D3
Opelousas	98	C3
Opheim	94	E1
Opochka	38	E3
Opoczno	18	K6
Opole	18	G7
Opornyy	44	J8
Opotiki	84	F4
Opp	98	D3
Opunake	84	D4
Opuwo	76	A3
Oradea	34	J2
Orahovac	34	H7
Orai	56	C3
Oran	28	K9
Oran	110	J3
Orange	76	C5
Orange, Australia	82	J6
Orange, France	26	K9
Orange, United States	98	C3
Orangeburg	98	E3
Orangemund	76	B5
Orangeville	96	D2
Oranienburg	20	J4
Orapa	76	D4
Orăştie	34	L4
Oraviţa	34	J4
Orbec	26	F4
Orbetello	32	F6
Orco	30	C5
Ordes	28	B1
Ordes Santa Comba	28	B1
Ordu	60	G3
Ordway	94	F3
Öreälven	16	K4
Örebro	16	H7
Oregon	94	B2
Oregon	96	A3
Orekhovo-Zuyevo	38	G3
Orel	38	G4
Orem	94	D2
Ören	36	L6
Orenburg	38	L4
Orestiada	36	J3
Orewa	84	E3
Orford Ness	22	D2
Orhei	34	R2
Orihuela	28	K6
Orillia	96	E2
Orinoco	108	D2
Orinoco Delta = Delta del Orinoco	108	E2
Orissaare	16	M7
Oristano	32	C9
Orivesi	16	Q5
Orkla	16	F5
Orkney Islands	24	K3
Orlando	98	E4
Orléans	26	G6
Orlik	46	F6
Orly	22	E5
Ormara	58	H4
Ormoc	52	G4

Ormos Almyrou 36 G9
Ormos Mesara 36 G9
Ornans 26 M6
Ornö 16 K7
Örnsköldsvik 16 K5
Orocué 108 C3
Orofino 94 C1
Oromocto 96 G1
Orona 80 J6
Oronoque 108 F3
Oroqen Zizhiqi 46 L6
Orosei 32 D8
Orosháza 34 H3
Oroszlany 18 H10
Orotukan 46 S4
Oroville 94 B3
Orroroo 82 G6
Orsa 16 H6
Orsay 26 H5
Orsha 38 F4
Orsk 38 L4
Orşova 34 K5
Ørsta 16 D5
Ortaklar 36 K7
Orthez 26 E10
Ortigueira 28 C1
Ortisei 30 G4
Ortles 30 F4
Ortona 32 J6
Ortonville 96 A1
Orūmīyeh 60 L5
Oruro 108 D7
Orvieto 32 G6
Orville 26 L6
Ōsaka 50 H6
Osăm 34 M6
Osceola 96 B2
Oschatz 20 J5
Oschersleben 20 G4
O Seixo 28 B3
Osh 44 N9
Oshamambe 50 L2
Oshawa 96 E2
Oshkosh, *Nebr., United States* 94 F2
Oshkosh, *Wis., United States* 96 C2
Oshogbo 72 E3
Osijek 34 F4
Osimo 30 J7
Oskaloosa 96 B2
Oskarshamn 16 J8
Oslo 16 F7
Oslofjorden 16 F7
Osmancık 60 F3
Osmaniye 60 G5
Osnabrück 22 L2
Osor 30 K6
Osorno 110 G7
Osprey Reef 82 J2
Oss 22 H3
Ossa de Montiel 28 H6
Osseo 96 B2
Ossora 46 U5
Ostashkov 38 F3
Oste 20 E3
Osterburg 20 G4
Østerdalen 16 F6
Osterholz-Scharmbeck 20 D3
Osterode 20 F5
Östersund 16 H5
Ostfriesische Inseln 20 C3
Ostiglia 30 G5
Ostrava 18 H8
Ostróda 18 K4
Ostrołęka 18 L4
Ostrov, *Czech Republic* 20 H6
Ostrov, *Russia* 38 E3
Ostrova Arkticheskogo Instituta 44 P2
Ostrova Medvezh'I 46 T2
Ostrova Atlasova 46 S6
Ostrova Vrangelya 88 V4
Ostrov Ayon 46 V2
Ostrov Belyy 44 N3
Ostrov Beringa 46 V6
Ostrov Bol'shevik 44 V2
Ostrov Bol'shoy Begichev 46 J2
Ostrov Bol'shoy Lyakhovskiy 46 Q2
Ostrov Bol'shoy Shantar 46 P6
Ostrov Chechen' 60 M2
Ostrov Iturup 50 P1
Ostrov Karaginskiy 46 U5
Ostrov Kil'din 16 T2
Ostrov Kolguyev 44 H4
Ostrov Komsomolets 44 T1
Ostrov Kotel'nyy 46 P1
Ostrov Kunashir 50 P1
Ostrov Mednyy 46 V6
Ostrov Mezhdusharskiy 44 H3
Ostrov Morzhovets 38 H1
Ostrov Novaya Sibir' 46 S2
Ostrov Ogurchinskiy 58 F2
Ostrov Oktyabr'skoy 44 S2
Ostrov Onekotan 46 S7
Ostrov Paramushir 46 T6
Ostrov Rasshua 46 S7
Ostrov Shiashkotan 46 S7
Ostrov Shumshu 46 T6
Ostrov Simushir 46 S7
Ostrov Urup 46 S7
Ostrov Ushakova 44 Q1
Ostrov Vaygach 44 K3
Ostrov Vise 44 P2
Ostrov Vosrozhdeniya 44 K9
Ostrov Vrangelya 46 W2
Ostrowiec Świętokrzyski 18 L7
Ostrów Mazowiecka 18 L5
Ostrów Wielkopolski 18 G6
Ostuni 32 M8
Osum 36 C4
Ōsumi-shotō 50 F8
Osuna 28 E7
Oswego 96 E2
Oświęcim 18 J7
Otago Peninsula 84 C7
Otaki 84 E5
Otaru 50 L2
Oţelu Roşu 34 K4
Othonoi 36 B5
Oti 72 E3
Otira 84 C6
Otjiwarongo 76 B4
Otočac 30 L6
Otog Qi 48 D3
Otoineppu 50 M1
Otorohanga 84 E4
Otranto 32 N8
Otrøy 16 D5
Otrozhnyy 46 W3
Ōtsu 50 H6
Otta 16 E6
Ottawa 96 E1
Ottawa, *Canada* 96 E1
Ottawa, *Ill., United States* 96 C2
Ottawa, *Kans., United States* 98 B2
Ottawa Islands 90 Q5
Otterøy 16 F4
Ottobrunn 30 G2
Ottumwa 96 B2
Otukpo 72 F3
Ouachita Mountains 98 C3
Ouadâne 70 C4
Ouadda 74 C2
Ouagadougou 72 D2
Oualâta 70 D5
Ouallam 72 E2
Ouanda-Djalle 74 C2
Ouargla 70 G2
Ouarzazate 70 D2
Oudenaarde 22 F4
Oudenbosch 22 G3
Oudtshoorn 76 C6
Oued Laou 28 E9
Oued Tiélat 28 K9
Oued Zem 70 D2
Ouéléssébougou 72 C2
Ouésso 72 H4
Ouezzane 70 D2
Oujda 70 E2
Oujeft 70 C4
Oulainen 16 N4
Ould Yenjé 70 C5
Oulu 16 N4
Oulujärvi 16 P4
Oulujoki 16 P4
Oulx 30 B5
Oum-Chalouba 68 D4
Oum-Hadjer 68 C5
Ounarjoki 16 N3
Our 22 J4
Ouray 94 E3
Ourense 28 C2
Ouricurí 108 J5
Ourthe 22 H4
Oustreham 22 B5
Outer Hebrides 24 D4
Outjo 76 B4
Outokumpu 16 Q5
Out Skerries 24 M1
Ouyen 82 H7
Ovacık 36 R8
Ovada 30 D6
Ovalle 110 G5
Ovareli 60 L3
Overflakkee 22 G3
Overlander Roadhouse 82 B5
Overland Park 98 C2
Overton 94 D3
Övertorneå 16 M3
Ovidiopol' 34 T3
Oviedo 28 E1
Owaka 84 B8
Owando 72 H5
Owase 50 J6
Owatonna 96 B2
Owen River 84 D5
Owensboro 96 C3
Owens Lake 94 C3
Owen Sound 96 D2
Owerri 72 F3
Owo 72 F3
Owosso 96 D2
Owyhee 94 C2
Owyhee 94 C2
Oxford, *New Zealand* 84 D6
Oxford, *United Kingdom* 22 A3
Oxnard 100 C2
Oyama 50 K5
Oyapock 108 G3
Oyem 72 G4
Oyen 92 D1
Oyonnax 30 A4
Ózd 18 K9
Ozernovskiy 46 T6
Ozero Alakol' 44 Q8
Ozero Aralsor 38 J5
Ozero Aydarkul' 44 M9
Ozero Balkhash 44 N8
Ozero Baykal 46 H6
Ozero Beloye 38 G2
Ozero Chany 44 P7
Ozero Chernoye 38 N3
Ozero Il'men' 38 F3
Ozero-Imandra 16 R2
Ozero Inder 44 J8
Ozero Janis'jarvi 16 R5
Ozero Kamennoje 16 R4
Ozero Kanozero 16 T3
Ozero Khanka 50 G1
Ozero Kolvitskoye 16 S3
Ozero Kovdozero 16 S3
Ozero Kulundinskoye 44 P7
Ozero Kushmurun 38 N4
Ozero Lama 46 D2
Ozero Leksozero 16 R5
Ozero Lovozero 16 T2
Ozero Nyuk 16 R4
Ozero Ozhogino 46 R3
Ozero Pirenga 16 R3
Ozero Pyaozero 16 R3
Ozero Saltaim 38 P3
Ozero Sarpa 38 J5
Ozero Segozeroskoye 38 F2
Ozero Seletyteniz 44 N7
Ozero Srednyeye Kuyto 16 R4
Ozero Taymyr 44 U3
Ozero Teletskoye 44 R7
Ozero Tengiz 38 N4
Ozero Topozero 16 R4
Ozero Umbozero 16 T3
Ozero Vygozero 38 G2
Ozero Yalpug 34 R4
Ozero Zaysan 44 Q8
Ozero Zhaltyr 38 K5
Ozero Zhamanakkol' 38 M5
Ozersk 18 M3
Ozhogina 46 R3
Ozhogino 46 R3
Ozieri 32 C8
Ozinki 38 J4
Ozona 100 F2
Ozurget'i 60 J3

P

Paamiut 90 X4
Paar 20 G8
Paarl 76 B6
Pabbay 24 E4
Pabianice 18 J6
Pabna 56 E4
Pacasmayo 108 B5
Pachino 32 K12
Pachuca 102 E4
Pacific Ocean 10 B3
Pacitan 54 E4
Packwood 94 B1
Padalere 55 B3
Padang 54 C3
Padangpanjang 54 C3
Padangsidempuan 54 B2
Padborg 20 E2
Paderborn 20 D5
Padova 30 G5
Padre Island 98 B4
Padrón 28 B2
Paducah, *Ky., United States* 96 C3
Paducah, *Tex., United States* 100 F2
Padum 56 C2
Paekdu San 50 D3
Paeroa 84 E3
Pafos 36 Q10
Pag 30 L6
Pag 30 K6
Paga Conta 108 G4
Pagadian 52 G5
Pagai Selatan 54 B3
Pagai Utara 54 B3
Pagalu = Annobón 72 F5
Pagan 80 E4
Pagatan 54 F3
Page, *Ariz., United States* 100 D1
Page, *Okla., United States* 98 C3
Pagosa Springs 94 E3
Pagri 56 E3
Pahiatua 84 E5
Paia 100 (2)E3
Paide 16 N7
Päijänne 16 N6
Painan 54 C3
Painesville 96 D2
Paisley 24 H6
Paita 108 A5
Pakaraima Mountains 108 E2
Pakch'ŏn 50 C4
Pakhachi 46 V4
Paki 72 F2
Pakistan 58 J4
Pakokku 52 A2
Pakotai 84 D2
Pakrac 30 N5
Paks 34 F3
Pakxé 52 D3
Pala 68 B6
Palafrugell 28 P3
Palagonia 32 J11
Palagruža 32 L6
Palaiochora 36 F9
Palamós 28 P3
Palana 46 U5
Palanan 52 G3
Palanga 18 L2
Palangkaraya 54 E3
Palanpur 56 B4
Palantak 58 H4
Palapye 76 D4
Palatka, *Russia* 46 S4
Palatka, *United States* 98 E4
Palau 80 D5
Palau 32 D7
Palau 80 D5
Palaw 52 B4
Palawan 52 F5
Palazzolo Arceide 32 J11
Palembang 54 C3
Palencia 28 F2
Paleokastritsa 36 B5
Palermo 32 H10
Palestine 98 B3
Palestrina 32 G7
Paletwa 52 A2
Palghat 56 C6
Pali 56 B3
Palikir 80 F5
Palimbang 52 G5
Pālkohda 56 D5
Palk Strait 56 C7
Palma del Río 28 E7
Palma de Mallorca 28 N5
Palma di Montechiaro 32 H11
Palmanova 30 J5
Palmares 108 K5
Palmarola 32 G8
Palmas 108 H6
Palmas 110 L4
Palm Bay 98 E4
Palmdale 100 C2
Palmerston 84 C7
Palmerston Island 80 K7
Palmerston North 84 E5
Palm Harbor 98 E4
Palmi 32 K10
Palmira 108 B3
Palmyra Island 80 K5
Palojärvi 16 M2
Palopo 55 B3
Palu, *Indonesia* 55 A3
Palu, *Turkey* 60 J4
Palyavaam 46 W3
Pama 72 E2
Pamekasan 54 E4
Pamhagen 30 M3
Pamiers 26 G10
Pamlico Sound 98 F2
Pampa 100 F1
Pampas 110 J6
Pamplona, *Colombia* 102 K7
Pamplona, *Spain* 28 J2
Pana 96 C3
Panagjurište 34 M7
Panaji 56 B5
Panama 102 H7
Panamá 108 B2
Panama Canal = Canal de Panamá 102 J7
Panama City 98 D3
Panarea 32 K10
Panarik 54 D2
Panaro 30 G6
Panay 52 G4
Pančevo 34 H5
Panciu 34 Q4
Pandan 52 G4
Pandharpur 56 C5
Panevėžys 18 P2
Pangani 74 F5
Pangin 56 F3
Pangkajene 55 A3
Pangkalanbuun 54 E3
Pangkalpinang 54 D3
Pangnirtung 90 T3
Panguitch 94 D3
Pangutaran Group 52 G5
Panhandle 100 F1
Panipat 56 C3
Panjāb 58 J3
Panjgur 58 H4
Pankshin 72 F3
Pantanal 108 F7
Pantar 55 B4
Pantelleria 70 H1
Pantemakassar 55 B4
Paola 32 L9
Paoua 74 B2
Papa 100 (2)F4
Pápa 34 E2
Papakura 84 E3
Papantla 102 E4
Paparoa 84 E3
Papa Stour 24 L1
Papatowi 84 B8
Papa Westray 24 K2
Papenburg 20 C3
Papey 16 (1)F2
Papua New Guinea 80 E6
Papun 52 B3
Pará 108 G5
Para 108 H4
Parabel' 44 Q6
Paracatu 108 H7
Paracel Islands 52 E3
Paraćin 34 J6
Pará de Minas 108 J7
Paragould 98 C2
Paragua, *Bolivia* 108 E6
Paragua, *Venezuela* 108 E2
Paraguay 110 J3
Paraguay 106 F6
Paraíba 108 K5
Parakou 72 E3
Paralia 36 E8
Paralimni 62 A1
Paramaribo 108 F2
Paraná 110 J5
Paranã 108 H6
Paraná 110 L3
Paranã 108 H6
Paraná 110 K4
Paranaguá 110 M4
Paranaíba 108 G7
Paranaíba 108 G7
Paranavaí 110 L3
Paranestio 36 G3
Paraparaumu 84 E5
Paray-le Monial 26 K7
Parbhani 56 C5
Parchim 20 G3
Pardo 108 J7
Pardubice 18 E7
Pareh 60 L4
Parepare 55 A3
Parga 36 C5
Parigi 55 B3
Parika 108 F2
Parintins 108 F4

Paris, *France* 26 H5
Paris, *Tenn., United States* 98 D2
Paris, *Tex., United States* 98 B3
Parkersburg 96 D3
Park Rapids 96 A1
Parla 28 G4
Parma 30 F6
Parma, *Italy* 30 F6
Parma, *United States* 96 D2
Parnaíba 108 J4
Parnaíba 108 J4
Parnassus 84 D6
Pärnu 16 N7
Pärnu 16 N7
Paros 36 H7
Paros 36 H7
Parry Bay 90 Q3
Parry Islands 90 L1
Parry Sound 96 D2
Parsons 98 B2
Parthenay 26 E7
Partinico 32 H10
Partizansk 50 G2
Paru 108 G4
Parvatipuram 56 D5
Paryang 56 D2
Pasadena, *Calif., United States* 100 C2
Pasadena, *Tex., United States* 98 B4
Paşalimani Adası 36 K4
Pasawng 52 B3
Paşcani 34 P2
Pasco 94 C1
Pascual 52 G4
Pasewalk 20 K3
Pasig 52 G4
Pasinler 60 J3
Pasłęk 18 J3
Pasłek 18 J3
Pasleka 16 L9
Pašman 30 L7
Pasni 58 H4
Paso de Hachado 110 G6
Paso de Indios 110 H7
Paso de la Cumbre 110 H5
Paso de San Francisco 110 H4
Paso Río Mayo 110 G8
Paso Robles 100 B1
Passau 20 J8
Passo Fundo 110 L4
Passos 108 H8
Pastavy 16 P9
Pasto 108 B3
Pastos Bons 108 J5
Pasvalys 18 P1
Pásztó 34 G2
Patagonia 110 G8
Patan, *India* 56 B4
Patan, *Nepal* 56 E3
Patea 84 E4
Pate Island 74 G4
Paterna 28 K5
Paternò 32 J11
Paterson 96 F2
Pathankot 56 C2
Pathfinder Reservoir 94 E2
Patia 108 B3
Patiala 56 C2
Patmos 36 J7
Patna 56 E3
Patnos 60 K4
Patos de Minas 108 H7
Patra 36 D6
Patraikis Kolpos 36 D6
Patreksfjörður 16 (1)B2
Pattani 52 C5
Pattaya 52 C4
Patti 32 J10
Paturau River 84 D5
Pau 28 K1
Pauini 108 D5
Pauini 108 D5
Paulatuk 100 (1)N2
Paulo Afonso 108 K5
Pauls Valley 98 B3
Päveh 60 M6
Pavia 30 E5
Pāvilosta 16 L8
Pavlikeni 34 N6
Pavlodar 44 P7
Pavlohrad 38 G5
Pavlovsk 38 H4
Pavlovskaya 38 G5
Pavullo nel Frignano 30 F6
Paxoi 36 C5
Paxson 100 (1)H3
Payerne 30 B4
Payette 94 C2
Payne's Find 82 C5
Paysandú 110 K5
Payson 100 D2
Payturma 44 S3
Pazar 60 J3
Pazardžik 34 M7
Pazin 30 J5
Peace 90 H5
Peace River 90 H5
Peach Springs 100 D1
Pearsall 98 B4
Pebane 76 F3
Pebas 108 C5
Peć 34 H7
Pecan Island 98 C4
Pechora 38 L1
Pechora 38 K1
Pechorskoye More 44 J4
Pechory 16 P8
Pecos 100 F2
Pecos 100 F2
Pécs 34 F3
Pedja 16 P7
Pedra Azul 108 J7
Pedra Lume 72 (1)B1
Pedreiras 108 J4
Pedro Afonso 108 H5
Pedro Juan Caballero 110 K3
Pedro Luro 110 J6
Peel Sound 90 M2
Peene 20 J3
Peenemünde 20 J2
Pegasus Bay 84 D6
Pegnitz 20 G7
Pegu 52 B3
Pegunungan Barisan 54 B2
Pegunungan Iran 54 F2
Pegunungan Maoke 55 E3
Pegunungan Meratus 54 F3
Pegunungan Schwaner 54 E3
Pegunungan Van Rees 55 E3
Pehuajó 110 J6
Peine 20 F4
Peiraias 36 F7
Peißenberg 30 G3
Peixe 108 H6
Pekalongan 54 D4
Pekanbaru 54 C2
Peking = Beijing 48 F3
Pelaihari 54 E3
Peleduy 46 J5
Peleng 55 B3
Pelhřimov 18 E8
Pelješac 32 M6
Pello 16 N3
Pellworm 20 D2
Pelly Bay 90 P3
Peloponnisos 36 D7
Pelotas 110 L5
Pelym 38 M2
Pemangkat 54 D2
Pematangsiantar 54 B2
Pemba 76 G2
Pemba Island 74 F5
Pembina 94 G1
Pembine 96 C1
Pembroke, *Canada* 96 E1
Pembroke, *United Kingdom* 24 H10
Pembroke, *United States* 98 E3
Peñafiel 28 F3
Peñaranda de Bracamonte 28 E4
Peñarroya-Pueblonuevo 28 E6
Pendik 36 M4
Pendleton 94 C1
Pendolo 54 G3
Pend Oreille Lake 94 C1
Pen Hills 96 E2
Peniche 28 A5
Península de Azuero 102 H7
Península de Guajira 102 K6
Península Valdés 110 J7
Péninsule de Gaspé 90 T7
Péninsule d'Ungava 90 R4
Penmarch 26 A6
Penne 32 H6
Pennines 24 K7
Pennsylvania 96 E2
Penrith 24 K7
Pensacola 102 G2
Penticton 94 C1
Penza 38 J4
Penzance 24 G11
Penzhina 46 V4
Penzhinskaya Guba 46 U4
Penzhinskiy Khrebet 46 V4
Peoria, *Ariz., United States* 100 D2
Peoria, *Ill., United States* 96 C2
Percival Lakes 82 D4
Peregrebnoye 38 N2
Pereira 108 B3
Pergamino 110 J5
Périers 26 D4
Périgueux 26 F8
Peristera 36 G5
Perito Moreno 110 G8
Perleberg 20 G3
Perm' 38 L3
Përmet 36 C4
Pernambuco 108 K5
Pernik 34 L7
Péronne 22 E5
Perpignan 26 H11
Perrine 98 E4
Perry, *Fla., United States* 98 E3
Perry, *Ga., United States* 98 E3
Persepolis 63 E2
Persian Gulf 63 C2
Perth, *Australia* 82 C6
Perth, *United Kingdom* 24 J5
Pertuis Breton 26 D7
Peru 108 C6
Peru 96 C2
Peru-Chile Trench 106 D5
Perugia 32 G5
Pervomays'k 38 F5
Pervoural'sk 38 L3
Pesaro 30 H7
Pescara 32 J6
Pescia 30 F7
Peshawar 56 B2
Peshkopi 36 C3
Peski Karakumy 58 G2
Peski Kyzylkum 44 L9
Peski Priaral'skiye Karakumy 44 L8
Pesnica 30 L4
Pessac 26 E9
Peštera 36 G2
Petah Tiqwa 62 B4
Petalioi 36 G7
Petaluma 94 B3
Pétange 22 H5
Petare 102 L6
Petauke 76 E2
Peterborough, *Canada* 96 E2
Peterborough, *United Kingdom* 24 M9
Peterhead 24 L4
Peter I Øy 112 (2)JJ3
Petersburg 96 E3
Petersfield 22 B3
Petershagen 20 D4
Petit Mécatina 90 U6
Peto 102 G4
Petre Bay 84 (1)B1
Petrič 36 F3
Petrila 34 L4
Petrinja 30 M5
Petrolina 108 J5
Petropavlovka 46 H6
Petropavlovsk 38 N4
Petropavlovsk-Kamchatskiy 46 T6
Petrópolis 110 N3
Petroşani 34 L4
Petrovac 34 J5
Petrovsk-Zabaykal'skiy 46 H6
Petrozavodsk 38 F2
Petrun 38 M1
Petukhovo 38 N3
Pevek 46 W3
Pezinok 18 G9
Pfaffenhofen 20 G8
Pfarrkirchen 20 H8
Pflach 30 F3
Pforzheim 20 D8
Pfunds 30 F4
Pfungstadt 20 D7
Phalaborwa 76 E4
Phalodi 56 B3
Phan Rang 52 D4
Phan Thiêt 52 D4
Phatthalung 52 C5
Phet Buri 52 B4
Phichit 52 C3
Philadelphia, *Miss., United States* 98 D3
Philadelphia, *Pa., United States* 98 F2
Philippeville 22 G4
Philippines 52 G5
Philippine Trench 42 R8
Philips 90 K7
Phillipsburg 94 G3
Phitsanulok 52 C3
Phnum Penh 52 C4
Phoenix 100 D2
Phoenix 76 (1)B2
Phoenix Islands 80 J6
Phôngsali 52 C2
Phuket 52 B5
Phumĕ Sâmraông 52 C4
Piacenza 30 E5
Piadena 30 F5
Pianoro 30 G6
Pianosa 32 E6
Piatra-Neamţ 34 P3
Piauí 108 J5
Piazza Armerina 32 J11
Pibor Post 74 E2
Picacho del Centinela 100 F3
Picayune 98 D3
Pichilemu 110 G5
Pico 70 (1)B2
Pico Almanzor 28 E4
Pico Cristóbal Colón 102 K6
Pico da Bandeira 110 N3
Pico da Neblina 108 D3
Pico de Itambé 110 N2
Pico de Teide 70 B3
Pico Duarte 102 K5
Picos 108 J5
Picton, *New Zealand* 84 D5
Picton, *United States* 96 E2
Pic Tousside 68 C3
Piedras Negras 100 F3
Pieksämäki 16 P5
Pielinen 16 Q5
Pierre 94 F2
Pierrelatte 26 K9
Piers do Rio 108 H7
Piešťany 18 G9
Pietermaritzburg 76 E5
Pietersburg 76 D4
Pietrasanta 30 F6
Piet Retief 76 E5
Pieve di Cadore 30 H4
Pihlájavesi 16 P6
Pik Aborigen 46 R4
Piketberg 76 B6
Pik Kommunizma 58 K2
Pik Pobedy 44 P9
Piła 18 F4
Pilaya 110 H3
Pilcomayo 108 E8
Pilibhit 56 C3
Pilica 18 J7
Pimba 82 G6
Pimenta Bueno 108 E6
Pinamalayan 52 G4
Pinamar 110 K6
Pinang 52 B5
Pinarbası 60 G4
Pinar del Río 102 H4
Pinarhisar 36 K3
Pińczów 18 K7
Pindaré Mirim 108 H4
Pindos 36 D5
Pine Bluff 96 B4
Pine Bluffs 94 F2
Pine City 96 B1
Pine Creek 82 F2
Pine Creek Reservoir 96 A4
Pinega 38 H2
Pineios 36 E5
Pine Island Bay 112 (2)GG3
Pineland 98 C3
Pinerolo 30 C6
Pineville, *Ky., United States* 96 D3
Pineville, *La., United States* 98 C3
Pingdingshan 48 E4
Pingguo 52 D2
Pingle 52 E2
Pingliang 48 D3
Pingshi 48 E5
P'ingtung 52 G2
Pingxiang, *China* 52 D2
Pingxiang, *China* 52 E1
Pinhel 28 C4
Pini 54 B2
Pinka 30 M3
Pink Mountain 90 G5
Pinneberg 20 E3
Pinsk 38 E4
Pioche 94 D3
Piombino 32 E6
Pioneer 100 D2
Pioneer Mountains 94 D1
Pionerskiy, *Russia* 18 K3
Pionerskiy, *Russia* 38 M2
Piopio 84 E4
Piotrków Trybunalski 18 J6
Piove di Sacco 30 H5
Piperi 36 G5
Pipestone 96 A2
Pipiriki 84 E4
Piqua 96 D2
Piracicaba 110 M3
Pirin 36 F3
Piripiri 108 J4
Pirmasens 20 C7
Pirna 20 J6
Pirot 34 K6
Piru 55 C3
Pisa 30 F7
Pisa 18 L4
Pisco 108 B6
Písek 18 D8
Pīshīn 58 H4
Pishin 58 J3
Piska 18 L4
Pisticci 32 L8
Pistoia 30 F7
Pisz 18 L4
Pitcairn Islands 80 P8
Piteå 16 L4
Piteälven 38 C1
Piteşti 34 M5
Pithara 82 C6
Pithiviers 26 H5
Pitkyaranta 38 F2
Pitlochry 24 J5
Pitlyar 38 N1
Pitt Island 84 (1)B2
Pittsburg 98 C2
Pittsburgh 96 E2
Pitt Strait 84 (1)B2
Piura 108 A5
Pivka 30 K5
Placer 52 G4
Placerville 100 B1
Plaiamonas 36 E5
Plains 100 F2
Plainview 100 F2
Plampang 54 F4
Planalto Central 108 H6
Planalto da Borborema 108 K5
Planalto do Mato Grosso 108 G6
Plankinton 94 G2
Plano 98 B3
Plasencia 28 D5
Plast 38 M4
Plateau du Djado 70 H4
Plateau du Limousin 26 F8
Plateau du Tademaït 70 F3
Plateau of Tibet = Xizang Gaoyuan 56 D2
Plateaux Batéké 72 G5
Platinum 100 (1)E4
Plato 102 K7
Plato Ustyurt 44 J9
Platte 98 B1
Platteville 96 B2
Plattling 20 H8
Plattsburgh 96 F2
Plattsmouth 98 B1
Plau 20 H3
Plauen 20 H6
Plavnik 30 K6
Plavsk 38 G4
Playa de Castilla 28 D7
Playas 108 A4
Plây Cu 52 D4
Pleasanton 100 G3
Pleiße 20 H5
Plentywood 94 F1
Plesetsk 38 H2
Pleven 34 M6
Pljevlja 34 G6
Płock 18 J5
Pločno 34 E6
Ploërmel 26 C6
Ploieşti 34 P5
Plomari 36 J6
Plön 20 F2
Płońsk 18 K5
Plovdiv 34 M7
Plumtree 76 D4
Plungė 18 L2
Plymouth, *United Kingdom* 24 H11
Plymouth, *United States* 96 C2
Plyussa 38 E3
Plyussa 16 Q7
Plzeň 18 C8
Po 30 E5
Pocahontas 102 F1
Pocatello 94 D2
Pochet 46 F5
Pochinok 38 F4
Pocking 30 J2
Pocomoke City 96 E3
Podgorica 34 G7
Podkamennaya Tunguska 46 F4

Santa Rosa, *N. Mex., United States*	100	F2
Santa Rosa Island	100	B2
Santa Vitória do Palmar	110	L5
Sant Boi	28	N3
Sant Carlos de la Ràpita	28	L4
Sant Celoni	28	N3
Sant Feliu de Guixols	28	P3
Santiago	110	G5
Santiago, *Brazil*	110	L4
Santiago, *Dominican Republic*	102	K5
Santiago, *Philippines*	52	G3
Santiago, *Spain*	28	B2
Santiago de Cuba	102	J5
Santiago del Estero	110	J4
Santo André	110	M3
Santo Antão	72	(1)A1
Santo Antônio de Jesus	108	K6
Santo Antônio do Içá	108	D4
Santo Domingo	102	L5
Santo Domingo de los Colorados	108	B4
Santoña	28	G1
Santos	110	M3
San Vicente	52	G3
San Vincenzo	32	E5
Sanya	52	D3
Sao Bernardo do Campo	108	E4
São Borja	110	K4
São Carlos	110	M3
São Félix, *M.G., Brazil*	108	G6
São Félix, *Pará, Brazil*	108	G5
São Filipe	72	(1)B2
São Francisco	108	J6
São João da Madeira	28	B4
São Jorge	70	(1)B2
São José do Rio Prêto	110	L3
São Luís	108	J4
São Miguel	70	(1)B2
Saône	26	K7
São Nicolau	72	(1)B1
São Paulo	110	L3
São Paulo	110	M3
São Paulo de Olivença	108	D4
São Raimundo Nonato	108	J5
São Tiago	72	(1)B1
São Tomé	72	F4
São Tomé	72	F4
São Tomé and Príncipe	72	F4
São Vicente	110	M3
São Vicente	72	(1)A1
Sapanca	36	M4
Saparua	55	C3
Sapele	72	F3
Sapes	36	H4
Sapientza	36	D8
Sa Pobla	28	P5
Sapporo	50	L2
Sapri	32	K8
Sapudi	54	E4
Sapulpa	98	B2
Saqqez	60	M5
Sarāb	60	M5
Sara Buri	52	C4
Sarajevo	34	F6
Sarakhs	58	H2
Saraktash	38	L4
Saramati	56	G3
Saran	44	N8
Saranac Lake	96	F2
Sarandë	36	C5
Sarangani Islands	55	C1
Saranpul	38	M2
Saransk	38	J4
Sarapul	38	K3
Sarapul'skoye	46	P7
Sarasota	98	E4
Sarata	34	S3
Saratoga	94	E2
Saratoga Springs	96	F2
Saratov	38	J4
Saravan	58	H4
Sarawak	54	E2
Saray	36	K3
Sarayköy	36	L7
Sarayönü	36	Q6
Sarbāz	58	H4
Sarbīsheh	58	G3
Sárbogárd	34	F3
Sar Dasht	60	L5
Sardegna	32	E8
Sardinia = Sardegna	32	E8
Sardis Lake	98	B3
Sar-e Pol	58	J2
Sargodha	58	K3
Sarh	72	H3
Sārī	58	F2
Saria	36	K9
Sarıkamış	60	K3
Sarıkaya	60	F4
Sarikei	54	E2
Sarina	82	J4
Sariñena	28	K3
Sarīr Tibesti	68	C3
Sariwŏn	50	C4
Sarıyer	36	M3
Sark	26	C4
Sarkad	34	J3
Sarkand	44	P8
Sarkikaraağaç	36	P6
Şarkışla	60	G4
Şarköy	36	K4
Sarmi	55	E3
Särna	16	G6
Sarnia	96	D2
Sarny	38	E4
Sarolangun	54	C3
Saronno	30	E5
Saros Körfezi	36	J4
Sárospatak	18	L9
Sarre	26	M5
Sarrebourg	26	N5
Sarreguemines	26	N4
Sarria	28	C2
Sartène	32	C7
Sartyn'ya	38	M2
Saruhanli	36	K6
Sărur	60	L4
Sárvár	30	M3
Sarvestān	63	E2
Sarviz	34	F2
Sarykamyshkoye Ozero	44	K9
Saryozek	44	P9
Saryshagan	44	N8
Sarysu	44	M8
Sary-Tash	58	K2
Sarzana	30	E6
Sasaram	56	D4
Sasebo	50	E7
Saskatchewan	90	K6
Saskatchewan	90	L6
Saskatoon	90	K6
Saskylakh	44	W3
Sassandra	72	C4
Sassari	32	C8
Sassnitz	20	J2
Sasso Marconi	30	G6
Sassuolo	30	F6
Satadougou	72	B2
Satara	56	B5
Satna	56	D4
Sátoraljaújhely	18	L9
Satti	56	C2
Sättna	16	J5
Satu Mare	34	K2
Satun	54	B1
Sauce	110	K5
Saudi Arabia	58	D4
Sauk Center	96	B1
Saulgau	30	E2
Saulieu	26	K6
Sault Ste. Marie, *Canada*	96	D1
Sault Ste. Marie, *United States*	96	D1
Saumlakki	55	D4
Saumur	26	E6
Saunders Island	106	J9
Saura	44	J9
Saurimo	74	C5
Sauðhárkrókur	16	(1)D2
Sava	30	L5
Savaii	80	J7
Savalou	72	E3
Savannah	88	K6
Savannah, *Ga., United States*	98	E3
Savannah, *Tenn., United States*	98	D2
Savannakhet	52	C3
Savaştepe	36	K5
Savè	72	E3
Save	76	E4
Sāveh	58	F2
Saverne	20	C8
Savigliano	30	C6
Savona	30	D6
Savonlinna	16	Q6
Savu	55	B5
Sawahlunto	54	C3
Sawai Madhopur	56	C3
Sawqirah	58	G6
Sawu Sea	55	B4
Sayanogorsk	44	S7
Sayansk	46	G6
Sayhūt	58	F6
Sāylac	68	H5
Saynshand	48	E2
Sayram Hu	44	Q9
Say'ūn	58	E6
Say-Utes	44	J9
Sazan	36	B4
Sazin	58	K2
Sbaa	70	E3
Scafell Pike	24	J7
Scalea	32	K9
Scarborough	24	M7
Scargill	84	D6
Scarp	24	E3
Schaalsee	20	F3
Schaffhausen	30	D3
Schagen	22	G2
Scharbeutz	20	F2
Schärding	30	J2
Scharhörn	20	D3
Scheeßel	20	E3
Schefferville	90	T6
Scheibbs	30	L3
Schelde	22	F3
Schenectady	96	F2
Scheveningen	22	G2
Schiedam	22	G3
Schiermonnikoog	22	H1
Schiermonnikoog	22	J1
Schio	30	G5
Schiza	36	D8
Schkeuditz	20	H5
Schlei	20	E2
Schleiden	22	J4
Schleswig	20	E2
Schlieben	20	J5
Schlüchtern	20	E6
Schneeberg	20	H6
Schneeberg	20	G6
Schönebeck	20	G4
Schongau	30	F3
Schöningen	20	F4
Schouwen	22	F3
Schramberg	30	D2
Schreiber	96	C1
Schrems	30	L2
Schull	24	C10
Schwabach	20	G7
Schwäbische Alb	30	E2
Schwäbisch-Gmünd	30	E2
Schwäbisch-Hall	20	E7
Schwalmstadt	20	E6
Schwandorf	20	H7
Schwarzenbek	20	F3
Schwarzenberg	20	H6
Schwarzwald	30	D3
Schwaz	30	G3
Schwechat	18	F9
Schwedt	18	D4
Schweich	22	J5
Schweinfurt	20	F6
Schwenningen	30	D2
Schwerin	20	G3
Schweriner See	20	G3
Schwetzingen	20	D7
Schwyz	30	D3
Sciacca	32	H11
Scicli	32	J12
Scobey	94	E1
Scotia Ridge	110	K9
Scotia Sea	112	(2)A4
Scotland	24	H5
Scott City	94	F3
Scott Inlet	90	T2
Scott Island	112	(2)Z3
Scott Reef	82	D2
Scottsbluff	94	F2
Scottsboro	96	C4
Scotty's Junction	100	C1
Scranton	96	E2
Scunthorpe	24	M8
Seal	90	M5
Sea of Azov	38	G5
Sea of Galilee	62	C4
Sea of Japan	50	G3
Sea of Marmara = Marmara Denizi	36	L4
Sea of Okhotsk	46	Q5
Sea of the Hebrides	24	E4
Searchlight	100	D1
Searcy	96	B3
Seaside	94	B1
Seattle	94	B1
Sebeş	34	L4
Sebkha Azzel Matti	70	F3
Sebkha de Timimoun	70	E3
Sebkha de Tindouf	70	D3
Sebkha Mekerrhane	70	F3
Sebkha Oum el Drouss Telli	70	C4
Sebkhet de Chemchâm	70	C4
Sebnitz	20	K6
Sebring	98	E4
Secchia	30	F6
Sechura	108	A5
Secretary Island	84	A7
Secunderabad	56	C5
Sécure	108	D7
Sedalia	96	B3
Sedan	22	G5
Sedano	28	G2
Seddon	84	D5
Seddonville	84	C5
Sede Boqer	62	B6
Sedeh	58	G3
Sederot	62	B5
Sedico	30	H4
Sedom	62	C5
Seeheim	76	B5
Seelow	20	K4
Sées	26	F5
Seesen	20	F5
Seevetal	20	E3
Séez	30	B5
Seferihisar	36	J6
Segamat	54	C2
Segezha	38	F2
Seghnān	58	K2
Ségou	72	C2
Segovia	28	F4
Segré	26	E6
Séguédine	70	H4
Seguin	98	B4
Segura	28	H6
Sehithwa	76	C4
Sehnde	20	E4
Seiland	16	M1
Seiling	98	B2
Seinäjoki	16	M5
Seine	26	F4
Sekayu	54	C3
Sekondi	72	D3
Selassi	55	D3
Selat Bangka	54	D3
Selat Berhala	54	C3
Selat Dampir	55	D3
Selat Karimata	54	D3
Selat Makassar	54	F3
Selat Mentawai	54	B3
Selat Sunda	54	D4
Selawik	100	(1)F2
Selb	20	H6
Selby, *United States*	94	G1
Selçuk	36	K7
Selebi-Phikwe	76	D4
Sélestat	30	C2
Selfoss	16	(1)C3
Sélibabi	70	C5
Seligman	100	D1
Seljord	16	E7
Selkirk, *Canada*	92	G1
Selkirk Mountains	90	H6
Sells	100	D2
Selm	22	K3
Selmer	96	C3
Selpele	55	D3
Selvas	108	C5
Selwyn Lake	90	L5
Selwyn Mountains	100	(1)L3
Semanit	36	B4
Semarang	54	E4
Sematan	54	D2
Sembé	72	G4
Seminoe Reservoir	94	E2
Seminole, *Okla., United States*	94	G3
Seminole, *Tex., United States*	100	F2
Semiozernoye	44	L7
Semipalatinsk	44	Q7
Semiyarka	44	P7
Semois	22	H5
Semporna	54	F2
Sena Madureira	108	D5
Senanga	76	C3
Senatobia	98	D3
Sendai	50	L4
Senec	30	N2
Seneca	98	E3
Senegal	72	A2
Sénégal	72	B1
Senftenberg	20	J5
Sengerema	74	E4
Senhor do Bonfim	108	J6
Senica	18	G9
Senigallia	30	J7
Senj	30	K6
Senja	16	J2
Senlis	22	E5
Sennar	58	B7
Senneterre	96	E1
Sens	26	J5
Senta	34	H4
Seoni	56	C4
Seoul = Sŏul	50	D5
Separation Point	84	D5
Sepinang	54	F2
Sept-Îles	90	T6
Seraing	22	H4
Serakhs	58	H2
Seram	55	D3
Seram Sea	55	C3
Serang	54	D4
Serbia = Srbija	34	H6
Serbia and Montenegro	34	H6
Serdobsk	38	H4
Serebryansk	44	Q8
Sered'	34	E1
Şereflikoçhisar	36	R6
Seregno	30	E5
Serein	26	J6
Seremban	54	C2
Serenje	76	E2
Sergelen	48	E1
Sergeyevka	38	N4
Sergipe	108	K6
Sergiyev Posad	38	G3
Seria	54	E2
Serifos	36	G7
Serifos	36	G7
Serik	36	P8
Seringapatam Reef	82	D2
Sermata	55	C4
Seronga	76	C3
Serov	38	M3
Serowe	76	D4
Serpa	28	C7
Serpneve	34	S3
Serpukhov	38	G4
Serra Acari	108	F3
Serra Curupira	108	E3
Serra da Chela	76	A3
Serra da Espinhaço	108	J7
Serra da Ibiapaba	108	J4
Serra da Mantiqueira	110	M3
Serra de Maracaju	110	K3
Serra do Cachimbo	108	F5
Serra do Caiapó	108	G7
Serra do Dois Irmãos	108	J5
Serra do Roncador	108	G6
Serra dos Carajás	108	G5
Serra dos Parecis	108	E6
Serra do Tiracambu	108	H4
Serra Estrondo	108	H5
Serra Formosa	108	F6
Serra Geral de Goiás	108	H6
Serra Geral do Paranã	108	H7
Serra Lombarda	108	G3
Serra Pacaraima	108	E3
Serra Parima	108	E3
Serra Tumucumaque	108	F3
Serra da Estrela	28	C4
Serres, *France*	26	L9
Serres, *Greece*	36	F3
Serrinha	108	K6
Sertã	28	B5
Serui	55	E3
Servia	36	D4
Sêrxü	48	B4
Sese Islands	74	E4
Sesfontein	76	A3
Sesheke	76	C3
Sessa Aurunca	32	H7
Sestri Levante	30	E6
Sestroretsk	16	Q6
Sestrunj	30	K6
Sestu	32	D9
Sesvete	30	M5
Setana	50	K2
Sète	26	J10
Sete Lagoas	108	J7
Setesdal	16	D7
Sétif	70	G1
Settat	70	D2
Setúbal	28	B6
Sŏul	80	C2
Seurre	26	L7
Sevana Lich	60	L3
Sevastopol'	60	E1
Seven Lakes	100	E1
Sevenoaks	22	C3
Sévérac-le-Château	26	J9
Severn, *Canada*	90	P5
Severn, *United Kingdom*	24	K10
Severnaya Dvina	38	H2
Severnaya Osetiya	60	L2
Severnaya Zemlya	44	U1
Severn Estuary	24	J10
Severnoye	38	K4

Name	Page	Grid
Severnyy	44	L4
Severobaykal'sk	46	H5
Severodvinsk	38	G2
Severo-Kuril'sk	46	T6
Severomorsk	16	S2
Severoural'sk	38	M2
Severo-Yeniseyskiy	44	S5
Sevier Lake	94	D3
Sevilla	28	E7
Sevlievo	34	N7
Seward Peninsula	100	(1)E2
Seyakha	44	N4
Seychelles	76	(2)B2
Seychelles Islands	66	J6
Seydişehir	36	P7
Seyhan	60	F5
Seymchan	46	S4
Seymour, Australia	82	J7
Seymour, Ind., United States	98	D2
Seymour, Tex., United States	98	B3
Seyðhisfjörður	16	(1)G2
Sézanne	26	J5
Sezze	32	H7
Sfakia	36	G9
Sfântu Gheorghe, Romania	34	N4
Sfântu Gheorghe, Romania	34	S5
Sfax	70	H2
's-Gravenhage	22	G2
Sha'am	63	G3
Shabunda	74	D4
Shabwah	58	E6
Shache	44	P10
Shädegän	63	C1
Shadehill Reservoir	94	F1
Shagamu	72	E3
Shagonar	44	S7
Shag Rocks	110	N9
Shahbä'	62	D4
Shahdäb	63	G1
Shahdol	56	D4
Shah Fuladi	58	J3
Shahjahanpur	56	C3
Shahrak	58	H3
Shahr-e Bäbäk	63	F1
Shahrtuz	58	J2
Shakhrisabz	58	J2
Shakhtërsk	46	Q7
Shakhty	38	H5
Shakhun'ya	38	J3
Shaki	72	E3
Shakotan-misaki	50	L2
Shama	74	E5
Shamattawa	90	N5
Shamis	63	E5
Shamrock	100	F1
Shand	58	H3
Shandan	48	C3
Shandong Bandao	48	G3
Shangani	76	D3
Shangdu	48	E2
Shanghai	48	G4
Shanghang	48	F6
Shangqui	48	F4
Shangrao	48	F5
Shangzhi	48	H1
Shangzhou	48	D4
Shantarskiye Ostrova	46	P5
Shantou	48	F6
Shanwei	52	F2
Shanyin	48	E3
Shaoguan	48	E6
Shaoxing	48	G5
Shaoyang	48	E5
Shapkina	38	K1
Shaqrä'	63	A4
Sharga	44	T8
Sharjah = Ash Shäriqah	63	F4
Shark Bay	80	B8
Shark Reef	82	J2
Sharmah	68	G2
Sharm el Sheikh	68	F2
Sharürah	58	E6
Shashe	76	D4
Shashi	48	E4
Shasta Lake	94	B2
Shats'k	18	N6
Shatsk	38	H4
Shaubak	62	C6
Shawano	96	C2
Shaykh Miskin	62	D4
Shcherbakove	46	U3
Shchigry	38	G4
Shchuch'ye	44	L6
Shchuchyn	16	N10
Šid	34	G4
Sheberghän	58	J2
Sheboygan	96	C2
Sheffield, New Zealand	84	D6
Sheffield, United Kingdom	24	L8
Sheffield, Al., United States	96	C4
Sheffield, Tex., United States	100	F2
Shegmas	38	J2
Shelburne	90	T8
Shelby	94	D1
Shelbyville	96	C3
Shelikof Strait	100	(1)F4
Shenandoah	96	A2
Shendam	72	F3
Shendi	68	F4
Shenkursk	38	H2
Shenyang	50	B3
Shenzhen	48	E6
Shepetivka	38	E4
Shepparton	82	J7
Sherbro Island	72	B3
Sherbrooke	96	F1
Sheridan	94	E2
Sherkaly	38	N2
Sherlovaya Gora	46	K6
Sherman	98	B3
's-Hertogenbosch	22	H3
Shetland Islands	24	M1
Shetpe	44	J9
Sheyenne	94	G1
Sheykh Sho'eyb	63	E3
Shiant Islands	24	F4
Shibata	50	K5
Shibetsu, Japan	50	M1
Shibetsu, Japan	50	N2
Shibotsu-jima	50	P2
Shiderty	44	N7
Shihezi	44	R9
Shijiazhuang	48	E3
Shikarpur	58	J4
Shikoku	50	G7
Shikoku-sanchi	50	G7
Shikotan-tō	50	P2
Shikotsu-ko	50	L2
Shiliguri	56	E3
Shilka	46	K6
Shilka	46	K6
Shillong	56	F3
Shilovo	38	H4
Shimabara	50	F7
Shimla	56	C2
Shimoga	56	C6
Shimo-Koshiki-jima	50	E8
Shimoni	74	F4
Shimonoseki	50	F7
Shinäş	63	G4
Shīndan	58	H3
Shingū	50	H7
Shinjō	50	L4
Shinyanga	74	E4
Shiono-misaki	50	H7
Shiprock	94	E3
Shiquan	48	D4
Shirakawa	50	L5
Shīrāz	63	E2
Shire	76	E3
Shiretoko-misaki	50	N1
Shiriya-zaki	50	L3
Shīr Küh	58	F3
Shiv	56	B3
Shivpuri	56	C3
Shiyan	48	E4
Shizuishan	48	D3
Shizuoka	50	K6
Shkodër	34	G7
Shomishoko	44	K8
Shorap	58	J4
Shoreham	22	B4
Shoshone, Calif., United States	94	C3
Shoshone, Id., United States	94	D2
Shoshoni	94	E2
Shostka	38	F4
Show Low	100	E2
Shoyna	38	H1
Shreveport	98	C3
Shrewsbury	24	K9
Shuangliao	50	B2
Shuangyashan	46	N7
Shubarkuduk	44	K8
Shulan	50	D1
Shumagin Islands	100	(1)E5
Shumikha	38	M3
Shuqrah	58	E7
Shurchi	58	J2
Shür Gaz	63	H2
Shurinda	46	J5
Shuryshkary	38	N1
Shuya	38	H3
Shuyang	48	F4
Shwebo	52	B2
Shymkent	44	M9
Sia	55	D4
Sialkot	58	K3
Siatista	36	D4
Šiauliai	18	N2
Sibay	38	L4
Šibenik	34	C6
Siberia = Sibir	42	N3
Siberut	54	B3
Sibi	58	J4
Sibigo	54	B2
Sibir	42	N3
Sibiu	34	M4
Sibolga	54	B2
Sibu	54	E2
Sibuco	52	B2
Sibut	74	B2
Sicilia	32	G11
Sicilian Channel	32	F11
Sicily = Sicilia	32	G11
Šid	34	G4
Siddipet	56	C5
Siderno	32	L10
Sidi Barrani	68	E1
Sidi Bel Abbès	70	E1
Sidi Kacem	70	D2
Sidirokastro	36	F3
Sidney	94	F2
Sidoan	55	B2
Sidorovsk	44	Q4
Sieburg	22	K4
Siedlce	18	M5
Sieg	22	K4
Siegen	22	L4
Siemiatycze	18	M5
Siĕmréab	52	C4
Siena	30	G6
Sieradz	18	H6
Sierpc	18	J5
Sierra Blanca	100	E2
Sierra Colorada	110	H7
Sierra de Calalasteo	110	H4
Sierra de Córdoba	110	J5
Sierra de Gata	28	D4
Sierra de Gúdar	28	K4
Sierra del Nevado	110	H6
Sierra de Perija	102	K7
Sierra Grande	110	H7
Sierra Leone	72	B3
Sierra Madre	102	F5
Sierra Madre del Sur	102	E5
Sierra Madre Occidental	92	E6
Sierra Madre Oriental	100	F3
Sierra Morena	28	E6
Sierra Nevada, Spain	28	G7
Sierra Nevada, United States	100	B1
Sierra Vizcaino	92	D6
Sierre	30	C4
Sifnos	36	G8
Sig	28	K9
Sigean	26	H10
Sighetu Marmaţiei	34	L2
Sighişoara	34	M3
Siglufjörður	16	(1)D1
Sigmaringen	30	E2
Signal Mountain	96	C3
Siguiri	72	C2
Sihanoukville	52	C4
Siilinjärvi	16	P5
Siirt	60	J5
Sikar	56	C3
Sikasso	72	C2
Sikea	36	F4
Sikeston	96	C3
Sikhote Alin	50	H1
Sikinos	36	G8
Siklós	34	F4
Siktyakh	46	L3
Sil	28	C2
Šilalė	18	M2
Silandro	30	F4
Silba	30	K6
Silchar	56	F4
Şile	36	M3
Silhouette Island	76	(2)B1
Siliana	32	D12
Silifke	60	E5
Siling Co	56	E2
Silistra	34	Q5
Silivri	36	L3
Siljan	16	H6
Sillamäe	16	P7
Silsbee	98	C3
Siluas	54	D2
Šilutė	18	L2
Silvan	60	J4
Silver Bay	96	B1
Silver City	100	E2
Silver Lake	94	B2
Silver Plains	82	H2
Simanggang	54	E2
Simao	48	C6
Simav	60	C4
Simcoe	96	D2
Simeonovgrad	34	N7
Simeria	34	N12
Simeuluė	54	A2
Simferopol'	60	F1
Šimleu Silvaniei	34	K2
Simmerath	22	J4
Simojärvi	16	P3
Simpang	54	C3
Simpson Desert	82	G4
Sinabang	54	B2
Sinai	68	F2
Sinaia	34	N4
Şinak	60	K5
Sinalunga	32	F5
Sinanju	50	C4
Sinbaungwe	52	B3
Sincelejo	108	B2
Sinclair's Bay	24	J3
Sindangbarang	54	D4
Sindelfingen	30	E8
Sines	28	B7
Singa	68	F5
Singapore	54	C2
Singapore	54	C2
Singaraja	54	E4
Singen	30	D3
Sîngerei	34	R2
Singida	74	E4
Singkawang	54	D2
Singkep	54	C3
Singkilbaru	54	B2
Singleton	82	K6
Siniscola	32	D8
Sinj	34	D6
Sinjai	55	B4
Sinjär	60	J5
Sinkat	68	G4
Sinni	32	L8
Sinop	60	F2
Sinsheim	20	D7
Sintang	54	E2
Sinton	98	B4
Sinŭiju	50	C3
Sinyaya	46	L4
Sió	34	F3
Siófok	34	F3
Sion	30	C4
Sioux City	96	A2
Sioux Falls	96	A2
Sioux Lookout	92	H2
Siping	50	C2
Sipiwesk	90	M5
Sipura	54	B3
Sira	16	D7
Siracusa	32	K11
Sir Bani 'Yäs	63	E4
Sir Edward Pellew Group	82	G3
Siret	34	P2
Siret	34	Q4
Sîrğän	58	F2
Širia	34	L11
Siri Kit Dam	52	B3
Sirohi	56	B4
Sirsa	56	C3
Sirsi	56	B6
Sisak	34	D4
Sisian	60	L4
Sisimiut	90	W3
Sisŏphŏn	52	C4
Sisseton	94	G1
Sistema Central	28	E4
Sistema Iberico	28	H3
Sisteron	30	A6
Sitapur	56	D3
Sitasjaure	16	J3
Siteia	36	J9
Sitges	28	M3
Sithonia	36	F4
Sitka	90	D5
Sittard	22	H4
Sittwe	56	F4
Sivand	63	E1
Sivas	60	G4
Siverek	60	H5
Sivrihisar	36	P5
Siwa	68	E1
Siyäzän	60	N3
Sjælland	16	F9
Sjenica	34	H6
Sjenica Jezero	34	G6
Sjöbo	18	C2
Skädlderviken	18	B1
Skærbæk	20	D1
Skagen	16	F8
Skagerrak	16	D8
Skala	36	E8
Skantzoura	36	G5
Skardu	58	L2
Skarżysko-Kamienna	18	K6
Skaulo	16	L3
Skawina	18	J8
Skaymat	70	B4
Skegness	22	C1
Skellefteå	16	L4
Ski	16	F7
Skiathos	36	F5
Skibotn	16	L2
Skidal'	18	P4
Skien	16	E7
Skikda	70	G1
Skipton	24	L8
Skjern	16	E9
Škofja Loka	30	K4
Skopelos	36	F5
Skopje	34	J7
Skövde	16	G7
Skovorodino	46	L6
Skowhegan	96	G2
Skuodas	16	L8
Skye	24	F4
Skyros	36	G6
Skyros	36	G6
Slagelse	20	G1
Slagnäs	16	K4
Slaney	24	F9
Slano	34	E7
Slantsy	16	Q7
Slaný	20	K6
Slatina	34	M5
Slave	88	N3
Slave Lake	90	J5
Slavonska Požega	34	E4
Slavonski Brod	34	F4
Slavyanka	50	F2
Slavyansk-na-Kubani	60	H1
Sławno	18	F3
Sleaford	22	B1
Sleeper Islands	90	Q5
Slidell	98	D3
Sligo	24	D7
Sligo Bay	24	D7
Slite	16	K8
Sliven	34	P7
Slobozia, Moldova	34	S3
Slobozia, Romania	34	Q5
Slonim	16	N10
Slough	22	B3
Slovak Republic	18	H9
Slovenia	30	K4
Slovenj Gradec	30	L4
Slovenska Bistrica	30	L4
Slov''yans'k	38	G5
Słubice	18	D5
Slunj	30	L5
Stupca	18	G5
Słupsk	18	G3
Slussfors	16	J4
Slutsk	38	E4
Slyudyanka	46	G6
Smålandsfarvandet	20	G1
Smallwood Reservoir	90	U6
Smargon'	16	P9
Smederevo	34	H5
Smila	38	F5
Smirnykh	46	Q7
Smiths Falls	96	E2
Smoky	90	H6
Smoky Hills	96	B2
Smøla	16	D5
Smolensk	38	F4
Smoljan	36	G3
Smooth Rock Falls	96	D1
Smyrna	96	E3
Snæfell	16	(1)F2
Snake	94	C1
Snake River Plain	94	D2
Snåsavatnet	16	F4
Sneek	22	H1
Sneem	24	C10
Snezhnogorsk	44	R4
Snežnik	30	K5
Snina	18	M9
Snøhetta	16	E5
Snøtinden	16	G3
Snowdon	24	H8

Snowdrift	90	J4
Snowville	94	D2
Snyder	100	F2
Soalala	76	H3
Soanierana-Ivongo	76	H3
Soa-Siu	55	C2
Sobral	108	J4
Sochaczew	18	K5
Sochaux	30	B3
Sochi	60	H2
Socorro	100	E2
Socotra = Suquṭrā	58	F7
Socuéllamos	28	H5
Sodankylä	16	P3
Söderhamn	16	J6
Södertälje	16	J7
Sodo	74	F2
Soe	55	B4
Soest	22	L3
Sofia = Sofija	34	L7
Sofija	34	L7
Sofiysk, *Russia*	46	N6
Sofiysk, *Russia*	46	P6
Sofporog	16	R4
Sōfu-gan	48	L5
Sogamoso	108	C2
Sognefjorden	16	C6
Sogod	52	G4
Sog Xian	56	F2
Sohâg	68	F2
Soignies	22	G4
Soissons	22	F5
Sokch'o	50	E4
Söke	36	K7
Sokhumi	60	J2
Sokode	72	E3
Sokol	38	H3
Sokółka	16	M10
Sokolo	72	C2
Sokolov	20	H6
Sokołów Podlaski	18	M5
Sokoto	72	F2
Sokoto	72	F2
Sokyryany	34	Q1
Solander Island	84	A8
Solapur	56	C5
Sölden	30	F4
Solenzara	32	D7
Solhan	60	J4
Solikamsk	38	L3
Sol'-Iletsk	38	L4
Soliman	32	E12
Solingen	22	K3
Sollefteå	16	J5
Soller	28	N5
Solna	16	J7
Solomon Islands	80	F6
Solothurn	30	C3
Solov'yevsk	46	K6
Šolta	34	D6
Soltau	20	E4
Sol'tsy	38	F3
Solway Firth	24	J7
Solwezi	76	D2
Sōma	50	L5
Soma	36	K5
Somalia	74	H2
Sombor	34	G4
Sombrerete	100	F4
Somerset, *Australia*	82	H2
Somerset, *Ky., United States*	96	C3
Somerset, *Pa., United States*	96	E2
Somerset Island	90	N2
Someş	34	K2
Somme	22	E4
Sommen	16	H8
Sömmerda	20	G5
Sømna	16	F4
Sondags	76	D6
Sønderborg Ærø	20	E2
Sondershausen	20	F5
Sondrio	30	E4
Songavatn	16	D7
Songea	74	F6
Song Hông	52	C2
Songhua	48	H1
Songhua Hu	50	D2
Songhua Jiang	50	D1
Songkan	48	D5
Songkhla	52	C5
Songnam	50	D5
Songnim	50	C4
Songo	76	E3
Songololo	72	G6
Songpan	48	C4
Sonid Yuoqi	48	E2
Sonid Zuoqi	48	E2
Son La	52	C2
Sonneberg	20	G6
Sono	108	H6
Sonora	100	B1
Sonora	100	D3
Sonoyta	100	D1
Sonsorol Islands	55	D1
Sonthofen	30	F3
Sopot	16	K9
Sopron	30	M3
Sora	32	H7
Sorel	96	F1
Sorgun	60	F4
Soria	28	H3
Sorø	20	G1
Soroca	34	R1
Sorocaba	110	M3
Sorochinsk	38	K4
Sorong	55	D3
Soroti	74	E3
Sørøya	16	L1
Sorrento	32	J8
Sorsele	16	J4
Sorso	32	C8
Sorsogon	52	G4
Sort	28	M2
Sortavala	16	R6
Sørvagen	16	G3
Sŏsan	50	D5
Sosnogorsk	44	J5
Sosnovka	44	G4
Sosnovo	16	R6
Sosnowiec	18	J7
Sos'va	38	M3
Sos'vinskaya	38	M2
Soto la Marina	100	G4
Soubré	72	C3
Soufli	36	J3
Souilly	22	H5
Souk Ahras	32	B12
Sŏul	50	D5
Soulac-sur-Mer	26	D8
Soumussalmi	16	Q4
Soûr	62	C3
Soure	28	B5
Sour el Ghozlane	28	P8
Souris	92	G2
Souris	92	F2
Sousa	108	K5
Sousse	70	H1
South Africa	76	C6
South America	106	F5
Southampton, *Canada*	96	D2
Southampton, *United Kingdom*	22	A4
Southampton Island	90	Q4
South Andaman	56	F6
South Australia	82	F5
South Baymouth	96	D1
South Bend	96	C2
South Boston	96	E3
South Carolina	98	E3
South Charleston	98	E2
South China Sea	52	E4
South Dakota	94	F2
South Downs	22	B4
South East Cape	82	J8
South East Point	82	J7
Southend-on-Sea	22	C3
Southern Alps	84	B6
Southern Cross	82	C6
Southern Indian Lake	90	M5
Southern Uplands	24	H6
South Georgia	110	P9
South Harris	24	F4
South Haven	96	C2
South Hill	96	E3
South Island	84	B6
South Korea	50	D5
South Lake Tahoe	94	B3
South Orkney Islands	112	(2)A3
South Platte	94	F2
Southport	24	J8
South Ronaldsay	24	K3
South Sandwich Islands	112	(2)C4
South Sandwich Trench	106	H9
South Saskatchewan	92	D1
South Shetland Islands	112	(2)MM4
South Shields	24	L7
South Taranaki Bight	84	D4
South Uist	24	E4
South West Cape, *Auckland Islands*	84	(2)A1
South West Cape, *Australia*	82	H8
Southwest Cape	84	A8
South West Pacific Basin	80	L9
Southwold	22	D2
Sovata	34	N3
Soverato	32	L10
Sovetsk, *Russia*	16	L9
Sovetsk, *Russia*	38	J3
Soweto	76	D5
Sōya-misaki	50	L1
Sozopol	34	Q7
Spa	22	H4
Spain	28	F5
Spalding	22	B2
Sparks	100	C1
Spartanburg	98	E3
Sparti	36	E7
Sparwood	94	D1
Spassk-Dal'niy	50	G1
Spearfish	94	F2
Spencer	96	A2
Spencer Gulf	82	G6
Spetses	36	F7
Spey	24	J4
Speyer	22	L5
Spiekeroog	20	C3
Spiez	30	C4
Spilimbergo	30	H4
Spišska Nová Ves	18	K9
Spitsbergen	112	(1)P2
Spittal	30	J4
Split	34	D6
Spokane	94	C1
Spoleto	32	G6
Spooner	96	B1
Sprague	94	C1
Spratly Islands	52	E4
Spray	94	C2
Spree	20	K4
Spremberg	20	K5
Sprimont	22	H4
Spring	98	B3
Springbok	76	B5
Springe	20	E4
Springer	100	F1
Springerville	100	E2
Springfield, *Colo., United States*	100	F1
Springfield, *Ill., United States*	96	C3
Springfield, *Mass., United States*	96	F2
Springfield, *Mo., United States*	96	B3
Springfield, *Oh., United States*	96	D3
Springfield, *Oreg., United States*	94	B2
Springfield, *Vt., United States*	96	F2
Spring Hill	98	E4
Springs	76	D5
Springs Junction	84	D6
Springsure	82	J4
Springville, *Al., United States*	98	D3
Springville, *N.Y., United States*	96	E2
Spulico	32	L9
Squamish	94	B1
Squinzano	32	N8
Srbija	34	H6
Srbobran	34	G4
Srebrenica	34	G5
Sredenekolymsk	46	S3
Sredinnyy Khrebet	46	T6
Srednesibirskoye Ploskogor'ye	46	G3
Srednogorie	36	G2
Śrem	18	G5
Sretensk	46	K6
Sri Jayawardenapura-Kotte	56	D7
Srikakulam	56	D5
Sri Lanka	56	D7
Srinagar	56	B2
Stack Skerry	24	H2
Stade	16	E10
Stadlandet	16	C5
Stadskanaal	22	J2
Stadtallendorf	20	E6
Stadthagen	20	E4
Staffa	24	F5
Staffelstien	20	F6
Stafford	24	K9
Staines	22	B3
Stainz	30	L4
Stakhanov	38	G5
Stalowa Wola	18	M7
Stamford, *United Kingdom*	22	B2
Stamford, *United States*	96	F2
Standish	96	D2
Stanford	96	D3
Stanke Dimitrov	36	F2
Stanley, *Australia*	82	J8
Stanley, *Falkland Islands*	110	K9
Stanley, *United States*	94	F1
Stanovaya	46	T3
Stanovoye Nagor'ye	46	J5
Stanovoy Khrebet	46	L5
Staphorst	22	J2
Stapleton	94	F2
Starachowice	18	L6
Stara L'ubovňa	18	K8
Stara Pazova	34	H5
Stara Planina	36	F1
Staraya Russa	38	F3
Stara Zagora	34	N7
Starbuck Island	80	L6
Stargard Szczeciński	16	H10
Starkville	98	D3
Starnberg	30	G2
Starnberger See	30	G3
Starogard Gdański	18	H4
Staro Orjahovo	34	Q7
Start Point	26	B3
Staryy Oskol	38	G4
Staszów	18	L7
Statesboro	98	E3
Statesville	98	E2
Staunton	98	F2
Stavanger	16	C7
Stavoron	22	H2
Stavropol'	60	J1
Stavropol'skaya Vovyshennost'	38	H5
Steamboat Springs	94	E2
Steens Mountains	94	C2
Steenwijk	22	J2
Stefansson Island	90	L2
Stege	20	H1
Štei	34	K3
Stein	20	G7
Steinach am Brenner	30	G3
Steinfurt	22	K2
Steinhausen	76	B4
Steinjker	16	F4
Stenay	22	H5
Stendal	20	G4
Steno Antikythiro	36	F9
Stephenville	98	B3
Sterling	94	F2
Sterling City	100	F2
Sterling Heights	96	D2
Sterlitamak	38	L4
Sternberk	18	G8
Stettiner Haff	16	G10
Stevenage	22	B3
Stevens Point	96	C2
Stevens Village	100	(1)H2
Stewart	90	F5
Stewart	100	(1)K3
Stewart Island	84	A8
Steyr	30	K2
Stillwater	98	B2
Stinnett	100	F1
Štip	36	E3
Stirling	24	J5
Stjørdal	16	F5
Stockach	30	E3
Stockerau	30	M2
Stockholm	16	K7
Stockport	24	K8
Stockton, *Calif., United States*	100	B1
Stockton, *Kans., United States*	100	G1
Stockton-on-Tees	24	L7
Stœng Trêng	52	D4
Stoke-on-Trent	24	K8
Stokksnes	16	(1)F2
Stolac	34	F6
Stolberg	22	J4
Stolin	38	E4
Stollberg	20	H6
Stomio	36	E5
Stonehaven	24	K5
Stony Rapids	90	K5
Stör	20	E3
Stora Lulevatten	16	K3
Storavan	16	J4
Stord	16	C7
Store Bælt	20	F1
Støren	16	F5
Store Sotra	16	B6
Storjord	16	H3
Storlien	16	G5
Storm Bay	82	J8
Storm Lake	96	A2
Stornoway	24	F3
Storozhevsk	38	K2
Storozhynets'	34	N1
Storsjøen	16	F6
Storsjön, *Sweden*	16	G5
Storsjön, *Sweden*	16	J6
Storuman	16	J4
Storuman	16	J4
Stour	22	C2
Stowmarket	22	D2
Strabane	24	E7
Stradella	30	E5
Strait of Belle Isle	90	V6
Strait of Bonifacio	32	D7
Strait of Dover	22	D4
Strait of Georgia	94	B1
Strait of Gibraltar	28	E9
Strait of Hormuz	63	G3
Strait of Juan de Fuca	94	B1
Strait of Malacca	54	C2
Straits of Florida	98	E5
Strakonice	20	J7
Stralsund	16	G9
Strand	76	B6
Stranda	16	D5
Strandavatn	16	D6
Stranraer	24	H7
Strasbourg	30	C2
Strasburg	100	F1
Străşeni	34	R2
Stratford, *Canada*	96	D2
Stratford, *New Zealand*	84	E4
Stratford, *United States*	94	F3
Stratford-upon-Avon	22	A2
Strathroy	96	D2
Stratoni	36	F4
Stratton	96	F1
Straubing	30	H2
Straumnes	16	(1)B1
Strausberg	20	J4
Streaky Bay	82	F6
Streator	96	C2
Strehaia	34	L5
Strelka, *Russia*	46	E5
Strelka, *Russia*	46	S4
Strezhevoy	38	Q2
Strimonas	36	F4
Strjama	34	M7
Strofades	36	C7
Stromboli	32	K10
Strömsund	16	H5
Stronsay	24	K2
Stroud	24	K10
Struga	36	C3
Strugi-Krasnyye	16	Q7
Strumica	36	E3
Stryy	18	N8
Stryy	18	N8
Strzegom	18	F7
Strzelce Opolskie	18	H7
Strzelin	18	G7
Strzelno	18	H5
Studholme Junction	84	C7
Sturgeon Bay	96	C2
Sturgeon Falls	96	E1
Sturgis, *Ky., United States*	96	C3
Sturgis, *S.D., United States*	94	F2
Sturkö	18	E1
Štúrova	18	H10
Sturt Stony Desert	82	G5
Stuttgart, *Germany*	30	E2
Stuttgart, *United States*	98	C3
Stykkishólmur	16	(1)B2
Suai	55	C4
Suakin	68	G4
Subcule	68	H5
Subi Besar	54	D2
Sublette	100	F1
Subotica	34	G3
Suceava	34	P2
Suck	24	D8
Suckow	20	G3
Sucre	108	D7
Sudak	60	F1
Sudan	68	E5
Sudan	72	D2
Suday	38	H3
Sudbury, *Canada*	96	D1
Sudbury, *United Kingdom*	22	C2
Sudd	74	E2
Sudová Vyshnya	18	N8
Suez = El Suweis	68	F2
Suez Canal	68	F1
Suffolk	98	F2
Sugun	58	L2
Suḩār	63	G4
Suhl	20	F6
Suide	48	E3
Suifenhe	50	F1
Suigam	56	B4
Suihua	46	M7
Suippes	22	G5
Suir	24	E9
Suixi	48	E6
Suizhong	48	G2
Suizhou	48	E4
Sukabumi	54	D4
Sukadana	54	D3
Sukhinichi	38	G4
Sukhona	38	H3
Sukkertoppen = Maniitsoq	90	W3

Place	Page	Ref.
Sukkur	58	J4
Sula	38	K1
Sula	38	K1
Sula Sgeir	24	F2
Sulawesi	55	A3
Sulejówek	18	L5
Sule Skerry	24	H2
Sulgachi	46	N4
Sulina	34	S4
Sulingen	22	L2
Sullana	108	A4
Sullivan	98	C2
Sulmona	32	H6
Sulphur Springs	98	B3
Sultan	68	D1
Sultanhanı	36	R6
Sultanpur	56	D3
Sulu Archipelago	52	G5
Sulu Sea	52	F5
Sulzbach	22	K5
Sulzbach-Rosenberg	20	G7
Sulzberger Bay	112	(2)CC2
Sumatera	54	C2
Sumatra = Sumatera	54	C2
Sumba	55	A5
Sumbawa	55	A4
Sumbawabesar	55	A4
Sumbawanga	74	E5
Sumbe	76	A2
Sumeih	74	D2
Šumen	34	P6
Sumenep	54	E4
Sumisu-jima	50	L8
Sumkino	38	N3
Summer Lake	94	B2
Summerville	98	E3
Summit	90	B4
Šumperk	18	G8
Sumqayıt	60	N3
Sumter	98	E3
Sumy	38	F4
Sunbury	96	E2
Sunch'ŏn	50	D6
Sun City	76	D5
Sundance	94	F2
Sundarbans	56	E4
Sunday Strait	82	D3
Sunderland	24	L7
Sundridge	96	E1
Sundsvall	16	J5
Sundsvallsbukten	16	J5
Sungaipenuh	54	C3
Sungei Petani	52	C5
Sungurlu	60	F3
Sunnyvale	94	B3
Sun Prairie	96	C2
Suntar	46	K4
Suntsar	58	H4
Sunwu	46	M7
Sunyani	72	D3
Suomussalmi	38	E2
Suŏ-nada	50	F7
Suonenjoki	16	P5
Suordakh	46	P3
Suoyarvi	38	F2
Superior	92	H2
Supetar	34	D6
Süphan Dağı	60	K4
Süqash Shuyükh	63	B1
Suqian	48	F4
Suquţrā	58	F7
Sûr	58	G5
Sura	38	J4
Surab	58	J4
Surabaya	54	E4
Sürak	63	H4
Surakarta	54	E4
Šurany	34	F1
Surat	56	B4
Surat Thani	52	B5
Surdulica	34	K7
Sûre	22	H5
Surfers Paradise	82	K5
Surgut	44	N5
Surgutikha	44	R5
Surigao	52	H5
Surin	52	C4
Suriname	108	F3
Surkhet	56	D3
Sürmaq	63	E1
Surovikino	38	H5
Surskoye	38	J4
Surt	70	J2
Surtsey	16	(1)C3
Susa	30	C5
Şuşa	60	M4
Sušac	34	D7
Susak	30	K6
Susanville	94	B2
Suşehri	60	H3
Sušice	20	J7
Susitna	100	(1)G3
Susuman	46	R4
Susurluk	36	L5
Sutak	56	C2
Sutherland	76	C6
Sutlej	56	B3
Suusamyr	44	N9
Suva	80	H7
Suvorov Island	80	K7
Suwałki	18	M3
Suwannaphum	52	C3
Suweilih	62	C4
Suweima	62	C5
Suwŏn	50	D5
Suzak	38	N6
Suzhou, China	48	G4
Suzhou, China	48	F4
Suzuka	50	J6
Suzu-misaki	50	J5
Svalbard	112	(1)Q2
Svalyava	34	L1
Svappavaara	16	L3
Svatove	38	G5
Sveg	16	H5
Svendborg	16	F9
Šventoji	16	N9
Sverdrup Islands	112	(1)DD2
Svetac	34	C6
Sveti Nikole	36	D3
Svetlaya	46	P7
Svetlogorsk	18	K3
Svetlograd	60	K1
Svetlyy, Russia	18	K3
Svetlyy, Russia	44	L7
Svištov	34	N6
Svidník	18	L8
Svilengrad	36	J3
Svitava	18	F8
Svitovy	18	F8
Svobodnyy	46	M6
Svratka	18	F8
Svyetlahorsk	38	E4
Swain Reefs	82	K4
Swains Island	80	J7
Swakopmund	76	A4
Swale	24	K7
Swan	106	C2
Swan Hill	82	H7
Swan Islands	102	H5
Swan River	90	L6
Swansea, Australia	82	J8
Swansea, United Kingdom	24	J10
Swaziland	76	E5
Sweden	16	H6
Sweetwater	100	F2
Swider	18	L5
Świdnica	18	F7
Świdnik	18	M6
Świdwin	18	E4
Świebodzin	18	E5
Świecie	18	H4
Swift Current	92	E1
Swindon	22	A3
Świnoujście	16	H10
Switzerland	30	C4
Syalakh	46	L3
Syamzha	38	H2
Syców	18	G6
Sydney, Australia	82	K6
Sydney, Canada	90	U7
Syke	22	L2
Syktyvkar	38	K2
Sylacauga	98	D3
Sylhet	56	F4
Sylt	16	E9
Sylvania	96	D2
Sym	44	R5
Sym	44	R5
Symi	36	K8
Synya	38	L1
Syracuse, Kans., United States	100	F1
Syracuse, N.Y., United States	96	E2
Syrdar'ya	58	J1
Syrdar'ya	44	L8
Syria	58	C3
Syrian Desert = Bādiyat ash Shām	62	D4
Syrna	36	J8
Syros	36	G7
Sytomino	38	P2
Syzran'	38	J4
Szamos	34	K1
Szamotuły	18	F5
Szarvas	34	K11
Szczecin	18	D4
Szczecinek	18	F4
Szczytno	18	K4
Szeged	34	H3
Szeghalom	34	J2
Székesfehérvár	34	F2
Szekszárd	34	F3
Szentendre	34	G2
Szentes	34	H3
Szerencs	18	L9
Szigetvár	34	E3
Szolnok	34	H2
Szombathely	34	D2
Szprotawa	18	E6
Sztum	18	J4
Szydlowiec	18	K6

T

Place	Page	Ref.
Tab	34	F3
Tabarka	32	C12
Tabas	58	G3
Tabāsīn	63	G1
Taber	94	D1
Table Cape	84	G4
Tabong	56	G3
Tábor	18	D8
Tabor	46	R2
Tabora	74	E5
Tabou	72	C4
Tabrīz	60	M4
Tabuaeran	80	K5
Tabūk	58	C4
Tacheng	44	Q8
Tachov	20	H7
Tacloban	52	H4
Tacna	108	C7
Tacoma	92	B2
Tacuarembó	110	K5
Tacurong	55	B1
Tadjoura	68	H5
Tadmur	60	H6
Tadoussac	96	G1
Taech'ŏn	50	D5
Taegu	48	H3
Taejŏn	48	H3
Tafahi	80	J7
Tafalla	28	J2
Tafila	62	C6
Tafi Viejo	110	H4
Tagab	68	F4
Taganrog	38	G5
Taganrogskiy Zaliv	38	G5
Tagbilaran	52	G5
Tagul	46	F6
Tagum	52	H5
Tagus	28	B5
Taharoa	84	E4
Taheke	84	D2
Tahiti	80	M7
Tahoe Lake	90	K2
Tahoka	100	F2
Tahoua	72	F2
Tahrūd	63	G2
Tahuna	52	H6
Tai'an	48	F3
Taihape	84	E4
Taihe	48	E5
Taikeng	48	E5
Tailem Bend	82	G7
Tain	24	H4
T'ainan	48	G6
T'aipei	48	G6
Taiping	54	C1
Taipingchuan	50	B1
T'aitung	52	G2
Taivalkoski	16	Q4
Taiwan	52	G2
Taiwan Strait	52	F2
Taiyuan	48	E3
Taizhou	48	F4
Ta'izz	58	D7
Tajikistan	58	J2
Tajima	50	K5
Tajo	14	D3
Tak	52	B3
Takaka	84	D5
Takamatsu	50	H6
Takaoka	50	J5
Takapuna	84	E3
Takasaki	50	K5
Takayama	50	J5
Takefui	50	J6
Takengon	54	B2
Takestān	58	E2
Takum	72	G3
Talak	70	F5
Talara	108	A4
Talas	44	N9
Tal'at Mūsá	60	G6
Talavera de la Reina	28	F5
Talaya	46	S4
Talbotton	98	E3
Talca	110	G6
Talcahuano	110	G6
Taldykorgan	44	P9
Tālesh	58	E2
Taliabu	55	B3
Talibon	52	G4
Talitsa	38	M3
Tall 'Afar	60	K5
Tallahassee	98	E3
Tallaimannar	56	C7
Tall al Laḥm	63	B1
Tallinn	16	N7
Tall Kalakh	62	D2
Tallulah	92	H5
Tall 'Uwaynāt	60	K5
Tālmaciu	34	M4
Tal'menka	44	Q7
Talon	46	R5
Tāloqān	44	N10
Taloyoak	90	N3
Talsi	16	M8
Taltal	110	G4
Tama	96	B2
Tamale	72	D3
Tamanrasset	70	G4
Tamanthi	56	G3
Tamási	34	F3
Tamazunchale	92	G7
Tambacounda	72	B2
Tambey	44	N3
Tambo	82	J4
Tambov	38	H4
Tambu	55	A3
Tambura	74	D2
Tampa	98	E4
Tamp-e Gīrān	63	H3
Tampere	16	M6
Tampico	102	E4
Tamsagbulag	48	F1
Tamsweg	30	J3
Tamworth, Australia	82	K6
Tamworth, United Kingdom	22	A2
Tana, Kenya	74	G4
Tana, Norway	16	P2
Tanabe	50	H7
Tana bru	16	P1
Tanacross	100	(1)J3
Tanafjorden	16	Q1
Tanaga Island	100	(3)C1
T'ana Hāyk'	68	G5
Tanahgrogot	54	F3
Tanahjampea	55	A4
Tanahmerah	55	F4
Tanami	82	E4
Tanami Desert	82	F3
Tanaro	30	C6
Tanch'ŏn	50	E3
Tanda	72	D3
Tandag	52	H5
Tăndărei	34	Q5
Tandil	110	K6
Tanega-shima	50	F8
Tanew	18	M7
Tanezrouft	70	E4
Tanga, Russia	46	J6
Tanga, Tanzania	74	F5
Tanger	70	D1
Tangermünde	20	G4
Tanggu	48	F3
Tangmai	56	G2
Tangra Yumco	56	F2
Tangshan	48	F3
Tanimbar	80	D6
Tanjona Ankaboa	76	A4
Tanjona Bobaomby	76	H2
Tanjona Masoala	76	J3
Tanjona Vilanandro	76	H4
Tanjona Vohimena	76	H5
Tanjung	54	E4
Tanjungbalai	54	B2
Tanjung Cangkuang	54	C4
Tanjung Datu	54	E3
Tanjung d'Urville	55	E3
Tanjungkarang Telukbetung	54	D4
Tanjung Libobo	55	C3
Tanjung Lumut	54	D3
Tanjung Mengkalihat	54	E3
Tanjungpandan	54	D3
Tanjung Puting	54	E3
Tanjungredeb	54	E2
Tanjung Selatan	54	E3
Tanjungselor	54	F2
Tanjung Vals	55	E4
Tankovo	44	R5
Tankse	56	C2
Tanlovo	38	P1
Tanney	22	G5
Tanout	72	G2
Tanta	68	F1
Tan-Tan	70	C3
Tanzania	74	E4
Tao'an	48	G1
Taongi	80	J4
Taormina	32	K11
Taos	100	E1
Taoudenni	70	E2
Taourirt	70	E2
T'aoyüan	52	G2
Tapa	16	N7
Tapachula	102	F6
Tapajós	108	E5
Tapauá	108	E5
Tapolca	34	E3
Tappahannock	98	F2
Tapsuy	38	M2
Tapuaenuku	84	D6
Taquari	108	F7
Tara	44	N6
Tara	38	J2
Tarābulus	70	H2
Taraclia	34	R4
Taracua	108	E3
Tarāghin	70	H3
Tarakan	52	F6
Taran	44	N3
Taranaki = Mount Egmont	84	E4
Tarancón	28	H4
Taranto	32	M8
Tarapoto	108	B5
Tarare	26	K8
Tarascon	26	K10
Tarauacá	108	C5
Tarauacá	108	C5
Tarawa	80	H5
Tarawera Lake	84	F4
Tarazona	28	J3
Tarbert, United Kingdom	24	G6
Tarbes	26	F10
Tarbet, United Kingdom	24	F4
Tarcoola	82	F6
Taree	82	K6
Tareya	44	S3
Tarfaya	70	C3
Târgoviște	34	N5
Târgovište	34	P6
Târgu Frumos	34	Q2
Târgu Jiu	34	L4
Târgu Lăpuș	34	M3
Târgu Mureș	34	M3
Târgu-Neamț	34	P2
Târgu Ocna	34	P3
Târgu Secuiesc	34	P3
Tarhunah	70	H2
Tarif	63	E4
Tarifa	28	E8
Tarija	110	J3
Tarīm	58	E6
Tarim	44	Q9
Tarim Pendi	44	Q10
Tarīn Kowt	58	J3
Tariskay Shan	44	Q9
Taritatu	55	E3
Tarkio	98	B1
Tarko Sale	44	P5
Tarlac	52	G3
Tarn	26	H10
Tarn	18	K10
Tarna	18	H4
Tärnaby	16	H4
Tărnăveni	34	M3
Tarnogskiy Gorodok	38	H2
Tărnovo	36	K2
Tarnów	18	K7
Tarnowskie Góry	18	H7
Taro	30	E6

Name	Page	Grid
Ţārom	63	F2
Taroom	82	J5
Taroudannt	70	D2
Tarquinia	32	F6
Tarragona	28	M3
Tarras	84	B7
Tàrrega	28	M3
Tarso Emissi	68	C3
Tarsus	60	F5
Tartagal	110	J3
Tartu	16	P7
Ţarţūs	62	C2
Tarutyne	34	S3
Tarvisio	30	J4
Tasbuget	44	M9
Tashigang	56	F3
Tashir	60	L3
Tashkent	44	M9
Tash-Kumyr	44	N9
Tashtagol	44	R7
Tasikmalaya	54	D4
Taskesken	44	Q8
Taşköprü	60	F3
Tasman Bay	84	D5
Tasmania	82	H8
Tasmania	80	E10
Tasman Mountains	84	D5
Tasman Sea	84	B3
Tăşnad	34	K2
Taşova	60	G3
Tassili du Hoggar	70	F4
Tassili-n'-Ajjer	70	G3
Tasty	44	M9
Tasüj	60	L4
Tata, Hungary	34	F2
Tata, Morocco	70	D3
Tataba	55	B3
Tatabánya	34	F2
Tataouine	70	H2
Tatarbunary	34	S4
Tatariya	38	J3
Tatarsk	44	P6
Tatarskiy Proliv	46	P7
Tateyama	50	K6
Tathlina Lake	90	H4
Tatta	58	J5
Tatvan	60	K4
Tauá	108	J5
Tauberbischofsheim	20	E7
Tauern	30	J4
Taumarunui	84	E4
Taungdwingyi	52	B2
Taung-gyi	56	G4
Taungup	56	F5
Taunsa	56	B2
Taunton, United Kingdom	24	J10
Taunton, United States	96	F2
Taunus	22	L4
Taunusstein	22	L4
Taupo	84	F4
Tauragė	18	M2
Tauranga	84	F3
Tauroa Point	84	D2
Tavda	38	N3
Tavda	38	N3
Tavira	28	C7
Tavoy	52	B4
Tavşanli	60	C4
Taw	24	J11
Tawas City	96	D2
Tawau	54	F2
Tawitawi	54	F1
Taxkorgan	44	P10
Tay	24	J5
Tayga	44	R6
Taylorville	98	D2
Taym	58	C4
Taymä'	68	G2
Taymura	46	F4
Taymylyr	46	L2
Tay Ninh	52	D4
Tayshet	46	F5
Tayuan	46	L6
Tayyebād	58	H3
Taza	70	E2
Tazeh Kand	60	M4
Tazenakht	70	D2
Tāzirbū	68	D2
Tazovskaya Guba	44	N4
Tazovskiy	44	P4
Tazovskiy Poluostrov	44	N4
Tazungdam	52	B1
T'bilisi	60	L3
Tchamba	72	G3
Tchibanga	72	G5
Tchin Tabaradene	70	G5
Tczew	18	H3
Te Anau	84	A7
Te Araroa	84	G3
Te Aroha	84	E3
Te Awamutu	84	E4
Teberda	60	J2
Tébessa	70	G1
Tebingtinggi	54	B2
Téboursouk	32	D12
Techa	38	M3
Techiman	72	D3
Tecuala	100	D4
Tecuci	34	Q4
Tedzhen	58	H2
Tees	24	L7
Tegal	54	D4
Tegernsee	30	G3
Tegina	72	F2
Teglio	30	F4
Tegucigalpa	102	G6
Tegul'det	44	R6
Te Hapua	84	D2
Te Haroto	84	F4
Tehek Lake	90	M3
Teheran = Tehrän	58	F2
Tehrän	58	F2
Teignmouth	24	J11
Tejo = Tagus	28	B5
Te Kaha	84	F3
Te Kao	84	D2
Tekirdağ	36	K4
Teknaf	56	F4
Teku	55	B3
Te Kuiti	84	E4
T'elavi	60	L3
Tel Aviv-Yafo	62	B4
Telegraph Creek	100	(1)L4
Telén	110	H6
Teles Pires	108	F5
Telford	24	K9
Telfs	30	G3
Teller	100	(1)D2
Telsen	110	H7
Telšiai	18	M2
Teltow	20	J4
Teluk Berau	55	D3
Teluk Bone	55	B3
Teluk Cenderawasih	55	E3
Telukdalem	54	B2
Teluk Kumai	54	E3
Telukpakedai	54	D3
Teluk Sampit	54	E3
Teluk Sukadana	54	D3
Teluk Tomini	55	B2
Tema	72	D3
Tembenchi	44	T4
Temerin	34	G4
Temerloh	52	C6
Teminabuan	55	D3
Temirtau	44	N7
Temochic	100	E3
Tempe	100	D2
Tempio Pausania	32	D8
Temple	100	G2
Temryuk	60	G1
Temuco	110	G6
Temuka	84	C7
Tenali	56	D5
Tendaho	68	H5
Ten Degree Channel	56	F7
Tendo	50	L4
Tendrara	70	E2
Ténéré	70	G5
Ténéré du Tafassasset	70	G4
Tenerife	70	B3
Ténès	70	F1
Tenggarong	54	F3
Tenke	76	D2
Tenkodogo	72	D2
Tennant Creek	82	F3
Tennessee	92	J4
Tennessee	88	K6
Tenojoki	16	P2
Tenteno	55	B3
Tenterfield	82	K5
Teo	28	B2
Teófilo Otoni	108	J7
Tepa	55	C4
Tepehuanes	92	E6
Tepic	92	F7
Teplice	18	C7
Ter	28	N2
Terceira	70	(1)B2
Terek	60	L2
Teresina	108	J5
Tergnier	22	F5
Terme	60	G3
Termez	58	J2
Termini Imerese	32	H11
Termoli	34	C8
Ternate	55	C2
Terneuzen	22	F3
Terni	32	G6
Ternitz	30	M3
Ternopil'	38	E5
Terracina	32	H7
Terrassa	28	N3
Terre Haute	98	D2
Terry	94	E1
Tersa	38	H4
Terschelling	22	H1
Teruel	28	J4
Tervel	60	B2
Tervola	16	N3
Teseney	68	G4
Teshekpuk Lake	100	(1)F1
Teshikaga	50	N2
Teshio	50	L1
Teslin	100	(1)L3
Teslin	100	(1)L3
Tessalit	70	F4
Têt	26	H11
Tete	76	E3
Teterow	20	H3
Teteven	36	G2
Tétouan	70	D1
Tetovo	34	H8
Teuco	110	J3
Teulada	32	C10
Tevere	32	G6
Teverya	62	C4
Tevriz	38	P3
Te Waewae Bay	84	A8
Texarkana	98	C3
Texas	92	F5
Texel	22	G1
Teya	44	S5
Teykovo	38	H3
Tfarity	70	C3
Thaba Putsoa	76	D5
Thabazimbi	76	D4
Thailand	52	B3
Thai Nguyên	52	D2
Thal	56	B2
Thale Luang	52	C5
Thamarīt	58	F6
Thames	24	L10
Thamūd	58	E6
Thane	56	B5
Thanh Hoa	52	D3
Thanjavur	56	C6
Thann	30	C3
Tharad	56	B4
Thar Desert	56	B3
Thargomindah	82	H5
Tharwāniyyah	63	E5
Thasos	36	G4
Thasos	36	G4
Thaton	52	B3
Thaya	18	E9
The Bahamas	98	F4
The Bluff	98	F4
The Dalles	94	B1
Thedford	94	F2
The Fens	22	B2
The Gambia	72	A2
The Hague = 's-Gravenhage	22	G2
Thelon	90	L4
The Minch	24	F3
The Naze	22	D3
Thenia	28	P8
Theniet el Had	28	N9
Theodore Roosevelt	108	E5
Theodore Roosevelt Lake	100	D2
The Pas	90	L6
Thermaikos Kolpos	36	E4
Thermopolis	94	E2
The Sisters	84	(1)B1
The Solent	22	A4
Thessalon	96	D1
Thessaloniki	36	E4
Thetford	24	N9
Thetford Mines	96	F1
The Twins	84	D5
The Wash	24	N9
The Weald	22	B3
The Whitsundays	82	J4
Thief River Falls	96	A1
Thiers	26	J8
Thiès	72	A2
Thika	74	F4
Thimphu	56	E3
Phingvallavatn	16	(1)C2
Thionville	22	J5
Thira	36	H8
Thira	36	H8
Thirasia	36	H8
Thirsk	24	L7
Thiruvananthapuram	56	C7
Thisted	16	E8
Phistilfjördhur	16	(1)F1
Thiva	36	F6
Thiviers	26	F8
Þhjórsá	16	(1)D2
Tholen	22	G3
Thomasville	98	E3
Thompson	90	M5
Thompson	90	H6
Thompson Falls	94	C1
Thomson	98	E3
Thonon-les-Bains	30	B4
Þhórisvatn	16	(1)D2
Þhorlákshöfn	16	(1)C3
Þhorshöfn	16	(1)F1
Thouars	26	E7
Thrakiko Pelagos	36	H4
Three Forks	94	D1
Three Kings Island	84	C2
Three Rivers	96	C2
Throckmorton	98	B3
Thuin	22	G4
Thun	30	C4
Thunder Bay	96	C1
Thuner See	30	C4
Thung Song	52	B5
Thüringer Wald	20	F6
Thurso	24	J3
Thusis	30	E4
Tiāb	63	G3
Tianjin	48	F3
Tianmen	48	E4
Tianqiaoling	50	E2
Tianshifu	50	C3
Tianshui	48	D4
Tianshuihai	58	L2
Tianyang	48	D6
Tiaret	70	F1
Tiassalé	72	G3
Tibati	72	G3
Tibboburra	82	H5
Tibesti	68	C3
Tibet = Xizang	56	E2
Tiburón	102	B3
Tichīt	70	D5
Tichla	70	C4
Ticino	30	D4
Ticul	102	G4
Tidjikdja	70	C5
Tieling	50	B2
Tielongtan	56	C1
Tielt	22	F3
Tienen	22	G4
Tien Shan	44	Q9
Tien Yen	52	D2
Tierra Amarilla	94	E3
Tiétar	28	E4
Tiflis = T'bilisi	66	H1
Tifton	98	E3
Tifu	55	C3
Tighina	34	S3
Tignère	72	G3
Tigre	108	B4
Tigris	60	K6
Tijuana	92	C5
Tikanlik	44	R9
Tikhoretsk	38	H5
Tikhvin	38	F3
Tikrīt	60	K6
Tiksi	46	M2
Tilburg	22	H3
Tilichiki	46	V4
Tillabéri	72	E2
Tillamook	94	B1
Tilos	36	K8
Timanskiy Kryazh	38	K2
Timaru	84	C7
Timashevsk	38	G5
Timber Creek	82	F3
Timerloh	54	C2
Timimoun	70	F3
Timişoara	34	J4
Timmins	96	D1
Timon	108	J5
Timor	55	C4
Timor Sea	82	E2
Timor Timur	55	C4
Tinaca Point	80	C5
Tin Alkoum	70	H4
Tinchebray	22	B6
Tindivanam	56	C6
Tindouf	70	D3
Tineo	28	D1
Tinfouchy	70	D3
Tinglev	20	E2
Tingo Maria	108	B5
Tingri	56	E3
Tingsryd	18	E1
Tiniroto	84	F4
Tinnsjø	16	E7
Tinogasta	110	H4
Tinos	36	H7
Tinos	36	H7
Tinsukia	56	G3
Tintâne	70	C5
T'i'o	68	H5
Tipperary	24	D9
Tirana = Tiranë	36	B3
Tiranë	36	B3
Tirari Desert	82	G5
Tiraspol	34	S3
Tire	36	K6
Tiree	24	F5
Tiroungoulou	74	C2
Tirschenreuth	20	H7
Tit	32	C9
Tiruchchirāppalli	56	C6
Tirunelveli	56	C7
Tirupati	56	C6
Tiruppur	56	C6
Tiruvannamalai	56	C6
Tisa	34	H4
Ţisīyah	62	D4
Tišnov	18	F8
Tisza	18	M9
Tiszaföldvár	34	H3
Tiszafüred	34	H2
Tiszaújváros	18	L10
Tit-Ary	44	Z3
Titel	34	H4
Titlagarh	56	D4
Titova Korenica	30	L6
Titovo Velenje	32	K2
Titu	34	N5
Titusville	98	E4
Tivaouane	70	B6
Tiverton	24	J11
Tivoli	32	G7
Tiyäs	62	E2
Tizi Ouzou	70	F1
Tiznit	70	D3
Tjeldøya	16	H2
Tjørkolm	16	D7
Tlemcen	70	E2
Tmassah	68	C2
Toad River	90	F5
Toamasina	76	H3
Tobago	102	M6
Tobelo	55	C2
Tobermorey	82	G4
Tobermory, United Kingdom	24	F5
Tobermory, United States	96	D1
Tobi	55	D2
Toboali	54	D3
Tobol	38	M4
Tobol	28	M4
Tobol'sk	38	N3
Tobseda	38	K1
Tocantins	108	H5
Tocantins	108	H5
Toce	30	D4
Tocopilla	110	G3
Todeli	55	B3
Todi	32	G6
Tofino	94	A1
Togo	72	E3
Toimin	32	H2
Toi-misaki	50	F8
Tōjō	50	G6
Tok	100	(1)J3
Tokar	68	G4
Tokat, Sudan	58	C6
Tokat, Turkey	58	C1
Tokelau	80	J6
Tokmak	44	P9
Tokoroa	84	E4
Tokounou	72	C3
Toksun	44	R9
Tok-tō	48	J3
Toktogul	44	N9
Tokushima	50	H6
Tokuyama	50	F6
Tōkyō	50	K6
Tolaga Bay	84	G4
Tôlañaro	76	H4
Tolbo	44	S8
Toledo, Brazil	110	L3
Toledo, Spain	28	F5
Toledo, United States	96	D2
Toliara	76	G4

Name	Page	Ref
Tolitoli	55	B2
Tol'ka	44	Q5
Tol'ka	44	Q5
Tollense	20	J3
Tolmezzo	30	J4
Tolmin	30	J4
Tolna	34	H5
Tolosa	28	H1
Tol'yatti	38	J4
Tolybay	44	L7
Tom'	44	R6
Tomah	96	B2
Tomakomai	50	L2
Tomamae	50	L1
Tomar, *Brazil*	108	E4
Tomar, *Portugal*	28	B5
Tomari	46	Q7
Tomaszów Lubelski	18	N7
Tomaszów Mazowiecki	18	K6
Tombouctou	70	E5
Tombua	76	A3
Tomé	110	G6
Tomelloso	28	H5
Tomini	55	B2
Tommot	46	M5
Tomo	108	D2
Tompo	46	P4
Tom Price	82	C4
Tomra	56	E2
Tomsk	44	Q6
Tomtor	46	Q4
Tomu	55	D3
Tonalá	102	F5
Tondano	55	B2
Tønder	20	D2
Tonga	80	J7
Tonga	74	E2
Tonga Islands	80	J8
Tongareva	80	K6
Tonga Trench	80	J8
Tongbai	48	E4
Tongchuan	48	D4
Tongduch'ŏn	50	D5
Tongeren	22	H4
Tonghae	50	E5
Tonghua	50	C3
Tongliao	48	G2
Tongling	48	F4
Tongshi	52	D3
Tongue	94	E1
Tongyu	48	G2
Tónichi	92	E6
Tonj	74	D2
Tonk	56	C3
Tonkābon	58	F2
Tônlé Sab	52	C4
Tonnay-Charente	26	E8
Tönning	20	D2
Tonopah	94	D2
Tooele	94	D2
Toora-Khem	44	T7
Toowoomba	82	K5
Topeka	92	G4
Topki	44	R6
Topliţa	34	N3
Topock	100	D2
Topol'čany	18	H9
Topolobampo	92	E6
Torbali	36	K6
Torbat-e Heydarīyeh	58	G2
Torbat-e Jām	58	H2
Tordesillas	28	F3
Töre	16	M4
Torelló	28	N2
Torgau	20	H5
Torgelow	18	C4
Torhout	22	F3
Torino	30	C5
Tori-shima	50	L8
Torneälven	16	L3
Torneträsk	16	K2
Tornio	16	N4
Toro	28	E3
Toronto	96	E2
Tororo	74	E3
Toros Dağları	60	E5
Torquay	24	J11
Torrance	100	C2
Torreblanca	28	L4
Torre de Moncorvo	28	C3
Torrejón de Ardoz	28	G4
Torrelapaja	28	J3
Torrelavega	28	F1
Torremolinos	28	F8
Torrent	28	K5
Torreón	100	F3
Torre-Pacheco	28	K7
Torres Strait	82	H2
Torres Vedras	28	A5
Torrevieja	28	K6
Torrington	94	F2
Tortolì	32	D9
Tortona	30	D6
Tortosa	28	L4
Tortum	60	J3
Torüd	58	G2
Toruń	18	H4
Tory Island	24	D6
Torzhok	38	G3
Tosa-wan	50	G7
Tostedt	20	E3
Tosya	36	S3
Totaranui	84	D5
Tôtes	22	D5
Tot'ma	38	H3
Totora	108	D7
Tottori	50	H6
Touba, *Côte d'Ivoire*	72	C3
Touba, *Senegal*	72	A2
Tougan	72	D2
Touggourt	70	G2

Name	Page	Ref
Tougouri	72	D2
Touil	70	C5
Toul	26	L5
Toulépleu	72	C3
Toulon	26	L10
Toulouse	26	G10
Toummo	70	H4
Toungoo	52	B3
Tourcoing	22	F4
Tournai	22	F4
Tournon-sur-Rhône	26	K8
Tours	26	F6
Touws River	76	C6
Tovuz	60	L3
Towanda	96	E2
Towari	55	B3
Towcester	22	B2
Towner	94	F1
Townsend	94	D1
Townshend Island	82	K4
Townsville	82	J3
Toxkan	44	P9
Toyama	50	J5
Toyohashi	50	J6
Toyooka	50	H6
Toyota	50	J6
Tozeur	70	G2
Tqvarch'eli	60	J2
Trâblous	62	C2
Trabzon	60	H3
Tracy	96	A2
Trail	94	C1
Traiskirchen	30	M2
Trakai	16	N9
Tralee	24	C9
Tralee Bay	24	B9
Tramán Tepuí	108	E2
Tranås	16	H7
Trancoso	28	C4
Trang	52	B5
Trangan	55	D4
Transantarctic Mountains	112	(2)B1
Trapani	32	G11
Trappes	22	E6
Traun	30	K2
Traunreut	30	H3
Traunsee	30	J3
Traversay Islands	106	H9
Traverse City	96	C2
Travnik	34	E5
Trbovlje	30	L4
Trebbia	30	E6
Třebíč	18	E8
Trebinje	34	F7
Trebišov	34	J1
Trebnje	30	L5
Trebon	30	K1
Tregosse Islets	82	K3
Trélazé	26	E6
Trelew	110	H7
Trelleborg	16	G9
Tremonton	94	D2
Tremp	28	L2
Trenčín	18	H9
Trent	24	M8
Trento	30	G4
Trenton, *Canada*	96	E2
Trenton, *United States*	96	F2
Trepassey	90	W7
Tres Arroyos	110	J6
Três Corações	108	H8
Tres Esquinas	108	B3
Tres Lagos	110	G8
Trespaderne	28	G2
Treuchtlingen	30	F2
Treviglio	30	E5
Treviso	30	H5
Triangle	76	E4
Tricase	32	N9
Trichur	56	C6
Trier	22	J5
Trieste	30	J5
Triglav	30	J4
Trikala	36	D5
Trikomon	62	A1
Trilj	30	M7
Trincomalee	56	D7
Trinidad	108	E1
Trinidad, *Bolivia*	108	E6
Trinidad, *United States*	100	F1
Trinidad, *Uruguay*	110	K5
Trinidad and Tobago	108	E1
Trinity Islands	100	(1)G4
Trino	30	D5
Tripoli	98	D3
Tripoli, *Greece*	36	E7
Tripoli = Trâblous, *Lebanon*	62	C2
Tripoli = Tarābulus, *Libya*	70	H2
Trischen	20	D2
Tristan da Cunha	66	B9
Trivandrum = Thiruvananthapuram	56	C7
Trjavna	36	H2
Trnava	34	E1
Trogir	34	D6
Troina	32	J11
Troisdorf	20	C6
Trois Rivières	96	F1
Troitsk	38	M4
Troitsko-Pechorsk	38	L2
Trojan	34	M7
Trollhättan	16	G7
Trombetas	108	F4
Tromsø	16	K2
Trona	94	C3
Trondheim	16	F5
Trondheimsfjörden	16	E5
Troodos	60	E6
Trotuş	34	P3
Trout Lake, *N.W.T., Canada*	90	G4
Trout Lake, *Ont., Canada*	90	N6
Troy, *Al., United States*	98	D3

Name	Page	Ref
Troy, *N.Y., United States*	96	F2
Troyes	26	K5
Trstenik	34	J6
Trudovoye	50	G2
Trujillo, *Peru*	108	B5
Trujillo, *Spain*	28	E5
Truro, *Canada*	90	U7
Truro, *United Kingdom*	24	G11
Trusovo	44	J4
Truth or Consequences	100	E2
Trutnov	18	E7
Trzcianka	18	F4
Trzebnica	18	G6
Tržič	30	K4
Tsetserleg	46	G7
Tshabong	76	C5
Tshane	76	C4
Tshikapa	74	C5
Tshuapa	74	C4
Tsiafajavona	76	H3
Tsimlyanskoy Vodokhranilishche	38	H5
Tsiroanomandidy	76	H3
Ts'khinvali	60	K2
Tsuchiura	50	L5
Tsugaru-kaikyō	50	L3
Tsumeb	76	B3
Tsumkwe	76	C3
Tsuruga	50	J6
Tsuruoka	50	K4
Tsushima	50	E6
Tsuyama	50	H6
Tua	28	C3
Tual	55	D4
Tuân Giao	52	C2
Tuapse	60	H1
Tubarão	110	M4
Tubas	62	C4
Tübingen	30	E2
Tubize	22	G4
Tubruq	68	D1
Tubuai	80	M8
Tubuai Islands	80	L8
Tucano	108	K6
Tuchola	18	G4
Tucson	100	D2
Tucumcari	100	F1
Tucupita	108	E2
Tucuruí	108	H4
Tudela	28	J2
Ţufayḩ	63	C3
Tuguegarao	52	G3
Tugur	46	P6
Tui	28	B2
Tuktoyaktuk	100	(1)L2
Tula, *Mexico*	100	G4
Tula, *Russia*	38	G4
Tulare	94	C3
Tulcea	34	R4
Tulkarm	62	B4
Tullamore	24	E8
Tulle	26	G8
Tulln	30	M2
Tuloma	16	S2
Tulsa	92	G4
Tulsequah	100	(1)L4
Tulun	46	G6
Tulung La	56	F3
Tulu Welel	74	E2
Tumaco	108	B3
Tumān	58	H2
Tumen	50	E2
Tumereng	108	E2
Tumkur	56	C6
Tumut	82	J7
Tunceli	60	H4
Tunduru	76	F2
Tundža	34	P8
Tungir	46	L5
Tungku	54	F1
Tungsten	100	(1)M3
Tungusk	44	S5
Tunis	70	H1
Tunisia	70	E2
Tunja	108	C2
Tupelo	98	D3
Tupik	46	L6
Tupiza	110	H3
Tupper Lake	96	F2
Tuquan	48	G1
Tura, *India*	56	F3
Tura, *Russia*	46	G4
Turan	44	S7
Turangi	84	E4
Turayf	68	G1
Turbat	58	H4
Turbo	108	B2
Turda	34	L3
Turek	18	H5
Turgay	44	L8
Turgay	44	L8
Turgayskaya Stolovaya Strana	44	L7
Turgutlu	36	K6
Turhal	60	G3
Turin = Torino	30	C5
Turinsk	38	M3
Turiy Rog	50	F1
Turka	46	H6
Türkeli Adası	36	K5
Turkestan	44	M9
Turkey	60	D4
Turkmenbashi	58	F1
Turkmenistan	58	G2
Turks and Caicos Islands	102	K4
Turks Islands	102	K4
Turku	16	M6
Turma	46	N6
Turnhout	22	G3
Turnov	18	E7
Turnu Măgurele	34	M6
Turpan	44	R9
Turpan Pendi	44	S9

Name	Page	Ref
Turquino	106	D2
Turtas	38	N3
Turtkul'	58	H1
Turtle Island	82	K3
Turu	44	U5
Turugart Pass	44	P9
Turukhan	46	C3
Turukhansk	44	R4
Turukta	46	K4
Tuscaloosa	98	D3
Tuscola	98	D2
Tuticorin	56	C7
Tutonchany	46	E4
Tutrakan	34	P5
Tuttle Creek Reservoir	98	B2
Tuttlingen	30	D3
Tutuila	80	K7
Tuvalu	80	H6
Tuxpan, *Mexico*	92	G7
Tuxpan, *Mexico*	92	E7
Tuxtla Gutiérrez	102	F5
Tuyên Quang	52	D2
Tuy Hoa	52	D4
Tuymazy	38	K4
Tuz Gölü	60	E4
Tuz Khurmātū	60	L6
Tuzla	34	G3
Tver'	38	G3
Tweed	24	K6
Twentynine Palms	100	C2
Twilight Cove	82	E6
Twin Buttes Reservoir	100	F2
Twin Falls	94	D2
Twizel	84	C7
Two Harbors	96	B1
Tyachiv	34	L1
Tygda	46	M6
Tyler	92	G5
Tylkhoy	46	U4
Tym	44	Q6
Tynda	46	L5
Tyne	24	K6
Tynemouth	24	L5
Tynset	16	F5
Tyra	44	S7
Tyrifjorden	16	F6
Tyrnavos	36	E5
Tyrrhenian Sea	32	F8
Tyry	46	P4
Tysa	18	N9
Tyukyan	46	K4
Tyumen'	44	M6
Tyung	46	K3
Tyva	46	F6

U

Name	Page	Ref
Uarini	108	D4
Uaupés	108	D3
Ubá	108	J8
Ubaitaba	108	K6
Ubangi	74	B3
Ube	50	F7
Úbeda	28	G6
Uberaba	108	H7
Uberlândia	108	H7
Überlingen	30	E3
Ubon Ratchathani	52	C3
Ubrique	28	E8
Ucayali	108	B5
Uchami	44	T5
Ucharal	44	Q8
Uchiura-wan	50	L2
Uchkuduk	44	L9
Uckermark	20	J3
Ucluelet	94	A1
Uda, *Russia*	46	F5
Uda, *Russia*	46	N6
Udachnyy	46	J3
Udagamandalam	56	C6
Udaipur	56	B4
Uddevalla	16	F7
Uddjaure	16	K4
Udine	30	J4
Udmurtiya	38	K3
Udon Thani	52	C3
Udupi	56	B6
Uecker	20	J3
Ueckermünde	20	J3
Ueda	50	K5
Uele	74	C3
Uelen	46	AA3
Uel'kal	46	Y3
Uelzen	20	F4
Ufa	38	L4
Ufa	38	L3
Uganda	74	E3
Ugep	72	F3
Ugine	30	B5
Uglegorsk	46	Q7
Uglich	38	G3
Ugljan	30	L6
Ugol'naya Zyryanka	46	R3
Ugol'nyye Kopi	46	X4
Ugulan	46	S4
Uh	34	K1
Uherské Hradiště	18	G8
Uherský Brod	18	G8
Uiju	50	C3
Uil	38	K5
Uil	38	K5
Uinta Mountains	94	D2
Uitenhage	76	D6
Újfehértó	34	J2
Ujiji	74	D4
Ujjain	56	C4
Ujung Pandang	55	A4
Ukerewe Island	74	E4
Ukhta	44	J5

Name	Page	Grid
Ukiah	94	B3
Ukmergė	18	P2
Ukraine	14	G3
Ulaanbaatar	46	H7
Ulaangom	44	S8
Ulan	48	B3
Ulan Bator = Ulaanbaatar	48	D1
Ulan-Ude	46	H6
Ulaş	60	G4
Ulchin	50	E5
Ulcinj	34	G8
Uldz	46	J7
Ulety	46	J6
Ulhāsnagar	56	B5
Uliastay	44	T8
Ulindi	74	D4
Ullapool	24	G4
Ullŭng do	50	F5
Ulm	30	F2
Ulog	34	F6
Ulongue	76	E2
Ulsan	50	E6
Ulu	46	M4
Ulubat Gölü	36	L4
Uluqqat	58	K2
Ulukışla	60	F5
Ulungur Hu	44	R8
Ulunkhan	46	J5
Uluru	82	F5
Ulu-Yul	46	D5
Ulva	24	F5
Ulverston	24	J7
Ulya	46	Q5
Ul'yanovsk	38	J4
Ulytau	44	M8
Umag	32	H3
Uman'	38	F5
Umanak = Uummannaq	90	W2
Umarkot	58	J4
Umba	38	F1
Umeå	16	L5
Umeälven	16	J4
Umfolozi	76	E5
Ummal Arānib	70	H3
Umm al Jamājim	63	A3
Umm Durman	68	F4
Umm Keddada	68	E5
Umm Lajj	68	G3
Umm Qaşr	63	B1
Umm Ruwaba	68	F5
Umnak Island	100	(1)E5
Umtata	76	D6
Umuarama	110	L3
Unalakleet	100	(1)E3
Unalaska Island	100	(1)E5
'Unayzah	62	C6
Underberg	76	D5
Ungava Bay	90	T5
Ungheni	34	Q2
Ungwana Bay	74	G4
União da Vitória	110	L4
Unije	30	K6
Unimak Island	100	(1)D5
Unim Bāb	63	D4
Unini	108	E4
Union	96	B3
Union City	102	G1
Union Springs	98	D3
United Arab Emirates	58	F5
United Kingdom	24	G6
United States	88	M5
Unna	22	K3
Unraven	100	E1
Unst	24	M1
Unstrut	20	G5
Unzha	38	H3
Upernavik	90	W2
Upington	76	C5
Upolu	80	J7
Upper Hutt	84	E5
Upper Klamath Lake	94	B2
Upper Lake	94	C2
Upper Lough Erne	24	E7
Upper Sandusky	96	D2
Uppsala	16	J7
'Uqlat al 'Udhaybah	63	B2
Urad Houqi	48	D2
Urakawa	50	M2
Ural	38	K5
Ural Mountains = Ural'skiy Khrebet	14	L1
Ural'sk	38	K4
Ural'skiy Khrebet	14	L1
Urambo	74	E5
Uranium City	90	K5
Uraricoera	108	E3
Uraricoera	108	E3
Uray	38	M2
Urbana, Ill., United States	96	C2
Urbana, Oh., United States	96	D2
Urbania	30	H7
Urbino	30	H7
Urdzhar	44	Q8
Uren'	38	J3
Urengoy	44	P4
Urgench	58	H1
Urho	44	R8
Uritskiy	38	N4
Urla	36	J6
Urlaţi	34	P5
Uroševac	34	J7
Uro-teppa	58	J2
Urt	48	C2
Uruaçu	108	H6
Uruapan	102	D5
Urucurituba	108	F4
Uruguaiana	110	K4
Uruguay	110	K5
Uruguay	110	K5
Ürümqi	44	R9
Urus Martan	60	L2

Name	Page	Grid
Uruti	84	E4
Uryupino	46	L6
Uryupinsk	38	H4
Urzhum	38	K3
Urziceni	34	P5
Usa	44	L4
Usa	50	F7
Uşak	60	C4
Usedom	20	J3
Useless Loop	82	B5
Usfān	58	C5
Ushtobe	44	P8
Usingen	20	D6
Usk	24	J10
Usman'	38	G4
Usol'ye Sibirskoye	46	G6
Ussel	26	H8
Ussuri	50	G1
Ussuriysk	48	J2
Usta	38	J3
Ust'-Alekseyevo	38	J2
Ust'-Barguzin	46	H6
Ust' Chaun	46	W3
Ústí	18	F8
Ustica	32	H10
Ust'-Ilimsk	46	G5
Ústí nad Labem	18	D7
Ust'-Ishim	44	N6
Ustka	18	F3
Ust'-Kamchatsk	46	U5
Ust'-Kamenogorsk	44	Q8
Ust'-Kamo	44	T5
Ust'-Karenga	46	K6
Ust'-Khayryuzovo	46	T5
Ust'-Kulom	38	K2
Ust'-Kut	46	G5
Ust'-Kuyga	46	P3
Ust'-Labinsk	60	H1
Ust'-Maya	46	N4
Ust'-Mukduyka	44	R4
Ust'-Muya	46	K5
Ust' Nem	38	K2
Ust'-Nera	46	Q4
Ust'-Nyukzha	46	L5
Ust'-Olenek	46	K2
Ust'-Omchug	46	R4
Ust' Ozernoye	46	D5
Ust' Penzhino	46	V4
Ust'-Pit	46	E5
Ustrem	38	N2
Ust'-Sopochnoye	46	T5
Ust' Tapsuy	38	M2
Ust'-Tarka	44	P6
Ust'-Tatta	46	N4
Ust'-Tsil'ma	44	J4
Ust' Un'ya	38	L2
Ust'-Urkima	46	L5
Ust'-Usa	38	L1
Ust'-Uyskoye	44	L7
Usu	44	Q9
Usuki	50	F7
Utah	92	D4
Utah Lake	94	D2
Utata	46	G6
Utena	16	N9
Uthal	58	J4
Utica	96	E2
Utiel	28	J5
Utrecht	22	H2
Utrera	28	E7
Utsjoki	16	P2
Utsunomiya	50	K5
Uttaradit	52	C3
Utva	38	K4
Uummannaq	90	W2
Uusikaupunki	16	L6
Uvalde	102	E3
Uvargin	46	X3
Uvat	38	N3
Uvinza	74	E5
Uvira	74	D4
Uvs Nuur	44	S7
Uwajima	50	G7
Uy	38	M4
Uyar	44	S6
Uyuk	44	N9
Uyuni	110	H3
Uzbekistan	44	L9
Uzgen	44	N9
Uzhhorod	34	K1
Užice	34	G6
Uzunköprü	34	P8

V

Name	Page	Grid
Vaal	76	D5
Vaasa	16	L5
Vác	34	G2
Vacaria	110	M4
Vachi	58	E1
Vadodara	56	B4
Vado Ligure	30	D6
Vadsø	16	Q1
Vaduz	30	E3
Værøy	16	G3
Vaganski Vhr	30	L6
Vagay	38	N3
Váh	18	H8
Vakh	38	Q2
Valbonnais	30	A6
Valcheta	110	H7
Valdagno	30	G5
Valday	38	F3
Val-de-Meuse	30	A2
Valdemoro	28	G4
Valdepeñas	28	G6
Valdez	90	B4
Valdivia	110	G6
Val-d'Or	96	E1

Name	Page	Grid
Valdosta	92	K5
Valdres	16	E6
Valea lui Mihai	34	K2
Valence	26	K9
Valencia, Spain	28	K5
Valencia, Venezuela	108	D1
Valencia de Alcántara	28	C5
Valenciennes	22	F4
Vălenii de Munte	34	P4
Valentia Island	24	B10
Valentine	94	F2
Valenza	30	D5
Valera	108	C2
Valga	38	E3
Val Horn	92	F5
Valjevo	34	G5
Valka	16	N8
Val'karay	46	X3
Valkeakoski	16	N6
Valkenswaard	22	H3
Valladolid, Mexico	102	G4
Valladolid, Spain	28	F3
Valle	16	D7
Valledupar	108	C1
Vallée de Azaouagh	70	F5
Vallée du Tîlemsi	70	F5
Vallée-Jonction	96	F1
Vallejo	94	B3
Vallentuna	16	K7
Valletta	32	J13
Valley City	94	G1
Valley Falls	94	B2
Valley of the Kings	68	F2
Valli di Comacchio	30	H6
Vallorbe	30	B4
Valls	28	M3
Valmiera	16	N8
Valognes	22	A5
Val-Paradis	96	E1
Valparai	56	C6
Valparaíso, Chile	110	G5
Valparaíso, Mexico	100	F4
Valsad	56	B4
Val'tevo	38	H2
Valuyki	38	G4
Valverde del Camino	28	D7
Vammala	16	M6
Van	60	K4
Vanadzor	60	L3
Vanavara	46	G4
Van Buren	96	G1
Vancouver, Canada	94	B1
Vancouver, United States	94	B1
Vancouver Island	90	F7
Vandalia	98	D2
Vanderbijlpark	76	D5
Vanderhoof	90	G6
Van Diemen Gulf	82	G7
Vänern	16	G7
Vangaindrano	76	H4
Van Gölü	60	K4
Van Horn	100	F2
Vanimo	55	F3
Vanino	46	Q7
Vankarem	46	Y3
Vanna	16	K1
Vännäs	16	K5
Vannes	26	C6
Vanrhynsdorp	76	B6
Vantaa	16	N6
Vanua Levu	80	H7
Vanuatu	80	G7
Van Wert	96	D2
Vanzevat	38	N2
Vanzhil'kynak	46	C4
Varāmīn	58	F2
Varanasi	56	D3
Varangerfjorden	16	R2
Varaždin	34	D3
Varazze	30	D6
Varberg	16	G8
Varda	36	D6
Vardar	36	E3
Varde	16	E9
Vardenis	60	L3
Vardø	16	R1
Varel	20	D3
Varéna	18	P3
Varese	30	D5
Vârful Moldoveanu	34	M4
Vârfurile	34	K3
Varginha	110	M3
Varkaus	16	P5
Varna	60	B2
Värnamo	16	H8
Varnsdorf	20	K6
Várpalota	34	F2
Varto	60	J4
Varzi	30	E6
Varzy	26	J6
Vasa	34	K1
Vasilikos	62	A2
Vaslui	34	Q3
Västerås	16	J7
Västervik	16	J8
Vasto	32	J6
Vasvár	30	M3
Vathia	36	E8
Vatican City	32	F7
Vatnajökull	16	(1)E2
Vatomandry	76	H3
Vatra Dornei	34	N2
Vättern	16	H7
Vaughn	100	E2
Vawkavysk	18	P4
Vayuniya	56	D7
Vazhgort	38	J2
Vecht	22	J2
Vechta	22	L2

Name	Page	Grid
Vecsés	34	G2
Vedaranniyam	56	C6
Vedea	34	N6
Vedi	60	L4
Veendam	22	J1
Veenendaal	22	H2
Vega	100	F1
Vega	16	F4
Vegreville	90	J6
Vejen	20	E1
Vejer de la Frontera	28	E8
Vejle	16	E9
Vel'	44	G5
Vela Luka	34	D7
Velenje	30	L4
Veles	36	D3
Vélez-Málaga	28	F8
Velika Gorica	30	M5
Velika Plana	34	J5
Velikaya	46	W4
Velikiye Luki	38	F3
Velikiy Ustyug	38	J2
Veliko Târnovo	34	N6
Vélingara	72	B2
Velingrad	34	L7
Velita Kladuša	30	L5
Velké Meziříčí	18	F8
Velký Krtíš	18	J9
Velletri	32	G7
Vellinge	18	C2
Vellore	56	C6
Velopoula	36	F8
Vel'sk	38	H2
Velten	20	J4
Velva	94	F1
Venaria	30	C5
Vence	30	C7
Venda Nova	28	C3
Vendôme	26	G6
Venev	38	G4
Venezia	30	H5
Venezuela	108	D2
Vengurla	56	B5
Veniaminof Volcano	100	(1)F4
Venice = Venezia, Italy	30	H5
Venice, United States	98	D4
Venlo	22	J3
Venray	22	H3
Venta	38	D3
Venta de Baños	28	F3
Ventimiglia	30	C7
Ventotene	32	H8
Ventspils	16	L8
Vera, Argentina	110	J4
Vera, Spain	28	J7
Veracruz	102	E5
Veraval	56	B4
Verbania	30	D5
Vercelli	30	D5
Verdalsøra	16	F5
Verde	108	G8
Verden	20	E4
Verdun	22	H5
Vereeniging	76	D5
Vereshchagino	46	D4
Verín	28	C3
Verkheimbatsk	46	D4
Verkhne-Imbatskoye	44	R5
Verkhnetulomskoe Vodokhranilishche	16	R2
Verkhneural'sk	38	L4
Verkhniy Baskunchak	38	J5
Verkhnyaya Amga	46	M5
Verkhnyaya Toyma	38	J2
Verkhnyaya Tura	38	L3
Verkhovyna	34	M1
Verkhoyansk	46	N3
Verkhoyanskiy Khrebet	46	M3
Vermillion	94	G2
Vermont	92	M3
Vernal	94	E2
Verneuil	22	C6
Vernon, France	22	D5
Vernon, United States	98	B3
Vero Beach	98	E4
Veroia	36	E4
Verona	30	F5
Versailles	22	E6
Verviers	22	H4
Veselí	34	N2
Vesijarvi	16	N6
Vesoul	20	B9
Vesterålen	16	G2
Vestfjorden	16	G3
Vestmannaeyjar	16	(1)C3
Vestvagøy	16	G2
Vesuvio	32	J8
Veszprém	34	E2
Vet	76	D5
Vetluga	38	J3
Vetluga	38	J3
Veurne	22	E3
Vevey	30	B4
Vezirköprü	60	F3
Viana do Castelo	28	B3
Vianden	22	J5
Viangchan	52	C3
Viareggio	30	F7
Viborg	16	E8
Vibo Valentia	32	L10
Vibraye	26	F5
Vic	28	N3
Vicenza	30	G5
Vichuga	38	H3
Vichy	26	J7
Vicksburg	98	C3
Victor Harbor	82	G7
Victoria, Argentina	110	J5
Victoria, Canada	94	B1
Victoria, Chile	110	G6
Victoria, Malta	32	J12

Victoria, *Romania* 34 M4
Victoria, *Seychelles* 76 (2)C1
Victoria, *United States* 98 B4
Victoria de las Tunas 102 J4
Victoria Falls 76 D3
Victoria Island 90 J2
Victoria Land 112 (2)W2
Victoria River 82 F3
Victoria Strait 90 M3
Victoriaville 96 F1
Victoria West 76 C6
Vidalia 92 K5
Vidamlja 18 N5
Videle 34 N5
Vidin 34 K6
Viedma 110 J7
Vienenburg 20 F5
Vienna = Wien 30 M2
Vienna 96 C3
Vienne 26 K8
Vienne 26 F7
Vientiane = Viangchan 52 C3
Vierzon 26 H6
Vieste 32 L7
Vietnam 52 D3
Viêt Tri 52 D2
Vigan 52 G3
Vigevano 30 D5
Vigia 108 H4
Vigo 28 B2
Vigo di Cadore 30 H4
Viho Valentia 32 L10
Vijaywada 56 D5
Vík 16 (1)D3
Vikna 16 E4
Vila do Conde 28 B3
Vilafranca del Penedès 28 M3
Vila Franca de Xira 28 A6
Vila Nova de Gaia 28 B3
Vilanova i la Geltru 28 M3
Vila Real 28 C3
Vila-real 28 K5
Vilar Formoso 28 D4
Vila Velha 108 G3
Vilhelmina 16 J4
Vilhena 108 E6
Vilija 16 N9
Viljandi 16 N7
Vilkaviškis 18 N3
Villa Ahumada 102 C2
Villablino 28 D2
Villacarrillo 28 G6
Villach 30 J4
Villacidro 32 C9
Villa Constitución 92 D7
Villa de Cos 102 D4
Villafranca de los Barros 28 D6
Villafranca di Verona 30 F5
Villagarcía 28 B2
Villagrán 100 G4
Villahermosa 102 F5
Villa Huidobro 110 J5
Villalba 28 C1
Villaldama 100 F3
Villalpando 28 E3
Villamartín 28 E8
Villa Montes 110 J3
Villanueva 100 F4
Villanueva de Cordoba 28 F6
Villa Ocampo 100 E3
Villaputzu 32 D9
Villarrobledo 28 H5
Villa San Giovanni 32 K10
Villavelayo 28 H2
Villavicencio 108 C3
Villaviciosa 28 E1
Villazon 110 H3
Villedieu-les-Poêles 22 A6
Villefranche-de-Rouergue 26 H9
Villefranche-sur-Saône 26 K8
Villena 28 K6
Villeneuve-sur-Lot 26 F9
Villers-Bocage 22 B5
Villers-Cotterêts 22 F5
Villerupt 22 H5
Villeurbanne 26 K8
Villingen 30 D2
Vilnius 16 N9
Vilsbiburg 30 H2
Vilshofen 30 J2
Vilvoorde 22 G4
Vilyuy 46 L4
Vilyuysk 46 L4
Vilyuyskoye Vodokhranilishche 46 J4
Vimoutiers 22 C6
Vimperk 30 J1
Viña del Mar 110 G5
Vinaròs 28 L4
Vincennes 98 D2
Vineland 96 F3
Vinh 52 D3
Vinkovci 34 F4
Vinnytsya 38 E5
Vinson Massif 112 (2)JJ2
Vinstri 16 E6
Vinzili 38 N3
Viöl 20 E2
Vioolsdrift 76 B5
Vipava 30 J5
Vipiteno 30 G4
Vir 30 L6
Virac 52 G4
Viranşehir 60 H5
Virawah 56 B4
Virden 94 F1
Vire 22 B6
Virginia 92 L4
Virginia, *United States* 96 B1
Virginia Beach 96 E3
Virgin Islands, *United Kingdom* 106 E2
Virgin Islands, *United States* 106 E2
Virihaure 16 J3
Viröchey 52 D4
Virovitica 34 E4
Virton 22 H5
Virtsu 16 M7
Virudunagar 56 C7
Vis 34 D6
Visalia 94 C3
Visby 16 K8
Viscount Melville Sound 90 J2
Viseu, *Brazil* 108 H4
Viseu, *Portugal* 28 C4
Vişeu de Sus 34 M2
Vishakhapatnam 56 D5
Vishera 44 K5
Vishnevka 44 N7
Visoko 34 F6
Visp 30 C4
Višegrad 34 G6
Visselhövede 20 E4
Vistula = Wisła 14 F2
Viterbo 32 G6
Vitez 34 E5
Viti Levu 80 H7
Vitim 46 J5
Vitolište 36 D3
Vitória 110 N3
Vitória da Conquista 108 J6
Vitoria-Gasteiz 28 H2
Vitré 26 D5
Vitry-le-François 22 G6
Vitsyebsk 38 F3
Vitteaux 26 K6
Vittel 30 A2
Vittoria 32 J12
Vittorio Veneto 30 H5
Viveiro 28 C1
Vivi 44 T4
Vivonne 26 F7
Vize 36 K3
Vizhas 38 J1
Vizianagaram 56 D5
Vizinga 44 H5
Vizzini 32 J11
Vjosë 36 C4
Vladikavkaz 60 L2
Vladimir 38 H3
Vladivostok 50 F2
Vlasotince 34 K7
Vlasovo 46 N2
Vlieland 22 G1
Vlissingen 22 F3
Vlorë 36 B4
Vltava 18 D8
Vöcklabruck 30 J2
Vodice 30 L7
Vodnjan 30 J6
Vogelsberg 20 E6
Voghera 30 D6
Vohipeno 76 H4
Vöhringen 30 F2
Voi 74 F4
Voinjama 72 C3
Voiron 26 L8
Voitsberg 30 L3
Vojens 20 E1
Vojmsjön 16 J4
Vojvodina 34 G4
Volary 20 J8
Volcán Antofalla 110 H4
Volcán Barú 102 H7
Volcán Cayambe 108 B3
Volcán Citlaltépetl 88 L7
Volcán Corcovado 110 G7
Volcán Cotopaxi 108 B4
Volcán Domuyo 110 G6
Volcán Lanin 110 G6
Volcán Llullaillaco 110 H3
Volcán San Pedro 110 H3
Volcán Tajumulco 102 F5
Volga 38 J5
Volgodonsk 38 H5
Volgograd 38 H5
Völkermarkt 30 K4
Volkhov 38 F3
Völklingen 22 J5
Volksrust 76 D5
Volochanka 44 S3
Volodarskoye 38 N4
Vologda 38 H3
Volonga 38 J1
Volos 36 E5
Volosovo 16 Q7
Volta Redonda 108 J8
Volterra 30 F7
Voltri 30 D6
Volzhskiy 38 H5
Voorne 22 F3
Voranava 16 N9
Vorderrhein 30 E4
Vordingborg 20 G1
Voreios Evvoïkos Kolpos 36 E6
Voreria Pindos 36 C4
Vorkuta 38 M1
Vormsi 16 M7
Vorona 38 H4
Voronezh 38 G4
Vorstershoop 76 C5
Võru 16 P8
Vosges 30 C2
Voss 16 D6
Vostochno-Sibirskoye More 46 U2
Vostochnyy Sayan 44 T7
Vostok Island 80 L6
Votkinsk 44 J6
Vozhgora 38 J2
Vraca 34 L6
Vranje 34 J7
Vranov 18 L9
Vranov nad Toplau 34 J1
Vrbas 34 G4
Vrbas 34 E5
Vrbovsko 30 L5
Vrendenburg 76 B6
Vriddhachalam 56 C6
Vršac 34 J4
Vryburg 76 C5
Vryheid 76 E5
Vsetín 18 G8
Vstrechnyy 46 V3
Vućitrh 34 J7
Vukovar 34 G4
Vuktyl' 38 L2
Vulcăneşti 34 R4
Vulcano 32 J10
Vung Tau 52 D4
Vuollerim 16 L3
Vuotso 16 P2
Vyatka 38 K3
Vyazemskiy 46 N7
Vyaz'ma 38 F3
Vyborg 16 Q6
Vychegda 38 K2
Vyksa 38 H3
Vylkove 34 S4
Vynohradiv 18 N9
Vyshniy Volochek 38 F3
Vyškov 18 G8
Vytegra 38 G2

W

Wa 72 D3
Waal 22 H3
Waalwijk 22 H3
Wabē Shebelē Wenz 74 G2
Wabush 90 T6
Waco 98 B3
Wad Banda 68 E5
Waddān 68 C2
Waddeneilanden 22 G1
Waddenzee 22 H1
Wadena 96 A1
Wādī al Fārigh 68 C1
Wādī al Hamīm 68 D1
Wadi Halfa 68 F3
Wādi Mūsā 62 C6
Wad Medani 68 F5
Wadsworth 100 C1
Wafangdian 48 G3
Wager Bay 90 P3
Wagga Wagga 82 J7
Wahai 55 C3
Wahiawa 100 (2)C2
Wahpeton 94 G1
Waiau 84 D6
Waiblingen 30 E2
Waidhofen 30 K3
Waidhofen an der Ybbs 34 B2
Waigeo 55 D3
Waiheke Island 84 E3
Waihi 84 E3
Waikabubak 55 A4
Waikaia 84 B7
Waikaremoana 84 F4
Waikato 84 E4
Waikawa 84 B8
Wailuku 100 (2)E3
Waimana 84 F4
Waimate 84 C7
Waingapu 82 B1
Wainwright 100 (1)F1
Waiouru 84 E4
Waipara 84 D6
Waipawa 84 F4
Waipiro 84 G4
Waipu 84 E2
Waipukurau 84 F5
Wairoa 84 F4
Waitakaruru 84 E3
Waitaki 84 C7
Waitangi 84 (1)B1
Waitara 84 E4
Waitotara 84 E4
Waiuku 84 E3
Wajima 50 J5
Wajir 74 G3
Wakasa-wan 50 H6
Wakayama 50 H6
Wakeeney 100 G1
Wakefield 24 L8
Wake Island 80 G4
Wakkanai 50 L1
Waku-Kungo 76 B2
Wałbrzych 18 F7
Walcheren 22 F3
Wałcz 18 F4
Waldmünchen 20 H7
Waldshut-Tiengen 30 D3
Walen See 30 E3
Wales 24 J9
Wales Island 90 P3
Walgett 82 J6
Walker Lake 100 C1
Walkerville 82 J7
Wall 94 F2
Wallaceburg 96 D2
Walla Walla 94 C1
Wallis et Futuna 80 J7
Walpole 82 C6
Walsall 24 L9
Walsenburg 94 F3
Walsrode 20 E4
Waltershausen 20 F6
Walvis Bay 76 A4
Wamba 74 D3
Wana 58 J3
Wanaaring 82 H5
Wanaka 84 B7
Wandel Sea 88 A1
Wandingzhen 52 B2
Wando 50 D6
Wanganui 84 E4
Wanganui 84 E4
Wangen 30 E3
Wangerooge 20 D3
Wangiwangi 55 B4
Wan Hsa-la 52 B2
Wanxian 48 D4
Wanyuan 48 D4
Warangal 56 C5
Warburg 20 D5
Ward 84 E5
Wardha 56 C4
Waregem 22 F4
Waremme 22 H4
Waren 20 H3
Warendorf 22 K3
Warka 18 L6
Warmandi 55 D3
Warminster 24 K10
Warm Springs 94 C3
Warren, *Mich., United States* 96 D2
Warren, *Oh., United States* 96 D2
Warren, *Pa., United States* 96 E2
Warrensburg 96 B3
Warrenton 76 C5
Warri 72 F3
Warrington, *United Kingdom* 24 K8
Warrington, *United States* 98 D3
Warrnambool 82 H7
Warroad 96 A1
Warsaw = Warszawa 18 K5
Warstein 20 D5
Warszawa 18 K5
Warta 18 F5
Warwick 24 L9
Wasatch Range 100 D1
Wasco 100 C1
Washap 58 H4
Washburn Lake 90 K2
Washington 94 B1
Washington, *N.C., United States* 96 E3
Washington, *Pa., United States* 96 D2
Washington, *Ut., United States* 94 D3
Washington D.C. 88 J6
Wassenaar 22 G2
Wasserburg 30 H2
Watampone 55 B3
Watansoppeng 55 A3
Waterbury 96 F2
Waterford 24 E9
Waterloo, *Belgium* 22 G4
Waterloo, *United States* 96 B2
Watersmeet 96 C1
Watertown, *N.Y., United States* 96 E2
Watertown, *S.D., United States* 94 G1
Watertown, *Wis., United States* 96 C2
Waterville 96 G2
Watford 22 B3
Watford City 94 F1
Watmuri 55 D4
Watrous 90 K6
Watsa 74 D3
Watseka 98 D1
Watson Lake 100 (1)M3
Wau 74 D2
Waubay Lake 94 G1
Waukegan 96 C2
Waukesha 96 C2
Waurika 98 B3
Wausau 92 J3
Waverley 84 E4
Waverly 96 C3
Wavre 22 G4
Wawa 96 D1
Wāw al Kabīr 68 C2
Waxxari 44 R10
Waycross 98 E3
Waynesboro, *Ga., United States* 98 E3
Waynesboro, *Miss., United States* 98 D3
Waynesville 96 D3
Weaverville 94 B2
Weber 84 F5
Webi Shaabeelle 74 G3
Webster 94 G1
Weddell Island 110 J9
Weddell Sea 112 (2)A2
Wedel 20 E3
Weed 94 B2
Weert 22 H3
Węgorzewo 18 L3
Wei 48 D4
Weichang 48 F2
Weida 20 H6
Weiden 20 H7
Weifang 48 F3
Weihai 48 G3
Weilburg 20 D6
Weilheim 30 G3
Weimar 20 G6
Weinan 48 D4
Weinheim 20 D7
Weining 48 C5
Weipa 82 H2
Weiser 94 C2
Weißenburg 20 F7
Weißenfels 20 G5
Weißwasser 20 K5
Weixi 52 B1
Wejherowo 18 H3
Welkom 76 D5
Welland 22 B2
Wellawaya 56 D7
Wellesley Islands 82 G3
Wellingborough 26 E1
Wellington, *New Zealand* 84 E5
Wellington, *Colo., United States* 94 F2
Wellington, *Kans., United States* 98 B2
Wells, *United States* 94 C2
Wellsboro 96 E2

Wellsford 84 E3
Wellton 100 D2
Wels 30 K2
Welshpool 24 J9
Welwyn Garden City 22 B3
Wenatchee 94 B1
Wenchang 52 E3
Wenga 74 B3
Wenman 108 (1)A1
Wentworth 82 H6
Wen Xian 48 C4
Wenzhou 48 G5
Werdër 74 H2
Werder 20 H4
Werl 22 K3
Werneck 20 F7
Wernigerode 20 F5
Werra 20 F6
Wertheim 20 E7
Wesel 22 J3
Wesel Dorsten 20 B5
Weser 20 E4
Wessel Islands 82 G2
West Antarctica 112 (2)GG2
West Bank 62 C4
West Branch 96 D2
West Cape 80 G10
West End 98 F4
Westerland 20 D2
Western Australia 82 D5
Western Cape 76 B6
Western Ghats 56 B5
Western Reef 84 (1)B1
Western Sahara 70 C4
Wester Ross 24 G4
Westerschelde 22 F3
Westerstede 22 K1
Westervoort 22 J3
Westerwald 22 K4
West Falkland 110 J9
West Frankfort 98 D2
West Glacier 94 D1
West Lunga 76 C2
West Memphis 98 C2
Weston 96 D3
Weston-super-Mare 24 K10
West Palm Beach 98 E4
West Plains 96 B3
Westport, *New Zealand* 84 C5
Westport, *Republic of Ireland* 24 C8
Westray 24 J2
West Siberian Plain =
Zapadno-Sibirskaya Ravnina 44 P5
West-Terschelling 22 H1
West Virginia 96 D3
West Wendover 94 D2
West Yellowstone 94 D2
Wetar 55 C4
Wetaskiwin 90 J6
Wete 74 F5
Wetumpka 98 D3
Wetzlar 20 D6
Wewak 55 F3
Wexford 24 F9
Wexford Harbour 24 F9
Weyburn 92 F2
Weymouth 24 K11
Whakatane 84 F3
Whale Cove 90 N4
Whalsay 24 M1
Whangamata 84 E3
Whangamomona 84 E4
Whangarei 84 E2
Wharfe 24 L7
Wheeler Peak 100 E1
Wheeler Ridge 100 C2
Wheeling 98 E1
Whitby 24 M7
White, *Nev., United States* 94 C3
White, *S.D., United States* 90 L8
White Bay 90 V6
White Cliffs 82 H6
Whitecourt 90 H6
Whitefish Point 96 C1
Whitehaven 24 J7
Whitehorse 100 (1)L3
White Island 84 F3
Whitemark 82 J8
White Mountain Peak 94 C3
White Mountains 90 S8
Whitemouth 94 G1
White Nile = Bahr el Abiad 68 F5
White River, *Canada* 96 C1
White River, *United States* 94 F2
White Sea = Beloye More 38 G1
White Sulphur Springs 94 D1
Whiteville 98 F3
White Volta 72 D3
Whitney 96 E1
Whitstable 22 D3
Whyalla 82 G6
Wichita 98 B2
Wichita Falls 98 B3
Wick 24 J3
Wickenburg 100 D2
Wicklow 24 F9
Wicklow Mountains 24 F8
Widawka 18 J6
Wieluń 18 H6
Wien 30 M2
Wiener Neustadt 30 M3
Wieringermeer Polder 22 G2
Wiesbaden 20 D6
Wiesloch 20 D7
Wiesmoor 20 C3
Wigan 24 K8
Wiggins 94 F2
Wil 30 E3
Wilbur 94 C1
Wilcannia 82 H6
Wildeshausen 20 D4
Wilhelmshaven 20 D3
Wilkes-Barre 96 E2
Wilkes Land 112 (2)U2
Willapa Bay 94 B1
Willemstad 108 D1
Williams, *Australia* 82 C6
Williams, *Ariz., United States* 94 D3
Williams, *Calif., United States* 94 B3
Williamsburg 96 E3
Williams Lake 90 G6
Williamson 98 E2
Williamsport 96 E2
Willis Group 82 K3
Williston, *South Africa* 76 C6
Williston, *Fla., United States* 98 E4
Williston, *N.D., United States* 94 F1
Williston Lake 90 G5
Willmar 96 A1
Willow 100 (1)H3
Willowmore 76 C6
Willow River 96 B1
Willow Springs 96 B3
Wilmington, *Del., United States* 96 E3
Wilmington, *N.C., United States* 98 F3
Wilson 96 E3
Wilson Reservoir 98 B2
Wilson's Promontory 82 J7
Wiluna 82 D5
Winamac 96 C2
Winchester, *United Kingdom* 24 L10
Winchester, *Ky., United States* 96 D3
Winchester, *Va., United States* 96 E3
Windhoek 76 B4
Windischgarsten 30 K3
Windom 96 A2
Windorah 82 H5
Windsor, *Canada* 96 D2
Windsor, *United Kingdom* 22 B3
Windsor, *United States* 98 F2
Windward Islands 102 N6
Windward Passage 106 D2
Winfield, *Al., United States* 98 D3
Winfield, *Kans., United States* 100 G1
Wingate Mountains 82 E2
Winisk 90 P5
Winisk 90 P6
Winisk Lake 90 P6
Winnemucca 94 C2
Winner 94 G2
Winnfield 92 H5
Winnipeg 90 M7
Winona, *Minn., United States* 96 B2
Winona, *Miss., United States* 98 D3
Winschoten 22 K1
Winsen 20 F3
Winslow 100 D1
Winston-Salem 96 D3
Winterberg 20 D5
Winter Harbour 90 J2
Winterswijk 22 J3
Winterthur 30 D3
Winton, *Australia* 82 H4
Winton, *New Zealand* 84 B8
Wisbech 22 C2
Wisconsin 92 H2
Wisconsin 96 B2
Wisconsin Dells 96 C2
Wisconsin Rapids 96 C2
Wisil Dabarow 74 H2
Wisła 18 H8
Wisła 18 H4
Wisłoka 18 L8
Wismar 20 G3
Wissembourg 20 C7
Witney 22 A3
Witten 22 K3
Wittenberge 20 G3
Wittenoom 82 C4
Wittingen 20 F4
Wittlich 22 J5
Wittmund 20 C3
Wittstock 20 H3
Witzenhausen 20 E5
W. J. van Blommesteinmeer 108 G2
Wkra 18 K5
Władysławowo 18 H3
Włocławek 18 J5
Włodawa 18 N6
Wodzisław Śląski 18 H7
Wohlen 30 D3
Wokam 55 D4
Woking 24 M10
Wolf Creek 94 D1
Wolfen 20 H5
Wolfenbüttel 20 F4
Wolf Point 94 E1
Wolfratshausen 30 G3
Wolfsberg 30 K4
Wolfsburg 20 F4
Wolgast 20 J2
Wollaston Lake 90 K5
Wollaston Peninsula 90 H3
Wollongong 82 K6
Wołomin 18 L5
Wolsztyn 18 F5
Wolvega 22 J2
Wolverhampton 24 K9
Wŏnju 50 D5
Wŏnsan 50 D4
Woodbridge 22 D2
Woodburn 94 B1
Woodland 94 B3
Woodstock, *Canada* 96 G1
Woodstock, *United Kingdom* 22 A3
Woodstock, *United States* 96 C2
Woodville, *New Zealand* 84 E5
Woodville, *Miss., United States* 98 C3
Woodville, *Tex., United States* 98 C3
Woodward 94 G3
Woody Head 84 E3
Woonsocket, *R.I., United States* 96 F2
Woonsocket, *S.D., United States* 94 G2
Worcester, *South Africa* 76 B6
Worcester, *United Kingdom* 24 K9
Worcester, *United States* 92 M3
Wörgl 30 H3
Workington 24 J7
Worksop 22 A1
Worland 94 E2
Worms 20 D7
Wörth 20 D7
Worthing 24 M11
Worthington 92 G3
Wosu 55 B3
Wotu 55 B3
Wowoni 55 B3
Wrangell 90 E5
Wrangell Mountains 90 C4
Wray 92 F3
Wrexham 24 K8
Wrigley 90 G4
Wrocław 18 G6
Września 18 G5
Wu 48 D5
Wubin 82 C6
Wubu 48 E3
Wuchang 48 H2
Wuchuan 48 E2
Wuday'ah 58 E6
Wudu 48 C4
Wuhai 48 D3
Wuhan 48 E4
Wuhu 48 F4
Wüjang 56 C2
Wukari 72 F3
Wuli 56 F2
Wunsiedel 20 G6
Wunstorf 20 E4
Wuppertal 20 C5
Würzburg 20 E7
Wurzen 20 H5
Wushi 44 P9
Wusuli 48 J1
Wutach 30 D3
Wuwei 48 C3
Wuxi 48 G4
Wuxu 52 D2
Wuyuan 48 D2
Wuzhong 48 D3
Wuzhou 52 E2
Wye 24 J9
Wyndham 82 E3
Wynniatt Bay 90 J2
Wyoming 92 E3
Wyszków 18 L5
Wytheville 98 E2

X

Xaafuun 74 J1
Xábia 28 L6
Xaçmaz 60 N3
Xaidulla 44 P10
Xainza 56 E2
Xai-Xai 76 E4
Xam Nua 52 C2
Xankändi 60 M4
Xanten 22 J3
Xanthi 36 G3
Xapuri 108 D6
Xar Moron 46 K8
Xátiva 28 K6
Xi 48 E6
Xiahe 48 C3
Xiamen 52 F2
Xi'an 48 D4
Xiangcheng 48 E4
Xiangfan 48 E4
Xianggang 52 E2
Xianghoang 52 C3
Xianghuang Qi 48 E2
Xiangtan 48 E5
Xianning 48 E5
Xianyang 48 D4
Xiaogan 48 E4
Xiao Hinggan Ling 46 M7
Xiaonanchuan 56 F1
Xichang 52 C1
Xigazê 56 E3
Xilinhot 48 F2
Xincai 48 E4
Xingcheng 48 G2
Xinghe 48 E2
Xinghua 48 F4
Xingtai 48 F3
Xingu 108 G5
Xingyi 52 C1
Xinhe 44 Q9
Xining 48 C3
Xinjie 48 D3
Xinjin 48 G3
Xinmin 50 B2
Xintai 48 E3
Xinxiang 48 E3
Xinyang 48 E4
Xinyu 48 F5
Xinyuan 44 Q9
Xinzhou 48 E3
Xinzo de Limia 28 C2
Xique Xique 108 J6
Xi Ujimqin Qi 48 F2
Xiushu 48 E5
Xiwu 56 G2
Xixia 48 E4
Xi Xiang 48 D4
Xizang 56 E2
Xizang Gaoyuan 56 D2
Xuanhua 48 E2
Xuchang 48 E4
Xuddur 74 G3
Xuwen 52 E2
Xuzhou 48 F4

Y

Ya'an 48 D3
Yabassi 72 F4
Yabēlo 74 F3
Yablonovyy Khrebet 46 J6
Yabrūd 62 D3
Yabuli 50 E1
Yacuma 108 D6
Yadgir 56 D5
Yagel'naya 44 P4
Yagodnyy 38 N3
Yahk 90 H7
Yakima 94 B1
Yako 72 D2
Yakoma 74 C3
Yaksha 38 L2
Yakumo 50 L2
Yaku-shima 50 F8
Yakutat 100 (1)K4
Yakutsk 46 M4
Yala 52 C5
Yalova 36 M4
Yalta 60 F1
Yalu 50 D3
Yalutorovsk 38 N3
Yamagata 50 L4
Yamaguchi 50 F6
Yamarovka 46 J6
Yambio 74 D3
Yamburg 44 P4
Yamdena 55 D4
Yammit 62 B5
Yamoussoukro 72 C3
Yampa 94 E2
Yampil' 34 R1
Yamsk 46 S5
Yana 46 N3
Yan'an 48 D3
Yanbu'al Baḩr 58 C5
Yancheng 48 G4
Yandun 48 A2
Yangambi 74 C3
Yangbajain 56 F2
Yangdok 50 D4
Yangi Kand 60 N5
Yangjiang 52 E2
Yangon 52 B3
Yangquan 48 E3
Yangshuo 52 E2
Yangtze = Chang Jiang 48 D4
Yangzhou 48 F4
Yanhuqu 56 D2
Yani-Kurgan 44 M9
Yanji 50 E2
Yankton 94 G2
Yano-Indigirskaya Nizmennost' 46 N2
Yanqi 44 R9
Yanqing 48 F2
Yanshan 52 C2
Yanskiy Zaliv 46 N2
Yantai 48 G3
Yantarnyy 18 J3
Yaoundé 72 G4
Yap 80 D5
Yapen 55 E3
Yaqui 92 E6
Yaraka 82 H4
Yaransk 38 J3
Yardımcı Burnu 36 E8
Yare 22 D2
Yaren 80 G6
Yarensk 38 J2
Yari 108 C3
Yarkant 58 L2
Yarkovo 38 N3
Yarlung Zangbo 56 F3
Yarmouth, *Canada* 90 T8
Yaroslavl' 38 G3
Yar Sale 38 P1
Yartsevo 38 F3
Yashkul' 38 J5
Yasnyy 38 L4
Yāsūj 63 D1
Yatağan 36 L7
Yathkyed Lake 90 M4
Yatsushiro 50 F7
Yatta 62 C5
Yavari 108 C5
Yawatongguzlangar 44 Q10
Yaya 44 R6
Yayladaği 60 F6
Yazd 58 F3
Yazdān 58 H3
Yazd-e Khvāst 63 E1
Yazoo City 98 C3
Ydra 36 F7
Ye 52 B3
Yea 82 J7
Yecheng 58 L2
Yecla 28 J6
Yefremov 38 G4
Yegendybulak 44 P8
Yei 74 E3
Yekaterinburg 38 M3
Yelets 38 G4
Yelizovo 46 T6
Yell 24 L1
Yellowknife 90 J4
Yellow River = Huang He 48 C3
Yellow Sea 48 G3
Yellowstone 94 E1
Yellowstone Lake 94 D2
Yeloten 58 H2
Yelva 44 J5
Yelwa 72 E2

Name	Sym	Pg	Ref
Yemen	A	58	D7
Yemetsk		38	H2
Yenakiyeve		38	G5
Yengisar		58	L2
Yenihisar		36	K7
Yenisey		44	S6
Yeniseysk		44	S6
Yeniseyskiy Kryazh		44	S5
Yeo Lake		82	D5
Yeovil		24	K11
Yeppoon		82	K4
Yeraliyev		44	J9
Yerbogachen		46	H4
Yerevan		60	L3
Yerington		94	C3
Yerkov		36	S5
Yerkoy		60	F4
Yermak		44	P7
Yermitsa		38	K1
Yerna		44	J5
Yershov		38	J4
Yerupaja	▲	108	B6
Yerushalayim		62	C5
Yesil'		38	N4
Yeşilhisar		60	F4
Yeşilköy		36	L4
Yessey		44	U4
Yevlax		60	M3
Yevpatoriya		38	F5
Yeyik		44	Q10
Yeysk		38	G5
Yibin		48	C5
Yichang		48	E4
Yichun, China		48	H1
Yichun, China		48	E5
Yilan		48	H1
Yıldız Dağları		36	K2
Yıldızeli		60	G4
Yinchuan		48	D3
Yingcheng		48	E4
Yingkou		48	G2
Yingtan		48	F5
Yining		44	Q9
Yirga Alem		74	F2
Yitomio		16	M3
Yitulihe		46	L6
Yiyang		48	E5
Yli-Kitka		16	Q3
Ylivieska		16	N4
Ylöjärvi		16	M6
Yoakum		98	B4
Yoboki		68	H5
Yogyakarta		54	E4
Yohuma		74	C3
Yokadouma		72	G4
Yoko		72	G3
Yokohama, Japan		50	K6
Yokohama, Japan		50	L3
Yokosuka		50	K6
Yokote		50	L4
Yola		72	G3
Yonago		50	G6
Yonezawa		50	L5
Yong'an		52	F1
Yongdeng		48	C3
Yŏnghŭng		50	D4
Yongren		52	C1
Yongxiu		48	F5
Yonkers		96	F2
York, United Kingdom		24	L8
York, Nebr., United States		94	G2
York, Pa., United States		96	E3
Yorkton		90	L6
Yoshkar Ola		38	J3
Yōsu		50	D6
Yotvata		62	C7
Youghal		24	E10
Youghal Bay		24	E10
Youngstown		96	D2
Youvarou		72	D1
Yozgat		60	F4
Yreka		94	B2
Ystad		18	C2
Ytre Sula		16	B6
Ytyk-Kyuyel'		46	N4
Yuan		52	C2
Yuanjiang		52	C2
Yuanmou		52	C1
Yuanping		48	E3
Yucatán		102	F5
Yucatan Channel		102	G4
Yuci		48	E3
Yudoma		46	Q4
Yuendumu		82	F4
Yueyang		48	E5
Yugorenok		46	P5
Yugo-Tala		46	S3
Yukagirskoye Ploskogor'ye		46	S3
Yukon		100	(1)E3
Yukon Territory		100	(1)K2
Yukorskiy Poluostrov		44	L4
Yüksekova		60	L5
Yukta		46	H4
Yuli		44	R9
Yulin, China		52	E2
Yulin, China		48	D3
Yuma		100	C2
Yumen		48	B3
Yumin		44	Q8
Yunak		60	D4
Yuncheng		48	E3
Yun Xian		52	C2
Yuogi Feng	▲	44	R8
Yurga		44	Q6
Yurimaguas		108	B5
Yurla		38	K3
Yuroma		38	J1
Yur'yevets		38	H3
Yu Shan	▲	52	G2
Yushkozero		16	S4
Yushu, China		48	B4
Yushu, China		48	H2
Yusufeli		60	J3
Yutian		44	Q10
Yuxi		48	C6
Yuyao		48	G4
Yuzawa		50	L4
Yuzhno Kuril'sk		50	N1
Yuzhno-Sakhalinsk		46	Q7
Yuzhno-Sukhokumsk		60	L1
Yuzhnoural'sk		38	M4
Yverdon-les-Bains		30	B4
Yvetot		22	C5

Z

Name	Sym	Pg	Ref
Zaandam		22	G2
Ząbkowice Śląskie		18	F7
Zabok		30	L4
Zábol		58	H3
Zabrze		18	H7
Zacatecas		100	F4
Zadar		30	L6
Zadonsk		38	G4
Zafora		36	J8
Zafra		28	D6
Zägheh-ye-Bälä		60	M6
Zagora		70	D2
Zagreb		30	L5
Zagyva		18	K10
Zähedän		58	H4
Zahirabad		56	C5
Zahlé		62	C3
Zahrän		58	D6
Zaječar		34	K6
Zakamensk		46	G6
Zäkhö		60	K5
Zakopane		18	J8
Zakynthos		36	C7
Zakynthos		36	C7
Zala		30	M4
Zalaegerszeg		30	M4
Zalakomár		34	E3
Zalari		46	G6
Zalaszentgrót		30	N4
Zalău		34	L2
Zalim		58	D5
Zalingei		68	D5
Zaliv Aniva		50	Q7
Zaliv Kara-Bogaz Gol		58	F1
Zaliv Kresta		46	Y3
Zaliv Paskevicha		38	L5
Zaliv Shelikhova		46	T5
Zaliv Terpeniya		46	Q7
Zamakh		58	E6
Zambezi		76	C2
Zambezi		76	E3
Zambia	A	76	D2
Zamboanga		52	G5
Zambrów		18	M5
Zamora		28	E3
Zamość		18	N7
Zanda		56	C2
Zandvoort		22	G2
Zanesville		98	E2
Zangguy		58	L2
Zanjän		60	N5
Zannone		32	H8
Zanzibar		74	F5
Zanzibar Island		74	F5
Zaouatallaz		70	G4
Zaozernyy		44	S6
Zapadnaya Dvina		38	E3
Zapadno-Sibirskaya Ravnina		44	L5
Zapadnyy Sayan		44	S7
Zapata		100	G3
Zapolyarnyy		16	R2
Zaporizhzhya		38	G5
Zaprešić		30	L5
Zaqatala		60	M3
Zara		60	G4
Zarafshan		44	L9
Zaragoza		28	G3
Zarand		63	G1
Zaranj		58	H3
Zarasai		38	P9
Zaraza		108	D2
Zarechensk		16	R3
Zaria		72	F2
Zărnești		34	N4
Zarqä'		62	D4
Zarqän		63	E2
Žary		18	E6
Zarzadilla de Totana		28	J7
Žatec		18	C7
Zavetnoye		38	H5
Zavidovići		34	F5
Zavitinsk		46	M6
Zayarsk		44	U6
Zaysan		44	Q8
Zayü		52	B1
Zazafotsy		76	H4
Zbraslav		18	D8
Žebák		58	K2
Žēbār		60	L5
Zeebrugge		22	F3
žefat		62	C4
Zehdenick		20	J4
Zeilona Góra		18	E6
Zeist		22	H2
Zeitz		20	H5
Zelenoborskiy		16	S3
Zelenograd		38	G3
Zelenogradsk		18	K3
Zelenokumsk		60	K1
Zelina		34	D4
Zella-Mehlis		20	F6
Zell am See		30	H3
Zémio		74	D2
Zemlya Alexsandry		44	G1
Zemlya Frantsa-Iosifa		44	J2
Zemlya Vil'cheka		44	L1
Zempoalteptl	▲	102	E5
Zenica		34	E5
Zerbst		20	H5
Zermatt		30	C4
Zeta Lake		90	K2
Zeulenroda		20	G6
Zeven		20	E3
Zevenaar		22	J3
Zeya		46	M6
Zeya		46	M6
Zeydäbäd		63	F2
Zeyskoye Vodokhranilishche		46	M5
Zgharta		62	C2
Zgierz		18	J6
Zgorzelec		18	E6
Zhailma		38	M4
Zhaksy		38	N4
Zhaksykon		38	N5
Zhaltyr		38	N4
Zhambyl		44	N9
Zhanatas		44	M9
Zhangbei		48	E2
Zhangguangcai Ling		48	H2
Zhangjiakou		48	E2
Zhangling		46	L6
Zhangwu		48	G2
Zhangye		48	B3
Zhangzhou		52	F2
Zhanjiang		52	E2
Zhaodong		46	M7
Zhaoqing		52	E2
Zhaosu		44	Q9
Zhaotong		48	C5
Zhaoyuan		48	H1
Zharkamys		44	K8
Zharkent		44	P9
Zharma		44	Q8
Zharyk		44	N8
Zhaxigang		56	C2
Zheleznogorsk		38	G4
Zhengzhou		48	E4
Zhenjiang		48	F4
Zherdevka		38	H4
Zhetybay		44	J9
Zhezkazgan		44	M8
Zhigalovo		46	H5
Zhigansk		46	L3
Zhilinda		46	J2
Zhob		58	J3
Zholymbet		44	N7
Zhongba		56	D3
Zhongdian		48	B5
Zhongning		48	D3
Zhongshan		52	E5
Zhongze		48	G3
Zhoukou		48	E4
Zhuanghe		48	G3
Zhucheng		48	F4
Zhumadian		48	E4
Zhuo Xian		48	E3
Zhytomyr		38	H9
Žiar		18	H9
Zibo		48	F4
Zichang		48	D3
Zierikzee		22	H4
Zighan		68	D2
Zigon		52	B6
Zigong		48	C5
Ziguinchor		70	B6
Zikhron Ya'aqov		62	C4
Zillah		68	C2
Zima		46	G6
Zimbabwe	A	76	D3
Zimmi		72	B3
Zimnicea		34	N6
Zinder		72	F2
Zinjibär		68	J5
Zinnowitz		20	J2
Zirc		18	G10
Žirje		32	K5
Zistersdorf		30	M2
Zitava		18	H9
Zittau		20	K6
Ziway Häyk'		74	E1
Zixing		52	E2
Zlatá Moravce		18	H9
Zlatoust		38	L8
Zlín		18	G8
Zlïţan		70	H2
Zlocieniec		18	F6
Zloczew		18	H6
Złotów		18	G4
Zmeinogorsk		44	Q7
Znamenskoye		44	N6
Žnin		18	G4
Znojmo		30	M2
Zoigê		48	C4
Zolotinka		46	M5
Zomba		76	F3
Zongo		74	B3
Zonguldak		36	P3
Zouar		68	C3
Zouérat		70	C4
Žovka		18	N7
Zrenjanin		34	H4
Zschopau		20	J6
Zug		30	D3
Zuger See		30	D3
Zugdidi		60	E1
Zugspitze	▲	30	F9
Zuid-beveland		22	F4
Zuni		100	E1
Zunyi		48	D5
Županja		34	G5
Zürich		30	D3
Zuru		72	F2
Žut		32	K5
Zutphen		22	J2
Zuwärah		68	B1
Zuwevka		44	J6
Zvishavane		76	E4
Zvolen		18	J9
Zvornik		34	G5
Zwedru		72	C3
Zweibrücken		22	K5
Zwettl		30	L2
Zwickau		20	H6
Zwiesel		20	J7
Zwoleń		18	L6
Zwolle		22	J2
Zyryanka		46	S3
Zyryanovsk		44	Q8
Żywiec		18	J8